SAILING TRACKS

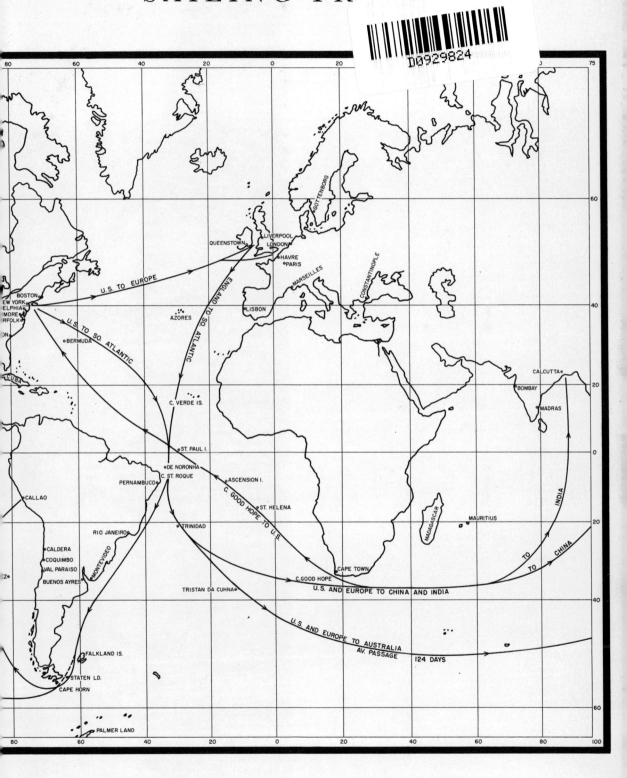

OF MAURY'S SAILING DIRECTIONS

GREYHOUNDS OF THE SEA

THE STORY OF
THE AMERICAN CLIPPER SHIP

CLIPPER SHIP "DAVID CROCKETT."
FROM PAINTING BY CHARLES R. PATTERSON.
Courtesy of Frank N. Brooks, Jr.

GREYHOUNDS OF THE SEA

THE STORY OF
THE AMERICAN CLIPPER SHIP

───────────────────────────

BY CARL C. CUTLER

WITH A FOREWORD BY

CHARLES FRANCIS ADAMS

SECRETARY OF THE NAVY

1929–1933

───────────────────────────

ANNAPOLIS • MARYLAND

UNITED STATES NAVAL INSTITUTE

*Printed in the United States of America
by the George Banta Company, Inc., Menasha, Wisconsin*

PUBLISHER'S NOTE

The Naval Institute is pleased to make available once again Carl Cutler's *Greyhounds of the Sea,* a book which has become a classic in its field since its original publication in New York in 1930.

Since this book's first appearance the author and others have continued their inquiries into the thoughts and activities of the men who designed, owned, and sailed the clippers. As a result of this scholarly activity over three decades, new information has come to light and has been incorporated into the present edition.

Three new illustrations, of the *Ino, Andrew Jackson,* and *Young America,* have been added to the original selection, as well as the *Rainbow's* lines and sail plan and the lines of the record-breaking *Lightning.*

Additions and corrections aside, the book has been printed from the original plates.

Grateful acknowledgement is made to those persons who made possible this new edition and to those whose searching through ancient files has made possible the publication of a more perfect work than might otherwise have been. Foremost among these, of course, is the author himself. Others are Vernon D. Tate, librarian at the U. S. Naval Academy; Miss Ethel M. Ritchie, formerly of the Fairburn Marine Educational Foundation, Inc., of Center Lovell, Maine, who ran down many small errors of fact in the original edition; Howard I. Chapelle of the Smithsonian Institution in Washington, D. C., who executed the new drawings of the old ships' lines; the staff of The Peabody Museum in Salem, Massachusetts; and the staff of The Marine Historical Association, Inc., of Mystic, Connecticut.

United States Naval Institute
Annapolis, Maryland
May, 1961

FOREWORD

We have all to some degree known of the romance of the development of American sailing ships and of the exploits of the hardy men who took them over the world. Some have vaguely realized that sea life profoundly affected the civilization of the Eastern States. Yet that vital and romantic history reached its climax and began to fade more than three-quarters of a century ago, and, till now, no one has undertaken with the thoroughness of the historian a complete study of these ships; how and by whom their design was developed, and what they accomplished.

In fact, strangely little had been written till some twenty years ago Captain Clark's "Clipper Ship Era" told of the men and the ships he commanded as a youth and later saw disappear from the sea. Since then studies of parts of this history have appeared, but no history of the whole.

That an achievement, great in its day, should have escaped the attention of the trained historian, indicates the extent to which a once well-nigh universal maritime interest passed from men's minds. It may suggest, too, that history has awaited proper perspective—a perspective in which failure is forgotten and success appears again. However this may be, the beginnings which have been made indicate that it is of importance that there should be a broader understanding of the significance of the growth and decline of an industry so great that it long occupied the center of the world's economic stage.

The life that engaged the labors of a large part of a people; that colored their speech; vitalized their commerce, industry and literature, and shaped to an extent their morals and ethics, has passed away forever. Whether there remains anything of permanent value to be saved from that rugged period, is a question the reader of these pages may answer for himself.

A thorough accurate study from original sources, bristling with news of forgotten sailors, their ships and their records, has a dramatic appeal to every reader. Perhaps, too, the student will find here something to complete and explain the picture of the development of our country.

C. F. Adams

Washington, D. C., June 30, 1930.

PREFACE

The story of the rise and decline of the American clipper ship is epic in quality, significance and proportions. A writer in this hurried age can scarcely hope to do full justice to such a theme, much less cut through the sea change of a century and make a dead past live again. The following account is no ambitious fling at the impossible, but an attempt to arrive at the truth underlying vague tradition and disputed fact. Accordingly other considerations have been subordinated to the careful verification of such data as seemed of consequence, and to the task of selecting from a mass of available material the facts which appeared most significant.

A generation since, the mind of the ordinary New England boy was well steeped in sailing ship lore through the medium of a seafaring ancestry, and this preliminary education was frequently supplemented by a voyage or two "deep water." The writer did not wholly escape these experiences, and while lessons learned on kicking yards by well-chilled "r'yal boys" may be easily overvalued, they possibly have a place in the equipment of one who essays to write on nautical subjects.

The collection of source material for the following account was undertaken shortly after the close of the late war. As a preliminary step the marine columns of the principal Boston and New York papers from 1800 to the outbreak of the Civil War were thoroughly combed, and the way prepared for a somewhat definite appraisal of the period. Subsequently thousands of scattering newsprint issues of the coastal towns of the present United States from 1770 onward were consulted. Collections of Americana, historical societies, athenæums, custom house records and Congressional Library contributed nuggets of information from pamphlet and manuscript. Upwards of five thousand logs were examined. In the foreign field frequent reference was had to early files of Australian and Hong Kong papers and other scattering issues, and considerable work done among the archives of the British Museum.

An important part of the data thus acquired, although constituting but a fraction of the total, is set forth in the following pages. In handling such a mass of material it seems inevitable that errors should appear, but it is believed that they will be traceable to inadvertence rather than to reckless assertion and, what is more, that they will not sensibly affect the final appraisal of the period.

It has been thought advisable to cite authority only for the more important items of information. On the other hand, no facts are included which are not supported by contemporary records and—possible error aside—all specific statements may be readily checked by any person interested in doing so. Virtually all arrivals and departures mentioned will be found in the marine columns of papers published at the port involved, usually within a day or two after the event.

It will be recognized that not all marine reports, even when contemporary, are equally reliable. Many errors have been detected through comparisons with log books; others are corrected in later issues of the offending publication, or indicated by a consensus of other reports. It is the writer's impression that where log books and shipping reports conflict, the former are almost invariably dependable. Personal recollections, memoirs and the like, compiled years after the events, have been found untrustworthy as to details, although usually furnishing invaluable impressions of a period.

Such conclusions as are drawn—and there are several which differ radically from current impressions—are made on the authority of the writer. On the evidence cited the reader may find himself unable to accept particular deductions, but it is hoped he will receive, on the whole, a definite conception of the part played in American history by fast sailing craft, and that he will here find the answer to not a few of the doubts which have hitherto assailed many lovers of the old ships. It is not important now perhaps that this ship or that individual should receive credit for some long-forgotten feat, but it is of moment that the measure of a past generation be taken with fair regard for accuracy. Above all, it is of vast practical value that the motivating forces involved in this achievement be understood.

Perhaps no branch of the merchant marine has been the subject of more profuse and effective illustration than the clippers, but a painting even when entitled to high rank in artistic achievement falls something short of disclosing the remarkable individuality which distinguishes each of these craft and sets it definitely apart from its fellows. Because it was found that essential characteristics could not be clearly indicated by paintings, however faithfully and skillfully executed, it has seemed proper to include herewith a number of photographic reproductions of builders' models and sail plans.

These photographs not only convey a reasonably accurate impression of the appearance of particular ships, but afford a means for comparing the lines of some of the most famous clippers. In selecting the models to be shown, an effort has been made to include such as would illustrate the course of development of the clipper ship from early fast sailing types to the thoroughbred racer of the late fifties.

The time may come when the real value of these few remaining old clipper half-models will be more generally recognized. There are, doubtless, occasional pieces from the hands of early workers in wood which compare in beauty with the rare, restrained sweep of their marvellous lines, but few that embody a tithe of the intricate technical and practical knowledge that plotted their curves. When historic value alone is considered, one may be pardoned for doubting whether there is an existing example of American handicraft which surpasses in significance the original model of the old *Samuel Russell* or the *Red Jacket* or half a dozen others. However this may be, it is believed that the photographs of these models will have a certain appeal to those who saw some of the clippers while they were still afloat.

No one can be more sensible than the writer, of the imperfections which mark the text. Nevertheless, since this older and possibly more interested generation is passing rapidly away, it has seemed advisable to assume the risks incident to somewhat premature publication of the collated material rather than to postpone the issue for the time necessary to complete a more satisfactory study.

But twenty years have elapsed since Captain Clark penned the closing lines of *The Clipper Ship Era*. In this brief interval the few remaining figures in that historic pageant of the fifties have all but disappeared. Seventy years in the life of man, as of ships, is a long time.

To the captain and his generation the clippers were a reality. Many of the important facts regarding them—their appearance, their records, their handling, the thousand and one details of their construction and rig, the character of the men who sailed them—were to him commonplace matters, as they still were to a considerable body of elderly mariners, merchants and shipping men. In outlines only slightly less clear, this picture was also familiar to an even more numerous body—descendants and younger associates of these men.

Accordingly Captain Clark could and did address himself primarily to readers who already knew by experience or first hand tradition much that was of general interest pertaining to ships of the sail. His task was to recall, rather than to inform; to reminisce, rather than to explore. In carrying out this undertaking he produced a most valuable record. As time goes on, it becomes increasingly evident that his account of the clipper ship is destined to remain unique—the last word of the last actor in a great scene.

Today the birthright of the nation has passed to alien lands, and with it has dissolved a mass of fact and tradition that was implicit in the mental background of yesterday. The strange, mysterious beauty of the ships, once so real, is gone, leaving only dim outlines to shadow forth the haunting loveliness that once held a world in thrall. For those who would in some measure know the ships their fathers knew and loved, other canvases must be painted, the details of which can no longer be drawn from living sources, but must be gathered from long-forgotten records and painstakingly fitted into place. Much has been lost beyond the possibility of recovery, but much has been and can still be made accessible.

Contributions to this work have already been made. The value of the task Howe and Matthews, Davis, Morison, Putnam, Magoun, Bradlee and others have completed can hardly be overestimated. That their work has involved years of unremitting toil is evident. Such labors would be impossible if they were not impelled by a genuine love for the beautiful old craft, and a profound appreciation of the men who sailed them as ships were never sailed before or since.

Achievements of this character, coupled with the work of Captain Clark and some others, might seem to make further effort gratuitous were it not apparent that the subject is far from exhausted. A substantial quantity of long-buried records still await the light—records of as intensely dramatic interest as any that have yet been made known. Forgotten tales of deep-sea races, as thrilling as the most hardly fought contests of clipper ship history, lie buried in ancient chests and wormeaten files. Unsuspected errors remain to be corrected, that the humblest of those who, as a class, were once the pride and glory of the nation, may have their due. Even in picturing the ships themselves, there is much that can be done. Cheap prints and paintings, of modest merit for the most part, were sufficient for those who through them could visualize the glorious originals, but they no longer suggest to unfamiliar eyes a tithe of the stately beauty that was once the toast of the world.

These are matters of interest to every American, for once again history is to repeat itself. The greatest triumphs of this country in peace and war, were won upon the sea, and already the nation is turning with fresh vigor to that great breeding place of the strong free races of every age. Her efforts will be in vain unless she relearns the essential lesson of the ancient craft. Times change—the verities remain.

They were more than things of wood and hemp—those old ships. They were at once the flower and symbol of all that was true and great and fine in a passing civilization. In them the varied threads of more than three centuries of the pioneer activities and hopes and aspirations of a world were woven into a pattern of surpassing beauty—an exquisite miniature, shadowing forth the soul of a civilization that was presently to disappear from the scene.

Even now we understand but imperfectly what was taking place in the early part of the nineteenth century—what it was that comprised the peculiar glamor and glory of the clipper ship era. Since time began, the elements had ruled the earth, and man had pitted his strength unaided against them, all too often in vain. The unequal battle was ending. New mechanical and physical devices and forces were being put to work which were presently to give man the advantage. Engine and propeller were about to replace mast and sail. Uneasy, and as if impelled by a premonition of coming change, the stalwart representatives of the vanishing order gathered themselves for one supreme gesture of defiance to the elements. How they succeeded is engraved in records that will endure unbroken while time lasts.

The story of the clipper ship can never be completely—perhaps never adequately—told. Today's standards are changed and shrunken. After the lapse of three quarters of a century, the men who played a part in that drama seem cast in an Homeric mould. Their deeds assume gargantuan proportions that baffle comparison. Rough Viking voyages become leisurely pilgrimages in the ruthless light of the terrible man killing drive of the clipper. Bold Elizabethan navigators lose something of color, matched with the seasoned clipper ship sailor, smashing his relentless way against masthead surges through inconceivable gales. One can only strive, in the light of new facts, to indicate a little more clearly the part he played in the march of events—to paint a picture of his achievements comprehensible to the present generation, to the end, perhaps, that when America's time of trial comes, as come it will, there may still remain a leaven of that old sea dog spirit which knew no fear and recognized no limitation.

More than this, we cannot hope. One can no longer write to quicken old memories. It is now too late to sense that keen, though homely, satisfaction. The burly figures that yesterday stamped the streets of our little seaport towns have vanished. Their stentorian tones are silenced. One cannot always walk the quarter deck making new records for an applauding world. Along with the beautiful, beautiful ships, the last living representatives of an age-old era are gone, and with them, an irreplaceable something of beauty and courage, of quaintly mingled courtesy and bluff heartiness, and a vast store of practical knowledge and shrewd wisdom dearly bought with fifty centuries of hardships.

CONTENTS

CONTENTS

ILLUSTRATIONS IN COLOR

ILLUSTRATIONS

ILLUSTRATIONS

ILLUSTRATIONS

SHIP AND SAIL PLANS, APPENDIX VII

"A NEW SONG"

FORTON PRISON, ENGLAND
May, 1778

Cease Rood boorous clustring railer,
    Listen, you Landsmen, all to me;
Messmates, here a brother sailor
    Sings the dangers of the sea
From Bowling bellows first in motion,
    When the distant Whirlwinds rise,
To the tempest troubled Ocean,
    Where the Seas contend with Skies.

Hark, the Boatswain loudly baling,
    By top-sail-sheets and halyards stand,
Down top-gallants quick be halling,
    Down your stay-sails, hand, boys, hand.
Now it freshens sett the braces,
    The lee-top-sail sheets let go—
Luff, boys, luff, don't make wry faces—
    Up your top-sails nimbly clew.

Now to you in down beds sporting,
    Fondly locked in Beauties arms—
Fresh Enjoyments wanton courting,
    Free from all but loves alarms:
Round us roars the tempest louder,
    Hark ye now, what fears enthrawls—
Harder yet it blows, yet harder,
    Now again the Boatswain calls.

Your top-sail yards point to the wind, boys,
　　See all clear to reaf each course;
Let your fore sheet go, don't mind, boys,
　　Though the weather should be worse.
Fore and aft your sprit-sail yard gett,
　　Reaf your Mizen; see all clear,
Hands at each proventor brace sett,
　　Man the fore yard: cheer, lads, cheer.

Now the dreadful thunder rattles,
　　Peal on peal contending clash,
On our heads fears rainfall powering,
　　In our eyes blew lightning flash,
One wide water all around us,
　　All above us one black sky—
Different deaths at once surround us,
　　Hark, what means that dreadful cry—

The fore Mast's gone, cries every tongue out,
　　O'er the lee 12 feet above deck.
A leak beneathe the Chestrees sprung out,
　　Call all hands to clear the wreck,
Quick the lanyards cut to pieces,
　　Come, my hearts, be stout and bold—
Plumb the well, the leak increases,
　　Four foot water in the hole.

While o'er the ship the wild Seas beating,
　　We for wives and children mourn.
Alas to them there's no retreating,
　　Alas to them there's no return.
Still the leak is gaining on us,
　　Both chain Pumps is choaked below,
Heaven have mercy here upon us,
　　Only he can save us now.

On the lee beam is the land, boys,
　　Let the guns o'erboard be thrown,

To the pumps come every hand, boys,
　　See the mizen mast is gone.
The leak we found it cannot pour fast,
　　We have lightened her a foot more,
Up and rigg a jury fore mast,
　　She rights, she rights, boys, we are off shore.

Now once more on joys we're thinking
　　Since kind Forton hath saved our lives,
Come the can, boys, lett's be drinking
　　To our Sweethearts and our wives.
Fill it up, about ship wheel it,
　　Close to lips the brimmers join,
Where's the tempest, now who feel it,
　　All our Dangers are drowned in Wine.

FINIS

GOD SAVE THE CONTINENTAL CONGRESS AND
THE HONOURABLE JOHN HANCOCK, ESQ.

"A NEW SONG"

To the pumps come every hand, boys,
See the mizen mast is gone.
The leak we found it cannot pour fast,
We have lightened her a foot more,
Up and rigg a jury fore mast,
She rights, she rights, boys, we are off shore.

Now once more on, boys we're thinking
Since kind Fortion hath saved our lives,
Come the can, boys, let's be drinking
To our Sweethearts and our wives,
Fill it up, about ship wheel it,
Close to lips the brimmers join,
Where's the tempest, now who fed in,
All our Dangers are drowned in Wine.

Then

GOD SAVE THE CONTINENTAL CONGRESS AND
THE HONORABLE JOHN HANCOCK, ESQ.

AMERICAN CLIPPER SHIPS

CHAPTER I

COLONIAL CONDITIONS

I N such "rood" phrase did young John Rogers, sometime Yankee privateersman in the war for independence and temporary recipient of the hospitality of King George the Third, scrawl a not unfitting overture to the long sea drama then opening and destined to culminate a lifetime later in one of America's most notable achievements—the clipper ship.

It is difficult now to visualize the situation in which the American colonist found himself, about the middle of the eighteenth century. He had made good his stand on a rocky, poverty-compelling coast. Behind him stretched the uncharted wilderness and the red man; before him the British Navigation Acts, aided and abetted, so far as a direct-reasoning race of amphibious farmers could judge, by a choice array of tall Spanishers, Portingales, Barbary lateeners, buccaneers and quasi-privateersmen, backed by the solid wall of European nations, each with its peculiar interpretation of honor on the high seas.

To the colonial mariner the Pacific was a name—nothing more. He was as definitely debarred from the rich trade of India and the Orient as though he had been a resident of Mars. The doors of Africa, with certain unpleasant exceptions, and of South America, were closed. Subject to orders in council, embargoes, rights of seizure, prohibitions and restrictions in never ending succession, he might visit scattering ports in the West Indies and on the continent of Europe and borders of the Mediterranean with a carefully restricted invoice of merchandise.

It was illegal for him to export certain staples (of which tobacco was the most important) to any country but England, where it was sold in a "buyer's market" for whatever it would bring, irrespective of its value just across the Channel. It was equally illegal for him to purchase a return cargo from other than British sources, unless he required certain merchandise such as Swedish iron or Russian hemp produced in the country where his outward voyage terminated. He could, it is true, obtain various other articles outside the British dominions provided he paid a prohibitive duty thereon, and he had other privileges of a similar nature.

The British Acts of Trade and other statutes regulating commerce and shipping constituted but one of the many handicaps under which colonial enterprise struggled, and on the whole their effect was probably less galling than other methods of interference which did not enjoy the distinction of being embalmed in statutes. They are too numerous and too lengthy to be considered in all their ramifications, but their general purport was simple.

> "In the making of these laws (always looked upon as the bulwark of the English commerce) Great Britain had two vast objects in view. One, the increase of her naval power (by making her own people the sole carriers of the whole British Commerce:) the other, the appropriation and securing to herself, and her own subjects, all the emoluments arising from the trade of her colonies; well knowing the importance of these two great sources of her wealth and power."
>
> (Pamphlet: *A Short View of the Smuggling Trade,* p. 3. London, 1732.)

Our American colonist could have found small quarrel with this statement of purposes had it not been for the fact that, in practice, "all the emoluments" were secured to Englishmen resident in England. However obscured by legal verbiage and the interpolation of lofty sentiments, the effect of this legislation was to make the English merchant an unwanted and expensive middleman in the field of colonial commerce. Long before the Revolution the operation of the resulting system of privilege and monopoly had brought the majority of the colonists to a state of chronic bankruptcy.

There was, it is true, a modest degree of prosperity in America, in which the owners of shipping seem to have shared to a greater extent than the planters and other members of the producing classes, who had to take what they could get for their exports. Shipowners and master mariners could, and occasionally did, avoid some of the more onerous provisions aimed at their activities, thereby adding somewhat to a painfully acquired competency, but on the whole the population was enured, in a land of plenty, to long hours of grinding toil and every species of petty economy.

"Cute Yankee skipper!" indeed. Good need had he to be cunning. For nearly two centuries he paid the tribute and endured the infinite harassments that all civilization laid upon an helpless continent. Whatever his defects, it has yet to be written that he whined because Europe held the purse strings. There are those still living who well remember the burdens their fathers shouldered, long after weightier foreign exactions were removed. If the early Yankee, blood brother to the Briton, seemed at times to carry shrewdness to excess, it is possible that he was merely displaying a family trait somewhat sharpened on the grindstone to which his nose was pressed in true brotherly fashion.

Legally, and otherwise, by one government or another, the colonist was excluded from nearly every source of lucrative maritime trade. Wherever he went, with the exception of a few places and commodities, he was either a virtual wage slave without the possibility of real profit, or he was a law-breaker under the imminent necessity of running or fighting. To his honor, possibly, he was not averse to doing both, as occasion served. Since broken spars and raw bones paid no dividends it can be surmised that there was a natural gravitation toward faster sailing ships, as the least of a choice assortment of evils.

It would be interesting, if it were within the scope of this account, to make a more careful examination of the conditions under which the early American merchant marine was developed. Smuggling, particularly of rum, sugar and "melasses" from the French and Danish West Indies, appears to have been a common and respectable occupation after the Peace of Utrecht, in 1713. Since successful smuggling left no trace, its extent will probably never be accurately measured, but there is no doubt of its importance. In like manner, the depredations on colonial commerce by warring powers and the omnipresent guerillas of the sea, cannot now be definitely estimated. Nor is accuracy in these respects important. For our purpose the salient fact is that the American pioneer was at all times subjected at sea to indignities and dangers which tended to keep alive in his mind the vision of an unbeatable sailing ship, and, incidentally, fostered the habit of pushing such craft as he had to their utmost speed.

There is risk of under-, rather than overvaluing a factor of this sort in tracing not merely the progress in shipbuilding, but in accounting for the remarkable urge for speed which distinguished the early American sailor to such an extent as to excite the astonishment of foreign writers like De Toqueville and others. The French—a people modestly equipped by nature and inclination for success in naval pursuits—became noted as the designers of fast vessels. If they had been natural seamen, they would possibly have become equally noted as "drivers." One cannot even hazard a guess at the number of Frenchmen sold into slavery before they built craft to compete with the swift feluccas of their neighbors, the Moors. "Sweet are the uses of Adversity." In like manner, the earliest voyagers discovered that remarkably fast craft had been developed in the pirate infested waters of the Orient. Down to the era of peaceful competion, deviltry and swift ships sailed the seas together.

It is uncertain when the colonist began to build sharp modelled vessels. There is a tendency of late to give the French the credit for directing his earliest efforts in this direction, when their fleet was sent over during the Revolution.

Apparently unwarranted conclusions have been drawn from the circumstances of this association. There is abundant collateral evidence that colonial mechanics and mariners were reasonably familiar with all classes of merchant ships long before the Revolution. To assume the contrary is to predicate a mental attitude on their part which is altogether foreign to pioneer institutions. Not only were such men extensive travellers (many shipbuilders being themselves able seamen), but for more than a century the fast craft of all nations—Spanish polacres, Mediterranean feluccas, French luggers and the like—had been familiar sights in American ports. There can be no doubt that swift sailing vessels were built in America long prior to the arrival of the French Fleet in 1778. One did not go a smuggling or venture into piratical waters in "slow coaches."

The log of the little colonial schooner *John*, commanded by Joshua Riggs, which left Cape Ann the 16th of February, 1762, bound for Lisbon, records a speed of 9 to 9½ knots on several occasions, and a noon to noon run of 208 miles. Nearly a decade earlier the schooner *Eagle* was on a voyage from Salem to Fayall and Madeira. Her master, Ebenezer Bowditch, Jr., on the 31st of October, 1753, noted that she logged from 9 to 9½ knots for ten consecutive hours. Similar instances might be cited. There is nothing in the logs or in contemporary newspaper reports of such voyages to indicate that this sailing was then regarded as remarkable. Altogether it is obvious that the colonist who could turn out a tiny craft in 1750 capable of making from 9 to 10 knots when loaded, must have had more than an elementary knowledge of the principles of fast-sailing design.

At this time, and indeed prior to the opening of the American Revolution, French naval vessels do not seem to have been regarded as possessing sailing qualities superior to those of the British. So far as the writer has been able to discover it was not until the Revolution was well under way (in 1779 to be exact) that English officers began for the first time to report their ships were being outsailed and outmaneuvered by French war vessels. There is an interesting letter still extant, signed "Publicola" and addressed to the editor of *Lloyds Evening-Post* (London) under date of September 25, 1779. After referring to the remarkable despondency and inactivity which had lately characterized the conduct of English naval officers, the writer continued: "If the enemy can maneuver better than last war, then there is more glory in beating them. The enemy is said to be much superior in forming a quick line of battle; the fast sailing of their ships; the better quality of their powder; to be sure, these are great advantages, but the late engagement proves that they would soon have been rendered of no use by the superior valour and perseverance of the British sailors."

The French margin of superiority was so slight, however, that another British writer was of the opinion that the "excellent scheme of Lord Sandwich in sheathing most of our ships with copper" would more than overcome this handicap, since it would keep English craft clean while French ships would speedily become foul. At this time American vessels were not coppered, but energetic Yankee skippers on long cruises offset this deficiency by putting their boats over in calm weather and engaging in scrubbing the vessel's bottom—an operation quaintly described as "hogging the ship." Anyone who has noted the activities of a familiar barnyard animal will appreciate the metaphor. But however arduous the process, it had the effect of keeping a vessel clean without the aid of copper.

It would seem, therefore, on the whole, that even during the Revolution, American shipwrights had comparatively little to learn from French draftsmen, although French technical knowledge may well have been valuable in designing frigates and ships of the line capable of carrying the heavy batteries of the period.

However this may be, long before French naval designers were in a position to instruct American shipbuilders, the vessels of the colonies had demonstrated a notable superiority in sailing and fighting ability over British craft. When the frigate *Raleigh,* launched at Portsmouth, New Hampshire, in May, 1776, was captured, the English were sufficiently impressed with her sailing qualities to put her in dry dock and take off her lines. There can be no doubt that Brother Jonathan had learned his lesson well under England's repressive measures. No other assumption is possible in view of the fact that during the entire period of the Revolution, before the entrance of the French, as well as after, a people untrained in sea fighting and with a fleet far inferior in numbers, not only captured more prizes than did the British, but took a surprisingly large number of ships vastly superior in tonnage and armament. It may well be doubted whether the Revolution would not have collapsed prior to the entry of the French if it were not for the shiploads of clothing, supplies, arms and ammunition captured by American privateers.

There are several logs of fast American privateers in existence which had completed cruises "against the enemies of the United States" before France came to their assistance. One of these, the letter of marque schooner, *Success,* Captain Phillip Thrash, which left Cape Ann harbor on the 4th of October, 1778, made 10 knots and a distance of 200 miles her third day out. Several months earlier, the schooner *Scorpion,* which sailed from Salem March 18th, 1778, maintained a speed of 10 knots for 6 successive hours while cruising and not in chase, after which Captain Brooks records: "We stood to the S. E. and ketched a plenty of mackrel." On the 6th of the same month John Adams and the boy John Quincy Adams paced the quarter-deck of the little frigate *Boston*—an all-American product—while she logged 210 miles in a noon to noon run, which occupied less than 24 hours.

If it be objected that 10 knots is not fast, it must be remembered that this was a full generation before the larger and longer

12-knot craft of the Federalist period. There is ample reason for thinking that the above vessels could have sailed it out mile for mile under ordinary conditions with any craft then afloat, while there can be little doubt they were superior in speed to the great majority of ships in either the French or British navy. Several of the Continental frigates built by the American rebels in 1776, soon made enviable reputations for speed. Through the tiny news sheets of the day one catches brief glimpses of the little *Boston* or the *Deane,* hanging on the outskirts of British convoys dodging the lofty two deckers, and cutting out fat transports, deep-loaded with the all-essential munitions of war. More than once these nimble craft were reported as having sailed several times around warships convoying hostile fleets without once coming within gun shot.

A striking instance of this superiority in speed is revealed by the log book of the *Pickering* (sometimes referred to as the *General Pickering*), a Salem ship of 180 tons and 14 guns, commanded by Jonathan Haraden. During the Revolution Haraden, with this and similar modest equipment, is said to have captured vessels mounting over 1000 guns.

One of the most remarkable sea fights of all time was his self-sought encounter with the ship *Achilles* of London, a vessel nearly three times his tonnage and carrying exactly three times as many guns. In full sight of thousands of spectators on the Spanish coast, June 4th, 1780, Haraden engaged this vessel of frigate calibre, his tiny craft looking "like a long boat beside a ship," beat her off and forced her to seek safety in flight. There was a man and there, too, was a ship. It is no disparagement to say that John Paul Jones faced smaller odds in the *Good Man Richard* when he took the *Serapis.* Nevertheless the fight would never have occurred if Haraden had not known beforehand that his superior speed would enable him to out-maneuver his opponent, and inflict a maximum of damage with a minimum of risk.

After refitting at Bilboa, Haraden set out for Salem on the 1st of August. His homeward bound log indicates the possibilities of "action" which a sea voyage at that time held for romantically inclined youth:

"Aug. 5th.   All Light sails out.   At 3 P.M. took in St.g sails.   The Dutchmen in sight.   Also discover another sail to Windward.   4 P.M.   She bore down upon us:—got all ready for Engaging—at 8 P.M. lost sight of her.

Aug. 6th.   Saw a brigg on our Lee Quarter; likewise a cutter in chase of us under our Lee quarter.

Aug. 7th.   8 A.M.   Saw a Sail ahead which appears to be a large ship.   10 A.M. took in St.g sails and hauled our wind. Merid^n she tack^d and gave us chace.

Aug. 8th.   The ship in chace rather gains on us—All sail out which we can set upon a wind.   At 5 A.M. saw the ship on our Lee quarter, haul^d to, to keep all sails drawing—she haul'd to after us.   10 A.M. bore away before the wind.   Light breezes.   Got out our Oars and by Row^g rather gain from her.

Aug. 9th.   The ship still in chace and we keep on Row^g. 7 P.M.   She haul^d to the Southw^d—we left off Rowing and took in Larboard St^g S^s and set Staysails.

Aug. 10th.   Saw a cutter on our Lee bow standing for us; clear^d ship for Engag^mt.

Aug. 11th.   At merid^n bore away a little for the cutter. She haul^d close upon the wind.   From 4 P.M. to 6 she made several short Tackes to Windw^d and outwinded us, though we tack'd after her.

Aug. 17th.   At 10 A.M. tack ship to Now^d.   Saw a sail bearing down upon us.   Merid^n tack^d to Southw^d—got ready for Engageing.

Aug. 28th.   Took an Eng. Brigg prize and ordered her for Salem.

Sept. 3rd.   Took an Eng brigg prize.   (Set Std^g Sls and T. G. Sls, fore and aft, also M. T. G. Royal, Driver, Spritsail and Spritsail T. S.)

Sept. 13th—at 8 A.M. took a reef in M.S. found his upper clew gone.   Spliced in a cringle immediately and set him."

The following day Cape Ann hove in sight to the W.S.W.

and thus ended one of the most noteworthy, and as it happens, one of the most obscure voyages of the Revolution.

The *Pickering* was a "fast" ship in her day. This does not mean that she possessed a marvellous turn of speed, but merely that she was faster than the great majority of ships of her class, a fact which enabled her to outmaneuver them by a margin which, though slight, nevertheless turned the scales of victory in her favor, where a slower vessel would have been doomed.

Hardly less notable was the encounter of the American ship *Thorn*, commanded by Daniel Waters with the brigantines *Tryon*, 16 guns and 86 men, and *Sir William Erskine*, 18 guns and 85 men, the latter under the command of a Captain Alexander Hamilton. This meeting took place on the 24th of December, 1779. In the words of Captain Waters: "A warm engagement commenced on both sides for about two glasses, when the largest brig laid us on board, on our weather quarter, whilst the other amused us on our weather bow, who kept up a regular fire; but she upon our quarter was soon convinced of her error, receiving such a warm and well directed fire from our marines, and seeing his men running about deck with pikes in their backs instead of their hands, were undoubtedly glad to get off again."

In the end the *Thorn* performed the difficult task of fighting and defeating two strong and determined assailants simultaneously.

Instances of this sort might be multiplied indefinitely. There was the privateer sloop *Revenge* of ten guns, commanded by Joseph Sheffield, which on the 20th of January, 1777, attacked two heavy English ships of 14 guns each, the *Thomas* and the *Sarah*. The *Thomas* was captured and the *Sarah* was saved from a similar fate only by the approach of darkness, in which she escaped. When John Paul Jones in the *Ranger*, 18 guns and 123 men, fought and captured the *Drake* sloop-of-war of 20 guns and 156 men sent to take him outside of White Haven in the Spring of '78, he raked her seven times in 65 minutes.

Bravery there undoubtedly was in Yankee ships, but it was a quality with which British cruisers were plentifully stocked.

The fact is that bravery and superior weight of metal availed nothing against an antagonist who could choose and maintain an advantageous position at will. When Jones brought his vessel across the stern of the *Drake* he converted a 20 gun opponent into a relatively helpless two gun craft. Without detracting in the least from his skill and courage, there is a vast deal of credit due the quick moving ship under him.

It would be misleading, however, to give American genius the credit for originating at this time the basic principles of the fast-sailing ship. The Dutch certainly had made great progress in this direction prior to the restoration in the 17th century when Charles the Second returned to the throne of England and incidentally introduced the Dutch "yacht" to the sporting bloods of his day. There is evidence pointing to the possibility that the ship *Thorn*, above referred to, was a captured British war vessel. Certainly some of the early American privateers were captured from the enemy in the first instance.

It is indeed altogether probable that the elementary principle of speed construction, viz., that to get a faster vessel it was necessary to build her relatively longer and sharper, has been an open secret for centuries. The evidence ranges from the ancient Fjords of Norway to the Straits of Malacca. Capable designers, everywhere, from the days of Cleopatra's barge, have been able to lay down swift craft. It is America's distinction, not that she alone possessed the secret, but that at an early date she took, and on the whole successfully maintained, a position of world leadership in the development of vessels of this type.

Early merchants, however, were usually more interested in cargo space than speed; hence relatively few fast vessels were constructed prior to the nineteenth century. On long voyages in the bulky carrying trades, sharp built ships were justly regarded as "pick pockets." The major achievement of clipper shipbuilders was the development of a type which proved to be very fast and at the same time provided a maximum of stowage room. For many years, however, progress was painfully slow.

CHAPTER II

THE YOUNG REPUBLIC

LONG before the new fast-sailing ship *Astrea* of 360 tons, Captain John Derby, arrived at Salem on the 4th of April, 1783, in the then remarkable and still excellent time of 22 days from France, bringing the declaration fixing the dates for cessation of hostilities, the bustle of preparation for new and far-reaching commercial adventures had begun. With an eye to profit rather than glory, Captain Mooers of Nantucket, left port in the ship *Bedford*, late in 1782, deeply loaded with oil. On the 6th day of February, following, a London paper said:

> "Yesterday the *Bedford*, Captain Morris (sic) from Nantucket, made entry at the Custom-House: this is the first vessel that has entered the river, belonging to the United States. It is said she touched at some port in France, and hearing of the peace, immediately proceeded to a market. She is loaded chiefly with oil."

Within a few days three American vessels were lying in the river Thames "with the thirteen stripes flying." The foreign trade thus begun was prosecuted with all the resources and energy the young nation could command.

Energy there was and to spare, but resources were painfully lacking. Seven years of hostilities had virtually destroyed the colonial merchant marine and most of the ships which survived were better adapted to privateering or coasting than to foreign commerce. With the end of the war also came scores of French, British and other vessels, glutting American markets with goods of every description before the assurance of peace had fairly reached this country.

Poverty was acute; conditions everywhere were unsettled. Royalists, baited on all sides, were fleeing in shiploads to "Nova Scarcity" and other places of exile. Former tory newspapers were executing a right about face. Well-known names disappeared from shops and counting houses and new ones took their places. The once feared if not respected forces of King George became the subject of universal jest. When the officers of a British war ship applied to the authorities for permission to bury one of their comrades the *Boston Evening Post* furnished the gratuitous epitaph:

> "Here lies, retired from busy scenes,
> A first Lieutenant of Marines,
> Who lately lived in peace and plenty,
> On board the ship the *Diligente;*
> Now stripped of all his warlike show,
> And laid in Box of elm below,
> Confined in earth in narrow borders,
> He rises not till further orders."

Amid scenes of confusion and widespread unrest and with every prospect of a long, uphill struggle, Brother Jonathan took up his task of organizing a new and self-sufficient merchant marine in direct competition with immensely wealthy firms having all the advantages accruing from century-old connections and monopolistic privileges.

There was no hard and fast line of demarcation between foremast hand and aristocratic merchant. Most of the latter, in fact, like John Derby above, began their career on the sea. With such men, to act was instinctive. As the little privateers and letters-of-marque came flocking home to disgorge their swarms of pigtailed gunners and top-men in the seaports of the Atlantic, they found their owners already occupied with new plans.

The China teas, India piece goods, Manila sugars, the drugs, spices and the innumerable articles of commerce which the colonists had formerly received from England, or smuggled from her competitors, could now be secured directly from the countries of their origin, with the prospect of greatly increased profits. Strange seas therefore must be sailed, new ports entered, and the dangers and endless labors incident to the establishment of a new, far-flung commercial empire, undertaken. The war had been fought and won. It remained to be seen whether the erstwhile colonist could reap any practical benefits therefrom, or whether the British middleman would be able to retain command of the situation.

It was doubtless all in the day's work to tough, sea-stomached ex-privateersmen, but, from the vantage point of the present few scenes in American history present a more valiant picture than the sailing of the earliest of these small, ill-found craft for virtually unknown seas. The first ship to arrive in China under American colors was the *Empress of China,* commanded by Captain John Green. Her log begins, appropriately enough, on the 22nd of February, 1784.

Light on the character of her venture is given by the following item which appeared in the *Maryland Journal and Baltimore Advertiser* for March 5th, 1784:

"On Sunday last sailed from New York, the ship *Empress of China,* Captain John Green of this port" (New York) "for Canton in China. On passing the garrison at Fort George, she fired with great regularity, the United States salute which was returned from the fort. This handsome, commodious and elegant ship modelled after and built on the new invented construction of the ingenious Mr. Peck, of Boston, is deemed an exceeding swift sailer. The Captain and crew, with several young American adventurers, were all happy and cheerful, in good health and high spirits; and with a becoming decency, elated on being considered the first instruments, in the hands of Providence, who have undertaken to extend the commerce of the United States of America to that distant, and to us unexplored, country."

The *Empress* arrived at Macao on the 23rd of the following August, her passage occupying six months. A probably accurate impression of the appearance of Whampoa and the character of the shipping she found there may be gained from the reproduction of a pen sketch of the port taken from the log book of the ship *Ceres* for 1797 and shown in the illustrations. The return passage was accomplished in 134 days, while the round voyage occupied 14 months and 24 days.

The trade thus inaugurated grew slowly for several years. Both capital and ships were lacking for adventures of this sort. Nevertheless, the trade did grow and it is worthy of note that during the next decade America and England were the only two countries to show an increase in tea imports from China. All others showed a loss. (See note.)

Much of this traffic followed a route which took the vessels around Cape Horn to the Northwest Coast for furs, thence to Whampoa to exchange their furs for tea, silks, etc. The voyage of the ship *Columbia* which left Boston in 1787 and was the first to complete a voyage of this character and, incidentally, the first to carry the American colors around the globe, has become a classic instance of Yankee enterprise. One can hardly conceive of the Lewis and Clark expedition without the preliminary work of these early Cape Horners, and yet the major credit for extending the territory of the United States beyond the Rockies is usually given to the overland explorers.

During the last decade of the eighteenth century American commerce expanded rapidly. The annual exports jumped from seventeen millions in 1791 to fifty millions in 1795, whereupon the *Columbian Centinel* complacently remarked that "the exports of Great Britain in 1791 were not more."

It is difficult to overestimate the effect on the American mind of such a growth. Fortunes, small it is true, but of a size undreamed of a few years before, were being rapidly accumulated. There is some evidence that by 1800 the United States was becoming "money mad." This cannot be regarded as strange when one considers the situation in those times of a person without means. Gloss it over as one will, the condition of the majority of slaves in 1860 was heaven itself compared with that of the early Yankee laborer. The Massachusetts and New Hampshire insurrections of 1787 were symptomatic, merely, of wide-spread conditions. Accordingly, the sudden distribution of an unheard of amount of wealth among a population accustomed to the most rigid economies could have no other effect than to stimulate the commercial activities in which it had its source. Despite the pessimistic prophecies of the pro-British element, Jonathan was finding that he could stand alone, if, indeed, he was not accomplishing the miraculous feat of lifting himself by his boot straps.

Shipping was increasing at a tremendous rate. At the close of the Revolution, Philadelphia, New York and Newport (which formerly had been one of the most important ports in America) were virtually without vessels of any sort, and other cities were in not much better case. Philadelphia was not long in taking the lead in commerce. For a number of years her ships were reputed to be the largest and finest craft built in America.

After 1800 New York and New England forged rapidly to the front. At the close of 1809 New York boasted a registered tonnage more than double that of her former rival. The figures for the more important ports are as follows:

New York	243,638	tons
Boston	133,257	"
Philadelphia	121,445	"
Baltimore	102,434	"
Salem	43,537	"

(Ming's *New York Price-Current*, Feb. 9, 1811)

By this time also, the average size of ships engaged in foreign trade had greatly increased and their quality improved.

There remained, however, the ancient fly in the amber. From the time that Genet, in 1793, began to outfit privateers at Philadelphia to prey on British and American shipping alike down to 1812, one can find scarcely a daily paper which fails to record fresh seizures of men and vessels, the lists sometimes comprising twenty or more ships in a single issue. France, England and the Barbary pirates were the worst offenders but other nations, particularly Spain and Denmark, were by no means guiltless. In addition, scores of good ships disappeared without a trace, the prey of piratical craft from the Spanish Main to the China Sea.

Virtually all of South America still remained closed to Yankee ships. It was difficult, and for the most part impossible for them to obtain access to ports under British control in the West Indies, South Africa and elsewhere. They were absolutely cut off from the large islands in the Far East under the dominion of the Dutch. In these respects they were no worse off than the traders of many other nations, but the facts are essential to an understanding of the general conditions under which the commerce of the United States developed.

Much has been written regarding the extent of impressment of seamen and seizure of ships during the Federalist period, and considerable stress has been laid upon the conflicting testimony given before congressional committees in this connection. Reputable and undoubtedly honest shipowners stated that they, personally, knew of but one or two instances of impressment of American seamen over a long period of years, and evidence of this character is cited as proof of extraordinary exaggerations regarding the extent of the practice. One can only state that an examination of the marine columns of the press of the times discloses thousands of reports by returning shipmasters of the impressment of American sailors, and in view of this, the conflicting evidence before Congress would seem to be of questionable value.

The log of the ship *Benjamin Morgan,* which arrived at Philadelphia on September 30th, 1803, from Bordeaux, throws light on the conditions then existing, and it may be said to be a fair picture of the difficulties to which American vessels were subject during the entire Napoleonic period. The *Morgan* sailed from Bordeaux on the 5th of August. She was boarded by the *Diamond*, British frigate, on the 6th, detained from 9 A.M. to 7 P.M., and ordered in to Plymouth for condemnation. On the 9th of August the French privateer *L'Aventure*, 16 guns, boarded her, taking off the British midshipman and seamen and setting her at liberty. Three days later two privateers of Guernsey, the *Lion*, cutter, and *Speculation*, lugger, brought her to and after considerable delay permitted her to proceed. Thereafter she was examined by the British sloop-of-war *Wasp*, which allowed her to proceed after a careful search, and on the 23rd of August she was boarded by the French privateer brig *Alert*, which put a Captain Cummings and one seaman from a captured American brig on board and allowed her to proceed. The *Morgan* appears to have reached Philadelphia without further molestation, having been on the whole better treated than many American vessels which had the misfortune to be boarded only once.

Depredations by the French appear to have excited more widespread indignation than the activities of the British during the early part of the Federalist period. Americans were divided between French sympathizers (Jacobins) and the pro-British element, but, on the whole, merchants and mariners, particularly those of New England, preferred John Bull's "right of search" to the downright piracy of the French.

The fluid state of public opinion about this period and the slowness with which the colonists, long accustomed to monarchical ideas, were finding their political legs, is indicated by the frequent publication of argumentative verse and prose of which the following is a sample:

Tune: "Come listen ye crimps and ye spies."

"You boys who do doat on a king
    Attend and I'll sing you a song.

You must very well know 'tis a maxim,
    Our monarch *can never do wrong.*

But as it is known he did *never*
    For his people a praise-worthy thing,
Won't it open your eyes to discover,
    That a Log *is as good as a King?*" etc.

French aggressions reached the point finally where President Adams appointed Washington Commander-in-chief of all armies raised or to be raised for the service of the United States, and Washington accepted the post on July 13th, 1798. But long before this, the country was aroused as it had not been since '76. On June 4th, 1798, the *Boston Price-Current* recorded that:

> "Capt. George Crowninshield & Sons have offered to the Government, the loan of the ship *America,* of 700 tons, at a valuation to be made by appraisers to be appointed by Government. She is a fine vessel, sails fast, and will carry 28 guns.
>
> The subscription at Newburyport for building a ship of war is filled, and the contracts made. She will be launched in 90 days.
>
> The ship *Herald,* of Boston, is purchased by the Government, to be fitted for sea immediately as a cruiser."

The Newburyport ship turned out to be the *Merrimack,* carrying 20 nines and 8 sixes. She was launched on the 12th of October, fully coppered, having been built in 74 working days. The *Portsmouth,* a 20 gun ship, had already been launched the previous day at Portsmouth, while another 36 gun frigate was to be built at once at Portsmouth, a 32 at Salem and a frigate called the *Philadelphia* on the Delaware—all by subscription. On the 13th of the following November, the pugnacious Newburyport *Herald* announced:

> "Capt. Thorndike has arrived at Beverly, from Copenhagen, with 80 pieces of cannon, 200 muskets, 20 pair of

pistols, and other articles suitable to the present and approaching seasons."

France, however, saw fit to moderate her actions and claims, and after many warlike acts, including the capture of *L'Insurgente* by the *Constellation*, the crisis passed without an actual declaration of war. It did not, however, lead to any permanent improvement in French manners, and many a slow sailing Yankee craft went, an unwilling "prize" into French or neutral ports during the incumbency of Napoleon. The name of Napoleon has a glamour today that it failed to have for the citizen of the youthful United States, to whom it meant little but a trail of ruined homes and broken shipmasters.

It must be remembered that at this period, and indeed for some thirty years thereafter, American crews were recruited from a very different class of men from that which later composed the merchant marine. The majority of them were not only American born but came from families of standing in their respective communities. Several contemporary newspapers were accustomed, as late as 1830, to prefix the title of "Mister" to the names of common sailors, when listing crews of merchantmen—a fact which indicates their status ashore if not afloat.

If France showed small indication of remorse, England showed less. Impressment and seizure went merrily on, usually under a pretence of right, but sometimes on the ground of necessity, as one British officer put it baldly to an unwilling Yankee: "We are fighting all creation, and we will take men where we find them." There were plenty of "down-easters" at the guns of Trafalgar, and not all of them were enthusiastic servants of His Majesty, as may be gathered from the fact that on the 12th of July, 1805, young Isaac Van Dyckman was hanged from the yardarm of Nelson's ship *Victory* for drinking the toast "that the Liberty Tree might be planted down the main hatchway and its branches spread through the British Navy." The fact that Van Dyckman's "release" had been on board the *Victory* for eleven months seems to have aggravated his offence in the eyes of his superiors.

Incidents of this character were, from their very nature, comparatively rare. Nevertheless, England had approximately a thousand warships in commission and in ordinary during this period, and according to contemporary accounts many ships had several impressed Americans on board. There are reports of as many as thirty-five on a single vessel. The actual total will never be known, but it is probable that the number amounted to several thousands, first and last, while estimates in excess of 20,000 have been made. At all events, most issues of daily newspapers during some twenty years recorded fresh outrages on our vessels, accompanied occasionally by acts of excessive brutality. It is altogether unlikely that the men of that day would have been stirred to measures like the embargo and non-intercourse acts and to actual war, by sporadic instances of oppression.

When war finally came not a few of these repatriated "British" sailors set to work with genuine enthusiasm to collect their back pay. Perhaps none were more successful than Jeremiah Holmes of Stonington, Connecticut, who had been detained for three years as gunner on one of his Majesty's men-of-war. It is said with at least a suspicion of truth that after young Jeremiah had finished sighting the guns of the little battery defending his native town in 1814, from an attack by the British fleet, it cost the Crown £10,000 to stop his shot holes.

CHAPTER III

DEMOCRACY AFLOAT

INNUMERABLE reported aggressions similar to those mentioned in the preceding chapter might be culled from the columns of the early press. The bare recital would fill a substantial volume —a matter which now concerns us only incidentally, since it would be a fruitless and unpleasant task, in this present day, to balance the evils of that strange world. The important thing to note is that, up to the close of the war of 1812, American ships were under a constant threat from immensely superior naval forces, in the presence of which they could only submit or seek safety by running or fighting. The evolution of the early fast-sailing ship cannot be understood without keeping this in mind.

Other factors affected the result, none more vitally than the new leaven of democracy that was working in America. The influence of independence on the government of the colonists was of minor significance compared to the sweeping changes it inaugurated in their lives. The war had substituted one form of government for another and, taken by and large, the change was essentially superficial. But in the realm of economics, more particularly in the domain of commerce, the effect was immediate and vital. Where formerly there had been restriction piled on restriction and monopoly within monopoly, now, temporarily at least, all restraints were removed.

Almost overnight the colonists entered into a freedom which changed their very philosophy of life. Henceforth it was not merely "America for Americans," but, having overturned by however slight a margin seemingly impregnable European institutions, they acquired the habit of scanning critically everything that bore the tag of the old régime. In practice, as in theory, blind subordination to authority gave place to a growing confidence in the ability of the individual to meet every situation. Such an attitude was bound, sooner or later, to make itself felt in the matter of shipbuilding, since it was already evident in 1783 that America's destiny lay on the sea.

It has become somewhat the fashion of late to speak slightingly of the quality of early American democracy—one view being that it was merely ancient aristocracy under a new cloak and that its achievements were those of class and privilege. The point is an interesting, but not a vital one. It would seem, however, that those who assume American society of, let us say the year 1800, was not essentially Democratic, lay more stress on manners than principles. It may be that breezy conduct, general back-slapping, shirt-sleeve hospitality and a thirst for neighborly gossip, are the hall marks of true democracy. If so, there was little of it in the counting houses or on the ships of the Federalist period.

Pure democracy is, and in the nature of things must be, a theory of human relationships rather than an institution of government; nevertheless its fundamental tenet that every man is capable of rising to higher levels and that it is natural and right that he should so rise, was probably more universally approved during the first fifty years of the American republic than at any later period. In an aristocracy, oligarchy or monarchy it is, or was, presumption for a man to attempt to rise. In a democracy, though by courtesy only, it is deemed a shame when he fails to do so by his own efforts, rather than by a gracious dispensation of favor from above. There is much evidence that this was the general feeling on early Yankee ships.

De Tocqueville undoubtedly had something of this sort in mind when he wrote concerning the American seamen: "I am of opinion that the true cause of their superiority must not be sought for in physical advantages, but that it is wholly attributable to their moral and intellectual qualities."

There are records of voyages where nearly every man jack on board ultimately commanded his own vessel. Tiny ships, in the course of their existence, "graduated" scores of masters and mates with a liberal sprinkling of naval architects, merchant princes and government officials. Men still living recall the bond of mutual respect which normally—rather than exceptionally—characterized the relations of man and employer of that generation.

It was a life of danger and subject to harsh, unexpected emergencies. Only those rose to command, who early demonstrated a capacity for absolute fearlessness, coupled with rare initiative and business shrewdness. However sheltered his environment on land, once at sea, a master, though a boy in years, became of necessity as impersonal as the elements and a shade more ruthless on occasion.

When 19 year old Zachariah F. Silsbee took command of the fast sailing Bryant & Sturgis ship *Herald* in 1803 and set out for Batavia, he was doing nothing remarkable, and the situations in which he presently found himself were no worse than those into which a thousand boys of his day were pitchforked by no cold blooded inhumanity, but by the iron law of necessity. A generation later Dana spent two years before the mast in just such another Bryant & Sturgis vessel.

Silsbee records that he sailed from Boston on the 18th of August, 1803.

"At 4 P.M. my brother and Mr. Bryant & the pilot left us just outside the Lighthouse & after exchanging three hurras with them made all sail Steerᵍ sails, Royals &c."

"Aug. 27. Am sorry to find our M. topmast back stay stranded. People employed fitting a standing preventer back-stay."

"Sept. 2. Am still mortified with a head wind, no prospect of a change; my patience is nearly exhausted.

Three weeks later there was wind and to spare. Young Silsbee's decks were swept and his close furled sails blown to shreds in their gaskets. For hours the *Herald* lay on her beam ends, the crew momentarily expecting the masts to go by the board. After 72 hours of this the weather moderated, but the day "closes with cloudy, squally threatening weather, God only knows what we are to have next—getting the T'galt masts aloft and fidding them, let the reefs from the Topsailes—bent mizen."

Every line of the water stained old manuscript is instinct with the driving force of a character but nineteen years in the making. It took something more than greed or a humdrum sense of duty to "sett Steering sails, Royals, etc.," at midnight in squally weather, or to hang on to encumbering masts hour after hour while the ship lay with her gunwale under water. Better sink than break the voyage.

If the American seaman dared more than the European, it was because he had the greater incentive. It required no miracle of circumstance or favor of the great to make him successively a shipmaster, shipowner and successful merchant. Those were normal phases of existence and while, as a foremast hand he jumped to the word of command, he was respected by captain and officers as a man who would shortly stand on his own quarter deck.

Yankee ships made faster passages than others because their masters knew they could be driven safely long after the crews of alien vessels could be depended on to save canvas. The same principle held throughout the ranks of builders and merchants. Faster models were originated because a new sense of personal worth led to the questioning of long established and seemingly infallible rules. Every branch of industry responded to the stimulus of the newly accepted theory of human relations, but none more than commerce on the high seas, since that commanded the attention of a majority of the keenest minds and most energetic men.

Within a few years from the signing of peace the most important invention in the history of wooden shipbuilding was perfected in the maritime towns of Massachusetts. This was the water-line or "lift" model, as it was sometimes called. Prior to this discovery, whenever an important vessel was to be constructed, it was usual to build either a miniature ship with frames and planking, or a solid block model which could be sawed into cross sections. (See illustration). From hulls such as these measurements were taken, the necessary calculations made, and the lines of the proposed ship laid down. Such methods were productive not only of gross inaccuracies, but afforded scant means for studying the effect of the various lines of the model. The water-line model, on the other hand, not only greatly reduced the margin of error, but afforded a new and valuable means of studying and improving the lines of vessels, and ultimately paved the way for a new era in naval design. It is doubtful whether the clipper ship would have attained anything like the degree of perfection it eventually did, without the assistance of this invention.

The model, which was never patented, has been ascribed to various individuals. John W. Griffiths, a prominent naval architect of clipper ship times, stated that the principle was known and used in eastern Massachusetts as early as 1790. However, the two earliest lift models in existence appear to have been made about 1794, and possibly as late as 1796. Both are shown here for the purposes of comparison.

Opposite page 28 is the model of the ketch *Eliza* built by Enos Briggs at Salem. This model is preserved in the Peabody Museum. The *Eliza* was said to have been very fast, and is reported to have run from the Massachusetts coast to the Equator in the remarkable time of 17 days, but trustworthy proof of this is lacking. It is, however, definitely established that she made a round voyage from Salem to the Isle de France in 7 months and 22 days, including detention in port—very fast time in 1797. Mr. Briggs is said to have built the famous frigate *Essex* from her model.

The other model, which is illustrated opposite page 28, is in the possession of the New York Historical Society, by whose courtesy it is here reproduced. This model was made not later than 1796 by Orlando Merrill, a young shipbuilder of Newburyport, and from it he built the sloop-of-war *Wasp*, which proved to be fast, and incidentally did yeoman service in the war of 1812.

Mr. Merrill lived to the green old age of 94, and saw the clipper ships in all their glory, after witnessing the passing of ancient craft which would not have loomed strangely to the eyes of Drake and Frobisher. Shortly before his death he gave the model in question to Mr. David Ogden, who exhibited it "on 'change" in New York as the model of the "first clipper ship," thus adding another to the list of ships competing for the honor.

As a matter of fact, both models, while presenting very different features, indicate that definite progress had been made at an early date in the direction of fast sailing design. They may profitably be compared with some of our crack cruising models of the present day. It is obvious that in several respects, they stand between the fast ships of Revolutionary days and the later speedy Baltimore clipper. Moreover, since vessels of this type could not possibly compete in carrying capacity with the ordinary merchantman of the time, it is clear that American insurance policies were beginning to take speed into account.

Speed, of course, was not the sole protection of the Yankee mariner. During the Federalist period hardly a foreign bound ship sailed that was not armed. The newspapers were full of advertisements of "remarkably fast-sailing" ships and brigs for sale or charter, mounting from six to eighteen guns "compleate with britchins and tackells" and, in the significant phrase of the times, "with men answerable." "Exercised the guns this day" is an entry to be found in the log of many an old merchantman, and a goodly proportion of the safe arrivals had to report more than one sailing match with suspicious craft, or an actual brush with a letter of marque. "Chaced by a privateer"; "robbed by an armed schooner heavily manned with a dark skinned crew"; "Boarded by His Majesties corvette," which perhaps took three men—these and similar items appear in the marine columns with remarkable regularity.

Harsh, yet strangely stirring days. The flavor of Elizabethan England still lingered. Side by side with the smart rakish brig which Master Cheeseman launched yesternoon near where Brooklyn Bridge now stands, could be seen the lofty poop and cumbersome spritsail topsail of an ancient Indiaman, which might well have carried troops to the siege of Louisburg. Everywhere a note of modernism contrasting with customs and ways inconceivably old. The ship *Adventure* in which Captain Cook circumnavigated the globe was still afloat, meeting her end in the "Gulph" of St. Lawrence on May 24th, 1811.

Here is the log of Commander Richard Dale, of the ship *Canton*, of 518 tons, built in Brooklyn in 1799, "on a voyage from China toward Philadelphia" at the very beginning of the 19th century. Dale, later a prominent shipowner of Philadelphia, had "lifted his warp" at Whampoa on the 3rd of December, 1799, and was now working cautiously in toward Cape Henlopen.

> Apr. 6, 1800. "At nine saw a sail to wind'd. At 10 spoke her—ye sloop Hannah of and for Boston 7 days from ye Island of Cuba—informs that no actual declaration of war has taken place between us and France—that our beloved Washington is no more & that the Constitution frigate, Capt. Talbot has sunk a French frigate, and was towed disabled into Jamaica."
>
> Apr. 11. "Anchor of Cape Henlopen Light. Our pilot as usual tells us a heap of news. From his conversation

can perceive him to be a Jacobin. His name is Higgins. At 7 strong breese. reefed ye topsails. Down T'gt yards and launched ye masts. At 10 moderating—Fidded Top G't masts. Turned a reef out of the main topsail. So ends."

Captain Dale's 130 day passage indicates that his ship was not in the class of the newer and sharper ships which America was beginning to turn out in considerable numbers.

It was not only lines which were improved. The new craft were sparred out of all proportion to the usual rig of merchantmen. Long, raking masts, an inordinate length of jib-boom, spritsails, ringtails, and huge steering (studding) sails from courses to topgallants, were the order of the day. But above all, the natural propensity of the Yankee shipmaster for "dragging on to her" was cultivated to the nth degree during this period, a fact which played its part in developing a thoroughbred racing type of sailor, without whom the later clippers would never have attained the speed they did.

Many remarkable records were handed down by these early ships, few of which exceeded 300 tons burthen, or attained a length of 90 feet. Some large ships were built, it is true. Philadelphia, regarded until the beginning of the 19th century as the most important shipbuilding center on the coast, produced several large vessels. The *China*, Captain McPherson, which was lost near Cape Henlopen in 1805, measured 1000 tons according to a contemporary report. If this report is correct she was an enormous merchant ship for those days. Several other ports launched ships ranging from 400 tons to the 661 ton *Manhattan* belonging to the Rhinelanders of New York. But for the most part, until some time after the war of 1812, the bulk of the American merchant marine was composed of vessels under rather than over 200 tons. Several of the largest craft were converted war vessels, frigates, etc., disposed of by the United States and individual States after the Revolution.

It is obvious that the report which has received wide circulation in recent years to the effect that when the *Manhattan* sailed she drained New York of its seamen, is an exaggeration. Her complement was 48 men, and several ships of peaceful intentions carried forty or more men, while numerous privateers sailing about that time carried many more than the *Manhattan*. As a matter of fact, the *Manhattan* was not the first merchantman of her size built in America. A ship of 700 tons was launched in the present town of Groton, Connecticut, as early as October, 1725. Shortly before the *Manhattan* was built, Newport had witnessed the launch of a ship only slightly smaller, the *Mount Hope* of 601 50/95 tons, mounting 14 carriage guns.

CHAPTER IV

THE EARLY FEDERALIST PERIOD

TOWARD the close of the eighteenth century, it was already evident to the casual observer that something unusual was afoot in Brother Jonathan's shipyards. His Majesty's ships, of whatever royal navy, were returning to port with strange tales of Yankee upstarts refusing to heave to for the most imperative signals. It was even reported that they trimmed their yards as they infernally pleased, and actually sailed away from the crack racers of the imperial navy, accompanying this act of defiance with insulting signals, performed with the most primitive instruments of mankind.

However this may be, after a temporary and expensive reversion to the traffic speed of Europe, American commerce suddenly began to hang up new and remarkable sailing records. By the time "Madison's war" was well under way, marks had been established which were to stand until bettered by the brief reign of the clipper.

On Sunday, the 26th of July, 1796, Captain George Crowninshield arrived at Salem "in the beautiful ship *Belisarius,* in the remarkable passage of 70 days from the Isle of France—having completed his voyage in seven months and a half." Joshua Humphrey, Jr., designer of the *Constitution* and other ships of the first American navy, states that the *Bellesarius* (sic) was "reconed one of the fastest sailing ships that swam the Sea's."

Among the many other excellent passages of this period, one of the earliest was that of the brig *Rose*, Captain Meany, which arrived at Philadelphia on the 8th of June, 1796, from the Isle of France, 68 days out. She had made the round voyage from her home port in 6 months and 19 days, including a lengthy stay at Mauritius. This voyage was little short of marvellous in that day, and would have been considered a good passage sixty years later for clipper ships five times her size.

As an indication of what it meant in 1796, it may be noted that before she left Port Louis the brig *Georgia Packet* arrived, 209 days, or nearly 7 months out from Philadelphia. On this voyage the *Rose* ran from the Cape of Good Hope to the Delaware in 43 days. More than forty years later, shipmasters were claiming longer voyages as records over this route.

In March, 1800, the well-known 700 ton ship *America*, under Captain Crowninshield, arrived in Boston 103 days from Calcutta, which established another record. Forty years later a passage of 104 days was claimed as the record, although in the interval, many faster runs than that of the *America* had been made and forgotten. Among them may be numbered that of the *Indus* commanded by Captain Chapman, which arrived in Boston on the 9th of April, 1801, only 96 days from Sand Heads.

The ship *Severn*, one of the Astor fleet, under the command of Captain Cowman, came ramping in by Sandy Hook on the 9th of March, 1805, 100 days from Canton, which seems to be the shortest passage that had ever been made. She had gone out and back in 9 months and 9 days, and brought back the news of her own arrival in Canton in the very good time of 118 days from New York. The *Severn* was built in New York, being one of a number of fast vessels built there prior to 1800, the period when New York began to take the lead over Philadelphia in the construction of fine ships.

Her run was not equalled for four years, when the *Asia*,

REEFING.

FROM PAINTING BY W. N. WILSON.

"Cœur de Lion."
Entering Boston.

ROUNDING CAPE HORN.

FROM PAINTING BY W. N. WILSON.

UPPER. CAPT. HENRY W. JOHNSON of the clipper *Invincible*.

LOWER. CAPT. ROBERT H. WATERMAN of the clippers *Sea Witch, Challenge,* etc.

UPPER. CAPT. OLIVER R. MUMFORD of the clipper *Tornado*. Courtesy of his niece, Mrs. A. C. Howland.

LOWER. CAPT. ARTHUR H. CLARK. Courtesy of the Peabody Museum, Salem, Mass.

Captain Williamson, arrived at Philadelphia on the 24th of March, 1808, in a passage of 100 days from Macao to the Delaware Capes, a record which was destined to stand until after the close of the war of 1812.

One day astern of the *Asia* came Girard's ship, the *Montesquieu,* commanded by Captain Wilson. She had made the excellent time of 86 days from Madras. Three days later the *Pekin,* under Captain Swain, took her pilot off Cape Henlopen, after a passage of 102 days from Calcutta.

Another ship which made excellent passages about this time was the *Oliver Ellsworth,* of New York. Under Captain Bennett she was said to have run from New York to Liverpool in 14 days during 1804, carrying away her main topmast on the trip. After a careful search a contemporary account of this voyage is lacking and we are unable to verify the report. It is quite possible that the passage was made as claimed, or the figures may refer to a run from New York to a point just outside Liverpool, where it was not uncommon for ships to be held up several days by unfavorable weather.

The record of the Philadelphia built and owned ship, *Rebecca Sims,* is likewise open to question. She was a ship measuring 400 15/95 tons, launched early in 1807 at the yard of Samuel Bowers. She is said to have taken her departure on the 10th of May, 1807, from Cape Henlopen and to have picked up her Liverpool pilot off the mouth of the Mersey on the 24th. If this run of 14 days can be substantiated, it would still stand as virtually equivalent to the record between the two ports.

Like her contemporary, the *Rousseau,* which rounded out 97 years of service afloat, the *Rebecca Sims* was a stout ship. Fifty-two years later Captain Charles P. Low, racing up the South Pacific bound for San Francisco in the clipper *N. B. Palmer,* entered in his log for the 3rd of September, 1853:

"At 6 P.M. was boarded by Captain Parsons of the whale ship Rebecca Sims of N. Bedford 35 months out; 1500 Bls. Sperm."

As a commentary on the early transatlantic trade it may be noted that the feat of the ship *Minerva*, Captain Turner, which landed her passengers in England 23 days from Boston in the Spring of 1796, was considered a very exceptional performance.

At this time nearly every port in America had its fast ships, a somewhat prevalent impression to the contrary notwithstanding. The statement that this or that locality was the original home of swift vessels stands on insecure foundations. It would seem to be nearer the truth that so long as the general demands of trade required smart sailing craft, virtually every master builder in the country was able to produce them.

Salem had her candidates. Witness the ship *Hazard*, Captain Burril, which arrived home on the 17th of January, 1805, only 64 days from Bourbon, near Mauritius.

There was the fast brig *Ida*, of Baltimore, commanded by Captain Pawson. She made the very remarkable run of 74 days from Batavia to Baltimore, arriving at the latter place on the 15th of October, 1806. Her round voyage occupied only seven and one-half months, of which 50 days were spent in port.

The ship *Fanny*, Captain Taylor, made the run from Greenock to New York in 23 days. Her arrival on the 29th of May, 1806, marked the completion of a 77 day voyage to Scotland and back—"a rate of dispatch said to be unequalled since the American War." The *Fanny* made many fast runs and did much to establish the reputation of Samuel Ackerly, her builder.

One frequently hears the remark that these early "fast" ships were not fast, but on the contrary were rather dull sailers. The point is well made if their speed is to be compared with that of the later clippers, but if it is measured by the performance of ordinary merchantmen, even the powerful ships at the end of the 19th century, they may well be regarded as fast.

The ship *Herald* referred to in the preceding chapter recorded a speed of 11 knots on several occasions, and in the New York *Commercial Advertiser* for December 26th, 1809, we find the following item:

"To decide a bet that the distance between the Battery and the Light-house at Sandy Hook could not be run by any vessel in one hour and a half, the pilot boat *New Thorn* started on Saturday last, and accomplished it in one hour and twenty minutes. The distance is universally admitted to be from twenty-one to twenty-two miles, and by the least calculation she must have sailed at the rate of sixteen miles an hour."

As a matter of fact the distance sailed was approximately 19 miles, and the vessel was undoubtedly assisted somewhat by an ebb tide, so that her speed through the water was probably under rather than over 13 knots.

The privateer schooner *Rollo*, of Bristol, R. I., commanded by James Dooley, noted in her log for the 29th of November, 1812, a speed of 12 knots, and entries of 9 or 10 knots are common.

Several years later the sloop *Juno* entered at New York March 24th, 1815, in 17 hours from Newport, and there are many similar performances recorded throughout the period. Not remarkable sailing, to be sure, but nevertheless rarely beaten by the crack yachts of a hundred years later.

As throwing additional light on this subject, the voyage of the ship *Anacreon*, Captain Fletcher, may be mentioned. During 1805–6, the *Anacreon* went from Newburyport to Virginia; thence to Cork and London; thence to the West coast of Florida; thence to Boston, and from there to the Cape of Good Hope and back to Newburyport, having been 262 days at sea. She averaged 144 miles for the first 200 days and 128 miles for the last 62 days. This was hailed in the papers of the time as "a remarkable passage." In other words, it was very exceptional then for a vessel to average six miles an hour over a period of several months and it remained exceptional down to the end of sailing ship days.

By 1801, if not earlier, the restless activity of the young Republic had brought out a new type of sailing craft; the three masted schooner, "the American three-masted schooner *Success*" being reported at Kingston, Jamaica, on March 3rd of that year, bound to St. Domingo. This development has frequently been ascribed to the period of 1850 by government documents and old sailors alike, but by 1804 the "nutmeg" state boasted a three masted schooner, the *Urania*, Captain Aldridge, hailing from Norwich, and by 1806 the three masted schooners *Nimrod*, *Orestes* and *United States* were in active service, occasionally making foreign voyages. The well known Captain Rosseter arrived at New York on the 28th of July, 1807, in the three masted schooner *Asenath*, 143 days from Canton with teas and nankeens, in time to see a little steamboat sometimes inaccurately called the *Clermont* puffing up and down the North River— the vessel referred to being registered under the name of the "North River Steamboat" of Clermont.

The smashing victory of Trafalgar late in 1805 might have been expected to result in curtailing the activities of both French and English against American shipping, but this was not the case. France had lost a large part of her battle fleet, but she continued to commission hosts of privateers, which lay just outside American ports, boarding every vessel they could overhaul and taking prizes almost under the guns of the forts. A British squadron lay off Sandy Hook, sending its tenders in pursuit of all vessels entering or leaving port, and many an exciting chase enlivened the day's work. Happy the master who had a fast ship under him and could report, as Bennett, of the *Oliver Ellsworth*, did on one occasion, that he had run a pursuing British war vessel "hull down in an hour and forty minutes" to the music of her bow-chasers.

Seized ships were condemned and sold whenever there appeared to be an excuse for so doing, under the elastic regulations prevailing. In general, legal resilience seems to have been nicely proportioned to the richness of the cargo involved. When, after costly delays, no excuse for forfeiture could be found, it frequently happened that a looted vessel was returned to her captain subject to the payment of a substantial sum "for heating the poker."

As time went on and the European conflict became more bitter, America's confusion increased. During 1807 Burr's case was dragging its tense coils through court and press. The country was becoming more and more sharply divided into the rival camps of French and British sympathizers. In December Congress adopted its first prohibitory measure under the title of the "Embargo Act"—a piece of legislation which seems to have excited remarkably little enthusiasm among historians.

With few exceptions it forbade American ships to leave port except for coastwise voyages and made it unlawful for foreign ships to take on cargo in the United States. The object was to save our ships and their crews from capture and to force both England and France to respect our rights by cutting off supplies of food and material. The American Government was thus added to the foes of the hard pressed merchant service. Nor was the situation materially improved when the Embargo Act was repealed in 1809 and the Non-Intercourse Act substituted, which forbade trade with France and England only. Our merchants and mariners were not of the kind to sit down idly and submit to fate. They had been accustomed to "illegal" trade in their early youth, and they met the new situation by lengthening stuns'l booms and gunter poles and dodging the half hearted United States forces along with the rest.

The act outlawing the slave trade in 1808 furnished another source of demand for fast vessels, and for another half century ships continued to be fitted out and financed in this trade by many a respectable citizen in the majority of American ports. Newspapers of the fifties contain occasional references to the number of ships sailing from the various cities in this traffic. One account stated that as late as 1859 there were seven slavers regularly fitted out in New York, and many more in all the larger ports.

While such conditions prevailed, it is evident there could be no intermission in the attempt to produce faster ships. As lines were fined out and spars lengthened there was many a new record hung up. That of the brig *Fox,* of 225 tons, is perhaps the most notable of the entire period. She was built by Henry Eckford in New York, and performed the very remarkable feat of running from Calcutta to New York in 90 days, arriving home on the 26th of December, 1809. To fully appreciate what this meant, one need only recall that the record for all time is the 81 day passage of the extreme clipper, *Witch-of-the-Wave,* a craft of five times her tonnage. Moreover, the *Fox* had established a new mark for the round voyage, having been absent from New York only 7 months and 14 days. It has been stated that Captain Cannon, "the King of captains," commanded her, and Augustus De Peyster, later a well-known packet master and long the Governor of the Sailors Snug Harbor, was her second officer, but in contemporary reports Cowman is mentioned as master.

Another experimental craft designed about this time by Christian Bergh was less fortunate. This was the brig *Gipsey.* She was built during 1809 for General Stevens, one of the forward-looking men of the day. The *Gipsey* was a vessel of about 300 tons, and so sharp that she could not carry her register.

In the absence of any precise data, it seems probable that in her design the principle of the convex bow was abandoned, without, however, perceiving the necessity of moving her spars sufficiently far aft to relieve the pressure of canvas forward. At all events, on a voyage to the Orient in 1810, under command of Captain Main, while scudding before a heavy gale, she ran under, drowning half her crew and carrying away her masts and bowsprit by the board, eventually reaching Manila, where permanent repairs were made. Later, rigged as a schooner, she was reported lost with all hands in a squall off the coast of France, while attempting to escape from a British blockader.

A very fine run of 33 days from New York to Rio Janeiro was made just prior to the war of 1812 by a fast sailing ship, *Eugene,* which arrived at her destination on the 5th of February,

1812. Although similar or better passages may have been made before that time, the writer has been unable to find any recorded.

The predecessors of the packet ships—the "regular traders"— were invariably modelled and rigged for speed. Among these was the ship *Alert*, of Boston. Under the command of Captain Nichols she arrived in Boston during April, 1811, "in the extraordinary short passage of 20 days from Liverpool." This feat was somewhat overshadowed by the arrival at Philadelphia a few days before of the brig *Osmin*, Captain Whelden, in 19 days from Rochelle. Both passages, however, appear to establish new records for their respective ports.

Another very fast vessel was the ship *Milo* of 397 tons, built at Newburyport in 1811. Under Captain Glover, who supervised her construction, she made many excellent voyages, and was said to have gone from Boston to Liverpool on one occasion in 15 days. As in the case of the *Oliver Ellsworth*, I have been unable to find this run in contemporary reports, but the fact is by no means conclusive that the run was not made, for early records are fragmentary and she was a very fast ship. In February, 1812, she arrived in Liverpool in 18 days from Boston. As late as 1829, she averaged approximately 8 miles an hour for nine successive days, covering 42 degrees of easting on a voyage from Boston to Hamburg. At times, of course, she must have greatly exceeded her average rate.

On the Canton run passages slightly in excess of 100 days were becoming more common. In the Spring of 1811, the ship *Atahualpa*, commanded by Captain Bacon, made the passage in 106 days, and about this time other vessels reported equally good or better runs. The *Atahualpa* still followed the Cape Horn and Northwest coast route to China—a run which demanded good sailors and hard fighters, and got them. They were no tinselled mannikins, these men of the old breed.

The year 1812 saw the westward Atlantic record lowered another day, when the *Lady Madison*, Captain Swaine, arrived at New York on the 4th of April "in the unprecedented time of

18 days." She was on the Grand Banks in 9 days. This passage does not appear to have been equalled again during the next seven years.

Many another fine run might be cited. Enough has been said, however, to indicate that during the Federalist period a higher degree of speed and all-around efficiency was attained than had ever been known before. They were not large ships which made these records that would do credit to the sailing craft of any day and age. Few of them measured over three hundred tons. All of them, in spite of widely differing features, and irrespective of their place of construction, belonged to the general type known later as the Baltimore clipper. In the North they were described merely as "fast-sailing" ships and were usually "pilot boat built"; *i.e.*, of the flush deck type, more of which in another place.

In general, the fast vessels carried much larger crews than ordinary merchantmen of the same tonnage. Thus a sharp ship of 300 tons would have from 20 to 26 men before the mast, while a full-built vessel of equal size was handled by 12 or 14 men at most. Wherever available, therefore, the crew lists of the period throw considerable light on the sailing qualities of merchant ships.

CHAPTER V

FAST SHIPS AND THE WAR OF 1812

IT has been said that the phrase "clipper ship" made its appearance during the war of 1812. The writer has been unable to discover any instance of its use in newspapers prior to 1835, but its appearance in works of fiction and books on travel indicate that it was a common expression at this time. Whatever its early history, there can be little doubt that originally it was a mere slang expression. As such, it may well have been one of many nautical colloquialisms which were in vogue for years before they attained sufficient currency to attract the attention of the press. War conditions are proverbially favorable to popularizing such expressions and giving them a definite meaning.

One would hardly expect to find a phrase of this sort rigidly applied at the outset, either to a definite class of vessels or to the productions of a special locality. There can be very little doubt, for example, that the men of the privateer *America*, with her lofty spars and remarkable speed, frequently asserted that she was the contemporary equivalent of a "clipper," with all the necessary qualifying adjectives. The mere fact that such expressions as "Baltimore clipper" were developed favors the assumption that it was originally convenient to distinguish one class of clippers from another. Even today the word is loosely applied to a wide variety of sailing craft.

But for a time, embracing roughly the period from 1845 to 1860, the phrase had a very definite meaning in the minds of deep-water sailors and dignified merchants alike. To be called a "clipper ship" was the highest honor that could be bestowed on a vessel. It was only to the thoroughbred racer of the seas they applied the term.

> "Clean, long, smooth as a smelt. Sharp arching head. Thin, hollow bow; convex sides; light, round and graceful stern. A genuine East Indiaman or Californian. Aloft, large built, iron-banded lower masts; taunt tapering smaller masts, long-proportioned spars from lower to skysail yards. Above board, she towers up with strong, fibrous arms spreading a cloud of canvas to the gale."

This was what the mariner of the fifties had in mind when he spoke of clippers. In the course of time there came to be a confusion between such ships, built primarily for speed, and the so-called "clippers" which followed them. These later ships were fine, heavily-sparred craft. Some of them were remarkably handsome, but they were relatively burdensome, carried much less canvas in proportion to their tonnage, and lacked the extraordinary turn of speed of the genuine clipper of the fifties.

It is evident, that the name has little value unless its meaning is definitely fixed. For the purposes of this account, it may be assumed that when the term clipper is applied to a ship, that ship is supposed to have possessed two prime essentials. First she was "sharp built"—designed as to hull for speed rather than cargo space—and in the second place, she was extremely heavily sparred, in order to spread a far larger area of canvas than ships of equal size were accustomed to spread.

And there was a third essential, without which the other two were of little use. Her captain must be a "driver." The soul of the clipper was her master. Unless she were commanded by a "horse"—a thorough dare-devil with a mania for speed, who left nothing undone to strengthen his rig and extend his spread of canvas, and then hung on until spars began to go and the head knees cracked, the finest ship that ever floated was a beautiful fabric and nothing more.

There are varying degrees of sharpness and varying proportions of sail and tonnage, and somewhere between sharp and full and heavy spars and light, there is a dividing line between the ship that is a clipper and one that is not. Unfortunately, there is no satisfactory way to fix such a line. Some of the old log books furnish evidence that at times the very master of a ship was in doubt whether to rate her as a clipper or not.

During the late fifties vessels which had any pretensions to clipperly qualities and many which had none, were classified roughly as "extreme" clippers, and medium or half-clippers. Admitting that many of the vessels listed as medium clippers properly belonged with the less pretentious ordinary merchantman, it seems, nevertheless, that this general method of classification is more satisfactory than any other, and an attempt will be made to use it wherever such a course seems likely to be of value.

The question of the invention or origin of the clipper ship is closely connected with the question of the origin of the name. The name preceded the thing itself, as we now know it. Numerous accounts of the development of the clipper ship have been put forward, none of which are wholly satisfactory. The truth seems to be that its origin—like the definition of philosophy—can be explained satisfactorily only by outlining its history. Any attempt to treat it as the creation of some tough-handed genius of the sea, or as the legitimate off-spring of an earlier fast-sailing type, falls of its own weight.

One may regret the loss of the dramatic element, but the perfected clipper ship of the eighteen-fifties appears to owe to the mysterious 18th century draftsman and to earlier fast sailing models—Mediterranean felucca, Singapore "fast boat" or what not—precisely what it owes to the frankly clump-built craft of an earlier day, and no more. Each in turn served, where it served at all, as the temporary basis of an experiment. And, in turn, the characteristic features of each were not merely modified, but were actually discarded and something different in principle incorporated in a long succession of models. In the end, the fastest sailing ships the world has ever seen were evolved, but in the final result every important theory of naval design which had prevailed up to 1830 and later was either scrapped completely or put to uses which its originators could not possibly have pre-visioned.

Take, for example, the French frigate, since this design is frequently mentioned as the inspiration of the Yankee clipper. The essential features were a rounding bow; a long and frequently hollow run; very great dead-rise; the greatest beam well forward of amidships, and by far the greatest depth of hull at the stern.

The American clipper ship in its final and most efficient form had eliminated every one of these features. Its bow was long and sharp, sometimes hollow but never rounding. The run was clean but full and comparatively short; while the sharp dead-rise was replaced by a relatively flat floor which would have been deemed fatal to the sailing qualities of a frigate. The greatest breadth was moved to a point almost exactly amid-ships, and in some cases slightly farther aft. The corresponding proportions of bow and stern had been transposed so that the depth of hull at the bow was now much greater than at the stern. In fact, the changes which had taken place would have been described more accurately as a reversal, rather than a modification of previous theories.

An inspection of the model of the *Lightning*, to cite an extreme instance, shows that her underbody would have resembled that of a fast French frigate far more closely if it had been turned end for end, and the bow placed where the stern was intended to be. Even the lines of the more typical clippers, such as the *Sovereign of the Seas, Red Jacket, Belle of the West* and others reproduced herein indicate a complete departure from the frigate principles. The essential features of the frigate type combined to produce a form which, under no conceivable conditions, could have been forced through the water at a speed greatly exceeding 14 knots.

American privateers of the Napoleonic period have a fairly consistent record of outsailing and outmaneuvering both French and English craft of the same class, yet an examination of a number of their logs fails to reveal a single instance where a speed greater than 13 knots was developed.

On the 3rd of January, 1813, the privateer *America*, built at Salem in 1804, Joseph Ropes, master, recorded 13 knots for two consecutive hours, which is the fastest rate mentioned in any of her available logs. The *America* was not only sharp built but, in proportion to her size, 331 tons, as altered for a privateer by the removal of her upper deck, she probably spread as much canvas at that time as any ship ever sent to sea.

At the outset of a later cruise the clerk of the *America* notes in his log for Wednesday, the 2nd of November, 1814:

"Com^s this 24 Hours with a plesant Breeze and cloudy. At 1 (PM) the pilot come on board. Orders was given to git the Ship underway, hove up our Larboard anchor and stowed him on the Gunnel, slip our starboard Cable and proceeded to sea."

The best speed recorded during the ensuing cruise was 12 knots on the 17th of March, 1815, after attaining which they were forced to "hand the Ryalls."

Among other smart craft of the 1812 period the *Fame*, of Salem, occasionally made 11 knots; the *Herald* and *Glide*, both noted ships, a similar rate, and the frigate *Essex* a speed slightly in excess of 12 knots. In view of this performance of the *Essex* her later reputation for dullness must have been established under exceptionally unfavorable circumstances. The *Constitution* has been credited with 13½ knots, but the date and circumstances of this performance are not available. During a cruise in 1815 the sloop-of-war *Wasp* never attained a speed much in excess of 10 knots, although there is little doubt she was capable of more. All these performances, it is to be noted, were recorded at a time when the ships were very heavily sparred and manned.

This is not to say that ships did not sail faster, but if they did the occasions must have been extremely rare, and the margin of superiority minute. During a voyage across the Atlantic just before her capture off Tripoli, the frigate *Philadelphia* is said to have made the unprecedented run of 337 miles in 24 hours—a rate just exceeding 14 knots. In all probability her speed through the water was somewhat less, since vessels going to the eastward were usually helped by favoring currents and long, following seas, but even so this run is not approached by any other early craft so far as the writer is aware. Since the *Philadelphia's* log was probably lost when she was taken by the Moors and at all events is not now available, this record cannot now be officially verified, but the report is no doubt substantially correct.

The *Philadelphia*, designed by Joshua Humphreys, the designer of the *Constitution* and the four other frigates of the United States Navy built just prior to 1800, was launched in 1799, near Philadelphia. She was similar to the *Constitution* in size and general appearance. Her length was slightly less but she was narrow and shallow in proportion, and her lines were finer. From this and other evidence (admittedly circumstantial) the writer is inclined to think that she is entitled to the rating claimed for her as the fastest ship of her day.

Granting to vessels of this type the rare speed of 14 knots, it is obvious that between ships limited to a maximum of 14 knots, and that at an inordinate sacrifice of cargo space, and those capable of 18, 19 and even 21 knots with ample stowage room, there is a gulf which no mere refinement of modelling can pass. This being so, one may well ask what the American designer owed earlier draughtsmen, except the presentation of models to be avoided.

It is true that many of the earlier clippers did show a tendency to revert to characteristics of the old frigate. There were two fairly distinct classes of clipper ships in the beginning. Among the vessels which in part embodied older theories were many fine, able craft, which made excellent passages but never—even after making due allowance for size—developed the extreme speed of the perfected type of the fifties. The *Sea Witch* is the classic example of this early type, but there does not appear to be any record of her having exceeded a speed of 15 knots, although she was marvellously fast under general sailing conditions, and was undoubtedly the fastest merchantman afloat when launched. All ships with the excessive dead-rise and long hollow run of this class showed a decided tendency to bury when driven, and consequently never attained the extreme swiftness of the later type, while in all around efficiency they were at a great disadvantage. Nevertheless, some of the daintiest models that ever floated are to be found among the first clippers, and occasionally, as in the case of the *Hurricane,* a happy combination of the early and later theories produced remarkably fast ships, at, however, a considerable sacrifice of cargo space.

An ingenious variant of the theory which credits the French with the invention of the clipper ship, suggests that after receiving Gallic instruction during the Revolution the Americans outstripped their teachers. Thereafter, following the war of 1812 (it is asserted), the French took the improved American models and again developed them to a point approximating clipper ship perfection.

Part of this statement is true. The French undoubtedly did experiment with ship models of American, and particularly Baltimore origin, after the 1812 War (see, *e.g.* report of M. Marestier on the Baltimore clipper, Paris, 1824), but that their experiments had any material effect on the evolution of the American clipper ship, is open to serious doubt. The French theory errs by seeking to prove too much. Not only do we fail at all times to find French ships that are superior in sailing qualities to existing American vessels, but a step by step examination of the history of American shipbuilding discloses the fact that explanations of this character are not merely superfluous, but that it is only with the greatest difficulty they can be fitted in to an orderly account of the industry.

Anticipating somewhat, the course of this narrative, it seems fair to describe the development of the American clipper as evolutionary rather than revolutionary in character. Accordingly, the postulation of a vaguely defined foreign genius to explain its major achievement, bears certain marks of kinship with the familiar primitive hypothesis that the earth was supported by a huge tortoise standing on a rock. Briefly, it may be said that if French ships were built at any period from 1782 to 1860, which outsailed existing American craft, a careful search of contemporary records has failed to disclose their identity to the writer.

Other claims for the credit of originating the clipper ship might be considered, but as already intimated, more satisfactory results will be attained by examining the history of the American merchant marine. One searches in vain for some heroic, outstanding figure as the "inventor" of the clipper and misses the thrill of being able to point to some beautiful vessel and say: "Here is the first true example." There seems to have been no "first clipper ship." Model shaded imperceptibly into model: new "improved rig" followed old "improved rig" until men felt it could serve no useful purpose to attempt to gain a further increase in speed. Somewhere between the first uncertain steps and the last glorious creation is the "first clipper."

Even the honored tradition that Baltimore was first to build small "clipper" craft is not a simple matter to maintain. There can be no doubt that Baltimore craftsmen won, and for many years worthily upheld a reputation for designing the fastest brigs and schooners afloat. In this respect, however, they appear to have reached the zenith of their fame during the third decade of the 19th century rather than earlier, during the Federalist period. We have already noticed that vessels ranking with the fastest afloat were being built everywhere along the Atlantic coast in the closing years of the eighteenth century. If, there-

CLIPPER SHIP "CHALLENGE."

FROM PAINTING BY GORDON GRANT.

Courtesy of Howard Young Galleries.

CLIPPER SHIP "RAINBOW."
FROM PAINTING BY CHARLES R. PATTERSON.
Courtesy of Roswell Parish, Jr.

fore, a claim for priority is to be maintained by any locality, the proponent must be fortified by a microscopic search of the records prior to 1790 and possibly far back into colonial times.

Fortunately one can speak with certainty regarding the type of these early fast vessels. By 1800, if not earlier, their general lines were fixed and though modifications and refinements were introduced from time to time there was no variation in principle between the small clippers of that day and the pilot boats of 1850. The yacht *America*, to mention a well known example, differed from them only in having her point of greatest beam moved farther aft. Whether we are considering the northern "Pilot boat built" brig or schooner or the Baltimore clipper, we are dealing with the same design. All these vessels had the easy lines, long bow and deep drag aft which is associated with the Baltimore clipper. As a rule they drew from two to four feet more aft than forward. In large craft the difference might occasionally be greater. All were closely akin to the fast French naval vessels, of 1776 and thereabouts, a fact which provides no answer to the question whether the type followed or preceded the French craft.

The fast armed topsail schooners of the 1812 war were fine examples of this design. Armed with from ten to sixteen guns they performed for the navy much the same functions that the destroyer performs today. They were sparred to the limit of safety, sometimes carrying a standing fore royal yard and a long coach whip stick of a main topmast. They sailed mostly under water and their officers were as choice a collection of reckless youngsters as the navy afforded. Perhaps not as particular as their successors to "bend a clean shirt every day," but equally at home chasing "pirates, slavers and other vigrom men," or "in the lee of a can of the right stuff." A wonderful service. It lasted as long as ships were stationed off the slave coast.

For all practical purposes, the close of the war of 1812 terminated the construction of this type of merchantman in northern waters. It was a natural result of changed conditions. With the signing of the peace, privateering, impressment and embargoes were believed to be things of the past—gone with other picturesque but unpleasant institutions to join the relics of barbarism. Henceforth, broadly speaking, speed was to be balanced with carrying capacity in the design of ships.

There remained certain limited fields in which the demand for speed outweighed all other considerations. Among these were the now outlawed slave trade; the market for fast craft suitable for war ships, particularly in South American waters, and light, smart merchantmen for use in the fitful airs of the tropics in the coffee and fruit trades.

Partly by virtue of her position as the largest shipbuilding center near the tropics, and partly because of the character of her trade, Baltimore continued to produce clipper schooners and brigs long after other places had ceased to build them, aside from an occasional pilot boat or yacht. There can be little doubt that the model served her needs admirably, while for the most part, it would have been unsuited to the requirements of northern commerce. For many years she was regarded as the clipper port of America.

At the same time, it should be noted that Baltimore vessels, generally, did not differ in size or quality from those of other important shipbuilding centers. There is a somewhat prevalent impression that she turned out only small craft. This is not the case. Throughout the entire era of wooden ships, Baltimore kept fairly even pace with other ports. When New York and Philadelphia launched 400 ton ships, she met the challenge, and when, after the War of 1812, New York built 500 ton packets, Baltimore responded with the 529 ton *Superb* in 1818 and others only slightly smaller. During the thirties she built such ships as the *Leila*, of 613 tons, and *The Sea*, of 807 tons. Very few American built ships larger than the latter were afloat at the time.

CHAPTER VI

THE speed of ordinary as opposed to fast-sailing 18th century merchantmen was a wallowing maximum of five or six knots. As competent an authority as Lieutenant Maury stated that during that period the average rate of a British merchantman on a long voyage did not exceed two or three knots. On the rare occasions when five knots was attained the fact was specially noted in the log. Well into the 19th century, even, their progress much resembled that of a certain appropriately named ship *Globe* which "would beat her head three times against a billow and then fall off and sail around it."

Two centuries of exploitation, however justified by European statesmen, had left its mark on America. The close of the War of 1812 found the Yankee mariner with a respect for speed that amounted to reverence. For as many years as they could remember, several thousand men had regarded swift ships as synonymous with life, liberty and the pursuit of happiness. During the three years of naval warfare some fifty thousand more, from first hand contact with the hazards of the sea, had become so convinced of the superior virtue of speed, either in pursuit or flight, as to become worshippers at its shrine.

With the close of the war, the stage was set for a new and

important development. Notwithstanding the three years of conflict and the preceding twenty years of legalized and illegal robbery to which the merchant marine had been subjected, there had been a substantial increase in the wealth of the United States. Yesterday's pioneers were becoming habituated to the comforts and even the luxuries of life. By 1815 the fortunes of many of the country's leading families had been placed on substantial foundations. It was obvious they would not long endure the risks and discomforts of the antiquated method of ocean transportation.

Moreover the hinterland was opening up. Not only from coastal towns but from the interior as well, were coming new demands for finer goods and greater luxuries than ever before. Remarkably fast river steamers were being built to whet the appetite for speed. New York had a dozen or so, ranging up to 399 tons and more. There was a growing desire on the part of the American public to travel; to see continental battlefields, cities, cathedrals and markets; to study abroad and to establish new contacts of trade. Conversely, there was evidence of a gathering of the forces in Europe for a renewal of the tide of emigration westward—a tide which was to swell year by year, to culminate finally in the tremendous rush of '48.

To meet the situation the merchant marine of 1815 had few vessels measuring 400 tons; the majority fell far below this mark. Such larger ships as there were, for the most part were full-built, slow-sailing craft designed for freight and not for passenger traffic. The fast-sailing ships were not only small but their cabins were mere closets, dingy, ill ventilated and uncomfortable beyond description. Many of them were so sharp that they were able to stow little cargo, and their between decks so low (less than five feet in height, usually) as to be unsuitable for steerage quarters. Steerage ventilation was unheard of. The size and character of the regular trading ships had changed very little since the close of the Revolution. With slight alteration the advertisement of the ship *Liberty*, burthen 350 tons, which was appearing in the New York *Gazette* during 1783, would describe the majority of packets at the close of 1818.

> "She has a spacious cabin of six feet in height, with excellent accommodation for passengers, also five feet in height between decks, which will be commodiously fitted up for such passengers as may wish to go at an easy rate."

Bad as these vessels were, they seem to have been superior to the British and French "packets"—so called from the fact they were regularly selected to carry the monthly or periodical packets of mail, papers as well as letters being included. The monthly packet service from England was perhaps most unsatisfactory of all. Not only were the British vessels small, but they touched either at Bermuda or Halifax going in either direction, thus greatly prolonging the voyage. A crossing to the westward on these ships usually occupied more than two months and might require 90 days, but in spite of the superior service of the better class of American vessels it was soon apparent they were not good enough.

As in critical periods of the 18th century, merchants and master builders again began to take counsel among themselves. It must have been clear to them that the possibilities of speed design along recognized lines had been nearly, if not quite, exhausted. For more than a score of years they had built ship after ship to get still another fraction of a knot. Models made prior to 1812 are still in existence to prove that every consideration of comfort and capacity had been sacrificed to sailing qualities. During the war their efforts had been redoubled. They had drawn upon every possible resource their ingenuity could devise to improve upon previous attempts. Ships were built with finer lines and rigged with loftier spars than ever before and sailed to the limits of recklessness—and beyond. It seemed as though human skill could go no farther in the direction of speed, and now the demand was not merely for faster travel, but for greater comfort and cargo space.

There was then as always a very considerable trade in which the question of dispatch played no part in time of peace. With the arrival of a condition approaching equilibrium throughout the world, speed retired from the field of "enemy insurance" and was relegated to its proper place in the department of economics. Certain commodities, such as oriental luxuries and valuable South American products could afford to pay a premium for rapid transportation, but by far the greater number could not. The majority of new ships were accordingly designed to evade, so far as possible, the artificial and stupid tonnage laws then in force throughout the world. They were intended to carry two tons of merchandise while paying dues on one. As a result, the bulk of the American marine gradually became floating monstrosities—great, wall-sided craft that could sail little better than the merchantman of a hundred years before—fitting monuments to the smug legislators responsible for their being.

The "kettle-bottoms" and their ilk, however, had no effect on the progress of shipbuilding except to retard it and, incidentally, by their general inefficiency, to cost the world untold millions during the years they were in service. Such progress as was made in naval design took place only in the trades where conditions enabled merchants to disregard legislative restrictions, that is, where speed and all-around efficiency were at a premium.

These conditions had always prevailed in the China trade, where the cargoes were not only of immense value and large profits awaited the owners of the first ships home, but where also speed was good pirate insurance. It remained for a small group of clear-sighted, straight-thinking New Yorkers to decide, in 1817, that for very different reasons a similar condition prevailed, or would shortly prevail in the transatlantic passenger traffic. The result was the establishment of the first "Line" of regular sailing packet ships between the United States and Europe. This was the famous "Black Ball Line" running between New York and Liverpool. It was founded by Isaac Wright & Son, Francis Thompson, Jeremiah Thompson and Benjamin Marshall.

This movement, more than any other in our history, brought fame and prosperity to the entire United States.

The various accounts of the inception of this service abound in inaccuracies. Even the newspaper sketches of the forties, compiled from memory while most of the original actors were still living and many of them still engaged in sailing or operating packet ships, are misleading in important particulars. For this reason it seems advisable to review as briefly as possible the principle facts regarding the early years of the world's first "ocean liners."

Among the impressions which have survived is the belief that the line was founded in 1816, and that it was composed of specially built ships, considerably larger than other vessels in the packet service, and superior to them in appointments. This is not the case. The first "regular sailing" packet ship did not leave New York until January 5th, 1818 (the corresponding ship sailing from Liverpool on the first of January), and the line was composed of ships none of which measured 400 tons, and all of which had been constructed and were in the transatlantic trade long before the line was established.

Of the four ships composing the original "Black Ball Line" the *Pacific*, of 384 tons, had been built prior to the War of 1812. Before 1811 she was being operated as a "regular trader" between New York and Liverpool by Isaac Wright and Francis Thompson. As soon as the war was over she again sailed for Liverpool under Captain William Bowne, on the 27th of March, 1815. She was, therefore, only a few days behind the fast sailing *Milo*, still under Captain Glover, which left Boston March 12th and was the first ship to sail for and return from England after the close of the war.

It is worthy of note that for several years thereafter both Isaac Wright & Son and Francis Thompson were conducting separate and apparently competitive operations, sometimes sending British as well as American ships to Liverpool. The first expansion in their joint business came with the addition of the new ship *Amity*, of 382 tons burthen, which first sailed in May, 1816, under the command of John Stanton, sometimes referred to as the "commodore" of the packet service. In 1817, the new ship *Courier* was added, sailing for Liverpool on the 15th of May under Captaine Bowne, Captain John Williams taking the old *Pacific*. The firm now had three ships of substantially the same size, and was ready for its great experiment.

On Friday, October 24th, 1817, the *Commercial Advertiser* of New York, carried the first advertisement of the proposed first "regular sailing" line of packet ships between the new and the old world, to begin operations in January, 1818.

This advertisement, with suitable variations to record the advent of new ships, changes in sailings, etc., appeared almost continuously in New York papers for several years. Its initial publication produced the usual head shaking among the practical old fellows along South and Front Streets, but it also seems to have produced a very different effect on the minds of at least two New Yorkers, for the next day the names of Benjamin Marshall and Jeremiah Thompson were added to those of Isaac Wright & Son and Francis Thompson, the original signers of the notice. A little later the fourth ship of the line, the *James Monroe*, was placed under the command of James Watkinson. All four vessels were built in New York.

The "Black Ball Line" differed from other packet fleets in one particular only—whereas none of the others had a definite date of sailing, but left port when they were loaded and had obtained a quota of passengers, and frequently went to other ports to complete loading, the new line undertook to sail direct from New York on a fixed day of the month, irrespective of cargo or passengers. In no other respect did they furnish better accommodations or superior service. There were in fact several other packet ships then in the Liverpool trade larger and more comfortable than the original Black Ballers. Among these were the *Ontario*, of 523 tons, and the *Nestor*, of 481 tons.

On the whole, however, the vessels of the new line were somewhat above the average in size. They were faster than the majority of the ships then on the run (Captain James Rogers, retired and living in Jersey City in 1851, was accustomed to say that the little *Pacific* would be considered fast among clippers), and it was unquestionably an advantage to both shippers and travellers to be able to depend on a definite sailing date.

CHAPTER VII

THE "RAILROAD ROUTE" TO EUROPE

ASIDE from the question of historical accuracy, the career of the packet ships is worth following in some detail, both for the remarkable records made by the vessels themselves, and for the reason that the type of ship eventually developed in that service appears to be the immediate ancestor of the clipper ship. It is true that the earliest craft to be generally acclaimed as clippers, with the exception of the *Ann McKim* and several other early Baltimore vessels, were built primarily for the China trade; but it is equally true that they derived their chief inspiration indirectly from the later packets, which by that time had sloughed off most of the early frigate influence.

But this is anticipating. Long, weary years of experiment and hardship were to intervene between the sailing of the first Black Ball liner in 1818 and that day in the forties, when the first beautiful creation "every inch a clipper" took the water.

After the war of 1812, America stood like a young cockerel in the pride of her second "victory" over England—a victory, by the way, that was undiluted glory for top-men afloat and parlously near a sound thrashing for buck privates ashore. Victory or drawn battle (according to one's point of view), it had nevertheless whipped up the confidence of Jonathan's sea-going population to a point where they believed they could out-fight and outsail the whole hide-bound, precedent-ridden, slow-motioned creation.

As a philosophy, the belief had its faults, but it had the advantage of simplicity. It could be grasped in a moment by all but the most stupid and even to those it could be taught quickly by judicious use of belaying pin or sea boot. The American merchant marine of the second quarter of the 19th century was probably the hardest school the world has ever seen. And of all divisions of this school, until the advent of the clippers, none could compare with the old packets. They were driven to the extreme of safety at all times. They carried sail until it was worth a man's life to go aloft. Liner after liner came in to report men lost off the yards, reefing and furling—not helpless greenhorns, but hard-salted, cat-like sailors, as much at home handing a split topsail as a "monkey in the mizen rigging." Speed meant not only money for owners and fame and future patronage for the ship, but it was the all important factor in keeping out foreign competition.

Year after year, therefore, the lofty, massive-timbered craft drove back and forth across the Atlantic—nerve-shattering, record-breaking runs. "Reef and turn 'em out." The "old man" who got his thirty dollars a month (with perquisites) and was, not infrequently, a youngster in his later twenties, paced the quarter or dozed alternately in his lashed armchair the entire passage. Mates bellowing: clamoring, cursing men clawing canvas in freezing winter gales or white summer squalls: there was never the slightest relaxation from the moment the anchor rose to the tuneful strains of "Sally Brown" until the hilarious bellow "Leave 'er, Johnny," shattered the morning stillness of the East River or the Mersey. Every nerve was strained to get the utmost ounce out of spars and canvas. Everywhere the same note of competent self-reliance in the most desperate situations.

Marine columns of the thirties and forties contain scores of reports of ships dismasted and leaking, but refusing every offer of assistance. When Captain Hawkins of the ship *Hercules* of Saco, spoken on the 26th of February, 1810, with rudder and sails gone, shouted his determination to stay with her "as long as there was a timberhead of her left," he was doing the normal, not the exceptional thing. So long as a packet master could salvage enough from the wreckage of his spars for any kind of a jury rig, he would patch things up somehow. Trouble at sea meant not merely hard work and exposure: it meant driving exhausted frames to the last gasp of endurance. More than one log records the deaths of hardy mates and men from "over-work."

Thirty years of this man-killing drive, which none but the strongest and most active could survive, and then, when the clippers came in the late forties, there were men to sail them as ships have never been sailed before or since.

It took a hundred years to build the clippers. It took a generation of undiluted hell to develop the men to sail them. Out of the storm and stress and terrible drive came the fine gold of the sea—quiet-spoken, self-possessed men, under whose un-ruffled surface played panther sinews and whip-cord muscles, and in whose hearts the thought of fear had never wakened—men who, by sheer vital force could cow a score of the most desperate characters that ever wasted good salt horse. Such were the men who sailed the clipper ships, although not all clipper captains were packet ship men. Some came from independent "regular traders." Some had spent most if not all their time on long foreign voyages in the Canton and East India trades. Here again, speed was a prime consideration, and the seamanship was of the highest order; and as practical navigators, the officers developed in this service were possibly superior to any in the world of their day.

Whirling, biting snow ushered in that long ago morning of the 5th of January, 1818, which was to witness the sailing of the first "ocean liner." About the little *James Monroe,* Captain

James Watkinson, at the steamboat wharf in New York, there was the bustle and din of the thousand and one last minute errands. The eight important cabin passengers eager to share in this lively experiment, were arriving and pridefully inspecting their tiny quarters. Astute owners and even more astute subordinates were busy on the scene. The ever present onlookers were gathering by tens and hundreds. Predictions were freely made that she would not sail on schedule. No packet ever had.

As sights go, it was a modest spectacle. The *Monroe* was a ship of less than 400 tons—a trim looking, well-sparred craft measuring approximately one hundred feet from knightheads to taffrail. Yet, spick and span in new paint and snowy canvas, to the eye of the New Yorker she appeared to be and was, in fact and phrase, a "floating palace." And "floating palaces" each succeeding "liner" continued to be in newsprint and after-dinner oratory to the present day.

Finally all was in readiness. The letter bag—tiny ancestor of the mail sack—from the "T. C." (Tonine Coffee) House had long been aboard. The last belated and overstimulated passenger had stumbled his erratic way down the wharf, attended by amiable and luggage laden friends. The tide was at the turn. Shirt-sleeved sailors jumped aloft in the brisk air to cast off the gaskets. Topsails were mastheaded to a stamping chorus: the lines hauled in, and the *Monroe* slid out beyond the pier-head amid the cheers of passengers and spectators. The fore topmast stay-sail was hoisted smartly and the sheet hauled to windward. As her bow paid slowly off toward Bedloes, the yards were swung and the guns rang out a parting salute. The first "liner" had sailed.

Down the bay she drove, booming past "Captain" Vanderbilt's "ferry," slowly beating up against the tide. By four o'clock she had crossed the bar. Already, in the gloom men were laying out on the yardarms, running out steering sail poles. Blow high or low, they were there to drive that packet. Far beneath, on deck, Messrs. Daniel Fisher, of Montreal; Hugh McNeil, of

Kentucky; A. Spooner, of Boston, and the rest of the eight cabin passengers, experiencing the first qualms of a sensation commonly supposed to be reserved for the humble steerage, found the experiment considerably livelier than they had bargained for.

Another innovation of far-reaching consequences was inaugurated at almost the same moment when the little steamer *Nautilus* began operations as the first commercial tow-boat in America, bringing in-coming packets up from Sandy Hook.

During the summer of 1820, the Black Ball Line acquired its first large vessel, "the superior coppered ship *Nestor*," of 481 tons, built at New York in 1815 and since operated as a regular trader. J. Pierpont was one of her early owners. Her first commander as a Black Baller was Jonathan Holdredge, after which she was taken by Seth C. Macy. She had the reputation of being a smart ship. In the summer of 1817 she was reported at Liverpool "in the remarkably short passage of 18 days from New York."

1821 marks the real beginning of a new era in transportation. All along the coast from Wiscasset to Baltimore, ship yards were booming—none more so than those of New York. There was a decided increase in the number and size of ships built, especially for the transatlantic route.

During the year a round dozen vessels measuring up to 500 tons had been launched in New York. The list included the *James Cropper*, for the Black Ball Line; the *William Thompson* and *Orbit*, later acquired by the same line; the *Ajax*, a fine skysail yarder, and such well known names as the *Hannibal*, *Columbia*, *Maria* and others.

Years later, Captain Hammond was having his troubles in the *Maria*, then operating as an Indiaman. His log for December 29th, 1838, records:

"A dead sulky thing for a mate worse than useless as usual. Mere lumber on board. May the person who recommended him have no worse punishment than such a one to depend upon in his station. Like a scabby ram which poisons the whole flock."

Since the *Maria* warped into her dock at New York Friday morning, February 15th, 1839, only 63 sailing days from Mauritius, one may conclude that the New York builder had not lost his cunning when he laid down the lines of the little packet, or the "old man" was something of a driver and irascible, to boot. Possibly both elements affected the performance. Mates had their sorrows, too, in those days.

There was plenty of competition for the Black Ball Line from the start, but for nearly three years there seems to have been no attempt to imitate her in the establishment of a fixed sailing schedule. It was not until toward the close of 1821 that Byrnes, Trimble & Company adopted definite sailing dates for their four packets: the *Manhattan*, Captain Tarr; *Meteor*, Captain N. Cobb; *Hercules*, under Captain Gardner, and the *Panthea*, commanded by Captain Bennett. As a matter of fact the new line, which became known as the "Red Star Line," had difficulty in maintaining its schedule, and it was not until the summer of 1822 that it actually began to live up to its representations.

By this time everyone wanted a "Line." During February, 1822, announcement had been made by the Black Ball firm of their intention to institute fortnightly sailings, on the 1st and 16th of each month, and the passage was reduced to thirty-five guineas. The innovation produced a sensation. "Decidedly, there must be something in a regular sailing date."

To make their new service effective, they added the *William Thompson* to the Black Ball fleet, and started construction on two immense new ships, the *New York* and the *Liverpool*, measuring 614 tons each. Another ship, the *Canada*, was to be constructed later in the year by Brown & Bell and put in service early in 1823.

The average passage of the Black Ballers from New York to Liverpool for the first six years, from 1818 to 1823 inclusive, was 23 days to the eastward and 40 days to the westward. This was at a period when the usual reported passages exceeded 30 and 45 days, respectively, while passages of from 60 to 90 days to the westward were so common as to excite no attention. Owing to the prevailing westerly winds the passage to the eastward was usually much shorter than the westward run. In the phrase of the day "it was all downhill going to the east'ard and all up-hill coming back."

During these early years, the palm for the best passage from New York to Liverpool was held by the ship *New York*. She was a large vessel for her day, measuring as we have seen, 614 tons, a product of the famous Brown & Bell yard. Under the command of Captain George Maxwell she sailed from New York on the 16th of December, 1823, and landed her passengers at Liverpool on the morning of January 1st, making the run in the unprecedented time of 15 days and 16 hours, a record that stood for a number of years.

This passage, through some oversight, has been credited to the *Canada* by subsequent accounts. The *Canada*, a sister ship of the *New York*, was one of the fastest of the early packets and for a number of years made the best average crossings, but she is not entitled to this record. The credit, however belated, belongs to Captain Maxwell and the gallant *New York*.

Immediately following the expansion of the Black Ball Line in 1821 and doubtless stimulated by it, individuals and firms which had long been giving irregular sailing to Liverpool and London began to advertise their ships to sail on a day certain. There was not much publicity about it—merely a slight change in the wording of the stilted little notices which had filled the news sheets for a century past. Many of the concerns which gave the new idea a trial abandoned it shortly under the stress of competition and eventually drifted into the lines of general trade. A few persisted and gradually built up wealthy and effective concerns.

John Flack, with the new 500 ton *Hannibal*, built by Fickett

"NORTHERN LIGHT."

PAINTED BY CHARLES R. PATTERSON.

Courtesy of the New York, New Haven & Hartford Railroad Company.

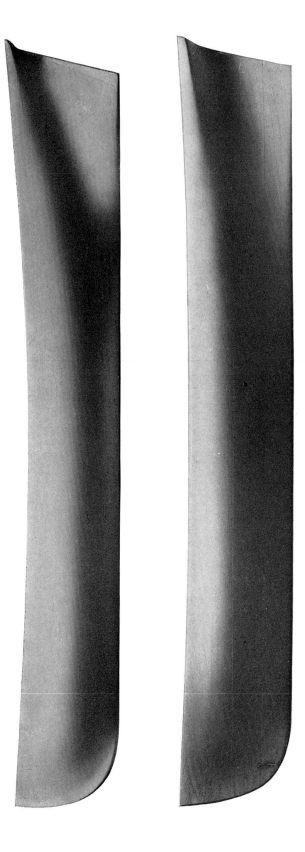

UPPER: Original model of the ketch *Eliza* built by Enos Briggs in Salem in 1795. The *Eliza* was very fast, as her lines in App. VII indicate. This model is said to have been the first water line or "lift" model made. Model in the possession of the Peabody Museum, Salem, Mass., by whose courtesy it is here reproduced.

LOWER: Original model made by Orlando Merrill, of Newburyport, Mass., at about the same time the model of the *Eliza* was made and said by the maker to have marked the discovery of the "lift" model. The sloop-of-war *Wasp* was built from this model. It will be noted that neither of these models show the bulwarks; being raised only as far as the spar deck line. Original model in the possession of the New York Historical Society, by whose courtesy it is reproduced.

"ELIZABETH F. WILLETTS."

PAINTED BY FREDERICK ROUX.

Courtesy of Mrs. Ethel S. MacMullen.

UPPER: Very old water line or "lift" model of a ship built in Connecticut in the vicinity of Clinton. Tradition says it was the model of a "frigate." It is unusually wide and shallow with decks obviously planned for fighting. The type belongs to the period of the Revolutionary War, although it may have been used later. The existence of models of this type raises the question whether "lift" models were not known prior to the time of the Merrill and Briggs models.

LOWER: Old sectional model of a type commonly used in the 18th century before the "lift" model was discovered. Each section represents a separate frame. It will be noted that both models shown here have an after-drag, a feature of the Baltimore vessels, and an almost universal feature of ships built with "easy" lines prior to 1830.

& Crockett at Corlear's Hook, appears to have obtained a brief recognition as the operator of a "Line." The *Hannibal* was commanded by Captain Watkinson, formerly of the Black Ball Line. Another ship of this line was the fast-sailing *Ann-Maria*, under Captain Waite.

On July 30th, 1822, Fish & Grinnell and Thaddeus Phelps & Company announced the formation of a "Fourth Line of Liverpool Packets" to sail regularly on the 8th of each month. To initiate this service, Captain Henry Holdredge, long an outstanding figure in packet ship circles, was to leave New York on the 8th of August in the *Robert Fulton,* a ship of less than 400 tons. The *Cortes,* Captain N. De Cost, was second, while for the October sailing it was announced that "a good ship would be provided." The fourth vessel was in process of construction and would be commanded by Henry Stoddard. With the institution of this service, New York had four sailings each month to Liverpool, in addition to a large number of irregular sailings.

Griswold & Coates, who had long been operating regular traders between New York and London, began to give regular service at this time also. They had the ships *Cincinnatus,* commanded by H. L. Champlain; the *Comet,* Captain Griswold; the *Robert Edwards,* under Captain Sherburne, and were building the *Hudson,* destined for many years to be a favorite London packet. Washington Irving has graphically described a voyage on this vessel.

Among other New York firms which operated packets in the transatlantic trade at this time, A. Gracie & Company had the *Braganza,* of 469 tons, commanded for a time by James Rogers, formerly of the *Pacific.* This firm also had the *America,* Captain Wallace. S. Hicks & Company had the *Florida* and the *Orbit* in the Liverpool trade. Jacob Barker had the *Caledonia;* Hicks, Jenkins & Company, the *Mohawk, Edward* and the second *Manhattan* (not the large *Manhattan* of the forties).

Francis Depau, John R. Skiddy and G. G. & S. Howland had long been interested in Havre packets, and all were important figures in shipping circles for many years. Depau, Isaac Bell, and Miles R. Burke founded the first regular sailing line between New York and Havre in 1822, with the little *Stephania, Helen Mar, Montano* and *Henry IV,* ships rating not much over 300 tons.

Other shipping firms in New York at this time were Franklin & Minturn and N. L. & G. Griswold. There were also N. Haven, E. Morewood, Thomas C. Butler, Jr., N. Scovill, Jun., J. & R. Loines and many more. Among the many well known masters active in the earlier years of the packets, David Wagstaff, Samuel Avery, S. G. Reid, William Lee, Jr., T. Delano, R. R. Crocker and William Sketchley may be listed. Many of them were to continue in service until they saw the clipper ships in all their glory, slipping easily and gracefully through seas against which their bluff little craft would have battered in vain.

The experiment was soon tried elsewhere, but apparently without success, with the notable exception of the Cope Line between Philadelphia and Liverpool, founded in 1821. Its real importance, however, dates from 1833, when the fine new ships *Montezuma* and *Susquehanna* were added. The *Susquehanna,* of 583 tons, was a very sharp model and was so rated by the American Lloyds as late as 1869, and it is at least debatable whether she was not entitled to a rating among the early clippers. She was scheduled to sail on her first voyage on the 20th of April, 1833, with Captain Dixey in command. Her record is one of consistently fine passages with many runs of 20 days and less from the Capes to Liverpool.

Boston, through the efforts of the Appletons and approximately fifty more of her leading merchants, organized the Boston & Liverpool Packet Company in 1821, gradually acquiring the ships *Sapphire, Topaz, Amethyst* and the famous *Emerald,* but the line was unsuccessful and the packets drifted into other channels of trade. A second attempt to establish a line with fixed sailing dates was made in 1827 with eight ships built at Medford by Thatcher Magoun, but after an unsatisfactory service of four or five years the enterprise was abandoned. Owing to her inability to attract large shipments of food stuffs from the West, Boston ships found it difficult to get a paying freight for England without going south for cotton, which of course precluded their building up a passenger business.

After the abandonment of the second line, Boston was without regular sailings until the Cunard Line commenced operations there in 1840, and with the assistance of a huge government subsidy was able to solve the problems which confronted the sailing packets.

Train's Line did not appear on the scene until 1844, and for several years thereafter Bostonians seem to have regarded its performance with mixed emotions. However, Train's persistence and business ability eventually gave to New England a direct sailing connection with Europe second to none.

CHAPTER VIII

SAILING RECORDS AFTER 1815

MEANWHILE general trade had not waited upon the formation of packet lines. Peace was no sooner assured in 1815 than the shuttle renewed its interrupted journey back and forth across the Atlantic. Captain Stephen Glover, "of the extraordinary quick sailing ship, *Milo*," looked to his ballast and backstays and was off past Boston Light on the frosty morning of the 12th of March. Eighteen days later he was walking the streets of Liverpool. Thirty-five days from the time he left Boston he was loaded and ready for sea again, but was detained in port for eleven days by heavy weather. On the 3rd of June, the *Milo*, 37 days out, poked her nose into Boston harbor, "the first American vessel which arrived in England after the peace, and the first which has arrived back."

It was another four years before the pre-war record of the *Lady Madison* to the westward was equalled. On the 23rd of April, 1819, the *Triton,* Captain Holcomb, arrived in Boston 18 days from Liverpool. Her run was possibly less striking than the longer passage of the *Madison* to New York, but she had the distinction of having performed the round in the then unequalled sailing time of 37 days, an achievement which has been rarely surpassed since.

The 18 day mark of the *Triton* stood for a few months only. On the 5th of the following December, Captain Fox, of the *Herald,* weighed anchor at Liverpool and drove for Boston, arriving there on the 23rd with a new 17 day record, in ample time to dock his ship and ride down to Cohasset, where the Christmas dinner was spread on the old table in the home kitchen.

The *Herald* was a new ship, built in Newburyport. She measured about 300 tons and was, therefore, smaller than the new packets, but was sharp built and commanded, moreover, by a man who, even in those days, had earned a reputation as a "hard customer." Nothing is better evidence of this than the fact his record stood for five years, to be beaten at last only by Fox himself, when he brought the packet *Emerald* into Boston harbor on the 9th of March, 1824, a few hours under 17 days from Liverpool. Nor is this elapsed time a complete indication of the quality of his performance. He is stated to have actually arrived outside of Boston Light in the remarkable time of 15 days and 14 hours, only to run into a calm which prevented his entering port until the following day. This report is confirmed, in a measure, by the fact that all the papers announcing his arrival state that his passage was made in the shorter time.

Two days before the *Emerald* reached port her sister ship, the *Topaz,* Captain Callender, arrived from Liverpool in a 42 day passage, and two days later the ship *America,* Captain Turner, arrived from the same port, 47 days out.

In some respects the westward run of the *Emerald* in less than 16 days from Liverpool to the Massachusetts coast, is one of the most remarkable old Neptune ever witnessed. Here was a short clumpy vessel of less than 400 tons (she measured 359 tons), shipping it green, every mile of the way across the broad Atlantic, on the wings of a roaring easterly. It was a breeze such as one might not meet in a century, and doubtless men like Captain Fox were almost as rare.

To appreciate the feat one has only to recall that the record passage for all time from Liverpool to New York is the 15 day run made in 1860 by the *Andrew Jackson,* more than four times the size of the *Emerald,* under command of Captain Johnson. Normally the *Andrew Jackson* was commanded by Captain Jack Williams, himself a product of the packet service, and with possibly one or two exceptions, the hardest "driver" that ever walked a quarter-deck. His name and something of his quality have been permanently enshrined in an old deep sea chanty:

> " 'Tis larboard and starboard on deck you will sprawl,
> For kicking Jack Williams commands that Black Ball."

With men of this stripe, carrying sail was more than an occasional whim. For them, every passage was a record, in effort, if not in time. After his world beating run Captain Fox remained in Boston only long enough to discharge and reload the *Emerald,* and then sent her back to Liverpool in 23 days, making the round voyage in the excellent time of less than 40 days at sea.

During this period several vessels hailing from the Chesapeake made exceptionally fine passages. The brig *Findorf* of 216 tons, built in Virginia in 1813, was one of the fastest among these of which there is any reliable record. Under Captain M. P. Cottle, she ran from the Baltimore capes to Sand Heads in 1816, in the very excellent time of 97 days. Continuing in this trade, she appears to have made consistently fine passages. She turned up at Baltimore on the 4th of February, 1819, in 99 days from Sand Heads, "having performed her voyage in seven months, and bringing back the news of her own arrival out."

Several years later, the little Baltimore schooner *Amanda,* under Captain Gibbs, ran from Valparaiso to Cape Henry in the then remarkable time of 65 days, arriving home in July, 1822. She was 46 days from off the Horn, and 30 days only from a position opposite Rio Janeiro. This is, perhaps, the best passage that had been made over the course up to that time. At all events, it sets a high standard of performance by which later runs may be measured.

A notable reduction in the time of the westward packet run to New York was made in 1829. Under the command of the able and deservedly popular Joseph C. Delano, the little 400 ton *Columbia* backed her main yard off Sandy Hook at 6 o'clock in the morning of April 17th. She had left Portsmouth at noon April 1st, and had therefore made the distance in 15 days and 18 hours, having been up with the Banks of Newfoundland in ten days.

This unparalleled passage was almost equalled a few hours later by the arrival of Captain James Rogers in the *Caledonia*, off the Highlands below New York in 15 days and 22 hours from Liverpool. Both these runs established new records between their respective ports. Captain Rogers, however, had lowered the time for the round voyage another day, for he had gone to Liverpool and back in 59 days, 23 of which had been spent in port. He had accomplished the trip in the then record time of 36 sailing days, on one of which he had been completely becalmed.

Another excellent run made about this time was that of the *Josephine* from Belfast to New York in 15 days and 12 hours. She was handled by Captain Thomas Britton, a brother of the somewhat more widely known John Britton, who later had the Liverpool packet Rochester and other ships of the "New Line." Captain John Britton and Joseph Delano are well remembered by many persons still living, since both survived their exploits by more than fifty years—the last living representatives of the early packet service. Their later "fourteen day passages" eastward in the larger ships of the thirties and forties kept them long in the public eye.

The remarkable and consistent performance of the packet ships played no small part in stimulating American commerce. The year 1830 witnessed a veritable boom in shipbuilding which, in turn, succumbed to the long depression preceding the panic of '37. Subsequently and for a considerable period during the thirties many of the transatlantic lines could not earn actual expenses. Depressions, however, had no effect on the service save to redouble the effort to make rapid passages. "To carry sail New York fashion" was becoming a byword on the seven seas.

All this time the increasing demands of freight and passenger traffic were working a gradual transformation in the packet ships themselves. By the early thirties they had not only doubled in size, but their very shape was changing. To accommodate the hundreds of immigrants which now swarmed into the steerage, they were designed with the greatest possible deck space—straight sided and almost rectangular above the water line. Below, the round bow and long, lean run was giving place to short, sharp ends and a long, full midships section, with great stowage capacity. The former extreme dead-rise was modified. (See note.) This change involved the almost complete elimination of the after "drag" characteristic of all early fast-sailing ships. The result was a more comfortable ship, dry and easy in a sea way, but more dependent on her lofty rig and the ceaseless activity of her officers for her ability to make good passages.

One of the most famous, as well as one of the largest of the new liners, was the *Independence*, of 732 tons and a length of 140 feet. She was designed and built by the well known firm of Smith & Dimon, and was launched in 1833. Captain Ezra Nye, a Cape Codder with a marked predilection for carrying sail, commanded her.

It was said of him that "he had a way of his own that always gave him a fair wind, and he would ever be seen with a topmast studding sail abroad, whether, by so doing, he could head his regular course or not." Ezra had his counterpart later in the occasional clipper ship captain, who, with reckless disregard of gear, set his studding sails when braced sharp on the wind. It would seem that masters who indulged their passion for fast sailing to such an extent, were indeed hopeless. However, Nye and the *Independence* earned a reputation, not only for general excellence of passages, but for record breaking runs that is almost unique in the packet annals of the thirties.

Even before he took the *Independence*, Nye had made some fast trips. On the 12th of May, 1829, he appeared in Boston harbor in the *Amethyst*, a sister ship of the *Emerald*, 20 days out from Liverpool, having made the round in 71 days, including a long detention on the other side. Seven years later, in the *Independence*, he lowered the round trip record by a notable margin. On June 14th, 1836, he arrived at New York, 20 days from Liverpool. This was by no means a record, but as the *Independence* had made the outward run in 14 days and 12 hours, the voyage occupied only 34 days at sea—the shortest that had ever been known.

By this time the era which, for convenience, may be designated "the early packet ship period," was drawing to a close. Developments of the utmost importance to the future of American commerce, and to shipping the world over, were already impending. Before discussing these, however, it is well to notice other events which had taken place in several other branches of the deep water trades.

CHAPTER IX

SIDE by side with the rapidly developing trans-Atlantic packet service another deep-sea traffic was writing a spectacular record. This was the trade between America and China, by way of the Cape of Good Hope and the Indian Ocean. The East India fleet comprised not only the most aristocratic branch of the merchant marine, but its influence on the evolution of the clipper ship was hardly less important than that of the packets. In general, its requirements called for the same type of fast sailing vessel and throughout the history of both trades the interplay of the same influences may be traced.

By 1825, or thereabouts, it was common practice to divert superannuated packets to the Canton route. Well known 400 ton craft like the *York*, *Silas Richards* and *Champlain* did excellent work in the tea trade long after their usefulness as crack passenger liners had ended. During the late 30's and early 40's larger packets were occasionally tried out. One of the best known of these was the *Sheridan*, rising 800 tons. The statement has been made that when she was built she was found too large for the transatlantic service and was therefore put on the China run. This statement is incorrect and gives a wrong impression of the relative importance of the two trades. She was actually smaller than several other successful Liverpool packets of her day. Neither at this period or any other did the trade with the Orient grow more rapidly than that with Europe. No other foreign commerce has ever compared in bulk or tonnage with America's European traffic.

Among the requirements which the two trades had in common was the combination of speed with large carrying capacity. Both services paid magnificent premiums for efficiency. Both were characterized throughout their history by the same incessant, relentless "driving" to the very limits of human endurance. Both were marked by a lengthening trail of broken records, culminating on the one hand in Waterman's strangely overlooked Canton passage of 1849 in the *Sea Witch*, and on the other, in the *Andrew Jackson's* westward run in the Liverpool trade just prior to the civil war.

For the moment, however, in 1815, there was little to indicate the remarkable era of change just ahead. Fine, full-flavored days! When 18th century knee breeches still held favor with conservative elders, and leeching and cupping went on unabated. Wig makers 'prentices still dreamed of long, prosperous years at their trade. Bostonians dutifully attended town meeting, and gossiped the while about the latest news from the prospective resident of St. Helena.

Precocious ship-boys, not yet in their 'teens, frolicked and fought below decks and betimes concentrated such attention as ship-boys might give on the three principles of existence; "to strive to cat the anchor; to haul out the weather earring, and ever to be the first to ship a hand-spike." Early they learned the first, and incidentally the last, lesson of a foremast hand— that to him who manifested a pleasing agility, much would be forgiven.

Out in the harbors, wall-sided, lofty-pooped Indiamen bristling with gun ports swung at anchor, side by side with low, lean brigs and schooners, yesterday's privateersmen, now ready to start for the musky middle passage. Deep waisted lumber droughers from the Provinces, polacres, snows, a snaky felucca or two, pettiaugers, pinks, Dutch galliots, turpentine-sided ships, brigs with yellow mouldings and white boot tops, pompous Philadelphia built merchantmen sporting the three broad mouldings peculiar to their kind, bright-waisted ships, red ships, green ships, pea-soupers, ships of every color, all mingled to comprise the arrivals at any of the larger ports in the second decade of the 19th century.

On their manifests were items which have long since disappeared from the merchant's shelves or are there today under quite different descriptions. Muscavado and brown clayed sugars; Company's long and short yellow nankeens, Chattabilla baftas, Gurrapore cossas, winter and summer sperm, callimancoes, shalloons and a bewildering array of pipes, puncheons, hogsheads and half-barrels, marked the rapid increase in the importation of luxuries as well as necessities.

Almost every foreign voyager carried a few carriage guns, "double reinforced" sixes, with a long nine or two, and muskets, cutlasses and boarding pikes for all hands and the cook. Husky, pig-tailed sailors who had laid many a gun on privateer or hardly pressed Indiaman without a qualm, but found it impossible to keep their eye scuppers free when listening to the little feminine tragedies of Cherry Street, eddied about the water front.

Here might be seen the redoubtable skipper of a clump brig, his hair tied with a rope yarn, pumps a-clanking and a bad list to larboard, recounting to his pursy lipped owner how he had "prepared a sail with thrums and oakum and fothered the vessel," but could not find the leak. Not far away might be a coffee trader from Rio—half her spars gone along with the camboose house and cook in a white squall ten days back.

On all sides the wail of deep sea shanties, like nothing else on earth, as anchors were hove short and tops'ls sheeted home, mingled with the grunting yo-ho-ing of a trio or two at work with handy-billy or warping a vessel along a dock. Countless sloops and schooners threading in and out of the welter of shipping—packets from up the Sound or down "Chesapeake way," each with its grave eyed urchin, an embryo seaman on his first voyage bound for the quarter deck of the tallest Indiaman he could descry. Here the *Slow-and-Easy* sloop rubbed sides with the *Lovely Matilda* brig, and there the prolifically named *Eleven Brothers* with anchor head and load of plaister made a pilot's luff to escape an imminent encounter with the squat and dingy *Who-would-have-thought-it,* whose squinting helmsman remained ruminatively oblivious to a running fire of critical comment.

Not far away is a little topsail schooner, deep-loaded with salt—two-thirds of her crew licked off the roundhouse several nights before while furling the mainsail, leaving the mate, peg-legged cook and boy to work her home. Down the harbor, signals flying, a Liverpooler 59 days out was coming in, reporting 84 steerage, three deaths and two births.

Across the street from the docks, under the very ends of the slim, incredibly long, flying jib-booms, mine host was waxing eloquent over "as good ale as ever mantled in a beer glass." Sailors drinking and paying with helpful nautical ejaculations out of handfuls of coin from every mint under the sun. "Good brown Jamaica rum, yes, but none of this new fangled gin that rotted a man's innards—a dutchman's drink."

Strange harsh days, and yet the sailor's golden age. Busy, hustling ports, seething with activity. As it had been since the days of Tyre, so it would be always. Not one of the countless merchants, builders, riggers, seamen gave any other possibility a thought. Even if a few years earlier they had seen queer Oliver Evans trundling through the streets of Philadelphia in his amphibious steam boat, it would never have occurred to them that the curious invention might sometime touch their ships. "Ships? There would always be ships." And what were ships without sails?

But the last sea war was over and in that long-ago summer of 1815 the race to the swift was already on. Within a brief four years a steamship had crossed the Atlantic and the *Robert Fulton* of 750 tons, a huge craft and the first large ocean steamer, was afloat. In Europe, early in 1816, the first channel steamer, the *Eliza,* had crossed to Havre in 20 hours, continuing thence up the Seine to Paris, to the amazement of thousands of Parisians attracted by the spectacle.

The China run, later the scene of the first great triumphs of the American clippers, was in some respects an unsatisfactory test of a ship's speed. It was a course in which much light, variable weather was apt to be met. The fitful monsoons, changeable currents, uncharted reefs and fearful typhoons of the China Sea proved the undoing of many a noble ship and the nemesis of many a veteran shipmaster. Piratical activity, well down into the third quarter of the last century, kept every crew alert and anxious until the dreaded "Streights" had been passed, after which the tension lessened but by no means disappeared.

After a smashing run across the Indian Ocean a ship might find herself fighting westerly gales for weeks off the Cape of Good Hope, with all prospect of a fine passage spoiled, or spend precious days "humbugging" about in doldrum weather in the "horse latitudes," or on the other hand, might fetch Bermuda in record time only to meet heartbreaking month-long delays beating up against wintry Nor'westers.

Such conditions as these obtained to a certain extent over every ocean course, but they were more uniformly met with in the tea trade than elsewhere. The result was the breeding of a class of officers there that for resourcefulness, alertness and superseamanship could not be surpassed the world over. For a score of excellent reasons speed had become the fetish of America. The Canton route appealed most strongly to venturous spirits afloat, for it could afford to pay well for dispatch besides holding out enticing pictures of the dangers and glamours of a different world.

Prior to the war of 1812, a run of 125 days from Canton to New York in the favorable monsoon constituted a good passage, while six months was so common as to excite little remark. Twenty to thirty days longer were required for vessels leaving during the unfavorable season, embracing generally the period from March to November. One of the earliest recorded races throws some light on the subject. It was the 13th of April, 1810, when Boston was treated to the unprecedented sight of three of her finest Indiamen sailing into port together. They were the *William*, Captain Emery, the *Mandarin*, Captain Nash, and the *Atahualpa*, under Captain Sturgis. All were from Canton, and they were respectively 128, 129 and 130 days out—fine, close sailing, and a finish to be talked about when the sleek California thoroughbreds were furnishing similar sights half a century later. Much better passages had been made, it is true, but they were the exception and the above voyages may be taken to represent fairly the standard of the period.

The news from Ghent had not reached Canton, however, when a new mark was set up in the China run, demonstrating possibly that fear or necessity had again wrought its perfect work. It was no tall Indiaman either that broke the century mark of the *Severn*. On the 30th of March, 1815, the schooner *Russell*, commanded by Captain Vibberts and owned by Minturn & Champlin, of New York, reached up Buzzards Bay, 96 days from Lintin, only to find that the war was over and that she would have been perfectly safe in making directly for New York. A couple of days later the brig *Sphynx*, Captain Brevoort, came to off Sandy Hook, 98 days from the same port.

The two vessels had sailed in company from Canton during the night of December 22nd, running the blockade maintained by His Majesty's *Grampus*, 50 guns, and the *Owen Glendower*, *Theban* and *Doris*, frigates. It is recorded in the log of the *Russell* that she had two close calls. In running out in the dark she passed within pistol shot of the *Grampus*, which gave chase, but at daylight was five miles astern. Again on March 1st, just below the Line, she was chased by a frigate and a brig which had the advantage of possessing "engines" (force pumps) with which to wet their sails. In the end the *Russell* was compelled to throw over her carriage guns and shot "when she easily left them."

A year later the feat of the *Russell* was virtually duplicated by the Baltimore ex-privateer brig *Chasseur* under Captain Davy. She arrived at Baltimore on the 9th of April, 1816, in a passage of 95 days from Canton to the Capes, a feature of the voyage being her run of 84 days from Java Head. Her time would seem to be virtually on a par with that of the *Russell*, distance considered. It surpassed by a liberal margin that of the "elegant fast sailing brig *Seneca*," Captain Depeyster, which had arrived at New York a few days earlier, 103 days out from Macao. The *Seneca* was one of John Jacob Astor's vessels, as was also the *Beaver*, which came in three weeks later from Canton, having been absent nearly five years, during three of which she had been at Whampoa waiting for news of peace.

Another excellent run made about this time was that of the ship *Ida*, Captain Dorr, which arrived at Boston on the 31st of March, 1819, 101 days from Canton.

There followed a long interval, during which many excellent voyages were made, but few of striking importance until the fine 60 day run of the old "regular trader" *Milo*, from Rio Janeiro to Canton, made while under the command of Captain Sever in 1831. About the same time the *Clematis* arrived out 95 days from Boston. It was not until the 26th of March, 1832, that the marks of the *Russell* and *Chasseur* were again approached. On that date the Philadelphia built ship *Atlantic* passed Cape Henlopen, 98 days from Macao, under command of Captain McCall.

His glory was short lived. Ships already afloat were destined to make "90 day passages" with a certain degree of regularity. One of them eventually set a mark beaten but once and equalled by only two ships in history.

The long distance world's championship race was now on in earnest. The above passages had the effect of thoroughly arousing a maritime world which was accustomed to regard with complacency any trip to China which occupied less than a year. Round voyages of slightly more than 8 months' duration were now indicated as a possibility with the attractive prospect of profitable side trips during the balance of the year. The attention of every ambitious master and merchant henceforth was focussed on the tea trade. "Speed to China" became a slogan.

Within two years the number of ships engaged in the trade had nearly doubled and a score of new names had appeared in the already long list of captains. Many of the new-comers and some of the old were to attain world-wide fame later in the clippers. China passages of 100 days or so now caused little comment. A Philadelphia ship, the *Commerce*, under Captain Fleming, came home during the Spring of '33 in 96 days. Even the remarkable time of the *Russell* did not long remain the criterion. On the 21st of March, 1834, the *Sabina*, Captain McEwen, backed her main yard off Sandy Hook Light, reporting a new record of 90 days—fast clipper time.

Good runs to and from Canton were now the rule rather than the exception. Among the better voyages made about this time were those of the *Clematis*, Captain Evans, 100 days; the *Horatio*, Howland, 98 days; the *Eliza*, 106 days, and the *Liberty*, Captain Davis, 109 days, all in 1834. The year following, the old packet *York*, under Captain Sterling, made the run in 104 days; the ship *Morrison*, Lavender master, in 99 days; the barque *Cynthia*, of Salem, Captain Graves, 102 days; the *Sachem*, commanded by Captain Brown, 96 days; the *Roman*, Captain Benson, 101 days; while the *Paris* distinguished herself in another way by taking 180 days, practically six months, to go from Canton to Boston.

Other fine passages followed in rapid succession, without, however, reducing the record. The *Silas Richards*, another old packet, made the homeward run in 98 days in the Spring of '36, while in command of Captain Rosseter. A year later she cut her time to 94 days, under Captain Pearce. Griswold, still in the *Panama*, made a satisfactory trip of 94 days in 1836. Deliverance Benjamin, later one of the prominent early clipper ship commanders, then took her and brought her home in 99 days. Meanwhile the brig *Richard Alsop*, under McMichael, also destined to become well known in clipper ship circles, made a passage in 96 days in 1836.

It is impractical to give anything like a complete record of the faster voyages over the China course during this early packet period. Remarkable as they were in their day, none of these achievements stands as a record now. Nevertheless, if they are matched with the average performances of the clippers—admittedly larger, faster and more powerful craft—it is obvious that their crews must have performed almost incredible feats of seamanship to keep them moving as they did.

In the Calcutta and Manila trade, on the other hand, speed was not so imperative. India was a land of bulky freights and few of her cargoes compared in value with those of China. Nevertheless some of the passages during the period just noticed were remarkable even when matched with later clipper ship runs.

The first noteworthy voyage from Calcutta to be completed after the 1812 war was made by the "fast sailing ship" *Trident*. Like other vessels of her day and class she was heavily manned and carried steering sails on the fore and main from courses to topgallants. Commanded by Captain Rae, she arrived at New York in November, 1816, exactly 102 days from Sand Heads, bringing among other items of merchandise, an elephant. This run was especially good for the season in which it was made, since the Northeast monsoon, which is the favorable period for the Bay of Bengal, begins as a rule in October and ends in March.

Two years later the *Glide* of Salem, Tucker master, made the run in 98 days, arriving at Salem on the 3rd of January, 1818, just as the first ocean liner was preparing to sail from New York. The next year this time was reduced one day by the ship *Cririe*, of 353 tons, owned by Robert Lenox, which arrived at New York on the 3rd of April.

Following the *Cririe,* the famous old ship *George,* "the Salem packet," proceeded to hang up a record that stood undefeated and but once equalled until the day of the clippers. Leaving Salem on May 25th, 1822, Samuel Endicott, her master, "discharged Perkins the pilot" at 2 P.M. She was 24 days to the line and passed the Cape of Good Hope at 2 A.M., July 15th, "fifty-one days and 1 hour from Salem."

Running up the Indian Ocean she met with a series of fine breezes and in the 15 days from July 24th to August 7th, inclusive, she logged 3118 miles, or an average of nearly 208 miles a day, her best day being 240 miles and her best speed 11 knots. At 5 P.M. on the 22nd day of August she was boarded by the pilot off Sand Heads and at 6 P.M. she anchored and furled all sail. Her passage of 89 days 4 hours was the best by a margin of many days that had ever been recorded. Continuing in this trade she made a number of runs well above the average, including three of 97, 100 and 101 days respectively.

The ex-packet *Emerald* also did excellent work over this course. Her best run appears to have been made in 1829, when she arrived off Boston Light at noon, the 20th of April, under the command of that fine old master mariner, Augustine Heard, exactly 91 days and 20 hours from Sand Heads. The time reported by contemporary writers was 90 days, but an examination of her log shows that she left Sand Heads at 4 P.M., January 18th, so that Captain Heard's own statement of the longer passage is correct.

This performance was somewhat overshadowed several years later by the voyage of the ship *America* in the opposite direction which is normally a longer passage. Under command of Captain Eldridge she arrived off Sand Heads on the 28th of July, 1833, only 89 days from Boston. This remarkable run, equalling that of the *George* and scarcely three days longer than the record for all time made by the clipper *Beverly,* marks the zenith of the Calcutta trade during the packet period.

The two passages stood unapproached for many years, although a decade later marine writers were claiming a run, longer by a full fortnight, as the best passage ever made, a circumstance which may possibly throw some light on the origin of not a few legendary "records."

CHAPTER X

THE BALTIMORE CLIPPER

WHILE the Northern ports were expanding their packet business and far Eastern trade and thereby developing a new, larger and more burdensome type of fast carrier, Baltimore in response to equally imperative demands, continued to specialize in small, rapid sailing vessels. She built other vessels also, but it was in the early clipper type that she excelled. Little by little minor refinements and improvements were introduced into the model, without, however, affecting its essential nature—that of the "pilot boat built" craft of the late 18th century. In particular the run was made fuller, and the flatness under the counters relieved, while at the same time the forward lines were sharpened.

It cannot be said that the *Ann McKim* was the final and highest expression of this evolutionary process, but her model (shown opposite page 72) indicates that Baltimore architects had made long strides in their profession since the day of the apple bow and hollow ground run of forty years earlier. Even before she was launched, they seem by common consent to have been awarded the leading position in America as designers of swift craft.

As we have already noticed, the model was not well adapted to carrying bulky cargo, and it further lacked certain desirable heavy weather qualities which the later packets possessed. Nevertheless, so long as small ships satisfied the requirements of trade, the Baltimore vessels not only paid well but made their full share of the records.

One of Maryland's most famous productions during the early packet period was the brig *John Gilpin,* of 282 tons, built at St. Michaels, Maryland, and owned by Richard Alsop and others of Philadelphia. The *Gilpin* was launched in 1831 and sailed for Batavia and China in May, 1832. She passed Cape Henry on May 20th; crossed the Line June 17th, and anchored off Anjier 82 days out, on the 10th of August, having logged 15,261 miles, an average of 186 1/10 miles a day.

She remained in the Pacific for a number of years, trading between Valparaiso and Canton. Her best run during this period appears to have been her passage of 56 days and 4 hours from Callao to Lintin, in 1837. On this occasion she left Callao September 30th at 5 P.M., and anchored at Lintin on the 26th of November, at 9 in the evening. This run established a transpacific record which stood until the pre-clipper *Helena's* 51 day crossing in 1843.

From the time of her departure from Cape Henry in 1832, until her arrival at Canton on December 12th, 1839, the *Gilpin* spent 1443.23 days at sea, logging 228,553 miles, an average of 159 5/100 nautical miles a day, during which time she was frequently becalmed. This calculation is subject to minor errors in the logs, but it is altogether probable that such errors could not materially affect the above figures. Nothing more is necessary to show that the *Gilpin* was very fast.

There were many other well known Baltimore clippers during the thirties, among which may be noted the brig *Lady Adams,* which spread the black main royal of Wilson & Company. The brigs *Argyle, Troubadour,* and *Tweed,* and the schooner *Yellot* were also very smart craft. The brig *Troubadour,* measuring 197 tons, under Captain Robinson, made the run from Montevideo to Cape Henry in 37 days, in 1834. A year later, under the same commander, the *Tweed* came around the Horn from Coquimbo in 76 days, arriving at Baltimore on the 9th of June. The *Lady Adams,* Captain McGill, is credited with the very fine passage of 70 days from Gibraltar to Valparaiso in 1837, while the *Argyle* arrived at Baltimore on June 22nd, 1838, from Canton 90 days out—a remarkable run for the season of the year. Altogether, the performance of their vessels gave Baltimore merchants excellent reason for satisfaction until the tremendous expansion of the forties made small cargoes unprofitable.

By far the most noted Baltimore vessel was the ship *Ann McKim,* the finest, although, as we shall see, by no means the only ship rigged vessel of this type launched at Baltimore, during and prior to the thirties. But as she is sometimes called "the first clipper ship," it seems advisable to examine her record with some care.

Probably few ships have been the subject of so many conflicting statements. In recent years, the impression has become somewhat prevalent that she was not only an experiment, but an unsuccessful one, as well. Neither assertion appears to be substantiated by the record. If, for example, she had embodied any new principles of design, some suggestion of the fact would probably have been noted in contemporary accounts of the ship and her launching. The following extract from the Baltimore *Republican and Commercial Advertiser* of June 3rd, 1833, is typical:

"The splendid ship *Ann McKim* will be launched from the ship yard of Messrs. Kennard & Williamson tomorrow afternoon at half past four o'clock. She is a hundred and forty-three feet in length, being the longest merchant ship in the United States, built by Messrs. Kennard & Williamson, who are among the most skillful mechanics in our country, and of the very best materials which have been selected with the greatest care, and at great expense, under the immediate supervision of Captain James Curtis, for the Hon. Isaac McKim.

"Her fastenings are altogether copper, no iron having

been used in her construction. The bills for copper alone amount to upwards of nine thousand dollars; and her whole cost when completed will fall little if anything short of fifty thousand dollars. The carving of the figure head and upon the stern, which is designed by Messrs. Kennard & Williamson, displays great taste, and is admirably executed. The lower masts are fitted in their places, the standing rigging is attached, and the top gallant masts are raised at the top to serve as flag staffs, and being painted with much taste and beauty, she presents a grand and imposing appearance."

Here is no word of novel design—no intimation that the *McKim* differed in principle from a hundred Baltimore craft before her. And, in fact, there was no difference. She was merely larger, slightly sharper and far more expensively finished. Perhaps the last person on earth to engage in the construction of an experimental ship was old Isaac McKim, himself a practical sea dog of many years' service.

If, on the one hand, the *McKim* was not an experiment, neither is there anything in her record to indicate that she was regarded as a failure by her contemporaries. All shipping suffered in the panic of '37, but aside from this she appears to have been actively employed during her entire career. The list of her passages shows that her speed compared favorably with the fast ships of the forties. Long before it became necessary to replace her, however, ships like the China packet *Helena* had demonstrated their ability to sail as rapidly and at the same time carry nearly twice as much cargo per ton register as vessels of the Baltimore design.

Even the opinion sometimes expressed that no other clipper of the *McKim* class was ever built at Baltimore or elsewhere, is open to doubt. Many a sharp ship rigged craft was built there between 1800 and 1840. Five years after the *McKim* was launched the fine corvette *Venus* was built. She was a true Baltimore clipper measuring 465 tons, only 28 tons less than the *McKim* and contemporary accounts assert that she was the sharpest ship ever built at Baltimore, although statements of this character are to be accepted with reservations. She was constructed with the intention of selling her to some South American country to be converted into a war ship.

Stress has been laid upon the fact that her later owners, Howland & Aspinwall, never had another ship built like the *McKim*. It would have been remarkable if, in that age of rapid development, they had copied a vessel more than ten years old and already small for the trade for which she was designed. As a matter of fact, the firm owned and operated several Baltimore vessels including the fast barque *Valparaiso*, and their later course, far from indicating dissatisfaction, shows that they were sensibly influenced by the design. One cannot say that their fine clippers *Rainbow* and *Sea Witch* were slavish copies of the type, but they owed at least as much to it as to the more recently developed fast packet ship.

Whether the *McKim* is entitled to be regarded as the first clipper ship is a question of another sort. On the one hand we have the negative evidence that aside from the greater size and more expensive finish she did not appear to impress her contemporaries as in any way different from other sharp built Baltimore vessels. On the other we are forced to conclude that she was not the first sharp built craft to be rigged as a ship.

There was, for example, the ship *Paul Sieman* of 443 tons built in Matthews County, Virginia, in 1800 and described in her register at Baltimore as "sharp built."

The *Congress* built at Baltimore in 1807 and measuring 363 tons, was so sharp that when launched she capsized and sank. She was heavily rigged as a ship and there is no doubt that she deserved the title of "Baltimore clipper" as much as any brig or schooner afloat at the time. Among other ships expressly registered as "sharp built" may be mentioned the *Meridian* of 387 tons built in Anne Arundel County, Maryland, in 1812, and the *Corinthian* of 503 tons and therefore a larger ship than the *McKim*. The *Corinthian* was launched at Baltimore in 1822 and acquired a reputation as a very fast sailer. When ten years old she was purchased by Wm. H. DeWolf of Bristol, R. I., through the agency of a ship master who bore the wistful cognomen "Golden Dearth."

It would be possible to mention other large, sharp, ship rigged vessels built in and around Baltimore before the *Ann McKim* but the foregoing examples are sufficient to indicate that the task of selecting the first clipper is not wholly devoid of pitfalls. It seems reasonably clear that many of these vessels differed only slightly from the *Ann McKim* in model and spread of canvas, and not at all in principle. While, therefore, it may be convenient to regard the *McKim* as the first clipper, it should be recognized that long before she was laid down, Baltimore ships of substantial size were built which were as definitely entitled to be described as clippers as any brig or schooner then in existence.

The *Ann McKim* sailed on her first voyage "for South America and a market," under the command of Captain Walker, on the 30th of August, 1833. The principal part of her cargo consisted of 3500 barrels of flour. She arrived at Callao on the 3rd of December in the short, but not remarkable passage of 89 days. Returning, she took her departure from Huasco, and made the run to Cape Henry in 72 days, arriving at Baltimore on the 16th of June, 1834.

Among the best of her passages on the Cape Horn run was her record of 59 days from Valparaiso to the Capes in 1837. On this occasion she made the very fine time of 42 days from off the Horn. This performance was completely overshadowed the following year when she came home from Coquimbo in 60 days; the remarkable feature of this run being her passage from off the port of Valparaiso, "land in sight" to Baltimore in 53 days. The Baltimore *Sun*, of November 7th, 1838, reported her arrival as follows:

"A BALTIMORE CLIPPER.—The ship *Ann McKim* at this port from Coquimbo, South America, made the run from

Valparaiso here in FIFTY-THREE days, said to be quicker time by nine days than was ever made before. The *Ann McKim* is a Baltimore vessel out and out, built and owned here. Baltimore ship builders against the world for building fleet craft."

The *Sun* was in error as to the margin of the *McKim's* victory but it was nevertheless a victory and a notable one.

On her next voyage Captain Martin took her to China around the Horn and across the Pacific from Valparaiso, and made the long out of season passage home from Canton to New York, her time being 150 days. She continued in this trade during the rest of her career as an American ship, her passages on that run being noted in the chapter devoted to the China records of the late pre-clipper period. Long before that time, however, developments were taking place which were destined to end forever the reign of the beautiful Baltimore clipper over the cargo carriers, although their influence still persists in the design of fast fishermen and deep water sailing yachts.

CHAPTER XI

EVOLUTION AND INFLUENCE OF THE PACKET

SUCH, in general, however imperfectly sketched, is the story of America's "fast sailing" vessels from the close of the Revolution to the end of the early packet period. It is obvious that the improvement noted in speed during this time could not have taken place without a corresponding improvement in ships. A better knowledge of navigation doubtless helped, but the majority of new records were made over routes which had remained substantially unchanged since the 18th century. Therefore one must look mainly to the ships and the men who sailed them for the real explanation of these passages.

Definite dates for the successive changes in the theory of packet design cannot be assigned. Progress did not follow a steady upward course. Even today vessels are occasionally to be seen which embody naval principles more or less discredited a century ago.

By 1836, however, it was apparent that the old fashioned rounding bow and extremely long run were giving place in the more pretentious ships to short, sharp ends. The bow, except at the deck, was becoming decidedly wedge shaped with an occasional tendency toward hollow lines. Aft, the great "drag" was being slowly eliminated, although to the end of sailing ship days some ships trimmed slightly by the stern—the fast clipper *North Wind*, for example, drawing two feet more aft than at the bow. The midship section was greatly elongated and the excessive dead rise modified, changes which resulted in flatter sides and a somewhat fuller run. As a necessary corollary the center of the ship was being moved farther aft, an innovation which necessitated placing the foremast away from its early position in the extreme bow of the ship.

About this time another influence resulted in important changes in naval design. The trade between New Orleans and the North Atlantic states, always important, had of late witnessed a tremendous growth. Owing to the bar at the mouth of the Mississippi it had been necessary to build a special type of shallow draft vessel for this commerce. These ships were almost perfectly flat on the floor, a feature which had always been considered detrimental to sailing qualities. But as no other kind of vessel could have negotiated the bar at the Balize they were built and it soon appeared that the flat floor was not so great a disadvantage as had been anticipated.

It so happened that Captain N. B. Palmer took command of one of these New Orleans packets in the early thirties, the *Huntsville*. She is said to have been a sister ship of the *Natchez* which later became famous under Waterman in the China trade, and it is quite probable that the vessels were similar. The *Huntsville* belonged to E. K. Collins & Co., one of the enterprising firms of the day, and later the founder of the magnificent Collins line of steamships. Mr. Collins was anxious to start a new Liverpool line and he called on Captain Palmer to assist in designing several vessels for that purpose.

The new venture was to be called the "Dramatic Line," possibly because Collins already owned the *Shakespeare*, of 827 tons. With Palmer's advice the ships *Garrick* and *Sheridan* were designed and launched in 1836, and the *Siddons* in 1837. All were of the same model and all measured 895 tons. A fourth of slightly improved model, the *Roscius* of 1009 tons, the largest packet ship that had yet been built and the largest merchant-man in America, was added in 1839.

All these ships adopted the most noteworthy innovation which had yet been developed in American naval architecture, the long, flat floor of the New Orleans packets. Heretofore all vessels which were designed for fast sailing had in greater or less degree the sharp V-bottom of the frigate. In spite of a considerable modification in theory, ship builders generally believed that speedy craft could not be built without a substantial dead rise. Even Brown & Bell, who constructed the Dramatic ships, shook their heads, while scores of old masters and builders declared "they'd never make a passage to the west'ard." However, both Collins and Palmer had learned a thing or two about the old cotton droughers, and they bided their time.

The results proved an unpleasant revelation to the established lines. In 1839 the four ships made twelve westward runs from Liverpool to New York in the average time of 28 days. It will be remembered that the average of the first Black Ballers over the same course was 40 days. Packet sailing had improved considerably in the interval but the new flatbottoms had set a much better average than any line in existence, and in addition had increased measurably their cargo capacity—a most important consideration.

One of the first of the new ships to distinguish herself was the *Garrick*. Under "Cap'n Nat" she left New York on the 1st of November, 1837, in company with the packet *England* also bound for Liverpool in command of Captain B. L. Waite. On this passage the *Garrick* made the then unprecedent run of less than 12 days to Cape Clear, thereafter meeting with contrary winds in the Irish Channel so that she did not dock until the 17th, a passage of 16 days. The *England* arrived the same day. Thereafter both ships sailed for New York on the same day and arrived off Sandy Hook a few hours apart, having made substantially the same time out and back. Both masters drove their ships to the utmost on these runs. Captain Waite being determined to show up the short-comings of the new droughers of the Dramatic Line, while Palmer had something quite different in mind.

Captain Palmer had the *Siddons* in 1839 and fell in with the frigate *United States,* then acknowledged to be the fastest sailer in the navy, and ran her, hull-down, in a short encounter, beating her 10 miles in 10 hours with perfect ease, although the frigate was a much larger vessel. Commodore Hull of the Ohio, 74, declared that the *Siddons* and *Roscius* would outsail any vessel in the American Navy. Since men-of-war with their enormous crews were able to carry sail far beyond the point where slenderly manned packets could cope with the situation, it is evident that the Dramatic liners represented something new and superior in the way of design. Little of the old theory of speed construction was embodied in them except the rule placing the point of greatest beam forward of amidships. During the next ten years even that rule was abrogated.

The *Roscius,* and to a slightly less degree the other ships of the Dramatic Line, had a most important influence on future packet design. This, parenthetically, is equivalent to saying that they had a most important influence on clipper ship design. From the time of their first successful voyages until the advent of the clippers and later, no liners were built which did not follow or improve upon their new points of excellence.

As a specimen of marine architecture the *Roscius* was the most remarkable ship of her day. Her cabins were finished in the most expensive woods. She cost $100,000.00 as compared with the $60,000.00 which marked the extreme limit of cost of the other packets. Her spread of canvas was immense. She swung a main yard 75 feet in length, as compared with the 82 foot yard of the *Flying Cloud,* an extreme clipper more than 700 tons heavier. Her main mast towered to the height of nearly 160 feet above her deck, again almost equivalent to the spars of the *Flying Cloud.* These facts are recorded, not to detract from the achievements of later builders, but as matters essential to sailing ship history. They had lofty ships and men to sail them long before the first clippers raced around the Horn.

A blunt, chunky craft by modern standards, the *Roscius* was nevertheless built "to go" by past masters in the art of calculated recklessness, and "go" she did. Her first three runs to the westward were made in an average of a few hours over 26 days—two days better than the already excellent average of the other Dramatic liners.

The model of the packet *Yorkshire* shown on another page represents with reasonable fidelity the new type of liner introduced by Palmer and his associates. A study of her lines reveals a virtually complete abandonment by her designers of the theories peculiar to earlier fast sailing craft. She was built by William Webb in 1843 and was acclaimed "the fastest packet of her time," although it is evident that today she would be termed an exceptionally full built ship. However, she has to her credit some of the best runs ever made by a packet.

The advent of the new models of the Dramatic Line may be taken to mark the period which definitely separated the old packet service from the new. It ushered in an era of remarkable improvement in size, design and equipment that did not cease until the liners of the sail exceeded 2000 tons register and provided a degree of comfort that made them in many instances preferred to the steamers as late as Civil War days. In fact, at intervals during the early 50's one finds editorials seriously asserting that the sail had definitely won the decision over steam; that steam was too dangerous, too uncomfortable, too expensive, and above all too slow! "It could never become anything more than an humble auxiliary to the sail."

It would be erroneous to ascribe the remarkable activity of the American merchant marine which followed the success of the Dramatic Line solely to the influence of those ships. They merely pointed the way for future development. For several years the manufacture of new records on the western ocean and Far Eastern courses had been at a standstill, indicating the need

"Game Cock" Entering San Francisco

Painted by Charles R. Patterson.

Courtesy of the New York, New Haven & Hartford Railroad Company.

UPPER: Half model of the Baltimore clipper ship *Ann McKim*, showing clearly the extreme dead-rise (or sharp, wedge-like shape of her bottom) and the deep after-drag common to all early fast ships.

LOWER: Half model of the "Canton packet ship *Sea Witch*" built from the table of measurements given by Griffiths, her designer. Built more than ten years later than the *Ann McKim*, it is evident that great changes were taking place in fast sailing theory. Her bottom is much flatter, her after-drag much less and her bow sharper (with concave, instead of convex lines) than the corresponding features of the *McKim*.

UPPER: CAPT. SAMUEL SAMUELS, of the clipper packet *Dreadnought*. Courtesy of the Peabody Museum of Salem.

LOWER: CAPT. JOHN E. WILLIAMS, of the clipper *Andrew Jackson*. Courtesy of Mr. Samuel Haley.

UPPER: CAPT. PEREZ NATHANIEL BLANCHARD, a master and shipbuilder of Yarmouth, Maine. Courtesy of William Hutchinson Rowe.

LOWER: CAPT. JOHN ROBERTS of the clipper barque *Storm*. Courtesy of the Peabody Museum of Salem.

CLIPPER SHIP "SEA WITCH."

PAINTED BY A CHINESE ARTIST IN HONG KONG ABOUT 1855.

From the collection of Charles R. Patterson. This picture was for many years the property of Mr. F. C. Matthews, the marine historian.

for a new principle of naval design. The *Roscius* had uncorked a new burst of speed, a very important thing it is true, but if there had not been other weighty interests involved, the matter would have ended there.

Steam, on land and sea, was becoming a factor. For two years prior to the launching of the *Roscius,* Palmer and everyone else in America had been hearing about the monster steamships building in England which were to revolutionize ocean travel. In the Spring of 1838 they had ocular proof of a new competitive force when the little *Sirius* steamed in by Sandy Hook, 17 days from Cork, followed in a few hours by the *Great Western,* 15 days from Bristol, the shortest passage that had ever been made.

Other influences were at work. Immigration was increasing tremendously. Oriental trade of all sorts was expanding, its most valued prizes going as ever to the swift. The slower, older vessels had been unable to average more than two round voyages to China in three years, involving long expensive layovers in China, the costly wear and tear of beating for weeks and sometimes months against the monsoon, with the practical certainty in the end of arriving home at a time when the market was glutted with tea and other Chinese goods. The day for that sort of thing was past.

Despite however the varied influences at work, there is a certain significance in the fact that about the time the Dramatic packets had demonstrated their value, several new Canton traders very like them in general characteristics, but with sharper lines and greater dead rise, were laid down at New York and in Massachusetts. One of the earliest of these ships was the *Akbar* built in 1839 by Samuel Hall at Medford. She measured 650 tons and was owned by John M. Forbes and others of Boston. On her first voyage, under Captain James Watkins, she went to Canton in the very fine time of 109 days against the monsoon.

Jotham Stetson built the *Probus* of 656 tons at Medford

in 1841. She was owned by Daniel P. Parker of Boston and Wm. S. Wetmore of New York, and appears to have been the first "Eastern-built" ship to establish a new record in the tea trade. Her exploit is recounted in the New York *Herald* of March 19th, 1842, as follows:

"The *Probus*, the finest and fastest ship ever in the China trade, will sail today for Canton. This clipper was built under the superintendence of Captain Sumner, her commander, at the East, and the first voyage she made out and home was performed in the almost incredible short space of eight months and fifteen days, including the time of discharging and reloading at Macao.—

"We believe this to be the quickest passage to the Celestial Empire and back on record, and indeed it equals the speed of the English Steamships."

As a matter of fact, the *Probus* had made the fine but not remarkable out of season run of 123 days home from Canton, leaving Macao on October 4th, 1841, and arriving at New York on the 4th of the following February. Her time for the round trip, however, seems to have established a new record.

Another important ship built about this time was the *Helena*, of 598 tons. She was built at New York by William Webb in 1841 for N. L. & G. Griswold. Her model is shown elsewhere in this book and her close resemblance to the Liverpool packet *Yorkshire* may be noted. She differed from the *Yorkshire* only in being sharper and more heavily rigged, tonnage considered. Like the *Probus* she enjoyed the distinction of being referred to as a "clipper," although it is obvious that vessels of this class were clippers in rig only, and not in mould.

The *Helena* sailed on her first voyage for Canton via Valparaiso on the 30th of October, 1841, commanded by the veteran master, Deliverance P. Benjamin. On the 4th of December, south of the Line, her log records that she came up with and passed the U. S. ship of the line *Delaware*, and 24 hours later the

Delaware was out of sight astern. A few days later the worthy Deliverance writes: "Fresh breezes with much rain. House all afloat. Not a dry spot in it. I wish the Devil had all such houses."

A perusal of the log indicates that the *Helena* did not have especially favorable weather on this voyage, but she made the fair run of 83 days to Valparaiso. In 1843 she covered the same course in 77 days. Benjamin's entry for May 19th of that year indicates that he had remarkably good fortune rounding the Horn:

> "Lat 52.25 S. Lon 79.09 W. Fine breeze S. E. & cloudy weather. Studdingsails set below and aloft. This is the most remarkably good fortune I have ever heard of in doubling the Cape in the Winter. We have had continued Easterly winds now for four days and the breeze is still fresh from the S. E. and the weather pleasant. The Lord be praised."

In 1845, still under Captain Benjamin, the *Helena* broke the transpacific record of the *John Gilpin,* by running from Callao to Hong Kong in 51 days. The following year, commanded by Captain Eyre, formerly of the *John Gilpin,* she established a new record from New York to Anjier. Eyre wrote from Anjier to the *U. S. Gazette:*

> "I am most happy to inform you of my safe arrival here, after a short passage of 73 days and 20 hours to Java Head, the shortest on record by three days. The *Helena* is a very fast ship and I have had very good luck.—The following is a summary of the points of our passage, viz: 23 days to the Equator, 29 to the Island of Trinidad, 47 to the Cape of Good Hope, 60 to the Island of St. Paul, and 73 days 20 hours inside Java Head.
>
> "The shortest passage ever made heretofore was 77 days by the *Montauk* from America and 75 by a British frigate from Portsmouth, England, which I consider not so good as 77 days from the United States. We made an average of

183 miles per day for 73 days, our maximum speed per day was 275 miles, and our minimum 60 miles. So that you can see that I had not strong fair winds all the time."

A few instances of this kind were sufficient to demonstrate that the earlier fast sailing design could not surpass the newer model even in speed, under all the trying conditions of the Canton course, while in carrying capacity they were hopelessly inferior. Slowly, very slowly indeed, naval designers were learning the lesson compressed half a century later into the homely statement: "Anyone can build a fast ship by cutting her bottom to pieces, but it takes a good man to build a 'carrier' and a 'racer' at the same time." Wherein—it is submitted—lay the crux of the clipper ship problem.

In the interval between the launching of the *Akbar* and the above passage of the *Helena* a considerable number of new vessels had entered the China trade. Some of these like the *Montauk* and *Paul Jones* were especially built for it. Others, of which the *Natchez* was one, were old ships diverted from other runs.

To command this rapidly growing fleet of Indiamen it was necessary to draw heavily on other trades. The work called for exceptionally able men—men who were not only good merchants but were even better seamen. Of all possible sources for such material the western Ocean "wind packets" held the greatest promise, and in truth the call came to willing ears. Many of the packet captains had worn dull the keen edge of their youthful enthusiasm for ramping back and forth across the Atlantic, facing freezing winter gales and blistering summer calms, confronted day and night with the necessity of quelling crews that were yearly becoming more ruffianly, and handling passengers of the lowest type under conditions of indescribable filth. By 1840, many of these captains had formed the habit of returning during midwinter to their Connecticut farms, or down on the "Cape," where the weather "was a coat warmer" than in bleak

Boston, to reappear in the early Spring, ready once more for the old grind on the "rail road route to Europe."

To men such as these, the wonderful records that were being made on the China and Calcutta runs held a special appeal. They could visualize long voyages over summer seas, through the snapping trades and droning monsoons, and there were doubtless few of them who did not ache for a chance to beat the last record of some old friend and shipmate in the China trade.

Among the old packet men who felt the lure of the Far East—to mention only two, of several outstanding figures—were Captains Robert H. Waterman and our old acquaintance, Nathaniel B. Palmer. In an age and service famous for supermen, these two would have made a very creditable clipper ship era by themselves. There were many remarkable men already well known, and destined to become better known in the China trade—men like Low, Dumaresq, Benjamin, Griswold, Lockwood, Land, Henry, McMichael, Hayes, Hallet and Cunningham.

Waterman and Palmer in some respects best represent the two leading but essentially different types developed in the hard school of the American merchant marine. Both were absolutely fearless "drivers," but where Waterman was wholly reckless of life and limb, Palmer felt his way carefully to the extreme edge of safety and stayed there. Waterman was all sailor. Palmer was that and a shrewd business man besides, and something more than an average good ship designer. By a coincidence the China career of the two men started about the same time. Captain Palmer cleared from Boston, on January 4th, 1843, for Canton, in the new ship *Paul Jones*, belonging to Robert B. Forbes. The very day before Captain Palmer cleared, Captain Waterman arrived at Canton in the old *Natchez* then about 12 years old, and a vessel of 523 tons measurement. He had gone out to Canton around the Horn, via Valparaiso and Mazatlan. Incidentally, he had made the run across the Pacific from Mazatlan in the remarkable time of 41 days, good clipper ship sailing. It was comparable to the record of 51 days from Valparaiso to

Canton established two years before by Benjamin in the "pre-clipper" *Helena.*

It has been frequently stated that before Waterman got the *Natchez,* she had acquired the name of being an uncommonly slow ship. As we have seen, however, she was similar to the *Huntsville, Nashville* and other flat floored New Orleans packets which were far from slow. Nor does the early record of the *Natchez* herself appear to bear out the contention of extraordinary dulness. For example, she sailed from Havre on the 25th of July, 1835, and arrived at New York August 27th, following. This was not only a good mid-summer passage, but she arrived in port the same day as the fast packets *Great Britain* and *Scotland,* which had sailed from Liverpool two and nine days respectively, before she sailed from Havre. It was something in those days to beat the crack liners.

Again, in 1840, Hays sailed the *Natchez* from Valparaiso to New York in 74 days, which was by no means slow time, and the following year, he took her over the same course in 64 days time which in later years was considered remarkable even for the fastest clippers. The fact seems to be that Howland and Aspinwall were not in the habit of buying uncommonly slow ships, and if they had gotten hold of one by chance they would doubtless have proceeded to get rid of it immediately. The *Natchez* had made the run more than once from New York to New Orleans in twelve days, as a packet ship, and while this is not record time—the record being apparently held by the old packet *Shakespeare* in her eight day passage in 1845—it is fast for the course. The *Huntsville* made the run in nine days in 1832, and the *Nashville's* run the latter part of February 1842, of 8 days and 15 hours from Sandy Hook to the Mississippi Bar is substantially equal to that of the *Shakespeare.*

On this run the *Nashville* set her studding sails the first night out from the Hook and did not take them in until she was ready to anchor at the Balize. It was a chance such as occurred to few men in a lifetime.

It is, of course, easy to over estimate the importance of mere modelling in the performance of a sailing ship. Under some cautious captains, the finest clipper that ever floated would make longer passages than a stubby cargo tub, while a Waterman could take a coal barge to sea and bring her home in creditable time looking, aloft, at least, like a clipper. There is no doubt that men like Hayes and Waterman fairly transformed the rig of the *Natchez*. Given a few spare spars, plenty of stuns'l poles, and an extra bolt or two of canvas, men of their terrific energy would not rest until they had every foot of canvas drawing that they could get to stand, the whole slender fabric one of symmetry and beauty.

This individuality or initiative, on the part of American seamen may not have been peculiar to the United States during the first half of the 19th century, but it appears to have been a quality more generally and generously distributed there than elsewhere. Even down to the closing years of the last century the driving propensity of Yankee masters was a by-word among sailors, while an American ship in a foreign port could be recognized as far as she could be seen. Her trim spars, taut rigging and neatly furled sails set her apart from all others, in no matter what welter of shipping.

CHAPTER XII

1840–1845

THE NEW CHINA PACKETS

IT CANNOT be said that either Waterman or Palmer were products of the packet service. In an age which bred no specialists, both men had accumulated experience in every variety of maritime trade, yet both were finished packet masters. At the age of twenty-one Waterman was first mate in the old Black Ball *Britannia*, under the veteran master Charles Marshall, and in 1833, when only twenty-four years of age, he was given the fine, fast *South America*, one of the newest and largest of the Black Ballers, a position demanding the highest grade of seamanship and unusual business ability. It was possibly a coincidence that he received his promotion just in time for the cold midwinter run.

Waterman remained in the *South America* nearly four years, or until he left the packet service in the early winter of 1836–7. This period covered the least profitable years in the history of the packet service. As might be expected no records were broken by the liners during the entire time and relatively few noteworthy passages were made. On the other hand, remarkable runs were being made to and from the Orient, as well as to the west coast of South America and it was evident to all that "something was doing" in those quarters.

These facts may have caused Waterman to leave the Liverpool Line. At any rate, he appears next, about the middle of November, 1837, bound from Boston to Valparaiso. The *Natchez* had just been taken off the New Orleans run by Howland and Aspinwall, and since Boston was then as now interested in copper and hides, it was natural that she should take on her cargo there. This service appears to have suited Waterman and he remained in it for some years, in command of various ships, eventually prolonging his voyage from Valparaiso to Canton for the first time in the year 1842–3, as we have seen. During this intermediate period the best run he appears to have made was his 70 day passage from Coquimbo to New York in the Spring of 1840. This was a fine showing but by no means a record. The *Ann McKim* as we have seen, had already bettered this time on several occasions, having made the run in 1837 in only 59 days.

Soon after this remarkable exhibition, the *McKim* was sent to China for the first time. She arrived back in New York on the 23rd of November, 1840, the year of the "opium war," after a tedious out-of-season passage, bringing the news of the arrival off Macao of the British fleet.

> "And the commencement of that outrage upon national justice and the rights of humanity which England, in the pride of her strength, meditates consummating at the expense of the ancient Empire of China."

The *McKim* made another rather long China voyage the following year. Then, in 1842, she ran from New York to Anjier in 79 days, the shortest passage on record at that time, and capped this achievement by returning home in the early Spring of 1843 in the excellent although not record time of 96 days. These voyages undoubtedly had some influence on the decision of Messrs. Howland and Aspinwall to extend their operations in the Canton trade, and helped pave the way for a series of the most remarkable records the world has ever witnessed. Incidentally, also, Howland & Aspinwall had in Hayes, Land and Waterman perhaps the most extraordinary triumvirate that ever walked the quarter deck of a sailing ship.

It was a notable period. *Dana* had recently immortalized the coast of California and the little brig, *Pilgrim*. Captain Freeman Hatch was out there in Boston ships laying the foundation for his later world famous clipper records. Ashore, Christopher Lilly and Thomas McMorrow were settling the title to a purse of $200.00 by fighting bare knuckles for 120 rounds, McMorrow dying on his feet in the ring after nearly three hours of punishment. Niblo was serving turtle soup daily at 10 o'clock at the Union races. Dumaresq, after a fling at the opium business, was slamming the old *Great Britain* out to China and back, "full sail in double reef gales." Howland in the famous *Horatio*, a Grinnell-Minturn ship, had just embellished a long list of notable achievements by making four successive out-of-season passages to and from Canton in the average time of 104 days, incidentally in 1843 claiming a round voyage record of 8 months and 20 days although it exceeded that of the *Probus* in 1842 by five days. At New York, the packet service was meeting the new steam competition by a tremendous expansion, with huge three deckers building, anticipating somewhat the first Boston ships of this class. The opium trade was attracting a good deal of attention, and in Boston the honest and always philanthropic Captain Forbes was getting ready to engage in the traffic in the fast sailing armed brig *Antelope*.

Nothing better illustrates the conditions which then prevailed than two remarkable incidents which took place about this time. One was the tragedy of the *William Brown* which struck an iceberg in the winter of '41 while loaded with immigrants. After a few hours in the long boat loaded with 31 of the passengers and crew, the mate proceeded to throw overboard sixteen of the passengers including several young girls amid scenes

that are too horrible to describe. He was later tried and con-
victed of manslaughter. The story set forth in detail by the
newspapers of the day forms a remarkable contrast to an almost unbroken series of tales of bravery and chivalry on the
high seas.

The other incident was the affair of the United States brig
Somers which arrived at New York toward the close of 1842,
from a cruise on the Atlantic with a crew of upwards of 100 men
and boys, mostly boys. Her captain electrified the world by
calmly announcing that a few mornings before he had hung at
the yardarm a midshipman and two boys, none of whom was
more than seventeen years old, for attempted mutiny. A court
martial followed, with disclosures which sickened people everywhere—a tale of brutality that remains one of the most revolt-
ing records in history; that pictured a little vessel manned principally by boys less than 14 years of age, drifting aimlessly about
the Atlantic, the scene of hourly brutal floggings, mere children
loaded with irons, thrust into the bowels of the ship and fed
on bread and water—the whole horrible story culminating in
the early morning hanging, at the instance of a uniformed
megalo-maniac.

Few men at sea were like the mate of the *William Brown*
or the captain of the *Somers* but the most kindly shipmaster
afloat was compelled to recognize the fact that such men and
the conditions that nourished them might be encountered anywhere. It was a soil in which strange inconsistencies of character grew and flourished. After all, seamen were men of action,
not greatly skilled in mapping out principles of conduct.

Strangely conflicting ethical standards were the rule, therefore, when Palmer, Waterman, Hayes and a round dozen others
started to break into the tea trade, in 1843, and thereabouts,
Captain Land had already grown old in the service, but he was
to remain active for many years, to die at last in the harness
after having commanded some of the noblest clippers that ever
sailed blue water.

Still in the old *Splendid,* a Baltimore ship of not unclippery qualities, launched early in 1832 and measuring 473 tons, he came home from Canton in the Spring of '43 in 102 days. Waterman brought the *Natchez* back in 92 days and this was claimed as a record, the 90 day run of the *Sabina* in 1834 apparently having been overlooked. Palmer, in the *Paul Jones,* did not reach New York until the following October, having made the run in 118 days, very fair time for an out-of-season passage. His 79 days from Anjier was excellent sailing.

Waterman, then a powerful man of 35 in his very prime, was bubbling over with elation at his successful passage, and keen for another try at the record. Palmer, who was 44, had been impressed with the possibilities of trade in fast-sailing ships in the Far East, particularly in the opium business, and he spent his spare time on the voyage home making a model for a new ship, designed to outsail anything afloat. Into it he wrought with critical eye and mind the sea experience of thirty years, embracing a practical acquaintance with every known fast sailing type from pilot built craft and Liverpool liner to the latest China packet. It so happened that Captain Palmer had as a passenger on the homeward voyage of the *Paul Jones,* William H. Low, who became much interested in Captain Nat's model and ideas and agreed to take a three-quarter interest in the proposed ship, and when they arrived in New York he took Palmer at once to see his brothers.

The result was that the ship *Houqua* was started for A. A. Low & Bro. early in November at the yard of Brown & Bell, in New York, within a few days after the arrival of the *Paul Jones.* Before her keel was cogged and fastened, an event of major importance in America's history had been celebrated a few blocks away, viz., the "First Monster Meeting of the American Republican Party" which occurred on the evening of November 20th, 1843, at the corner of Hudson and Christopher Street. Like many another happening of the period this meeting has since been ascribed to later times and other places. Nevertheless the workmen who talked the meeting over on the morning of the 21st as they clipped away at the timbers of the new craft, gave it small thought and missed no stroke of the adze. Well they knew that men like Palmer and A. A. Low brooked no loss of time when they had once arrived at a decision.

The *Houqua* when finished was 142 feet long, 32 feet wide and 17 deep, a flush decked ship measuring about 600 tons. While she was building, the *Helena,* still under Captain Benjamin, came home from Canton in 90 days, beating Waterman's run by two days, reaching New York, April 4th, 1844.

Three days after the *Helena* arrived, Webb launched another "China Packet" of 500 tons called the *Montauk,* a very handsome sharp ship. It was evident that the China trade was looking up. Six ships had already arrived that Spring from the Flowery Kingdom. The *Houqua* was launched less than a month after the *Montauk,* on Friday, the third of May, 1844, and in the interval between the two launchings, Waterman completed his second homeward run in the *Natchez,* making a 94 day passage.

The arrival of the *Houqua* on the scene was the signal for the appearance of the first of a series of semi-poetical effusions that were to greet the more noteworthy of the new ships for the next decade, and were to herald more than a hundred of the most beautiful craft the world has ever beheld. Bennett's article in the young and vociferous *Herald* is typical, and we quote it in part:

"One of the prettiest and most rakish looking packet ships ever built in the civilized world is now to be seen at the foot of Jone's Lane on the East River. . . .

"We never saw a vessel so perfect in all her parts as this new celestial packet. She is about 600 tons in size—as sharp as a cutter—as symmetrical as a yacht—as rakish in her rig as a pirate—and as neat in her deck and cabin arrangements as a lady's boudoir.

Her figure head is a bust of Houqua, and her bows are as sharp as the toes of a pair of Chinese shoes."

She had, moreover, high man-of-war bulwarks, pierced on each side for eight guns, sixteen in all, and she was six feet between decks, an unusual height for this trade.

Palmer sailed in the *Houqua* for Canton on Friday, May 31st, 1844, slightly more than six months after he had stepped ashore with her little wooden model under his arm. She arrived at Macao in 95 days, a very fine run.

About the time the *Houqua* was laid down, a larger ship, the *Rainbow*, was started by Smith & Dimon at their yard a short distance away. She was ordered by Howland & Aspinwall from a design by John Willis Griffith, a very able young naval architect in the employ of Smith & Dimon. Years after the *Rainbow* had reached the port of all good ships a tale, spun from slender material, gained circulation which in effect pictured her as "an original" springing full rigged and all a tanto from the mind of a youthful genius. It is no discourtesy to the memory of Griffiths whose reputation and achievements stand on secure foundations, to say that the story is overdrawn.

The *Rainbow* represented a certain departure from fast-sailing models of her day but she was far from being a radically new type. She differed from former vessels merely in the manner in which she combined existing principles of design—a statement which holds equally true for every successful ship of the period. However, her appearance as she gradually took shape on the stocks aroused so much criticism that her owners delayed her completion for more than a year. She was, perhaps, the first large ship of the extremely hollow bow type, and in spite of the fact that very similar lines had been incorporated in pilot boats for years, old wiseacres grumbled that her bows were "turned inside out." She was finally launched on Washington's Birthday, 1845, and the *Herald* welcomed her:

> "This morning at nine o'clock, the *Rainbow*, a new clipper ship for the China trade, will be launched from the yard of Smith & Dimon. She is seven hundred and fifty tons in size, and will be commanded by Captain Land, who,

for several years, very splendidly navigated the *Splendid,* in the same trade that is to receive the new ship. The *Rainbow* holds out a promise, we should judge by her model, of great speed."

While diplomatic conversations between Howland & Aspinwall and the young Griffiths were being held, two other fast ships were building for the tea trade, both of which were launched in 1844. One was the *Panama,* of 670 tons, constructed by Wm. Webb for N. L. & G. Griswold. The other was the barque *Coquette,* of 420 tons built at East Boston by Samuel Hall for Russell & Co. The *Coquette* was first commanded by Oliver Eldridge, a Cape Cod boy and a brother of Asa Eldridge, afterwards lost in the steamer *Pacific,* but not before he had established some notable records in the clipper service.

It can readily be seen, therefore, that the desire to build Canton packets of a faster type than existed must have inspired several people about the same time, and while the actual launching of the ships took place on different dates, they were all in process of construction together. Too much stress, however, cannot be laid upon the fact that long before this time—certainly after the Dramatic packets were built, if not before—all the essential features of the later clipper had been tested in one combination or another.

Individual claims for the prior invention or construction of the clipper ship were not made until years afterward. A careful study of the marine items of the day seems to establish the fact that the only thing in the minds of the designers and builders of these early ships was the simple desire to attain a greater sailing speed, and to this end they progressed slowly and carefully, testing every step of the way. It is doubtful whether anyone had the slightest idea that ships could be built to sail faster than 15 knots until the big California clippers began to appear in 1850. At all events the most fulsome yellow journal reporter of the period never mentioned any faster rate of sailing as the goal of a newly launched vessel. Buried in the marine columns of the press from 1820 to 1850 one dimly perceives the outlines of a vast moving picture—a procession of hundreds of seamen, merchants, naval architects and builders, moving step by step toward an ultimate goal which none of them consciously visualized. If one happened to take a longer step or attain a more striking success than another, it may well have been that he merely analyzed new features a trifle more clearly or rapidly than another.

By 1845, however, it was evident that our naval architects and seamen were on the track of new possibilities in the way of sailing ship speed. A. A. Low & Company's new ship, the *Montauk,* under McMichael, came home from Canton in 94 days, not a remarkable run, in itself, but she had made the passage from China to Cape Hatteras in 87 days. Hepburn, in the *Cohota,* another Griswold ship, made it in 100 days. Bucklin & Crane's barque *Grafton,* Captain Gardner, reported 96 days.

The day after the *Grafton* arrived, the old *Natchez* under Waterman, came romping up the Narrows in the world beating time of 78 days, having left Macao on the 14th of January, and arriving at New York the 3rd of April, 1845. The sensation created by this run can easily be imagined. Waterman, strange as it may seem to those who are familiar with the fo'c'sle gossip sometimes served up as authentic history, walked the streets of New York a hero. Every one wanted to shake his hand, and if there was any talk of arrests, the proponents were undoubtedly in too hazy a state of mind within an hour after reaching port to carry out that or any other intention. The glamour of a China only eleven weeks distant absorbed every one's thoughts to the exclusion of all else.

Howland & Aspinwall were delighted. Not only had their ship made an immensely profitable voyage but their firm had received an incredible amount of free advertising the world over. They made plans to build the largest and swiftest ship in the China trade for Waterman.

In a little more than a month Waterman was off again in the *Natchez* for Canton, close on the heels of the *Houqua*. The following June, Conklin brought the *Stephen Lurman* of Baltimore home in 95 days, having made the round to Canton in 8 months and 10 days.

On the 9th of August, Grinnell & Minturn sent Captain James F. Creesy to Canton in the *Oneida*, a fine packet of 420 tons, which had been built in 1832 for Francis A. Hathaway and others of New Bedford and Gideon Nye, Jr., of New York.

By the autumn of 1845, there were no less than 44 ships and two barques owned in America regularly engaged in the China trade, besides others which made occasional passages. Practically all these ships brought their cargoes to New York, although more than half of them were owned in Boston and elsewhere. New York was now the home of the Canton specialist as Boston was of the Calcutta trade. In addition there were twelve other American owned vessels permanently employed on the China coast, some of which were trading with South America regularly.

The *Rainbow* returned to New York on the 19th of September, in the unfavorable season run of 105 days. She had, however, made the new record of 7 months and 17 days for the round trip. Captain Land had driven the top gallant masts out of her four days after leaving New York, incidentally driving her under and nearly losing her. On the return voyage he lost his only remaining sails and it took ten days and nights and a rich vocabulary to repair and replace them.

Benoni Lockwood, a veteran in the East India trade, and later master of the beautiful *White Squall*, made a Bombay passage this year that still ranks with the best. On a voyage from Liverpool to Bombay he took his departure from off Holy Head on the 4th of April and hove to for a pilot off Bombay on the 19th of June, having made the passage in the then record time of 77 days. He had the new Philadelphia built ship *Tartar* of 573 tons.

Aside from the Canton and India trade, the year 1845 was

a notable one for the shipping industry. It was marked by a slight falling off in new construction due to the apprehension of war with England over the Oregon question, and with Mexico over the location of the Texas border. On the other hand, Brown & Bell launched the *Henry Clay*, of 1402 tons, 189 feet 6 inches long and having the astounding depth of 30 feet. She was considered to be the largest merchant ship afloat.

In Boston, Train was trying to get his Liverpool Line under way—an effort which seems to have been productive of much local criticism, if one can judge from caustic comments of *"Boston Correspondent."* He had four ships, "only one of which, the *Joshua Bates*, built by Donald McKay, could sail." Even at that the line might have given satisfaction of a sort, were it not for the fact that "sailing day" as often as not saw the ship starting for a southern port to fill up, instead of leaving for Liverpool.

The glamour of Train's espousing the cause of young McKay is dimmed by the suspicion that Train was operating "on a shoestring" at the time, and probably needed McKay even more than McKay needed him. However, time and a native business ability remedied that.

There is little doubt that at this period Boston built ships were inferior in size, model and strength to the New York vessels. This was not the fault of the builders, for they knew how to build fine ships. The fact seems to be that Boston merchants did not want to invest the money in a single hull that the New York firms did. Probably, owing to local conditions, which included the competition of the Cunard steamers, a liner which cost around $100,000.00—the price of a first class packet—could not have earned her way at the time in the Boston-Liverpool trade.

This year also saw the beginnings of the first regular packet line between Baltimore and Liverpool, which advertised active operations in 1846 with three old packets—the *Emerald* and *Rhone*, formerly on the Havre run, and the *Roscoe*, a Liverpooler.

E. K. Collins also felt the call of steam this year, and put up the Dramatic Line for sale. Eventually he built four of the largest steamers in the world, all side-wheelers, and started the famous Collins Line.

Long before this time, the fast river and sound steamers had been developed on a scale which had no equal the world over. It was true they were not very safe. The inland and coastal waters from Maine to the Mississippi echoed to the popping of over-distended boilers, and many a grim shower rained into the racing waters. Nevertheless, there was progress, and the year 1845 saw side-wheelers 300 feet and more in length and capable of a speed of considerably over 20 miles an hour, covering the distance between New York and Albany in less than eight hours.

On the first day of October, for instance, while the stevedores were lowering the last of the *Rainbow's* second cargo into her hold, the new *Oregon* ran from New York to Albany in seven hours and a half. Her average speed as far as Hudson was 23½ statute miles per hour.

Steam shovels and steam winches had been in operation for the past two years. Apparently the first steam winch for loading a ship was used on the ship *Russell Glover* at Pier 4, North River, New York, in October, 1843.

Railroads also were playing their part in titillating the great American mania for speed. When the anxiously awaited Cunarder arrived in Boston, her mail bags would be hurried to the new Providence & Boston depot and rushed to Stonington at the eminently unsafe rate of 48 to 50 miles an hour, there to be thrown on to the New York boat which lay at the wharf, paddles slowly turning and safety valve popping. It was not unusual for the European mail to be delivered in New York within twelve hours after the liner docked in Boston—an achievement which modern methods have improved upon only slightly.

CHAPTER XIII

1845–1846

THE CLIPPER PACKETS

I F 1845 had dragged a trifle after the unwonted
activity of the previous two years this could not
be said of 1846. Before it was over the Mexican
war was in full swing, and the failure of Euro-
pean crops and partial repeal of British corn laws had started a
demand for new ships which was to continue almost unabated
until the first requirements of the Australian gold miners were
satisfied eight years later.

It was the year which saw the installation of telegraph service
between Washington, New York and Boston. Leeching and cupping were going out of style. Here and there an advanced
modernistic couple talked daringly of installing a bath tub. "The
Havana" became plain Havana, although ships were still clearing to the "Spanish Main" and voyages were still made to "the
Brazils." Wig-makers' advertisements had lingeringly disappeared from the press. More people than ever were buying the
New York *Herald* and chuckling over its Elizabethan witticisms.
The first American-built steamer had gone to China, equipped
with special facilities for handling opium, including an 8 inch
howitzer and 6 inch rifle.

Forbes had turned from the business to build the first large ocean-going tug in the country—the *R. B. Forbes,* a twin-screw, double-engined, iron steamer measuring 300 tons. Busily engaged laying down her lines and working out her specifications was a boy of twenty named Samuel Harte Pook. He will be heard from again.

Eighteen forty-six, and forty-six ships dotting the waters between Canton and New York. At least twice that number of the "fittenest" masters and mates that ever walked a quarter-deck unwittingly making ready for the hardest, fastest service under sail the world has ever seen. Names even now to conjure with: Cressy, Nickels, Kinney, Lovett, Easterbrook, Crocker, Hepburn, Lockwood—some of whom have already been noted.

The year began ominously for ships of the sail. The *John Minturn* coming up from New Orleans in the dead of winter in the clutch of a howling northeast snow storm brought up on Barnegat with several other ships. While a New Jersey pastor and his flock greedily looted the drifting wreckage, Captain Stark, his wife and children and some 36 others of the passengers and crew slowly froze to death in the rigging, victims to the confused ethics of the times. A few days later the magnificent *Henry Clay,* with our old friend Captain Nye, went ashore where the *Minturn's* timbers still strewed the beach, but Nye was more fortunate and got his ship off with the loss of only six lives.

In the interval the *Houqua,* still under Cap'n Nat, had completed her second round to Canton, returning in 94 days.

Wm. McMichael, in the *Montauk,* distinguished himself next by arriving at New York on the 8th of April, 87 days from Macao. He was only 10 days to Anjier, and 42 days from Macao to the Cape of Good Hope. The *Montauk* is said to have been a vessel after the model of the *Helena,* but was somewhat smaller and sharper, measuring 550 tons. This was her fourth trip between New York and Canton, in none of which had she been more than 90 days at sea—a remarkable record.

Right on the heels of the *Montauk* was the *Rainbow,* 79 days out. Captain Land was only 60 days from Macao to the line, and had, moreover, completed his round voyage in the unprecedented time of 6 months and 16 days, including his detention in port.

Captain Land celebrated the event by breaking a life long reputation for taciturnity. "The *Rainbow*," he declared, "was the fastest ship that had ever sailed the seas, and, moreover, the ship couldn't be built to beat her."

The astute old captain may be pardoned for this boast. His sailing days began and were mostly lived in old bluff bowed ships like the *Globe*.

Justus Doane was out in the South Seas in the old *Congaree* from Boston, acquiring the experience that was later to assist him in taking the smart clipper *R. B. Forbes* from Boston to Honolulu in record time. His log of 1846 carefully notes the removal of his chafing gear as soon as he reached port and stowed his sails. A fine man and a thorough seaman—no dutchman's pennants decorated his ship in harbor or at sea.

Waterman got back to New York on the 14th of June in the *Natchez*, after an out-of-season passage of 103 days. He turned the *Natchez* over to Land, and Hayes took the *Rainbow*, sailing for Canton the 18th of May, via Valparaiso.

Another sharp-built ship, the *Ariel*, 570 tons, was being constructed "down east," by Currier & Townsend at Newburyport, for the Canton trade. She was owned by Minot & Hooper, Josiah Bradlee and Captain Macondry, and was launched on the 18th of October, two weeks before the *Yorkshire* left Liverpool on her record run of 16 days to New York. While apparently not in a class with the *Rainbow*, the *Ariel* made several very excellent passages.

Less than two months later, on the 8th of December, to be specific, the famous *Sea Witch* took the water from Smith & Dimon's yard at the foot of Fourth Street, New York, and the *Herald* gave the following account of her:

"The splendid ship *Sea Witch,* whose peculiar model and sharp bows have for the past few months attracted so much attention, was launched yesterday from the yard of Smith & Dimon, foot of Fourth Street.

"She was built for Messrs. Howland & Aspinwall, for the Canton trade, and is to run in connection with the fast sailing ship *Rainbow,* also owned by the same gentlemen.

"The *Sea Witch* is, for a vessel of her size, the prettiest vessel we have ever seen, and much resembles the model of the steamer *Great Britain,* only on a smaller scale. She is built of the very best material, and, although presenting such a light appearance, is most strongly constructed. Her figure head is intended to represent the black dragon—the symbol of the Chinese Empire.

"Capt. R. H. Waterman, of the ship *Natchez,* who, like Capt. Bailey of the *Yorkshire,* is celebrated for quick passages, is to have command.

"Her length is 192 feet over all, 34 feet beam, 19 hold, and 900 tons burthen, making as fine a specimen of New York shipbuilding as we have seen in a long time."

She sailed for Canton December 23rd, 1846. Thus started a sea career of less than ten years, by all odds the most remarkable ten years of sail in the history of the world. Before her brief life had ended, the *Sea Witch* had broken more records than a ship of her inches had ever broken and in company with other clippers had established the majority of sailing records that still survive. She was the first vessel to go around the Horn to California in less than one hundred days. Twice she broke the record for speed from Canton to the United States, and neither of these passages have ever been equalled by any ship under sail.

In 1847, Europe was no place for a poor man. The potato crop failed. There was actual famine in Ireland and a shortage of food stuffs everywhere. England was being forced to open the ports for grain. Ships were wanted. Emigrants were coming to America in hordes. New York could not begin to supply her merchants' demands for tonnage and they went East for more ships. The yards of Medford, East Boston, Newburyport and a dozen other places began to hum with redoubled activity.

Another winter of disaster on the sea. Captain John Rathbone's career had started with an attempt to torpedo the British fleet off Stonington in 1814. A big, kindly man. The fine new mammoth packet *Columbia* was swept by a giant wave on the 13th of January, washing away her wheelhouse with Captain Rathbone, his first and second mates, five men and a boy, leaving the body of the third mate jammed under the tiller, and the ship officerless. A drunken orgy followed, the crew of packet rats plundering ship and passengers, while they drifted helpless in the gale. Not a bad essay on the qualities required in a ship's officers in that day.

Captain Wm. H. Hayes slithered in by the Hook the last day of February, 85 days from Canton. "The magnificent clipper ship *Rainbow*," said the papers.

Captain Palmer was superintending the construction of the *Samuel Russell*, designed to be the fastest and most powerful ship in the China trade.

Nickels, destined to become a clipper racer of renown, drives the none too speedy *John Q. Adams* from Canton to New York in 97 days—a remarkable feat, all things considered.

The *Panama*, still under Griswold, came back in 91 days, and the *Natchez* in 95.

China is yielding to foreign influence, forcefully expressed. Shanghai is open and the *Huntress*, Captain Gillespie, makes what is, perhaps, the first passage from that port to New York, in 110 days.

Smith & Dimon were building a ship "of clipper mould" to measure a thousand tons. She proved to be the *Memnon*, the first clipper to round the Horn in the imminent rush to California, a vessel somewhat resembling the *Sea Witch*.

The *Sea Witch* herself gets back to New York the 25th of July, a trifle over 81 days from Canton, *against the monsoon*—a record. But she has too many records for one more or one less to matter. On her outward passage she passed the Cape of Good Hope 42 days out, having sailed 8894 miles, an average of 206 miles a day for six consecutive weeks—a record. She passed Java Head 70 days and 10 hours out—a record. Her best day's run up to that point was 302 miles, and she had averaged 248 miles a day for 10 days.

On her return she ran from Anjier to the Cape in 26 days, another record. Her best day's run was 312 miles. She took her New York pilot on, 62 days from Anjier, again a record, and during that run she had averaged 264 miles a day for 10 days. It does not appear that Waterman avoided either publicity or the police on his return.

A few days of feverish activity and the New York *Herald*, under date of August 15th, published the following:

"REMARKABLY QUICK SAILING—The Canton Packet *Sea Witch*, as the whole world knows, has made a remarkably quick passage to China; but the rate at which she sailed yesterday beat anything she ever performed.

"She left our port in charge of Mr. John Hyer, of the New York pilot boat *John E. Davison*; and, incredible as it may appear to persons not acquainted with her, she got to sea, a distance of nineteen miles in the extremely short time of one hour and three minutes."

Doubtless the tide helped, but it was "sailing some."

The day that the *Sea Witch* gave to New Yorkers this remarkable exhibition of speed, the new clipper *Samuel Russell* was launched. She measured 174 feet in length and 34 feet 4 inches in breadth and her depth of hold was 20 feet, giving her 50 tons greater register than the *Sea Witch*. One of the papers of the times commented on her appearance as follows:

"The external appearance of the vessel is strikingly beautiful; her great length, towering and well proportioned spars, her sharp bows and clean, graceful run, give her a dashy, man-of-war air. Her bow is formed according to the new style, no lumbering heavy cut-water, the planking running chuck up to the stem, and is ornamented with a finely carved billet head, and gilded carved work along the trail board.

.   .   .   .   .   .

"The hull is black with a narrow red and white ribbon streak around her waist. The yards, black, the jib and flying jib-booms varnished and tipped with black."

Her deck was nearly flush, clear and unencumbered. Her cabin was in a half-poop lighted by a sky-light and 7 square stern windows. She had no house on deck except one to hold the long boat, galley and fowl coop. The crew slept below, and she had Robinson's patent steering apparatus.

The *Russell* was undoubtedly one of the best examples of marine architecture then in existence. That she won and kept the love of men who sailed on her may be gathered from the following letter published in the New York *Herald* on the 23rd of September, 1851:

"A Clipper as Is a Clipper"

"To the Skipper of the New York *Herald:*

"Hope you will excuse the liberty an unlearned fo'castle salt takes in presuming to pay his services to your honor after this fashion; but d'ye see there's no help for it, seeing as how the beautiful yarn in Saturday's *Herald* about Yankee pilot boats, and Yankee yachts and Yankee steamers, and Yankee clippers, was very awkwardly spun, in one respect, as it seems to me; and that was in neglecting to include among your list of clipper ships, the name of one of the sweetest crafts that ever danced through old Neptune's dominions. I mean the clipper ship *Samuel Russell*, of this port, built by Westervelt & McKay.

"O, sir, you may safely believe it, she is indeed some, and a plain tar begs you will excuse a wholesome jealousy he feels for the reputation of a craft his heart is somewhat bound up in. Why, sir, though nearly every one of the clippers in your long list has been built since the *Russell*, and of course all supposed to be on Brother Jonathan's scale of gradual improvement, yet I would be glad to stake the wages of a twelve months' voyage, that throughout John Bull's wide extended kingdom, either in his navy or among his merchantmen, no matter what the size or rig, he has not a vessel among the whole crowd that could successfully compete with the *Samuel Russell*.

"When I made a voyage to China in that 'ere ship, under command of old Captain Nat. Palmer (a captain, let me tell you, as is a captain), we had an experience of so wonderful a character that it has often been a wonderment to me, that the ship's owners, or some of her relations, did not blow on it through the newspapers. Scores of vessels, on the same tack with ourselves, were overhauled and ran away from with just the same ease as the America beat the Royal yachts of England. Occasionally, to be sure, some brother Yankee would put the good ship to her mettle before we could shake her off; but as to anything foreign—whether English, or French, or Dutch, or what not, and we had chances with all sorts of them—why, Lord bless you, sir, it was the merest baby play in the world.

"But, lest you should consider this only a sailor's yarn, also to give you a more definite idea of her performances on that voyage, allow me to state one fact that may be proved by her log-book. One day, we took a pretty smart breeze upon our starboard quarter, and it continued to blow tolerably steady for the space of ten days. At the end of that time we had skimmed upwards of forty-five degrees, making, as you will perceive, hard on to three thousand two hundred miles in ten days. The handsomest run, in any one day, was three hundred and twenty-eight miles. Now, sir, I humbly submit, if that is not a feat to boast of? If that is not an achievement to entitle a ship to be classed among the clippers? But the most astonishing fact of all remains to be told, and I tell it to you upon the word of an honest sailor, that, from the time we left Sandy Hook until our return (being the first to report our own arrival in China), I never saw scarce a gallon of water on her deck that did not either come from the clouds or was drawn up by the bucket rope.

"I could tell you many interesting facts connected with

the history of this favorite ship—how, on a subsequent voyage, all hands wrote home from Hong Kong, by a ship that sailed nearly a month before us, and how beautifully we overhauled and passed her, having thereby to deliver the contents of our letters by word of mouth. How—but I must haul in the slack, as your time is too important to be taken up with a rough sailor's yarn. But I will say, however, with your permission, that, in my humble opinion, if the *Russell* were somewhat more heavily sparred, there is not a ship afloat, in the world that could outsail her. You may, perhaps, judge of the correctness of this opinion, when informed that while she is sixty tons larger than the *Sea Witch*, and is, in all respects, fully her equal, yet she carries one-fifth less canvass than that justly celebrated clipper.

"Hoping that you will excuse this boldness, and that you may shortly herald the arrival of Capt. Limeburner, now in command of the *Samuel Russell*, I remain your very humble servant,

ROBERT STEIGH,
nicknamed by my messmates 'Bob Stay.' "

"September 22, 1851."

A comparison of the models of the *Samuel Russell* and the *Sea Witch*, the two most advanced ships of their day, suggests that the *Russell* was capable of holding her own with any ship afloat. She sailed for Canton on the 13th of September, 1847, under command of Captain Nat Palmer, sometime blockade runner, sealer, explorer, packet autocrat and China trader. Her first voyage is sufficiently described in the letter given above.

The lines of the *Russell* indicate unmistakably her close kinship with the later Liverpool packets. Her essential difference was in the degree of sharpness and in the further fact that she embodied the pronounced dead-rise of the earlier packets. This, however, was a concession to the nature of the China passage, which as a rule involved an unusual amount of close-hauled sailing in light variable airs. It was as well understood then as now, that in cargo carriers the wedge bottom type of ship was far better adapted to this kind of sailing than the flatter type.

Most of the vessels which made notable records on the Canton run were of this V-bottom sort—an almost invariable feature of the British tea ships twenty years later. Hence the *Samuel Russell* is not an example of an ill-considered reversion to an earlier type, but a well-planned combination of the most desirable sailing qualities, with reference to anticipated weather conditions. The bump of practicality was most highly developed in the sailor of '45.

This matter of designing a ship to meet particular conditions has been practiced from time immemorial, and it is the explanation underlying many conflicting claims as to the relative speed of famous craft. In light, leading airs, for instance, Webb's sharp bottomed *Gazelle* could have sailed all around the *Sovereign of the Seas,* while in heavy following gales the relatively flat floored *Sovereign* would have travelled three feet to the *Gazelle's* two, and carried sail long after the *Gazelle* was stripped to bare poles.

In this connection, too, the matter of loading, trim, condition of the bottom, etc., were often the deciding factors. The great records of the clippers were often made with the vessel badly out of trim, or deeply overloaded, or with bottoms foul from a year or more spent in warm waters. Yet, compared with later voyages of ships carefully trimmed to an inch with moveable weights and with light tea or wool cargoes putting them down to their best sailing marks and sharpest water lines, with bottoms cleaned and freshly painted, the early clippers show to marked advantage. The driving force of the old sea-toughened clipper captains seems never to have been equalled by the younger breed. Or it may have been merely that the day when owners were willing to pay for glory and split sails was past.

CHAPTER XIV

1847–1849

BOOM DAYS IN AMERICA

AMERICA in 1847 was the granary of the world. The railroads were feverishly hauling wheat from the Middle West, charging what the traffic would bear, reaping a harvest of dividends that was to end in an orgy of construction, and the panic of '57. Bigger and faster packets. Swifter clippers. Steamships that astounded the world.

The new Griffiths clipper, the *Memnon,* was launched by Smith & Dimon. The *Samuel Russell,* embodying Cap'n Nat Palmer's latest theories, had been built by Brown & Bell. Probably no two men contributed more toward working out the practical details of early clipper design than Griffiths and Palmer.

Westervelt & Mackay were at work on the 1700 ton side-wheelers *Washington* and *Hermann* for the Ocean Steam Navigation Company. The *United States,* 2600 tons, was laid down in the yard of Wm. Webb for Charles H. Marshall & Company. Dozens of smaller steamers of all descriptions were on the stocks, to be followed within two years in Jacob Bell's yard by the huge *Pacific* and *Baltic,* of 3600 and 3700 tons, carpenter's measure, launched in 1849 and 1850 respectively, for the new E. K. Collins Line.

The "Down-Easters" were busy. Donald McKay had already put over the *John R. Skiddy*, 930 tons, and the *New World*, the latter a monster of 1404 tons and very sharp for a packet, "having" one contemporary account said, "been intended for a frigate." Her launching was delayed until the 9th of September, 1846, "as the workmen had religious scruples against working on the Sabbath."

Samuel Hall, of East Boston, was building sharp fast ships. New vessels were sold abroad in large numbers. "Europe wished to avail herself of the benefit of our skill in naval architecture." "There was a perfect mania for building ships."

Train withdrew the *Joshua Bates* from the Liverpool run and sent her to Canton, under Stoddard, to reap some of the fabulous profits of the new style tea trade. She made a rather long homeward passage of 120 days, Palmer bringing in the *Houqua* a few days later in 101 days, possibly affording a basis of comparison between the two ships, rather than their commanders.

Perine, Patterson & Stack, a new yard established in 1845, launched the packet *Jamestown* at the head of Water Street, New York, on the 9th of November, 1847. She rated 1300 tons, and was at once loaded for Liverpool. They also built the *Senator*, a portly packet of 1250 tons, for Slate, Gardiner & Company, owners of the Jamestown.

Four "canvas back liners," all over 1300 tons, were brought out the same year by Wm. Webb, master builder—the *Isaac Wright, Ivanhoe, Yorktown* and *London*.

The *Devonshire*, rising 1200 tons, was being built by Westervelt & Mackay for Griswold's London Line, to be commanded by Captain E. E. Morgan, who later owned the Morgan Line.

Down in Portsmouth, George Raynes was building the *Columbus* for D. & A. Kingsland, of New York. She was another of the three-deckers, and measured 1307 tons. She was very much like the *Constitution*, of 1333 tons, which Brown & Bell had built the year before for Woodhull & Minturn. Neither were as sharp as the *New World*.

1847 passed into history. Texas had been made safe for Democracy and the land scrip looters. The squabbling generals were preparing to return from Mexico. Lieutenant Grant said goodby to his mules. The picks and shovels were already on their way around the Horn to dig the grave of an ancient civilization.

The voice of the abolitionist was heard in the land, rising now to a shriller note. In Europe—mutterings of the coming Revolution.

It was truly a boisterous America in the Roaring Forties. Dickens and Trollope may be excused for embroidering their American Notes with pleasantries grateful to British ears. They saw a superficial frenzy, marked the boastings, heard the hysterial bellow of prophecy, soon to burst into the great crescendo of the fifties, turning the whole nation into a speed mad, money drunk mob.

"Of course America was an aggregation of noisy braggarts. How could it be otherwise? Listen to them."

Nevertheless, the mills of the gods were turning in the late colonies of His Britannic Majesty. Dickens and those who followed heard the sound of the gears and did not see the grist.

For a glorious thirty years every last Yankee had drunk the new wine of freedom and democracy. He had measured his own or his neighbor's skill or shrewdness or science against that of the world—a somewhat superior world—and what he saw made him throw up his hat and whoop with the exuberance of a boy out of school. Mistakes enough and to spare, but much may come even from mistakes.

The years just before 1850 were extraordinarily colorful years. They gave to the world much that held implicit the boasted achievements of our own day—gave also the most poignantly beautiful pageant the world has ever seen, when the clipper ships, visions of almost ethereal loveliness, moved on the face of the waters.

Five years of high pressure sailing ship construction had pro-

"STAG HOUND."

REPRODUCED BY COURTESY OF THE ARTIST, MR. CHARLES R. PATTERSON.

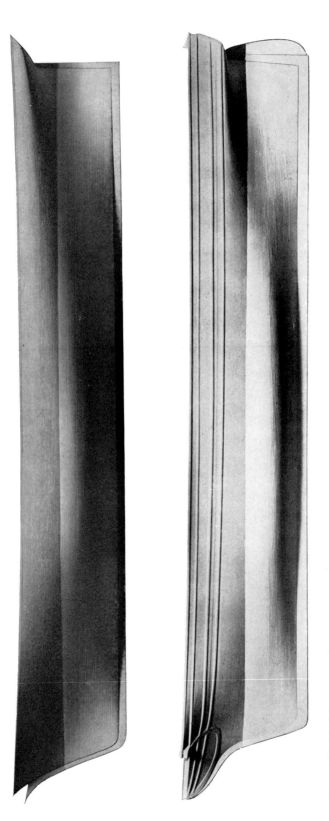

UPPER: Model of the extreme clipper *Nightingale* from lines taken from *The Monthly Nautical Magazine*, 1855.

LOWER: Model of the extreme clipper *Samuel Russell*. Reproduced from the original builder's model by the courtesy of Mr. John T. Coolidge, in whose possession the model now is. These two models illustrate the divergent tendencies of clipper ship design during the early clipper period, from 1845 to 1850. Except for her sharp bottom the *Samuel Russell* is Liverpool packet from bow to stern, while the *Nightingale* clings to many of the features of the earlier theory, having abandoned the after-drag and the rounding bow, but retaining much of the rest.

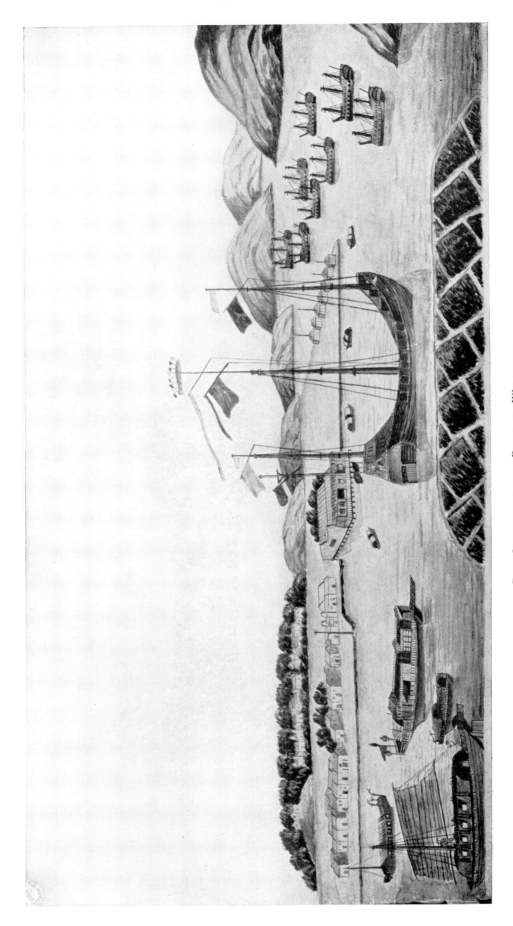

Pen Sketch of the Port of Whampoa.

CLIPPER SHIP "FLORA TEMPLE" OF BALTIMORE.

From a very old photograph for many years in the possession of a sailor of the *Flora Temple* and by him given to Capt. Nils Sjoberg, of Baltimore, through whose courtesy it is here reproduced. Owing to the faded condition of the picture it was necessary to retouch it, but it is believed that it gives a reasonably accurate image of that famous ship.

duced a temporary surplus. The year 1848 opened with eleven steamers on the stocks in New York and but one sailing vessel. Besides the two mammoth Collins steamers, the list included two for George Law's Panama Line, of 2000 tons each. Fortunately for England, they were all paddle wheel boats.

Possibly the fact made little difference in the final result. The Cunard Line was getting a subsidy of $800,000.00 a year, and viewed in that light, a mere problem in the mechanics of propulsion becomes pale and colorless.

Baltimore moved toward the front rank in clipper construction, bringing out three sharp models this year: the *Architect* of 520 tons, launched in August, 1848; *Grey Eagle*, 478 tons, completed the following December, and the *Grey Hound*, measuring 536 tons, finished a few days later. All these ships proved to be fast, although the *Architect* had by far the most spectacular career.

It was leap year, and the "fine clipper ship *Rainbow*" reached New York on the 29th of February, 88 days from Canton. The passage was not specially noteworthy, except for the fact that Captain Marshall had beaten out of Sunda Straits under double reefed topsails—a feat that very few square riggers of that or any other time could have duplicated.

On the heels of the *Rainbow*, the *Sea Witch* staggered up past Hatteras against a heavy Northwest gale driving sheer poles under, *77 days from Canton*. She had run from Java Head to the Cape of Good Hope in 25 days, better time than any yet reported, and had made St. Helena 46 days, from Macao. This is the run that is usually referred to as the record for all time from Canton to the United States.

The day she arrived Hayes left on what was destined to be the *Rainbow's* last voyage. She is thought to have been lost off the Horn, but whether she ever reached there is not known. She simply left New York and vanished.

John Jacob Astor passes from the scene, pursued by an extremely uncomplimentary obituary notice attributed to Bennett, of the *Herald*. Evidently the old trader had dealt in mortgages as well as furs. Years later his ship *Beaver* was broken up and part of her live oak frame put into a new ship. Better than most, Astor would have appreciated the news that reached New York from his old northwest country barely five months after his funeral. On Tuesday, the 19th of September, 1848, the Washington *Union* printed the following:

"We noticed in our last the arrival of Mr. Edward Fitzgerald Beale (the grandson of Commodore Truxton), a passed midshipman, who arrived on Saturday evening, in the steamer *Augusta*. He is just from Commodore Jones' Squadron; and he has performed the most rapid journey that has ever been known from the Pacific to Washington.

"He left Commodore Jones at La Paz, on the first of August, came by Mazatlan and arrived at the port of San Blas on the 10th, and pushed his way by horses and mules across the country to the City of Mexico, where he arrived on the 17th. He was detained three days by Mr. Clifford for dispatches, and in forty-eight hours passed from Mexico to Vera Cruz, about 275 miles, sleeping not more than ten minutes at a time. From Vera Cruz he sailed to Mobile, and arrived here on Saturday evening.

.   .   .   .

"But the most extraordinary intelligence which Mr. Beale brings is about the real EL DORADO, the gold region in California. His accounts of the extraordinary richness of the gold surface, and the excitement it had produced among all classes of people, inhabitants of the country and of the towns, and among the seamen and the soldiers, are confirmed by letters from Commodore Jones and from Mr. Larkin, the United States naval agent at Monterey, California.

"Mr. Beale states that the whalers had suspended their operations—the captains permitting their seamen to go to the gold region upon condition that every ounce of gold the seamen obtained should be given to the captain for $10.00, the captain making six or seven dollars by the bargain. The towns were being evacuated—mechanics, etc., going to the attractive spot. The two newspapers had been suspended—the compositors going off to gather gold for themselves.

"The danger in California is from want of food for the residents, and still more for the stream of emigrants. Would not some of our merchants find it profitable speculation to send cargoes of biscuit, flour, etc., round to the Pacific Coast?"

Further particulars and letters from California followed in rapid succession, confirming the news and creating an interest, skeptical at first, but soon to flare into intense excitement.

It so happened that Howland & Aspinwall had already built the steamer *California,* of 1200 tons, for their newly organized Pacific Mail Steamship Company. Of all American merchants, they, literally, "fell into the new gold mine." Within three weeks from receipt of the first news, the *California* was off round the Horn, sailing the 6th of October.

The government had already chartered three ships to transport troops and stores to San Francisco, and others were loading on private account. One of the first to leave, aside from the government vessels, was the barque *J. W. Cater,* Captain Hoyt, who sailed October 18th, 1848. Another early departure was the fine fast sailing ship *Sea Queen,* under command of George F. Manson. She sailed from New York the 13th of December and dropped anchor opposite the motley collection of San Francisco shacks at 4 A.M., April 30th, following. Her net sailing time of 125 days was probably the best passage that had ever been made to California up to that time.

Thereafter sailings came thick and fast. Before long there was hardly a little seaport on the coast from Calais to New Orleans that did not have its quota of shipping "up for California."

By December, scores of glowing circumstantial accounts of the new discoveries had reached the East, and excitement knew no bounds. Every harbor on the coast seethed with the preparation of expeditions. In the little port of Mystic, Connecticut, there were two full rigged ships and five schooners fitting out for the "gold coast" to sail early in January.

The New London *Chronicle* of December 29th contains the following, under the head of "Mystic" items:

"The vessels now advertised and fitting for California from this port are the ship *Mentor,* a large and fine vessel, owned by the Messrs. Brown, in great forwardness with a large number of cabin and steerage passengers with a full freight engaged. In this ship Mr. George Brown will embark himself, and she will carry out some of the most active and energetic young men in the country. She will be capitally commanded by Captain Howard, a first rate whaling master of long experience in the navigation of the Pacific, and will be fitted out in complete order in all respects.

"The schooner-smack *Mary Taylor,* of nearly 90 tons burthen, goes out, excellently well commanded also, and will be manned by a joint stock company of first rate men, who will not fail of finding gold either by digging, or otherwise, before they come back.

"The schooner Velasco, another first rate vessel, will sail soon with a joint stock company of the 'right sort,' from Groton, who will come home, 'high hook' in the gold line, or we are very much mistaken in the men.

"The schooner smack *Mount Vernon* is also advertised; and will sail under equally favorable auspices; and next, we have the schooner *Heroine,* of which staunch vessel there is no danger in saying 'ditto.'

"In addition to these, the smack *Sea Witch,* of this port, is fitting out for the 'gold coast,' from New York. The ship *Trescott* is fitting out at Mystic with the utmost dispatch, by Mr. Mallory, whose business character is sufficient guarantee of the energy with which the enterprise will be conducted. The ship will be commanded by a man of experience, and if the adventurers of the *Trescott* do not bring home their full share of the golden fleece, we have overestimated the qualities of the Argonautes. That is all.

"There is likewise a large schooner of something like two hundred tons, 'up to California,' from Mystic. This vessel is fitting out by a joint stock company and will sail soon.

Whether other enterprises of the sort are in contemplation from this neighborhood, we know not, but we dare say there may be. Success to them all."

The scenes at Mystic were being duplicated in every port on the coast.

Sailings "round the Horn" became a matter of daily occurrence, and many were the humorous and pathetic scenes enacted as the vessels cast off for the long passage.

The Boston *Bee,* under date of December 26th, gave an account of the sailing of one of these ships, the barque *Eliza,* from Salem, quoting in full the well known "humorous ditty" entitled "The California Emigrant," and beginning:

"I come from Salem City, with my wash-bowl on my knee,
I'm going to California, the gold dust for to see."

On the 13th of the following month the *Tarolinta,* commanded by Captain Cave, left New York for San Francisco with 85 cabin passengers and 40 in the steerage. In the cabin were Caleb Lyon, of Lyonsville, a popular poet of the day, and Frederick Jerome, "the gallant sailor with his world wide reputation." Lyon wrote a song to commemorate their departure, the first verse of which is as follows:

"Where the Sacramento's waters roll their golden tide along,
  Which echoes through the mountains like a merry drinking
      song;
  Where the Sierra Nevada lifts its crests unto the sky,
  A home for freedom's eagles when the tempest's sweeping by,
  Where the bay of San Francisco—the Naples of the west—
  Lies sleeping like an infant beside the Ocean's breast,
  There we go with dauntless spirits, and we go with hearts elate,
  To build another Empire—to found another State."

Brave, thoughtless lads, outward bound for old "Cape Stiff" and a hard, alien life. Their wreckage marked every league of the long 17,000 miles, and death and disease claimed them in every intervening port. The tale of the argonauts of '49 will never be told.

Events marched quickly. By the third week of February, 1849, no less than 141 ships of all descriptions had left Eastern ports for California around the Horn, and 37 for Chagres on the Isthmus. They carried out more than 11,000 prospective settlers, miners and adventurers. Hundreds were being dumped at Chagres and other points along the Isthmus, to make the remainder of the journey as best they could, an appalling percentage to perish from tropical scourges.

The story of the gold rush is not altogether pleasant reading. Execrations not entirely undeserved were called forth by the attempts of "respectable" business men to reap a harvest of easy passage money. An effigy was carried around San Francisco streets, placarded "Vanderbilts Death Line." Others would have been paraded in person with special rites to follow in the sand lots if their victims could have laid hands on them.

Bennett, of the *Herald*, was advertising "maps" of the gold diggings at six pence each. One can imagine their real value.

In February, Aspinwall sent a party of thirty-nine men to Chagres to survey a railway line across to Panama.

An old tea ship, the *Loo Choo*, sailed early in March for San Francisco. Another tea ship, the *John G. Coster*, was also "up for California." Men were dickering for super-annuated packets—the *Sheridan*, *Saratoga*, *St. Patrick* and others. Editorials and leaders sounded a high note of optimism. The New York *Herald*, always in the van, blossomed out in black letter "scare heads" fully three-eighths of an inch in height:

"We are only in the commencement of a great and startling commercial period in the history of this mighty Metropolis."

Cows were still being pastured around 23rd street, and the daintily be-whiskered "Broadway Exquisite" in corset and pegtop pantaloons still paraded mincingly the incredibly filthy sidewalks of the present financial district.

Not many sailing ships had been built around New York this year. The ending of the Mexican War had released a large tonnage from the government service and there was a temporary surplus. Then, too, the spectacle of the huge Collins steamers on the stocks, together with a number of others of the largest size, was calculated to cause any but the most optimistic to have doubts as to the future of sail transportation. A few barnacled old captains stuck to their guns, but on the whole the year started badly for the "canvas backs."

The Canton trade was going its way almost unnoticed in the general excitement of the gold discoveries, but Captain Robert Waterman was not letting California gold affect his destiny.

It was Sunday afternoon, the 25th of March, 1849, when the watcher at the Sandy Hook telegraph station descried a large, heavily-sparred ship in the offing, coming up wing and wing before a spanking breeze from the south-southeast. As she drew near, it became plain to the operator that here was an Indiaman of the extreme clipper type. But there was no vessel of that description due. The swift sailing ships of the tea fleet were not expected to leave Canton before the 5th of January, if then, and at best would not reach port for a fortnight.

Nearer and nearer she came, breasting the sagging tide, her studding sails crumpling one by one as the light canvas was taken in. Long before her private signal went fluttering up from the little group on the quarter deck, the watcher knew that she was indeed the *Sea Witch,* and that Bob Waterman had set another mark for the Canton packets to shoot at. Waterman himself could not even dimly foresee that he had participated in the making of a record which would never be broken by any ship of the sail, for at that time there was no imaginable limit to the possibilities of clipper ships.

The next morning the newspapers of the city blazoned forth the fact that the *Sea Witch* had arrived the preceding afternoon, breaking all China records by a notable margin. *She had come home in 74 days and 14 hours!*

By some strange twist of circumstance, this passage has been recorded by later writers as occupying 79 days, and the *Sea Witch's* passage of 77 days in 1847 has been cited as the world's record to the present time.

Nevertheless, evidence in favor of Waterman's claim in 1849 is as conclusive as any that can be adduced in substantiation of any of the early records, and the passage cannot be stretched to 79 days without a grotesque distortion of every shred of evidence.

On the negative side there appears to be no suggestion that the record was ever disputed by any contemporary report, although there were many rivals in the China trade whose ships were arriving almost daily, who would undoubtedly have been glad to set "Bob Waterman" down a bit. Two fast ships are definitely known to have sailed from Macao for New York on the 5th of January, the last day for Waterman's departure, if his passage was to occupy 79 days. These were the *Oneida*, commanded by Creesy, and the *Carrington* under Abbott. Although fine ships, neither were in the class of the *Sea Witch*. The *Oneida* passed Anjier nine days later on the 14th, one day ahead of Waterman.

Aside from the possibility of accident—of which there is not the slightest hint in the marine records of the times—it is unthinkable that the comparatively slow sailing *Oneida* could have beaten the *Sea Witch* on the run to Anjier. It is far more likely that the *Sea Witch* beat the time of the *Oneida* on this leg by at least two days, *since she arrived at New York 26 days before the Oneida.*

The *Carrington* also arrived at New York 19 days after the *Sea Witch*. Both the *Oneida* and *Carrington* were reported as sailing in company on the 5th, but nothing was said of the *Sea Witch*. If there had been any doubt about the time of the *Sea Witch*, it would surely have been raised by the arrival of the two later ships, if not before. Nothing would have been simpler than for Creesy, for example, to have reported that he had sailed in company with the *Sea Witch,* if such had been the case. It appears to be the fact that the question was never raised by any of the numerous shipmasters who lay at anchor at Whampoa with Waterman, or, for that matter, by any contemporary writer, in this country or elsewhere.

The log of the *Sea Witch* was evidently open to inspection, as witness the following particulars published in the New York *Commercial Advertiser* three days after the arrival of the ship:

"The splendid ship *Sea Witch,* Capt. Waterman, arrived here on Sunday in seventy-five days from China, having performed a voyage around the world in 194 sailing days.

"During the voyage she has made the shortest direct passages on record, viz.: 69 days from New York to Valparaiso; 50 days from Callao to China; 75 days from China to New York. Distance run by observation from New York to Valparaiso, 10,568 miles; average, 6 2/5 miles per hour. Distance from Callao to China, 10,417 miles; average, 8⅝ knots per hour. Distance from China to New York, 14,255 miles; average, 7⅞ knots per hour. Best ten (consecutive) days' run, 2,634 miles; average, 11 1/10 knots per hour."

This passage of the *Sea Witch,* in some respects the most remarkable voyage of the entire clipper ship age, received, relatively, as much publicity as the famous 89 day run of the *Flying Cloud* in 1851. Thereafter it vanished, unaccountably, from the lists of record passages, a curious and not uninstructive example of historical vagaries. "Fables agreed upon."

It seems altogether probable that subsequent writers were misled by the statement that Captain Waterman brought China papers to the 4th of January, and concluded from this he sailed either on the 4th or 5th of the month. As a matter of fact, the papers referred to were issues of the *China Mail,* published every Thursday. The issue of January 4th therefore was followed by that of the 11th and this number records the information that, far from sailing for New York from Macao on January 5th, *the*

Sea Witch's departure was actually taken from Hong Kong on the 8th, a fact which definitely clinches Waterman's claim.

In other words, after clearing from Canton on the 4th, Waterman ran over to Hong Kong, a few hours distant, and sailed or was scheduled to sail from there on the 8th. In the absence of his log it is possible that he did not leave until the early morning of the 9th. Whether he delayed his sailing a few hours after he was scheduled to depart or not, the fact is obvious that a small deduction for time spent at anchor at Anjier and St. Helena in accordance with the custom of that day would in any case, account for the net sailing time of 74 days and 14 hours reported.

It is interesting to note that on this voyage the *Sea Witch* made a shorter mileage from Hong Kong to New York than the regular sailing ship course, on this occasion. Her run of 14,255 miles is more than a thousand miles shorter than the best recommended route in the Northeast Monsoon, and is the shortest that has ever come to the writer's attention, while her passage as a whole may well be rated as the most spectacular achievement in the entire history of sail. IT WAS THE WORLD'S FIRST PERMANENT SAILING RECORD.

During the year 1849, someone discovered that more Liverpool packets were needed. The *Constitution* and the *Guy Mannering*, 1600 ton vessels, the largest merchant sailing ships in existence, were launched in March. They were approximately 2000 tons, carpenter's measure.

Before the year closed the *Jacob A. Westervelt*, of 1400 tons, was ready for Taylor and Rich's Liverpool Line; the *Washington*, 1650 tons, was launched in Williamsburg for Frost & Hick's Line, while in Boston, Donald McKay had finished the *Anglo-Saxon* and the *Parliament*, both slightly under 1000 tons, for Train's White Diamond Line.

There were other large packets, the *Gallia* and the *Albert Gallatin*, the one 1300 and the other 1600 tons, finished by Wm. Webb. The new Black Baller *Manhattan*, 1600 tons, under the veteran Hackstaff, was getting ready for her first voyage as the year closed. Other large vessels, including the *Isaac Webb* and the *American Congress,* were nearing completion. Captain Jack Williams, the terror of slow-moving sailor men, was to have the *American Congress,* and while he commanded never did ship more belie her name.

Smith & Dimon, builders of the *Sea Witch,* were laying down the 1300 ton packet *Universe* for Williams & Guion's Liverpool Line. She was said to be the first "clipper packet" for the transatlantic service, but was not so sharp a vessel as many subsequent "Liverpool clippers."

The year that had started so badly for ships of the sail was to close with a new mark for tonnage constructed, and a speed record that is still unbroken.

CHAPTER XV

1849

THE rush to California went feverishly on. Early in March, '49, crippled ships were crawling into Rio Janeiro by the dozen. Between a thousand and twelve hundred Americans were stranded there, not knowing when their vessels would continue their voyage, or whether they would ever sail.

Our old acquaintance, the ship *Mentor,* from Mystic, had made one of the best passages to Rio, 38 days, justifying the prophecy of the New London *Chronicle.*

Complaints from the gold seekers were drifting back—stories of hardships, sickness, unlivable quarters, uneatable food. "God sends provisions, but the devil sends cooks."

Lieutenant Beale arrives from California in 44 days by way of the Isthmus, the fastest time on record. His reports add to the already hysterical excitement. James Gordon Bennett dashes off an "editorial" predicting "a commercial revolution."

Gold was coming in from San Francisco in large quantities. Also reports of unparalleled lawlessness. Underneath all, a deep, insistent muttering: "The whole country is getting crazy on the subject of slavery."

One of the first clipper ships to clear for the gold fields

was the *Architect*, Captain Gray, a Baltimore design of 520 tons. Although a fast craft under certain conditions, she sailed from New Orleans, January 16th, 1849, and did not arrive out until the 28th of the following June, having put into Port twice and making the long run of 160 days, elapsed time. The other little Baltimore clippers, *Grey Hound* and *Grey Eagle*, went to California about the same time, the *Grey Eagle* under Captain Bower, clearing from Philadelphia the same day the *Architect* left New Orleans while the *Grey Hound* left Baltimore January 10th "for Valparaiso and a market." They were later reported in contemporary accounts as having made the passage in 119 and 117 days, respectively. The same accounts credited the *Architect* with 120 days' actual time at sea, remarkably consistent, even sailing.

Closely following the *Architect* was the *Memnon*. She was a fine, sharp, heavily-sparred clipper of 1000 tons, built by Smith & Dimon, with the idea of improving, if possible, upon the *Sea Witch*. Reports said she resembled the *Sea Witch* in appearance. Her first commander was Captain Benjamin, who had been making clipper time in the *Helena*.

The *Memnon* had already proved her mettle. On the 6th of November, 1848, she left New York for Liverpool, and arrived off Point Lynas on the 20th, having made the run in fourteen days and seven hours, incidentally breezing past the steamship *Europe* on the way at 13 knots an hour. Many a packet ship equalled or closely approached this time, but their records were isolated instances taken from scores of long, tedious voyages. Like some of the later clippers, the *Memnon* made her record with but a single chance.

Captain Joseph R. Gordon took the *Memnon* out. She left Sandy Hook about 3 P.M. on the 11th of April, 1849, and made the fine passage of 19 days to the Line. She was off Rio Janeiro in 32 days and put into Montevideo May 26th, 45 days out, hand spikes and belaying pins flying—"all hands refusing duty." Thus were heard the first murmurings of a rising gale of discontent that was to blow around Cape Horn for fifty uninterrupted years.

Captain Gordon seems to have neglected to get a "hand-picked" crew, or possibly he was one of the first to set out for California with a record in mind. If so, his ambition was realized, for he passed the Golden Gate on the 28th of August, 123 sailing days from New York. Aside from the little Baltimore clippers, this was the best run that had been reported up to that time. Most passages exceeded 150 days.

This year saw the completion of other excellent California passages by well known masters and ships. Captain Wm. C. Rogers, later of the beautiful *Witchcraft,* took the *Thomas Perkins* around in 126 days, arriving off the Heads on the 21st of November. Few of the older generation of Boston merchants would require further information about Rogers or the *Thomas Perkins.* The *Probus,* under Deverie, and the *William Sprague,* Captain Chase, are also numbered among the '49ers.

Meanwhile McKay was building the *Reindeer* at East Boston. She was launched on the 9th of June, in the presence of "a large concourse of people." "Finest in model and strength McKay has yet built," said the Boston papers. She had Forbes double topsail rig, measured 770 tons, and was owned by George Upton and R. B. Forbes.

As yet none of the larger eastern-built vessels approached the New York clippers in sharpness of model, or in sailing qualities. Samuel Hall's China packet for the year, the *Lantao,* was sharper than the average, but she was a relatively full model. Hall, however, launched the barque *Hazard* on the 13th of March this year, in rig at least, an extreme clipper. She was less than 400 tons register and only 122 feet in length, yet her mainmast, exclusive of doublings, was 130 feet long. The criticism was made that she was badly oversparred. Nevertheless she was a very successful ship in the coffee trade, surpassing in some respects the exploits of the famous *Courier.* She is stated by Maury to have made six passages to Rio in her first three years, in which her runs to the Equator averaged twenty-six days—a truly remarkable record for a vessel sailing in and out of season.

Samuel Hall, as a matter of fact, was an unusually competent builder and designer, as a reference to the work of his later clippers will show. Nevertheless the Boston merchants were not yet convinced that speed would pay, at the expense of carrying capacity, and it was not until the following year that they began to build sharp ships in earnest.

New York merchants had fewer doubts. A. A. Low & Brother and "Cap'n Nat" were building their third clipper—the *Oriental*. She was a beautiful ship of 1050 tons, the largest Canton trader yet constructed, a product of the same yard that had built the *Houqua* and *Samuel Russell*, now operated by Jacob Bell, who had succeeded Brown & Bell.

In the New York *Commercial Advertiser* of Monday, August 6th, 1849, there appeared the following description of the *Oriental*:

> "The *Oriental*, a splendid vessel for the China trade, and to be commanded by Capt. N. B. Palmer, was launched on Saturday morning, from the yard of Mr. Jacob Bell, at the foot of Stanton Street. She is owned by A. A. Low & Brother. She is a two decked vessel, burthen 1050 tons, length 175 feet, breadth of beam 30, and depth of hold 21 feet. She is built of white oak, live oak, locust and cedar; her flooring being of white oak.
>
> "Her model gives promise that she will be both a safe and fast ship; and Capt. Palmer is a gentleman likely to do the *Oriental* justice in both respects, being well known as a cautious and enterprising officer. Her launch was exceedingly beautiful. She was taken to the dry dock to be coppered."

The 10th of September saw the *Oriental* on her way to Canton. It was Palmer's last long voyage as commander. He was 50 years of age—an old man for the clipper service, yet his gigantic frame and iron constitution were still capable of standing hardships such as few men now afloat could endure. He proved his metal by bringing the *Oriental* home in the Spring of 1850 in 81 days—a proud and fitting climax to the career of one of the most worthy representatives of the old sailing ship days.

While the *Oriental* was outward bound "Cap'n Nat" crossed the track of his brother Theodore homeward bound in the *Samuel Russell*. The *Russell* had left Canton on September 1st. She made the remarkable out-of-season run of 90 days to New York, while her time of 64 days from Java Head on this occasion has rarely been beaten.

Following close on the heels of the *Russell* was the Medford built *John Quincy Adams*, Captain Nickels, from Manila. She reached New York on the 18th of December, having made the round trip to Manila and back in 7 months and 25 days, said to have been the shortest time on record.

Both ships were immediately put up for San Francisco. The advertisements of the *Adams* were characteristic of the times, and read as follows:

> "For San Francisco, California,—Dispatch Line.—The elegant clipper ship *John Q. Adams* will have immediate dispatch for the above port, has just arrived from Manila, being absent from New York seven months and twenty-five days only, the best time on record. This ship is guaranteed to make a shorter voyage to California than any other vessel.
>
> "E. B. Sutton, 84 Wall St., or
> John Ogden, 116 Wall St."

As a matter of fact, the *Adams*, while a fine, able and relatively fast vessel, was far from being a clipper in the sense that ships like the *Samuel Russell* and *Sea Witch* were. She was not greatly different from the China packet *Helena*, but in those booming days, as in later times, merchants allowed themselves a certain latitude of poetic license in advertising their sailings.

1849 ended with Maine strongly in the lead in shipbuilding. During the year she had constructed craft aggregating 82,256

Clipper Ship "Flying Fish."

From Painting by Frank Vining Smith.

Courtesy of the Artist.

Charles Robert Patterson

CLIPPER SHIP "YOUNG AMERICA."
FROM PAINTING BY CHARLES R. PATTERSON.
Courtesy of Logan G. Thomson, Esq.

tons, none of which appear to have been clippers, while New York held second place with 44,104 tons. Pennsylvania ranked next, and Massachusetts was fourth on the list with a tonnage of 23,888. But in the size and quality of her new ships, New York undoubtedly was entitled to first honors by a good margin.

In addition to clipper ships, a number of very fast barks, many of them with clipper lines, had been set afloat during the forties. Among these were the *Inca*, of Baltimore; *Isabelita Heyne*, built at Philadelphia in 1846; the *Ocean Wave* and the *Mimosa*, both of Boston; the *Hazard* of Salem, a very heavily sparred craft; the *Jennette*, built at Essex, Connecticut, in 1847, and the *Candace* of 398 tons, built at Warren, Rhode Island. The last two appear to have had rather full lines, but they spread a cloud of canvas and made excellent passages.

The great steamers of the Collins Line, the *Arctic* and the *Baltic*, were almost ready for launching, and the *Pacific* and *Atlantic* had been launched before the end of the year. Each of these vessels was nearly 300 feet in length and about 3000 tons, government measure. These were the largest, but there were several others of 2000 tons and upwards. Their advent was hailed as an indication that the United States, which had lagged far behind Great Britain in steamship development, was more than able to hold her own against this form of foreign competition.

They were all paddle-wheel boats and this was probably unfortunate for the future of steam navigation in America. Ericsson's propeller was still a fertile subject for the "wits" of the waterside. The paddle wheel had the merit of being "fool proof," but events were to prove that in steam as in sail, the race was not to the fool.

In all, 775 vessels had cleared from Eastern ports for California during 1849, the list including 242 ships and 12 steamers, besides a large number of barques, brigs and schooners. More than 90,000 passengers from all over the world had been landed at San Francisco. The closing days of the year saw more than 450 ships, roundly speaking, on their way to the land of gold, a goodly proportion of them deeply laden with merchandise that was unsaleable in the East.

Large as this fleet was, the early days of 1850 were to see its numbers augmented beyond belief. The results were apparent a few months later when the procession of ships entering the Gate was virtually continuous. The scene is described in the issue of the Pacific *News* for November 20th, 1850:

> "The number of vessels entering our harbor is really a matter of wonder. Within the forty-eight hours ending on Sunday night, nearly sixty sail entered the Golden Gate. The history of the world presents no comparison. The arrivals yesterday were between twenty and thirty sail."

Long before the above paragraph was penned, however, San Francisco had more than once received ocular proof of the fact that the California clipper era was under way.

CHAPTER XVI

1850

THE FIRST CALIFORNIA CLIPPERS

THE year 1850 witnessed the first of the most re-markable voyages under sail that the world has ever seen—remarkable not merely for speed, but for the extraordinary difficulties under which they were made.

The story of the Cape Horn clippers can never be told, or even dimly pictured to a generation that never rounded the Cape. Through the mists of the years and the yellowed salt stained pages of old logbooks, one catches fleeting glimpses of beautiful, gallant ships urged by relentless masters of the quarter deck, fighting through indescribable conditions for another mile of westing. There are brief sketches of icy infernos, in which are mingled confused impressions of steep decks, cascading water, milky white; of ponderous yardarms slashing through heaving crests; of lofty spars whipping and buckling under an insane spread of rigid canvas that fairly hurled the groaning hull at the seas; of stout shrouds threshing slackly to leeward, while weather stays drum like bars of steel.

Manikin figures of that long ago dart alertly about decks between seas waist deep; strain at yanking wheels; pull in yelping chorus at a myriad of ropes; crawl numbly aloft to be whipped, it may be, like ripe fruit from flailing spars. Stifle that last involuntary wail! One cannot even hear the roar of the hurricane, so deep there is no such thing as sound; nothing but a never ceasing pressure on one's soul.

Always the agony of endless nights—the ceaseless freezing torture, when it seemed the day would never break again. Crippled, half-delirious men, racked with suffering, reeling aft for another trick at the wheel. Stark, frozen corpses in the bunks. But never a faltering—never a thought but to drive that clipper round the Cape, though fifty ships should turn and run for their lives.

The price of those incomparable records was paid in full in human wreckage on those gallant Cape Horners. Yet there was no true sailor who did not glory in the part he played in those man-killing drives. Men of the old packet breed sailed for more than fame or fortune.

American clippers have been criticized by those whose duty it is to know better, as being frail-built, soft-wood ships. It is easy to point to wracked hulls and twisted spars and attribute them to poor construction. The fact is that never in the history of the world, before or since, have ships been rigged so heavily or driven so relentlessly as were American clippers in the early California trade. One has only to read the details of construction to know that in their day better ships were not built. Many a "soft wood" ship was oak or better from shoe to broad teak rail, while few clippers had less durable stuff than the heavy hard pine of Georgia with generous white and live oak timbers at the critical points. Far weaker ships came through without a mark, but they never had to beat past St. Diego against gales of hurricane force. The wracking below and the wreckage aloft were not the result of faulty construction, but of the conditions under which these ships sailed in the hard journey around the Horn.

The first vessel of importance to sail for San Francisco in 1850 was the old *Natchez,* Captain Duryee. She cleared at New

York, on the 31st of December, 1849, and while her actual sailing date is not reported, she was still at anchor in the North River on January 3rd and it is probable that she left within a day or two thereafter.

She was closely followed by Low, in the *Samuel Russell,* who left New York on the 15th of January. The *John Q. Adams,* Captain Nickels, sailed exactly a month later. Oliver Mumford left in the *Wisconsin* on the 21st of February, while Daniel McKenzie took his departure in the *Houqua* on the 15th of March, crossing the bar at 4 P.M. with a moderate northwest breeze.

Wm. B. Gerry, just returned from Calcutta to Boston in a hundred day passage in the *Cohota,* next took her out around the Horn. He dropped his pilot off Boston Light at 3 P.M. the 6th of April and took a pilot off the Heads at 6 P.M. August 11th. His passage of 126 days was excellent, considering the fact that it was made during the unfavorable season of the year.

The *Sea Witch* had just arrived from Canton in 85 days, and she was next put up for San Francisco, Waterman turning her over to his old mate, George Fraser, a "driver" after his own heart. She sailed from New York on the 13th of April.

The *Memnon,* which had already made one trip to San Francisco and home by way of Canton, making the run from Macao to New York in 89 days, sailed again for San Francisco on the 28th of May, discharging her pilot outside the Hook at 1:30 P.M., and the contest which was to revise sailing ship history and the very ships themselves, was on. The queens of the Canton trade were "off to Californy."

In the meantime, McKay's new product, the *Reindeer,* Captain Lord, arrived at San Francisco on April 2nd, in 122 sailing days from Boston. Her passage was made notable by the fact that she put into Valparaiso, and ran from there to her destination in 36 days, said to be the shortest time that had been made between those ports.

To the little brig *Eagle,* of Gloucester, possibly, belongs the honor of making the first voyage under 110 days. She arrived inside the Golden Gate on the 18th of March, reporting a passage of 106 days. The ship *Argonaut,* which was considered a very good sailer, had arrived several days earlier in a run of 133 days from Boston.

While these records were being made, Captain Low was putting the *Samuel Russell* through her paces. He was spoken when only 32 days out, in latitude 32.11 South, longitude 45 West, well down toward Montevideo. It developed later that he had crossed the line in 20 and was off the Horn in 44 days—the latter a record that has been rarely improved upon.

He arrived out on the 6th of May, in a passage of 109 days. On the following day, the *Daily Pacific News* noted the *Russell's* arrival with the remark that she "is one of the most beautiful specimens of naval architecture afloat."

One of the older stars that failed to shine in the Cape Horn passage was the *Natchez.* She did not arrive at San Francisco until the 3rd of June, reporting a passage of 150 days, while just behind her came the little old *Severn,* eight months out.

A very good passage of 113 days from Philadelphia was made by the *Thomas Wattson,* Captain Thomas. She arrived out on June 25th, just one day later than the fine, fast-sailing *Wisconsin,* 123 days from the Hook. While the passage of the *Wisconsin* did not equal that of the *Wattson,* it was a very creditable one. Mumford pridefully records in his log that he anchored at 3:15 P.M. on June 24th in San Francisco harbor, "ahead of all the ships that sailed 30 days before us."

The *John Q. Adams* arrived next, on the 1st of July, having made a passage of 136 days, although there was probably little to choose between Nickels and Low as navigators and hard driving sailing masters. Both were seamen of the first rank.

Following the *Adams* came the *Houqua,* on the 23rd of July, 130 days out. The very next day the *Sea Witch* came romping in through the gate, in the record time of 97 net sailing days. She had rounded to off the port at 8 P.M. the night before. To the *Sea Witch,* therefore, belongs the honor of being the first ship to break the century mark on the California run. She was destined to make three successive voyages to San Francisco from Eastern ports in three successive years, none of which exceeded 110 days in length. Other clippers were later to duplicate this feat, but, with the exception of the *Andrew Jackson,* which made four successive voyages in four years, well within the above time limit, none appears to have exceeded it. Moreover, in addition to setting a new standard for the San Francisco run, the *Sea Witch* had made the last leg of her voyage, from Valparaiso to the Golden Gate, in 37 days, very close to the record for loaded ships.

Standards are not lacking by which the achievements of these early California American clippers may be judged. A contemporary account in one of the New York papers stated that between June 26th and July 28th, 1850, seventeen New York vessels arrived at San Francisco in the average time of 157 days. Sixteen Boston vessels arrived with an average of 168½ days, while twenty-four other vessels from other eastern ports averaged 190 days. As will be seen by inspection of the California passages in 1849, listed in the appendix, 23 vessels arrived at San Francisco from eastern ports during the first two weeks in September of that year. Their runs varied from 160 to 240 days in length, the average of the fleet being some hours over 199 days.

In the light of such performances, the work of the *Samuel Russell* and the *Sea Witch* appears, and indeed was, little short of marvellous. They were small vessels, lacking the power of the later clippers. All the more honor therefore is due to the courage and skill of the men who sailed them.

New contenders for the honors of the sea were now constantly appearing. By mid-summer, the *Celestial* and the *Mandarin,* clippers which were to lower old records on more than one hard course, were rigged, coppered and on their way around the Horn.

It was a year of experiments. The steam schooner *Ohio*, under command of George N. Brown, the first of her kind to appear on the Pacific, left New York on the 7th of August, 1850, arriving at San Francisco after a passage little short of five months, letting go her anchor at 5 o'clock on the afternoon of the 30th of December. Steam was 48 days slower than the best clipper in the journey from New York to San Francisco.

Shipbuilders and merchants everywhere were waking up. The seventy-odd thousand dollar freight money earned by the *Samuel Russell* on a single voyage was something decidedly objective. Against this golden wall the arguments in favor of full bellied ships for the California trade might beat in vain. When clipper ships could earn their cost in a voyage of less than four months, hard-headed experience must needs keep silent.

Early Monday morning, the 10th of June, 1850, was the time set by Wm. H. Webb for launching the *Celestial*. She was built for Messrs. Bucklin & Crane, of New York, and Captain E. C. Gardner was selected for her commander. Her model showed in every line her close kinship with the later packets, although she was much sharper than any of them—considerably sharper, in fact, than the *Helena*, which she resembled superficially. Compared to the *Samuel Russell* she was relatively flat-bottomed, showing thus early the divergent tendencies of clipper ship theory.

Commenting on her appearance, the New York *Herald* of June 9th, 1850, said:

"The *Celestial* has been built for Messrs. Bucklin & Crane, and is intended for a Canton trader, under the command of Captain Gardner. She is 155 feet long, 35 feet beam and 19 feet hold. The model of this craft differs somewhat from the ordinary wedge bottom clippers built for the same trade, and it is thought, by competent judges, to be superior, by enabling the vessel to keep up on the water, preserving a buoyancy which is very desirable and very rarely met with in this class of vessels."

On the Saturday following the launch of the *Celestial*, Smith & Dimon launched the famous *Mandarin* from their yard at the foot of 4th Street, East River. She was somewhat smaller than the *Celestial*, measuring 776 tons as against the 860 tons of the latter. Moreover, as her lines shown in Appendix VII indicate, she was as nearly flat floored as it was possible to build a ship, while her sides were almost perpendicular. She had every requisite of a large carrier and her lines were clearly adapted to strong breezes rather than light, close-hauled work.

The construction of this type of vessel by the builders of the *Sea Witch* and *Rainbow* indicates the ceaseless quest for faster sailing principles. The latter ships, except for their diminished "after drag," were not greatly different in principle from the Baltimore clippers, which, it will be remembered, were closely related to the fast frigate type. On the other hand, it is worth remembering, in view of her later performance, that the *Mandarin* abandoned the hollow bow of the *Sea Witch* and *Rainbow*, and the excessive dead rise of the Baltimore clippers, and reverted almost entirely to the latter Liverpool Packets for her inspiration, while at the same time greatly lengthening and sharpening their lines.

No time was lost by the owners of these two ships. Little more than a month elapsed before both were rigged, loaded as deeply as it was possible to load them, and off for the long grind around the Horn.

The *Celestial* cleared for San Francisco on the 15th of July, while the *Mandarin* sailed on the 25th. The sailing date of the *Celestial* does not appear in the New York papers, but it was stated on her arrival to have been the 16th of July. If she did actually sail on that date, it is evident that owing to weather conditions then prevailing she must have been nearly a week getting an offing. All in all, the two vessels were off to a fairly even start, and the results should have given some conception of their respective merits.

As a matter of fact, if one can judge by subsequent performances, the race gave no reliable indication whatever. The *Celestial* arrived out on October 30th (some accounts give November 1st) in the excellent time of 104 days, while the *Mandarin* took 128 days to cover the course. The full-built but fast ship *Carrington*, under Captain Abbott, reached port a few days later in the same time.

This sound beating seems the more remarkable when one considers that two years later the *Mandarin* was to establish a record of 70 days from New York to Melbourne—a passage that has never been equalled to this day. Whatever the explanation, it seems probable that the merits of the ships were not so much involved as weather conditions and possibly the relative loads carried by the two vessels.

But no time was lost in speculation about the runs of these two ships. The clipper rush was on in deadly earnest. The demand was for "ninety day ships," and the merchants of the East were scouring the Atlantic ports for men who could turn out fast ships in four months or less. Nothing approaching it had been known in shipbuilding since the days of the Spanish Armada.

In Baltimore, during the summer of 1850, Bell & Co. turned out the *Seaman*, rising 500 tons, while the *North Carolina*, of 600 tons, was launched on the 17th of August. The *Sea Nymph* was also built here, and sailed on her first voyage from New York for San Francisco on the 15th of December.

The diminutive *Seaman*, under Captain Myrick, left New York on the 16th of November and arrived at San Francisco, in the remarkably fine passage of 107 days, on March 10th. It was stated that she ran from the latitude of Valparaiso to her destination in 30 days and from the line to San Francisco in 14 days, both runs very close to the present record. She is reported as making 1508 miles in five days during the voyage, excellent sailing for a ship of three times her tonnage.

At New York the yard of Jabez Williams, in Williamsburg,

was finishing the *Eclipse,* a noble 1300 ton clipper for T. Wardle & Co., of New York. Jacob Bell was putting the final touches on the beautiful *White Squall,* a 1200 ton ship for Platt & Co., of Philadelphia, preparatory to her launching early in August.

Smith & Dimon were having a busy year. Aside from the *Mandarin,* they had built the first clipper packet, the *Universe,* for Williams & Guion's Liverpool Line. She was a fine ship of 1300 tons, carpenter's measure, and while she would not compare with the later clippers, was much the sharpest packet ship that had yet been built.

To Smith & Dimon also—if one excepts early Baltimore vessels—apparently belongs the honor of building the first clipper ship for foreign account. This was the *Nicholas I,* built for the Russian American Fur Company. She had 26 inches dead rise and measured about 600 tons. Captain Leach, an old "down east" driver, who took her to Cronstadt for the company in the summer of 1850, said she was an excellent sea boat and very swift, and that he considered her comparatively flat floor a great improvement.

By mid-summer, the urge to build clippers had extended to Maine. The yard of Metcalf & Norris, at Damariscotta, evidently one of the most progressive in the State, seems to have turned out the first veritable clipper from that section. She was the *Alert,* a fine ship of 764 tons, owned by Crocker & Warren, of New York. The *Grey Feather,* measuring 610 tons, and sometimes classed as a clipper, was built about the same time by C. S. Husten of Eastport. The *Alert* was launched in November, and arrived in New York to load for San Francisco on the 29th of December. The *Grey Feather* also loaded in New York and sailed for California on the 11th of January, 1851.

Several clipper barques, including the beautiful *Black Squall,* were built in Maine during the year, but it was not until 1852 that the Pine Tree State began to turn out clipper ships in earnest.

In and around Boston activity was increasing. During the first half of the year, Samuel Hall built at East Boston the barque

Race Horse of 512 tons for Goddard & Co., a well known firm of Boston. She loaded in Boston and sailed for San Francisco on the 4th of August, under command of Captain Babcock. Fifty-two days later she was 20 miles south of the Horn, and on October 20th her log records: "at 11 P.M. made the Farralones Rocks, one hundred and eight days from Cape Cod Light. So Ends."

To Hall also belongs the honor of constructing the first large clipper ship built outside of New York. This was the *Surprise,* of 1261 tons, designed by Pook for A. A. Low & Brother, and commanded by Captain Philip Dumaresq. She was launched on October 5th, and left New York for San Francisco December 13th, two days later than the little Baltimore clipper *Sea Nymph,* under Captain Philip Hale. The *Surprise* arrived out in the record time of 96 days and 15 hours, beating the *Sea Nymph* 61 days on the passage.

The next important vessel to be launched in New England was the *Sea Serpent,* built by George Raynes, in Portsmouth, New Hampshire. Under date of November 20th, the Boston *Atlas* printed the following:

"THE CLIPPER SHIP SEA SERPENT.—This is the second clipper on a large scale which has been built in New England this season; the *Surprise,* built at East Boston, was the first. The *Sea Serpent* is about 1300 tons. She is 212 feet long over all, has 39 feet 3 inches extreme breadth of beam, and 21 feet depth of hold. She is very sharp forward and beautifully proportioned aft, without being cut up like a center-board, and broadside on she looks rakish and saucy.

"To use a nautical phrase, 'her model fills the eye like a full moon,' and her strength and workmanship are of the highest order. She is owned by Messrs. Grinnell, Minturn & Co., of New York, and was built at Portsmouth, N. H., by Mr. George Raynes, under the superintendence of Capt. Howland. She will be launched this day from the ship yard of Mr. Raynes. A large number of gentlemen from this city and New York will be present to welcome her on the waters."

After the *Sea Serpent* arrived at New York, the *Herald* had the following to say about her:

"Her bow partakes of the wedge in appearance, and she is very sharp, but her lines are nearly all rounded. Her bow is tastefully ornamented with a large gilded Eagle, with outstretched wings, beautifully carved, and has a simple and very neat appearance. Her hull is entirely black, excepting a narrow yellow line which relieves the sameness and looks much smarter than the white streak, so common on other vessels.

The model of the *Sea Serpent* is one that the greatest grumbler would be at a loss to find the smallest fault with. Head on she has a most rakish appearance, and her lines swell along the bow into their utmost fulness, and then taper off again into the clean run, they show incontestably that 'the line of beauty' has been made the guide in her construction. They are as perfect as perfection itself.

"Her stern is most beautifully proportioned, and is tastefully decorated with two carved full length representations of the Great American Sea Serpent."

The *Sea Serpent* was said to have been very much like the *Witch-of-the-Wave,* a later and larger production of Mr. Raynes the model of which is shown on page 158. Both ships were very sharp and both had the very extreme dead-rise of 40 inches, exceeding that of the *Nightingale,* which was built a few months later at Portsmouth by Samuel Hanscomb, Jr., and only slightly less than that of the famous *Hurricane's* forty-one inches.

There followed in rapid succession the famous *Stag Hound,* 1534 tons, launched by Donald McKay, at East Boston, on the 7th of December. The *Witchcraft,* built by Curtis & Taylor at Salem, rating 1310 tons, and the *Game Cock,* of 1392 tons, also a product of the yard of Samuel Hall. Both the latter ships were launched on December 21st.

The *Witchcraft* was modelled by Pook and owned by W. D. Pickman and Richard S. Rogers, of Salem. A crouching tiger formed her figurehead and she was richly decorated about the bow. Her name was much criticized by the superstitious and many predictions of ill-fortune were made, but she seems to have encountered no greater difficulties than the majority of the clippers.

Pook is also said to have been responsible for the design of the *Game Cock*. She was built to the order of Daniel C. Bacon, one of the well-known merchants of Boston, and himself a veteran sea captain who had proved his mettle on more than one perilous adventure. Although expressly modelled for speed, it is interesting to note that the *Game Cock*, like many another early "extreme clipper," was classified as "medium built" by later shipping lists.

It is difficult to describe the impression created by the appearance, in rapid succession, of these ships. By the standards of any age or place they were things of consummate beauty. They took the water amid the cheers of thousands, and wherever they went, the world over, unstinted praise was heaped upon them by the foreign press. They compelled praise, even from the most unwilling competitors.

Once fairly started, the pace of construction increased rather than abated. Even while these ships were being built, other keels were being laid of larger and more powerful clippers, and the contracts for still greater and more speedy ships were being signed.

In October, the announcement was made that Wm. Webb was to lay the keel of the largest merchantman that had ever been built. This was the magnificent *Challenge*, possibly the most extreme clipper that was ever built, all things considered. She was the first three deck clipper to be laid down. She measured over 2500 tons, carpenter's measure, and under the rules then existing registered 2006 tons, and was more than 27 feet longer than the 120 gun line-of-battle ship *Pennsylvania*. For her tonnage, she appears to have been the loftiest vessel that was ever rigged. Her mainmast towered above her deck to the height of almost 190 feet, or approximately 200 feet above the water. Her mainmast, after making the proper deduction for doublings, was 210½ feet in length from heel to truck. This was 18¾ feet longer than that of the *Sovereign of the Seas,* a ship more than 400 tons larger than the *Challenge,* and herself considered to be very heavily sparred.

Her lower studding sails stretched 160 feet from leach to leach. Some idea of the enormous spread of her canvas may be gained from the fact that her spar plan was reduced three times in succession before it met the approval of the captains who sailed her after Waterman left her.

It must be borne in mind, moreover, that this enormous fabric was sustained by a ship which under the revised tonnage laws, rated only 1375 tons. One occasionally notes comment to the effect that the sail area of the clippers has been greatly exaggerated, and that they were not nearly as heavily sparred as has been supposed. Material for revision of such statements in part at least is not lacking, nor is it necessary to resort to the more extreme instances presented by ships like the *Challenge* or the *Young America.*

The closing days of 1850 was a period of intense activity. Webb alone was building three ships besides the *Challenge*—the *Gazelle, Comet* and *Invincible*—all ships of the very highest type. Like the *Challenge,* the *Comet* and *Invincible* were iron braced. They measured about 1800 tons each and made records that have withstood the assaults of the years.

All the other New York firms were busy. Westervelt & MacKay were building the *N. B. Palmer,* of nearly 1500, and the *Eureka* of 1100 tons, while Perine, Patterson & Stack had the beautiful *Ino* almost completed. To the eastward the activity was quite as pronounced.

At Portsmouth, Fernald & Pettigrew were building the *Typhoon,* of 1600 tons. Captain Hood had the smart little *Raven* nearly completed at Somerset, and the 1400 ton *Rip Van Winkle* well under way. James O. Curtis had the *Shooting Star,* the first of the Medford clipper ships, nearly finished. At East Boston, McKay, destined to become the most famous clipper ship builder of all time, had commenced work on the *Flying Cloud*, rating nearly 1800 tons. Currier & Townsend, at Newburyport, were preparing to lay down the *Racer*, another three decker, measuring nearly 1700 tons.

On every hand, contracts were being closed for ships ranging from one to two thousand tons. Every yard of importance was represented, and the merchants were searching for other builders who might possibly supply the demand, daily becoming more insistent, for speedy sailing ships.

"YOUNG AMERICA" IN A HURRICANE.

Photo by Louis S. Martel, courtesy, The Marine Historical Association, Inc.

A Journal of the Transactions and Remarkable Events on board the

H.	K.	F.	Courses.	Winds.	L.W	THERMOMETER Air.	Water	Transactions and Remarkable Events
1	14		E.	S.W.				Friday, 18th.
2	14							Throughout this 24 hours strong breezes
3	16							and rough sea. At 10 A.M. took in
4	17							royals.
5	17							2 3.14
6	17							W.N.Dis.
7	17							9 26.32 Dine.
8	17							5.42 correctd.
9	17							9 32.14
10	18							3 31.00
11	18							6.01.06
12	17							N.N. Dis.
1	17							90.16 Long at 3 P.m.
2	18							1.12
3	18							91.28 " " 12°
4	18							3.22.56
5	18							0.12
6	18							3.31.00 Dine at Ship.
7	18							
8	19							
9	19							
10	18							
11	15							

Courses.	Distance.	D. Lat.	D. Lon.	Winds.	L.W	Lat. by D.R	Lat. by Obs.	Diff. Long.	Long. in.	Long. per L.	Variation.
E ¼	436 miles	110 miles		S.W.		52.12	52.12	6.30 miles			91.30

FACSIMILE OF A HALF-PAGE OF THE OFFICIAL LOG OF THE EXTREME CLIPPER *Sovereign of the Seas* ON HER RECORD RUN FROM HONOLULU TO NEW YORK, GIVING THE ENTRY FOR MARCH 18, 1853, AND RECORDING THE RATE OF 19 KNOTS FOR THREE CONSECUTIVE HOURS.

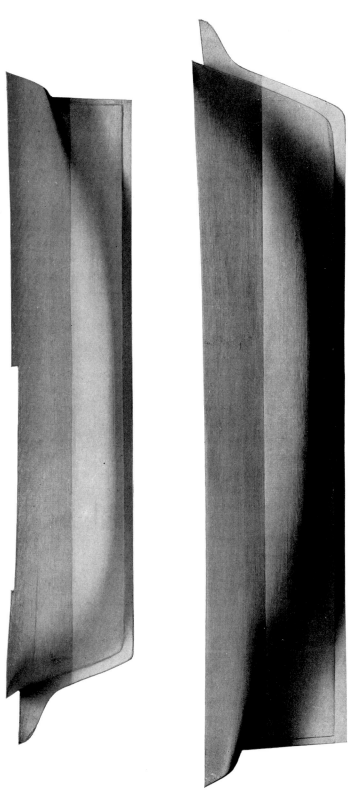

UPPER: Model of the Liverpool packet *Yorkshire*—"the fastest packet of her day." Her bottom was almost flat, a feature of the New Orleans packets, and her ends were short but sharper than usual in vessels of her time in the packet service. Reproduced by courtesy of the Webb Institute of Naval Architecture, New York City.

LOWER: Model of the China packet *Helena*. Her close kinship to the above type of Liverpool packet may be observed. She differs from them principally in having a somewhat sharper bottom and ends. Built in 1841, she proved to be one of the fastest ships of her day. Reproduced by courtesy of the Webb Institute of Naval Architecture, New York City.

CHAPTER XVII

1850

THE BRITISH TEA TRADE

AMONG all the men engaged in designing and building clippers, none stood out at the close of 1850 in any spectacular way. Here and there one attracted special attention for a time, but his brief notoriety was swiftly eclipsed by the launching of another and greater or more striking model. In mere volume of large tonnage, Webb, in New York, was doubtless holding the lead by a respectable margin, but it was by no means certain that he would not be eclipsed even in this respect within a few months.

As the year drew to an end and clipper keels were laid down in rapidly increasing numbers, popular interest reached a pitch of enthusiasm that can be appreciated only with difficulty today. The press devoted more and more space to the subject. Editorial comment and lengthy descriptions of the latest masterpieces were the order of the day. On every hand the statements were made and repeated that here, there or elsewhere, the largest, sharpest, speediest, or most advanced type of clipper was being constructed or projected.

It is not surprising that wholly extravagant claims were made at this time by writers of the period, many of whom had seen only the ship they were praising. Nor is it strange that many of these claims have persisted to this day, although modifying facts have long been accessible.

After the lapse of eighty years, one can obtain a more comprehensive view of the whole situation and form perhaps a truer conception of the significance and value of the various contributions which eventually blended into the most beautiful and powerful ship of the sail which the world has ever seen.

Foremost among the facts which appear to run counter to certain popular beliefs, is the one already touched upon, namely, the absence of any acknowledged leader in the actual development of the clipper ship. Notable men there were—men who, in any time and place would have been persons of mark, but the great master designer, the man whom, by the force of his superior ability and accomplishment all others were forced to follow, is conspicuous by his absence. Unfortunately for the historian who, humanly enough, delights in such figures, such a person cannot be discovered.

It should not be understood by this that there were no individuals who made striking contributions to the development of the clipper. Aside from practical seamen like Palmer and builder-designers like Webb, two names stand out with especial prominence—Griffiths in New York and Pook, who did most of his work in Boston. Griffiths has already been noticed as the most successful designer of the earlier type of clipper, in which he combined the old frigate theory and the later packet lines with remarkable results.

Pook, on the other hand, seems to have sensed very early the shortcomings of the Griffith's models as cargo carriers, and devoted his efforts toward evolving a more burdensome and even swifter type of ship from the flat-floored packet lines. In the end, as we shall see, his theories—or rather the theories he sponsored—triumphed, and with few exceptions the great racing prizes of the century were carried off by lineal descendants of the Western Ocean packets. After 1852 very few large American ships were built which did not embody the principles followed by Pook. Neither Griffiths nor Pook, however, developed a school of slavish imitators.

If there is one thing which appears to stand out in this connection, clear and incontrovertible, it is that the clipper ship was a composite creation—the product of literally scores of the keenest minds in America, afloat and ashore, none of whom considered himself too great to learn and each of whom would have scorned to apply that learning without attempting to add something of himself. There is the greatest secret and glory of the clipper era—that it was the achievement of normal, self-reliant, forward looking men.

If the age produced no acknowledged leader, it was nevertheless marked by an extraordinarily high level of intelligence. Merchants, master mariners, designers and builders formed a body of men of wide knowledge and unusual ability. There were few specialists among them. The merchants were not only versed in the intricate art of handling ships, but on occasion could design and rig them. In like manner the captains, architects and shipwrights were past masters in all the allied branches of their respective vocations. To paraphrase a contemporary saying: "wherever they fell, they lit on their feet."

These men took, and were not ashamed to take, the best that could be found in new design and theory. Naturally, they tried to guard their own work as today one guards a business secret, but on the whole with slight success. The lines of nearly all the more noteworthy ships were available to prominent builders, even before the ships were in frame. Every large yard had its corps of designers and draughtsmen and it was virtually impossible to preserve secrecy. Even if it had been possible it would have had little practical effect, since where tracings were not available, the huge frames of the ships themselves, naked to all observers, yielded up perforce their secret to the keen eye of the expert builder.

In fact, the chief source of secretiveness seems to have been the desire of the merchants who ordered the ships that their plans should not become known to business rivals in advance. A case in point is an incident attending the construction of the *Stag Hound*. Just before the keel was laid, McKay gave an interview to newspaper men and others in which he showed the model of the *Stag Hound*, and pointed out her characteristics without any attempt at concealment. He did, however, state that she was to be a vessel of 1200 tons, about 180 feet long on the keel and 185 feet on deck. This interview took place on August 25th and a long account of it was published in the Boston *Atlas* the following day.

The *Stag Hound* was laid down almost immediately and when she was launched on the 7th of December, it was discovered that she was a ship of nearly 1600 tons, with a keel of 207 feet in length and correspondingly broad and deep. In the meantime, several of the business rivals of George B. Upton and Samson & Tappan, of Boston, owners of the *Stag Hound*, proceeded with their plans to build clippers of twelve or thirteen hundred tons, with the result that several months later, they found themselves second rankers.

So far as the models themselves were concerned, all the interested parties understood that their new features were experimental, the practical value of which could be demonstrated only at sea. They knew, moreover, that a rival builder would do no more than attempt to incorporate certain selected features in a new and different model of his own. The truth of this statement is strikingly borne out by the fact that, except in the rare instances where an owner ordered a duplicate of his own ship, there are no two clipper ships to be found which are alike in dimensions or characteristics.

In that day and age imitation was regarded as a confession of incompetence.

McKay himself stated, in the apparently authentic interview above referred to, that before making the model of the *Stag Hound* he had become familiar with "all the celebrated clipper models." The *Stag Hound* differed in several features from any of the clippers built at the time, but the difference was not radical. McKay's chief claim to distinction, like that of most remarkable men, rests on the fact that he was able to select the best from the combined experience of others, and add to it something of his own of permanent value.

The years 1849 and 1850 had witnessed a tremendous activity in the construction of large ocean steamships—beautiful vessels, with thin arched bows and long, slinky lines. Since they were not intended to carry the immense press of canvas that sailing ships did, they could be, and were, built much sharper than any sailing ships had ever been designed.

One cannot help associating these fine-lined, inordinately sharp steamers with the development, toward the middle and latter part of 1850, of the clipper model of a hitherto unheard-of sharpness. It is impossible that there should not have been an interplay of forces here. If time and space permitted it would be interesting to trace the influence of steam on the clipper model, and vice versa. That there was such an influence is sufficiently obvious, for all the large yards in New York were building clipper steamers side by side with clipper sailing ships.

Altogether, during 1850, not less than 20 sharp flyers had been launched, in addition to 4 barques of clipper lines.

During the year, in addition to the new records on the California run, several excellent passages were made in other trades. The ship *Magellan*, under command of Captain Millet, arrived at Boston on the 28th of May, from Talcahuano, March 28th, having made the run from land to land in 59 days. In the transatlantic lines, Captain E. E. Morgan set a new record. He left Sandy Hook in the *Southampton* at 11 P.M., the 8th of June and landed his passengers at Falmouth in 13 days and 12 hours, the best passage that had ever been made over that course, and one that is comparable with the famous run of the *Red Jacket*.

Meanwhile, Cap'n Nat's brother, Theodore, had been writing a new chapter in the history of America's foreign relations.

Leaving New York in the *Oriental*, a larger and sharper edition of the *Samuel Russell*, he made a most remarkable series of runs which are summarized in the New York *Herald* for Friday, November 8th, 1850.

> "The ship *Oriental*, owned by A. A. Low & Brothers, made the trip to Hong Kong from this port, in less than eighty-one days. Her average speed on the voyage was two hundred miles a day. Her greatest speed in one day was three hundred and two miles. For thirty-three days in succession she averaged two hundred and thirty-nine miles per day, and in twelve days she ran 3119 miles—equal to two hundred and fifty miles per day.
>
> "She has secured a freight to London at £6 per ton, which is from two to three pounds per ton more than other vessels are receiving."

In passing it should be noted that this 81 day run of the *Oriental* is still the record from New York to China. Moreover, her time is shorter by several days than the record from Great Britain to China, although—due to the prevalence of fair winds from England to the Equator—that run is regarded as normally somewhat shorter than the passage from America.

Thus with a single chance, the *Oriental* not only established a new record to Hong Kong, but she made daily runs very close to the best previous work of the *Sea Witch* and *Samuel Russell*. Her work was far from finished, however.

The final abrogation by Great Britain in 1848 of the remaining provisions of the old Navigation Acts, left the way open for the first time in history for American ships to engage in commerce of foreign origin with Great Britain on equal terms with British ships. Accordingly, when the *Oriental*, after this unprecedented passage, rounded to in the harbor of Hong Kong, with flying sheets and smoking halliards, there was a rush for her charter.

Nor was the interest confined to the *Oriental*. Yankee skippers everywhere had a well earned reputation for speed. Within a few weeks seven American ships had been loaded with English owned tea and were on their way to London.

The part which America was to play in the British tea trade for the next ten years has never been comprehensively treated. Its extent and importance seems never to have been adequately appreciated. Up to the time of the Civil War no less than 139 cargoes of tea were landed in Great Britain by American ships— an average of more than twelve ships a year. These passages are listed in Appendix II and, in view of the many errors and omissions in Chinese marine reports, it is quite possible that the list is incomplete.

Statistics therefore do not bear out the impression, however unintentionally created, that American vessels played a brief and unimportant part in the English tea trade, and that after the first year or two they were employed in rapidly diminishing numbers. This was so far from being the case that in 1855, five years after the *Oriental* broke into the trade, twenty-four American ships carried tea to England, securing not merely the bulk, but the cream of the trade, while, as late as 1859, no less than fourteen were chartered in the same service. It is to be regretted that no authentic account of this splendid rivalry has yet been published.

While deservedly holding the post of honor by virtue of her unrivalled performance, the *Oriental* was not the first ship to sail from China with tea for England. The little barque *Jennett*, under Captain Ward, left Whampoa on August 25th, 1850, three days before the *Oriental*. She did not arrive at London until the 20th of the following January, while the *Oriental* had reached port on the 4th of December, forty-seven days earlier, in the unprecedented passage against the monsoon of 97 days from anchor to dock.

Other American ships chartered this year to carry British teas were the *Argonaut*, under Captain Nott, the *Roman*, in command of Captain William E. Putnam; the *Wisconsin*, Captain Oliver R. Mumford, later master of the clipper *Tornado*;

the *Susan G. Owens*, Captain Barclay; *The Mohawk*, Captain Morrison, and the *Carlo Mauran*, under Captain Tillinghast, of Providence. The *Susan G. Owens* did not get away for London until the 11th of January, 1851, but is mentioned here because her charter was made in 1850, and she would have sailed earlier but for delays in loading.

Next to the *Oriental* the *Wisconsin*, a full built ship of 925 tons, made the best passage. She got under way at Hong Kong at 7 A.M. December 4th, and anchored in the Downs at 10:30 P.M. on the 10th of March, 1851. Her time of 96 days was therefore virtually the same as that of the *Oriental* to this point, but her run of course was in the favorable monsoon.

Possibly as creditable, considering the season, was Putnam's work in the *Roman*. He left Macao the 13th of September, and had a long beat of 25 days down the China Sea. Taking his departure from Anjier at 1 o'clock on the afternoon of October 8th he ran 1757½ miles in the next seven days, an average of slightly more than 250 miles a day. The day after Christmas he made the Scilly lights 75 days from Anjier and 100 days from Canton. There followed another round in the British tea trade and on the 22nd of February, '51, as Putnam slammed his little packet down the Channel we find in his log the simple entry "old England on our lee." As in the case of many another exile, something antedating the Boston Tea Party—older, perhaps, than the circle of Stonehenge—tugged at the heart strings of the Yankee skipper as he swept past the white cliffs and smooth fields lying fair on his starboard beam.

None of the ships above mentioned were out-and-out clippers, with the exception of the *Oriental*. The *Argonaut* has sometimes been rated as a clipper, but, strictly speaking, she belongs like the *Roman* and the *Wisconsin* to the class of fast-sailing Canton traders which preceded the clippers, and which derived their speed from the quarter deck rather than from their lines. The *Argonaut* was, nevertheless, an excellent craft and made a number of very creditable passages.

Both in England and America the performance of the *Oriental* caused a tremendous sensation. In England, the news of the arrival of the *Oriental* was received with mixed emotions. In his *Clipper Ship Era,* Capt. Clark makes the broad statement "that the arrival of this vessel in London with her cargo of tea in this crises of 1850, aroused almost as much apprehension and excitement in Great Britain as was created by the memorable Tea Party held in Boston harbor in 1775." Her London passage by no means tells the story. On the 30th of January, 1850, the *Oriental* was in China preparing to sail to New York. She went to New York, returned to China again in 81 days, the record to this date, and was in London before the end of the year, having made three profitable voyages between North Atlantic ports and China in the space of 10 months and 8 days.

It is sufficient to say that her performance was a powerful factor in America in shifting the attention of ship owners back from steam to the old and tried "canvas back." Few of those afloat, either seamen or masters, had a good word for the "smelly, noisy old tea kettles."

CHAPTER XVIII

1851

FAST CALIFORNIA PASSAGES

AS though it were the signal for a concerted demonstration in behalf of ships of the sail, the passing of 1850 marked the beginning of a prolonged outburst of popular enthusiasm which was strikingly reflected in the press. Nothing like it had happened before and, such is the complexity of modern society that in all probability, nothing like it will ever be seen again. News space was far more valuable in 1851 than today, yet for two years and more the great dailies snatched with avidity at every scrap of clipper ship information.

Encomium piled on encomia. The descriptions of the new favorites touched at times the border lands of poetry. The popular excitement which greeted the arrival of a fleet racer with another record: the cheers which sped them on their course when two or more of them weighed anchor for a contest over the long Cape Horn route: the complacent satisfaction, the oratory and dripping "luncheons" which marked each launching of "the largest and sharpest yet," are all imperishably embalmed in a thousand musty old files. One may turn those pages and be transported to a world that has long ceased to be—a world in which crudity, coarseness and ineffable beauty are strangely mingled.

One reads and long dead men come to life again, and bustle about queerly shrunken, yet strangely familiar streets, fussily intent on droll errands which somehow manipulated the strings of empire.

In the great yards one sees huge timbers stretched; massive frames rise in place one after another, cinema fashion; white glistering oak planking mysteriously surrounds the whole; lofty spars stretch fibrously toward the clouds—a moment's shouting; the glimpse of an important personage lending tone to the occasion, white wings flutter out, and the massive hull, unbelievably small under that snowy pile, moves seaward. Another clipper has sailed. Another voyage has begun that will be boisterously told in the halls of Valhalla and will become a not forgotten part of the tradition of the sea.

Toward the end of 1850, men saw the new version of the clipper ship for the first time and their eyes were opened. Larger, loftier, more powerful than any merchant ships men had ever looked upon, they embodied at the same time a new and unimagined conception of form. And, pressing closely behind each proud debutante were scores of clippers in the making, ever larger, loftier and more powerful, giving promise of a rare, exotic beauty that the humblest might feel but the most gifted could not describe. The streets and counting houses reverberated with excited talk about the all-engrossing subject and reporters exhausted their adjectives and space in lengthy accounts of the latest masterpiece, and in wild prophecies for the future.

For the moment steam was "finished." It had "reached the limit of its possibilities" and, on the whole, had proved a disappointment. J. G. Bennett, never restrained, opined it not only too expensive but "too slow!" On the other hand, the new, huge packets were never more prosperous. One after another they were coming into port with 800, 900, nearly a thousand passengers at a time. They were making remarkably fine passages. They were more comfortable than the noisy throbbing steamships, which were still in the experimental stage. The disaster to the new propeller, the *Helena Slowman*, the lingering memory of the mysterious disappearance of the ill-fated ship *President* and others, the poor financial returns, the remarkable speed shown by the new clippers, all contributed to a sudden reversion of interest to the old and well-tried method of transportation.

Whereas, at the beginning of 1850 far more steam than sailing tonnage was being constructed in New York, the early days of 1851 witnessed exactly the opposite situation. This condition was temporary, for, as the rush to California continued, the demand for rapid and luxurious facilities for travel by way of the various land routes over the Isthmus and through Central America increased. By the end of the year approximately fifty steam vessels were reported in course of construction in and near New York. Many of these were small craft, but a fair proportion were large, ocean-going vessels. At the same time popular interest in the clipper ships grew rather than diminished.

An article in the New York *Herald*, on Sunday, January 19th, 1851, indicates the extent of the appeal made by these beautiful vessels to persons in every walk of life:

"There is great anxiety manifested, and much speculation indulged in, by a great many persons interested in ship-building, concerning the respective sailing qualities and sea worthiness of the various beautiful clipper ships that have left and are preparing to leave this port for California and China. Each vessel, as she is launched from one of the ship yards of our city, and every one that comes to our port, from some Eastern yard, has its separate admirers. The various points of beauty, whether of hull or spars, are marked and descanted upon with a critical eye. Some one, probably a New York shipbuilder, with sparkling eye and animated countenance, among the groups that are generally assembled in the neighborhood of the docks where these ships lie, will point out to you, what, in his opinion, are the masterpieces of the art.

"The *Eclipse,* with her signal flying, 'Through by Daylight,' sailed on Wednesday for California and China, and the *Ino,* now receiving freight for the same destination, will be considered by him as combining all the elements of a vessel never to be excelled, and but on rare occasions to be equalled

by any craft hailing from any other than a New York ship-
yard. From stem to stern—from keel to masthead—their
various powers for skimming the waters or withstanding the
anticipated heavy weather to be met with in weathering the
Cape, and the qualities of their commanders to bring all the
vessel's powers into play, are talked of with as much earnest-
ness as if the speaker had embarked his all in the voyage; and
sanguine assertions are made that either of his favorites will
beat anything that the Eastern States can ever produce in the
shape of a sailing vessel.

"But the Eastern built vessels are not without their friends
and backers. The *Sea Serpent,* which left on the 11th, and
the *Stag Hound,* now receiving her cargo, are cited as proud
monuments of the skill of our Eastern brethren, each, in its
turn, warranted as sure to take the starch out of anything
afloat; and though admitting that for beauty of model and
sailing qualities the New York vessels may probably have
some claim to perfection, a confident guess is rendered that
the results of the voyage will prove that the East have as
good, if not a better claim to superiority in ship building
than their New York competitors.

"Among so many vessels it is impossible to select one as
superior, where all are beautiful. If this one has a neater or
more beautiful stem, that has a more elegantly turned stern
and a cleaner run; if one has a greater capacity for stowage
and better bearings, another has a greater rise of floor, with
its accompanying lightness of appearance. The trips, however, of the *Eclipse* and *Sea Serpent* will probably go some
ways toward settling the matter in dispute, as each is of a
different model, and one a New Yorker and the other an
Eastern vessel, and each commanded by a man celebrated for
his energy and great seaman-like qualities. It will be a neck
and neck race—they having sailed within four days of each
other, and are looked upon by the two parties as the champions of their different ideas of clipper ships.

"Success to the winner!"

By 1851 popular interest had largely centered on the California run. All the larger and most of the smaller clippers were
going around the Horn with the intention, if it should prove

feasible, of crossing to China for a tea cargo and thence going to England or home direct.

At the time the *Sea Serpent* and *Eclipse* sailed on the 11th and 15th of January, respectively, three other clippers left Boston and New York practically in company with them. The *John Bertram* under Captain Frederick Lendholm sailed from Boston on the 11th, while the *Grey Feather*, Captain Daniel McLaughlin, and the little Philadelphia built clipper barque *Isabelita Hyne* commanded by Samuel F. Dewing were reported as sailing in company from New York on the 12th. The log of the *Grey Feather*, however, gives her sailing date as the 14th. Here were five ships, four of which were brand new, all commanded by men keyed to the situation and resolved, blow high or low, to be the first to pass the Golden Gate.

There was no hilarious rushing forth to unregarded dangers. The master mariner of 1851 understood as no person now living could possibly understand, the exact extent of the risks that confronted him. It was no small thing in the closing days of sail, with light top hamper, a third less canvas, tonnage considered, and all the safeguards of wire rigging, turnbuckles and patent devices of all sorts, to take a new ship to sea. In clipper days it was a far more serious matter. Many a new racer towed down the harbor with the riggers still on board, feverishly at work setting up shrouds and backstays until the last moment when the pilot should turn the ship over to the captain and the tug ran alongside to pick them off and take them back to other half rigged vessels.

The master who took his ship out with her towering spars and immensely square yards wholly dependent for their support on elastic hemp which would stretch with the first blow and let the whole enormous weight of yards and masts come tumbling about their ears unless prevented by sheer force of seamanship, knew exactly what to expect. He knew, moreover, that if he were to make a record passage he must of necessity handle his ship as a scant dozen living men were able to do.

The tragedy of commanders who had courage without the requisite skill or physical endurance, or who had skill without the courage at critical moments, would fill many books. The pity is that most of the failures were fine, upstanding men of undoubted ability who would have made a success anywhere and in any field but that of the terrible Cape Horn course. The poorest of them were better than the best need be today.

It was in no idle humor that the thoroughbreds flew the banner "Eighty Days to the Golden Gate" at the wharves of Boston and New York. That the goal was never attained was due to the chance of wind and weather and not to faltering determination. "Light flattering breezes" and "Heavy head gales with bad sea" were entries that spelled many a deep sea tragedy.

One is all too apt to forget the price paid for every day saved on the long run. Experienced Cape Horn shipmasters in the closing days of sail were often heard to say that the use of stay-sails did not reduce the passage more than two or three days at most, while studding sails as a rule effected no greater saving. Undoubtedly the relatively small spar plan and full lines of the later ships had much to do with it, but the above opinion, however mistaken, indicates in some small measure the herculean efforts necessary to reduce the average time by weeks and months rather than days.

Everything considered, the five ships above mentioned made excellent passages. That of the *Grey Feather*, 136 days, was the longest in actual sailing time, while the 112 days, net, of the New York built *Eclipse* was two days shorter than the time of her closest rival, the *Sea Serpent*, representing Portsmouth. All the larger ships, the *John Bertram*, *Eclipse* and *Sea Serpent* lost and sprung spars and were forced to put into Valparaiso for repairs. As one by one they reached their destination and rounded to at their anchors, their crews gazed open eyed at the blackened expanse of San Francisco's business district stretching for three quarters of a mile along the waterfront, leveled to the ground by the great fire of May 3rd. A few nights later (at 1.00 A.M.

the 11th of June), sailors from the recently arrived *John Bertram* witnessed the first "execution" by the Vigilance Committee when an Englishman named Jenkins from the Australian convict settlements was hanged from the gable of "the old adobe" in Portsmouth square. Fifteen years earlier a humble foremast hand named Richard Dana had noted this building as the only structure of importance then standing in San Francisco.

McKay's new ship, *Stag Hound*, commanded by Josiah Richardson, sailed 17 days after the *Eclipse* and reached port five days after the arrival of the latter. Leaving New York on the 1st of February, her log records that she discharged the pilot and made all sail outside Sandy Hook at 3.15 P.M. Six days later she lost her maintopmast and three topgallant masts, in spite of which she crossed the line a few hours less than 21 days out. On March 23rd, fifty-one days from the Hook, she was up with the Horn at midnight bucking a Southwest gale. Richardson anchored in the harbor of Valparaiso at 3 P.M. on the 8th of April and sailed again on the evening of the 13th. On the morning of May 25th he sailed into San Francisco harbor, letting go his anchor at half past ten.

Deducting the five days spent at Valparaiso the *Stag Hound*'s sailing time from New York was less than 108 days. In estimating the quality of this achievement the shortened spars and partly disabled condition of the ship must be taken into consideration.

March witnessed the sailing of four clippers from New York and one from Boston. Two of these, the *Gazelle* under Captain Henderson and the *Ino*, Captain R. E. Little, left New York on the 4th and 12th of the month respectively. Both were extreme clippers, and although the tonnage of the *Gazelle* was nearly twice that of the *Ino*, both made the same passage, 134 days. It is probable that the *Gazelle* would have made better time but for the fact that Captain Henderson was sick the entire trip and was totally blind for the last fifty days. As a result Captain

Dollard, one of the owners, went post haste from New York by the Isthmus to take over the command at San Francisco.

The *Gazelle* was a very beautiful craft. She had, however, an extreme dead rise which Mr. Webb, her builder, considered excessive, and later stated that this feature was dictated by the owners who were old sea captains, a circumstance which possibly accounted for the persistence of Baltimore clipper features in more than one of the new ships. Like many vessels possessing this feature, she was very fast in moderate weather, but was no match for the flat floored clippers when it came on to blow.

Immediately following these two came the Maine built *Alert* under Captain Bartlett on March 15th, the little Baltimore clipper *Architect,* Captain Caspar, on March 20th, and the *Shooting Star,* which left Boston on the 22nd in charge of Judah P. Baker, who died a couple of years later in command of the *Flying Dragon.*

Of the three the *Architect* made the best time, 116 days, allowing for a detention of 13 days at Talcahuano. The *Alert* made a long passage of 150 days. Baker, in the *Shooting Star,* was partly dismasted in the South Atlantic and put back to Rio Janeiro. He sailed from Rio on the 11th of May, which would give him the long run of 95 days, thence to San Francisco. Elsewhere he is erroneously credited with making this part of the trip in 90 days. The entire passage occupied to his chagrin 124 sailing days. However, he thoroughly redeemed himself by taking her out the next year in a smashing passage of 105 days around the Horn in the dead of winter, after she had been re-rigged in stronger fashion.

Boston and Salem were represented in the April contest. The *Game Cock,* of Boston, one of Daniel C. Bacon's ships, and one of the earliest examples of Pook's draftsmanship, in command of Captain Hollis, sailed from New York on the 3rd, followed by the *Witchcraft* of Salem under William C. Rogers, on the 4th of April. They were evenly matched as to tonnage, rating somewhat over 1300 tons, the *Game Cock* being 82 tons heavier than the *Witchcraft*.

Both ships were driven clipper fashion, with the result that they turned up in Rio harbor in May, the *Game Cock* with her mainmast sprung and the *Witchcraft* minus her mizzen. The *Game Cock* had to discharge at a ruinous expense to replace her mainmast. She was detained 57 days and her net time to San Francisco was 128 days.

The *Witchcraft* effected her repairs in a much shorter time, getting away nearly a month earlier, and made the then record run of 62 days from Rio to the Golden Gate. Her net sailing time of 103 days was the best of the year, aside from the record run of the *Flying Cloud* later in the season. All in all, it was a good showing for Captain Rogers, who had come in through the cabin window as an owner's son instead of crawling through the hawse pipe in the good old way.

It may be noted that these passages, although for the most part far from being records, were remarkable compared with those of the full built ships made about the same time, some of which consumed more than six months on the voyage while the majority took from forty to fifty days longer. Even the *Joshua Bates*, McKay's early fast sailing model, under the very able command of Easterbrook, which sailed in company with the *Ino*, was 156 days on the run.

It should be remembered that almost without exception the clippers were not merely deeply loaded but were badly overloaded, a fact which put them well down below their best sailing marks. One has only to examine their models to appreciate the reason for this.

The case of the *Witch of the Wave* is an illustration. She was not only a very sharp and heavily sparred ship but a remarkably beautiful craft as well. Her model, shown in this book, gives a faint idea of the perfection of her lines which seem to have left a vivid impression on the people of her day. Under the later tonnage rules she rated only 975 tons, yet on her first voyage around the Horn in the Southern mid-winter she carried a cargo of 1900 tons, and to the distant observer, as she towed down the harbor, her deck seemed barely afloat. In spite of this handicap she arrived out in 121 days, being one of the few clippers of the year which were not dismasted.

Charles P. Low, who sailed from New York in the *N. B. Palmer* on the 7th of May, just two weeks before the *Witch of the Wave* left Boston under the command of J. Hardy Millet, made a fine passage of 107 days. Both ships made good runs on the first part of the voyage. The *Palmer* was 26 days to the Equator while the *Witch* made the crossing in 25 days. Thereafter they were respectively 60 and 63 days to the Horn, and Millet had the rare experience of going around in dead of winter with a breeze fair from the East Northeast and all studding sails set. In the North Pacific his luck deserted him and his log records day after day of flat calm. On the 7th of September, after eight consecutive breezeless days, his goosequill viciously splutters:

"Flat calm—How much more of this (God only knows)."

In spite of this the *Witch of the Wave* administered a beating to the clippers *Eureka* and *Southern Cross*, which sailed about the same time. Although expressly designed for speed the *Eureka* seems to have fallen far short of the hopes of her owners. She was a very sharp, handsome ship. Nevertheless Captain Benjamin F. Cutler of Stonington, who had her before he took the Baltimore clipper, *Mary Whitridge*, always said she was an uncommonly dull sailer for a clipper.

The *Southern Cross*, however, handsomely atoned for her perverseness in this instance, by a complete reversal of form. Under Captain Levi Stevens she left San Francisco on the 24th of October, following, and went to Calcutta in 56 sailing days, arriving there on Christmas day. Her time to Hong Kong was only a couple of days over the record, while to Singapore it was 43 days.

It may be noted that on the same day the *Southern Cross*

sailed, the fine full built *Buena Vista,* of Boston, also left for the same destination with Captain Eben Linnell in command. Captain Linnell, who later had the beautiful extreme clipper *Eagle Wing* and also invented a variation of Howes double topsail rig, which was used on many well known vessels, made a race of it with the result that he arrived at Sand Heads in a passage of 60 days, net.

CHAPTER XIX

1851

FLYING CLOUD **AND** *CHALLENGE*

IN May, 1851, the eyes of the marine world were fixed on two ships, at the time the largest of their kind. These two ships were destined to have the most remarkable, yet widely different, careers of any ships that ever sailed the seven seas.

The *Flying Cloud* was loading at pier 20, East River, in New York. A mile or so farther up the river, in the Webb yard, the finishing touches were being put upon the *Challenge,* preparatory to her launching on the 24th of the month. For the moment the *Flying Cloud* was the largest merchant ship afloat, and would continue to be until the *Challenge* took the water. Both vessels were centres of attraction to all interested in nautical affairs, and in 1851 that included all the men and boys and a generous sprinkling of the women and girls of the Atlantic coast.

One of the leading New York papers printed, on May 20th, the following description of the hospitality dispensed by the owners of the *Flying Cloud,* an incident typical of clipper days and ways:

"GRINNEL AND MINTURN'S FLYING CLOUD.—Hundreds of people have visited this beautiful and unique clipper built vessel, which will sail this day week, we believe, for California and China. She is nearly full, vast as is her capacity of tonnage.

"We dined on board yesterday with as fine a 'band of brothers' as any man could desire for companions in a *Flying Cloud*. Indeed, so familiar were the voices of many that we could not realize that we had mounted to the nebular regions. Yet all admitted that we actually were inside a *Flying Cloud* whose destination was California, and of which Capt. Cressy, over whose keen eye and intelligent face there was assuredly no mist, had command; and we can only say that more table luxury, more tasteful and costly furniture, more ample ventilation and comfort of every kind, we never knew even in an earth-built packet ship or steamer.

"The *Flying Cloud* is just the kind of a vehicle, or whatever else it may be called, that a sensible man would choose for a ninety days voyage."

Five days after the above incident, the *Challenge* was launched in the presence of one of the largest and most vociferous crowds that had ever attended a launching in New York. There was ample in the immediate vicinity to stir the enthusiasm of the spectators, aside from the *Challenge* herself. On either side were the beautiful clippers, *Comet* and *Invincible*, nearly completed and only slightly smaller than the *Challenge* herself. Nearby was the *Sword Fish*, already in frame and partly planked. Not far away, in the yard of Westervelt & MacKay, the great bulk of the *Hornet* could be seen rearing itself maternally above three smaller clippers. Beyond, in Jacob Bell's yard, the huge *Trade Wind* stood, while across the river, in Williamsburg, could be seen the forms of the *Eagle* and *John Stuart* amid an assortment of small fry. From these and lesser neighboring yards came the incessant music of a thousand mauls and the screech of saws.

It was a picture to stir the pulse of the average man of any time. One has only to remember that most of the onlookers could readily recall the days when the largest of these yards considered it a good year's work when they launched one or two

chunky little vessels, a third the size of the *Challenge,* with perhaps two or three small schooners or brigs thrown in for measure.
Many, indeed, could look back to the days when it taxed the
facilities of any yard in the land to launch more than a single
ship of four hundred tons in a given year.

As her model, illustrated in this book, shows, the *Challenge,*
with the possible exception of the *Stag Hound,* had the sharpest
entrance lines of any large ship that had been built up to that
time. Add to that the further fact, already noted, that she was
probably the loftiest clipper that ever sailed blue water, irrespective of size or period, and one can gather some conception of
the immense strides that had been made in designing and building
ships during the previous two years. In all probability the
launching of a hundred thousand ton steamer would seem less
spectacular today than the construction of a two thousand ton
clipper did to the citizen of 1851.

The *Flying Cloud* sailed on the 2nd of June. Everyone
knows what she accomplished, but none are left to recall that
31st of August when she slipped through the Gate, eighty-nine
days twenty-one and a half hours from New York. Her log,
reprinted in Appendix V, tells the story of a passage that was at
once the wonder and admiration of old sailors and mariner merchants to the end of their days.

She was ably sailed and nobly manned by a cursing, competent crew. America owes not a little of her glory to those
hard, salt-toughened fellows who handed her canvas and fished
her buckling spars on that icy winter passage 'round the Horn—
men of the breed that fought the privateers of 1812 and laid
broad the foundations of this present prosperity in the years that
followed.

With the *Challenge* the situation was different. Her story
is neither so glorious nor so clear as that of the *Flying Cloud,*
muddied as it has been of late by a choice mess of fo'c'sle gossip
which bears the earmarks of having been in circulation and un-
laundered since Drake worried the Armada.

The *Challenge* dropped down from New York and anchored at the South West spit on the 13th of July. All marine reports seem to agree that she sailed the same day, but from the fact that the wind was easterly from the 13th to the 15th it is at least doubtful whether she made an offing for 48 hours. The matter is unimportant except in its bearing on the exact length of the passage from land to land.

Much has been made of the fact that Waterman's crew was made up of the jail sweepings of the Atlantic ports, as indicating that he had a reputation as a killer. The true explanation is much simpler. Not only had the California mines drained the seaports of thousands of able seamen, but literally hundreds of large ships requiring large crews had been built and sent around the Horn and elsewhere during the previous months. Sailors are not made overnight. As the records of mutinies about this time would indicate, many crews were made up of poor characters, with a sprinkling of able seamen. On smaller ships it did not matter so much. A few good sailors could handle things in a pinch. In a huge, tremendously over-sparred clipper like the *Challenge* it was a very serious matter.

One may comb the papers and other records of the forties, including those of the courts, with the utmost care, without finding the slightest suggestion either that Waterman had ever killed a man or that a complaint of any character had ever been lodged against him. It is difficult to think that if he had to avoid the police after his various China trips, some mention of the fact that warrants were out would not have appeared in the press. It is, further, extremely improbable if an unsavory odor attached to him that a firm so eminently respectable as N. L. & G. Griswold would have sought him out to take charge of the ship which was the apple of their eye.

Waterman undoubtedly was a hard man to sail under, but he shared this trait with every noted clipper captain who ever sailed, in the sense that any ship which was out to make a record was no ship for either a lazy or an incompetent man, or a weakling.

Only the hardiest could do a man's work on a clipper and like it. Even in those days it was no shame for a good, husky all-around sailor man to admit that he steered clear of clippers. Life is sweet and laying out on a yardarm in a hurricane is not conducive to health or long life.

The machine took its toll, and Waterman was as much a creature of the machine as the humblest sailor under him. He had no choice but to drive. Is it entirely to his discredit that he ranks among the three or four past masters of the art that the world has produced?

But he was more than a driver; more, even, than a first-class seaman. There are mathematical geniuses who have rated in tests a thousand per cent above the point that marks perfection—men who seem gifted with some strange clairvoyance, which undoubtedly has a physical explanation, but which is none the less abnormal. Some such power as this seems to have belonged to Waterman at times. Be that as it may, he brought to his work an alert, anticipatory intelligence that is rarely matched on land or sea. If there is such a thing as a wind sense, he had it. It is something to come home from China followed every inch of the way by a favoring gale, and over a course shorter by a thousand miles than the usual one. "Taking a chance" may explain the thing once, but when it occurs several times in succession, one must look further. A fourteen thousand mile voyage is no turn of the dice.

The *Challenge* fanned her way slowly down the Atlantic in light winds and calms; bucked the heavy Cape Horn gales for twelve days, and moved leisurely up the Pacific. She entered San Francisco harbor on October 29th, 108 days from New York—an excellent passage considering the season. It appears to have been beaten only once by a ship sailing from the East in July. Nevertheless, it was a tremendous disappointment to Waterman and to his employers, who had sunk a fortune in the ship to beat the world.

It is clear now that the *Challenge* did not have a chance on this voyage. The experience of the next few years was to establish the fact that she sailed at the most unfavorable season of the year for a fast passage. Waterman reported that he was able to make 300 miles in 24 hours only once during the trip. This, in spite of the fact that the *Challenge* later proved herself phenomenally fast, and even in her old age, after her spar plan had been cut down three successive times, was able to record 300 mile runs with astonishing ease and frequency.

But the *California Courier* of November 1st tells the story:

"The ship *Challenge* has arrived, and Capt. Waterman, her commander, has also—but where are nine of his crew? And where is he and his guilty mate? The accounts given of Captain Waterman towards his men, if true, make him one of the most inhuman monsters of this age.

"If they are true, he should be burned alive—he should never leave this city a live man. Nine of his men are missing, and the sailors who are here declare that four were shaken from the mizen-topsail yard into the sea, where they were drowned, and five of them died from the effects of wounds and ill treatment.

"The scene at this time on board of the ship beggars all description. Five of them are mangled and bruised in the most shocking manner. One poor fellow died today, and five others, it is expected, will soon be in the embrace of death. One of the men now lying on his deathbed has been severely injured in his genitals, by a kick from this brute in human form. Had these poor men been put in a den with bears and panthers, they could not have been much more inhumanly and shockingly maimed. They are all now lying in the forecastle of the ship. The captain, the vile monster, has made his escape, and so has his brutal mate.

"It is an infamous outrage to have such a bloody murderer to command a ship. He is noted for his cruelty everywhere, and in the streets of New York he dare not show himself, nor dare he hereafter show himself in this city. We hope the respectable house to which he is consigned here will not only disavow his conduct, but if they have the power, remove him from command. If he is not removed, we hope this community will not permit such a monster to sail out of this port as captain of any vessel. In all sincerity, we hope the monster may be caught, and dealt with in the severest manner. We did hear last night, that the mate had been taken, and now we trust that all humane men will turn out and pursue the captain until he is captured and punished."

Aside from the remarkable incoherencies of the above and the amazing alternative suggestions that Waterman be either burned alive or deprived of his command, one can readily read between the lines the true story of the situation.

The *Challenge* had arrived on the 29th of October. The article quoted did not appear until the first of November. What was happening during the intervening two days? To old sailors this is a rhetorical question. To others it may be explained that the men had been duly paid off; Waterman and his officers had gone leisurely and unmolested about their business; Waterman had given his report of the trip to the newspaper, and—the sailors were getting drunk.

Even the most incompetent sailor can get reasonably drunk in twenty-four hours. Then, and not till then, did they begin to think of their disease ridden comrades still in their bunks on the *Challenge*, where some of them had been since the ship left Sandy Hook. After that it was simply a matter of making as lurid a story as possible for their new found drinking companions.

What followed is a matter of history and may be read in all the newspapers of the period, without resorting to fiction compounded of the grog shop and fo'c'sle sweepings of three centuries past.

After the above article appeared on the morning of November first, a mob gathered whose numbers eventually increased to about two thousand partially sober men. They first searched the offices of Alsop & Co., the agents for the *Challenge*, and failing to find either Waterman or the mate they took old Captain

Land, who was there; accused him of secreting the mate, and threatened to hang him. At this stage of the affair the mayor called upon the Vigilance Committee by tolling the bell of the Monumental Fire Company and

> "in five minutes 600 members of the Committee were upon the ground, presenting a most sublime spectacle, and placing the committee for the first time in its proper position—that of friendship to the authorities. The appearance of the Vigilance Committee had the desired effect; for, after cheering the Committee, and groaning the captain and mate of the *Challenge,* the mob quietly retreated. And thus ended, after a three hours siege, a most disgraceful affair, an insult put upon the commercial community of the grossest character; their buildings and counting rooms searched by a vagabond mob, simply for the reason that their Captain was a brute."

In due time Waterman received a trial, at his own request, and was completely exonerated by the testimony of his passengers and sailors from his own crew. In the interval before the trial the true facts began to come out, which induced a complete reversal of public opinion. Several days after the above occurrences one of the San Francisco papers printed the following:

> "We are informed that a state of feeling exists among a portion of the sailors who came out with Capt. Waterman in the *Challenge,* different from that which has generally been supposed to have existed among them unanimously. A gentleman of this city informs us that nine of the seamen who have just arrived in her, have waited on the consignees of this ship, and informed them that they were willing to make a voyage to China, in the *Challenge,* with Capt. Waterman as master. Five of these seamen are Americans and four are foreigners. The same gentleman states that the passengers are unanimous in justifying the course pursued by the captain on the way out."
>
> (See also manuscript of Thomas G. Cary: "Vigilance Committee in 1851." Congressional Library.)

Severity there undoubtedly was. In no other way could the over-sparred, ill-manned ship have been brought to port as Waterman brought her, without losing a spar or splitting a sail. In no other way could he have saved the life of his mate when he was attacked by a crowd of sailors armed with knives. But that there was unnecessary cruelty, in view of the circumstances, may be doubted when the testimony of the passengers is considered. In such matters passengers are, and always have been, somewhat squeamish.

By all odds the closest and most interesting race to California completed during the year was that of the *Sea Witch, Typhoon* and *Raven*. The *Sea Witch* under Fraser sailed from New York on the 1st of August, followed the next day by the 1600 ton *Typhoon* commanded by Charles H. Salter of Portsmouth. The *Raven*, smallest of the three, sailed from Boston on the 5th in charge of Captain William W. Henry.

It was a hard fought contest in which first one ship and then another had the advantage. On the 28th of August, off the Brazils, the *Typhoon* came dead into the wake of the *Raven*. Both ships made all possible sail and the *Typhoon* gradually drew ahead. As they closed in on Cape Horn the *Raven* and *Sea Witch* were sailing on even terms with the *Typhoon* two days astern. Off the Horn the two little clippers fought it out tack by tack, with the *Typhoon*, helped by her greater size, slowly drawing up on them. Up the Pacific they went, both ships gaining again on the *Typhoon*, and the *Sea Witch* increasing her lead over both. They crossed the Equator with the *Sea Witch* two days ahead of the *Raven* and four days ahead of the *Typhoon*.

On the long close-hauled stretch from the Line to the Golden Gate the *Raven* and *Typhoon* began to overhaul the *Sea Witch*. Nevertheless it was a race right up to the San Francisco Heads. Five hundred miles from port the luck of the *Sea Witch* deserted her. She ran into a belt of calms and light airs which resulted in her taking five days to cover a distance she should have made in two. At the last moment both her competitors slipped by her, the *Typhoon* entering the harbor on the 18th, the *Raven* on the 19th and the *Sea Witch* on the 20th of November.

By virtue of her later start the *Raven* emerged the winner, her time being 106 days, as against the 107 and 110 days of the *Typhoon* and *Sea Witch*, respectively. It was a notable victory, since the *Typhoon* was not only double her size but had already proved herself to be of championship calibre, as her record run to Liverpool testified, while it seems to have been the only instance where the *Sea Witch* was ever headed by a ship approaching her own tonnage. Moreover the *Raven's* margin of victory would have been even greater if she had not lost her maintopmast three days before reaching her destination. It was estimated that this accident cost her two full days.

No apology need be made, however, for any of the ships. Some conception of their feat, which was performed during the worst season of the year for a good run may be gained from the fact that the clipper barque *Fanny*, Captain E. Spicer, Jr., left New York six days after the *Raven* and arrived out more than two months after she had passed the Golden Gate. Yet the *Fanny* was a very smart craft and Spicer was a hard-driving sailor man, as officers raised a stone's throw from Nat Palmer and Dave Babcock were apt to be.

Not all the good sailing of '51 took place in the races. There was many a fine lone run made against time. One of the most striking was that of the diminutive Baltimore clipper *Seaman*, commanded by Joseph Myrick. She left San Francisco bound for Valparaiso on the 18th of April and crossed the Line on her 15th day out. On the 23rd of May she reached her destination 36 days from the Heads, "having" as her log states, "had a passage of 7 days less than any on record."

From Valparaiso she sailed at noon the first of June for Rio Janeiro, arriving there on the 28th of the month, a run of 27 days. In the interval Myrick had sustained a good dusting off the Horn. His log for the 13th contains the following entry:

"made sail, having been 3½ days with close reefed topsail and reefed foresail. Out of 13 times I have passed and repassed Cape Horn, never have seen so hard a gale or one of so long continuance, neither have I seen it so cold. Much snow and ice upon the ship, the latter making freely upon deck at midday."

Continuing, the *Seaman* ran from Rio to Cape Henry in 30 days, a smart but not a record passage. Her entire running time of 94 days from San Francisco was one of the best eastward voyages up to that time, if indeed it was not the best.

Meanwhile other fine clippers were coming along. A round dozen and more were to be completed and sail for California before the end of the year. Among these were the *Hornet, John Wade, Comet, Trade Wind, Wild Pigeon, Golden Gate, Flying Fish, Northern Light, Seaman's Bride, Swordfish, Hurricane, Invincible* and others. Noble ships all. Hardly a one but made day's runs or passages which are, or closely approach, the present records. Just behind them a score of other fine clippers were receiving their finishing touches preparatory to sailing early in '52.

Aside from the clipper ships large and small, two diminutive craft from Boston made remarkable passages. These were the pilot boat schooner *Fanny,* commanded by William Kelly, and the brig *Sussex,* Captain Bagley. The *Fanny,* 84 tons and less than 75 feet in length, went out in 108 days' sailing time, arriving at San Francisco February 18th, 1851. The *Sussex* arrived on the 5th of the following April after a passage of 106 days. A generation or so ago the mere mention of such records would have been sufficient. Today the perspective is changed and 17,000 mile drives around the Horn "under water" are reduced to a couple of dates and a mis-spelled name.

CHAPTER XX

1851

ORIENTAL TRADE EXPANSION

S the clippers reached California they were un-
loaded and sent on their way with all possible
dispatch. Those whose connections warranted
it, sailed for the Orient to load teas and silks for
England or America. Others ran to Manila or Calcutta, while
not a few hurried back to the East coast for another profitable
San Francisco charter.

Among those which left for Hong Kong was the *Raven*. She
purchased her anchor and squared away on the 19th of December. Old man Land, some time of the *Helena* and the still smaller
and tubbier *Splendid,* stood on the magnificent flush deck of the
largest clipper in the world, his white hair stirring in the breeze,
and watched her as she went—her crew sheeting home and walking noisily away with the halliards. The next day he was out in
hot pursuit.

He caught her as she was entering the harbor of Hong Kong.

Fifteen Yankee ships sailed for London or Liverpool with tea
during 1851. Of these only four rated as clippers: the *Surprise,*
Memnon, Oriental and *White Squall.* The *Memnon* was lost in

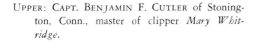

UPPER: CAPT. BENJAMIN F. CUTLER of Stonington, Conn., master of clipper *Mary Whitridge*.

LOWER: CAPT. JOHN ELDRIDGE of Yarmouth Port, Mass., master of packet ship *Liverpool* and clipper *Young Brander*.

UPPER: CAPT. THOMAS F. HALL of East Dennis, Mass., taken at the age of 20 when first mate of the clipper *Belle of the West*.

LOWER: CAPT. THOMAS F. HALL at the age of 83. Capt. Hall was one of the last living officers of the extreme clipper period. After leaving the *Belle of the West* he commanded the barque *Egypt*.

"DREADNOUGHT."

PAINTED BY CHARLES R. PATTERSON.

Reproduced by courtesy of the New York, New Haven and Hartford Railroad Company.

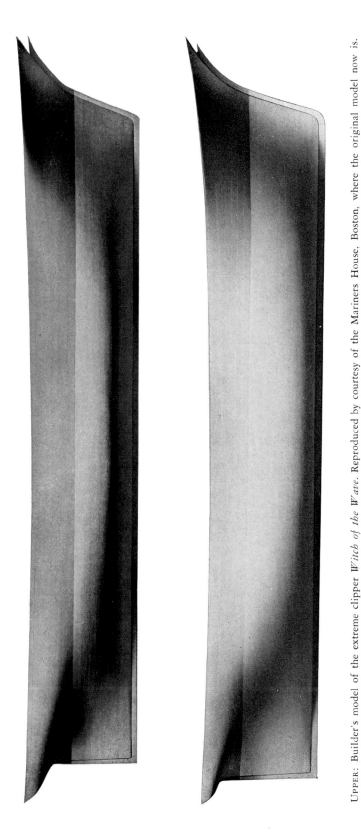

UPPER: Builder's model of the extreme clipper *Witch of the Wave*. Reproduced by courtesy of the Mariners House, Boston, where the original model now is.

LOWER: Builder's model of the extreme clipper *Morning Light*. Reproduced by courtesy of the Mariners House, Boston, who have the original model. Excellent examples of the two schools of fast sailing design; the *Witch*, with her sharp bottom and long, graceful ends, being one of the best products of the Griffiths school, and the *Morning Light*, with her long, flat floor and wedge bow, being a handsome and burdensome model of the Pook school.

EXTREME CLIPPER "INO."

The smallest of the extreme clippers, and so sharp she could not carry her registered tonnage, she set an all-time record during the Civil War between Boston and Cadiz, making the port-to-port run in thirteen and a half days and the land-to-land run in twelve and a half days. She logged 16 knots for hours at a time. Note the rarely seen moonsail on her mainmast. Photo by Louis S. Martel, courtesy, The Marine Historical Association, Inc.

Gaspar Straits a few days out from Whampoa, leaving only three clippers to complete their passages this year.

By a coincidence all three of these ships, in spite of their youth, were holders of as yet unbeaten world's records. Those of the *Oriental* are well known. Dumaresq, in the *Surprise*, had the latest position of honor in the California run with his passage of 96 days and 15 hours before noted, while old Captain Lockwood in the *White Squall* had just lowered to 39 days the time from 50 South Pacific to the Golden Gate. His time of 38 days and 22 hours from San Francisco to Hong Kong, moreover, was good enough to receive special mention.

The *White Squall* was the largest ship that had yet appeared on the China coast, and her arrival excited considerable interest among the British merchants there, as will be seen from the following item which appeared in the Hong Kong *Register:*

"The new American clipper ship *White Squall*, Captain Lockwood, anchored in our harbour on Saturday evening, after a passage of 39 days from San Francisco. We believe she is the longest and the sharpest ship of the new class that has yet been launched. She is a beautiful specimen of naval architecture. The extreme symmetry of her masts & spars conceals the appearance of her great length. The round stern, while it doubtless adds to her strength and durability, to our eye, rather detracts from her appearance. Her speed is most extraordinary—15 knots being registered in the log.

"The *White Squall* is about 200 ft. long, but ship owners seem to have a most insuperable objection to giving length to their ship, without which it is useless to look for speed. We understand that ships are building in New York for the California and China trade, 230 and 240 feet long. We confess we cannot look upon such ships as the *White Squall* without a feeling of apprehension for our carrying trade. We have had a deal of writing lately about the relative speed of the new class of ships built in England and America, and fortunately the tests of their speed and capacity as evidenced in late passages from China to England do not lead us to doubt of the ability of our ship builders to hold their own with

Brother Jonathan. But if they mean to do so, after seeing the *White Squall,* we tell them they had better be about it, and that speedily.

"The Seamen on board the Vessel speak in the highest terms of their Commander and his officers; and we learn that yesterday evening, to show their admiration of Captain Lockwood, and in honour of this being his thirtieth voyage to these Seas, they gave a handsome ball on board the Vessel."

It is with a feeling of regret that we record the fact that sturdy and beloved old Captain Lockwood sailed away from Hong Kong to his last port. The old timbers that seemed so sound were weakened by the strain of hard usage, and a few weeks after the events above described his men carried him out to the little English cemetery in Bombay and left him there.

All the China clippers sailed during the unfavorable season for fast runs. The *Surprise* left the 28th of July from Macao and arrived at London on the 12th of November in the fair time, everything considered, of 106 days and 12 hours.

The *Oriental* sailed from the more distant port of Woosung on the 15th of July and entered in at London on the 20th of November, a passage of 128 days.

Captain Goodwin, who had succeeded to the command of the *White Squall,* appears to have made the best passage of the year to England, irrespective of season. He left Whampoa on the 8th of September, ran into a wicked typhoon almost immediately and had a long passage down the coast. He was at anchor off Anjier for two days and lost a topmast off Madagascar: nevertheless he arrived in the Downs on the 18th of December after a passage of 101 days elapsed time or 99 sailing days.

The best British time of the year seems to have been that of the *Chrysolite,* which was reported as sailing from Whampoa on the 18th of August and arriving at Liverpool on the 1st of December, which would make her run 105 days if the reported dates are correct.

Among the full built American tea ships perhaps the best work, all things considered, was that of the *Roman*, still under Putnam. She left Woosung on the 23rd of July, exactly thirteen days after the little British clipper *Reindeer* is reported as having left, and arrived at London on December 1st, five days after the arrival of the *Reindeer*. For a ship of her type, her passage of 120 days against the monsoon must be considered good. It will be remembered that Woosung is nearly 850 miles farther up the coast than Canton. In the favorable monsoon this usually involves only four or five days' sailing at the most, but with the monsoon ahead it may extend the passage for weeks. In the latter part of 1851 the *N. B. Palmer* is said to have run from Woosung to Hong Kong in seventy hours.

The *Chrysolite* was a new ship of 471 tons. She was built by Hall, in Aberdeen, and was intended to meet some of the new competition initiated by the *Oriental* and other American ships. She was slightly smaller than the *Stornoway,* launched from the same yard the year before, but was a very smart ship.

On her maiden voyage in 1851, she ran from Liverpool to Anjier in 80 days. This was good sailing, but it was not a record. In fact, it had been beaten several times by British ships by a considerable margin, and could not be considered a national, let alone an international, record. However, her backers assumed it was, and that was sufficient to start a controversy that occupied the newspapers for several months, until the facts finally found a proper lodging place. After an interment of more than half a century, the corpse has been recently dug up and paraded as the first noteworthy victory of the British over the American clippers.

When the news of the *Chrysolite's* arrival in China filtered back in the Fall of 1851, the British papers published articles, of which the following seems to be typical:

"THE QUICKEST VOYAGE TO CHINA.—Our Aberdeen correspondent says: The *Chrysolite*, a clipper ship, built at Aberdeen, by Messrs. Hall, for the Liverpool and China trade, has just made the voyage from Liverpool to Anjier in 80 days. This is the quickest voyage on record. The *Oriental* made the same passage out in 89 days, and that was without precedent; but for the present the *Chrysolite* has the palm. This ship, we understand, was built expressly to contest the voyage with the *Oriental*, and no expense was spared to make her worthy of the British name. She is, we believe, of 500 tons, per register, but carries nearly 900 tons of tea, and this is the desideratum which this new build has realized, and which promises soon to be generally adopted."

These statements brought forth a series of replies in the American press, the burden of which was that the shorter of two long voyages did not establish a new record. On her previous voyage, the *Oriental* had run from New York to Anjier in 71 days. The voyage from New York to China, it may be said, has always been considered several days longer, under ordinary conditions, than that from England, owing to the fact that English craft usually meet with more favorable winds running down to the Line, while American ships are compelled to make a point near the Cape Verde Islands before meeting the northeast trades. Previous to 1851 a dozen American ships had sailed from New York to Anjier in passages averaging less than seventy-five and one-half days.

It could not, therefore, be seriously considered that the *Chrysolite* had broken any records, her time being longer, even, than former British voyages, although her passage was good and she eventually did better. For many long years neither the *Chrysolite* nor any other foreign built clipper permanently lowered an American record over any course which the ships of the two nations travelled in common. This is merely restating an historical fact which no amount of present day debate over particular voyages in a given year can wholly obscure, and which, it may be said, to the credit of British sportsmanship, was freely and generously admitted by those most vitally interested at the time.

As we have seen, it took half a century of hard driving service in packet ships and China traffic when the ships of other nations neither required or desired speed, to teach Americans how to build and sail ships "clipper fashion." It would be manifestly absurd to expect any people, however skillful or adapted to the work, to master it in two or three years. A stern chase is a long chase.

Aside from the Cape Horn run and the British tea trade, 1851 witnessed many excellent passages.

One of the most notable was that of the *John Bertram,* which left San Francisco on the 5th of July, and arrived at Rio Janeiro the 2nd day of September, in the record run of 58 days. All through her career she proved to be a very fast vessel. Built at East Boston in the remarkably short space of sixty-one days, she was, nevertheless, so well designed and constructed that she survived over thirty years of hard driving, and when she finally foundered at sea in 1883, she had to her credit a considerable number of passages and runs which were close to record marks.

No passage appears to have been made from San Francisco to China this year which equalled the thirty-five days' record of the *Memnon* made late in 1850. On the other hand, the little schooner *Sierra Nevada,* of Sag Harbor, commanded by Captain L. B. Edwards, crossed from Shanghai to San Francisco in the then record time of 34 days. She arrived in port on the 25th day of January, 1851.

In her hold was a chest of choice tea, a present for President Fillmore, which was trans-shipped by way of the Isthmus and arrived at New York exactly sixty-nine days from Shanghai.

"The Railroad Route" to Europe was marked this year by the fine passage of the packet ship *Danube,* Captain Chase, which arrived in New York on the 24th of April in the very short run of sixteen days from Havre. A few days before, the *Gallia* had arrived, in command of Captain Richardson, from Havre, and fifteen days from off the Lizard. She ran from the Lizard to the Grand Banks in six days.

All runs to the eastward across the Atlantic were eclipsed this year by the passage of the *Typhoon,* in command of Captain Charles H. Salter, of Portsmouth. She left Portsmouth on the 12th of March, and arrived at Liverpool in a passage reported to be 13 days 12 hours. She is sometimes said to have been the first American clipper to enter that port, but such statements overlook the arrival of the *Memnon* at Liverpool in 1848. Captain Salter said he was off Holy Head in less than 13 days, but was detained ten hours by fog. He recorded a speed of fifteen and one-half knots and a day's run of 346 miles.

The *Typhoon* was launched at Portsmouth by Fernald & Pettigrew on the 18th of February, 1851. The owners were D. & A. Kingsland, of New York. She was an extreme clipper of 1611 tons, with a dead-rise of 30 inches. Her record is one of consistently fast passages.

No new records were made this year from China to America. In fact it may be said that the Canton records terminated for all time with the 75 day passage of the *Sea Witch.*

The best run from Canton appears to have been made by the *Samuel Russell.* Captain Low arrived at New York on the 27th of January in 88 days, and reported the very fine run of 17 days from the Line. The *Samuel Russell* and the *Candace* performed the unusual feat of appearing twice this year at New York with Canton teas, the *Russell* arriving home the second time on October 20th in a fine out of season passage of 102 days, after an absence of 7 months and 7 days.

The little barque *Candace,* under Captain Arquit, completed an equally fine achievement. She arrived at New York from Shanghai on December 29th after an absence of nine months and five days. In a period of nineteen months and seventeen days she had delivered three full cargoes of teas at New York from the far north port of Shanghai, besides making several intermediate voyages on the China coast. None of her passages were remarkably fast, but all were consistently good.

As one of the New York papers remarked:

"The same can be done by any of the famous clipper fleet, no doubt, but until it is, Captain Arquit deserves praise for accomplishing more than any other vessel yet has done."

It is a pleasure to note that Captain Arquit later commanded the beautiful clipper *Comet*, a ship more than three times the size of the *Candace*, and one of the finest sailing ships ever built.

McKenzie, in the *Houqua*, made the best passage of the year home from Shanghai, entering New York harbor on the 20th of January, 1851, 88 days out. But for the fact that he was detained four days north of Hatteras by northwest gales, he would have made an even better showing. As it was, the run was an excellent one. The *Oneida*, Captain Creesy, which left Shanghai five days after, took 106 days to cover the route. It will be remembered that the *Oneida*, while not a clipper, was noted for her consistently good China passages.

Another of the shorter runs was that made by the *Ariel*, under Captain Brewster. She arrived at New York from Canton early in the year, on February 17th, in 90 days. A feature of her voyage was her run from the Cape of Good Hope in 39 days, and the very fine time of 17½ days from the Line.

In the field of steam, the big Collins liners were scoring new honors. The *Pacific*, under Captain Ezra Nye, of *Independence* fame, has the distinction of being the first vessel of any description to cross the Atlantic in less than ten days. Her achievements in this direction gave rise to an early example of the "Englishman jokes."

"A Yankee merchant told an Englishman that Captain Nye intended to alter the *Pacific*.
"'Alter her! My word! We thought she had been altered already.'
"'Oh, yes, but Capt. Nye intends to make a day boat of her.'"

CHAPTER XXI

1851

AUSTRALIAN GOLD

EPTEMBER MORN! The first September morn, in fact, of 1850. Beautiful Jenny Lind steps ashore from the great Collins liner *Atlantic*, surrounded by a cheering throng and P. T. Barnum. She was a success before she opened her mouth. After her first song in Castle Garden, she was a riot. Two things that year in America turned the heads of young reporters and elderly gentlemen alike—the new clippers and Jenny Lind. "The Swedish Nightingale!" "The Golden Voice!" "The Soul of Song!"

Down in Portsmouth, N. H., Sam Hanscom laid a new keel and on the 16th of June, 1851, the *Nightingale* was launched—one of the loveliest of all the clippers, and finished like a yacht. Even today the name brings a mist before aged eyes which saw the ship and the singer in all their youthful glory.

Trickling through, in the early fall of "Fifty-one," by the Isthmus, from England, and on whalers ramping home from the South Seas deep with "grease," came strange whisperings from Australia. In a few weeks the whispers became a shout. Gold again!

Red shirted miners from the "played out" diggings of the Sacramento began to crowd the ships leaving San Francisco for

Sydney and Melbourne. Pay dirt was harder to find along the creek bottoms of California. Astute eastern merchants rubbed their hands and ordered another clipper.

The first flyer to get away for Australia was the *Nightingale,* under the command of Captain John Fiske. She left Boston on the 18th of October. The voyage gave little promise of the great turn of speed which she developed on later passages. She was 90 days to Melbourne, and from there she went to Shanghai, making an exceptionally long run against the monsoon in 1852, from Woosung to London, where Captain Fiske resigned his command in disgust. In justice to both the *Nightingale* and her captain it should be said that the best route to Australia was not so well known in 1851, as it was later, when the labors of Maury and others began to bear fruit. Even the following year the English papers hailed the passage of the Quebec clipper ship *Gipsey Queen* from London to Sydney in 102 days as one of the shortest runs known. On this occasion the *Gipsey Queen* was stated to have beaten the Scotch clipper *Phœnician* by a margin of five days.

With the sailing of the *Nightingale,* the rush to the new gold fields was on, a rush which was to develop, among others, the firm of R. W. Cameron & Company, the only one of all the great clipper ship houses now left in America. Many, alas! were to fall by the wayside during the dark days of "57." The Civil War and '73 took their toll, although many of the houses, of course, retired voluntarily from the field, as the old men grew weary and the young heeded the call of the new west.

But in the closing days of 1851, the sun had never shone more brightly on America.

Forty fine clipper ships, and four smart clipper barques, besides countless fine, large ships and steamers, had been built and launched during the year, and the yards from Baltimore to Eastport were full of new keels, longer and heavier than ever before, their keyed, white oak scarpings models for the cabinet maker of any age.

Nineteen American ships and barques had loaded in China

with tea for the British Isles. Perhaps double that number had loaded in India, Manilla and other Far Eastern ports for the same destination. It was a most profitable business—all velvet—after the rich California run. Best of all, there was every indication that the future would be even better.

The stage was set for the "Golden Year" of the clippers— the year that was to see the launching of some of the most beautiful ships that ever skimmed the waves—the year when freights were still at their peak, and more plentiful than the ships—when the merchants were without a care, except to find a means to reap the profits that lay ready for the taking, and even humble "Jack" found flattering friends on every street corner.

1853 was to see more clippers launched than '52, and witness a greater number of fast passages. Freights were still to be high, and the volume of business larger. But with the passing of '52, there passed also something of the careless, confident optimism that had characterized the two previous years. An intangible something was creeping into the business atmosphere—a something that was to take form as fifty-three wore on and crystallize into the genuine depression of 1854.

But in '52 the rush was on, merrily and madly as ever. In '53 ships were lying in port a little longer. Freights showed a sagging tendency. Numbers of fine large clippers took their turn at the despised guano business. There were whisperings that the clipper ships had been overdone.

All this, however, was beneath the surface. Outwardly, in numbers, size and achievement, 1853 was the grand climacteric of the clipper ships. But—1852 was the golden year, and its like never came again.

Beautiful beyond compare were the ships of '51, ranging from the exquisite loveliness of the *Witch of the Wave* and *Nightingale,* to the queenly grace of the *Challenge* and stately ruggedness of the *Flying Cloud*.

None were alike. Each made its separate appeal to the eye

and mind, yet, whatever characteristic might predominate, all were beautiful.

Properly understood, each in her respective sphere was final. Whatever might be added in years to come of size or swiftness, power or finish or convenience, the pioneer work was ended. Thenceforth, there could be only refinement or a more efficient combination of lines and principles already embodied in living ships. The data had been gathered; the analyses were complete; the principles established. The rest was synthesis, which is, perhaps, to original work what the fitting of puzzle pictures is to art. Fine, useful—on occasion, even noble work, but calling for a keen sense of discrimination rather than a highly developed inventive faculty. The one impossible except to altruistic natures—the other impossible where the altruistic sense predominates. One forward looking, the other exploitive.

As the new conceptions took form and shape in 1851, they excited a remarkable interest on the part of the public, which was reflected in the press. Many of the lengthy descriptions which then appeared have already been reprinted. Many others are worthy of preservation, in part, at least.

"NEW CLIPPER SHIP INO.—This beautiful craft, having been coppered, is now lying at her berth, at the foot of Maiden Lane, loading for San Francisco. Her capacity for stowage is estimated at from 6,800 to 7,000 barrels only; whereas many vessels of the same tonnage (879 tons, Custom House) will carry from 11,000 to 12,000—her stowage capacity being thus much reduced to increase her sailing powers. Under full sail, she will spread no less than 9491 1/3 square yards of canvas. Her model is faultless, strength of hull not having, in any particular, been lost sight of in the determination to make her a fast-going vessel. In both these qualities she will bear a strict comparison with any vessel afloat. We understand she is liberally equipped with spare spars, besides being furnished with an entire duplicate set of sails, and will also carry an extra number of men—thus providing, so far as human foresight can, for any emergency that may occur from accident or bad weather.

"Her dimensions correspond with those of the clipper ship *Celestial*, celebrated for her short passage to California, and as like in dimensions as she is expected to be like in speed, to that favorite vessel.

"Messrs. Perrine, Paterson & Stack, of Williamsburg, have the credit of building the *Ino*, and never have they turned out of their yard a vessel that does them more credit, or of which New York may be more proud. The following are her dimensions: Length on deck, 160 feet; breadth of beam, 38 feet; depth of hold, 19 feet. She is owned by Messrs. Siffkin & Ironsides, and commanded by Capt. Robert E. Little."

From the foregoing it will be seen that the *Ino* could carry little more than 700 tons dead weight, less than 80 per cent of her registered tonnage.

On Thursday, the 30th of January, James Gordon Bennett walked down by the waterside. While the entertainment afforded in the cabins of a clipper ship did not then possess the unique value that it would today, Bennett seems to have combined business with pleasure in a satisfactory manner. He records:

"We yesterday paid a visit to this beautiful craft (the clipper ship *Gazelle*), lying at Peck slip, where she will take freight for California and China. We have seen many of this kind of vessels lately and all of the first class; but we have never met with one that came nearer to our idea of a skimmer of the wave than does the *Gazelle*. She was constructed upon the same principle as the far-famed *Celestial*, and by the same builder (Mr. Wm. H. Webb, of this city), but is much sharper—everything, excepting the due and proper regard for strength, being made secondary to speed.

"Shippers by the *Celestial* were able to make their payments from returns for goods sent out, before their bills became due—such is the extraordinary speed of that vessel; and yet the *Gazelle's* trip to San Francisco is confidently expected by many to exceed that of the *Celestial*.

"The *Gazelle* has a dead rise of forty inches—nearly as much as any ship ever built—with very fine lines below;

which gives her the power of sailing very fast in light winds, at the same time that her great breadth at deep-load line, carried well forward and aft, combined with her deep keel, will enable her to carry a very great press of canvas in strong winds, at the same time keeping her well above water, and preventing her pitching deep in heavy weather, and enabling her to scud at all times.

"She has a very small and short cutwater, or head, totally different from the old style—which, on account of the great length, was very objectionable—and has but little ornamental carving. The cutwater is fitted or framed in the ship in so strong a manner that it will require an extraordinarily heavy sea to displace any portion of it. Her stern is very small, but carried high up out of water, and ornamented with a carved representation of a gazelle. She has but few mouldings outside, and her round, swelling sides, small and beautifully turned cutwater, and light, airy stern—the outline of which is perfection itself—gives her hull a most neat and graceful appearance."

The following description of the *N. B. Palmer* not only conveys an excellent idea of the ship herself, but throws light on the various questions of naval design which had agitated maritime circles since navigation began. It will be noted that the dimensions given differ somewhat from those reported elsewhere. This is by no means an uncommon occurrence, and accounts not only for variations in tonnage, but for many discrepancies in dates and other particulars.

"Our dimensions of this vessel, the other day, were somewhat erroneous. The following are her correct ones for Custom House tonnage: Length, 202½ feet; beam, 39.4; 1457 39/95 tons, and depth of hold, 22 feet. As we have already stated, this vessel will be commanded by Capt. Palmer, too well known to require any comment, and will sail soon for California and China.

"The proportions of the *N. B. Palmer* are not, perhaps, the most pleasing to the eye of a landsman, but will be admired by those versed in the art of marine construction, more

especially by those experienced old salts, who well understand
the necessity, in heavy weather, of a ship having not only
buoyancy to her mid-ship-body, but are also aware of the
fatal fallacy of having little or no buoyancy in the after body.
We have examined several vessels in this port lately, which
although extolled as pattern ships, may—like those of the
British navy, built by Sir Wm. Symonds, late surveyor of the
R. N.—disappoint their most sanguine admirers.

"The Baltimoreans, who have had the most experience in
clipper vessels, have found it necessary to give them invariably round load lines aft, and without these proportions they
are considered unsafe sea boats. Every person having sailed
in vessels with very hollow load lines aft, and flat counters,
must be aware of the many inconveniences and dangers they
are subjected to. Several of those we speak of are more faulty
in this respect than any that have come under our notice.

"Many persons appear very much pleased with the old-
fashioned overhanging English clipper, or snipe bow. Of all
bows this is the most objectionable; its great, useless, overhanging weight, having a tendency to weaken the ship, and
there is danger in heavy weather of spooning up an extra
quantity of sea water, and flooding the decks.

"The materials of which the *N. B. Palmer* is built are
white oak, live oak, locust and cedar (and not all white oak).
The treenailings of the plank on the bottom are through the
timbers and ceiling, and wedged inside and outside—(and not
driven blunt into the timbers). Inside she is square bolted
and fastened throughout, or two bolts in each timber in every
plank; her 'tween-decks ceiling is bolted with $\frac{7}{8}$-inch iron
driven in flush with the wood; and not, as formerly, blunt-
bolted with $\frac{3}{4}$-inch bolts, having little rings on them, giving
the appearance of being driven through from the outside and
clinched. Her lodging knees are of white oak, and overlap
each other—not short hacmatack knees, with a bosom piece
to scarf the butts. Her hanging knees are large white oak,
with long arms and long bodies—not hacmatack with short
arms and bodies.

"Her arrangements and solidity about decks are equal,
and will compare with the rest. Her lower masts are all
made masts, and well iron hooped, avoiding the difficulty of

procuring single sticks without sap about the head and hounds. All the masts and yards are well proportioned with good doublings, or long mast heads, insuring them more security. In fact, she must be acknowledged, up to the present, one of the most perfect specimens of naval architecture seen in this port.

"Mr. Westervelt, our old veteran builder, commenced his career when a boy, before the mast, and has had some experience at sea since. This circumstance, no doubt, greatly aids him in judging the requisites for a good sea boat."

Many of the *Boston* and other eastern built ships launched this year have been elsewhere described. Of the others, one of the handsomest was the extreme clipper *Telegraph.* Like the *Surprise* and *Game Cock,* she is said to have been designed by Pook. The Boston *Atlas* of May 25th contains a description of her, in part as follows:

"The design of this beautiful vessel may be said to embrace the most advantageous points contained in the ships *Surprise* and *Game Cock.* Her ends are sharper than those of the *Surprise,* and she has about the same fore rake or inclination of the stem, but more buoyancy of floor. Her dead rise is 27 inches, and her floor, owing to the uprightness of her stem, for she has only 5 feet fore rake, is carried well forward and aft, and is, therefore, available for speed and buoyancy almost the whole length of her keel.

"She has 24 inches sheer, and broadside on has somewhat the appearance of our fast vessels of war, but aft the outline of her stern is lighter, and is fashioned to carry along the line of the monkey rail, and below, to form a complete arch like the stern of the *Game Cock.* Her sides swell about four inches, but their fore and aft sweep is bold and easy. She has rounded lines and ends of great beauty."

Several so-called clipper packet ships had been constructed from time to time, but the first genuine clipper for the Liverpool trade was the *Racer,* built by Currier & Townsend, at Newburyport. She measured 1669 tons, and, at the time of her launching,

February 8th, 1851, was the largest ship that had been built on the Merrimac. A New York paper gives the following description:

"THE NEW CLIPPER SHIP RACER:—This vessel arrived at our port on Saturday last, from Newburyport, where she was built by Messrs. Currier & Townsend, under the superintendence of Capt. W. H. Steele, who commands her. She is owned by David Ogden and others of this city, and is intended for the St. George line of New York and Liverpool packets, being the first clipper ship ever built for that trade. The *Racer* was designed to combine the advantages of a strongly built freight ship, with that of a swift-going clipper, and, as far as can be judged from appearance, as she lies at the dock, she certainly posseses these qualities in an eminent degree.

"The dimensions of this vessel are: 200 feet long on the keel; 207 feet on deck; 42 feet 6 inches extreme breadth of beam; 28 feet depth of hold; 7 feet between decks; and she registers about 1650 tons. She is 26 inches through the side, and the same at light load line, and is a long looking craft, and pretty sharp, but at the same time showing great capacity for stowage. She has a dead rise of 10 inches, and has three decks, and her estimated load line is 20 feet draught.

"On deck, between the fore and main mast, is a large house, 47 feet long by 18 wide, containing apartments for cooking ranges for crew and passengers, hospital, etc. Forward, between decks, are the accommodations for the crew, fitted up with berths for forty-five men, and well lighted and ventilated.

"The cabins and staterooms are fitted up in a very handsome style, and furnished with all the modern improvements and conveniences for the comfort of her passengers. The decorations of the first cabin are very superb. The panellings, frame work, and a portion of the pilasters are of fine mahogany; the remainder of the pilasters and a part of the cornice are rosewood, richly ornamented to imitate inlaid gold. The two ends of the cabin have mahogany panels, and each is decorated with a superb English engraving; one representing a "Steeple Chase," and the other the "Start for the Derby."

The ceiling is pure white with handsome mouldings and beads, richly gilt. On each side of the cabin are three staterooms fitted up to correspond.

"The second cabin, which extends to the main mast, is handsomely grained to represent oak, and is well lighted and ventilated, as also are the state-rooms in both.

"Above the load line, the *Racer* is painted black, and her exterior appearance is clipper like and handsome. Her bow is ornamented with a carved and gilt figure of a race horse, and her name, *Racer*, is on the trail-boards. Her stern is round, and ornamented with a spread eagle, carved and gilt, and the vessel's name and port underneath. Taking this vessel as a whole, she will compare favorably, in strength and finish, with any vessel of her size and class afloat, and we hope, that under the guidance of Capt. Steele, we shall soon have the satisfaction of announcing that 'the shortest trip on record,' between New York and Liverpool, has been accomplished by the good ship *Racer*."

A very fine example of Baltimore shipbuilding, the *Seaman's Bride,* was completed this year. She registered 668 tons, and was 150 feet long between perpendiculars, 31 feet 6 inches beam, and 17 feet 6 inches deep. Her dead rise was 20 inches—three more than that of the *Seaman*. For some unfathomable reason contemporary reports said that her masts were shorter than usual in a ship of her size, but the yards were longer. As we have seen, her sail plan showed that she was one of a very few ships to carry three moon sails above her sky sails. She swung a main yard of 68 feet, and her main topmast was 40 feet long. She spread nearly 7000 yards of canvas. The newspapers of the period said of her:

"She is a very finely modelled craft, with sharp ends. Her stem is ornamented with a gilt eagle with wings thrown back, as though stooping for flight. The effect is improved by its being artistically placed in line with her stem, thereby obviating an ugly angle, that sometimes detracts from similar ornaments. She has a handsome, light, eliptic stern."

CHAPTER XXII

1852

CALIFORNIA RACES

ONE of the first, if not the first clipper ship to sail for California in 1852, was the *Eclipse*, under the able command of Captain Hamilton. There is some doubt as to the exact time of her leaving New York. She dropped down from the city on the 3rd of January, and anchored that night at the Southwest Spit. It is quite possible that she was held there for several days by the storm which delayed other vessels. The *Courser*, under Captain Cole, for instance, left Boston on New Year's day, but was forced back by the gale and did not leave port until some time subsequent to January 7th.

It is unfortunate that the exact dates of the sailing of these two ships are in doubt. But, in view of the weather and certain other circumstantial evidence, it seems probable that both sailed from their respective ports on January 8th, or a day or two later. They were well matched, although the odds were rather in favor of the *Eclipse*. She was the sharper vessel and was 201 tons heavier than the *Courser*, which registered 1024 tons. Both ships proved to be very fast, and subsequently made runs over various courses closely approaching the present records.

First to arrive at San Francisco was the *Eclipse*. Both vessels were forced to put into Valparaiso for repairs. The net sailing time of the *Eclipse* is variously reported—the time ranging from 104 to 109 days. In view of the uncertainty of her actual date of sailing from New York, it seems probable that the time of 104 days, given by Captain Clark, is correct. Captain Hamilton reported 64 days to Valparaiso, and there is no doubt that her passage from Valparaiso to her destination was within the limit of 40 days. Her best day's run was 325 miles. Like many another good ship of the period, she carried away her jib-boom the first night out of New York.

The *Courser* arrived six days later, on April 28th, in a passage reported as 108 sailing days. It was therefore a close race from every point of view, and a promising start for the new year.

In the meantime, the clippers which had sailed late in '51 were reaching port. A noteworthy percentage of smart passages had been made.

First to arrive was the *Comet*, Captain E. C. Gardner, anchoring on January 14th, in a passage stated as 103 days. Exactly two weeks later the *Wild Pigeon*, a vessel similar to but of somewhat fuller lines than the *Witch-of-the-Wave*, under George W. Putnam, let go her anchor after a run claimed in certain accounts to have been made in 102 days. Elsewhere, the passage has been given as 104 and 107 days. It is evident that as between the *Comet* and the *Wild Pigeon*, much depended on the correctness of these conflicting reports. There seems no doubt that the time of 107 days is incorrect, and it probably originated in the fact that the *Wild Pigeon* was first stated to have left New York on the 11th of October, when, as a matter of fact, she sailed on the 14th.

The evidence for the passage in 102 days is stated in the Boston *Atlas* of March 3rd, 1852:

"The new clipper ship *Wild Pigeon*, Capt. Putnam, which sailed from New York, Oct. 14, made the shortest passage to

San Francisco (102 days) of any vessel which sailed in October, having beaten the *Comet, Trade Wind* and *Golden Gate*, all magnificent New York clippers, the least of which is 500 tons larger than her. She sailed in company with the *Golden Gate*, and ten to one were staked in New York in favor of the latter, yet the *Wild Pigeon* never had wind enough during the passage to obtain her highest rate of speed.

"The most she made in twenty-four hours was three hundred miles, close hauled, carrying skysails. She had skysails set seventy-five days, and during twenty consecutive days carried royal staysails and skysails, without lowering one of them. Off Cape Horn she encountered a heavy gale, but carried sail, and she was not hove to during the passage.

"Captain Putnam writes that under every circumstance she proved to be a perfect vessel, so much so that he could not suggest an improvement in her. She was built at Portsmouth, N. H., by Mr. George Raynes, and is owned by Messrs. Oliphant & Son, of New York."

The logbooks, however, are available to settle the matter beyond dispute. This is not a suggestion that interested parties misstated the facts, but a recognition of the possibility that there may have been unintentional errors in computing the passage, or —as more frequently happened—in transcribing the record. There is also the possibility that either master in reporting his time may have stated the hour of arrival off the port, while the other gave his run from anchor to anchor. Occasionally, but not often, time appears to have been deducted for delays caused by calms, fog or other weather conditions. Instances of this sort, of however rare occurrence, may be of crucial importance in closely contested races and in some cases there seems to have been a failure to take such possibilities into account.

Reference to the log of the *Comet*, therefore, proves that she sailed the 2nd of October. At 4 o'clock in the afternoon the Highlands bore West, distant 25 miles. She was 24 days to the Equator and took her pilot outside the Heads on the 13th of January, 103 days from New York, having made 15,083 miles "on strait courses," an unusually short distance, since many ships were forced to cover more than 17,000 miles on the run.

On the other hand, the log of the *Wild Pigeon* shows that she sailed, as stated, in the above news item, and anchored in the harbor of San Francisco on the 28th of January. This would make her elapsed time 106 days, and while she experienced some delay in working into port, the wind being brisk from the Northwest and therefore not quite fair, there appears to be slight reason for calling her passage anything less than this. The greater honor therefore belongs in this instance to the *Comet*.

Meanwhile another race was under way. The 7th of November, 1851, had witnessed the start of what was to prove one of the most notable of all the Cape Horn contests. On that day the *Flying Fish*, McKay's new model, said to be sharper than any ship then afloat, sailed from Boston commanded by E. C. Nickels. At 8 o'clock that evening she was ten miles off the tip of Cape Cod and "going like a steam boat."

Five days later the *Swordfish*, a somewhat fuller clipper, built by Webb and commanded by David S. Babcock, of Stonington, left New York passing Sandy Hook at 3 P.M. It was a race from the start; Nickels against Babcock, Boston against New York and McKay against Webb. The event had been anticipated for weeks and probably no two ships ever left port with masters more thoroughly keyed up to the task in hand, or with a better appreciation of what was expected of them by their respective supporters.

In the light of present day knowledge it would be assumed that the *Flying Fish*, with her 500 tons heavier register than the *Swordfish*, had the odds greatly in her favor, and time allowances would undoubtedly be elaborately figured. The master mariner of '52 would have scorned such aid to his art. He would sail it out ship for ship and man to man or not at all, and generally speaking, the results of clipper ship contests justified the attitude. If greater length and weight counted off the Horn or running the Easting down, the smaller and lighter ship had a certain advantage in the light variable airs prevalent in the middle latitudes.

As it turned out, therefore, victory fell a second time to New York and Webb. The *Swordfish* made the best passage of the year and the fourth best for all time, arriving at San Francisco on February 10th after a passage of 90 days and 18 hours from Sandy Hook. Four days later the *Flying Fish* dropped her anchor on the bar, after a run of 100 days and 6 hours. It was a decisive victory for Babcock, yet it must be said that both ships rank among the fastest of the entire Cape Horn fleet, their average passages indicating that they were exceptionally well designed for the conditions of that run.

Nickels had made the Equator crossing on November 25th, a fine 19 day run, while the *Swordfish* did not reach that point until the 4th of December, the *Flying Fish* having increased her lead another four days. On the slant from the Line down to the Horn, however, the *Swordfish* did excellent work, reducing the nine day lead of her opponent to a scant three days. Up the Pacific they went, the *Swordfish* now gaining every day. At the Pacific crossing the *Swordfish* was two days ahead and moreover had the advantage of being ten degrees farther east. On the last stretch the *Swordfish* continued to increase her lead and on the 10th of February Babcock wrote his final entry: "12 noon passed the Fort—91 day passage."

The foregoing by no means tells the story of the quality of the performance of the *Swordfish*—a performance which she continued to maintain as she sailed for China and home. A brief summary of her work is contained in the following letter published a year or two later:

"MAY 18, 1853.

"*To the Editor of the New York Herald:*
SIR—In the *Morning Herald* of this date, I notice a statement of the comparative passage of clipper ships from New

York to California, in which the *Swordfish* is put down at 93 days.

"The *Swordfish* sailed from New York on the 11th of November, 1851, and arrived at San Francisco on the 10th of February, 1852, making the passage in 90 days, 18 hours. She crossed the Equator in the Pacific inside of 71 days and at the end of 89 days was within 100 miles of San Francisco, or 140 miles less than the *Flying Cloud* on her first passage.

"The time of the *Swordfish*, say 91 days to San Francisco, 46 from thence to China, and 89 from China home (against the monsoon), has never been equalled, and if the size of the ships is taken into consideration, her passage to California is far ahead of any other.

"Yours respectfully,

"D. S. BABCOCK."

Following the distinguished lead of the *Swordfish* came a notable procession of as fine a lot of ships as ever had entered the Golden Gate in an equal period. Three days behind the *Flying Fish* came B. G. Palmer, one of Captain Nat's cousins in the *Celestial*, 108 days from New York. The *Thomas Wattson*, under Captain Lyle, arrived the 6th of March in a run of 118 days from Philadelphia. Bailey Loring brought the soon-to-be-famous *Northern Light* up the bay two days later, after a passage of 110 from Boston. On March 26th, Lendholm in the *John Bertram*, also from Boston, completed a 106 day voyage. The big *Invincible*, another Webb clipper, under Captain H. W. Johnson, the story teller of the *Clipper Ship Era*, made the run from New York in 108 sailing days, having been forced into Rio Janeiro by a leaky water tank, entailing a delay of eight days. Two days behind her came the *Hurricane*, commanded by Samuel Very, Jr., in a passage which has been variously reported from 104 to 108 days.

Eleven clippers in all had entered the harbor of San Francisco within a space of four months, in passages of 110 days or less around the Horn—approximately twenty per cent of the entire clipper fleet of America afloat on the high seas. It was a record which had no parallel in sailing ship annals, and bespoke as nothing else could the grim determination and remarkable seamanship of those early clipper ship-masters.

Realism forsooth! The realities of hurricane and broad shouldered calm wrote their tough fibred story on many a rugged face. Common among the expressions of a generation ago were references to "steel trap jaws." It was no mere figure. The clipper captains were as individual as their ships, but in the matter of jaws there was no variation. They were all "steel traps" and when they clamped down on an order with a roar like a bull seal, forty men who feared God not a whit, jumped as though the devil were behind them.

By the time the *Courser* and *Eclipse* arrived in the latter part of April, as before noted, the season was becoming unfavorable for fast passages. An increasing number of vessels reported long detentions off the Horn in the antarctic autumn gales. Some runs were made which seem surprisingly long considering the ships and their officers and leaving weather out of account, but on the whole the balance of the year is marked by a high average of fast passages, showing that in '52 the "driving" tension on the California route was still abnormal, even for clippers.

Among the ships which reported good passages were the *Wisconsin*, 118 days; *Antelope*, 118 days; *Sea Serpent*, 113 days; *Ino*, 116 days; *Stilwell S. Bishop*, of Philadelphia, and later the *Grey Eagle* of Baltimore, 121 days; *Union*, of Baltimore, 120 days; *Messenger*, 124 days; *Grey Hound*, of Baltimore, 125 days; *Witch of the Wave*, 119 days; barque *Greenfield*, 122 days; *Mandarin*, 116 days; *Onward*, 120 days; *Raven*, 121 days; *Samuel Russell*, 119 days, and the *Winged Arrow*, 113 days.

Still better were the passages of the *Sea Witch*, 108 days, and the memorable run of 103 days made by the *Sovereign of the Seas* at the height of the unfavorable season, and which was to be surpassed only once by a ship sailing from the East coast during the month of August.

McKay pushed his ship from the start. The *Sovereign of the Seas* passed Sandy Hook on the 4th of August. On the following day she was met by the Packet *Nicholas Biddle*, Captain Caulkins, "going off under full sail when the *Biddle* was under reefed topsails. Captain Caulkins supposed she was going at the rate of 14 or 15 miles an hour."

This voyage of the *Sovereign of the Seas* ranks among the most notable in sailing ship annals. It would seem that not only is the ship herself entitled to a place among the five or six swiftest clippers ever built, but the seamanship of her commander on that occasion was of a remarkably high order, comparable, perhaps, with that of Cressy on his first record breaking, spar-smashing voyage in the *Flying Cloud*. One needs no further proof to maintain the thesis that many a fast clipper was a failure because of the failure of her commander to attempt the "impossible."

Theoretically, it was impossible in the heavy weather that existed, to save the massive spars when McKay was dismasted in the South Pacific. Such a thing had never been done before, and under anything like similar conditions, it has never been done since. It required herculean efforts merely to prevent the spars from pounding the ship full of holes, let alone getting the ponderous weight of spars and back stays on board again. One can only imperfectly imagine the effect on the record of the ship if McKay had followed the dictates of prudence and cut away the wreckage, worked his way into Valparaiso, and re-rigged there. Under more hopeful conditions, Napoleon turned his horse's tail on the battlefield of Waterloo.

Within 24 hours the fore and main topmasts and mizzen topgallant mast, with all the yards, sails and gear attached, were back on board and the work of re-rigging was under way. It was a task that involved every one engaged in it, in the utmost danger. The main topsail yard alone was a stick that must have weighed considerably more than three tons without the hamper attached to it, and the work of disengaging such a spar from the snarl of rigging in the heavy seaway that prevailed was a thing to tax the courage of the bravest and most active sailors afloat. There was something more than skill or activity or bravery at work on the *Sovereign of the Seas* then—something that for want of a better term, may be called greatness of soul.

One of the best contests of the year was that between the ill-fated *Staffordshire*, a huge McKay ship of slightly more than 1800 tons, and the *Shooting Star* of almost exactly half her tonnage. It was the second voyage around the Horn for both vessels, and both were thoroughly overhauled and re-rigged for the run.

They sailed in company from Boston on the 3rd of April. Late the same afternoon they were seen off Cape Cod, about ten miles apart, with every sail set and going like steam boats before a strong northerly wind. As they started, so they sailed. Neither ship appears to have gained a decisive advantage until they reached the Horn. Here the greater length and weight of the *Staffordshire* told, in the heavy winter gales, and she nosed out into the Pacific, ahead of the little *Shooting Star*. Finding favorable winds, she made the excellent run of 36 days from 50 S. to San Francisco, which seems to have been the record at the time. Once around, Baker sent the *Shooting Star* along at a remarkable pace, but the *Staffordshire* kept her lead and passed the Golden Gate on the 13th of August, 101 days out.

Four days after the arrival of the *Staffordshire*, the *Shooting Star* came in, having made the passage in 105 days. From every angle it was a fine, exciting contest, typical of the time and reflecting as much credit on the loser as on the winner.

As the above ships sailed from Boston, the *Flying Cloud* was loading in New York, also for her second California voyage. Cressy sailed on the 14th of May. Four days later, the *Gazelle*, under Dollard, followed her out by Sandy Hook, and four days after the *Gazelle* came Low, in the *N. B. Palmer*.

Whether Cressy was the victim of over-confidence, after his

remarkable record of the year before, or whether the following ships found better winds, it is a remarkable fact that both the *Gazelle* and the *N. B. Palmer* came up with the *Flying Cloud;* the *Gazelle* shortly after crossing the Line; the *Palmer* off the coast of Montevideo on the 1st of July. As this meeting was the occasion on which the *Flying Cloud* is said to have run the *N. B. Palmer* out of sight in a few hours, the following letter is quoted as, possibly, throwing light on the facts. The letter is dated at New Orleans, June 30th, 1854.

"*To the Editor of the Herald:*

"Reading the Boston *Semi-Weekly Atlas* of the 10th inst., I saw an account of the ship *Flying Cloud's* late passage to San Francisco; and in the remarks it says: 'We have upon a former occasion shown how the *Flying Cloud* once over-hauled the clipper *N. B. Palmer,* run her out of sight in less than twenty hours, and beat her from the latitude of Rio Janeiro to San Francisco, twenty-one days.'

"I was in the ship *Flying Cloud* on that voyage, and the two ships fell in company in the latitude of the Rio de la Plata—the *Palmer* being ahead, having sailed ten days after us in the *Cloud*. The wind was light at daylight, and we had been near Cuba all the night before. During the fore-noon the breeze sprang up from the Northeast, and both ships made sail for a race—the *N. B. Palmer* outsailing the *Flying Cloud* while the wind was exactly aft, and Capt. Low finding his ship outsailing the *Cloud,* hove to to speak. The *Cloud* came up and both masters bid each other success on the passage, and parted for a race just at twelve, noon. The *Palmer* hauled two points to the westward for a side wind; there Capt. Low missed, for that was just what the *Flying Cloud* wished for. During the night the wind freshened, so that by four in the morning the *Cloud* had all studding sails taken in; at eight o'clock (just good daylight) the *Palmer* was astern foot of her, foretopsail in sight, with his foretop-mast studding sail set. It shut in thick with rain before nine o'clock and of course she was lost to sight; and that is how the *Flying Cloud* outsailed her so fairly in less than twenty

hours. The *N. B. Palmer* put into Valparaiso and laid there
ten days. That is the way she was beat twenty-one days.

"The clipper ship *Gazelle* sailed from New York three
days after the *Flying Cloud*, on the same voyage. Came in
sight in our wake before we crossed the line, and I could just
see her from the mizzen topgallant yard at nine o'clock in
the morning, and at six o'clock the same evening could see
her hull from the deck of the *Cloud*; next day still nearer.
Shifted anchors on board the *Cloud*, guns, etc., and altered
our course and got out of sight as soon as possible.

"Let the New York clipper ships have their just due. Although I am a Bostonian and master of a Boston ship, and I
have been in two clippers of the late Jacob Bell's build, besides being in the *Cloud*, I go in for the second side of a story
and fair play.

"(Signed) P. W. G."

The *N. B. Palmer's* log contains the following reference to
the above incident:

"July 2. Lat. 36.01 S. Long 50.50 W. Moderate breeze.
At 2 P.M. spoke the *Flying Cloud* after heaving to for two
hours for her to come up. Stiff breezes and hauling to the
Southward, sent down skysail yards and royal stunsail
booms."

The following week as she drew near the cold latitudes of
the Horn the deck of the *Palmer* was the scene of one of those
unpleasant incidents destined to become increasingly frequent as
ships multiplied and able seamen drifted into more lucrative employment ashore.

"July 9, Lat. 47.59 S. Long. 56.27 W. Wind South and
variable. Close reefed Topsails. Midnight single reefed the
Topsails. At midnight on turning out heard some one say
call the Captain. Give me a pistol and I will shoot him. Met
Mr. Haines, who handed me a musket and told me not to go
on deck, that one of the men had a revolver and had shot

him through the leg. Went on deck the mates were armed with muskets and all hands were sent on the poop, where they were examined one by one and two of them were put in Irons, but soon after the man called Semons came & gave himself up as being the one that fired at the mate. I put him in Irons and let the other go. At 8 A.M., finding that Dublin Jack had knocked the 2nd & 3rd officers down with a hand-spike while engaged in placing Semons in Irons, I had him Ironed and then called all hands and flogged Semons and Dublin Jack, giving Semons a dozen and a half and Dublin Jack Twenty lashes. They were then placed in the Booby Hatch in Irons. Mr. Haines was shot in the leg about six inches above the knee. Light airs. Stiff Gales. Double Reefs."

Captain Low had the reputation, and deservedly so, of being a kindly, well-bred master, but it will be seen from the above that he did not hesitate to use energetic measures in emergency.

On the 9th of December, San Francisco was treated to the unusual sight of three clippers sailing into port one after the other and rounding to their anchors in the brisk fashion of the smartest ships of that or any other day. They were the *Sea Witch*, the *Samuel Russell* and the little *Seaman*, in 108, 119 and 129 days, respectively, from New York. Besides beating her two companions, the *Sea Witch* had administered a trouncing to the fine ships *Golden Fleece* and *R. B. Forbes*, which sailed some days before she did, and which did not arrive until later in the month.

The California clipper trade, relatively speaking, was probably never again so active as in the closing months of '52. Dozens of great clippers, many of which had never been to sea, were loading or fitting out for the Cape Horn run, while more than a score were on their way, outfooting on every day's mileage hundreds of slow, full-bodied ships bound for the same destination. The situation is graphically described in the news of the day:

"Yesterday the beautiful clipper ship *Wild Pigeon*, Captain Putnam, hauled out of her berth, at the foot of Wall

Street, and sailed for California. The bark *Salem,* Captain Millet, also cleared yesterday for the same destination. Both vessels have large and valuable cargoes. The agent of the first named vessel had to refuse some one thousand barrels, for want of room. The *Wild Pigeon* has only been in port twenty-nine days, and in the short space of twenty-eight working days discharged and received cargo, and is now again on her way to the Pacific.

"On the other side of the slip, just evacuated by the *Wild Pigeon,* lies the Boston clipper ship *Flying Fish,* Captain Nickels, also taking cargo for San Francisco. She arrived here some three weeks back, from Manila, and it is her first appearance in this port. She is of a similar model to the celebrated clipper ship *Flying Cloud,* and both constructed by the same builder (Mr. Donald McKay, of East Boston) but has sharper ends, and is stated to be the sharpest vessel he ever launched. Like all clipper ships, she is filling fast, and will leave on or about the 23rd inst.

"Independent of the above, there are seventeen other vessels up for the same port. Among these are the following beautiful new clippers yet untried: *The Flying Dutchman, Contest, John Gilpin* and *Tinqua.* The first two were built in this city—the *Flying Dutchman* by Mr. W. H. Webb, the other by Messrs. Westervelt & Sons; the *John Gilpin,* by Mr. Samuel Hall, of East Boston. The *Tinqua* was constructed by Mr. George Raynes, of Portsmouth, N. H. She has not yet arrived here, but will make her appearance shortly, to commence loading in Mr. John Ogden's line of clippers, to which the *Wild Pigeon* and *Flying Fish* also belong.

"The other clippers also loading here for San Francisco are the *Game Cock, Grey Feather* and *Trade Wind,* all first class vessels. The freighting business for California is at present very active, several of the new clippers having had a portion of their cargo engaged before they appeared at their berths.

"The clearances at this port for San Francisco, during the month of October, give one for every alternate day; and from the first of last month up to the present date, the number amounts to twenty, including the clipper *Comet,* and other first class ships. The whole number from all our Atlantic ports during that period is thirty-six; which shows the great preponderating commercial enterprise of New York, over all the other commercial cities of the Union combined." (N. Y. *Herald*, October 12, 1852.)

In all, ninety-five clipper ships and ten clipper barques had sailed from eastern parts for San Francisco during 1852. Seventeen of these made the passage in 110 days or less.

Many a beautiful, untried racer was to sail in the last days of '52 for the broad Pacific: the *Golden Eagle, Fleetwood, Jacob Bell, Winged Racer, Flying Childers, Golden West, Red Rover, Peerless, Bald Eagle*—names even now to conjure with, where elderly shipping men are gathered. And always in their wake the endless stream of new clippers: the *Rattler, Phantom, Flying Eagle, Golden State, Highflyer, Mystery, Radiant* and *Empress of the Seas*, each with her individual stamp of loveliness.

CHAPTER XXIII

1852

NEW CHINA RECORDS

S the thoroughbreds of '52 drove in through the
Golden Gate, there was a mad scramble to discharge and get away on the long westward sail
to the tea ports. A few clippers—their numbers
were to increase as the year wore on—started back around the
Horn, with the intention of stopping at the Chinchas for a load
of guano. The first straw indicating the beginning of the slow
decline from their royal state. But for the most part they were
bound for China and the aristocratic shores of the Indies.

First to sail with British teas in 1852 was the *Witch of the
Wave*. She had run over from California in the Fall of '51 and
left Whampoa on the 5th of January, at the height of the monsoon. Seven days later she was up with Anjier, and on the thirty-
seventh was off the Cape of Good Hope, her run to that point
being within a few hours of the record. She was in the chops of
the channel 86 days out, and from there had to beat up against
a strong head wind, passing some 400 sail on the way. At Dunge-
ness she took her pilot, 90 days from Whampoa, the record to
that date by several days. She brought 19,000 chests of tea.

The American clipper barque *Behring*, Captain Thompson,
which had sailed from Whampoa more than three weeks before

OLD SHIP'S FIGURE HEAD NOW STANDING OVER THE ENTRANCE TO THE
SAILOR'S HAVEN, CHARLESTOWN, MASS.

Representing Capt. Samuel Scholfield, a well known seaman and ship builder of Brunswick, Me., in
clipper days. Said to have been an excellent likeness and a fine example of the wood carver's art.
From a photograph furnished through the kindness of Mr. E. W. Longfellow of Boston and Lieutenant Lord, U. S. N., in charge of the restoration of the *Constitution*.

"TWILIGHT."

PAINTED IN CHINA.

Reproduced by courtesy of Mrs. N. Stanton Gates.

Charles Robert Patterson

The Clipper Ship "Great Republic" Becalmed.
Painting by Charles R. Patterson.

Shows this great vessel as she appeared after being re-rigged following the disastrous fire at New York, December 26th, 1853. Courtesy of Columbia Rope Co.

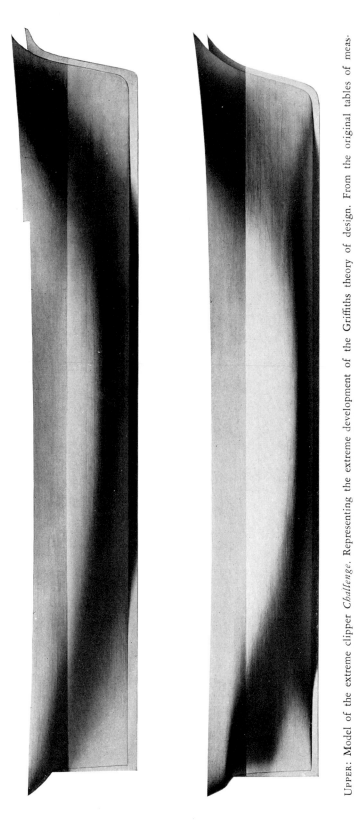

UPPER: Model of the extreme clipper *Challenge*. Representing the extreme development of the Griffiths theory of design. From the original tables of measurement in the possession of the Webb School of Naval Architecture, New York City.

LOWER: Original builder's model of the *Sovereign of the Seas*. Courtesy of the Mariners House, Boston. Very sharp, with long, flat floor. One of the fastest of the clippers. This model is not an accurate representation of the ship as built, owing to the fact that after the model was made the vessel was lengthened by the insertion of a number of frames amidships, making a relatively longer craft without, however, changing the other dimensions or the general appearance.

the *Witch of the Wave*, entered in at London only one day before the latter hove to off the pilot grounds.

It may be noted that the *Witch of the Wave* met with unfavorable winds after passing the Cape of Good Hope, causing her to make an unusually long run up the South Atlantic. Otherwise she would have arrived several days earlier. As it was, it proved to be many a long year before her passage was again equalled.

The next clipper was the *Telegraph*, Captain Harlow. She left Whampoa on the 24th of March and made the long run of 118 days to London. Following her, the *Celestial* made the out-of-season run of 137 days from Shanghai to Liverpool, arriving off the port on the 22nd of September. (N. Y. *Herald*, October 6, 1852.) Her time of 96 days, according to several reports, does not appear to be correct. Webb's fine new model, the huge *Invincible*, under Captain Johnson, made another out of season passage of 105 days from Whampoa to the Downs. She entered in at London on the 5th of January, 1853, having been delayed several days in the river, owing to her draft of water. Her best day's run on the voyage was 336 miles with three topsails set. It was reported at the time that she made the Downs in 40 days from the Cape of Good Hope, which is extraordinary sailing. Ranlett took the *Surprise* to London, entering in at that port on the 3rd of November, after a passage of 107 days. All three runs, of course, were made in the less favorable season.

Mild looking old Captain Land, with his deceptive white hair, had taken the *Challenge* after Waterman left her at San Francisco, and in her had renewed youth. Going over to Shanghai, he picked up a cargo of coolies, and ran back to California in 34 days. His time of 18 days from a point opposite the coast of Japan has never been beaten, although the run of the *Golden West* from Japan to San Francisco in 20 days during the summer of '56, is perhaps the record for the direct passage.

Returning, Land was eight days to Honolulu, and fifteen days later he was within 400 miles of Hong Kong, a run which has never been approached in those latitudes. But Land had made his last port. No man ever drove a ship more swiftly toward his waiting bride than Land drove his toward the grim figure waiting at the Hong Kong anchorage. There he died and Mr. Pitt, first mate of the *Witchcraft*, took command and the *Challenge* was put up for London. Land evidently knew how to get the best out of the *Challenge*, and it would have been interesting to see what he could have done with her on the London run.

Pitt, however, was a very able seaman, and as it was the *Challenge* eclipsed the time of every ship leaving Canton during the summer of 1852. She left Whampoa on the 5th of August and made the long run of 38 days to Anjier. Here Land's long experience in the China Sea would have been invaluable and might have resulted in a much faster passage. Leaving Anjier, she was only 65 days to Deal, arriving there the 18th of November, 105 days from Whampoa. She entered in at London on the 22nd of November, being detained at Gravesend three days because her great draft would not permit her to enter the docks earlier. While she was at Gravesend, the British clipper *Challenger* arrived and entered in at London on the 19th.

The *Challenger* had sailed from Shanghai on the 27th of July, nine days before the *Challenge* left Whampoa, and was reported as passing Anjier on the 4th of September, nine days before the *Challenge* arrived. A fictitious account of the "race" of these two vessels has recently been published, wherein it is made to appear that they left Anjier in company and the *Challenger* beat the *Challenge* two days on the passage. (See Basil Lubbock: "The China Clippers, p. 76.)

In this connection, it is worthy of notice that the *Nightingale* left Shanghai four days after the *Challenger* and arrived at Deal on November 18th, the day before the *Challenger* entered in at London. It is idle to assert that British built ships in 1852, or indeed for years later, were a match for the better type of American clippers, even though those ships were designed primarily for the very different conditions of the California trade. There were three or four smart British ships and they appear to have been very ably commanded. Men like Enright probably had no betters and few equals in the China trade, but the overwhelming superiority of the best American clipper passages compared with a similar number of the best British clipper runs during the fifties furnishes a criterion that cannot be gainsaid. Nor did the British merchant of the day fail to recognize and admit the fact. Nothing else will explain America's capturing and holding the cream of the China trade for a full decade. Other things being equal or even approximately so, British tea would have been carried in British ships.

Twenty-two American ships loaded tea for England this year, of which ten were clipper ships and three were clipper barques. More American ships, in fact, sailed for England from China than for the United States.

The challenge which the American Navigation Club, of Boston, had issued in the summer, through its president, Daniel C. Bacon, "to the shipbuilders of Great Britain," for a ship race to China and back, with cargo on board, for stakes of £10,000 a side, was ignored.

Among the many smart passages completed this year that of the *Game Cock,* Captain Hollis, presents some interesting features. The *Game Cock* arrived at Bombay on the 17th of January from San Francisco, November first. She had 16 days to Honolulu, which was only fair, but from there she ran to Hong Kong in the very exceptional time of 19 days, averaging 261 miles a day on this part of her voyage. From Hong Kong she went to Bombay in 33 days.

Another excellent passage was that made by the *R. B. Forbes,* under Captain Doane, of 21 days, 13 hours, corrected time, from Honolulu to Hong Kong. She left Honolulu on January 30th, at 3 P.M., and entered the harbor of Hong Kong at 10 A.M., February 20th. Her distance was 4500 miles, and she had therefore maintained an average speed of 10 44/100 miles an hour during the entire run, very fine work, and only a fraction of a mile under the *Game Cock's* record, a few weeks previous.

1852 was further marked by the claim for the first time in history, that the distance of 400 miles had been made in 24 hours by a sailing ship (N. Y. *Herald*, May 18, 1852). This was reported as the achievement of the new clipper *Hurricane* under Samuel Very, Jr., father of Admiral Very, U.S.N., which left New York on the 17th of December, 1851. In common with the majority of the extreme clippers this year the *Hurricane* was partly dismasted early on her voyage and put in to Rio Janeiro. Leaving there on the 8th of February, she was only 67 days to San Francisco. The run has been reported as 61 days, but her log gives the longer time. Unfortunately for the above claim, the same log seems to furnish conclusive evidence that the 400 mile run was not made. It does not appear, however, that the claim originally emanated from Captain Very, but, on the contrary, it seems to have been put in motion by one of the mates.

Few vessels were as lofty as the *Hurricane*. On her main she sported a moon sail, a feature which was shared only by the *Phoenix* and one or two other clippers at this period. All her officers appear to have agreed that she was "a noble sea boat and a very dry vessel."

Not long after the arrival of the *Hurricane* in San Francisco on this voyage, the *Defiance*, Captain Robert McCerren, arrived at New York fresh from Deacon Thomas' yard in Rockland. She had made the unprecedented speed of 20 nautical miles an hour on the run. It must be considered that she was in ballast at the time, a circumstance which undoubtedly affected her performance.

Nevertheless, the fact made a deep impression on the naval architects who had theretofore been unyielding advocates of the sharp wedge-shaped bottom. It was evident that the *Defiance* with her flat floor—she had but 10 inches dead rise—had travelled at a rate none of the other type had yet been able to attain.

Thereafter few American ships were laid down which did not accept this feature—a feature which, it will be remembered, was efficiently used by Palmer in the Dramatic packets years before.

An inspection of the models of the *Sovereign of the Seas* and all the later McKay clippers, as well as those of the great majority of American clippers wherever built, indicates the virtually complete elimination thereafter of the sharp bottom—the last important characteristic of the old frigate theory to be abandoned.

One of the most remarkable experiences of the year was that of the *Tornado,* under Mumford. In the early morning, August 7th, she got her anchor and commenced beating out of San Francisco harbor, dropping her pilot at one o'clock in the afternoon. Seventeen days later she crossed the line, and on August 31st her log records:

"Ship has sailed by log since the 7th inst. 4301 miles by obs 4169 miles."

Continuing toward the Horn the *Tornado* had reached the position on September 9th of 43.07 South, and Mumford's troubles were beginning. His entries for that and several successive dates are here given.

"Sept. 9—Weather very unsettled and wind very unsteady. Was struck aback twice during the night with the wind from SE sea all up in heaps. I would here state that I am compelled to keep the ship under short canvas as our crew is the most worthless lot I ever saw on board a ship. 4 PM bar down to 28.60 in 2 reefs furled jib and mainsail Middle bar 28.33 wind hauling Northerly a sharp lightning to the Northward. 2 AM wind hauling Easterly.

"Sept. 10—Lat 45.25 S. Lon 96.33 W. 4 AM wind ESE. 7 AM wore ship to the Eastward, wind hauling Southerly. Sea all in heaps. Bar 28.20 Noon Bar 28.50. dirty looking weather.

"Sept. 11—Begins with moderate Breeze from the South and squalls of sleet. Bar. 28.50.

"2 AM was struck by a whirlwind which carried away the bow sprit 3 ft. outside the night heads and landed it inside of the larboard anchor stock on the forecastle. The foremast also went close to the deck and fell upon the midship house. The foretopmast was broke in 3 pieces between the hounds and cap. At the time this occurred the wind was moderate and had been so before during the night. Ship had single reefed topsails upon her, except the mizzen which was close reefed. reefed mainsail & jibb & reefed spanker as when in lat. 46.35 S. Long. 95.08 West. from the low state of the Bar. though steady I had come to the conclusion that it was blowing hard to the South of us, and the storm was travelling partially to the East and as I could not depend upon our crew in an emergency I was going along easily, not wishing to overtake the storm if my supposition was correct, that it was travelling to the East from the South. there was not much sea and that was from the SE.

"The Foremast and bowsprit when (built) and was 36 inch in diameter. 4 AM hard gales and the sea rising very fast. 8 AM finding the gale increasing and the great weight upon the main stays and topmast stays was endangering the mast (maintopgallant mast carried away) I decided to cut clear from the wreck & at 10 AM finding the gale still increasing & the sea very heavy cut the lanyards of the fore rigging and let the wreck go. back the close reefed mizzen topsail and cleared it without much apparent injury to the side of the ship. by this time it was quite cold wind S. 8 of our crew was suddenly *taken sick* (from the cold) although they had as much hot coffee as they chose to drink it was kept hot for them in the galley and I would here enter my protest against the *Buncomb* speech of the ex commodore ———— he may be a sailor, but he wants to be President, and I wish I had one hand upon his throat and the other upon ———— senator for N. H. at the present moment, and I think I could squeeze them both with a good will.

"From the 11th to the 17th inst. we were hove too sometimes heading to the Northward and Eastward & then again to the SE. We have got up a studdingsail boom for a foremast for the present, and the only sail we are able to set upon it is a Fore stgsail. I am making a foremast out of a spare lower yard.

"Sept. 17. Lat. 46.36 S. Long. 94.51 W. Stepped our foremast 6 feet forward of the old one took a spare topmast & fitted it for a bow sprit. Ship under easy sail.

"Sept. 18. No obs. Unbent the main spencer and bent it on the foremast.

"Sept. 19. Lat. 49.43. S. Long. 91.71 W. fine breeze and heavy sea. fitting rigging for yards &c."

The above entry continued unchanged for the next five days, during which Mumford got up a fore topmast and fore yard and bent the crochet for a foresail.

"Sept. 25. Lat. 55.10 S. Long 77.42 W. Sent up fore topsail yard & bent the sail and set it. our fore top mast is a fore topgallant mast. Fore yard is a spare topsail yard. Fore topsail yard is a spare top gallant yard with a main top gallantsail bent for a fore topsail. Fair weather & smooth sea. made all possible sail for the first time since the accident. 3 PM spoke ship John Baring from N. Y. for San Francisco."

In spite of this delay and the obvious handicap of the above jury rig the *Tornado* arrived at New York after a passage of only 100 days from California. For his seamanship on this occasion Mumford was presented with a beautiful silver service by the insurance companies.

Another very fine run was that of the new clipper ship *Warner*, under command of Captain Carr. She had been out to San Francisco and, on the return voyage, made a 67 day passage from Valparaiso to New York, arriving the 9th of July. This run was stated at the time to be a record, but while this was an error, it was nevertheless a rare performance, and was marked, moreover, by the very extraordinary time of 27 days from latitude 36 south, which latter run appears never to have been beaten.

In common with a number of other fine clippers, the *Warner* appears to have suffered the fate of being omitted from all the recent lists of clipper ships, although there would seem to be but little question as to her clipper mould and rig. Throughout her short life her performance indicates that she possessed clipperly qualities in a high degree, and when she was posted as missing in March, 1854, the New York papers referred to her as "a full clipper." With her was lost the fine young master mariner, Luther Ripley, Jr.

One of the noteworthy short runs of the year was made by the beautiful new *Tinqua,* under the veteran driver, Jacob D. Whitmore. He left New York on the 24th of November, in a roaring nor'wester, bound 'round the Horn. On December 7th, he was spoken in latitude 2.33 north, longitude 31.10 west. He had run to within less than 200 miles of the Line in 13 days.

One can only dimly imagine the way the "old man" carried sail to accomplish this unprecedented feat. The *Tinqua* was a new ship very heavily rigged with the best Russian hemp by men who were masters of their art. Yet Whitmore drove her so hard that his rigging slacked off, not once, but several times, and each time he was compelled to heave to and set it up—a fact which must have cost many hours delay in the aggregate. It is no hasty job to set up a ship's rigging, even under the ordinary conditions of doldrum weather, where such work is usually done. Reading between the lines, it is altogether probable that the *Tinqua* was delayed a full 24 hours in this manner.

For half a century some of the finest sailing by American ships had been done by the coffee traders clearing to the Brazils. Many a smart passage had been made by such craft as the *Maria,* a succession of *Couriers,* a couple of *Hazards,* ships and barks, to say nothing of a lengthy list of Baltimore vessels, schooners and brigs with here and there a ship or two.

There had never been a contest or a race against time, however, over this course which equalled in dramatic quality or speed a brief dispute which took place between Maine and Baltimore in the Spring of '52. Maine was represented by the barque *Black Squall*, a craft of about 400 tons, built at Cape Elizabeth, and commanded by Captain J. Codman. The ship *Grey Eagle* of Baltimore, W. P. Whipple master, measured about 500 tons.

Codman took his departure from the Sugar Loaf at Rio on the 13th of May, and crossed the Line on the 25th at 9 A.M., having

> "made 1600 miles (229 per day on an average) in last week notwithstanding an average contrary current of 2 knots pr hour. So that our days works have averaged 277 miles."

The *Black Squall* took her pilot off Sandy Hook at noon June 9th, 15 days from the Equator crossing and 26 from Rio, having "run by daily observation 5136 miles average of 197½ miles pr day."

The *Grey Eagle* took her departure three days later on the 17th of May bound for Philadelphia. During the next fifteen days she made 3194 miles, an average of slightly less than 213 miles a day, very fine work for those latitudes. Thereafter the following entries appear in her log:

> "June 2—Spoke Bark *Black Squall* of and for New York flying light from Rio on the 13th ult. Noon she is about 6 mile ahead. We are very deep. She not copper too.
> "June 3—*Black Squall* in Co gaining on her.
> "June 4—Dropping the *B. Squall* rapidly.
> "June 5—Lost sight of *B. Squall* dead to leeward."

Eventually the *Grey Eagle* anchored at the quarantine grounds below Philadelphia on June 9th, 23 days from Rio, on the same day the *Black Squall* arrived at New York, the honors of the contest going to the Baltimore ship, which had established a new low record for the course.

Among the better passages between China and America this year was that of the smart little clipper barque *Mermaid*. Under the able guidance of Captain Forbes she romped home from

Canton in the very good time of 87 days, having left Macao March 13th, when the season was getting poor. We shall hear of the *Mermaid* more than once as the years roll on.

Of all the tea ships the *Atalanta*, under command of Captain Wallace, made the fastest passage from Southern China. She left Canton on the 16th of December, '52, and arrived off New York the 11th of March, following. Unfortunately she went on the Romer shoals in thick weather, getting off after some delay without damage, but her time of 84 days was unsurpassed by any of the clippers this year.

She had beaten, by a decisive margin, such fine ships as the *White Squall*, which sailed a day ahead of her and reached New York fifteen days later; the *Victory*, of Boston, which arrived off the Hook on the 12th of March, 100 days from Canton, and the *Hornet*, Captain Bunker, which arrived the night the *Atalanta* went on the shoals, after a passage of 113 days.

From Shanghai, the finest run was that of the *Panama*, one of the N. L. & G. Griswold ships. Under Captain Dearborn she entered New York harbor on the 2nd of February, '53, ninety days out. She had beaten the *Seaman's Bride*, *Witchcraft* and *Aramingo* by margins varying from 21 to 28 days. Her time was the best since the 88 day record of the little *Houqua*, in 1851.

Back from the scenes of her triumphs in the closing days of the year, came the *Oriental*, 106 days from Shanghai, against the monsoon. Two years and seven months had elapsed since she left Sandy Hook. In the interim she had sailed 97,000 miles, and earned tremendous sums for her owners, and, incidentally, had established new sailing records wherever she went. As she backed her long main yard off the Hook she looked "as trim as the day she left the riggers' hands," and as ready to set out for her second hundred thousand miles.

Altogether, Cap'n Theodore had a right to feel a certain complacency. Breaking the economy record of a lifetime, he passed his cable to the tug *Titan* and gave himself up to the pleasurable sensations of a "ride" up through the Narrows.

By this time numerous small ship building centers had representatives in the Clipper fleet. Mystic, Connecticut, had three, two of which ranked with the sharpest of the extreme clippers and were acclaimed as among the most beautiful. They were the *Alboni,* Captain N. R. Littlefield, and the *Charles Mallory,* commanded by Charles Hull. The third was the medium built *Eliza Mallory,* with the extreme clipper captain, Jack Williams.

On the 19th of July the *Eliza Mallory* was nearing the Horn bound for the Golden Gate and Cap'n Jack was meeting typical Cape Horn weather. His entry for the above date follows:

"First part light airs middle part strong and cloudy. Latter part thick and rainy. First part strong breeze from the Eastward and heavy rain squalls. Barometer going down very fast. At 8 AM close reeft and reefed the foresail at 9 PM furled the four and mizen topsails and foursails wether looking very bad glass still going down. Middle part wind canting to the NW still squally At 12 midnight cleared up stars out Glass 28.9 at 2 AM thick again wind holing to the Eastward. At 3.30 AM calm at 4 AM the wind came from the SSE in heavy squalls It bloud a hericane for about 4 hours At 4 the glass has gone up one tenth at 6 it stud 29.2 at 9 29.3 Latter part squalls not quite so hard At 9 Wind SSW. Wore ship to the Southward and eastward. Very heavy cross sea Ship Rouling Bad."

Such was the beginning for the *Eliza Mallory* of a long dreary midwinter passage around the Cape with its endless nights and days of beating back and forth. The old water stained logs keep the reckoning, but they yield their story only to the lessening numbers of those who have weathered the Cape.

Hull went around in the early Southern summer, but he had his difficulties. Sailing from New York on the 16th of September, 1852, on the wings of a fine N.N.E. wind, he was South of the Horn about the middle of November. He writes:

"Nov 15—57.23 S 67.42 W. Begins with Fresh breeze and squalls of hail and snow. Middle—wind hauls & blows up. In topgallant sail. Double reef'd Topsails and Reefe the courses. Strong gales with squalls of hail and snow. Latter the same heavy sea up. One ship and bark in Company. So ends.

"Nov 16—56.54 S 67.25 W. Begins with fresh gale and squalls, Hail and snow. Double reefs and reef's courses. At 4 PM clears off fine. Set Topgallantsails over single reefs. At 5 squalls of Hail—in topgallantsails. 2 ships in company astern. At 7 PM wind hauls to the SSW and blows up a strong gale. Double reef'd main, close reefed fore and mizen. Reef'd courses. At 9 a heavy sea and heavy gale. furled the courses. At 3 AM split fore topsail and furled it. At 6 AM heavy squalls. clewed down the maintopsail to reef it and split it and furled it, heavy sea and strong squalls. Ship laboring heavy. At 12 more moderate. All hands employed in bending new sails. this is Cape Horn that Capt. ———— calls a bug a boo. If he should pass it about ten times he might know more about it so he would not write and call it all moonshine. I have been off here about ten times and I have seen all kinds of weather. For the last 7 days it has blown a gale of wind with squalls hail and snow all the time, let the wind be where it would, and how much longer it will last I can not tell."

Altogether it was a busy 24 hours for Hull and his crew of Mystic boys. However, the brave little clipper eventually got around and in the pleasant waters of the North Pacific Captain Hull felt better. It would be no exaggeration to say that he assumed a slightly cocky attitude, as the following bears witness:

"Dec 23—15.24 N 115.43 W—Begins and ends with fresh Trade and pleasant wether. by the wind all drawing sail set. At 10 AM saw a large ship abeam, steering NW everything set. at noon hauled his wind 2 points on the wether bow 2 Leagues dist. See by his rig he is a clipper *come down to show himself.* In 24 hours we will see where he is.

"Dec 24—All this day a pleasant Trade from NE & fine wether. all sail set by the wind. One clipper in sight 2 points abaft the beam 10 miles to leeward. Can not see his courses from the deck. Passed him at 11 PM one mile to Leeward."

The *Charles Mallory* anchored in the harbor of San Francisco at 9 P.M. the 9th of January, having made her passage in 106 days, a shorter run than was made by any of the ships sailing about the same time: to that extent justifying Captain Hull's pride in his command. It is to be regretted that her life was so short. When she piled up on the coast of the Brazils on her homeward voyage in the grip of an unsuspected current, she broke her master's heart and he never sailed again.

CHAPTER XXIV

1852–3

A DEEP SEA DERBY

MEANWHILE one of the most remarkable Cape Horn races of all time was being sailed—remarkable not only for the number and character of entrants, but for tense, dramatic quality. Maury has given a vivid description of the work of four of the participants. He choose for this purpose the *Wild Pigeon, John Gilpin, Flying Fish* and *Trade Wind,* all of which left Eastern ports at intervals from October 11th to November 13th, 1852.

As a matter of fact if this period is extended three days only, it includes the start of no less than fifteen clipper ships, practically all of which ranked among the finest and swiftest craft afloat. The ships, their commanders and respective dates of sailing are as follows:

Wild Pigeon	George W. Putnam	N. Y.	Oct.	11
Flying Dutchman	Ashbel Hubbard	"	"	15
Dauntless	James Miller	Boston	"	15
Westward Ho	Joseph P. Johnson	"	"	16
Northern Light	Freeman Hatch	"	"	28
John Gilpin	Justus Doane	N. Y.	"	28
Flying Fish	Edward C. Nickels	"	"	31

Queen of the Seas	Elias D. Knight	Boston	Nov. 3
Grey Feather	Daniel McLaughlin	N. Y.	" 9
Whirlwind	Wm. H. Burgess	Boston	" 10
Trade Wind	Nathaniel Webber	N. Y.	" 13
Telegraph	George W. Pousland	Boston	" 15
Contest	W. E. Brewster	N. Y.	" 16
Game Cock	Lewis G. Hollis	N. Y.	" 16
Meteor	Samuel W. Pike	Boston	" 17

Months of careful planning could hardly have arranged a deep sea derby to compare with this impromptu affair. Here were fifteen ships and masters of comparable merit, although the size of the diminutive *Grey Feather* reduced her chances. It would have been difficult, if not impossible, to have picked an equal number to match them from the balance of the fleet. The names speak for themselves. A dozen records of these ships still stand and will remain to the end of time, so far as human foresight now extends.

It was the favorable season of the year. Vessels sailing in October and November were apt to meet with fine favoring winds in the North Atlantic and usually found Cape Horn easy to negotiate, and when arriving in the North Pacific generally made good runs to the coast. Little as they realized it, the men who paced the decks and handed the canvas of those brave clippers outward bound in the closing days of '52, were participating in the grand classic of the sea. It was the very crest of the clipper wave—the golden meridian of sailing ship days. Just ahead loomed the darkening shadows of a mechanical age: the long, losing fight against steam, the falling freights and glutted markets of punctured mining booms and fevered shipbuilding.

For the moment, however, no thought of this dulled the stern enthusiasm of Yankee mariners. For them the future stretched an unending summer sea filled with fair winds and ever swifter ships. Their undivided energies were bent on running every sail on the horizon out of sight astern in the shortest possible time.

As cotton canvas now whitened every sea, it gave them enough to do, in all conscience.

Fifteen ships and four hundred men—the very aristocracy of the world's men of action. They drove their clippers through the Golden Gate in an average of less than 112 days; less time than Lord Anson's *Adventure* spent between southern Argentine and Juan Fernandez. If one excepts the little *Grey Feather* and the *Queen of the Seas*, deep loaded and a foot by the head, the average of the remaining thirteen was less than 109 days. Six ships went around in less than 105 days, seven in 110 days or less, while two were under 94 days. It was such a record as was never made again by a competing fleet, in an equal period.

Among the contestants the shortest passages were made by the *John Gilpin* and the *Flying Fish*. The *Gilpin,* 1089 tons, fresh from the yard of Samuel Hall, was commanded by Justus Doane. The *Flying Fish* was a third larger. She had already proved her quality in a fine passage of 101 days the previous year, and was ably handled by Nickels, who three years earlier had made a record on the round between Manila and New York in the *John Q. Adams.*

The *Gilpin* sailed first, passing Sandy Hook on the 29th of October, sea time. At three that afternoon she was 15 miles East by North from the Highlands of Neversink. The *Flying Fish* followed two days later.

Words poorly describe the grim determination with which the ships were driven; the constant sleepless vigilance with which their sails were trimmed and sweated up to make the most of every vagrant puff of air; the untiring work of wetting down canvas to hold the wind. Catlike veterans of twenty handed their sails in whistling squalls that put polished teak rails three feet under swirling green water or took another "small pull on lee fore braces" as they smashed to windward under steel bellied topgallants past stout craft hove to under a goose winged topsail.

Before the Line was crossed the *Flying Fish* had passed the

CLIPPER SHIP "N. B. PALMER."

FROM PAINTING BY FRANK VINING SMITH.

Courtesy of the Artist.

CLIPPER SHIP "WESTWARD HO."
FROM PAINTING BY W. N. WILSON.
Courtesy of the Artist.

Gilpin only to find herself far to leeward and fighting desperately to weather Cape St. Roque. By the time the Horn was reached the *Gilpin* had regained the lead and was a day ahead. Meeting heavy westerly breezes there, she was retarded until the *Flying Fish* came up with her and Nickels humorously extended Doane an invitation to dinner. As it was hardly small boat weather, Doane was unable to avail himself of the opportunity. Here the greater length and power of the *Flying Fish* told and Nickels took the lead and for a time maintained it, despite the heroic efforts of the smaller ship. He was two days ahead at the Pacific crossing.

From there the *Gilpin* shot ahead again. She made the remarkable run of 15 days from the Line as against a few hours more than 17 days consumed by the *Flying Fish*. Reaching the Farallones on the 30th of January she took her pilot 93 days and 20 hours from Sandy Hook. She entered the harbor in company with the good ship *Milton*, 209 days from the same point of departure.

The *Flying Fish* swept in through the Golden Gate the next afternoon, coming to anchor at 4 o'clock, 92 days and 4 hours from New York, winning the race therefore on elapsed time. And here is a noteworthy fact: Nickels was a few miles off the land for three days in calms and light contrary airs. But for this he should have lowered the record of the *Flying Cloud* a full day. On his 88th day he was 156 miles nearer port than Cressy was on his famous passage. It was one of those heart breaking situations that wrung the very soul of many a clipper master whose well earned victory eluded his grasp at the last moment.

Nickels in fact had missed two chances. The three days he lost beating around Cape St. Roque as a result of failing to follow sailing directions in the Atlantic doldrums cost him, in all probability, the distinction of beating the *Flying Cloud's* mark, not by hours but by days. But for one rash attempt to evade the mathematics of wind and current records his name today might have occupied a place in Neptune's hall of fame, comparable with that of Waterman and the *Sea Witch*.

Just ahead of the *Flying Fish* as she crossed the bar, was the beautiful extreme clipper *Westward Ho*. From his quarter deck Nickels could see her stunsails crumpling like falling petals as Johnson's willing crew rolled her canvas up for the last time. She had left Boston the day following the departure of the *Flying Dutchman* from New York. Deducting a delay of four days, hove to off the Heads in fog and calms, her net sailing time was 103 days.

Hubbard had brought the *Flying Dutchman* in four days earlier, that is on the 27th of January, after a run of 104 days gross, which included a brief delay at Rio Janeiro. A feature of her passage was her record of 35 days from 50 South Pacific, which enabled her to tie the net sailing time of the *Westward Ho*. She was fortunate enough to escape the calm and fog which shut down immediately after her arrival and held up the other ships.

Two more clippers arrived in company on February 24th. The *Contest* was 100 and the *Trade Wind* 103 days from New York. The *Contest* had made a notable run of 42 days from the Horn.

A couple of weeks later blase forty-niners were treated to the sight of three large clippers roving in, bowsprit to taffrail. They were the *Meteor*, *Game Cock* and *Telegraph*, fresh from one of the closest three-cornered sailing matches of the course. A single day only intervened between their respective times of 113, 114 and 115 days. In common with many other ships shortly to arrive, they had experienced unusual delays off the Horn, the *Telegraph* and *Game Cock* having been delayed there two weeks, indicating very unseasonable weather conditions there.

One may read between the meager lines of Pousland's log the tenseness that pervaded the *Telegraph* as she drove for the Heads from the open Pacific, the snowy piled canvas of her rivals on either quarter.

"Mar. 4—Clipper in Co. on Larboard beam.

Mar. 5—The Two clippers in Co. out of sight astern.

Mar. 7—A clipper ahead—coming up with her.

Mar. 8—Come up with the clipper Game Cock, spoke her 112 days from Boston.

Mar. 9—Tacked ship Game Cock in Co. stormy breezes.

Mar. 10—Fresh breezes and passing squalls Layed to under double reefed topsails till four AM Made sail and took pilot at 6 AM. Ship Game Cock in Co. Arrived at San Francisco."

The following day the *Whirlwind* arrived closely followed by the *Queen of the Seas*. Their passages of 121 and 128 days had also been prolonged by extraordinary weather off the Horn. In the case of the *Whirlwind* the delay amounted to 18 days.

Three of the ships, the *Northern Light*—destined presently to establish the undefeated record from San Francisco to Boston —the *Wild Pigeon* and the *Dauntless*, soon alas! to sail for the port of missing ships, made the same run, 118 days. Altogether it was a contest that for number and character of ships and men engaged, consistent performances and high average of speed maintained, probably has no parallel in history. It formed a fitting prelude to the record smashing year of '53, which by now was well under way.

CHAPTER XXV

1853

FLOOD TIDE

THE year that had just closed witnessed a notable increase in the number and size of clipper ships. Altogether, sixty-six had been launched, fourteen of which were extreme models. This was as many as had been built in the two previous years.

In addition, a considerable number of lighter clippers (barques, brigs and schooners) were built. Several of the schooners were large three masters, one of which registered 600 tons.

The first "three masted brig," later called a "barkentine," seems to have appeared at Boston on February 18th this year from the California coast. She was a small vessel of 300 tons register called the *Carbon,* and was launched in Robbinston, Maine, in 1851. It is at present uncertain whether she was originally designed as a barkentine or was dismasted on her voyage around the Horn and re-rigged after the ingenious and economical ideas of her master, Captain John Valpey. However that may be, it was a rig that eventually proved both popular and advantageous on the broad reaches of the Pacific. The extreme clipper *White Squall* was re-fitted in this fashion in 1854, after having been badly damaged in the fire which burned the *Great Republic.*

Despite the tremendous increase in sharp ships during 1852,

the rage for them continued unabated. Persons of every condition were yielding to the lure of fabulous profits. Knowledge of nautical affairs was far more widely diffused in the fifties than at present, and hundreds of men who had never owned a share of shipping were investing their surplus in the new racers. Long after legitimate commercial requirements were satisfied, clippers were built to accommodate this uncritical demand.

Exact statistics are not available, owing to the fact that reports from small and remote shipyards were meager and unreliable. It is certain, however, that at least thirty-five of these vessels were in course of construction simultaneously on January 1st, 1853. Many of these were nearly completed. Eight of them were launched in January alone.

Signs—hardly as yet to be called ominous—were not wanting. Shipyard wages were rising to unheard of levels. Workmen were becoming a trifle difficult to suit and more than a trifle indifferent about suiting. Freights were still high, but it was already apparent to conservative merchants that the more pressing needs of California had been satisfied, and it was only a question of months, or possibly weeks, when speed to the Pacific would be important to the shipowner as a measure of economy, rather than to the shipper, as a means of filling the empty shelves of western wholesalers.

The magnificent *Sovereign of the Seas*, now loading at Honolulu for her record breaking run to New York, was to find it impossible to get another profitable charter to San Francisco, and had to be diverted to the Australian trade, which, later in the year, was to find itself in a similar situation—its warehouses crammed with merchandise, and its harbors bristling with the spars of deeply loaded ships. The days when speed was to be the paramount consideration in designing ships of the sail could have been quite definitely numbered by disinterested men of vision in the closing days of '52. Men of vision, however, were mostly "interested."

But whatever the future might hold, the new year dawned

upon a cloudless sky. The month of January was marked by the sailing of an unprecedented number of fine ships for California. Eighteen clippers in all left eastern ports within the 23 days from January 8th to 28th, inclusive. The following month sixteen more spread their wings for the Cape Horn route, thirty-five brave clippers in all, comprising some of the finest ships in the world, taking their departure within an interval of 49 days. Nothing like it had ever occurred before, and the world was never to witness such a sight again. By the time they reached their destination, whispers were already going the rounds that San Francisco markets were glutted.

The *Phantom*, a new Medford-built clipper of 1174 tons, old Sam Lapham's masterpiece, under command of Alvin H. Hallett, was the first to sail for California in '53. She left Boston on the 6th of January. The third day out she took the wind strongly from the South, and it held until she reached 29 North, 36.30 West, when it veered to the south and east. Hallett then stood to the south and west, and passed Rio on his twenty-third day out—a wonderful run, and one which seems never to have been surpassed.

He was off the Horn on the fifty-second day, encountering very heavy westerly gales. Smashing his way along, pitching bows under, he carried away his head and part of the stem, washed the moulding off the stern, stove his cabin windows, started ten channels and disabled fifteen men by washing them about the decks and under the spars, the seas making a clean breach over the ship the greater part of the time.

On March 24th the wind blew with hurricane force and continued for some forty hours, wrecking the patent steering gear. Hallett got six tackles on the rudder and mortised a hole in the rudder head and shipped a six foot tiller and rove steering tackles to it. It lasted one hour. He then secured the rudder until the hurricane abated and rigged a patent steering apparatus of his own which worked.

The *Phantom* arrived 104 days out from Boston, after a

summer passage that was fairly typical of a Cape Horn clipper in a hurry. Winter passages were another matter. One was apt to have trouble on them.

Among the reasons for Captain Hallett's haste was his knowledge that a couple of New York clippers were due to sail about the same time he did. The *Eagle*, Captain John S. Farren, and *Rattler*, Richard Brown, master, left Sandy Hook one and two days, respectively, after the *Phantom* sailed, but Hallett beat both of them by a liberal margin. Throughout her existence the *Phantom* had the name of being a very fast ship. The *Eagle* made the run in 111 days, while the *Rattler* took ten days longer. Even so, this was very good time in view of the conditions. The *Celestial*, under B. G. Palmer, who was not specially noted for slow passages, sailed in company with the *Rattler* and beat her by one day only.

Another *Rattler*, under Captain Stump, sailed from Philadelphia on January 14th, and made the run out in 133 days. It has been said that she was an old Baltimore ship, built in 1842. The fact is that she was a new ship on her first voyage, having been launched at Baltimore on the 27th of November, 1852. She registered 538 tons and was similar to the *Seaman* and other Baltimore clippers of the period.

Among the January departures the *Simoon* and *Typhoon*, both extreme clippers, sailed a very close race. The *Simoon* left New York on the 19th, followed by the *Typhoon* on the 22nd of January. A few nights later the *Simoon* lost her fore topgallant mast and swinging booms. She met with an unusual amount of adverse weather throughout her passage, incidentally having to beat around Cape St. Roque. Nevertheless she beat the *Typhoon* by approximately one day, elapsed time, entering San Francisco on the 1st of June. The *Typhoon* arrived off the coast three days later, having made the run to that point in the same time as her rival, but was compelled to stand off and on in a fog for four days before entering port.

Meanwhile the sailing clippers of '51 and '52 were chalking up their records. Andrew Barstow brought out the Westervelt & Mackay model, the *Golden Gate,* surpassing beautiful in form and finish, as were all the ships from that yard. He made the run in 104 days, arriving the 20th of March.

Dumaresq, veteran of the China and Calcutta trades, made the passage about the same time in 107 days 10 hours in McKay's smart new clipper, *Bald Eagle.* He rounded to just off Market Street wharf at half past ten the evening of April 11th, as the night life of the forty-niners was getting under way, and on the stage of one of 'Frisco's garish theatres Lotta Crabtree, the child actress, was smilingly acknowledging her initial shower of gold.

Barely a cable's length from him lay the little barque *Storm,* Captain John P. Roberts. She was the first clipper of Sag Harbor, which for a century and more had specialized in square ended "spouters." Leaving New York on the 21st of December she was on the line at midnight, January 8th, less than 18 days from the Hook. Here she carried away her larboard cathead and wrung the bowsprit cap in a squall. Roberts had already carried away all her trestletrees fore and aft, owing, he was careful to explain, to poor material. Thereafter the *Storm* proceeded somewhat more sedately with the result that she reached San Francisco the night before the *Bald Eagle* arrived, in a passage of 110 days, having, as Roberts' entry reads, "beaten every clipper that sailed about the time I did."

As the year wore on good passages became less and less frequent. The battered clippers crept in to Valparaiso to refit, reporting from 20 to 60 days off the Horn, or plunged doggedly on up the Pacific licking their wounds as best they might. C. A. Fletcher, sometime of the old Swallow Tail packet *Independence,* and now in the *Oriental,* carried her foremast away off the Cape. He managed to improvise a jury rig and arrived at San Francisco in the extraordinary time, circumstances considered, of 101 days. As a feat it was a tribute at once to the skill and courage of the master and to the designers and builders of the ship.

Closely contested races continued to mark the season. Two old rivals, the *Swordfish* and *Sea Serpent*, sailed from New York on the 12th of February just as the *Sovereign of the Seas* left Honolulu on her epochal voyage. Both ships were sailed for all that was in them. It was anybody's race up to the last few hundred miles, with almost equal honor to victor and vanquished. The *Swordfish* arrived out on the 30th of May in the excellent passage of 107 days, with the *Sea Serpent* less than 48 hours behind.

Weeks before this, however, the *Sovereign of the Seas* had reached New York, 82 days from the Sandwich Islands, with every existing record for speed and distance annihilated. Lt. Maury made the voyage the subject of a special report to the Secretary of the Navy and it was later commented on at length by Captain Clark.

It is to be regretted that neither Lt. Maury nor Captain Clark had the original log kept by Captain McKay when they made their analysis of the performance of the *Sovereign of the Seas*. Since both Maury and Clark were clearly under the impression that McKay had not reported a speed in excess of 18 knots, whereas his log notes the rate of 19 knots for three successive hours, it is obvious that both had access only to an imperfect abstract of the official record. The conclusive value of Maury's article is further weakened by the fact that it was issued from Washington on May 10th, while the *Sovereign* did not anchor in the East River at New York until 7:30 P.M., May 6th, a circumstance which gave him no time to communicate with Captain McKay on doubtful points.

Maury credited the *Sovereign* with a maximum day's run of 427.6 statute miles in 24 hours (approximately 374 nautical miles). This seems to have been unsatisfactory to McKay, whose official log had entered the run of 430 nautical miles, or slightly more than 495 statute miles, and as a result he appears to have sent in his original log to Maury for comparison. At all events it found its way to Maury's department, by which it was eventually turned over to the marine division of the weather bureau at Washington, in whose possession it now remains.

A recent analysis of this log by a group of navigation officers in the Navy department at Washington, D. C., establishes the conclusion that the noon to noon run of the *Sovereign*, Friday, March 18, 1853, was 410.7 miles (equivalent to 472.92 statute miles) in 23 hours and 18 minutes. As the ship continued to log 15 miles during the whole of the following day it is obvious that her actual distance for the full 24 hours would be slightly in excess of 421 nautical miles. Aside therefore from the possibility of deliberate falsification—an act, it may be said, which seems absolutely foreign to the character of Captain McKay, and one that is further disproved by an inspection of the log as a whole—it may be considered that the run of 421 nautical miles in 24 hours is established by the weight of the evidence.

From whatever angle considered, this passage of the *Sovereign of the Seas* must rank among the greatest of the world's voyages under sail, made as it was with a short handed crew composed mostly of greenhorns, and with a sprung foretopmast which prevented Captain McKay from carrying sail as he otherwise might. The *Sovereign's* runs of an average of 378 miles a day for four consecutive days and of 330 miles for eleven consecutive days set new records which have been rarely equalled since. By way of riveting down her new title the *Sovereign* immediately proceeded to lower the record from New York to Liverpool to 13 days and 23 hours, dock to dock in the month of June, a feat which has never been duplicated.

These performances had the effect of focussing the attention of the entire maritime world on Donald McKay, and from that time forward he appears as the dominating personality in the shipbuilding industry. This is not to imply that his contribution to the development of the clipper was of greater value than that of several others. Absolute fairness compels the statement that he did not lay a clipper keel until the new principles of design had been tested in all their essential features. But if it cannot be claimed that he stands first as the originator of the new type, there can be no question regarding his eventual leadership in its construction. No builder of any period turned out an equal tonnage of clipper ships, and no clippers were more uniformly successful than McKay's. Endowed with a most attractive personality, gifted with a remarkable sense of discrimination and a knowledge of the fundamentals of his profession, second to none, coupled with rare courage and a flair for the spectacular, it was inevitable that his name should become the synonym for the finest in men and ships during the clipper era. Donald McKay honorably won and richly deserved the place he now holds in America's heart.

In 1853, however, events marched rapidly. News of the latest accomplishment of his latest success had scarcely drifted back to America when public attention was fixed upon a passage which still stands as the closest sailing match in the history of Cape Horn.

On the 8th of April the *Hornet,* one of the finest productions ever put out by Westervelt & Mackay, commanded by Captain William Knapp, had left Sandy Hook followed a few hours later by the *Flying Cloud.* The race which ensued is partly described in the San Francisco *Herald* of August 13th:

"ARRIVAL OF TWO CLIPPERS.—EXTRAORDINARY COINCIDENCE.

"Yesterday the clipper ships *Hornet* and *Flying Cloud* arrived at this port in 105 days from New York. The *Hornet* came in about forty minutes ahead of the *Flying Cloud,* having left New York on the same day, the *Hornet* several hours ahead. Outside the Heads at New York she was becalmed until the *Flying Cloud* came up, when they started together, and have reached their destination almost simultaneously— an extraordinary coincidence.

"The *Hornet* was nineteen days in reaching the Equator, and the *Flying Cloud* seventeen. The *Flying Cloud,* it will be recollected, has made the quickest passage to this port on record. From the memoranda she appears to have encoun-

tered much worse weather than her rival, having had her jibboom carried away in a gale, as well as her chief officer and
one of her seamen washed overboard and lost. These passages are the best that have been made this season, and considering all the circumstances, they may be considered as
excellent."

Additional light is thrown on the incident by the following
extracts from the *Hornet's* log:

"Apr. 28—At 2 P.M. dischg pilot & tug off S Hook. Wind
S by E & Calm for 2 days.
"Apr. 29—Lat 40.20 N Lon 70.10 W—At meridian clipper
ship in sight to S.W. (presume to be the Flying
Cloud which intended leaving same day with us).
Later recognized the Flying Cloud bringing up
the breeze.
"Aug. 12—Com. moderate breeze & hazy 8 PM shorten sail
foggy—tacked ship. by calculation between the
Faralones & Point Reyes. 30 fathom water. Hove
to head off shore. 4 AM fog partly lifting saw
Point Reys bearing N by W distant 4 miles. 9 AM
took a pilot on the Bar. At 10 AM saw the ship
Flying Cloud coming up with fine breeze. 11½
AM anchored off the port of San Francisco 40
minutes ahead of the Flying Cloud."

As in the majority of close finishes the victory, in point of
elapsed time, has been claimed by admirers of both ships and
various accounts of the contest have appeared. The dispute does
not seem so important to us now as it did to the ardent contemporaries, but the foregoing evidence is conclusive of the fact
that both ships won the race. Whereas the *Flying Cloud* made
the shortest passage from anchor to anchor, the *Hornet* beat her
from the point of meeting just outside Sandy Hook to the San
Francisco anchorage.

Nor was it a disgrace to any clipper to be held by a ship like
the *Hornet,* for she was very fast. Immediately after the above
voyage she set a new record for the passage from San Francisco

to Callao, arriving at the latter port on the 7th of October, 34 days from the Golden Gate.

Winner or loser, as one's sympathies may incline, it would doubtless have been glory enough for any man now living to have stood on the deck of either ship that last exciting day, as with every inch of canvas set and the watches jumping at the braces, alert and tense with the strain of getting the last fractional knot out of their ship, they gazed to see whether they were gaining or losing. Glorious days! Now no more. All their wealth of craft and skill, specialized knowledge and tradition gone with "yesterday's seven thousand years."

For the most part the California passages ending in the summer of '53 were longer than usual. The old favorite, the *Stag Hound*, was 127 days making the distance while McKay's huge new clipper, *Empress of the Seas*, showed her black main royal to the watchers at Point Reyes on the 11th of July, 119 days from New York.

The *Empress*, commanded by W. E. Putnam, had sailed from New York in company with the *Surprise*, still under Ranlett, both ships drifting out past Sandy Hook with a light breeze shortly before noon, the 13th of March. That afternoon (March 14th, sea time) Ranlett whimsically observes of the *Empress*: "She is now bearing N ¼ W of us—*Bow first.*"

By the time he had reached the Line on the 1st of April Ranlett had increased his lead nearly five days. He was still four days ahead at the Horn, where he was held up by heavy westerly gales. On the 7th of May his log notes the following:

> "Lat 58.3 S. Lon 68.40 W. Everything wet and cold men almost ready to give up, in fact 2nd mate and Botswain & some 6 or 7 men have given out—two men for want of clothes."

To old time sailors of the sail, it is doubtless superfluous to add that mates of ships like the *Surprise* did not "give out" except for the best of reasons and when they did they had to be carried below.

While the *Surprise* was fighting for westing the *Empress of the Seas* was coming up hand over hand. She was off the Horn on the 9th of May, two days after the above entry was made. This seems to have been the extent of her gain, and the *Surprise* dropped her anchor at San Francisco in the late afternoon of July 9th, two days ahead of the *Empress* and 117 days from New York. Just outside the Heads she had passed the new Baltimore built ship *Sirocco,* the first large clipper launched there, 147 days from Sandy Hook.

A few weeks later the beautiful *White Squall* from Philadelphia, commanded by Samuel Kennedy, duplicated the 117 day passage of the *Surprise.* Passing Cape Henlopen May 10th Kennedy found himself on the 22nd of the following July well past Cape Horn in latitude 51.25 S., longitude 81.45 W. His log for that day records:

"Begins heavy gale 1 P.M. Bar. 28.87 Wind S.E. 4 P.M. very heavy gale. Furled the topsails. Ship running under her fore staysail only & going 13½ knots. The sea a perfect sheet of foam and the wind a tempest. At 5 P. M. the sea getting very heavy and breaking on board in all directions, let the ship come to the wind on port tack. Bar. down to 28.65. From 4 P.M. to 7 P.M. a most tremendous gale and sea."

Eventually Kennedy anchored in the harbor at San Francisco at 11 A.M. the 4th day of September.

New clippers were coming along. The workmen in the various yards in and near Boston assembled at noon Saturday, March 26th, to assist in launching five beautiful ships. One after another, in the space of an hour, the *John Land, West Wind, White Swallow, Star of Empire* and *Queen of Clippers,* took the water—every one a clipper of the finest mould and a marvel of workmanship and finish.

Long before the close of the year, all of them, with the exception of the *Star of Empire*, which was put up for Australia, had been around the Horn and were homeward bound again.

Two of the fleet of '53 never completed their first voyage. The beautiful *Golden Light* of Boston was struck by lightning and burned when only ten days out. Captain Winsor with the passengers and crew took to the boats, and all were saved with the exception of one boat's crew of seven men, which disappeared during the night and was never heard from.

The *Carrier Pigeon*, another new ship, owned by Reed, Wade & Co., of Boston, went ashore in the fog a few miles below San Francisco, and proved a total loss.

In addition to these, the *Flying Arrow*, also on her first voyage, was totally dismasted four days after leaving New York. Eventually she was towed into St. Thomas, having been saved from foundering only by superhuman exertions on the part of her crew and passengers. Repairs proved a long and difficult task, and many of the ship's company died of yellow fever before they were completed. The *Flying Arrow* proved to be an extremely unlucky ship. One accident followed another, including a partial dismasting and ending with her complete dismasting a second time off the coast of Australia. Captain Treadwell again saved his ship with great difficulty, but her career as an American vessel was ended. She was sold for salvage and some time later was rerigged as a British ship under the name of *Wings of the Wind*.

One of the most noted, as well as one of the most beautiful of the belles of '53, was the *Young America*. She was a Webb product and resembled in a general way several other of his later ships. Many of the features of the *Challenge* were reproduced in her design, in a modified form. In particular, the concavity of her bow and stern were less pronounced than in her famous predecessor, while her spars, though much heavier than the run of clippers, were less lofty than those of the *Challenge*. Nevertheless she was very heavily rigged and expensively finished and was generally regarded as Webb's finest clipper.

Her appearance made an excellent impression on nautically minded New Yorkers, and many laudatory comments were published, of which the following is typical:

"This beautiful clipper is now nearly filled up, and will probably spread her sails for San Francisco on Monday next. She is lying at pier 28, East River, with the clipper ship *Flying Dutchman,* but lately returned from her first voyage.

"They are both the production of Mr. Wm. H. Webb, and excite great attention from their matchless symmetry and finish. The *Young America's* arrival at San Francisco, will be anxiously looked for, and many anticipate that she will make a trip that will throw all previous short passages in the shade.

"She possesses every element of a fast sailer, being both sharp and buoyant, and if she has the luck to get an average share of fair wind and weather, aided by the well known skill of her commander, Captain Babcock, her trip to the Golden State will doubtless be the opening of a new book in the records of navigation. She is the Champion of New York, and to be in advance of all is *Young America's* 'manifest destiny.' "

Leaving New York on the 10th of June, she made the Cape Horn passage in 110 days—not a fast run unless one considers that it was made at the height of the unfavorable season. As it is, her run seems never to have been equalled or beaten for the month of June, except by the *Young America* herself and one other vessel.

The *Young America* was Webb's last extreme clipper, and something more than the apple of his eye. While she was loading for her first voyage, certain invidious comparisons were made between her model and that of the *Sovereign of the Seas,* just returned from her record breaking trip. As the remarks took concrete form in the newspapers, Webb's ire was kindled and he replied in kind:

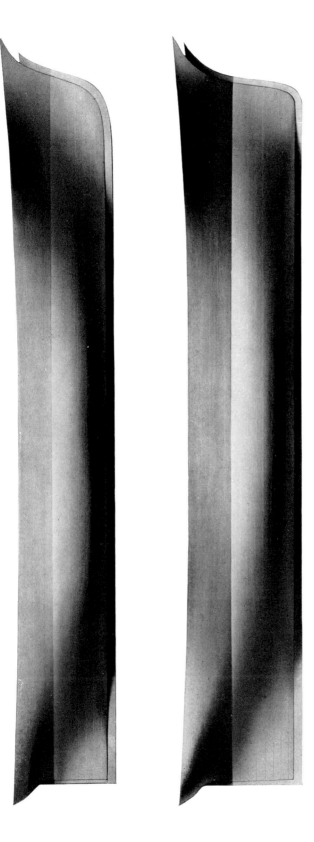

UPPER: The extreme clipper *Lightning*. Her long, hollow bow was probably the sharpest ever put on an American ship, but her flat floor and relatively full run gave her great stability and power.

LOWER: Builder's model of the *Red Jacket*. A very sharp, beautiful three-decker with flat floor and rounding sides and bilges. One of the speediest and most efficient of the clippers. The ships of this type proved superior in almost every way to vessels modelled after the theories of the earlier school, of which Griffiths was the outstanding representative.

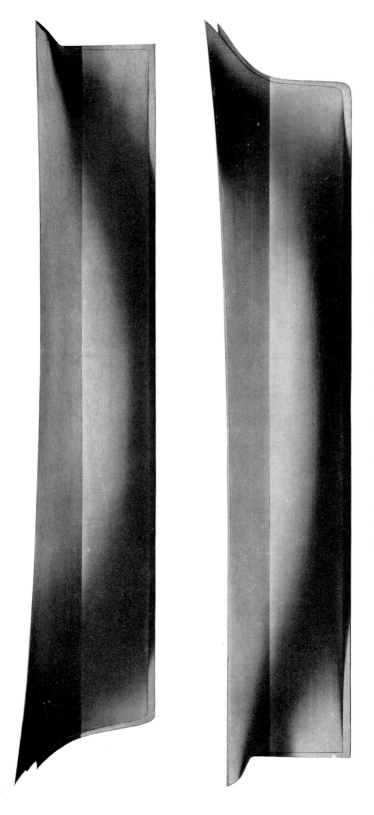

UPPER: Builder's model of the extreme clipper *Belle of the West*, designed by Pook. Courtesy of the Mariners House, Boston.

LOWER: Builder's model of the extreme clipper *Golden West*. Courtesy of the Mariners House, Boston. Both ships were fine examples of the California clipper of 1853, with long sharp ends, rounding sides and bilges and long, flat floors.

Two Views of the "Red Jacket."

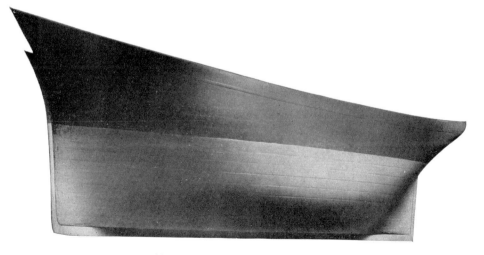

The "Belle of the West."

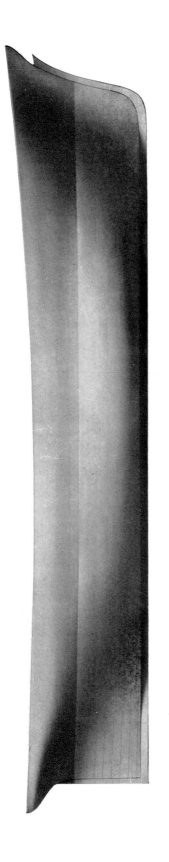
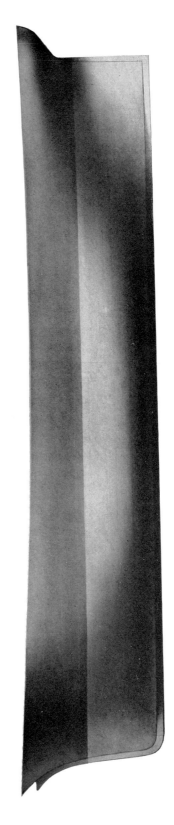

UPPER: Builder's model of the *B. F. Hoxie*, an example of the later medium clippers. Characterized by short but sharp ends and long, flat floor, they were both speedy and enormous cargo carriers.

LOWER: Builder's model of the ship *Garibaldi*, of the period of 1860. A good example of the moderately full built ship which followed the clippers. Both these models have the round stern peculiar to Mystic ships of that day. The lower model, in general appearance, is very much like that of the clipper *Andrew Jackson*, but her lines are fuller than those of the *Jackson*.

"NEW YORK, May 14, 1853.

"To the Editor of the New York Herald:

"DEAR SIR.—My attention having been called to an article in the *Evening Post,* of Thursday last, headed 'The Clipper Ship *Sovereign of the Seas*—A Challenge to the World,' I wish to state in reply that I am ready to bet the sum of ten thousand dollars on the ship *Young America,* Captain D. S. Babcock, the last ship of my construction, and now loading at the foot of Dover Street, East River, against the ship *Sovereign of the Seas.*

"The trial to be made on the terms proposed, viz., from New York to San Francisco, both vessels loaded and to sail together, or within thirty days of each other.

"Yours respectfully,

"WM. H. WEBB."

As a sequel to this, the *Herald* for May 19th, following, published this paragraph:

"We have received the following relative to the contemplated race between the clipper ships *Sovereign of the Seas* and *Young America.*

"'A CARD.—The owner of the *Sovereign of the Seas* begs to state, in answer to the letter from Mr. Webb in Monday's *Herald,* that, though he himself never challenged any ship to a sail against the *Sovereign of the Seas,* he would nevertheless have felt happy to take up the gauntlet, if the present state of the California freight market did not preclude the possibility of laying her on in that direction with any advantage. The *Sovereign of the Seas* will have to make, in all probability, an intermediate trip to England, and the owner can only hope that on her return the better feeling for California will enable him to lay her on again for San Francisco— and then, to sail her for the stipulated amount against any clipper which Mr. Webb is willing to match against her.'"

In spite of the *Young America's* excellent maiden run, however, Babcock seems to have missed several opportunities to shorten his voyage. His anxiety in the doldrums of the Atlantic seems to have led him off the recommended course more than once. Oddly enough, the log of the new ship *Windward* is the only record now available which throws any light on this phase of her voyage. The *Windward* was a small medium clipper with no special pretensions to speed, built by Trufant & Drummond of Bath, who also constructed the medium clippers *Mary Robinson*, *Viking*, *Monsoon* and others. She sailed from New York on the first of June bound for California under the command of Comfort Whiting, Jr. The following entries appear in her log:

"July 8—Lat 8.00 N, lon 29.46 W—A large clipper ship on my lee bow steering South, looks like the Young America left N. Y. shortly after I sailed. He went to E'ward.

"July 15—6 AM. Young America comes along again.

"July 16—Noon—Young America tacked to E'stw'd.

"July 21—Lat. 4.17 S. lon 32.40 W. At 5.00 the Young Am. comes along again & sails right away from me so did not gain anything by tacking to E'w'd.

"Sept. 2—58.58 S. 70.02 W—Ship Young America on my lee bow 2 or 3 miles dist. Hoist my ensign and then my private flags; he wont answer me: acts as though ashamed of the beat I have given him from the line up to here: If a breeze springs up he runs right away from me as he did before. If he does not look out sharp I shall be close on him at S Frisco.

"Nov. 2—12 noon, took a pilot and ran in. Every one complains of a long passage."

The *Windward* accordingly was 44 days longer on the voyage than the *Young America*, fairly conclusive evidence that she was a much slower ship, although she was only nine days behind the time of the larger vessel when off the Horn. It seems altogether probable therefore that if Babcock had followed sailing directions more closely during the first half of the trip, instead of trying to "raise a breeze," he would have made a shorter passage. As we have seen, it was a similar impatience which in all likelihood cost Nickels and the *Flying Fish* the championship of the world a few months earlier.

It is unfortunate that the *Sovereign* and *Young America* never had an opportunity to try their speed over the Cape Horn course. Such a race would undoubtedly have written one of the most interesting pages in marine annals, inasmuch as the two clippers represented the highest development of two different theories of naval design. The *Sovereign of the Seas* was an example of the wedge bow and long flat floor, while the *Young America* embodied in a modified form the hollow lines and rounding sides of the Griffiths' school of naval architecture. Both were extremely fast ships under all conditions, but in the light of present day knowledge, it seems probable that the *Sovereign of the Seas* would have proved somewhat faster in exceptionally heavy weather, while the *Young America*, with her finer lines and tremendous spars, might well have developed a higher rate of speed in light to medium breezes.

Altogether, numbers and records considered, it was the year of years on the California run. Not less than 145 fine clippers cleared from eastern ports for San Francisco between the first of January and the thirty-first of December, and in spite of the fact that a large proportion sailed in the unfavorable season, they made a far greater number of short passages than had ever been made before or would be again. On several occasions three beautiful clippers entered the Golden Gate during the course of a single day, while on two occasions five of them arrived within a period of forty-eight hours.

The following item taken from a San Francisco paper of the times, gives an excellent picture of one of these events:

"Yesterday afternoon, between four and five o'clock, our harbor presented rather an extraordinary, and certainly a most imposing spectacle—the entrance of no less than fourteen vessels: three clipper ships, six ships and barks, and five brigs and schooners. As the anchor of one was let go and she swung gracefully around with the tide, another and another were seen rounding the inner point of the Heads, keeping up a continuous line from North Point to the Golden Gate.

"To add to the liveliness of the scene, the fleet of river steamers left their berths at the same time, steaming gallantly by the vessels which were just coming to anchor.

"The three clippers were the *Grey Hound, Bonita* and *Mischief,* the first 139 days from Baltimore, the second 140 days from Boston and the last 172 days from New York, via Valparaiso, 42 days. They have all, as will be seen, had long passages, owing to the same causes which have delayed all the vessels arriving this season—light or adverse winds and calms."

The closing days of the year witnessed the finish of another contest between two old acquaintances. The *Mandarin,* under John W. C. Perit, and the extreme clipper *Hurricane* left New York on the 11th of August. Perit's log records:

"At 4 P.M. dischg^d the pilot abreast the light ship. The ship Hurricane ahead about 6 hours."

They passed the Golden Gate in reverse order—the *Mandarin* arriving on the 11th and the *Hurricane* on the 12th of December, in 123 and 124 days, respectively. It was a notable victory for the little *Mandarin,* although considering the unfavorable season, the passage reflected credit on both masters.

CHAPTER XXVI

1853

OMINOUS SIGNS

AS 1853 marked the zenith of the California clipper traffic it also witnessed a large but comparatively uneventful participation in the British tea trade. Twenty Yankee ships loaded this year at various China ports for England, eleven of which carried the lofty rig of the clipper. Included in the fleet were the *Challenge, Nightingale, Celestial, Golden State, Typhoon, Flying Childers* and *Mystery,* all large first class craft. With a single exception none of the finishers sailed at the favorable season, and but one short passage was made.

It was the last departure of the *Oriental.* She was lost coming out of Foo Choo Foo on the 25th of February in the treacherous chow-chow water of the River Min while in charge of a pilot, bringing to an untimely end one of the finest ships that ever engaged in the China trade—a trade for which she was specially designed and remarkably well suited. It is regrettable that she could not have completed this passage to London with a moderately favorable monsoon, in order to afford a basis of comparison with her previous record of 97 days against it.

With her loss there was small hope of establishing a new record during the remainder of '53. None of the other American clippers was so fortunate as to get away during the strength of the Northeast monsoon. Nevertheless the *Celestial* made a rather good run. According to marine reports she entered London on the 31st of January, 1854, from Foo Chow 96 days out. She was also reported loading at Foo Chow on the 4th of the previous November, which, if true, would make her passage within 86 rather than 96 days.

In any case her voyage appears to have been shorter by a full week than any made by either American or British ships. The four next shortest runs were those of the barque *Jeanette*, Captain Mix, 103 days from Hong Kong to London; the *Typhoon*, under Salter, which arrived at Deal in 104 days from Shanghai; the *Flying Childers*, commanded by Captain White, 106 days from Whampoa to London, and the *Architect*, under George Potter, 107 days from Macao to London. Apparently none of the British vessels made a passage in less than 108 days, although among the individual contests the British *Challenger* won a decision over the *Nightingale* by a margin of approximately 30 hours elapsed time. The *Nightingale's* run of 68 days from Anjier, however, was very good time.

Meanwhile the America bound tea ships were racing home. Jacob Bell's new clipper *Messenger*, a ship resembling the *White Squall* but sharper, made the run from Macao under the command of Frank Smith in 93 days. This was a passage noteworthy for the fact that she was only 15 days from the line to Sandy Hook, time which has seldom been beaten. In fact the run of the *Swordfish* over this course during the early part of 1860 in 16 days was erroneously considered a record at the time.

Comparatively few ships built were more extreme in design and rig than the *Messenger*. She was so sharp that she could not carry her registered tonnage in dead weight, and she was very heavily sparred with stunsails on the royals. Owing to her persistent ill fortune in encountering unfair winds on some portion of her voyages she never completed any voyages in record time, but she has to her credit a number of very fast day's runs over the various sections of her trips.

On the whole the work of the *Mandarin* was the outstanding feature of the year on the China-New York run. She left Shanghai on the 18th of February and arrived at New York on the 19th of May. Her 90 days equalled that of the *Panama* the season before and had been excelled only by the remarkable run of the little *Houqua* two years before.

In this connection it may be noted that the speedy *Hurricane* reached New York the day before the *Mandarin*, 95 days out from Hong Kong, a port some 800 miles nearer home than Shanghai.

In spite of the relatively long passages—long, that is, compared with the early records of the *Sea Witch* and others—there were many close and interesting finishes. The 21st of January, 1854, was marked by the arrival of three of the fastest of the clippers, the *Swordfish*, *Stag Hound* and *Surprise*, all of which had arrived off the Hook the previous evening. The *Swordfish*, 97 days from Whampoa, had been outsailed by the *Stag Hound*, which took only 87 days. On the other hand, the *Surprise* was 98 days from Shanghai, but her time from Anjier was within two days of that of the *Stag Hound*.

The relative speed of the *Samuel Russell* and *N. B. Palmer* had been a much discussed question. Some light was thrown on the problem this year. On the 27th of April five vessels were gathered at Anjier, bound for New York and Boston. Four of them were full clippers; the *Samuel Russell*, *N. B. Palmer*, *Wild Pigeon* and barque *Comet*. The fifth was the fast sailing pre-clipper ship, *Joshua Bates*. It was an ideal combination to test the qualities of five vessels of distinctive design and the outcome was in the nature of an "upset."

When the *Palmer* was laid down for A. A. Low & Brother she was not only larger but was intended to be faster than the *Russell*, as, under certain conditions, she undoubtedly was. However the cunning of Captain Nat, who designed the *Russell* strictly with a view to the Canton route, was in evidence here, for she arrived off the Hook on the 26th of July, two days ahead of the *Palmer*. Practically in company with the *Palmer* came the *Wild Pigeon*. For 12,000 miles the latter two had fought it out neck and neck, driving every inch of the way. Altogether it was one of the closest and, to the participants, one of the most exciting races of the China course. Five days later the *Joshua Bates* put in her appearance, a creditable performance, considering the measure of her competitors. The barque *Comet* arrived at Boston on the 29th of July.

If 1852 had been the golden, carefree year of reckless achievement and fabulous profits in the beautiful new clippers, 1853 was the year of records. Twelve months had been sufficient to double the number of swift ships afloat, while it had not as yet instilled the lesson of economy in spars and canvas to any perceptible extent. More important passages were made during 1853 than during any similar period of sailing ship history and a surprising number of the marks then set still stand, undefeated and unequalled. One of the best beats of the year was the run of the *Northern Light* against the clipper *Contest*.

Wm. E. Brewster of "Stunington" had the *Contest*, a beautiful ship later burned by the *Alabama*. At 3.00 P.M., Saturday March 12, he got under way at San Francisco and stood out to sea with a fine following breeze bound for New York. The next afternoon the *Northern Light* was off after him, having cleared for Boston, and Freeman Hatch notes that he dropped his pilot at 5 P.M. Accordingly the start of the ships from the Heads must have been almost exactly 24 hours apart. The result should have gone a long way toward burying the superstition against Sunday sailings.

Both ships had the very unusual run of 14 days to the Line. Thereafter the *Northern Light* gained one day on the *Contest* and on her 38th day out she was off the Horn with her opponent in sight, dimly discernible through the murk and snow of the early Antarctic winter. The encounter is thus referred to in the log of the *Contest*:

"Apr. 20—Lat 56.30 S. Lon 66.22 W—Comes in with moderate breezes, cloudy and light snow squalls (Latterpart) moderate breezes from SW with light snow squalls. Saw ship Northern Light.

"Apr. 21—Lat 54.09 S. Lon 60.40 W—Latter, fresh gales and good weather. in company with her.

"Apr. 22—Lat 50.57 S. Lon 54.20 W—Fresh gales and pleasant. Middle, very squally. Latter more pleasant but not suitable to carry light sails—24 miles current NNE. Northern Light two points abaft the beam.

"Apr. 23—Lat 48.32 S. Lon 50.16 W.—Comes in moderate—Latter squally with snow and rain. Northern Light 15 miles astern."

Apparently the two ships did not sight each other again during the voyage, but from this point to the Equator the honors were even. On the 12th of May the noon position of the *Contest* was 15 miles, and that of the *Northern Light* was 46 miles north of the Line, but the latter vessel was approximately 140 miles farther to the Eastward, a position which seems to have resulted in her getting better winds during the rest of the passage.

At 6.00 P.M., May 30th, the *Contest* picked up her pilot to the Southeast of the Jersey Highlands and an hour and a half later sighted the Highlands, 80 days from San Francisco. Two days earlier the *Northern Light* had picked up her pilot at 10 in the evening five miles outside of Boston Light, and Seth Doane, first officer, entered in her log:

"So ends this passage of 76 days and 5 hours from San Francisco."

It would have done no harm if young Doane had underscored the entry, for the run still stands as the sailing record between the two ports after the lapse of more than seventy-five years, while over the grave of his captain the mosses of forty summers obscure the legend:

"FREEMAN HATCH

1820–1889

"He became famous making the astonishing passage in clipper ship Northern Light, from San Francisco to Boston in 76 days, 6 hours—an achievement won by no mortal before or since."

Three weeks before the finish of this race another and only slightly less spectacular contest had ended off Sandy Hook. This was the match between the *Comet* and *Flying Dutchman*, both Webb ships. Captain E. C. Gardner in the *Comet* sailed from San Francisco on the 13th of February for New York, discharging his pilot at 6 P.M., just 23 hours behind Hubbard in the *Flying Dutchman*, bound for the same port.

Both ships had extraordinary runs to the Equator, that of the *Dutchman* being approximately 11½ days, apparently the record for this crossing, while the time of the *Comet* was a few hours longer. They were off the Horn only a few hours apart, the *Dutchman* in 37 days and the *Comet* in 38. At the Atlantic crossing the *Dutchman* was three days in the lead. Thereafter the *Comet* slowly closed up the gap, taking her pilot 33 miles from Sandy Hook at noon, May 7th. The *Dutchman* made the land at 3.00 P.M. the same day off Little Egg Harbor, the loser by some thirty hours.

A story of the race by a passenger on the *Comet* is extant which tells of repeated encounters between the two vessels on the voyage, with new prodigies of sail carrying to mark the meetings. No mention of this appears in the log of either ship. It was a fine piece of rivalry, however, and a worthy prelude to the run of the *Comet* over the same course in '55 when she lowered her time to 76 days, a mark which still stands as the record between San Francisco and New York.

Somewhat more than a month before the *Northern Light* established her record, the *Staffordshire* had entered Boston port, setting a new standard over the Calcutta course. Captain Richardson left Saugor on the 25th of January and arrived at his destination slightly more than 83 days later, although for some reason the passage is entered in the log as 82 days. It was remarkably fine sailing and the time has been equalled by only three or four of the many hundreds of fine ships which have since made the run. Nevertheless it stood for a few weeks only. The ship was already on her way which was to establish the record that has never been defeated.

On the 13th of April the *Witch of the Wave*, with Benjamin Tay in command, left Saugor, also bound for Boston. She reached port on the 3rd of July in the magnificent passage of 81 days. In the course of the voyage she ran from Sand Heads to the Cape of Good Hope in 37 days, equalling the time of the *Typhoon* the previous year and establishing a double record which appears never to have been equalled again by any ship under sail, although the *Hurricane* later matched her passage to the Cape.

One could go on to mention a host of other excellent records. There was the clipper barque *Nimrod*, which arrived at Port Phillip on August 21st in a passage from Rio, which Captain Nichols reported as 36 days. On the Pacific, the barque *Mermaid* had gone from Batavia to San Francisco in the then record time of 50 days, in the course of which she ran from the coast of China to the Golden Gate in 30 days, which would seem to be equal to the record. Her best day was 320 miles. Almost at the same time the three masted clipper schooner *Spray*, Captain Hall, arrived at San Francisco, 57 days from Hobart Town, stated to be the record at the time.

For the first time in history the New York-Liverpool run was made in less than fourteen days. As we have already noted, the honor belongs to the *Sovereign of the Seas*, still under Lauchlan McKay, and fresh from her 82 day triumph on the Honolulu run. Both passages have been described at length, and deservedly so, in articles on clipper ships. With her builder, Donald McKay, on board, the *Sovereign of the Seas* arrived at Liverpool on the 2nd of July, 13 days and 19 hours from Sandy Hook, or 13 days and 23 hours from dock to dock. Her time from the Banks to Cape Clear was six days. The run is the more remarkable for the reason that June is generally unfavorable for fast passages across the Atlantic.

It seems doubtful indeed whether the ship was ever built that could pass the *Sovereign of the Seas* under proper trim in strong plain sail breezes, with Lauchlan McKay in command.

Few tragedies of the sea made a deeper impression on contemporaries than the loss of the *Staffordshire* on the 30th of December, of this year. It was a gloomy ending to a year of unparalleled achievement by ships of the sail.

After her remarkable run from Calcutta, the *Staffordshire* had been put on the transatlantic route, owing to the stagnation of both the California and Australian trade. Returning from Liverpool in December with approximately 180 Irish immigrants, she encountered extremely heavy gales on the Banks. On the 24th of the month her steering gear was disabled, and a few days later she carried away her massive bowsprit with all the gear attached, and again smashed her temporary steering gear.

While directing the work of clearing away the wreckage, Captain Richardson fell from the fore rigging to the deck and injured his spine. Suffering intensely, he was placed on the cabin table, where he continued to direct the navigation of the ship. On the second night after the accident, as a result of a miscalculation of position, the ship struck on Blonde Rock, several miles from Cape Sable. She filled rapidly and went down with a loss of 170 persons, principally immigrants. Captain Richardson refused to be saved and went down with his ship. So died a brave man, one of the most accomplished seamen of his day, faithful to the high tradition of the sea.

A tragedy of another sort befell the beautiful *Golden Eagle*.

She was an extreme clipper, fresh from the yard of Hayden &
Cudworth, who turned out so many first class racing ships. Her
story is best told in the letter received early in March, 1853, by
her owners, Wm. Lincoln & Co., of Boston. Captain Fabens
wrote:

"OFF RIO JANEIRO, Jan. 20th.

"We had a favorable passage till our arrival in latitude
38.02 south, and longitude 48.14 west, 36 days out, when,
during a hard gale from the west and southwestward, we
shipped a tremendous sea forward, which instantly crashed
in the gratings over the head, breaking off or splitting all the
knees, breast hooks, etc., above the main deck, opening the
top gallant forecastle, tearing off the main rail, and stripping
all the outer planking above the main deck as far as the cat
heads. This unfortunate accident took place between 5 and
6 o'clock, A.M., and as I was on deck at the time, the ship
was at once put before the wind to examine the damage.

.   .   .   .

"We were doing exceedingly well, and at the time of our
accident, were four days ahead of the *Flying Cloud*'s first
passage, the shortest run known, and under usual circumstances should have reached Cape Horn in 43 days from
Boston."

Captain Fabens further reported that he found it was impossible to repair the ship at sea, and the wind being strong, dead
ahead, he put back to Rio. Mr. Gregory, the mate, relieved the
tension to his own satisfaction at least, if not to Captain Fabens',
by dashing off a poem:

"We were bound for California
For our pockets full of tin,
But we're putting back to Rio
With our bows stove in."

As Hayden & Cudworth's ships were noted for strength of
build and fastening, one can readily understand that Fabens must

have been carrying sail to wreck his ship in this manner. It is extremely unfortunate that the accident occurred, as it put an end to Fabens' hopes of making a new world's record—a feat he was in an excellent position to accomplish, since he was due to round the Horn in the season normally favorable for rapid passages. It was only another of the numerous heartbreaking experiences common to the life of every clipper ship and clipper captain.

Several weeks later another new California packet was undergoing a similar trial. She was the *Golden State*, like the *Golden Eagle*, an extreme clipper. Captain Doty also wrote his owners from Rio Janeiro:

> "RIO JANEIRO, March 18, 1853.
>
> "I have arrived here at anchor on the 16th at 5 P.M., and have the misfortune to inform you that on the night of 18th Feb., ten days out from New York, in a sudden whirlwind, carried away all three topmasts with everything attached.
>
> "This ship has proved herself a remarkably fast sailer, having made, the day previous to her disaster, 327 miles, good observation, under royals. The third day out from New York came up with and passed the ship *Northern Crown* (from New York for San Francisco) and in eight hours left her out of sight. Next day, wind S.E., fell in with ship *Ariel*, from New York for China, and in nine hours beat her out of sight to leeward.
>
> "In six days after losing spars had set all sail possible— nothing above fore and mizen topsails single reefed, as they were set on spare top gallant masts. Made Rio in 36 days, and would have made it in 26 if could have set sail, as weather was mild.
>
> L. F. DOTY."

A decided expansion, geographically speaking, had taken place in the building of sharp ships. Prior to '53 an overwhelming majority of clippers had been built in New York and Eastern Massachusetts, principally around Boston and on the Merri-

mac. Maine now entered the lists in a substantial way, con-
tributing no less than twenty-eight beautiful clippers during the
year, many of which later ranked high among the most famous
ships in history, and one of which, the *Ocean Herald* of Damariscotta, registered originally nearly 2400 tons.

Six ships were built in Connecticut—four of them in the
little village of Mystic; the *Electric, Pamparo, Hound* and *David
Crockett,* the latter of which was still in service as a coal barge
up to the very close of the last century. Three were launched
at Warren, Rhode Island. Baltimore produced six, three of
which, the *Flora Temple, Kate Hooper* and *Pride of the Sea,*
were ships ranging from fourteen to nineteen hundred tons.
East Dennis, Massachusetts, launched the beautiful *Belle of the
West* on a little tidal creek barely wide enough to float the ship,
and as these lines are penned, Captain Hall, her first mate, now
nearly 90 years of age, sits on the veranda of his summer home
overlooking the spot that gave her birth, perhaps the last sur-
viving officer of the veritable clipper ship period. *Neptune's
Car,* destined to become famous for a day, was built at Portsmouth, Virginia, the first and apparently the only large clipper
built in that state. The *Sea Nymph,* also the first vessel of this
type to be built on Buzzards Bay, was launched at Fairhaven.

Less than ten years had elapsed since shipbuilders from
Maine to Florida had chuckled over the temerity of New York
in laying down one small clipper for the China trade.

George Steers, who designed the *America,* was becoming interested in clipper ships. During '53 he made a model of a 2500
ton ship very much like the *America,* but improved in various
particulars, and calculated to sail at least twenty-two miles an
hour. A reporter for the New York *Herald* included a description of the model in a lengthy interview with the designer, published in the Sunday edition, November 6th, 1853. He says:

> "Like the *America,* her keel tapers from the stern to the
> stem, 'growing fine by degrees, and beautifully less,' and her

'fore foot' is cut away—that is, the angle formed at the bottom of the bow and junction of the keel in other vessels, is completely rounded off, and the entire line along the bottom of the keel, beginning at the helm, and ending at the top of her prow in nothing, is almost one beautiful curve. She is thus far deeper behind than before.

"Like the *America*, too, her stern is sharp and tapering as well as the bow, that being necessary for easy clearance of the water, as the sharpness of the bow is for easy entrance; but, though the portion of it under water is made quite thin, the edge is not raked or cut away underneath, like the bow, but is nearly straight up and down, thus presenting a large area of perpendicular surface as a balance of resistance to the water, for the resistance of the almost perpendicular surface of the side of her bow at the lee-side, caused by the pressure of the wind on the sails, aided by the fact of the weather bow being raised out of water when the ship is going fast, and therefore presenting little or no resistance to her tendency to turn round into the wind: what is cut away therefore from her bow is added to her stern. All this is contrary to the English models, which are nearly perpendicular in the stem, while the stern is raked. They are also bluff in the bows.

"Again, the model of the proposed ship is like the *America's* in being neither wall-sided and rounded at the bottom, nor bellied, but straight from the waterline to the keel, thus presenting the strongest kind of side resistance to the water. The model is also very wide and shallow, giving great stability. It tapers so beautifully from the center that the eye cannot find the exact central spot—'just like the well formed leg of a woman,' from which Mr. Steers says he borrowed his idea."

It is to be regretted that Steers never found a merchant sufficiently venturesome to build a ship from this design, since he had evidently retained many of the features of the Baltimore clipper type, and in addition had forecast much that is still embodied in modern yachts and fast fishing schooners. Such a ship would doubtless have proved remarkably speedy under normal weather conditions, whatever her capacities might prove to be when tested off Cape Horn or on the Australian turnpike.

Merchants, however, were becoming conservative. There was a vague feeling of uncertainty and unrest in the air. A tremendous tonnage of new clippers had been launched. By the end of the year the number of new ships of this type alone would total 120, while scores of clipper barques and smaller fry served to swell the tonnage of sharp ships, expensive to build and costly to operate.

The effect of this enormous output was strikingly illustrated in the harbor of New York toward the end of the year. On the 10th of November there were no less than twelve new clipper ships loading at the various piers, not one of which had ever been to sea. The list included such well known names as the *Chief of Clippers, Electric, Lightfoot, Edwin Forrest, David Crockett, Quickstep, Golden Fleece, David Brown, Dreadnought, Pride of America* and *Lookout*. There were also in port and loading at the same time a very considerable number of old clippers, some preparing for their second, others for their fourth or fifth voyage around the world. The *Great Republic,* 4555 tons, the largest clipper ever built, had been launched by Donald McKay on the 4th of October and was soon to begin loading. Her partial destruction by fire at New York the night after Christmas was the outstanding tragedy of the year in the marine world where tragedies were all too frequent. Among the ships to suffer with her was the beautiful *White Squall*.

The year had witnessed the clearing from eastern ports of 145 of these fine ships for San Francisco alone. Large numbers had also sailed for Australia. From both these points word had come back of most depressing conditions. It was evident that for some time only a very moderate amount of freight would be offered for those places. Meanwhile the ships had to be kept busy.

Warnings had not been wanting. Quite early in the year the clipper ships began to enter the detested guano trade on a large scale. The late Fall saw scores of them gathered in Callao or at the Chinchas, loading or waiting their turn at the chutes. Toward the end of the year it was reported that 130 ships, sharp and full built, were there at one time and that some of them would have to be there for months awaiting their turn. Among these were such beautiful creations as the *Flying Eagle, Radiant, Witchcraft, Hornet, Sirocco, Empress of the Seas,* and a score of famous princesses of the blood. Many other fine new clippers were put into the cotton or lumber trade on their first voyages. Fine, useful work, but—speed was a handicap.

Not even the diversion of some of these lovely craft to the wretched coolie trade, or the musky taint of the African slave trade, bespoke more clearly the end of the golden era of the Yankee clipper than this participation in the sordid guano business or the humdrum existence of lumber and cotton droughing. Whatever the future might hold of marvellous records, of unsurpassed and unsurpassable gallantry of ships and men—and much was still to come—the glorious, carefree days were over. Henceforth it was a struggle, the end of which became clearer with each passing year, in which speed and sheer beauty were penalized and the race went once more to the prosaic mud horse.

As in other developments since time began, nothing was to happen suddenly or in a spectacular way. Probably, as a matter of fact, nothing spectacular ever does happen, but events seem so only to the young and to those of limited mental outlook. The glorious pageant of ships of the sail was passing—a little nibbling here, a little undermining there by a power that did not have its source in the four winds of heaven—and the white sails would disappear entirely from all commercial lanes.

Steam was coming along. Griffiths was building a "seven day steamship" for the Galway run—a light, shallow craft, of wood and iron, called the *William Morris.* It was more prophetic than successful. Steers was trying to interest capital in a "six day boat" to be from 500 to 1000 feet in length. The difference of a few hundred feet, more or less, seemed less material then than now.

Slowly but surely concrete facts regarding steam power were coming to light. When the *Surprise* started on her homeward voyage from Shanghai this year the brand new tug *Confucius* passed her the bight of her unchristened hawser and started down the river with her first tow. The P. & O. steamship line had long since initiated and was maintaining a regular service to China from London. In England also a new steamship company had been formed called the "General Screw Steamship Company." It built two full rigged clipper ships and equipped them with feathering screws and auxiliary steam power. One of these, the *Harbinger,* went to Melbourne early in '53, in seventy days, including six days spent in re-coaling, so that her actual running time was sixty-four days—an unheard of thing. The second ship of the new line, the *Argo,* did even better. She went to Melbourne and back by way of the Cape of Good Hope in the actual running time under steam and canvas, of one hundred and twenty-one days. Her consumption of coal during the entire time averaged seventeen tons a day.

It was a challenge to sail, and one which was nobly met in '54. As a matter of fact, these first auxiliary vessels were both clippers and steamers, with all the expense of operation pertaining to both types. They were not a success, financially, and when the fine new clippers built by Deacon Thomas down in Rockland and Donald McKay, in East Boston, and others, were put in service the following year, it was evident their passages would fall little short of the steamship runs. The experiment, however, pointed the way, and eventually steamers were developed which were able to compete successfully with sailing craft on these long runs, in cost of operation as well as in speed.

There was also a growing dissatisfaction with sailing ships in the passenger trade.

Toward the close of 1853, the conditions of the transatlantic packet service were little short of appalling. The generally unpleasant features of this traffic—for it was nothing else—have frequently been referred to, but words give a pale conception of the facts. One can only faintly conceive the results of crowding a mass of humanity composed of from 700 to 1000 unwashed and unwashable individuals, on a deck less than 200 feet in length. In ideal weather, conditions were deplorable: in bad weather, with battened hatches, they were indescribable. The law allowed each passenger space of two by seven feet—barely enough from which to be buried.

In November, the fine packet *Constellation* arrived in New York, having lost exactly one hundred of her passengers at sea, out of a total of 922. Twenty-eight ships which arrived about this time, with passenger lists aggregating 13,762 immigrants, lost 1141 on the way over.

It is something of a commentary on the times that nothing was done about the matter, and what is, perhaps, more significant, the thought of adopting corrective measures appears to have occurred to no one. Nevertheless, such a condition was bound to affect unfavorably the future of the sailing packets. An immediate result was to increase the patronage of the steamships, which, because of their higher rates, were not so overcrowded, and which also made much shorter passages to the westward.

There were, it is true, several fine sailing packets put afloat this year, but there appears to have been no attempt in their design to alleviate the harsh conditions of steerage travel. By all odds the most noted of these new ships was the *Dreadnought* She was launched in October from the yard of Currier and Townsend at Newburyport. Her owners were E. E. Morgan, F. B. Cutting, David Ogden and others operating the "Red Cross" line between New York and Liverpool.

The *Dreadnought* was regarded as a clipper ship, although her claim to this classification appears to be based largely on her heavy rig and the qualifications of her commander, Captain Samuels, rather than her lines. In respect to hull she was more akin to the sharp built packets of the day rather than to the clippers. Her cargo capacity was 2000 tons, while her registry under the old rules was only 1413 tons, and, of course, considerably less under the new rules.

Captain Samuels was a driver, however, and the *Dreadnought* was built to carry sail "packet fashion." Reference to her logs shows that her long series of excellent passages was due to the ability of her master to maintain a good average speed rather than to any phenomenal runs. The writer has not noted any day's run exceeding 345 miles, and she has few runs of 300 miles to her credit—a thing which would hardly be expected of a true clipper ship operating year after year on the Western Ocean. Her first eight passages to the westward averaged 24½ days, as against the 26 day average of Palmer's old *Roscius* of 1839.

Few ships were better built or more ably commanded than the *Dreadnought*, and while she broke no records—her reputed 9 day crossing apparently having no foundation in fact (see note),—she maintained her schedule for years with greater regularity, perhaps, than any canvas-back liner then afloat. Even today her story, interestingly told in Captain Samuels' autobiography, remains one of the most colorful to be found in all the records of the sea.

CHAPTER XXVII

1854

COMMERCIAL DEPRESSION

THE pendulum which had started its upward swing a full decade before, came waveringly to a halt in '53, and by the beginning of 1854, had definitely reversed itself. In the ten year interval approximately 270 full rigged ships of clipper mould had been set afloat, besides a huge flotilla of barques and lesser craft. Of these, 125 or nearly half the total number of ships, and more than half the total in tonnage had been launched in '53.

When one considers that even now the volume of "express" is infinitesimal compared with the aggregate movement of commodities, it can readily be appreciated that this was a heavy increase in the facilities for handling merchandise which could afford to pay a substantial premium for speedy delivery. Under the conditions then prevailing, commerce was simply incapable of putting this tonnage to an efficient use. The surprising thing, to the casual observer from the vantage point of four score years, is that clippers continued to be built at all. Their initial cost was greater, their capacity smaller, and, since they required larger crews, and made use of an immensely greater quantity of canvas and cordage, their operation was far more expensive than that of full built ships. Why then should merchants continue to lay down clipper keels?

The answer is indicated by the fact that although the charges for fast freight were rapidly approaching the level of ordinary freight, merchants for several reasons still preferred the clipper, and between two available vessels other things being equal, chose the one they believed the faster. In times when charters were scarce, a chronic condition after the summer of '53, this was an obvious advantage. It was, however, far more of an advantage to the shipowner, whose craft combined in the highest degree the appearance and sailing qualities of a clipper, with the full bodied storage room of an ordinary freighter.

A fact of this sort was self evident to the merchant of 1853, faced with the loss of a large portion of his highly profitable California and Australian business. As frequently happens when new problems in efficiency present themselves, the first corrective impulse overshot the mark. The year 1854 was marked by the output of a considerable number of new ships "outfitted in mongrel fashion with clipper tops and full bottoms." Above the load line they presented the graceful sheer and attractive curves of a veritable clipper, but when it came to sailing they were little, if anything, better than the ordinary cotton or lumber drougher.

It did not take long for both shippers and builders to discover the fallacy in this particular example of applied logic and thereafter the designers once more devoted their efforts to a practical modification of the best clipper lines, rather than to beautifying the humble drougher. The result was the development during the next few years of a very fine type of vessel which combined to a rare degree, the beauty and speed of the extreme clipper with the huge stowage capacity of the old packet ships. Many of these later vessels, including the *Andrew Jackson* of Mystic, the *Mary Whitridge* and *Carrier Dove* of Baltimore, and *Flying Mist* of Medford, were not only very burdensome but very beautiful ships, which made runs that are records to this day.

All this, however, was something for shipowner, merchant and builder to wrack their brains about. However intimately it might concern the master in his capacity as agent and part owner while he lay in port and waited for laggard charters, once he was at sea, he had no thought but to send his ship along. The clouds were gathering; the long descent toward oblivion had begun, but the true situation was suspected by few and admitted by none. Superficially viewed, the ship of the sail was sweeping on to a glorious future. In a twelvemonth the number of clippers had almost doubled. American ships had never been so newly bright, so stout, so numerous, so marvellously lovely as in 1854. Half the clipper fleet had been less than a year at sea— barely long enough to set up their rigging and give them that indescribable appearance about which old sailors were to romance for many a long year, to the disgust of cocky younger knights of fid and hand spike.

Bright, new, taut and confident, the Yankee clipper of '54 swept the seas as they had never been swept since the triremes of Rome smashed Carthaginian galleys. Record fell before record. The most powerful sailing craft the world had ever seen had barely nailed her broomstick to the mast before another and seemingly more powerful ship appeared to excel her achievement.

The beautiful new *Red Jacket* led off with her still unparalleled performance, leaving New York on the morning of the 10th of January and arriving off the Bell Buoy on the 22nd— twelve days out. She anchored in Liverpool exactly 13 days, one hour and 25 minutes from New York.

In six consecutive days her poorest run was 300 miles, while her average for the period was slightly over 343 miles. On the 19th of January it was reported on excellent authority that

> "The main brace was spliced on the strength of four hundred and thirteen miles, being the greatest distance ever run in twenty-four hours by anything afloat."

In view of the previous performance of the *Sovereign of the Seas* it is doubtful whether the excuse assigned for the ceremony paid due regard to historical accuracy, but there is no question as to its being good and sufficient.

A Maine ship, the *Red Jacket*, built by good old Deacon Thomas and captained by a Cape Cod boy, Asa Eldridge, of the stout old packet *Roscius*, and soon to go down with the ill-fated *Pacific*, the pride of Collin's Line.

The Liverpool papers commented in generous terms on the *Red Jacket* and her remarkable exploit. Regarding the ship herself the Liverpool *Journal* of January 28 remarked:

> "The *Red Jacket* in general appearance of hull, spars, rigging and deck arrangements is very much after the style of the celebrated *Sovereign of the Seas;* but she appears to have rather more 'Spring' forward and she certainly has more outside ornament in the shape of a full length figure head, and an elaborate design in gilt work on her stern extending also down each side of the rudder."

All things considered, it was a triumph such as few ships or captains have enjoyed. Nevertheless, the ink was hardly dry on the news print of the details before another ship had surpassed the record in one important particular.

Donald McKay had made a sale. This was nothing new for him, but in the volume of tonnage and character of ships, it stands unique in clipper ship annals. In addition to a couple of fine medium clippers rising 2000 tons which he already had under construction, the *Japan* and *Commander Perry*, he contracted in 1853 to build for James Baines four clippers ranging from 2000 to 2500 tons in size, to be the swiftest ships under sail.

The first of these new ships, the *Lightning*, was launched at East Boston on the 3rd of January, exactly one week before the *Red Jacket* sailed. So far as may be gathered from a comparison of what appears to be a substantial majority of the extreme clipper lines and models in existence, the *Lightning* had the sharpest entrance lines of any clipper ever built in America. Her design was like that of no other large clipper ever built, but it may be noted from the reproduction of the model elsewhere in this book that several features of the entrance and run somewhat resembled lines of the yacht *America*. In other important respects, of course, there was no resemblance, since the heavy after drag of the *America* was lacking and her extreme dead rise had been eliminated.

When the *Lightning* followed the *Red Jacket* across to Liverpool in February she covered 436 nautical miles in 24 hours, surpassing the previous record of the *Red Jacket* by 23 miles. Although this often is accepted as the flood tide mark for ships of the sail, it had already been beaten by the *Marco Polo* and later by the 465 mile run of the *Champion of the Seas*.

More than a generation was to elapse before this run was equalled by a steamship.

In the Spring of '54, as Europe was setting the Crimean stage with its Sebastapol and Light Brigade, its pageantry of new untried fleets of steam frigates and glinting, golden thread of Florence Nightingale's sacrifice, the last of the Cape Horners of '53 came pouring through the Golden Gate—three, four, five and even six tall clippers in an afternoon. On the 25th of January, the *Onward* rounded the Heads followed closely by the *Ocean Pearl, Kingfisher, Bald Eagle, Courier,* and *Pampero,* fine ships, all. The *Kingfisher,* under Crosby, and the *Bald Eagle,* in command of Caldwell, had sailed a notable race. Caldwell had left New York on the first of October and Crosby passed Boston Light two days later. They fought it out almost jibboom to jibboom for 17,000 miles and entered San Francisco almost within hailing distance of each other.

A similar scene took place on the 8th of February when four of the smartest little clippers of the fleet romped in, yard arm to yard arm, in one of the most evenly matched contests ever staged. The *Matchless* under Symes Potter and the *Ringleader* under Matthews had sailed from Boston on the 21st of October. The *Golden City,* commanded by Richard Canfield, left New York two days later, followed by the beautiful new *San Francisco* under Captain Setzer on the 25th of the month.

Here were four ships, three of them new, and all exceedingly sharp, heavily sparred vessels leaving eastern ports within a period of 96 hours. They were frequently in sight of one another during the voyage and entered port at intervals of an hour or two apart. All that is, except the *San Francisco,* which had made the best run of them all, taking her pilot on the 105th day out. In entering the harbor she missed stays and went ashore, becoming a complete wreck. All four ships had made the passage in less than 110 days—a fact which indicates not only the extent of the rivalry between them, but serves to classify them among the speediest of the smaller clippers. The *San Francisco* was the largest of the four and, measured by modern methods, she would rate a scant thousand tons.

Two new champions appeared off the Golden Gate in March. They were the *Romance of the Seas,* built by McKay, and the *David Brown,* built by Roosevelt & Joyce, who had succeeded the famous Brown & Bell firm. Again it was Boston against New York and this time George Brewster against Dumaresq.

The ships were almost evenly matched as to size, the *Romance* being somewhat larger and of a slightly longer and leaner type than the *David Brown.* Brewster sailed from New York on the 13th of December at 8:00 A.M. and Dumaresq left Boston three days later. At the Horn the *David Brown* was four days in the lead, but thereafter the *Romance* gained steadily, catching up to her in the North Pacific and leading her into port by a margin of a few hours only. Both ships arrived out on March 23rd, the time of the *Romance* being 96 days, against 99 for *David Brown.*

It is interesting to note that in continuance of this rivalry, both ships sailed for Hong Kong on the 31st of March in company and arrived in port after a passage of 45 days with the *Romance* one hour in the lead. She had been able to cut in ahead of her rival by bringing up the breeze just off the port.

Some conception of the close competition which obtained between these two ships may be gained from the following entries in the log of the *David Brown* on the run across the Pacific:

"April 1—Small breezes. At 2.00 P.M. all hands and pilot being on board purchased our anchor and side by side with ship *"Romance of the Sea"* steamed down and at 5:30 found ourselves outside the Golden Gate and clear of the Bar. Having made sail while coming down the Bay and discharged steam tug before and worked the ship out over the bar under canvas. Tugg being too light to handle the ship— *Romance* having the best boat is now, as I discharge pilot (5:30 P.M.)—five miles ahead—braced forward on the wind and set all sail to the SSW. At 9:00 P. M. came up and kept off to pass under the lee of the *Romance* Midnight Foggy. At 9:00 A. M. (April 2) Fogg lifted when the *Romance* was discovered 12 miles astern. As we came out of port last evening and stood out from the land saw many right whales about.

"April 2—1st Small airs baffling WNW to WSW. 2 and 3 calm with Fogg. Ends light and pleasant from W by S. At 10:00 A.M. could just see the *Romance* from the miz. royal yard astern. At 12 M last sight of her. altogether. Several fin backs around.

"May 16—5:00 P. M. Made Padro Blanco N. 8 miles. At 1:00 A. M. passed in through Lema Channel. At 2:30 took pilot. At daylight off Lemma Cal. a large clipper ship (the 1st vessel we have seen since leaving San Francisco) was seen 4 miles astern coming up with a breeze while we were becalmed and at about 9:00 A. M. the above ship passed to windward of us while we were still becalmed and proved to be the *Romance of the Sea* who carried the breeze along with him while we were becalmed and anchored at Hong Kong at 11:45 A. M. At 12.15 to 12.30 we anchored close to her— all well."

Thereafter the *Romance* went to Whampoa and the *David Brown* to Shanghai, both ships loading for London. The *Romance* sailed June 9th, entering in at London on September 21st, a run of 104 days lacking a few hours. Brewster took his departure from Shanghai the 11th of July and on August 18th went hard and fast on a reef in the Straits of Sunda, running his bow three feet out of water and twisting his forefoot badly.

A few days later he writes:

"August 20—At Anjier—called on the Governor got recruits and went to sea.

"September 14—Lat 35, 19 S. Lon 19.51 E. Stood to West. More moderate but a very turbulent sea causing the ship to labor very heavy—*but she is a beauty in a gale.*

"October 1—Lat. 00.13 N. Lon. 28.07 W pass line at 10:45 A. M. 17 days from the Cape—Praise to God for all mercies.

"October 6—Trimmed sharp by the wind with F. topmost studding sail.

"October 28—Wind S. and latter part W. Brisk gales and fine clear weather all through this day with all sail driving up the channel. At 7:30 P. M. about off the Caskets in sight of Deal. At 3:30 A. M. Beachy Head light was seen from the masthead to the N—by which I find the tide has set me more to the South than I was looking for. At 6:30 Dungenness bore WNW 6 miles. At 7:30 took a Pilot and steered through the Downs and up the River.

"Thus ends up off Tounge Buoy 104 days from Saddle Isles, off the Yang Tse Kiang, 69 days from Anjier, 44 from the Cape and 27 from the Line—altho it is not quite what I was in hopes of doing yet it is not bad when we consider the monsoons against us and the ships forefoot athwartships and copper off and rough.

"To God be all the Praise, for his protecting care."

From which it will be seen that there was on the whole little to choose between the performance of the *Romance* and the *Brown.* Both were worthy good ships and ranked among the fastest of their day. Both were sailed by princes of the quarter deck, in a day when men were compelled to measure their strength and skill against the elements as well as against other individuals.

From the California route in 1854 comes the first clear indication of the slowing up of deep sea commerce, which was to become pronounced in 1855 and would eventually culminate in the debacle of 1857. Fewer clippers were built—69 as against 125 in the preceding year. General shipbuilding went on at a somewhat accelerated pace, but it was in response, largely, to plans and contracts already made.

In spite of the increase in the total number of clippers, only 111 of these ships cleared for San Francisco during the year, as against 145 in 1853. There were, however, many instances of remarkably close sailing.

The *Red Rover, Seaman's Bride* and *Winged Racer* sailed on the 22nd, 23rd and 24th of January respectively. The two latter ships arrived out on May 23rd and the *Red Rover* reached port on the following day, the race going to the *Winged Racer* by a margin of one day over the *Seaman's Bride* and three days over the *Red Rover*.

The *Golden Eagle,* under Fabens, sailed a dead heat with the old *Carrington,* commanded by Captain French. Fabens sailed from New York on March 21st and French left the following day, the ships arriving at San Francisco 124 days out on consecutive days in the order of their sailing.

Typical in the experience of shipmasters was the sailing of the new clipper *Viking,* Captain Linas Winsor, who describes his command as a half clipper drawing 21 feet. He left Boston on March 17th, civil time. His first entry in the log March 18th, sea time, reads:

"First day out all hands, nearly, drunk. At 8:00 the wind changed to Southeast with rain, thunder and lightning.

At 4:00 A.M., the wind changed suddenly to the NW. Shortened sail. Making ice fast. Ship under close reefs blowing a perfect hurricane. Ship all ice, everything, men most froze stiff. Rigging getting slack."

A very unusual run, considering the season, was made by the extreme clipper *Witchcraft*, under Benjamin Freeman. She sailed from New York the 9th of May and anchored in San Francisco harbor the 15th of August. Her run of 98 days has been beaten only once by a ship (the *Flying Cloud*) sailing from the East Coast in the unfavorable month of May and stands otherwise unequalled. It would have been shorter but for the fact she was held off the coast 9 days in calms and light winds.

Palmer, in the *Celestial*, and Kirby in the *Stingray* left Sandy Hook in company on the 29th of July, both ships anchoring at San Francisco on the 8th of December. Kirby sends in his log with the remark:

"Well the *Stingray* is in San Francisco at last after a passage of 129 days, the most tedious I ever made. You will find in some places I have growled a little. *The Celestial* sailed six hours behind me went farther East and beat me to the Equator two days. I caught him again off Cape Horn and both arrived in San Francisco within an hour of each other."

Almost as even was the work of the *Fearless* and the *Ocean Telegraph*, both very sharp extreme clippers, and both, as it happened, designed by Samuel H. Pook. The *Fearless* under Nehemiah Manson left Boston on the 18th of July, and the *Ocean Telegraph*, commanded by George H. Willis, sailed from New York on the 22nd.

The *Fearless* arrived out November 19th, five days before the *Ocean Telegraph*, beating the latter ship by the margin of one day only. A feature of this race was the run reported by the *Fearless* of 15 days from the Line to port. The winning time of 124 days was not remarkable unless one considers the unfavorable season. All the other ships sailing about this time took from four days to two weeks longer on the passage, the very speedy *Contest,* which sailed six days before the *Fearless,* being 128 days on the run.

Stagnation became pronounced in the shipping business during the summer. September saw New York harbor and wharves crowded with waiting vessels, 777 ships in all, including many clippers of the largest size. Similar conditions prevailed in Boston. All the time the shipyards were turning out new vessels. It was estimated that over 300,000 tons were on the stocks in various stages of completion in the early Fall.

As winter approached, there was a temporary revival. England and France—their hands occupied with the Russian Bear— found it expedient to charter American ships in large numbers. Sailings to California again became matters of almost daily occurrence. Petersen in the *Phantom* was off on the 26th of October, one day behind Lane in the *Sweepstakes.* The *Sweepstakes* registered a victory of 24 hours net for the run. Bearse, in the *Winged Arrow* made a remarkable run of 34 days from the Horn to within a day of San Francisco, and then lay for seven days in a dead calm. Richard Canfield, in the *Golden City,* beat Mumford in the *Tornado* one day only.

Canfield had made one false start. When he first sailed on November 25th, certain members of his crew held an informal conference and decided they did not like the looks of the lengthy spars and immensely square yards above them. By the time they were off the Highlands the deck presented an animated scene. Two perfectly good mates were used up, and when Canfield put back for recruits his crew had accumulated an assortment of contusions remarkable for number and quality even in those days.

Although a smaller number of fast passages were made in the California trade in 1854 than during 1853, the clippers actually

"ANDREW JACKSON."

Photo by Louis S. Martel, courtesy, The Marine Historical Association, Inc.

Abstract of a Voyage from New York Towards San Francisco

March		Dist	Latt	Long	Bar	Bar	Air	W	Winds	Winds	Winds
Monday	12		14,23	121,05	30,07	30,12	78		W S	NE to SE ½ E	NE ½ W
Tuesday	13		16,42	124,05	30,05	30,12	76		N N E	N ½ E	N N E
Wednesday	14		20,07	126,36	30,07	30,15	74		N N E	N E ½ W	N E & N E ½ W
Thursday	15		23,37	128,10	30,10	30,17	71		N E ½ W	N E	N E ½ E
Friday	16		24,52	129,26	30,10	30,20	68		N E to N E	N N E	N ½ E
		I am in hopes that to Do as well as the Flying Clouds time									
Saturday	17		26,50	131,46	30,15	30,22	64		N N E	N E ½ W	N ½ W to N E ½ E
Sunday	18		29,34	132,26	30,18	30,25	62		N ½ E	N E & N E ½ E	N E ½ E
Monday	19		32,49	133,56	30,20	30,26	60		N E	N E & N E ½ E	N E to N N E
Tuesday	20		34,05	134,50	30,24	30,26	61		N E to N N E	N E ½ N	N to N N E Calm
Wednesday	21		35,00	133,17	30,07	30,00	62			N N N to S N	S N
On the	22	we are good for the							Flying	Cloud	Yeah
Thursday	22		36,10	128,44	29,82	29,90	52		S N to N	S N & N	N ½ N
Sunday	23		37,24	124,35	30,05	30,15	54		N S N & N	N S N to S N	S N to south

89 Days and 4 hours from New York

FACSIMILE OF THE LAST TWO PAGES OF THE LOG BOOK OF THE CL[IPPER]
TO SAN FRANCISCO, DECEMBER 25, 1859, TO MARCH 23, 18[60]

Ship Andrew Jackson   J E Williams Master

First Part Strong Breeze and Bad Sea from the WNW Sky Sail in Sume of the time
Middle Part More Modrat Latter Part Modrat Breeze and Plesant Weather
First Part Modrat and Plesant Middle Part Strong Breeze Latter Part Strong
Breeze Not a Cloud to be Seene the Sun went Down & Came up Very Read
these 24 hours Strong Breeze and Clear Bad Sea from WSW Sky Sail in from 8 pm
First Part Strong Middle Part Modrat Latter Part Lights and Clouding up
First and Middle Part Very Light and Baffling Latter Part Breging up the Wind is going frost
First Part Modrat Breez & Bad Sea Coming from SW Middle Part Modrat and
Cloudy Latter Part Little Squally Very Bad Sea wind Baffling
First Part Fine Rain Squalls Middle Part Thick but more Steady Latter Part
Modrat and Clearing up Sum Bad Sea from WW and Long Roule from the West
First Part Breging up Strong at 8 pm furled Sky Sail Middle Part Strong Breeze with Bad
Sea Latter Part wind Baffling and Puffey I am in hopes the wind will Come to the west Soon
First Part Strong Breeze and Puffey and Baffling 3 points Middle Part Light and Baffling
at 3 Am backd to the S & E Latter Part Light Air and Calm
First Part Calm Middle Part Light Latter Part Breezing up Strong with Sum Rain
First Part Strong and Squally at 6 30 holed in Studing Sailes at 8 furled Royels and
Top G Sailes Blowing Strong in Squalles Middle Part Hard Squalles with Rain
Latter Part Modrating with Sum Hail Squalles Ends with Main Royal Set
First Part Modrat with Baffling Rain Squalles Middle Part Modrats
& Baffling Latter Part Modrat and Baffling from Courlord Very Light water at
First Part Modrat Breeze at 4 pm Made the Farallones Middle Part
Lights & Calme Latter Part Lights at 7 Am took Pilots

Andrew Jackson KEPT ON HER RECORD PASSAGE FROM NEW YORK
HANDWRITING OF CAPT. JOHN E. WILLIAMS.

"DASHING WAVE."

FROM A PHOTOGRAPH SAID TO HAVE BEEN TAKEN ABOUT 1910. ONE OF THE LAST OF THE CLIPPERS
TO CARRY SAIL.

Reproduced through the courtesy of Mr. Edward S. Clark.

engaged made a somewhat better showing. Approximately 19 per cent went around in 110 days or less, as against 17 per cent the previous year. The number of extremely short passages, moreover, that is, those occupying less than 100 days, totalled six—double the number of similar passages made in any other year. Included in this list was another eighty-nine day run by the *Flying Cloud,* her exact time on this occasion being given as 89 days 8 hours. Continuing her voyage to Hong Kong, the *Flying Cloud* was 37 days, or 127 sailing days from New York, this being the record to this day over this course.

Very, in the *Hurricane,* made a good passage in the poor season. He sailed May 26th, 12 hours behind Barstow in the *Golden State* and beat him 24 days. The last entry in his log reads:

> "September 4—passed between the 'Heads' just 100 days and 12 hours from anchorage in the East River and considering that we sailed on an 'unlucky Friday,' and also 'when the Sun was in the Eclipse,' I am very well satisfied."

It is worth noting that the *Hurricane* had crossed the tropics in the Atlantic in 15 days, 17 hours, and in the Pacific in 15 days 22 hours, averaging slightly more than 8 miles an hour through the latitudes where light breezes normally prevail. She was a very sharp bottomed craft, having 41 inches dead rise and being 9 feet 2 inches through the back bone. On this voyage she drew 21 feet 9 inches aft and 21 feet forward with 1700 tons of cargo weight and measurement, a cargo only slightly in excess of her registered tonnage, and of course considerably less than the nominal 1700 tons in actual dead weight.

Whatever the records of '54 may have lacked in quantity they generously atoned for in quality. It was evident that however discouraging the financial and commercial outlook might be, it could not daunt the tough grist of the old packets. Trained from their youth to buck head seas, foul winds and poverty, the clipper captains never for a moment lost sight of the great goal—a record passage.

Many ships in '54 did as good, but few did a better year's work than the *Swordfish*. Captain Horace Osgood had her. He left New York on the 3rd of April, facing the pleasant prospect of a midwinter passage around the Horn. On the 20th of May he was fighting for westing with one sail going after another, the forecastle battered down and the entire crew mustered in the safest possible place—on deck. When risk of drowning in a forecastle becomes greater than danger on deck, it may be safely assumed that the ship is, as one master mariner grimly noted, "very damp forward." He crossed the Line in the Pacific 78 days 4 hours out, 35 days under the average passage for that season of the year. From California he went to Manila and thence home to New York, anchoring inside the Hook at 11:00 P.M., February 13th. He had been 261 days at sea and had sailed 39,979 miles.

The China and India trade of 1854, affected by very different conditions from those prevailing in California, was eminently satisfactory to Yankee shipowners, however it may have impressed their British confreres. Fourteen American ships cleared this year from China for England, aside from the *Romance of the Sea* and *David Brown* already mentioned. The list included a smaller number than the preceding year, but 12 of them were clippers, such ships as the *Snow Squall, Flying Dutchman, Architect, Archer,* the huge *Lightfoot, Eagle Wing, Gravina* and last, but far from least, the *Golden Gate.*

It was a season unfavorable for fast passages on the whole. The *Snow Squall* made a very long run of 119 days from Shanghai to London during the northeast monsoon. Ships were scarce along the China coast and freights were high—7£ to London and $24.00 to New York. Ashbel Hubbard piloted the *Flying Dutchman* from Macao to London, anchoring at Gravesend at 6:00 P.M. the 24th of May, a run of 98 days. Most of the other ships made out of season passages varying in length from the 112 days of the *Architect* to the 121 days of the *Lightfoot*. The *Lightfoot* was one of the largest ships which had ever loaded tea and moreover was very lofty, carrying a main moonsail and royal stunsails. When she arrived at London drawing 20 feet, she was, in common with several other extreme clippers rigged with a spritsail. She had to anchor in the river several days before getting a tide sufficiently high to permit entering the dock.

Captain E. H. Linnell still had the beautiful *Eagle Wing*. He left Foo Chow July 31st for London. The 10th of the following month he shortened sail for an approaching typhoon and his log tells the story:

> "During the heaviest of the weather ran NE 38 miles, the sea being hove up in grate confushion. Ends more moderate—made low sail."

Linnell's spelling, like Grant's whiskey, may be forgiven him for somewhat similar reasons. He was soon to set a mark that many an able mariner, British and American, was to shoot at in vain.

To a world accustomed by now to spectacular achievements the American-British tea trade of '54 would have closed in rather a dull fashion, if it were not for the remarkable work of the *Golden Gate*, under Samuel F. Dewing. Her actual time under sail from Shanghai to Beachy Head was 86 days, a record that seems never to have been equalled.

She left Shanghai on November 22, was detained several days by a collision with the barque *Homer* in the China Sea, and was anchored for five days in the fog at Beachy Head. So far as available information shows, this run has never been equalled. It is especially worthy of note that on this voyage the *Golden Gate* was reported to have surpassed by a wide margin the run usually given as the best day's work ever performed in the China trade. (See *e.g. Encyclopædia Britannica*, 14th Ed., Article on clipper ships.)

A partial account of the trip is contained in a letter written by one of the officers of the ship:

"BATAVIA, Dec. 6. Since leaving Shanghai we have made three days runs of 350, 360 and 380 miles by observation. We sailed on the 22nd of November in company with the clipper ship *Surprise* for New York. Capt. Ranlett having charts that brought him into Formosa by a cut through the islands, the *Surprise* got the lead; but on the 24th the lookout sang out "Sail ho, right ahead, upper sails just above the horizon" at 9:00 A. M.

"We continued to gain on her; at 12 we made her out to be the *Surprise;* at Sundown she was about 8 miles ahead, with a fine fresh breeze, slightly quartering, carrying royal steering sails on both sides; at 10 P. M. we passed her close alongside (did not speak) and at 12 his lights were out of sight astern. When we passed the *Surprise* we were making a round 15 good making our 380 miles at meridian next day; had we not lost our jibboom &c., (she was fouled by another ship) "90 days would have been all the time we should have taken to reach London. Our ship was sailing against several English clippers, viz.: *Spirit of the Age, Lady Hotchkiss* and *Northfleet*—all crack vessels, who boasted they could beat us without difficulty."

As this was the occasion on which the *Surprise* made the run of 68 days from Shanghai to the Equator, it can be seen that the *Golden Gate* must have been exceptionally fast to pass her in the above manner. It may be said that if the *Surprise* had maintained the same rate of speed after passing the Line in the Atlantic as before, she would in all probability have equalled the record for all time on the Shanghai run. Her chance was spoiled by twenty days continuous head gales after passing Bermuda.

Another England to China record was hung up this year by the *Comet* under command of Captain Gardiner. She sailed from Liverpool loaded with coal for Hong Kong. Coal is perhaps one of the poorest cargoes imaginable to develop the speed of a ship. Nevertheless, the *Comet* made the run in five days less time than the previous record and only one day over the record for all time.

The Hong Kong *Register* contains the following account of her work:

"THE QUICKEST PASSAGE ON RECORD—The American clipper *Comet,* of 1836 tons, Capt. Gardiner coal laden, arrived in this harbor (Hong Kong) on Saturday, September 9, from Liverpool, having made the passage in less than 85 days —the fastest yet recorded. We have been furnished with the annexed particulars:

" 'The *Comet* left her anchorage on the 16th of June, at 1 P.M. and anchored in Hong Kong Harbor on 9th September at 1 P.M., making 86–16/24 days meantime from anchor to anchor, and 83–21/24 days from pilot to pilot. She sailed in straight course, from noon to noon, 17,500 geographical miles, making an average of about 215 miles per day, or a little more. The best day's run was 350 miles, geographical. The ship has made this run without losing a sail, spar or rope, and is as tight, staunch and strong as when she left Liverpool.' " (See note.)

So far as can be discovered this passage of the *Comet* from England to Hong Kong has been beaten by only one American ship and one British ship. On her return from London to China in 1855 the *Eagle Wing,* under the above mentioned Captain Linnell, sailed from the Downs on the 17th of April, dropping her pilot at 9:30 A.M. At 11 A.M., July 10th, she let go her anchor in the harbor of Hong Kong; "making," to quote her log, "the passage from pilot to pilot in eighty-three and a half days, being the shortest passage ever made from London to this port."

This run is believed to stand as the record between England and China. A voyage made by the British clipper *Ariel* has recently been advanced for this honor, the statement being made that she left Gravesend October 14, 1866, and arrived out on the 6th of January following in a run called 83 days. It will be noted, however, that the dates make a passage of 84 days. It was a performance of which to be proud, but on the facts stated it did not lower the record, although further particulars may indicate it was virtually equivalent to the *Eagle Wing's* performance. In this connection the writer responsible for the claim asserted:

> "It was an easy record for the run out to Hong Kong and has never been beaten since. There were many imaginative reports of better performances; there was even a rumour that an American clipper, the *Pride of the Ocean,* had run from the Lizard to Hong Kong in 69 days, but this, like all the others, was never substantiated. The nearest approaches to the *Ariel's* passages that I can find are two runs of the *Northfleet,* both just under 90 days, and one of *Robin Hood's* in 90 days." (Basil Lubbock: *The China Clippers,* p. 244.)

The quality of the "rumour" is somewhat impaired by the fact that there never was an American clipper, *Pride of the Ocean,* on the Hong Kong or any other run. A ship of that name which had scant claim to the title of clipper was built in 1853 and immediately sold abroad under another name, making no China voyages under American ownership or under the above name.

Few contests over the Canton route in any year afforded the human interest furnished by the giant *Sweepstakes* and the pigmy *Wild Pigeon*. The *Sweepstakes,* as we have seen, had made the run to California against the *Phantom* in 125 days and the *Wild Pigeon* came out in 126. On the 24th of January the *Pigeon* sailed for Hong Kong, followed by the *Sweepstakes* on the 2nd of February. The two ships met more than once on the passage as indicated by entries made in the log of the *Pigeon* by Captain Hanson:

> "February 25—Came up with and spoke the ship *Sweepstakes*. So far not a great beat. Ends fine breezes from North and clear. Parted company with the *Sweepstakes,* try it again."

"February 26—The *Sweepstakes* in sight about 10 miles to the Northwest, go it Capt. Lane. I will follow. Ends fresh breezes with passing clouds.

"March 15—At noon saw Pootoy ahead about 4 miles took a pilot. Pootoy bearing North 1 mile. At 4 P. M. came in to Hong Kong Roads, three hours after the clipper ship *Sweepstakes*. I saw her go in Simon passage. I came in Pootoy. Here ends this long passage.

"P. S. I understand from my friend Capt. Lane that he is bound to Whampoa to load for New York. I am glad to hear it. The *Pigeon* will also proceed to Whampoa to load for New York. We will I hope both sail about the same time. I mean for to try him again. The *Sweepstakes* is the fastest ship in strong breezes. She is also the largest ship some 1800 tons. The *Pigeon* is only 1,000 tons."

Leaving Whampoa the *Sweepstakes* got away first, sailing on the 1st day of April. The *Pigeon* sailed three days later and passed her rival on the way to Anjier. On the 26th of April, Pulo Leat, bearing N. by E., the *Sweepstakes* overhauled and spoke her. Nine days later they sailed from Anjier together. The story has arisen somehow that two ships sailed virtually a dead heat to New York, arriving there on the same day, 76 days from Anjier, in company with the *Flying Fish*, which passed Anjier four days ahead of them.

The log of the *Pigeon*, however, shows that she took her pilot off the Jersey Highlands at 3 P.M., the 18th of July, 74 days from Anjier, while the *Sweepstakes* anchored outside Sandy Hook at 11.30 P.M. on the 20th. New York papers reported the *Pigeon* as arriving at New York on the 19th and the *Sweepstakes* as arrived below on the 20th. The *Wild Pigeon* therefore won by a margin of four days at least from Whampoa and by rather more than one full day from Anjier.

The *Sweepstakes*, however, had proved to be a somewhat faster ship over the other courses. Sixteen days out from Anjier she caught and passed the *Flying Fish*, Captain Lane making the following entry in his log:

"May 21—'First part squally with slight showers. Wind very unsteady. Caught aback once in a squall. At 9:40 P. M. came up with and spoke clipper ship 'Flying Fish' 48 days from Manilla for Boston * * * at 12 meridian the F. F. 5 miles astern bearing E by N by compass. She is a fast ship, we dont beat her much. Have passed everything else easy."

It is only fair to say that the *Flying Fish* was deep with hemp and sugar from Manilla while the *Sweepstakes* was in fine trim with the lighter tea cargo.

Another fine bit of sailing was the out of season run of fine new clipper *Panama*, a Griswold vessel so sharp that she could not carry her registered tonnage in dead weight. She left Shanghai October 27th at daylight two days after the *Messenger* of Philadelphia, catching her at Anjier, both ships leaving there at the same time on the 15th of November. The *Panama* made the run home in 67 days from Anjier, her time from Shanghai being 85 days, 14 hours, one of the best passages ever made at that season of the year. The *Messenger's* time was 91 days. Captain Wm. P. Cave of the *Panama* said, "She is a very fast but not a dry ship and handles like a boat. She frequently runs 11 to 13 knots by the wind."

Although the first rush of Australian trade was over, the population of the country had greatly increased during the three years since the discovery of gold and continued to do so. After a period of uncertainty it was discovered that a demand existed for fast passenger and freight service to the colonies both from England and New York. Far sighted Donald McKay had planned the *Great Republic* expressly for this trade. The year witnessed not only the first steam packet sailings over this long route, but the first successes of the immense new clippers which were destined to add so much to the lustre of sailing-ship days.

Colonial commerce afforded the ideal sailing course of the world, no better evidence of which need be adduced than the fact it was the scene of the last stand of fast windjammers. More than half its distance lay through the steady westerly gales of the lower forties—the wind that blew around the world.

In America, R. W. Cameron, and in England, James Baines & Co. were Australian specialists. There were many others, but these names are associated in a large way not only with the earliest but the fastest passages of the period, and the most famous clippers. Three of McKay's great quartet, the *Lightning, James Baines* and *Champion of the Seas* made their initial runs to Melbourne this year, and the fourth, the *Donald McKay,* was nearing completion. They were all magnificent ships, the last three averaging about 2500 tons register. With the exception of the *Great Republic,* the *Donald McKay* of 2598 tons was for many years the largest sailing-ship in the world, although later superseded by the converted Vanderbilt steamer, the *Three Brothers.*

The *James Baines,* after establishing on her maiden voyage in September, 1854, the present record of 12 days, 6 hours from Boston to Rock Light near Liverpool, made the run from Liverpool to Melbourne in 63 days time, which has been equalled by one other ship, the British clipper *Thermopylae.* On her first outward voyage the *Lightning* made a longer passage than the *Baines,* but her homeward run from Melbourne to Liverpool was made in 63 days, also a record. Captain Read in the *Red Jacket* made the round voyage in 5 months, 10 days and 22½ hours, including detention in port, averaging over 203 miles a day for the entire passage.

Two ships from New York, the *Nightingale* and *Flying Scud,* also made excellent passages to Melbourne. The *Nightingale,* Captain Mather, set a record, later surpassed, by running to Melbourne in 75 days from pilot to pilot, carrying the mails. While this was much longer than the time of the *James Baines,* it may fairly be said that the relative performance of the two ships was much closer than the figures imply. Lt. Maury is authority for the estimate that Liverpool is ten days nearer Melbourne than New York, owing to the prevalence of more favorable winds on the early part of the voyage from England. While this may be considered an extreme statement by some, it must be remembered that Maury had the aid of statistics of several hundred voyages in developing this conclusion. In any case there can be no doubt whatever that Liverpool was substantially nearer Melbourne in sailing time than New York, whether the difference is regarded as one day or ten. For precisely the same reason it was a shorter run from Melbourne or China to New York than to Liverpool, a fact which must be considered when comparing records over the various courses.

Captain Warren H. Bearse of Cape Cod, a native of Hyannis, on the Cape, which produced many a smart captain, had the new ship *Flying Scud*. He came of the sort of family which was not unusual in those days. Two of his brothers were clipper captains and all had the reputation of being drivers of an advanced type. His brother Frank had the *Winged Arrow* and Richard commanded the *Robin Hood* and other fast ships.

The *Flying Scud* was "calculated" for speed. She was built by Metcalf & Norris of Damariscotta, which as we have noticed, appears to have been the first firm to lay down clippers in Maine. She was a large ship, registering 1713 tons and very sharp. The story is still told around Damariscotta that when she sailed from that port on her maiden voyage, her officers decided that her chronometers were out of order—being of the opinion that no ship could have run down the river and gotten to sea in the time they indicated.

R. W. Cameron, her agent, advertised her as the 18th ship for Melbourne in his Australia Pioneer Line and, with an optimism not entirely foreign to the times, promised a "sixty days passage" to prospective travellers. It is to be regretted that Mr. Cameron's judgment did not march with his imagination, for he sent the *Scud* on her way with her scuppers almost awash, a heavy deck load and trimmed two feet by the head. She was, therefore, extremely crank and in view of all the circumstances it is remarkable that she made the passage at all.

She sailed from New York September 29 and arrived at Fort Phillip Heads December 14, in a passage of 76 days. In addition to the handicap of being out of trim two feet by the head and overloaded, she was delayed several days by having her compass deranged by lightning.

Her log for the 6th of November contained the notation that on that day in lat. approximately 27.41 S. she ran 449 nautical miles. She further made 4620 miles in 16 days when running her easting down, a daily rate of nearly 289 miles. Further evidence that she was very fast is that in December, 1855, she went from New York to Marseilles in the record time of 19 days 20 hours deep loaded with grain and drawing 22 feet. She also has to her credit a very fine run to the East Indies, which will be noticed later.

It is to be regretted that the log of the *Flying Scud* is not available to throw additional light on the claim of 449 miles in a single day. If it can be reasonably authenticated it would stand as the best day's run ever made by a clipper. In the absence of the log or other corroborative evidence there is always the possibility of error on the part of Captain Bearse in figuring his distance. On the one hand, however, it must be assumed that it would be difficult to make an honest error which would seriously affect the above result, and on the other an investigation of Captain Bearse's reputation in the neighborhood in which he lived and died indicates it was highly improbable that he would make a dishonest report of any sort.

At the time of this passage he was already well along in middle life. He retired a few years later to the little white cottage in Hyannis, where he was born. When somewhat more than seventy years of age he married his housekeeper, an event which she celebrated by taking him to a church supper. The double ordeal was too much for the stout old captain and he "only lived a few days."

Among the ships diverted this year to the Australian trade was the *Grey Feather*. Captain Daniel McLaughlin still had her and this year he piloted her into the ranks of record makers. On June 8th he left Melbourne for Calcutta, discharging his pilot at 6 P.M. July 14th he makes the following entry:

"8:30 P. M. seen Fals Point bearing N by W, then shaped a course for the pilot station. At 11.45 took a pilot and proceeded up the River. This ends the abstract and also the quickest passage ever made between the 2 ports" (36 days).

The run to the colonies eventually produced a goodly proportion of the extremely fast-sailing records of clipper ship days. "Running the Easting down" in the strong westerly gales and long rolling surges with the "send" peculiar to seas of this character was the ideal track for a ship powerful enough to hold her course in the worst weather. More than one clipper recorded a speed of 20 or more knots in these latitudes, and the great majority of day's runs approaching 400 miles and upward were made here.

Hamburg was now the hailing port of the *Sovereign of the Seas* and she was sent to Sydney, New South Wales, under Captain Muller. Her voyage reported in the Sydney *Empire* of October 24th is in some respects typical of the course:

"The *Sovereign of the Seas*, Muller, arrived on the 22nd, having made the passage from London in 84 days. During the early part of her present voyage she promised to excell all her earlier performances. On the 40th day out she was off the Cape and but for a succession of Easterly gales would have made the passage in an unprecedented short space of time. The best day's run she made was 410 knots, and her log proves her to have travelled occasionally at the rate of *22 knots per hour*. On September 8 she met with a casualty that would have resulted in a serious detention had she not been well found and manned. At 3:00 P.M. of this day she was sailing comfortably under the easy canvass, the weather at the time being most auspicious, but by 3:30 so great a change had taken place that nothing above her three lower masts was standing, a sudden storm having denuded her of her topmasts and gear attached. In six days from the accident everything was repaired and the ship on her way at her usual speed."

Many a fine ship this year had a narrow escape under similar conditions. The *John Land* on her second voyage was missing for months, turning up finally on the beach at Tahiti, where truculent Captain Percival was heaving her down for repairs with native help, while his disillusioned, pump-weary crew sat in the hoosgow ashore in double irons until such time as he should need them again.

Donald McKay's first experiment in sharp craft, the little coffee trader *Courier*, which had made so many fine runs between Rio and New York under Captain Wolfe, piled up on the bleak shores of the Falklands. She was still owned by Andrew Foster & Co., the firm for which she was built.

The *Dauntless* was missing, with Captain Miller and all his boisterous dare-devil crew. Through all the years no word has come back to tell her fate, and now those who waited for the news are gone. The great three decker *Trade Wind* went down in heavy weather after a collision, with great loss of life. The bones of the beautiful *Eclipse* had long strewn the beaches of Ypala.

Steamship lines were suffering, too. The great Collins liner *Arctic* went down in a collision, carrying with her nearly 400 souls.

In January the steamer *San Francisco* had foundered after more than a week of terrible gales in which upper works and deck houses were completely stripped from the vessel, carrying with them over 150 of the passengers and crew. For seventy-five years thereafter, every Yankee school boy was to know and declaim "The good *Three Bells* of Glasgow shall stand till daylight by." The *Three Bells* and her wonderful crew did more, far more, than that. For a full seven days and nights her captain hung doggedly to windward of the wreck, without thought of ship or self, and when the *San Francisco* went down more than 200 survivors crowded the deck of the *Three Bells*. The annals of the sea contain no brighter, braver page than that written by the little 600 ton Scotch square rigger and her crew from the Land o' Cakes.

Three months later one of the worst hurricanes in years was raging on the North Atlantic. The clipper *Red Gauntlet* from Liverpool for Boston was in it for 56 hours on April 17 and succeeding days. She reported:

> "April 17—had hurricane, lasting 56 hours. Barometer at 27.5 for 40 hours. On 18th struck by a sea which carried away the fore channels and drew bolts of top gallant backstays out of sides, losing fore and main top gallant masts, and starting upper works forward. At 1 A. M., shipped a sea which went through the main spencer, taking larboard quarter and stern boats, staving bulwarks midship houses and taking everything moveable about decks, same time filling cabin and between decks with water. At 4 A. M., blew away a new main topsail from the close reef."

Almost identical conditions and results were reported by the ship *Constantine*, even to the sea through the main spencer at 1 A.M. The ships must have been a biscuit toss apart without knowing it.

Captain Holmes of the *Living Age*, of Boston, tried to ride out a typhoon in the Yellow Waters of the China sea under bare poles, all sail furled and secured with double gaskets. Nearly all his canvas was blown away, together with jibboom, fore top gallant mast, main topmast and other spars. In addition to this his main and mizzen masts were badly sprung.

Few of the ships that survived the perils of the deep were used more roughly than the little clipper barque *Storm*, still commanded by John P. Roberts. The *Storm*, deeply loaded, was bound from Manilla for New York and had reached the North Atlantic when she was struck by a hurricane. Captain Roberts' own log tells the story:

"Oct. 18 Lat. 25 30 N. Lon. 55 20 W. Exceedingly fine weather and steady breeze. Gulf Weed in profusion. At 11 A.M. made a sail ahead from the fore topsail yard, going same way. At noon could see her topsails off deck. Dist Obs'd 190 miles N 40 West. I am out of the usual track, but rely upon the chartes which are favorable to this track which is shorter than the common one. I fear calms more than anything else. At noon threw a bottle overboard with paper &c.

"Oct. 19 Lat. 26 58 N. Lon. 57 55 W. Fine weather and moderate breeze. At 2 P.M. spoke the British brig *Derwent* 15 days from Memerara for Liverpool. Reported very light winds. If the wind holds this way, I shall not be sorry for hanging to the eastward. Much weed about.

"Dist. obs'd 166 miles N 58 W.

"Oct. 20 Lat. 27 58 N. Lon. 60 00 W. First part fine, wind moderate. At 4 P. M. spoke and passed the Barque *Springbok* of and for Boston from Cape Town 48 days. Reported being becalmed as we were a few days ago. Said he never found it calmer there before. Middle part light air and rain. Latter part moderate breeze and fine weather. Wind hauled against the sun. Swell high from N.E.

"Dist obs'd 126 miles N 62 West.

"Oct. 21 Lat. 30 05 N. Lon. 63 22 W. First part fine, wind moderate. Middle part puffy. Latter part blowing a gale. Sky very murky. Under double reefs. A very heavy swell from S. W. and the barque rolling fearfully.

"Dist obs'd 197 miles N. 19 30 W.

"Ninety eight days out and 66 from Anjier.

"Oct. 22 Lat. 31 02 N Lon. 64 19 W. First part blowing heavy and an awful sea on. At 7 P. M. while close reefing the main topsail was struck by a perfect hurricane. The foremast was struck by lightning from the royal yard down to the eyes of the lower rigging where the mast snapped and went over the side and the barque broached to and went over nearly on her beam ends when the main top mast and mizen topmast backstays were cut away and both masts went, the mainmast close to the deck and the mizen in the eyes of the lower rigging. The barque righted and paid off with the wreck hanging under her stern and threatening every minute to knock the rudder off. With great exertions we finally cleared it without further damage. At this time it was blowing frightfully so that it was dangerous to expose ourselves to the force of the wind. The sea was beaten down quite moderate comparatively and was white with spray. After the wreck was cleared the barque behaved much better than I expected and shipped little water though wallowing badly. We heard no thunder and saw but the one flash of lightning that struck us. Latter part blowing heavy with a clear sky and the barque laying broadside to it with nothing standing but bowsprit and fore and mizen masts below the eyes of the rigging and poorly off for spare spars. However, it might have been worse.

"Dist. Obs'd 75 miles N. 41 West.

"Oct. 23 Lat. 31 09 N. Lon 63 48 W. Commences with fine weather and blowing fresh with a high sea. Set the fore top mast staysail on the fore stays and the triangular lower studdingsale for a mizen stay sail. Middle part wind and sea moderating. Later part fine and wind moderate. Got a spare topsail yard up for a foreyard and set a topsail single reefed for a topsail. Set the square lower studding sail on the mizen mast and at noon are going 4 knots.

"Dist obs'd 28 miles N. 75 East.

"Oct. 24 Lat. 32 20 Lon. 64 13. Fine weather and moderate breeze. Got a stump top gallant mast up for a fore topmast, and at 10 A. M. set the sail. It is astonishing how well the barque sails under such short sail. In the night, the wind was light so that the sails would not stand full and yet she went 2 knots. Ends fine, wind moderate. Getting a topmast rigged for a mainmast.

CHAPTER XXVIII

1855

LIQUIDATION BEGINS

AMERICA touched the zenith of her maritime achievements in 1855. Her shipping (5,212,000 tons, less than 15 per cent of which was in the form of steamers) was greater than ever before and relatively greater than at any time since. Her fleet was almost as numerous as Britain's, while, in size, condition and general efficiency of ships, it was far in advance. The enormous amount of 586,000 tons of new vessels had been added during the year ending June 30th, nearly three times the volume of the entire American merchant marine five years after the close of the Revolution.

No other nation shared so largely in the most desirable and profitable commerce of the world. In Chinese waters at the end of the year, for example, foreign shipping amounted to 58,000 tons, of which 24,000 tons flew the stars and stripes, 18,000 tons was British and the remainder represented the other maritime powers of the earth.

Viewed superficially, it was the moment of America's maritime supremacy—a supremacy which virtually everyone in the United States confidently expected to see maintained. Actually, the battle was already lost. Much of the new tonnage included in the statistical year of 1855 had already been laid down or completed during the calendar year of 1854. Construction around New York was at a standstill. Less than 6500 tons were on the ways in the early Spring.

Isaac Smith of Hoboken, who had built the *Hurricane* and other fine clippers, closed his yard and moved to Sing Sing. Other plants closed, never to reopen. In its review of the industry, on January 1st, the New York *Herald* said:

> "Experienced shipbuilders pronounce the depression and gloom of the past year to be unparalleled. . . . Gloom and total desertion still prevail in many of our neighboring ship yards."

In Maine, new ships were selling for 25 per cent less than in 1854. From this time forward construction declined until in 1859 it amounted to less than 163,000 tons. For more than twenty years thereafter, with the exception of sporadic upward fluctuations, the registered tonnage of America gradually declined until in 1880 it amounted to little more than 4,000,000 tons. Thereafter it climbed slowly, but the twentieth century was under way before it again attained the level of 1855.

Few commercial phenomena have attracted the attention or given rise to the debate which has been devoted to this remarkable rise and decline of American shipping. For the next seventy-five years Congressional records were to be filled with discussion, reports of investigations and proposals for the relief of shipping, while every old sea captain and shipping merchant had his pet theory and panacea, upon which he would discourse at length to all listeners.

It was a strange situation, but hardly so strange as the fact that among all the persons most interested, few if any seem to have grasped the true explanation or if they did, gave it small publicity. Possibly the causes were too fundamental; too deep-seated for contemporary comprehension.

At all events, public attention has been devoted principally to proposals for subsidies and changes in laws affecting registration of vessels, welfare of seamen, etc., unmindful of the fact that the American marine made its best growth under conditions infinitely harsher and more inequitable, and under far greater financial and legal handicaps than later prevailed. This is not to intimate that intelligent legislation could not have done much to prolong America's day in foreign trade, or that it can not still do much to give her a merchant marine adequate to her needs. Facts of this sort are too obvious to require restatement, but they should not be permitted to exclude, or even obscure factors of primary importance.

Other theories hark back to the Civil War, giving it credit for playing a major part in the downfall of American supremacy on the high seas, disregarding the fact that the deterioration of her shipping was already well under way years before the outbreak of that war.

The essential clue, without which the loss of America's nautical leadership cannot be understood, lies in the fact that even before the clipper ship period the United States had undertaken a far greater and (from a temporary point of view) more important task than the maintenance of a superior merchant marine. This was the opening and development of the West. It is no exaggeration to say that the doom of the American merchant marine was sealed with the Louisiana purchase. The work of making this territory accessible at first called merely for a few hardy axemen and trappers, but under the accelerating influence of steam, electrical inventions and the discovery of gold it eventually attracted the best brains and the most energetic and ambitious men of the century.

By 1850 the trail maker's work was done and the day of the builder was at hand. One may read between the lines of every newspaper article thereafter that where formerly the best young blood of the North went into shipping and allied industries as a matter of course, now it was going into railroad and engineering work and the development and application of new discoveries.

The boys who had no choice but to build and sail ships in the forties found it infinitely more profitable and interesting a decade later to build cities, and develop land transportation.

It was a stupendous task. America lacked both the man power and the wealth to carry on this work and at the same time to provide properly for the maintenance of her maritime position. Only within recent years have conditions reached a state approaching equilibrium. If the foregoing explanation (subject to a wide variety of qualifications which need not be set forth here) is approximately correct, one may look to see a gradual reversion to a greater and more intelligent interest in nautical matters in America.

In 1855 and later fine, able men still went to sea. But the opportunities were no longer in their favor and the old incentive to improve the service was lacking. Given equal energy and intelligence, the man who once commanded a ship or conducted a small overseas trading concern could with less risk and hardship control the destinies of a sizable inland empire. The old yard-stick of a ship of the sail was exchanged for a thousand miles of railroad, a Comstock lode or tentacled business.

The story of the clipper ship is the record of a losing fight. The significant fact is that after two or three years of the most intense and colorful competition the world had seen, the youth of the land tacitly abandoned the field for no other reason than that life had become easier, more interesting and more profitable elsewhere. Men who were too old to change or had no wish to do so, carried on. The era was closed by the men, for the most part, who saw it begin and not by a new generation of smart young sailors.

There was a chronic dearth of seamen as early as 1853. It had reached the proportions of an acute problem within a year and with brief respites it remained one as long as sailing ships were a factor. The "impolitic baby act" was much criticized in this connection, and without doubt it placed a burden on shipmasters who were willing to train boys. Boys were a burden anyhow. In a pinch, one able seaman was worth several youngsters and cost less to maintain. The chief useful function of a boy on shipboard was to assist in handling the lightest sails. On ships that carried boys able seamen were not supposed to go above the topgallant yards. To "ship as r'yal boy" was an ancient phrase known to every waterside youth half a century ago. Some ships would not carry boys at all, but most captains recognized that the supply of skilled sailors must be kept up, and did what they could in spite of hampering, useless restrictions.

Six extreme clippers, including three built by McKay for James Baines & Co., were launched in 1854. None were laid down in 1855 or ever again in America. Approximately 35 medium clippers were constructed, however, including several that became famous by establishing new world records. The list would be considerably longer if a number of rather full modelled ships were included which were usually described as clippers, but which belonged rather to the class of smart sailing craft which eventually succeeded the clippers.

Among the new vessels which became famous the *Andrew Jackson* of Mystic was prominent. Baltimore furnished two well-known ships, the little *Mary Whitridge* and the *Carrier Dove,* a very handsome 1700 ton ship. The latter made a run of 78 days from Liverpool to Melbourne in 1858.

E. and H. O. Briggs, of Boston, worthy descendants of the great Enos, of Salem, built the *Fair Wind,* a 1300 ton ship of medium model. She was owned by Henry S. Hallet & Co., of Boston, and in 1861 made the run from San Francisco to Honolulu in 8 days, 18 hours, which is close to the record.

Few of the other well-known builders, with the exception of McKay and Hayden & Cudworth, put out clippers this year.

Although the new fleet contained no extreme clippers, there were a number of remarkably finely modelled ships. The *Express* and *Golden Fleece* (2nd) from the yard of Paul Curtis were exceptionally handsome vessels. Hayden & Cudworth's *Electric Spark,* virtually a sister ship of the *Thatcher Magoun,* had very beautiful lines and very expensive fittings. Her cabin chairs cost $60.00 each, a large sum for the period.

John Brower & Co., of New York, purchased the *Andrew Jackson* from her builders, Irons & Grinnell of Mystic. She had a round stern of a type peculiar to Mystic ships, and so far as can be learned, never put on any other sailing ships until adopted by British iron ship builders. The stern of the *Andrew Jackson* was more heavily formed than that of later Mystic craft, but she was a handsome, powerful vessel.

Irons & Grinnell designed the *Andrew Jackson* for a fast clipper, but although she was heavily sparred, crossing a main skysail yard, she is said to have been somewhat of a disappointment at first. After a year or two Brower decided to re-step her masts and alter their rake. Whether it improved her speed or not, the move was followed by a remarkable series of fast passages, beginning with her hundred day run to San Francisco in 1857. It must not be thought, however, that the *Jackson* was a slow ship even at first. On the 22nd of August, 1856, for example, she was reported at New York, 23 days from Liverpool. This was not only a good midsummer passage but it was 10 and 11 days shorter, respectively, than the time of the packets *Silas Wright* and *Fidelia,* both smart sailing vessels of their type, which arrived the same day.

A Mystic built ship shared with the *Westward Ho* of Boston the honor of being the first of the Cape Horners to sail. Captain Charles Sisson in the medium clipper *Elizabeth F. Willets* left New York on the 13th of January; the *Westward Ho,* Captain Hussey, leaving Boston the same day. Follansbee in the barque *Greenfield* and Patten in *Neptune's Car* left New York the following day.

Sisson had the misfortune to run into a calm belt off the California coast and it took him 15 days to cover the last 800 miles. His entry tells the story:

"May 10—3 P.M. Anchored S.F. 118 days and 3 hours from New York, and found that I was the Black Sheep out of the fleet. The Neptune's Car 102 days, the Westward Ho 102 days and the bark Greenfield 110 days."

It is possible that Sisson was too preoccupied with a disciplinary problem to make a fast passage. Just before leaving home to join his ship on this voyage he had warned his small daughter that if she left the yard without permission he would punish her. Shortly before his departure the little girl was missing and he was compelled to leave before he had a chance to make good his word. On his return a year later his first act was to lay the culprit over his knee and administer a sound spanking.

The actual time of both Hussey and young Joshua Patten was better than reported by Sisson. *Neptune's Car* passed Sandy Hook at 4 P.M., January 14th, and on the 25th of April Patten made the following entry in his log:

"All of this Day fresh Breezes and Cloudy at 10 A.M. the water discollered. During this day passed large quantities of Celp. At 1 P.M. made the South Farlone barring N.N.E. Dis 10 miles at 2 do took a pilot on board and Proceed in. at 5 do passed through the Heads and at 6:20 came to anchor off North Point and furled Sails. Pilot left and Pirates came on board and commenced their work.

"So ends this Passage by J. A. Patten."

His passage from Sandy Hook to anchor, therefore, was 101 days, 2 hours and 20 minutes, while the time of the *Westward Ho* was said to be slightly less.

Both ships were up for Hong Kong and the elated Hussey offered to wager any sum on his ship that was agreeable to admirers of *Neptune's Car*. Fortunately for him there were no takers. Young Patten sailed the same tide with Hussey and beat him ten days on the crossing. This margin of apparent superiority over the *Westward Ho* won for Patten a London charter, while the *Westward Ho* found nothing better awaiting when she arrived than an offer of a cargo of coolies for the Chincha Islands —a business on the whole somewhat worse than the African slave trade.

W. E. Kingman had the little *Shooting Star* this year. He sailed for California on March 21st, dropping his pilot off the Hook at 4 P.M. A bad stretch of weather drove him around to the Eastward of the Falklands, yet on his 58th day out he was past the Horn and on the 15th of July he closed his log with the words:

> "4 A.M. got underweigh light air from S E and thick foggy weather. 11 A M took a pilot on the Bar. 1 P M came to anchor off North Point, and am happy to know that we have handsomely beaten the celebrated clippers *Swordfish, Witchcraft, Monsoon, Lookout, Queen of the Seas, Eagle* and several others."

Among the "others" which the little *Shooting Star*, racked by four years' driving, had defeated, was the beautiful, ill-fated new clipper *John Milton*, the *Polynesia* and the *Ellen Foster*, all of which had sailed from two to three weeks before her. Of all the ships which arrived about this time Griswold's *Panama*, commanded by Cave, was the only clipper to make a quicker passage, and her time was only two days less than that of the *Shooting Star*.

Shortly after her entry, San Francisco witnessed an event which was to occur but once in the history of any port. This was the arrival of seven clipper ships from the East in one day. On August 2nd the *Monsoon, Lookout, Ellen Foster, Queen of the Seas, War Hawk, Messenger* and *Cœur de Lion* passed the Golden Gate in stately procession and folded their wings one after another. Fine beautiful ships all. No other port or day was ever to behold a similar sight.

The best California passage completed during the year was the 99 day run of the *Herald of the Morning*. She was not a large ship, measuring less than 1300 tons, but she has been mentioned as one of the handsomest of the clippers, and her model indicates that she was entitled to a high rating in this respect. Pook, who had designed many of the most beautiful as well as the swiftest ships afloat, was responsible for her lines.

Everywhere she went to the end of her days the *Herald* excited admiration. On her first visit to Mauritius, where she went with guano following the above run, the Mauritius *Commercial Gazetteer* of December 7th, 1855, had this to say about her:

"IMPROVEMENTS IN SHIP BUILDING.—The rapid improvement made in ship building in recent years is in great measure due to America. It is there that the *elan* was given which has lately excited so much competition in England. Since the American yacht *America* beat the English yachts that were built with every possible perfection at hand without regard to cost, there has been a stir among shipbuilders and a different class of vessels are now built for the merchant service.

"But in the meantime such has been the activity, the enterprise and the ingenuity of the Yankees that they have continued to go ahead faster than the Britishers, and the fleetest vessels in our merchant service, the renowned clippers that make such remarkable passages to Australia, India and China, are built in America. Some American clippers have been attracted to this port that have excited general admiration. The *Kate Hooper* came and eclipsed them all. Now we have a specimen of a ship that leaves the *Kate Hooper* a very long way behind. The splendid American clipper *Herald of the Morning* arrived in our harbor on the 25th ult. She was reported to us as something very superior and we decided to visit her. Having done so we have little confidence in ourselves to be able to convey a correct idea of what we saw.

"Capt. Baker received us most cordially, and in giving us the information we asked for, avoided uttering a word in praise of his vessel. He was right. She spoke for herself.

"The *Herald of the Morning* was built at Boston and was launched in November, 1853, so that she is now two years old. She is 203 feet in length, 38 feet of beam, 24 feet hold and about 1300 tons register. Her bow is so sharp as to take the form of a razor, the keel forming the edge; there are no rails at the bow, which is quite unencumbered. Her yards are double, and the rigging is on a new principle which greatly facilitates the changes in the sails, &c. The poop deck is a fine promenade, and although guano is being discharged, everything on deck wore the appearance of order, neatness and cleanliness."

Many fine individual runs were made over the various sailing tracks in '55, the most striking of which was the 70 day passage of the *Mandarin* under John W. C. Perit, begun in 1855 and completed in 1856, which still stands as the record between New York and Melbourne. Perit sailed from New York December 21st, dropping his pilot off Sandy Hook at 4 P.M. He took a pilot at noon off Melbourne Heads, coming to anchor at 8 P.M. on the first day of March. His time from anchor to anchor was 70 days, 9 hours.

John Giet had taken the *Whirlwind* over the same course earlier in the year in 75 days, equalling the performance of the *Nightingale* already referred to; and a year later the *Panama* was to go out in a few hours over 74 days. Many other fine runs were made by such vessels as the *Flying Dutchman, Snow Squall, Invincible, Ringleader,* and others, but the above appear to be the shortest passages made between the two ports.

Only an Eldridge could whip an Eldridge. The Boston-Calcutta record of 89 days made by Captain Eldridge of the ship *America* in 1833 was still undefeated. Comes now the ship *Nor'-Wester,* a medium clipper owned by J. S. Coolidge & Company of Boston and commanded by Frank Oliver Eldridge.

The *Nor'Wester* hauled away from her wharf in Boston at 11 o'clock on the forenoon of June 22nd. At 3:30 A.M. on the 23rd Eldridge dropped his pilot four miles from Boston Lighthouse. On the 16th of the following September the *Nor'Wester* was lying at anchor becalmed a few miles from Sand Heads. The following morning she got under way, False Point bearing W.N.W. 15 miles, and at midnight, September 17th, Eldridge laid his main topsail to the mast to take a Hoogly pilot, 86 days 21½ hours from pilot to pilot. Remarkable as this passage is, an inspection of the log reveals that it would have been two and possibly three days shorter, but for the calms met in the "Bay." Nevertheless it was a fine performance and has been beaten only once, and then by another Boston ship, the *Beverly,* in 1857.

The *Nor'Wester* followed this performance by returning to Boston in 86 days, a run which strangely enough had been surpassed a few weeks earlier by the 83 day voyage of the *Beverly.*

Baltimore's new clipper, *Mary Whitridge,* set up a new transatlantic record this year in a remarkable midsummer passage to Helvoet. Cheesebrough drove her from the Baltimore Capes to the English Channel, landing her passengers there less than 12½ days out. It was a remarkable feat from any point of view and distance and season considered, it is doubtful if any transatlantic run has ever equalled it. Certainly none, not even the 13 day record of the *Red Jacket* from Sandy Hook to Liverpool, surpassed it. The latter passage, like that of the land to land run of the *Great Republic* in 12 days (also made this year) was shorter than the route covered by the *Mary Whitridge.*

In the China trade the British clippers were beginning to afford some competition; nevertheless twenty-four American ships loaded English teas during the year. With one or two exceptions all were clippers. It was the largest number of ships under the Stars and Stripes which ever participated in this trade in any one year, although, contrary to common impression, American vessels continued active in the business until the Civil War intervened.

There are indications that the nerves of an occasional Briton were reacting somewhat erratically to the presence of so many Yankee clippers. In October, the American barque *Reindeer,* Captain E. W. Nichols, was lying at Hong Kong with some twenty other American ships. One of the *Reindeer's* men deserted, and after a few days "on the beach" came back full of

Dutch courage and bad intentions. Captain Nichols found he was trying to stir up mutiny among his crew and placed him in irons.

British police came off and "rescued" the man, and then the local court issued a warrant for Nichols and gave judgment that he pay a fine of $50.00 to the Queen and $25.00 to the seaman. This was too much for the captain and he flatly refused to pay the fines or any sums whatever. The authorities came off to enforce their demands and Nichols took refuge in the U. S. steam frigate *Powhatan*.

Thereupon a strongly worded letter of protest to the authorities was signed by every American captain in port, representing such ships as the *Swordfish, Lantao, Boston Light, Samuel Willets, Stephen Baldwin, Houqua, Ellen Foster, Lookout, Helena, Nightingale, Meteor* and others. The matter was finally dropped; the authorities, true to British tradition from time immemorial, deciding to take a common-sense view of a relatively unimportant incident.

The list of ships sailing for London with tea in '55 reads like a roll call in the clipper's hall of fame. It included such craft as the *Nightingale, Stag Hound, Sovereign of the Seas, Neptune's Favorite, Storm King, Courser, Nabob, Wild Pigeon, Spitfire, Flying Dutchman, Neptune's Car* and *Romance of the Seas*. Few of these ships were of the type best suited to the China trade. None except the *Nightingale* got away in the favorable season, and she sailed from Shanghai February 16th, when the monsoon was becoming weak. She was 25 days to Anjier (the record for ships of her class in a strong monsoon being less than 12 days) and 74 days thence to Beachy Head, where she took her pilot.

Among the clippers leaving during the less favorable season the 96 day run of the *Kingfisher*, commanded by Crosby from Macao to Deal and the *Don Quixote's* 105 days from Foo Choo Foo to London, were the best reported. Many of the ships met with very unfavorable weather. The *Invincible* was in collision with the ship *A. Cheesebrough,* which was sunk, and the *Invincible* herself was beached near Hong Kong, with eleven feet of water in her hold.

Captain John Arey, who wanted his men to be able to jump over the foreyard before breakfast, was especially unfortunate. His ship, the *Spitfire,* was trimmed a foot by the head when he left Foo Choo Foo and later when anchored in the Straits of Allas the current brought the cable under ship's forefoot and strained her badly. For the rest of the voyage the pumps were going day and night and sail had to be shortened to keep the ship on her bottom and prevent wetting the tea.

In spite of this Arey managed to beat the *Wild Pigeon,* which had sailed 13 days ahead of him. He caught her the day after leaving the Straits of Allas, and beat her 10 hours to St. Helena and docked in London December 4th, two days in the lead.

Of the New York bound tea ships none equalled the work of the *Eagle Wing.* Captain Linnell had not made noticeable improvement in spelling since his last record, but in sailing he ranked well toward the head of the class. His log recorded:

"November 22 Got under weigh at Woosung. Dischgd pilot at 3 P.M.

"December 3 In the Strates of Sunday light baffling airs and light breezes . . . saw the ship Joshuway Bates for New York that left Shanghai Nov 1st.

"December 23 Spoke "the Romanse of the sea" whitch left Shanghai foreteen days previous to us She had lost a boat and 2 men the night previous."

Eventually Linnell took a pilot to the Southeast of Sandy Hook February 16th after a passage of 86 days from Shanghai, 75 from the "Strates of Sunday." Not a record, but better than the average time even for a clipper ship generation that celebrated in song the mythical passage of the "Flying Fish sailor, ninety days from Hong Kong." If it had been made a few weeks later in the full strength of the monsoon, it might well have been several days shorter.

CHAPTER XXIX

1856

EXTRAVAGANCE had never been a vice of Yankee sea captains, but probably none still in active service had ever experienced greater difficulty in earning bare expenses than in 1856. Not a few ships that had been driven at top speed to California, Melbourne or China lay at their destination for weeks, only to be forced to sail for other ports with all or a considerable part of their original cargo intact. Many of those fortunate enough to dispose of their merchandise found it almost impossible to secure profitable charters, and drifted into the wretched coolie or guano trade.

A large volume of shipping was released from transport service by the ending of the Crimean war with the Peace of Paris on March 30th. Several American clippers which, like the *Great Republic*, had been under charter to the French Government, were sold in France. Among these were the *Ocean Herald* and *Queen of Clippers*. Others had been lost. The extreme clipper *Highflyer*, Captain Gordon B. Waterman, had sailed late in '55 from San Francisco for Hong Kong and was never seen again. Years later vague rumors sifted down to Hong Kong of the wreck of a large ship on Formosa and the massacre of her entire crew by the natives, but nothing was definitely established.

The clipper packet *Driver* of the Red Cross line, owned by the same firm which had the *Highflyer*, was missing in February with her crew and passengers, 372 all told. One after another Red Cross ships disappeared until within the space of a few months only the *Dreadnought* was left. Severe storms along the Atlantic coast in January and February accounted for a large number of fine craft, fourteen being reported ashore near New York alone after one January storm, while many others were supposed to have foundered. The *Sea Witch*, barely ten years old, but long superannuated, met her end on a reef off the Coast of Cuba in April. A fine new medium clipper, the *Leah*, of Mystic, sailed out of New York January 4th on her maiden voyage and was never heard from. Her master, Captain John Latham, the mates and most of her 22 seamen were from Mystic and many a home there was left desolate.

Less than thirty new clippers were built this year, although a much larger number were called clippers. All were of the new type known as "half" or "medium" clippers—fine, sharp, fast ships, but cleverly designed to carry very heavy cargoes. Typical of these was the *Mary L. Sutton* of Mystic, a handsome round sterned craft of great capacity, which nevertheless made a number of smart Cape Horn passages, including three to San Francisco, in 110 days or less, while her run of 17 days from 50 South Pacific to the Equator is still the record.

Equally fine ships were the *Intrepid*, built by Webb, the *Florence* from Samuel Hall's yard in Boston, the *Flying Mist*, the second *Witch of the Wave* and McKay's new *Minnehaha*. Florida's first and only clipper ship was launched this year; probably also the only clipper to be built with mahogany timbers. She was the *Stephen R. Mallory* and was constructed at Key West by Bowne & Curry. These and many others were not only capable of making long passages in almost as good time as the extreme clippers but they could load from a third to a half more cargo per ton register. Since they were new ships they were able to get favorable charters more readily than the older ships.

Altogether the outlook in 1856 was sufficient to discourage the most optimistic of the extreme clipper masters, if they had been the sort that depended on optimism. Fortunately the old packet breed required no such windy support. His was a stamina nurtured in opposition; that never fully responded until the outlook was blackest. Some of the finest performances of all time were made by these men in the gloomy days that saw the end of the clipper era.

One of the best passages of the year was made by the *Surprise*, under Charles S. Ranlett. She left Shanghai on January 2nd at 2 P.M. and ran to Sandy Hook in a few hours over 82 days, notwithstanding the fact her copper was badly torn, this passage being equal to the record at that time. Her time to the Straits of Sunda was 12 days, during which she logged 2663 miles with her best day only 296 miles.

At the same time the *Sea Serpent* was making her record run from China. Under Captain Whitmore she left Hong Kong on the 3rd of January, passed Anjier on the 11th and crossed 20° North Atlantic on her 64th day out. From there she had light airs, but reached Sandy Hook two days ahead of the *Surprise*, 78 days from Hong Kong. This run had only been beaten twice in history. The time of the *Surprise* and *Sea Serpent* from Java Head was identical, 68 days, and everything considered, there seems to be little to choose between the performance of the two ships.

Captain Bradley, who now had the *David Brown*, figured in the keenest race of the year around Cape Horn. He sailed from New York the 15th of January, followed three days later by Peterson in the *Phantom*. Few ships are entitled to higher rank than these two in high average performance. They could sail in any weather, blow high, low or flat calm. There appears to

FACSIMILE OF LINES OF THE *Bellesarius* FROM THE NOTEBOOK OF JOSHUA
HUMPHREY, THE DESIGNER OF THE *Constitution*, ETC.

Reproduced from the original by courtesy of the Pennsylvania Historical Society. (Note: The angle
which the lower part of the 2nd frame makes with the horizontal line at 6 gives an excellent
illustration of the meaning of "dead-rise." The above lines indicate the very extreme dead-rise
of approximately 40 inches or 22 degrees.)

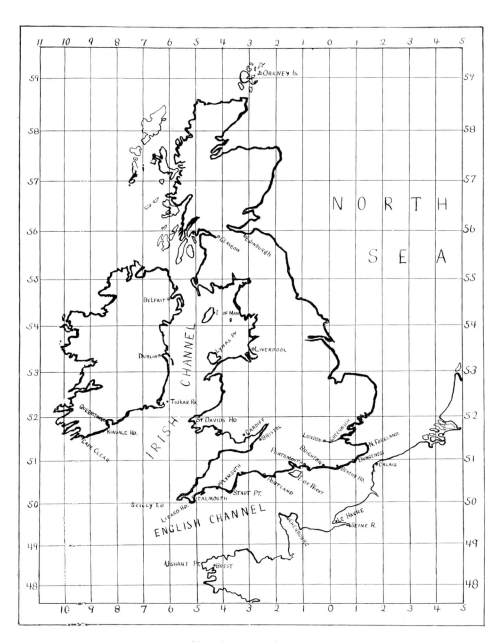

THE ENGLISH COAST

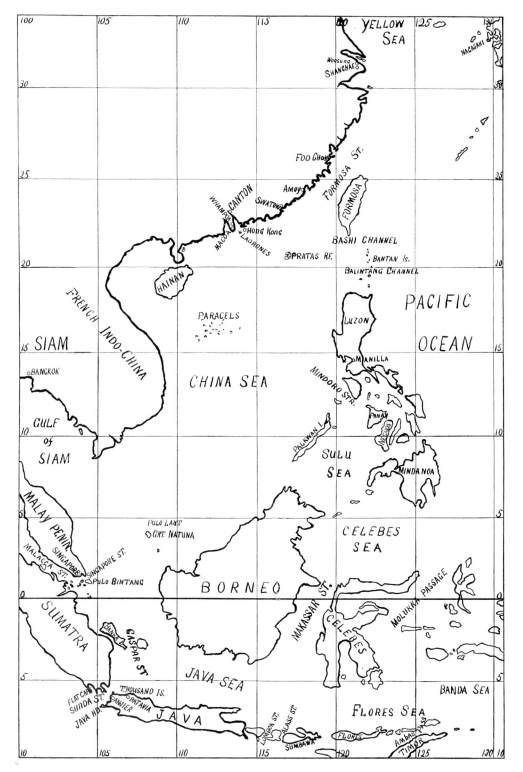

The China Coast

be no record of the ships sighting each other during the voyage. It was a race against time with grit for a pace maker. As it was the *Phantom* gained two days on the *Brown,* anchoring at San Francisco on the 29th of April, 101 days from New York, while the *Brown* reached port the day before in a passage of 103 days.

As so frequently happened, the two ships were not satisfied with this brush, but followed it up immediately with a race to Hong Kong. Again the *David Brown* sailed first, this time two days in advance of the *Phantom,* both ships being in light sailing trim. Peterson sailed the morning of May 16th, discharging his pilot at noon. On the 2nd of July he sighted the *David Brown* ahead, and two days later he took a pilot off Hong Kong at 6 A.M., drifting slowly in through the jabbering fishing junks over a sea covered with millions of floating cuttle fish bones, "the *David Brown* almost out of sight astern to leeward."

Aside from the above there were many fine close battles over the Cape Horn route this year, as exciting to the contestants as any of the more famous struggles, but the crowded grand stand of former years was emptying fast. Many of the picturesque figures in the shipping world had retired. N. B. Palmer had given up the sea. Waterman was fiddling around the San Francisco waterfront, buying a wreck and doing a little salvage work now and then. Stout old Captain Benjamin was out of the harness. Millet, of the *Witch of the Wave,* no longer figured in the reports. One by one the old China packet masters disappeared, and the rising generation had new matters to occupy their minds. Many an old seafaring family felt the lure of the West and transferred their interests to the prairies, farms and lumber camps of the Northwest.

Thousands of able seamen and hundreds of officers were scattered along the Pacific coast from the Mexican border to Nootka Sound. The bones of honest old barnacles were whitening in the gulches of the Sierras, along the dusty trails of the "Golden Caribou" or in the Australian bush.

Young A. G. Hamilton had the smart clipper *Wild Duck* in '53, a ship very similar to the *Wild Pigeon*. The grave of old "A.G."—some time miner and Indian trader—rests on a wild bank of the Fraser River, a scant fifty miles from the great Arctic Divide, far in the interior of British Columbia. Only an aged Chinaman mourned his departure.

With all the distractions of gold and railroad real estate booms, rich farm and timber land for the asking, a new insistent snarling note was dinning into the ears of North and South alike. The abolitionist joke was becoming a humorless reality written in border brutalities and sectional disturbances. Before the year was over the unpleasant aftermath of the Kansas-Nebraska Bill was sowing the seeds of bitter dissension throughout the land. Against these distractions the high, clean sport of clipper racing made small appeal to the younger generation.

It was a hard winter at sea. Ships coming on the coast were reporting forty to sixty days north of Bermuda. They staggered into port frozen masses of ice, sailors sick and dying in the forecastles, and often without sufficient man-power to let go the anchor. Formerly, survivors of such experiences had no choice but to ship again. Now they were thinking in terms of Sunny California or Australia, where men were in demand.

Few ships, since the voyage of the *Adventure,* had survived worse weather than the clipper *Rapid,* Captain Phineas Winsor, from New York May 26th, bound for Frisco. She arrived off the Horn in the dead of winter and encountered one head gale after another, with bitter cold; the wind sometime attaining hurricane force. Captain Winsor bucked sea and wind week after week until most of his sails were gone and out of his crew of twenty-four seamen, ten were dead and ten more lay absolutely helpless in the forecastle. Four only were able to hobble about the decks, the mates doing the steering. With no prospect of a break in the weather, and facing the practical certainty that another day or two would leave no men to handle the ship, he reluctantly turned back to Rio—the only instance, apparently, of a clipper ship that ever did so while still sound in hull and spars—but no other clipper had ever lost five-sixths of her effective foremast hands off the Horn before.

As Captain Winsor ran back from the Horn he crossed the track of young Joshua Patten, bound for California in the big extreme clipper, *Neptune's Car.* Patten and Gardner, who was in the *Intrepid,* sailed from New York the first of July. Winsor afterwards reported that he passed close to the *Intrepid* off the Horn and that she refused to acknowledge his distress signal. Gardner, however, showed by his logbook that he was not within a thousand miles of the *Rapid* on the day of this occurrence, so that it is evident Captain Winsor was mistaken.

It is possible that the ship referred to was the *Neptune's Car,* which, though a much larger ship than the *Intrepid,* and built in Virginia, was said to have been designed by Webb, the designer and builder of the *Intrepid.* If it was the *Neptune's Car,* no ship ever had better excuse for disregarding a distress signal, for Captain Patten lay sick of brain fever in his cabin. He was virtually insensible, being both deaf and blind. His first mate was under arrest for insubordination and the lofty, heavily sparred clipper was under the sole command of a nineteen year old girl, the wife of the Captain, and a competent navigator in her own right. How Mrs. Patten fought that ship to the westward while the *Rapid* turned and ran for sunny Rio to refit, and eventually brought her to port ten days ahead of the *Intrepid,* is a story that has no parallel in fiction. Patten was one of the younger masters in the service, in his 29th year at the time. He was nevertheless one of the ablest members of his profession, and a youth of excellent principles and sturdy character, as revealed by occasional entries in his log. Able commander though he was, few shipmasters then living could have excelled his wife, in seamanship or as a navigator, as Captain Gardner of the *Intrepid* and formerly of the magnificent clipper *Comet,* could testify.

Ordinary winter gales never troubled a seaman, as the log

of the ship *Boston,* Captain Jesse F. Potter, bound from New York for Acapulco, bears witness. Captain Potter wrote:

"Sunday, February 3rd—Sea acct. Noon had passed through the Narrows with a strong NW wind and very cold clear weather, under topsails and tow of steam tug *Hector,* Charles Wolsey, pilot. At 3 PM discharged the pilot ship in fair channel & just over Sandy Hook Bar. At 4.30 Highland Lighthouse bore NW dist. 15 miles. Continuous brisk gales throughout from 4 AM incessant snow squalls, and a dense vapor arising from the water which with the snow had the appearance of thick fog. SE course steered Monday.

"Feb. 4th. Throughout these 24 hours a continuation of strong NW winds with very squally weather, with an irregular but not a high sea. Squalls attended with snow til 8 PM after which hail and rain, the hail-storms in one squall the size of a Filbert and appeared like frozen wet snow. The Main Top gallant sail set. The atmosphere growing gradually milder. Obliged to keep the ship before the sea to avoid shipping water, still the decks are the most of the time flooded and considerable finds its way below. The pumps thawed out today after being frozen since the 5th of January. Found 2 feet of water in Pump well which was soon got out by rigging the double pump break. Ends cloudy and squally. S. E. course Steered.

"Tuesday, February 5th—A continuation of strong NW gales with frequent squalls of hail and rain, the sea increasing, deck flooded. At 4 AM squalls were severe, took in Main Top Gallant sail. At 9 AM passed a Barque hove to under close reefed Main Top sail head to the Northward. The sea running very irregularly.

"Feb. 28th—Crossed Line, 8 PM 25 d. 5 hrs. from Sandy Hook.

" 'Saw a bird called by sailors a Booby. His great propensity is that when his tail is down his head is asleep, like any other Booby.' "

Among the shorter runs the *Snow Squall,* Captain Girard, made a fine passage in the coffee trade, being 28 days from New York to Rio Janeiro and returning in 34 days. Her round trip of 79 days, including detention, was said to be equal to any that had ever been made.

The *Great Republic* broke the record from Sandy Hook to the Equator. Commanded by Limeburner, she left New York on the 7th of December and made her crossing on the 23rd. Her time of 15 days 19 hours was the shortest ever made up to that time.

On the run between Melbourne and Callao, the old *Governor Morton*, commanded by John Charles Berry, set up a new record. Berry sailed from Port Phillip on the 23rd of October and anchored at Callao November 19th at 7 PM:

> "and made my passage in 31½ days and think according to Lieut. Maury's sailing directions I made the quickest passage that was ever made from Australia to this port under Canvas."

Eight American ships loaded tea for England this year. The *Challenger*, Captain Burgess, got away January 10th and was 109 days to Deal. Barber was next in the *Galatea*. His run from Canton to Deal was 102 days, arriving there the 17th of May.

The only race of the year was that between the barque *Maury* and the British ship *Lord of the Isles*, which sailed on the 10th of June from Foo Choo Foo in company with the *Chrysolite* and *John Wade*. Charles E. Fletcher commanded the *Maury* and sailed one of the closest races in history with the *Lord of the Isles*, both ships being in company on several occasions. Crossing the Indian Ocean, the *Maury* made a series of fine runs. Her average daily work for the 12 days from July 28 to August 7th, inclusive, was 272¼ miles, with 370 miles as her best day. She arrived at Gravesend on the 15th of October with the *Lord of the Isles* in plain view a few minutes astern, 127 days out. Not a great victory as sailing matches go, but the *Lord of the Isles* was a much larger and longer vessel than the *Maury* and a very fast ship. She has a record of 91 days from Shanghai to London, which seems to be the best passage over that course ever made by a British ship.

Captain Harding had the *John Wade* and he drove her main mast out in heavy weather off the Cape, so she was eliminated. She limped into London under jury rig, just 38 days behind her rivals. A similar fate befell the *Chrysolite,* which took 144 days to make the passage.

The year witnessed many fine runs in time, closely approaching the record. It is impossible to notice many of them. Perhaps one of the best was the 81 days of the *Flying Scud,* Captain Rodman Baxter, from New York to Bombay, where she arrived on the 4th of July, the record at the time. *Treadwell* left San Francisco in December and sent the *Bald Eagle* through to Calcutta in 57½ days, truly remarkable time. The new medium clipper *Florence,* under Dumaresq, now an old man, as clipper masters went, made her début in a 91 day passage from Boston to Hong Kong. Dumaresq was still one of the hardest drivers afloat. His log is full of references to ships under double reefs passed by the *Florence* under topgallants, with occasionally a main royal for good measure.

On the 23rd of October, the *Carrier Dove,* Captain Corner, arrived at Valparaiso 30 days from Melbourne, a passage very close to the record. Another very fine run was that of the medium clipper *Wild Wave,* commanded by Captain Knowles. She left Callao bound for Havre with guano and arrived off Plymouth late in November, 70 days out. This time does not seem to have been equalled by any other ship before or after her.

None of the Indiamen reported a harder blow about this time than the old *Joshua Bates,* Captain D. S. McCallum, which was bound from New York to Shanghai and was in the Indian Ocean at the time. His log contains a graphic description of his experience:

"Thursday, Oct. 30th Begins with W-N. & N.W. by W. winds. Generally gloomy. 7 P M increasing breezes with rain—took in light and studg sails.

"11 PM very dark and blowing fresh—took in Fore Top Galt sail.

"Midnight in Main Top Galt Sail.

"Middle watch increasing squalls from the NW with light rain.

"Carried whole Top sails till daylight.

"Bart falling steadily.

"4 A.M. Daylight commenced to reef—wind and sea fast increasing—obliged to keep off before the wind to secure the sails—close reefed and furled the courses, also Fore and Miz. Top sails.

"8 A.M. rounded to on the Port Tack after having run to the Southard and southard and eastward for nearly three hours. I regretted we had to do so for I knew we were immerging deeper into the gale—and running across the face of it—for as we went to the southard the wind drew to the Northward.

"About 11 A M, Bart inch 29–10.

"In a violent hail squall—wind suddenly shifted 2 or 3 points to the westward blowing now a perfect *Hurricane*. The pressure of the wind must have been greater on the surface of the water than any other gale I ever experienced; for I never saw the Ocean present such a fearful appearance before. In some of the squalls we could neither see, hear, or speak. . . . After the shift to the westward the Bart started up a tenth and again depressed for a short time.

"Four P M now heading up North and North by West *blowing* if anything *harder* and *harder*. . . . Removed all the crew out of the 'Midship House' and kept everybody aft ready for any emergency.

"5 P M Bart again made an attempt to arise inch 29–20 air 50—'*Sun Set*' blowing fearfully and the wildest appearance I ever saw.

"7 P M no abatement. . . . Ship behaving admirably. 8 P M some signs of abatement. More moderate between the squalls. Bart rising fast. The greater portion of the storm has now evidently passed us and we are on the N.W. corner of it. . . . Throughout the 'tempest' we laid to under the lee clew of the Main Topsail. (A splendid new sail!) The Main spencer eased off against the main rigging—and a Tarpaulin in the Mizzen rigging.

"Midnight. Wind moderating. Set the weather clew of the main Topsail. . . . The highest sea I ever saw running.

"Oct. 31—Lat. 42.38 S. Lon 89.51 E.

"4 A M Bart inch 29–83.

"5 A M Squared away on our course with Main Royal set. An awful swell from the S.W.

"Thus we have weathered one of the most furious gales that the oldest seaman on board ever experienced (and certainly the hardest that I have ever seen) without the slightest damage."

Thanks to the carefully selected white oak and honest square fastening of Donald McKay, the *Joshua Bates* came through without a mark and Captain McCallum arrived at Shanghai in time to receive news of the first stages of a great anti-foreign movement that centered around Canton and proved to be the beginning of a three years war between the Chinese on the one hand and the British and French on the other.

CHAPTER XXX

1857

COMMERCIAL PANIC AND CIVIL STRIFE

LESS than a hundred clippers had taken the Cape Horn route to California in 1856. Even more marked was the decrease in '57 when only 68 sailed from eastern ports for the Golden Gate. The depression, first apparent in 1853, which had been growing more pronounced with each succeeding year, culminated during the autumn in a world wide financial debacle of unprecedented fury, which swept away thousands of firms and left the business world in a gloom which lasted for several years.

Even the laying of the first Atlantic cable failed to arouse an outburst of enthusiasm comparable with that which greeted the arrival less than twenty years before of the first transatlantic steamers at New York.

Buchanan and the Dred Scott decision came. John Brown was marching. Repercussions of the "War in Kansas" filled the air. Uncle Tom's Cabin started its peregrinations. Downright hatred or frenzied admiration were replacing the good-humored, patronizing tolerance with which anti-slavery orators had been regarded. The butt of North and South alike in 1850 was America's saviour or enemy in '57, depending largely on geographical considerations. Boys who had joked with their elders about "crazy abolitionists" were to lie in grim windrows at Antietam or Fredericksburg a few years later.

Reform by force is doubtless well enough, but it is rather hard on the contemporary younger generation. In the late fifties the young men who might have been filled with the fire of constructive enthusiasm, as were the boys of the three preceding decades, spent their surplus energy debating matters their predecessors without hesitation or courtesy had dubbed "crazy."

Possibly the circumstance had little to do with the result so far as ships were concerned, but unquestionably one misses the singleness of purpose, the driving force and creative enthusiasm of the "builder" during the later fifties and thereafter.

From 1857 until the Civil War was in full swing many of the famous old clippers were laid up for months on end. The *Flying Cloud* was idle two years and more. Many ships, among them the famous *Challenge,* were eventually dismantled in Chinese waters, where some of them were sold for a mere fraction of their original cost.

Relatively speaking, commerce was at a standstill. One would expect to see a corresponding failure of efficiency in sailing-ship achievements. On the contrary, taking into consideration the volume of commerce, a remarkable number of very fast runs were recorded. On the California course alone ten passages were completed which averaged less than 102 days each. Two of these runs were under 100 days, that of the *Flying Dragon* being 97 and the *Great Republic* 92 days.

In the Orient, England had a couple of wars on her hands, but they were on the whole the sort that improved a merchant marine. Her three year punishment of the Mandarins around Canton was in full swing. India was making a premature bid for freedom to go to the dogs as she chose. The Sepoy Mutiny was full of colorful incidents, but none more so than the races of the great McKay ships owned by James Baines & Co., and chartered by the Government as transports to India.

It is worth noting in this connection that the best time made by any of the great sailing transports was the 87 day run this year of the *Lightning* from Portsmouth to Sand Heads, a run which under normal conditions may be fairly considered several days longer than the 87 day record of the *Nor'Wester* from Boston a couple of years earlier.

British requirements provided almost the only profitable employment obtained by American clippers at this time, aside from the tea trade. A large number were put on the run between India and England. Among them were the *Sirocco, Hornet, Euroclydon, Defiance, Flying Scud, Typhoon, Mary Robinson, Bonita, War Hawk, Nor'Wester, Gamecock, Meteor, Rival* and *Belle of the West.* In the Australian service were to be found the *Governor Morton, Free Trade, Wizard King, Titan, Queen of the East, Neptune's Favorite* and a host of fine ships.

One of the best passages made from India to England at this time was that of the *Invincible*, Captain Johnson, 82 days from Bombay, May 14th, to Liverpool, August 4th. It was a good run, though not a record, and therefore hardly comparable with that of the *Beverly*, 676 tons, from Boston to Calcutta, completed a few months later. William Perkins of Boston owned the *Beverly* and Captain Chase commanded her. Chase sailed from Boston the afternoon of August 30th, sea time, and took his pilot off Sand Heads on the morning of November 23rd, "85 d. 16½ hrs. from pilot to pilot or from Boston Light to Sand Heads."

This was a record for the course, and, so far as can be ascertained, it has never been equalled since.

The year appears to have been favorable for good runs to India, for the present record between New York and Bombay, was also established at this time by the extreme clipper *Sweepstakes*. Still commanded by Lane, she left New York May 9th and anchored at Bombay, July 22nd, in a run of 74 days. The passage was no fluke, for Captain Lane immediately brought his ship back to New York in 80 days, establishing a round trip record of 154 days, which is believed to be still unbeaten.

William Appleton & Company owned the medium clipper *Nabob*, built by John Taylor of Chelsea, and perhaps the best ship from his yard, although the extreme clipper *Aurora* was a very handsome, able craft. Captain William Cole had made several very fine passages in the *Nabob*, but his run this year from New York to Hong Kong was the best of them all.

Cole left Sandy Hook about 6 o'clock on the evening of April 22nd, and anchored at Hong Kong at 4.30 P.M., July 17th. Deducting 18 hours' stop at Anjier, his net sailing time appeared to be 85 days, 4½ hours. In some way—possibly by making the permissible but unusual deduction of 12 hours and 33 minutes' difference between New York and Hong Kong time—Cole figured his passage as 84 days and entered in the log of the *Nabob*:

> "This is the shortest passage on record between the United States or Europe and any port in China. Dist. 17532.—daily av. 208.71—8.69 miles per hour. July 5th up with Java Head 74 days from New York."

It was, of course, very fine work, but hardly what Captain Cole considered it to be. He had apparently overlooked the 81 day run of the *Oriental* in 1850, which was still unequalled, and several other passages made prior to his own in somewhat better time. However, it was an excellent performance and Captain Cole was a thoroughly able seaman. It is to be regretted that he lost the clipper *Courser* on Pratas Shoals the following year, an event which resulted in his death from anxiety and overwork.

The *Comet*, now commanded by Arquit, loaded guano at Elide Island, lower California, from which she made the run of 92 days home to New York, where she arrived on the 19th of December. A feature of her voyage was her run of 14 days from the Equator to Sandy Hook, a performance that apparently still stands as the record. Indeed, it has been stated more than once that 16 days is the best time made over this course.

Eight Yankee clippers assisted this year in the British tea trade, precisely the same number the British themselves were able to muster. For the first time the new barkentine rig appeared in the trade. The little clipper barkentine *Fairy*, Captain Blish, sailing a remarkably even race with the barque *Maury*, both vessels loading at Foo Choo Foo. Captain Fletcher took the *Maury* out on the 3rd of July and entered in at London on the 17th of October. The *Fairy* sailed the following day and docked two days after the *Maury*, their respective runs being 106 and 107 days, very good out of season passages. One has only to refer to the lists of passages of the very efficient tea clippers from 1860 to 1880 to appreciate the quality of this performance.

Among the other American ships which carried tea to England were the *Swallow, Competitor, Neptune's Favorite, North Wind, Celestial,* and *Spit Fire.*

The best run was made by the *North Wind,* her time being 96 days from Hong Kong to London with the reported 98 days of the *Celestial* second best. Three of the American passages were shorter than the best reported British run. In this connection it is necessary to note that the passage of the British clipper *Northfleet,* Captain Freeman, from Hong Kong to Plymouth this year as given by an English writer is incorrect. The run is given as 82 days (Basil Lubbock: *"The China Clippers,"* p. 134), which, if correct, would stand as the world's record by a generous margin, but as a matter of fact, the *Northfleet* sailed from Hong Kong on the 8th of August and entered in at London on the 8th of December. Her passage therefore was 122 days, or if her passage is considered to end at Plymouth, 117 days. The same writer gives the passage of the *Celestial* as 141 days, possibly confusing her with a British ship of the same name. The American *Celestial,* credited with 98 days, actually took 137.

The sea again took its toll and two well remembered old ships disappeared. Captain Thompson sailed in the *Helena* from China for Havana with coolies and was never again reported. An old whale ship called the *Natchez* pounded her life out on the lonely shores of the Okhotsk sea.

The unfortunate *Flying Arrow* had again been totally dismastered in Australian waters toward the end of 1856 and was condemned. She was rerigged as the *Wings of the Wind* and auctioned off at London in January '57, going under the French flag, thus ending her career as an American ship.

Captain Andrew Barstow with the old *Lantao* was also numbered among the missing this year. He sailed from Caldera for Boston in October, 1856, and was never reported.

Forty-eight days from Liverpool came the clipper packet *Typhoon*, a mass of ice from jibboom end to taffrail. Captain Salter had a crew of forty hardened packet rats, only ten of whom were able to leave their sodden, steaming bunks. He had been stripped of every sail on the yards more than once, and had but one sail left on the main and mizzen masts—the main course. During the previous three weeks he had lost seven close-reefed, brand new topsails, blown out of the bolt ropes one after another. Taken all in all, it had been a fair sample of an Eskimo hell. Captain Salter was no slack baked sailor, but it is not surprising that he and the *Typhoon* next turn up in the hottest trade on Earth—the Calcutta run.

On New Year's day the *Surprise* had sailed from Shanghai for New York. Thirteen days later Ranlett passed Anjier, and on February 1st he was trying conclusions with a hurricane. He lost his foresail, reefed main topsail and larboard quarter boat and washed away the larboard topgallant bulwark, but he passed Sandy Hook on the 25th of March, in a passage of slightly more than 82 days, but little longer than the present record over the course. It was excellent hard driving under any conditions, but with a strained leaky ship and ragged copper it must be considered one of the best passages ever made from China. The old *Oneida,* under the able command of William A. Creesy, left Shanghai five days later than the *Surprise* and was 116 days on the run.

The *Surprise* went on the dry dock for a thorough overhauling and new copper, as did scores of other clippers about this time. From five to seven years hard driving had left their mark on the best of them. At this time also many of them were re-rigged in the interests of economy, their spars reduced and double topsails substituted for the huge old single topsails, but as yet the *Surprise* was not among this number. Having repaired his ship, Ranlett was off to Shanghai again. On the 1st of November he was busy snugging down for a typhoon. Extracts from his log give a graphic picture of experience of this sort in the China sea.

"Sept. 26th. working out the Great Lema Channel, good breeze and ebb tide in our favor. At 6 P M out clear of all the Lema Islands. Lots of fishing junks, hard to keep clear of them during the night. Ends with strong single Reefed Topsail Breeze. Making tacks From 2 to 4 hours long.

"Sept. 27th. Commences with good breeze and fine weather. Ex sig with Eng. Ship *Earl of Eglington* bound for Shanghai. From 1 to 5 A M very heavy squalls and enormous quantities of rain, plenty of lightning all round the compass. Lowered topsails down and hauled courses up Daylight made sail. Ex Sign with Eng. Ship *Admiral* bound for Shanghai. Ends with strong gale and very heavy head sea pitching bows under. Tacked ship 5 times and wore ship once. Land in sight.

"Sept. 28th. Heavy rain squalls throughout the twenty-four hours, and tremendous head sea from E Ne. Ship pitching bows all under, decks flooded with water. 4 P M saw Pedro Branco Rocks bearing NE just in sight off deck. Very few fishing junks round. 3 A.M. thick rain and blowing very hard, topsails on the Cap, courses hauled up, jib down. Ends strong double Reefed Topsail breeze. No alteration in weather, wind hauling more to the Nd. (Good)

"Sept. 29th. Strong breeze and heavy rain squalls. 4 P M. Tacked ship off Pedro Branco Rock, bearing N by E. 10 P M Strong gale and thick rain, with tremendous heavy head sea, ship pitching bows under, and flooded with water. Daylight not much wind, bad chop of a Sea. 11 A M a very heavy squall took in every rag of canvass except 3 close reefs. *Tremendous quantity Rain.*

"Sept. 30th. First part heavy squalls of wind & *rain* from

S.E. Middle part weather a little better. Latter part strong gale and dense black squalls of *rain*. Never saw such quantities of rain before. A very heavy sea. Ship rolling and straining badly. 7 A M. Got into 7 fthms water wore ship off shore. 9 A.M. saw a pt of land bearing North. Don't know anything about where we are.

"Oct. 1st. Lat 22.05 N. Commences with strong gale and storms. 4 P.M. Took in Fore Sail and Mainsail. 5 PM. A whirlwind passed over the Ship, parted Foot Rope of Miz Topsail. Weather looks *very bad but* the *Bar* does *indicate* the *approach* of a *cyclone storm*. During the night continual heavy squalls of wind and *immense quantities* of *rain*. Very heavy sea, put our *flying jibboom under water frequently*. Daylight moderate Made sail. Ends fine weather. During squalls Bar. vibrated 2/10ths. Coast land in sight.

"Oct. 2nd. Fine pleasant weather, all possible sail, *want our sky-sails* now. 8 P. M. Getting thick and rainy again from N. E. Strong southerly swell all day. 11 P. M. Breezing up from W S Daylight passed by Breaker Pt. Sea breaking high on it. Latter part very fine weather and good breeze. Sent up M Royal Yd and set sail also Fore Tp. M. Studg, Saw a Dutch barque going into Swatow behind *Namoa* Is. with this wind, we shall go up through Formosa Straights. (Risky.)

"Oct. 3rd. Fine beautiful weather and good breeze. Jibed ship and run down alongside of an *English Man of War Steamer*, using both sails and steam and kept company with her 4 hours when she slowly left us. We could sail as fast as she could with the wind a pt on the quarter. Mid Good breeze and clear moonlight. Latter part cloudy, all starboard studs set. Passed barque & brig bound same way. 12 Med. Oksuer Is bore N ½ W 13 miles.

"Oct. 4th. Light winds and fine weather. Haitan land is sight before dark. During the night light air and clear moonlight. Latter part calm and current setting us to the SW. Brig in company and a barque bound south. Turnabout just visible W by N. High Land of Formosa in sight.

"Oct. 5th. Commences with a light breeze springing up at N NW. Stood on port tack E by S. 11 PM blowing strong. Single reefed Topsails and at 12 mid Gale coming on

CLIPPER SHIP "JOHN BERTRAM."

FROM PAINTING BY LARS THORSEN.

Courtesy of the New York, New Haven & Hartford Railroad Company.

much faster. Close reefed the topsails and furled the jib mainsail foresail and spanker. 5 A.M. blowing a heavy gale and tremendous sea on. Ship made a heavy roll to starboard, carrying away Main Top Mast-head in the eyes of the Rigging and Miz Top Galt Mast in three pieces. Main Top Galt Mast and yard all down amongst our braces in great confusion. Cleared away the wreck. 10 A. M. saw Aligator Rock to windward of us. Ends with a tremendous gale of wind and very heavy sea. Running in for the White Dog Is's for an anchorage.

"Oct. 6th. Commences with tremendous heavy gale of wind and very heavy sea. 2 P. M. Bore up S W. for the White Dog Is. 3 P.M. Hauled round the S. E. end of the Eastern one. 3.30 P.M. Came too with both anchors just inside of the Breakwater Island, 60 fthms on one 35 fthms on the other. Brought up very heavy came near loseing both chains and anchors, tore all the whelps off one side of the windlass. Book of directions for entering Fou Chou for River Min, says this is a good anchorage, it *may* be close in where junks can anchor, but we find it very rough. Ship pitching bows under. During the night, blowing squalls of great violence and many whirlwinds coming down off the land. Ends moderate N W wind and fine rain. Hove up one anchor and catted it. Should go to sea now if we had any topsails bent, but they are all torn to pieces.

"Oct. 7th. Fine pleasant weather and very hot sun. Men employed shifting Topsails &c. Light breeze from N W all night. 4 A. M. Got underweigh and set all the sail possible and that is not much as we have no Top Galt. sails. 8 A. M. boarded by a China pilot for the River Min. Ends dead calm and ebb tide setting us down in the Islands again. Got all ready to anchor again in 24 fthms water. *Hard luck this.*

"Oct. 8th. 1 P. M. A light breeze sprung up from the East just in time as we must have anchored in an ½ an hour more or we should have drifted on Castle Rk. Floor tide sets Nd. We made several tacks this twenty four hours standing off shore on the floodtide and on when it ebbs. Latter part weather very fine. We do not gain any. Think the under current must set to the Sd and as we draw 21 ft it takes hold of us. Aligator Rk just in sight off deck. Very few clouds.

"Oct. 9th. Fine pleasant weather and moderate breeze but baffling two or three points all the time. Flurry during the night and very bright moonlight. Trying hard to fetch by the North End of Formosa but every time we get near it the wind heads us off. Current evidently setting strong to the Sd. Latter part wind and weather the same. North Cape bears S S E.

"Oct. 10th. Lat. 26.43 N. First part wind baffling two or three pts and getting light. Sea very smooth. appearances of a strong current setting us to the N E. Birds, Fish and drift stuff. 6 P. M. Pinsele Is bears S E by S & Agincourt Is bears E by N ½ N. Middle and latter part fine weather and light breeze. Set Fore Top Galt Sail, Getting Miz Top Galt Mast Rigged. Made a good day's work to the Nd.

"Oct. 11th. Fine pleasant weather light winds."

Other ships did not fare so well. The *Great Republic* running for London with guano had her hatches smashed and deck stove by tremendous Cape Horn combers dropping over the rail, and was forced into the bleak Falklands in distress and half full of water. Captain Cicero Brown in the S. *Gildersleeve,* another guano ship, took a pampero off the River Platte with all larboard studding sails set. Officers and men worked like Trojans up to their waists in water along the lee rail. The bark of orders: the electric thrill as the immense fabric bowed lower and lower, yard arms cutting the water, a mighty rushing wind: dull sounds of exploding sails: the machine gun racket of shredding canvas, sheets, halyards, down hauls and clew lines parting.

In five minutes it was over. Father Neptune had effectually snugged down Cap'n Cicero's canvas. Not a sail was left except the topsails and spanker hanging in voluminous folds where the halyards had been let go with a run. From great main course to skysails every inch of cotton was gone, with fore topgallant mast and the spare yards and boats from the midship house. Fore and main lower masts were sprung—almost broken through at the spider band—and the fore yard looked like a bent bow.

It was not that Captain Brown had been caught napping.

Only those who have been through a similar experience can appreciate his predicament. A bolt from the blue is the nearest approach in nature to this phenomenon of the Argentine coast. To the writer it seems more probable that such missing lofty clippers as the *Rainbow* met their end in pamperos rather than in heavier but slower rising gales of the Horn.

At all events there was Captain Brown and there was the *Gildersleeve,* reasonably sound from the spider bands down. Faced with the alternative of Rio and ruin, or getting up a jury rig, Brown went to work. How he fished his lower masts with spare topmasts and lower yards run up between "trussel trees" and secured with chains and wedges: fidded a new topgallant mast: crossed makeshift yards and patched split canvas is a story longer in the telling than the doing, but at last he was rigged and doing an easy seven knots for Havre. It was all in the day's work.

Captain Stoddard of the Clipper *Kathay* put in a busy week at the close of the year. He arrived at Bankok on December 31st in a run of six days from Hong Kong, the best run reported up to that time between the ports. The Captain was a bit of a driver in his way. Homeward bound a few months later, he lost a maintopmast and a Chinaman off Cape Horn.

One could not always judge a smart passage by the number of days it required. The extreme clipper *Wizard* made the fair but by no means record run of 45 days from Hong Kong to San Francisco with 700 prospective laundrymen thronging her decks. The *Alta California* of July 4th noted her arrival:

"The celebrated clipper ship *Wizard,* Capt. Slate, now discharging at Lombard Dock, is a noble specimen of American Clipper ships. Her fine appearance, 'alow and aloft,' bespeak a thorough seaman in command; and her splendid voyage of forty-five days from Hong Kong, coming in ahead of some six vessels which sailed before her, tells to the credit of the ship and her gallant captain."

It proved a worthy obituary for Captain Slate. He took his ship back to China and there received another and greater command. He died at Macao in November and his stalwart frame lies in Hong Kong, the eternal anchorage of so many once famous Yankee masters.

In a certain material sense the clipper ship era ended in 1857. No new clippers were launched thereafter in America. Ships of clipper form were built, it is true, fine smart looking sharp craft like the *Prima Donna* of Mystic, *Star of Peace* at Newburyport, the *Industry* at Medford, the second *Memnon* at South Boston in 1858, and the second *Shooting Star* and the *Maid of the Sea* in 1859.

They lacked, however, the lofty spars and immensely square yards of the clipper, having been planned at a time when a general reduction in the sail area of the older ships was already under way.

This reduction was only partly in the interest of economy. It was in a majority of cases a necessity, for most of the clippers had been wracked by hard driving to such an extent it was no longer safe to carry their original spars, many of which were considerably longer and heavier than the spars of men of war of the same tonnage. In this fact, also lies the explanation of the contention, so persistently made by the later shipmasters, that the clippers were not heavily masted. Seafaring men whose experience dated from 1860 never saw the clippers in all their glory.

A scant half dozen racers were launched in '57, including the barque *Dawn*, built at New York by Thomas Collyer, with her record of 36 days from Buenos Ayres to Sandy Hook in 1860. They were all clippers, however, the *Belle of the Sea*, built at Marblehead, in particular being credited with the very fast passage of 64 days from London to Melbourne. The others were the *Hotspur*, built by Roosevelt & Joyce at New York; *Richard Busteed*, by Emery Sawyer at Quincy; *Fortuna*, Paul Curtis' last clipper, and the *Twilight* from the yard of Charles Mallory in Mystic.

None of the new ships attracted more favorable attention than the *Twilight*. From her figure head of a woman in white holding a star in one hand and a flaming flambeau in the other to her exquisitely rounding stern with its plain gold beading, she was marvellously beautiful. The day following her arrival in New York the *Herald* said:

> "The new and magnificent clipper ship named the *Twilight,* has just been laid on the load for San Francisco in Coleman's California Line, and is well deserving a particular notice. She has been built with all the modern improvements, including the latest and most approved type of ventilation.
>
> "The ship is 200 feet in length, 40 feet beam, and 20 feet depth of hold, and registers 1482 tons—is of an extreme clipper model, a round stern with a long clean run; was built at Mystic, Conn., and was designed and modelled by Mr. Mason C. Hill. She is planked with selected white oak and is considered one of the best ships ever built.
>
> "Her model—for stability, capacity, and sailing qualities—is all that could be desired, combining strength and beauty, and looks to perfection the bold and dashing clipper. She is owned by C. H. Mallory and others of Mystic and Capt. Gurdon Gates, who commands her. We would advise all those who are admirers of, and take an interest in naval architecture, to pay her a visit at her pier at the foot of Wall Street."

Some vague beautiful premonition must have prompted the naming of the *Twilight*. It was in very truth the twilight of the gods, and the dusky half light of that dying day disclosed one of the loveliest, as she was the last of the clippers. Her model exquisitely carved, still hangs in the Mallory loft in the little village of Mystic, where old Charles Mallory laid it away more than 70 years ago.

Mystic days and Mystic ships. Many a gnarled old father and silent, unassuming mother paid heavy tribute that they might hand down new ideals of beauty, and new standards of efficiency. Hardly a little seaside cemetery along the Atlantic that does not hold its mossy slab like that in the old Elder Wightman burying ground at Center Croton, Connecticut:

SACRED TO THE MEMORY OF
JOHN LAMPHERE
BORN MAY 2, 1842, LOST IN
THE PACIFIC OCEAN FROM SHIP
MARY E. SUTTON, CAPTAIN SISSON,
JUNE 20, 1857.

Only fifteen, yet his farmer father, like many another poverty stricken parent of his generation, toiled grimly on to pay the heavy cost of the simple monument. It was a small part of the price of a single wintry passage around the Horn.

Going to sea in the smart clipper of the fifties was a serious business. Occasionally it displayed a lighter side, as when John Ropes entered in the log of the *John Gilpin* on the 6th of July: "Neptune came abord & shaved us 4 boys and pat." This horseplay apparently was rather rare, for the *Gilpin* arrived out at Honolulu the 30th of September following, 106 days from Boston—a good winter passage around the Horn.

CHAPTER XXXI

1858

EVEN commercial cataclysms have their limitations. In spite of unparalleled depression the quest for faster and more efficient communication went on unceasingly. Agitation for rail service to the Pacific, which had followed closely on the discovery of gold, was redoubled. Telegraph lines had netted the West as far as the Mississippi, and were rapidly pushing farther.

On the 10th of October, 1858, the first "overland mail" clattered down Market Street, San Francisco, just 23 days, 23½ hours from St. Louis. The Northwest Coast, through the medium of the "pony express," had moved perceptibly nearer Wall Street. With the aid of the new Atlantic cable, recently completed and ready for business, Europe was less than a month distant from the San Francisco merchant. If the burden of Atlas was no lighter it was definitely smaller.

California trade showed a slight improvement. Eleven clippers cleared from Eastern ports in January and during the year ninety sailed, a decided increase over the preceding twelve months. An interesting commentary on the sources of clipper ship development is that 11 of the 90 were from the little village of Mystic, and two of those headed the fleet. The 100 day runs of the *Twilight* and the *Andrew Jackson* were equalled by no other clippers arriving at San Francisco during the year. For two succeeding years thereafter Mystic ships made the best passages recorded by any of the Cape Horners, and when the 100 day mark was again broken in 1866 after a period of long passages, it was another Mystic ship, the *Seminole,* that turned the trick.

The nearest approach to the time of the leaders in 1858 was the 107 day voyage of the *Dashing Wave,* Captain Young, who left Boston on New Year's Day and arrived out on the 18th of April. Fernald and Pettigrew of Portsmouth, who built the *Typhoon* and a number of other clippers, were the builders of the *Wave* and so well did they do their work that with the exception of the old ship *Syren,* she appears to have been the last of the clippers in active service. It was stated that in 1920, while operating as a barge on the Pacific Coast, her hull was examined and found to be in sound condition, after nearly 70 years afloat.

Another Mystic ship sailed a close race against the *Stag Hound.* This was the Mallory built clipper, *Elizabeth F. Willets,* commanded by Captain Joseph Warren Holmes. Although less than 900 tons, she passed the Golden Gate on the 11th of June, 122 days from New York, while Hussey had brought the *Stag Hound* around from Boston four days earlier in 121 days. If Captain Holmes was disappointed, he nevertheless had the satisfaction of making a shorter voyage than the fine clippers *Flying Eagle, Phantom* and *Southern Cross* which sailed about the same time.

Just forty years later Holmes left San Francisco bound for New York on his *eightieth* passage around the Horn in sail—he was to make three more, a record that will probably stand unequalled to the end of time.

Another interesting character of the day was Captain William H. Nelson of the *Harvey Birch,* another Mystic production named after Washington's famous patriot spy of Revolutionary days. She was owned by John Brower of New York, and was later burned by the confederate ship *Nashville*. Nelson is said to have been a street waif of Boston, who was picked up and sent to sea at a very early age. Few of the ships that sailed this year had a harder time off the Horn than the *Harvey Birch*. Captain Nelson's log is a record of a mid-winter passage around the Horn in a deeply loaded ship.

"Have abt 3000 tons wt. & measurement gen. merchandise including 736 tons coal. Draws 24.6 aft—23.7 for'd. Crew of 28 all told (built for Liverpool trade).

"April 17. At 7 took tug off the Battery. 10.30 A. M. pass bar. 11.00 tug and pilot leave. Found ship very deep and wet.

"May 18. Cross Line at 6 P. M. (31 d and a few odd hours) 2 d ahead of last voyage and 9 behind first.

"(June 27. 50 South Atlantic Nelson had a series of head gales off the Horn and did not reach 50 South Pacific until July 24th).

"July 11. 59–35 S. 71–30 W. Comes in with heavy increasing gales from N. NW., very heavy sea on. Morning tremendous gale blowing and increasing. Latter part a Hurricane gale blowing in squalls came near losing foretopsail by the parting of the weather sheet. Tremendous sea running one of the heaviest I ever see. At meridian the sun broke through the clouds presenting the wildest scene the imagination could picture. A tremendous cross sea running, the water a blowing the scud a flying and to cap the climax a threatening looking squall rising in the west which broke upon us at 30 minutes P. M. with a force as though it would take all with it in its course. The Barometer commenced to rise and the wind canted W.N.W. wore ship as soon as we could. Fore part moderating gales from W. N. W. Ends with heavy snow squalls rising in S. W. but having no effect on the wind.

"July 19. 57–40 S. 78 W—I believe a ship never had such a time since Lord Anson's time. My ship shows it and feels it, although as good a ship as comes this way.

"July 21. The blackest and darkest squall I ever see

passed over blowing very heavy with snow and hail. A large ship in company An American I take her. The times are exciting *pulling cotton*. He has his match for today and more too."

It is a far cry from Nelson on the quarter deck of the *Victory* to Nelson the street waif urgently "pulling cotton" between squalls, in mid-winter Cape Horn clipper races, but no one can doubt that the two men spoke the same language, and would have rounded the Cape famously together.

A drawn battle was staged by the *Euterpe*, commanded by hard driving John Arey, from "down Frankfort way" and the Damariscotta clipper *Talisman*, under Captain Thomas. They sailed from New York on August 25th and 27th, respectively, the worst season of the year for fast passages, and arrived out in the same order exactly 135 days later.

Shortly before this the *Great Republic* had arrived 120 days from New York. The *Adelaide*, commanded by Captain Wakeman, had left the same day and the two vessels were in company for 10 days. Then the *Adelaide* drew ahead, making an excellent passage to the Equator, and it was not until she was off Cape St. Roque that the *Great Republic* caught her again. Eventually the *Great Republic* led her into San Francisco by a margin of nearly two weeks, but not before the *Adelaide* had demonstrated that under certain weather conditions she was somewhat faster.

On her return passage to New York the *Great Republic* had a brush with the *Talisman*. The *Alta California* of February 9th, 1859, describes the start of the race:

"On Thursday afternoon the clipper ships *Great Republic* and *Talisman* both started to sea bound for New York. A friend who went down to the Heads in one of the vessels, described the appearance of the ships as magnificent, covered as every mast and spar was by a cloud of canvas, and dashing away to the southward under a fine sailing breeze. As both are fast vessels and commanded by able and experienced captains we may look for some 'tall going' and short time between this port and New York."

Remarkable as it may seem, the pigmy overcame the giant; the *Talisman* reaching New York on the 18th of May in a run of 96 days, while the *Great Republic* did not arrive until the 22nd of the month.

Fine runs were made by a number of the old favorites. The *David Crockett*, Captain Spencer, homeward bound from California was up with Hatteras in 13 days from the Equator, and "like to break the record." The wind then hauling ahead she was four days thence to Sandy Hook.

More of the clippers made their last port. The *John Milton*, commanded by Ephraim Harding, racing up from the Tropics before a bitter Southeast snow storm went ashore near Montauk the night of February 20th. Morning revealed only a heaving sea of pulp wood with here and there a tossing frozen arm flung momentarily aloft. Twenty-six men—all were there, captain and cabin boy.

At the same moment the beautiful *Flying Dutchman* was breaking up on Brigantine Beach. An ice berg off the Horn in January accounted for the *John Gilpin*. The *Tropic Bird* dragged ashore in June at Inagua and went to pieces. In the South Pacific the *Wild Wave*, Captain Knowles, was lost on a coral island and for months her crew were given up as dead. The long story of their adventures and rescue is one of the epics of the sea, a brief but excellent version of which is to be found in Howe & Matthews' *American Clipper Ships*.

Only two American ships sailed from China for England this season. They were the barque *Snapdragon*, Captain Davis, and the new ship *Florence*, commanded by Phillip Dumaresq. The *Snapdragon* left Whampoa the latter part of April, passed Anjier on the 20th of May and entered in at London August 13th, after a long run even for the unfavorable season.

Dumaresq left Shanghai loaded principally with Japanese goods on the 26th of December, made Caspar straits in 12 days and passed Anjier the 8th of January. He was off Good Hope on his 44th day, crossed the Equator 68 days out, was on the Mother bank 92 days from Shanghai and entered in at London after a passage of 99 days. The *Florence* had light winds throughout, her best day being only 280 miles. In the China Sea she carried royal studding sails for 9 days.

It was the first time since the days of the *Oriental* that a Yankee ship had failed to hang up the record passage of the year from China to a port in England. Without disparaging the remarkable 89 day passage of the *Lord of the Isles* to Dover and the 92 and 93 day runs reported by two other British clippers (all achievements of the first rank), it should be pointed out that both the *Florence* and *Snapdragon* were relatively full built vessels. The *Florence* was so full that she stowed nearly double her registered tonnage, whereas an extreme clipper could barely carry the equivalent of her register and many could not do that. Her fine passages were due almost entirely to her commander's predilection for carrying sail, for the period had produced few harder drivers than Dumaresq. Instance after instance is recorded in her log of passing close-reefed ships while she went tearing by with royals and occasionally main skysail set.

Comparatively few American clippers were designed expressly for the China trade, and the majority of those that were, had been built for the tea merchants of Boston, New York and Philadelphia, who as a rule needed their services so imperatively that they were not available for charter. With the exception of a few clipper packets and small coffee traders all others were modelled for the harsh conditions of the Cape Horn and Australian runs. Their fine passages in the moderate airs of the China course were due to incessant driving and good seamanship rather than to their "fanning" ability in doldrum weather.

A full built ship of Dennis, the *Webfoot*, commanded by Captain Hedge, made the run from Calcutta to New York in

85 days, arriving at Sandy Hook on the 21st of March. At the same moment the *Surprise,* racing home from Shanghai, crossed the Equator in the Atlantic and Ranlett noted the vernal equinox with the entry:

> " 'Old Sol' crossed the line about 10 P.M., and the 'old Surprise' did the same thing at 6 A. M."

He laid his maintopsail to the mast for a pilot off the Highlands on the morning of April 10th, 92 days 22 hours from Shanghai, the finest passage of the season. His time of 13 days from Woosung to Anjier was unusually good.

The end of the year came. The trim clipper *N. B. Palmer* was smashing homeward from Shanghai, racing with death. Her young commander Higham, still in his twenties, paced her quarter deck day and night, his spare frame racked at intervals with paroxysms of coughing. From his drawn face, burning eyes roved incessantly from flat rigid canvas to the beautiful blue water just combing the lee rail. Oh the beautiful, beautiful blue of those tropic seas! As he gazed Higham knew it was for the last time. He was nearing the end of the passage. Well he would make it a good one. He turned to his first officer with a gesture. Orders barked: bare-footed men sprang to the braces to trim still sharper yards already on the slack lee backstays, until the cock of the watch, an ancient mariner of 30 summers, forehanding the brace should slue his weather eye and huskily report "two blocks, Sir."

Sunday morning, the 17th of January, 1859. The church bells of Brooklyn were ringing sharp and clear over the bay as the *N. B. Palmer* slipped into her dock, 82 days from Shanghai. Higham had won his race, and what was more to him, had equalled the world's record. In company with him came the smart clipper *Kathay* which had sailed from the nearer port of Foo Choo Foo exactly thirty days before he left Shanghai.

Five days later every flag in the harbor flew at half mast. In his Brooklyn home Captain Higham lay dead of consumption in the 28th year of his age. Somewhere beyond that harsh Cape all seamen weather, ship and master are sailing still. May they find "a smooth sea and a steady trade"—forever.

Old captains and old ships were passing fast. The *Flying Fish* was gone, another victim to the chow-chow water of the Min. The *Alert* disappeared under the yellow waves of the China Sea, carrying with her a couple mates and half her crew. Yellow fever was raging. Joseph Hamilton, formerly of the *Eclipse*, succumbed to it during the summer at Charleston, South Carolina. Men died like flies in southern waters. The *Sparkling Wave* of Boston arrived at New York on the 7th of August. In six months she had lost two captains, five mates, a stewardess and five seamen and six more of her crew were sick.

CHAPTER XXXII

1859

LAST GREAT VOYAGES

CLIPPER days were drawing to a close in America. By 1859 nearly all the more extreme ships had been dismasted, some of them several times. Many of them were leaky. Few vessels built of wood could survive the twisting, wracking leverage of the immense spars for more than a few years. As one by one they hobbled into port under jury rig, the lofty sticks were razed; the great yards sent down, shortened and refitted; swinging booms reduced and sometimes discarded altogether, while in many cases the huge single topsails gave place to the new Howes rig, which was rapidly gaining favor over the earlier but less handy Forbes rig. The ships were still fast. In a gale of wind they could sail almost as well as ever, but in light airs they were relatively sluggish.

Nothing illustrates this better than the California passages for 1859. In 1852, when the number of vessels bound from Eastern ports for San Francisco included an even 100 which were fairly entitled to be called clippers, 19 made the passage in 110 sailing days or less. During 1859 the number taking their departure was 85, of which only six made the run within the allotted 110 days. Much the same proportions hold good for the

three or four years when the clippers were in their prime, indicating that the above comparative performance was not the mere
chance of wind and weather.

It is, perhaps, a noteworthy fact that of all the clippers clearing for California this year prior to November—and this included 68 out of the total of 85—only one made the run within
110 days. This was the *Sweepstakes,* which still retained her
extreme rig, her time being 106 days.

Two races resulted in virtual ties. The *Ocean Express* and
the *Amos Lawrence* sailed from New York together on March
13th and entered the Golden Gate on the same tide August 1st.
Captain Limeburner of the *Great Republic* and James H. Little
of the *Ocean Telegraph* left New York in company on the 24th
of November and arrived out the 12th of the following March,
having made the passage in 109 days. It was fine even sailing
and the time was especially creditable for the *Telegraph* since her
log records that she was "very tender and deep, drawing 23 feet,
her exact depth of hold."

Captain Nat Brown, Jr., now had the *Young America.* He
left Sandy Hook on the 30th of January and two days later carried away his main topmast and mizen topgallant mast with all
gear attached. He put into Rio and repaired. His total elapsed
time on the passage was 174 days, but his run from Rio was only
a few days under the record. On his arrival the San Francisco
Times said:

> "She left Rio May 15, and has consequently made the
> passage in 70 days—the second best on record. On the pas-
> sage she spoke the *Orpheus, Elizabeth F. Willetts* and the
> *Belle of the West.*
>
> "The *Young America* presented a very fine appearance as
> she entered the harbor; her long low black hull gliding up
> against the tide like a huge serpent, surmounted by a pyramid
> of canvas."

More than seventy years have elapsed since the *Young
America* spoke the *Belle of the West* and of all the strong, proud

young men on those two ships only one is living today. Captain Hall of East Dennis, "down on the Cape," the very young and very proud first mate of the *Belle,* still recalls perfectly at 91 years of age the circumstance of this meeting.

Another Cape Codder, Laban Howes, had the *Orpheus* at this time. He sailed from New York on the 8th of April and after speaking the *Young America,* followed her into Frisco at the respectful interval of one week, in the very fair passage, nevertheless, of 115 days. Howes wrote of his command:

> "She is a medium sharp model, not to say the very clipper, but a handsome staunch vessel better adapted for strong winds than a light weather voyage like this. Crew 27 all told. Draws 21 ft. 5 in. aft, 20 ft. 6 in. forward."

On the 12th of June he was off the Horn and entered in his log:

> "First and middle parts fine breeze. Latter part moderate, water smooth, some light squalls of rain, but fine weather such as an 'Old Woman' might round the Horn with."

Laban little knew his fortune. How he got through as he did is one of the miracles of the Cape, for it appears to have been the worst winter off the Horn of the entire clipper period. The fine staunch ship *Golden Eagle,* Captain Luce, only a few weeks behind him, racked back and forth in those latitudes 88 days. When she finally reached Talcahuano in distress she had only one spar standing— a lower mast—that she had when she left Sandy Hook. Fifteen of her crew were down with the scurvy, some with complications in the shape of broken legs and arms.

Another fine medium clipper, the *East Indian,* Captain Lecraw, put into Talcahuano about the same time 94 days from the Straits of Le Maire. From August 13th to November 5th she had bucked month long westerly gales that blew without ceasing. The men had worn out what few clothes they had and the watch on deck was compelled to strip to the skin when they went below, in order to provide clothing so that the other watch could go on deck.

Many other ships rounding the Horn this winter reported terrible experiences. The little clipper *Fleetwood*, commanded by Captain Frank Dale, was lost in the ice in the latitude of 60 South, longitude 71 West, on the 4th of May. A boat with the mate and four seamen was picked up, but the captain's boat with 16 men and 1 passenger, besides the captain's wife and child was never reported.

A very close match was sailed over the China course this year between the *Romance of the Seas* and the *Snow Squall*. It was Caldwell and the big McKay clipper against Captain Lloyd and Alfred Butler's masterpiece, a thousand tons smaller. The ships left Shanghai late in March when the monsoon was dying. Caldwell sailed on the 21st, followed the next day by the little white clipper.

The *Snow Squall* gained the first advantage, catching her opponent off Anjier on the 9th of April. In the strong trades of the Indian Ocean the *Romance* pulled ahead again and passed the Cape of Good Hope May 7th, two days in the lead. The South Atlantic proved her undoing, however, for the *Snow Squall* gained four days on this leg, crossing the Line May 29th, two days ahead. They reached Sandy Hook in this order, the *Snow Squall* on the 22nd of June and the *Romance of the Seas* on the following day, 92 and 94 days, respectively, from Shanghai.

They were not record passages, but it was not the month for records, and few ships have made better time over this route at this season of the year. No ship could have done as well if she were not a first class clipper sailed for all there was in her. The fine three skysail yarder *Malay*, ably commanded by Captain Wilcomb, very heavily sparred and carrying royal studding sails on the fore and main, left Shanghai exactly two weeks before the *Snow Squall* and the two ships arrived at New York in company.

On the whole, small ships seem to have been better suited to the conditions of Oriental trade than the larger vessels. Most of the records in these waters were made by craft of a thousand tons or less. It is true that a vastly greater number of voyages were made by small clippers, which no doubt affects the result somewhat, but as a rule even when large and small ships of the same general type went over a course at the same time, the smaller vessel came out ahead.

In the British tea trade there appears to have been a striking return of American ships to favor. Possibly in '58 Yankee masters were still holding out for high rates and were underbid by their competitors. This year they loaded for London at £2 and £3 per ton, the lowest rate by far in their ten years' experience. Whatever the explanation, no less than 12 American ships stowed British teas in '59. Ten of them were clippers.

The fleet comprised the *Ringleader, Golden City, Charmer, Rapid, Sea Serpent, Grace Darling, Bald Eagle, Sultan, Florence* and *Alboni*. Of these only four sailed when the season was favorable and their passages were as follows: *Ringleader* and *Alboni*, 109 days from Foochow; *Sultan*, 103 days from Shanghai, and *Florence*, 102 days from Whampoa.

None of the British ships appear to have equalled the time of either the *Sultan* or the *Florence* or in fact, with the exception of the very fine 106 days of the *Falcon*, the time of any of the American clippers sailing at approximately the same date from the same ports. The *Sea Serpent* made the passage in from 3 to 15 days less time than her four nearest British opponents.

It was not, as has sometimes been stated, the last appearance of American vessels in this trade. Four ships participated again in 1860, and for several years thereafter an occasional charter was secured by a Yankee clipper. It was, however, the last year in which they figured in the trade to any considerable extent.

More of the clippers were meeting with disaster. In September the ship *Eloisa* was engaged in picking the bones of one of the noblest ships ever built, the *Sovereign of the Seas*, hard and fast on the treacherous Malacca reefs. While she was still engaged in this work another McKay ship, the medium clipper *Mastiff*, five days out from San Francisco for Hong Kong, was burned. All her passengers and crew, 181 in number, were rescued by the British ship *Achilles*.

On the 10th of August, Samuel A. Fabens, formerly of the extreme clipper *Golden Eagle* and now of the *Challenge*, passed the Golden Gate in the late afternoon bound for Hong Kong. From the first he experienced adverse winds and calms, and on the 17th of September he was in the midst of the worst typhoon of his life. The last observation of the *Challenge* was taken on the 15th, showing the position then to be latitude 20.36 North, longitude 129.07 West. Her log gives a brief description of the storm:

"Sept. 17. Laying too under main Spencer, all other sailes furled and extra gaskets (studding sail gear) passed. Typhoon in every sense of the word. At 3 PM the three Royal masts blew over the side at 7 PM all three lower mast heads were twisted off and the ship completely dismasted, the spars chafing the ship badly outside, tearing up the decks, etc., blew away one boat and injured five or six others, some copper torn off. The twisting off the masts was so sudden that not one Shroud Backstay or Stay gave way, but were obliged to cut away all our rigging to clear the wreck which hung alongside all night. Ends more moderate."

This was virtually the last of the *Challenge* as an American ship. Fabens worked her into Hong Kong and she was laid up until near the close of 1860 when she was sold to Captain Haskell. After knocking around Eastern ports for a few months she was again sold at Bombay, this time to a British firm, Thomas Hunt & Co., who renamed her the *Golden City*.

About the time that the *Challenge* was dismasted in the Pacific the *Tornado* was fighting a hurricane in the North Atlantic. At the height of the storm she was boarded by a huge roller which washed away her first and third mates, five seamen and all five boats.

The hurricane that proved so disastrous to her worked havoc with other craft. The mahogany clipper *Stephen R. Mallory*, Captain Seaman, from London bound for Key West, was passed October 14th with nothing standing but her fore lower mast. Her after house was stove, ballast shifted and she had a heavy list to starboard. With half her crew below trying to shovel her ballast back to windward and the rest on deck rigging shears to set up a spare topmast at the stub of the mainmast, her master signalled "do not want assistance."

Several days later the ship *Augustus* was in Lat. 42.30 N. Lon. 39 W., and we are indebted to Captain Kearney's log of October 19th for a vivid description of his experience:

"At 10 P.M. laid ship to, under bare spars. Wind S.W. thick & rainy with heavy squalls. At 12.30 A.M. barometer, 28.07 and soon fell suddenly to 28.04, and blew terrifically and the waves became greatly agitated and rapidly increased. At the same moment we discovered we were in the direct pathway of and near to the focus of the gale; and also a brilliant snow white semicircle appeared, apparently one mile distant, and 1⅛ mile across the base, with several very bright and clearly defined broad streaks of haze, reaching from outside points of the semicircle and from the base to the ship, down which the wind rushed with such tremendous fury, it was hopeless to expect a spar or even the ship itself could survive it from moment to moment, and the terribly agitated and fearfully increasing waves which constantly threatened to board her and inevitably sweep everything away, if no worse calamity happened. Every possible exertion to get ship out of these seas and off the streaks but she lay unmanageable for ½ hour when wind suddenly ceased and then blew gently from N.W. & sea became smooth. 4 or 5 miles further began to blow again violently from N.W. Seas struck under lea quarter so violently as to shake out oakum. It was my most dreadful experience in 40 yrs at sea."

During November the news reached New York of the loss of the *Queen of the Pacific* on a reef to the northward of Pernambuco. Captain Dubois saved part of her cargo of guano, but the ship proved a total loss.

Several excellent short runs had been made in the course of the year. On the Pacific, Captain Crowell in the *Boston Light* made a very good passage of 37 days from the Golden Gate to Hong Kong, arriving the 13th of April. One of the best transatlantic runs of all time was made by the lofty moonsail yarder *Phoenix*, under Captain John Hoxie. She arrived in Cork Harbor on the 24th of January, 14 days and 9 hours from Savannah. During the passage she had maintained an average of 352 miles a day for several successive days. It was said at the time that this run was equivalent to 13 days from New York to Liverpool.

Early in November the *Flying Cloud*, which had been lying idle at New York for nearly two years, was taken around to the sectional dock for repairs, preparatory to putting her in commission again under reduced canvas. As the weatherbeaten old clipper surged up the East River at the end of a tow rope she passed the spruce young *Andrew Jackson* lying opposite the house of her owners, John H. Brower & Company, 45 South Street, with the banner "up for California" flying at her fore. It was the course on which the *Flying Cloud* had won the highest honors yet accorded a ship, but never again would the stout McKay built craft buck the Cape Horn rollers. It remained to be seen whether smart new clippers could improve on the record she had established.

Since Noah squinted over his old cross staff from the top of Ararat no voyage has given rise to more debate than the one for which the *Andrew Jackson* was loading. If the discussion became at times a trifle acrimonious it was but natural, for the question as to whether the *Andrew Jackson* had beaten the time of the McKay clipper cannot be dismissed in a few words. The view favoring the claims of the *Flying Cloud*, or more precisely, opposing those of the *Andrew Jackson*, since neither owners nor officers of the *Flying Cloud* appear to have made any objection to the *Jackson's* record, is set forth in Howe and Matthew's recent valuable contribution to clipper ship literature, and one cannot do better than to quote their exact words:

"The *Jackson* broke no records, either on a whole passage or over any of its sections. It has frequently been published that her run from New York to San Francisco, in 1859/60, was 89 days, 7 hours (also given in some instances, 89 days, 4 hours) which would be eclipsing the *Flying Cloud's* two fastest runs, but these statements are proven to be mythical. On the passage in question, the *Jackson* hove up her anchor at New York at 6 A.M., Dec. 25th, and passed Fort Lafayette at 8.45; discharging her pilot at noon. She received her San Francisco pilot at 8 A.M., Mar. 24, 1860, and anchored in San Francisco Bay at 6 P.M. Thus her passage is 90 days, 12 hours, anchor to anchor; 89 days, 20 hours, pilot to pilot; which is the third fastest of record to this date. Distance sailed, 13,700 miles as against 15,091 miles covered by the *Flying Cloud* on the record run of 89 days 8 hours, anchor to anchor."

The writer then refers to other passages of the *Andrew Jackson* and continues:

"It appears that the fast passages of the *Jackson* were due to hard driving and also to a succession of winds favorable to her running near to a direct course, rather than to her ability to move through the water rapidly and there is no record of any great day's run to her credit."

Passing for the moment the general comments regarding the sailing ability and records of the *Andrew Jackson*, it may be said that the foregoing, so far as it goes, appears to be a correct summary of her performance on the voyage in question. A contemporary newspaper account states that Captain Williams was reported passing Sandy Hook at noon, Christmas Day, 1859. This is by no means conclusive evidence as to the exact hour of his departure, for newspapers have no special interest in precision in such matters. Nevertheless it is altogether probable that he made sail, if not at noon, at least during the early part of the afternoon, at which time his "sea day," December *26th*, began. The distinction between sea and civil time is of some importance to bear in mind in this connection.

There is, furthermore, no doubt but that the *Jackson* took a pilot off San Francisco Heads not later than 8 A.M., March 24th, civil time. This would make the longest possible calculation of her passage from Sandy Hook to pilot, 89 days and 20 hours, assuming she crossed the bar at New York at noon, exactly—a point which has never been disputed. Thus far there appears to have been no material discrepancy in the published accounts of the voyage.

The essence of Captain Williams' claim, however, was that he arrived on the pilot grounds off the San Francisco Heads, where he was becalmed, 89 days and 4 hours after taking his departure from off Sandy Hook, and that no pilot was available until the following morning. If this claim is substantiated it is obvious that the *Andrew Jackson* will be in the position of having made the best passage at sea under sail from the New York to the San Francisco pilot grounds, while the *Flying Cloud's* sea passages would be somewhat longer and her claim to the record would rest on the fact that her time consumed in working in and out of harbor was shorter than that of the *Jackson*. Save that the point is one of interest to all lovers of the old ships, there can be no object in discussing it at this late day. Of those primarily involved, mariners and owners alike have long since passed to their reward. It remains only to add whatever fragments may be gathered to the meagre store of information heretofore available, to the end that the measure of honor due the clippers and the men who sailed them may be increased rather than diminished.

Passing for the moment such positive evidence as may be available, there are several collateral matters which seem worthy of mention. The imponderables have a certain relevancy even when seemingly conclusive facts are adducible.

There is then the negative fact that the claim appears to have been undisputed for more than a generation, and indeed as we shall see, was assumed by Grinnell & Minturn, owners of the *Flying Cloud*, to have been proved as recently as 1892.

There is the further circumstance that whether the ship deserved the honor or not, it was awarded her apparently without a dissenting voice by the merchants' associations of San Francisco. Not only did they present the commander of the *Andrew Jackson* with a commodore's pennant for the shortest voyage from New York to the Golden Gate, but they attempted to parade him around the city in a victoria with the object of banqueting him afterwards; honors, which, on the authority of the Captain's sister, as stated to the writer, he was too modest to accept.

It can hardly be assumed that the merchants' committee acted without evidence in the matter. From comments in the various papers it is clear that the *Jackson's* log was available for examination, and that the people of San Francisco were satisfied that a record passage had been made. In some respects their sources of information were superior to those of the present generation. They knew as much about the time the *Jackson* sailed from New York as can be ascertained now, and they undoubtedly could have obtained detailed information about the arrival of the ship off the Heads. It is well to remember that the San Francisco committee were concerned with a matter that happened less than 24 hours earlier, and the men were walking the streets who could have challenged their award, and who might well have been interested in doing so if they felt the *Jackson's* claims were false.

On the *Jackson's* return to New York much was said of her exploit in the papers, including an account of the presentation of a chronometer watch by John Brower to Captain Williams with the time of her run, 89 days, 4 hours engraved in it. Even here no doubting voice was raised, although the friends of Captain Creesy and the *Flying Cloud* were as warm blooded as they were numerous. Many years later in reply to a question from the Hon. Thomas L. James, of Providence, R. I., Messrs. Grinnell, Minturn & Company wrote:

> "The passage of the 'Flying Cloud' from New York to San Francisco in 1851 was made in about ninety days, eighty-nine days and eighteen hours exactly, we believe. The passage of the 'Andrew Jackson' in 1860, we understand, was somewhat faster than that of the 'Flying Cloud,' but we cannot give particulars at the moment."
>
> (From a manuscript copy of letter given by Mr. James to Mr. Charles Stark of Providence, R. I., in 1892.)

It cannot be said that circumstances of this sort, in themselves, constitute proof that the run was made as claimed, but if the credibility of Captain Williams and his officers is involved, they possibly have a moral value.

There is danger in speaking too dogmatically on the matter, but it would seem to have been remarkably easy at the time to have pieced together the facts invalidating Captain Williams' claim if it had been false. If the passage was not made as stated it is obvious not only that the Captain was an untrustworthy character, but that the people of the time, including many admirers of the *Flying Cloud*, must have been strangely credulous. Furthermore it involves the assumption that if Captain Jack were bluffing he was willing to assume the very real and imminent risk of making himself the laughing stock of the world. All these things are possible, but whether they are probable is a matter the reader is competent to decide for himself.

After he retired from the sea Captain Williams lived at Mystic, Connecticut, until his death in 1905, where a great many of his friends and business associates still live. Of the people now living some liked and others disliked him. The Captain was an outspoken man and made enemies, but friends or enemies, all are agreed that he was not a man to tamper with the truth. It has been stated emphatically to the writer by a number of acquaintances that, whatever his faults, "Cap'n Jack" was not that kind of a man. As one man put it: "If he said a thing was so, you could depend upon it whether it hurt him or helped him." Another old shell-back remarked: "Cap'n Jack was never a man to claim anything which did not belong to him." There is no doubt but that to the day of his death he asserted and firmly believed he had made the run from the New York pilot grounds to those off San Francisco in the time above stated.

Fortunately for the historian, the record no longer need depend on newspaper reports and circumstantial evidence. After the lapse of seventy years the original log of the *Andrew Jackson*, in the crabbed hand and simplified spelling of Cap'n Jack, has come to light. It is reprinted in full in the appendix, and since the hour of arrival at the San Francisco pilot grounds is the mooted point, the last page of the log with the master's "89 Days and 4 Houers from New York" is here reproduced in facsimile.

The log tells a significant story. Briefly, at noon the 23rd day of March, 1860, and precisely 89 days, flat, from Sandy Hook bar, the *Andrew Jackson* was 71 miles from the Southeast Farallon, or approximately 96 miles from the bar off the harbor entrance. In the days of sail the San Francisco pilot grounds occupied, roughly speaking, the area between the Farallones and the bar. At four P. M. Captain Williams records that he made the Farallones and was still going along with a light but fair breeze. Assuming that the log is a correct record of the events of the voyage, it is obvious that approximately 89 days and 3 hours from the time of taking his departure off New York (*i.e.*, after dropping his pilot), or 89 days and 4 hours after passing Sandy Hook, Captain Williams was on the San Francisco pilot grounds ready to receive a pilot if one had been available. The wind was falling, however, and there was no pilot to be had. Accordingly the *Jackson* remained all night between the Farallones and the bar and did not secure a pilot until seven o'clock the following morning.

This, it is submitted, is a summary of the evidence at present available. It is unlikely that anything of importance will be added to the record in the future, although old letters and manuscripts may yet appear to affect the situation. The reader may, therefore, draw his own conclusions from the foregoing, with the consciousness at least that his data is more complete than any hitherto available.

Whatever decision one may reach, the situation is unchanged in one important particular. The *Flying Cloud* undoubtedly still holds the record for the shortest passage from anchor to anchor. Since, however, the performance of a ship behind a tug or working in and out of port under command of a pilot is not the true criterion of her sailing ability, it would seem that the better test is her run from pilot to pilot. If this measure is accepted it may be regarded as probable that the record for the passage under sail belongs to the *Andrew Jackson*.

Be that as it may, the honors are virtually even between the two ships. The difference of a few hours in a 15,000 mile voyage is in itself a slight matter, however important it may be in determining a record. Both were noble, good craft, and both were commanded by men who are entitled to be numbered among the first dozen of the hardest driving sailor men the world has produced.

The statement that "the *Jackson* broke no records either on a whole passage or over any of its sections" appears to be due to an oversight, since the ship undoubtedly holds two world's records of prime importance. One is the present mark of 15 days from Liverpool to Sandy Hook, a course which possibly has been traversed by more fine sailing ships than any other deep sea route since the world began. The other is the round voyage record from New York to Liverpool and return. Setting world's records for all time over this much travelled course is no small matter.

It is a fact worth noting that no ship which sailed in company with the *Andrew Jackson* ever equalled her time to their common destination. On the occasion when she lowered the record from Liverpool to New York to 15 days, the very fast extreme clipper *Invincible*, which had already reported a run of 400 miles in one day, left the Mersey about the same hour on the 3rd of November, 1860. Captain Johnson, who commanded the *Andrew Jackson*, arrived at the bar off Sandy Hook on Sunday night, November 18th, having passed Cape Race on the 8th day out and the Nantucket Shoals, 200 miles from New York on the 13th day. The *Invincible*, a slightly larger ship, did not arrive until the 20th after a passage of 17 days. Since the *Invincible* was unquestionably speedy, and was commanded by Captain Hepburn, one of the best known and ablest clipper masters, there would seem to be no doubt that the *Jackson* had demonstrated her ability to travel in fast company.

The other *Jackson* record is referred to in the following excerpt from the New York *Herald* of November 20, 1860:

"This renowned ship arrived yesterday A. M. from Liverpool in 15 days passage, with a full cargo. She also made the run to Liverpool (grain laden) in 15 days, and on the voyage out and home has been *only 30 days at sea*, including two days calms, and sailed over 6500 miles, thus averaging nearly 220 miles a day throughout—a rate of speed rarely, if ever, equalled, continuously in a sailing vessel before. The *Andrew Jackson* arrived at the bar on Sunday Night."

So far as can be discovered this time of a few hours over 30 sailing days from Sandy Hook to Liverpool and return constitutes a record which has never been equalled, much less surpassed. The nearest approach to it is the 30 day round trip of Captain Judkins, between Boston and Liverpool, in the winter of 1839–40, when he went out in the *Britannia* and returned in the *Columbia*. Since Boston is considerably nearer Liverpool than is New York, this voyage cannot be considered equal to that of the *Jackson*, even waiving the fact that it was made by two ships. If the *Jackson* had sailed from Boston her passage over, other things being equal, would have been a day shorter, while on her return, as we have seen, she was up with Nantucket—that is, beyond Boston—on her 13th day from Liverpool.

Another fact intimately bound up with the question of the sailing ability of the *Jackson,* is the impression that her model was so full that she could not have been a fast ship. As a matter of fact, her lines, which are reproduced in Appendix VII, show her to be a very powerful craft, with a somewhat heavy looking top, but an underbody that compares favorably with some of the fastest of the clippers. She is for instance virtually as sharp as the extreme clipper *Swordfish,* which made several fine records. This is not to argue that she was as fast a ship as the *Flying Cloud* under general conditions, but it is quite possible that under certain heavy weather conditions she might have proved a match for the Boston clipper. The *Flying Cloud* was a wonderful ship, but no less an authority than Donald McKay himself considered that he had built ships to beat her. There can, moreover, be no question as to her virtual defeat by the *Hornet,* as we have seen, even though the margin of victory was scant, and the *Flying Cloud* scored a technical, or anchor to anchor, victory on that occasion.

Perhaps no better commentary on the early merchant marine of America and the quality of men engaged therein, can be suggested than the remarkable part played by tiny villages and men of obscure origin. From Maine to Georgia few localities failed to produce ships or men or records which added measurably to the glories of the day of the sail. Frankfort, Damariscotta, Cape Elizabeth, Medford and Mystic were small communities, yet all produced not one but many ships whose names were once familiar the world over. In the matter of men no similar area produced more deep water masters of outstanding ability than Cape Cod, although here again comparisons are of little value, since scores of smaller districts supplied far more than their quota.

CHAPTER XXXIII

CONCLUSION

AMERICA, always effervescent, was never more vociferous than in 1860. The sonorous periods of Webster no longer resounded from the halls of Congress, and Clay had long since been gathered to his fathers, but they were scarcely missed. A thousand elbowing partisans shrilled where the lions had thundered.

Everywhere groups of excited men engaged in endless discussion, interminable argument interspersed with unpleasant recrimination and fringed with fisticuffs. Strange names and alien principles filled the air—talk of force and threats of violence, issuing strangely from lips fashioned to speak of liberty.

A decade earlier there had been the same tensity—a similar high note of rivalry—but with what a difference! Where formerly the press had little space save for the new mysterious beauty of the ships, and men no thought save friendly debate upon their points of loveliness, excellence and speed, now all was bitterness and wrangling. America had been intensely constructive; she was now preparing to try her hand at destruction. It was a transition as portentous as that from the golden age of Pericles to the Eagles of Rome.

Doubtless politics furnished in some measure a safety valve to men exasperated by ruined enterprises and enveloped in the gloom of post panic days. No one was satisfied in 1860, least of all the shipyard worker, who had earned the remarkable pay of three and a half or four dollars a day and suddenly found himself reduced to a beggarly dollar and a quarter, or the merchant who saw the accumulations of a lifetime swept away in a few hours, or the youth by now acquainted with the disappointments and hardships of life on the frontier. The nation was ripe for the harvest.

Whether any man or group of men could have restored a measure of sanity to the country, and substituted a fair-minded exchange of ideas and equitable proposals for the intolerant bickering and unfair attitude that characterized both North and South is extremely problematical. The point to be noticed is that in a situation of dwindling maritime resources and vanishing prestige, America was dissipating vast stores of energy and thought that should have been productively employed if her sea power was to be maintained, much less increased.

As we have seen, nothing, in all probability, could have kept the United States in her position of leadership. The mere opening of the West called for too great an effort, and drained too completely the mental and financial resources of the East. There can be no doubt, however, that the internal strife which preceded the Civil War and continued for many years thereafter accelerated the downfall of the merchant fleet and effectually retarded its revival.

America, which had been sea-minded for two centuries, was nautically decadent in 1855. By 1860 the process could go little farther. There was an utter lack of anything resembling public interest in matters pertaining to shipbuilding or in the exploits of the ships themselves. New records escaped notice entirely or obtained a scant paragraph in almost unreadable marine columns instead of bold faced editorials on the news page.

The year was marked by the smallest participation in the California clipper traffic since 1850. Sixty-three clippers cleared from Eastern ports and of these only seven made the passage in 110 days or less. Two of the best runs were made by a single

Mystic built ship, the *Mary L. Sutton*, which, commanded by Captain Spicer, appeared twice during the year in San Francisco harbor in 103 and 110 days. The *Sutton's* 103 day run was the best of the year, being one day shorter than that of the *Great Republic*, Captain Limeburner.

Two of the races were as close as deep sea contests could well be. The *Golden Fleece*, under Captain Manson, and the *Golden State*, commanded by Ranlett, sailed from New York in company on the 22nd of June. They entered the port of San Francisco October 29th, a few hours apart, their passage of 129 days being among the shortest made about that time.

Another dead heat was sailed later in the more favorable season by the *Spitfire*, commanded by Captain Leach, and the *Black Hawk*, Captain Bowers. The *Spitfire* left Boston on December 21st and the *Black Hawk* passed Sandy Hook the same day. Both ships arrived out on the 8th of April in a passage of 107 days. Five days behind them came the beautiful *Romance of the Seas*, Captain Clough, in the excellent run of 105 days.

The *Black Hawk* above mentioned was not the Newburyport ship of that name. The latter vessel was a new craft of 941 tons. She was on her first voyage to Calcutta and was homeward bound in April. On the 8th of the month, while still in the Bay of Bengal, she was seen to capsize in a squall and go down with all hands.

Several fine clippers were lost this year, among them the magnificent Baltimore ship *Flora Temple*, bound for Havana with 800 coolies, wrecked in the China Sea. The *Phœnix* was burned in February at Melbourne. The old pre-clipper, *Esther May*, was wrecked early in the year in the Yang Tse Kiang River, and the medium clipper *Intrepid* went to pieces on Belvidere Shoals near the entrance of Gaspar Straits.

Another old packet met her fate in the North Atlantic when the *Roscius* foundered on August 26th while under the command of Captain Hallett.

Four American ships carried tea to England this year. Of

these, two, the *Lawrence Brown* and the barque *Saxonville*, were full built ships. The other two were the *Flying Cloud* and the barkentine *Fairy*, both of which sailed early in August during the unfavorable season. Captain Winsor had the *Flying Cloud* under greatly reduced spars and left Foochow on the 6th of August. He entered in at London December 7th after a passage of 123 days. The *Fairy*, Captain Blish, was reported from Hong Kong August 10th and arrived at London December 3rd, 115 days out. Although an occasional Yankee clipper thereafter made the run, it was virtually the last of their competition. War was just around the corner, and the ships were wracked and old.

As the *Flying Cloud* raced up past St. Helena, Lincoln was elected—"the Prince of Rails." Newspapers had space for little else than secession news, threats and counter threats. Even if America had had the ships, the cost of war insurance and the imminence of war risks would have made it difficult for her to get foreign charters in '61. As a matter of fact she no longer had the ships. The great majority of the extreme clippers were from seven to ten years old, and of these all but two or three were operating under greatly reduced canvas. The *Flying Cloud*, originally less heavily sparred than a great many others, had been cut down twice. Wooden ships could not be built to carry the tremendous leverage of the extreme clipper rig more than five or six voyages without being rebuilt. Few merchants in 1860 could afford to rebuild their ships, and none could operate them to advantage if they had been rebuilt. The only alternative was to recalk and cut down the rig to the point where a badly strained clipper could safely carry it.

Good passages were becoming increasingly rare. It is therefore somewhat remarkable that the record from Shanghai to New York should be lowered this year. The *Swordfish*, Captain Joseph W. Crocker, left the former port on the 12th of December, 1859, and arrived at Sandy Hook on the 2nd of March, her passage of 81 days being the shortest on record, in spite of the fact that she was becalmed 5 days on the equator in the Atlantic.

Another American ship, the *North Wind*, Captain W. S. Morton, made a 66 day passage from London to Australia. She left the Downs on the 10th of November and reached Port Phillip January 15th.

On Eastern waters the *Mary Whitridge*, under Wm. A. Creesy, formerly of the Oneida, made a very fine run from Melbourne to Batavia. She left Port Phillip on the 15th of April and arrived at her destination on the 3rd of May. Her record of 18 days over the course was said to be the best up to that time.

Several excellent passages were made from South American ports. The *Andrew Jackson* made the very good run of 61 days from Callao to New York, following her 89 day passage to San Francisco. The *Wild Pigeon* made a remarkable passage of 50 days from Talcahuano to New York, arriving at Sandy Hook on the 28th of April. This is apparently the record for the course. None of the clippers made a better showing on the whole than the new clipper barque *Dawn*, built by Thomas Collyer. She was on the run between Buenos Ayres and New York, the sailing distance on the Northward run between these ports being 6500 miles in round figures. Commanded by Captain Chase, the *Dawn* arrived in New York on the 2nd of November, 38 days from the South American port. It was her third successive voyage between the two ports in less than 40 days, the other two passages having been made in 36 and 39 days. On the occasion of her arrival at New York on the 11th of June in 36 days, it was stated that the passage constituted a record between the two ports. The time from a point off Buenos Ayres has been bettered by several vessels homeward bound from San Francisco, but the three successive runs in an average of approximately 37 days 16 hours seem never to have been approached by any other ship.

With the close of 1860 we may bid farewell to the American clippers. Few indeed were left which retained a fraction of their early grace, or whose sailing qualities were not impaired by reduced canvas and worn rigging. The day was at hand when the last beautiful creation was to spread her broad pinions and sail away into the blue never again to be seen by the eye of man in the full glory of unshorn power and beauty.

Brave ships, beautiful ships, were still to come in seemingly endless procession. The long powerful cargo carriers—"California clippers" and "Wool clippers"—and the trim yachtlike British clippers, were still in the future, and fine craft they were. For their work and day no better craft were ever built, but ton for ton they were not the lofty racing queens of the fifties, nor were they handled by men of the clairvoyant intuition and reckless skill that marked several of the masters of the earlier clippers.

In one sense the American clipper was neither a national nor racial achievement. The men who played the leading rôles came from every important maritime country of Europe. Some of the ablest shipwrights and seamen hailed from Canada. Even more liberal quotas were furnished by the Scotch, Irish, Welsh and English from the British Isles. Scandinavians, French and Dutch contributed able representatives. In this respect the clipper ship was a product of the "melting pot," but the fact remains that it was developed and perfected in America. Other nations might later "gild the lily" to their individual or racial liking. Their achievements included much work, ably done. The men who built and sailed the later ships deserve greater praise than we are worthy to bestow, but it can serve the purpose of neither truth nor justice to credit them with the task their fathers completed.

While they were active the old captains had accomplished more, perhaps, for their nation than any similar number of men before or since. They had found her the gibe and prey of every navy of Europe. They had made her for the moment the greatest and most efficient maritime power in the world. With one or two possible exceptions they had written, or were presently to write, every important sailing record which endures to this day. Other beautiful craft were still to come—other remarkably able seamen were yet to do the impossible with the means at their disposal. It is no disparagement to either to assert that the brilliance of the American clipper era has been dimmed by not so much as a single candle power in all the years since 1860. Certainly no substantiated records have appeared which surpass the records of that day, and among the thousands of later passages the number which equal them in intrinsic importance may be tallied on the fingers of a hand.

In the field of design, they had finished their task. When the last American clipper left the ways every important feature of the fast sailing merchantman had been fully developed and tested, and blind indeed is he who cannot see in their lines something more than a promise of today's sleek ocean greyhounds. Aside from the use of a new material—steel for spars, rigging and hull—little creative work remained to be done. The story of the clipper since 1860 is the story of repeated refinements of this or that example of earlier modelling to meet the demands of changing conditions—evidence of which fact still exists in a hundred builders' models at home and abroad.

And so we leave them—the bones of the gallant *Sovereign of the Seas* bleaching on Mallacan reefs—the marvellous *Phantom* under young Sargent, soon to sail away never to return, booming up the Southeast trades, 75 days from Shanghai—the *Sea Serpent* and *Swordfish* just astern, homeward bound from Hong Kong— sharp across their track the *Eagle Wing* and *Northern Light* and a dozen more driving for the Golden Gate. In their home ports the peppery *Spitfire*, the dainty *Belle of the West* and lovely *Romance of the Seas*, a trifle wistful now, awaiting the freights which came so slowly.

One by one they were meeting the common fate of ships and men. Those who built and owned and sailed the clippers were still vigorous, although no longer in the early prime of life; still keen intellectually, but no longer forward looking. They might still have done much toward meeting England's challenge by a comprehensive attack upon the problem of steam. But already they were beginning to look backward—to resail old voyages—

to live, ever so slightly at first, in the past. Like sailors before them since time began, they were finding "it was hard to put new kinks in old standing rigging." And so, perhaps, it will ever be. Men, like ships, never quite live out their days. Now both men and ships are gone.

How still they lie—the dead captains who were so alive—on their quiet New England hillsides, overlooking the white flecked waters for which they held a love passing the love of woman. How languidly they dream away the hours, who once lived years in moments; whose souls clashed with the lightning and hurricane, and gloried in the tempest with a strange, calm glory. Gone are the mountain surges, the greybeards of the sea; the steady drone of the storm; the mighty rushing waters; the shrill of orders, bugle clear above the gale; the call to more than human deeds. In their place the softly falling snow; the grasses slowly stirring; the sound of gently rustling leaves, and friendly wrens to mock the stately albatross. The old captains are dreaming now. Their ships are outward bound.

ACKNOWLEDGMENTS

I am indebted for facilities and assistance afforded in the collection and preparation of material contained herein to the following historical societies, libraries, governmental departments and institutions:

The British Museum; United States Weather Bureau; Bureau of Construction and Repair, U. S. Navy Department; United States Naval Library; Smithsonian Institution; Congressional Library; United States Bureau of Navigation, Department of Commerce; The Customs Division of the United States Treasury Department; Maryland Historical Society, Baltimore, Maryland; The Department of History, University of Pennsylvania, Philadelphia; The Free Library of Philadelphia; The Genealogical Society of Pennsylvania, Philadelphia; The Pennsylvania Historical Society, Philadelphia; The New York Yacht Club; The New York Public Library; The New York Historical Society, New York City; The New Haven Public Library, New Haven, Connecticut; New York, New Haven & Hartford Railroad, New Haven, Connecticut; Yale University Library, New Haven, Connecticut; New London Historical Society, New London, Connecticut; The John Carter Brown Library, Providence, Rhode Island; The Shepley Library, Providence, Rhode Island; The Providence Public Library, Providence, Rhode Island; Hyannis Public Library, Hyannis, Massachusetts; Museum of Fine Arts, Boston; Boston Marine Museum, Boston; Mariners House, Boston; Boston Public Library; The American Antiquarian Society, Worcester, Massachusetts; Peabody Museum, Salem; Essex Institute, Salem; Portsmouth Athenæum, Portsmouth, New Hampshire; The Maine Historical Society; Portland Public Library, Portland, Maine; The Rockland Public Library, Rockland, Maine.

In addition to the foregoing, I am under obligations to the following persons whose co-operation and assistance has in many cases extended over long periods of time and, moreover, has been characterized by a cordial and generous interest which has lightened appreciably the work of preparing the manuscript:

Mr. Sherman R. Peabody, American Trade Commissioner, Melbourne, Australia; Mr. J. H. Gray, Secretary, Geelong Harbor Trust Commissioners, Geelong, Australia; Prof. R. J. Duval, U. S. Naval Academy, Annapolis, Md.; Dr. W. T. Howard, Mr. George Rohde, Mr. Micajah W. Pope, Mr. Charles Fickus, Acting Librarian, Maryland Historical Society, Mr. Henry P. Janes, Mr. John Wesley Brown, Mr. Walter Stone, Asst. Collector of Customs, Captain Nils Sjoberg and Mr. James H. Woodall, of Baltimore, Maryland; Mr. John T. Coolidge, Mr. Asa W. Longfellow, Pres., Boston Marine Museum, Mr. Nathaniel F. Emmons, Secretary, Boston Marine Museum, Mr. Malcom B. Stone, Mr. Roswell Parish, Jr., and Mr. Wilton G. Smith of Boston; Mr. C. P. Wright, of Cambridge, Massachusetts; Mr. Frank W. Brooks, Jr., of Detroit, Michigan; Mr. Frank Vining Smith and Mr. Ray Baker Taft, of Hingham, Massachusetts; Mr. Fred Scudder, of Hyannis, Massachusetts; Mrs. Agnes Farnsworth, Mr. George Greenman, Mr. Gurdon Gates and Dr. Charles K. Stillman, of Mystic, Connecticut; Mr. Charles R. Patterson, Mr. James Suydam, Albert Reese, Esq., Mr. Gordon Grant, Mr. Richard C. McKay, Truman Henson, Esq., Mr. W. N. Wilson and Mr. Louis H. Fox, of New York City; Mr. Brower Hewitt and Mr. Leslie H. Tyler, of New Haven, Connecticut; Captain Wilson Brown, U. S. N., New London, Connecticut; Mr. Lars Thorsen, Noank, Connecticut; Captain Thomas F. Hall, of Omaha, Nebraska; Prof. A. E. McKinley and Prof. A. C. Howland, University of Pennsylvania, John Ashurst, Librarian, the Free Public Library, Mr. W. A. Dobson and Mr. Richard S. Griffith, of Philadelphia; Mr. Edward S. Clark, Piedmont, California; Mr. A. S. Brownell, of Providence,

Rhode Island; Mr. Lawrence W. Jenkins, Asst. Director, Peabody Museum, and Harriet S. Tapley, in charge of the library of the Essex Institute, Salem, Massachusetts; Dr. Richard Alston Metcalf, Richmond, Virginia; Captain Willis Snow and Mr. H. W. Thorndike, of Rockland, Maine; Mr. T. Whitridge Cutler, of Stonington, Connecticut; Prof. Charles F. Marvin, Chief of the United States Weather Bureau, Captain Young, Mr. Franklin G. Tingley and W. E. Hurd of the Marine Division of the Weather Bureau, M. H. Avery, Esq., of the U. S. Shipping Board, Captain H. C. Cocke, U. S. N., Supt. of Naval Records and Library, Captain W. P. Roberts, U. S. N., Acting Chief of Bureau of Construction and Repair, Navy Dept., Carl W. Mitman of the Smithsonian Institution, Captain C. S. Kempff. U. S. N., Hydrographer, The U. S. Hydrographic Office, Captain Gershom Bradford, U. S. N., of Washington, D. C.; Mr. George Wharton Rice, of West Southport, Maine; Judge Ellery Bowden, of Winterport, Maine; Mr. Clarence Brigham, Librarian of the American Antiquarian Society, Worcester, Mass., and Mr. William Hutchinson Rowe, of Yarmouth, Maine.

It seems not unfitting here to mention the influence on this work of my father, Gilbert B. Cutler, an old sailor-preacher, now in his eighty-third year of active life. As a boy I derived from his teaching and example a love for the sea that has never failed.

It also seems appropriate to record here the sense of personal loss experienced by the many friends of Nathaniel F. Emmons, former secretary of the Boston Marine Museum, to whose assistance and suggestions this volume owes not a little. His untimely death a few weeks since will long be regretted by those who knew him. The cordial enthusiasm and keen, discriminating sense of values he brought to matters pertaining to sailing ship history will be missed by many, and for some the place he left vacant will never be filled.

I am especially indebted to Mr. Charles R. Patterson for valuable co-operation in the matter of illustrations. Mr. Patterson's long experience at sea before the mast in the old square-riggers has enabled him to portray with remarkable fidelity ships of the sail and their environment, and in doing so, perform a notable service for future generations.

NOTES AND REFERENCES

ABBREVIATIONS: A. G. A.—*Aurora General Advertiser* (Phila.); B. A.—*Baltimore American;* Bos. E. P.—*The Boston Evening Post* and the *General Advertiser;* Bos. Gaz.—*The Boston Gazette* and *Country Journal;* Bos. P. C.—*Boston Price Current;* C. C.—*Columbian Centinel;* C. M.—*The China Mail* (Hong Kong); Cont. Jour.—*The Continental Journal* and *Weekly Advertiser* (Boston); D. A.—*The Daily Advertiser* (New York); E. I.—Essex Institute, Salem, Mass.; I. L. N.—*Illustrated London News;* Ind. Gaz.—*The Independent Gazette* or the *New York Journal Revived;* Lon. N. Y. P.—*London's New York Packet;* L. L.—*Lloyd's List;* M. A.—*Melbourne Argus;* Ming.—*Ming's New York Price Current;* N. E. P.—*New England Palladium* (Boston); N. Y. A.—*New York American;* N. Y. E. P. —*New York Evening Post;* N. Y. C. A.—*New York Commercial Advertiser*—Also at intervals entitled *Commercial Advertiser;* P. M.—Peabody Museum, Salem, Mass.; W. B.—Marine Division of the United States Weather Bureau.

Page 7, line 21 et seq. Schooners *John* and *Eagle.* See logs in possession of E. I.

Page 9, line 22 et seq. Schooners *Success, Scorpion* and frigate *Boston.* See logs in possession of E. I.

Page 10, line 16. Ship *Pickering.* See log in possession of E. I.

Page 12, line 10. Ship *Thorn.* Cont. Jour. Feb. 24, 1780.

Page 12, line 25. Sloop *Revenge.* Bos. Gaz. Feb. 24, 1777.

Page 12, line 30. Ship *Ranger.* Bos. Gaz. July 6, 1778.

Page 14, line 1. Ship *Astrea.* Bos. E. P. Apr. 12, 1783.

Page 16, line 20. Ship *Empress of China.* See also Ind. Gaz.

Feb. 26, 1784 and Lon. N. Y. P. May 12 and 16, 1785. Fragment of ship's log in possession of the Marine Division, U. S. Weather Bureau.

Page 17, line 17. Tea imported from China, 1776-1795, incl. See Sir George Stanton's "An Authentic Account of an Embassy from the King of Great Britain to the Emperor of China." App. VII. Printed at Philadelphia, 1799. Statistics of American importations seem to be of doubtful accuracy.

Page 19, line 34. Log of ship *Benjamin Morgan*. D. A. Oct. 3, 1803.

Page 22, line 31. Execution of Isaac van Dyckman. American Citizen (N. Y.) Oct. 31, 1806. Affidavit of David Brown.

Page 26, line 24. See log of ship *Herald* in possession of E. I.

Page 30, line 21. See log of ship *Canton* in possession of W. B.

Page 34, line 4. C. C. June 18, 1796.

Page 34, line 23. A. G. A. Apr. 17, 1801.

Page 35, line 11. It is possible that the record run of the *Oliver Ellsworth* was made in Nov.–Dec., 1805. She cleared for Liverpool at New York, Nov. 15, and arrived at Liverpool Dec. 8. She was, however, advertised to be sold at New York at auction, Nov. 22, so that it is possible that she did not sail until the 23rd, in which case she would have made the run claimed.

Page 37, line 35. Three masted schooner *Success*, A. G. A. Apr. 29, 1801.

Page 38, line 10. Three masted schooner *Asenath*—voyage to China. N. Y. E. P. July 28, 1807.

Page 40, line 3. Ninety day record of brig *Fox* from Calcutta to New York. N. Y. C. A. Dec. 26, 1809.

Page 40, line 18. Dismasting of brig *Gipsey*. Ming. Apr. 13, 1811.

Page 41, line 5. Transatlantic record of ship *Alert*. C. C. Apr. 6, 1811.

Page 41, line 9. Transatlantic record of brig *Osmin*. C. C. Feb. 20, 1811.

Page 46, line 13.   Dead-rise.   See lines of *Belisaurius*.

Page 47, line 9 et seq.   See logs of *America, Herald, Glide, Wasp* and *Essex* in possession of E. I.

Page 48, line 8.   For record run of frigate *Philadelphia* see Memoirs of Charles H. Cramp by Augustus C. Buell.

Page 63, line 35.   For account of sailing of the "first liner" see N. Y. C. A. Jan. 6, 1818.

Page 64, line 10.   For further particulars of ship *Nestor* and others mentioned in the succeeding pages, see alphabetical lists of ships in App. I.

Page 66, line 1.   Average passages of early packets.   N. Y. H. Dec. 31, 1852.

Page 66, line 10.   Record run by Liverpool packet ship *New York*.   N. Y. C. A. Feb. 14, 1824.

Page 70, line 17.   Record of the *Triton*.   C. C. Apr. 24, 1819.

Page 71, line 3.   Record of the *Herald*.   C. C. Dec. 25, 1819.

Page 72, line 28.   Record of the *Amanda*.   N. Y. E. P. July 13, 1822.

NOTE: In general the record runs mentioned are reported in New York, Boston, Philadelphia or Baltimore papers within a day or two after date of arrival. Except in special cases, therefore, it can serve no purpose to cite such sources of authority for such runs.

Page 80, line 3.   First channel steamer *Eliza*.   N. Y. C. A. May 9, 1816.

Page 83, line 15.   China record of *Sabina*.   N. Y. C. A. Mar. 22, 1834.

Page 85, line 1.   Record run of the *George* from Salem to Sand Heads.   See log in possession of E. I.

Page 85, line 28.   Voyage of *America*.   N. Y. C. A. Nov. 27, 1833.

Page 88, line 5 et seq.   Records of brig *John Gilpin*.   See logs in possession of W. B.

Page 92, line 26 et seq.   Passage of *Ann McKim* in 1837.   B. A. Aug. 3, 1837.

Page 96, line 25 et seq. Race of *Garrick* and *England*. N. Y. A. Jan. 6th, 12th and 26th, 1838.

Page 100, line 21 et seq. Voyages of *Helena*. See logs in possession of W. B.

Page 104, line 27 et seq. Record of *Shakespeare*. N. Y. H. Nov. 10, 1845. Record of *Nashville*. New Orleans Bee, Mar. 3, 1842.

Page 107, line 31. Record run of *Ann McKim* to Anjier. N. Y. C. A. Aug. 15, 1842.

Page 108, line 17. Fast passages of ship *Horatio*. N. Y. C. A. July 26, 1843.

Page 111, line 26. Description of ship *Houqua*. N. Y. H. May 22, 1844.

Page 115, line 19. Record voyage of *Rainbow*. N. Y. H. Sept. 19, 1845.

Page 116, line 8. On Boston packet service see, *e. g.* letters in N. Y. H. May 11th and July 27th, 1845.

Page 116, line 31. First Baltimore-Liverpool packet line. N. Y. H. Feb. 28, 1846.

Page 119, line 7. N. Y. H. Sept. 30, 1845, printed a list of American vessels engaged in the China trade.

Page 120, line 1. Record run of the *Rainbow*. N. Y. H. Apr. 17, 1846.

Page 128, line 8. On ship building activity see, *e. g.*, long article in N. Y. H. Mar. 13, 1847.

Page 136, line 4. List of vessels for California, N. Y. H. Feb. 20, 1849.

Page 143, line 20. Run of ship *Memnon*. N. Y. H. Dec. 16, 1848.

Page 146, line 34. Ship building statistics. N. Y. H. Jan. 1, 1849.

Page 151, line 29. Voyage of *Reindeer*. N. Y. H. May 29, 1850.

Page 156, line 27. Voyage of *Seaman*. N. Y. H. Apr. 22, 1851.

Page 158, line 1. *Racehorse*. See log in Possession of W. B.

Page 164, line 27. Pook. History seems to have done scant

justice to the work of Samuel Hartt Pook, naval architect. As a young man he designed a large number of the most successful of the clipper ships, among them the *Red Jacket, Game Cock, Northern Light, Surprise, Ocean Telegraph, Ocean Chief, Telegraph, Fearless, Herald of the Morning, Belle of the West* and *Challenger*. It is doubtful whether any single individual did more to develop a beautiful and successful merchant marine in America than Pook. After the outbreak of the Civil War he had a long and eventful career as designer of ships for the Navy. His achievements deserve far greater attention than can here be given them.

Page 167, line 29. Record of *Southampton*. N. Y. H. June 25, 1850.

Page 169, line 25. *Jennett*. Sometimes called *Jeanette*. N. Y. H. Apr. 9, 1851.

Page 170, line 7. Voyage of *Wisconsin*. See log in possession of W. B.

Page 170, line 14. Voyage of *Roman*. See log in possession of W. B.

Page 176. Logs of *John Bertram, Sea Serpent* and *Grey Feather* in possession of W. B.

Page 180, line 30. Log of *Witch of the Wave* in possession of W. B.

Page 181, line 6. Log of *N. B. Palmer* in possession of W. B.

Page 192, line 26. Voyage of *Seaman*. See log in possession of W. B.

Page 195, line 15. *Hong Kong Register*, Apr. 17, 1851.

Page 196, line 30. *White Squall*. N. Y. H. Jan. 8, 1852.

Page 197, line 34. *Chrysolite*. See N. Y. H. Oct. 16, 1851.

Page 200, line 2. *Typhoon*. N. Y. H. Apr. 11, 1851.

Page 207, line 20. Description of *N. B. Palmer*. N. Y. H. Feb. 9, 1851.

Page 210, line 4. Description of *Racer*. N. Y. H. July 29, 1851.

Page 214, line 19. Log books of *Comet, Swordfish, Flying Fish* and *Wild Pigeon* in possession of W. B.

Page 219, line 1. *Sovereign of the Seas.* N. Y. C. A. Aug. 7, 1852.

Page 220, line 7. Log of *Staffordshire* in possession of W. B.

Page 226, line 10. Run of *Witch of the Wave.* I. L. N. May 1, 1852.

Page 227, line 27 et seq. Record runs of *Challenge.* See N. Y. H. May 31, June 4, Sept. 2 and Sept. 10, 1852.

Page 228, line 22. China clipper race. See *e. g.,* N. Y. C. A. Dec. 4, 1852.

Page 229, line 17. Challenge of American Navigation Club. N. Y. H. July 10, 1852.

Page 229, line 31. Record of *R. B. Forbes.* N. Y. H. May 6, 1852.

Page 230, line 25. For record and description of *Defiance* see N. Y. H. May 27, 1852.

Page 231, line 10. Log of *Tornado* in possession of W. B.

Page 235, lines 2 and 3. Logs of *Black Squall* and *Grey Eagle* in possession of W. B.

Page 237, lines 5 and 7. Logs of *Charles Mallory* and *Eliza Mallory* in possession of W. B.

Pages 240-241. Logs of *Wild Pigeon, Flying Dutchman, Westward Ho, John Gilpin, Flying Fish, Trade Wind, Telegraph* and *Contest* in possession of W. B.

Page 246, line 11. "Three masted brig" *Carbon* was built in Robbinston, Me., in 1851. She was commanded by John Valpey and owned by N. M. Brewer of Robbinston and E. R. Rice of Wilmington, Del. I have not been able to learn whether she was barkentine rigged originally, or not

Page 248, line 12. *Phantom.* See N. Y. H. May 26, 1853.

Page 260, line 3. Log of *Windward* in possession of W. B.

Page 262, line 15. Logs of *Mandarin* and *Hurricane* in possession of W. B.

Page 264, line 2. *Celestial.* N. Y. H. Feb. 18, 1854.

Page 268, line 11. See logs of *Comet* and *Flying Dutchman* in possession of W. B.

Page 269, line 21.   Barque *Nimrod.* N. Y. H. Nov. 18, 1853.

Page 269, line 23.   Barque *Mermaid.* N. Y. H. May 24, 1853.

Page 271, line 4.   *Golden Eagle.* See also Journal of Benj. A. Pettingill, in possession of E. I.

Page 275, line 12.   New Clippers in New York. N. Y. H. Nov. 10, 1853.

Page 277, line 16.   Voyage of the *Argo.* N. Y. H. Nov. 18, 1853.

Page 278, line 10.   Mortality on packet ships. N. Y. H. Dec. 5, 1853.

Page 279, line 17.   *Dreadnought.* Two voyages have been mentioned as passages on which the *Dreadnought* made the run of 9 days to Cape Clear. In his article "The Dreadnought of Newburyport" F. B. C. Bradlee cites the occasion when the ship left New York, Feb. 27th, 1859, and quotes Captain Samuels' letter dictated in 1908 as authority for the statement that she was off Queenstown 9 days and 17 hours out. Captain Clark disposes of this claim in a seemingly conclusive manner (see page 246, *Clipper Ship Era*) giving the abstract of the *Dreadnought's* log and showing that when 9 days and 21 hours from Sandy Hook she was more than 400 miles from Queenstown.

The other passage is referred to by Howe & Matthews on page 145 of their work on American Clipper Ships. Here it will be noted that the possibility that the *Dreadnought* made the run in question involves the assumption that she did not leave New York until June 17, 1859. It appears to be conclusively established, however, that she left port the previous day, *i. e.*, on the 16th, and crossed the bar at Sandy Hook at 12.30 P. M., with a light Southwest wind. (See, *e. g.*, N. Y. H. June 17, 1859). On the evidence available, therefore, we are reluctantly compelled to conclude that the passage is not sufficiently authenticated, although further and more favorable evidence may be uncovered.

Page 285, line 23.   Log of *David Brown* in possession of W. B.

Page 293, line 23. *Golden Gate* record. See, *e. g.*, N. Y. H. Mar. 19, 1855.

Page 295, line 13. *Comet.* The 86-16/24 days is obviously a misprint for 84-16/24 since the dates given by the paper show clearly that the anchor to anchor run was made in 84 and not in 86 days.

Page 300, line 18. *Flying Scud.* Full particulars of her voyage in the *Melbourne Argus,* Dec. 20, 1854.

Page 303, line 27. Loss of *San Francisco,* N. Y. C. A. Jan. 14, 1854.

Page 305, line 1. Log of barque *Storm* in possession of W. B.

Page 313. Logs of *Elizabeth F. Willets* and *Neptune's Car* in possession of W. B.

Page 317. Logs of *Nor'Wester* and *Beverly* in possession of Boston Marine Museum.

Page 319, line 20. For record of *Eagle Wing* see log in possession of W. B.

Page 327, line 20. Barque *Maury.* See log in possession of W. B.

Page 328, line 22. *Wild Wave.* N. Y. H. Dec. 12, 1856.

Page 333, line 30. Record of *Sweepstakes.* N. Y. C. A. Sept. 15, 1857.

Page 335, line 18. *Northfleet.* For departure from Hong Kong see C. M. Aug. 13, 1857. For arrival at Plymouth see L. L. Nov. 30, 1857.

Page 346, line 29. Captain Joseph W. Holmes Cape Horn passages. See Connecticut Magazine, Aug. 1899, p. 409.

Page 355, line 21. For report of voyages of *Eagle Wing* and *East Indian* see N. Y. H. Dec. 29, 1859.

Page 360, line 10. *Phœnix* record. N. Y. H. Feb. 20, 1859.

Page 373, line 1. *North Wind* record. N. Y. C. A. Apr. 24, 1860.

Page 373, line 5. *Mary Whitridge* record. N. Y. H. July 4th and 11th, 1860.

Page 373, line 13. *Wild Pigeon* record. N. Y. H. Apr 29, 1860.

APPENDIX I

(In Three Parts)

(a) A selected list of fast sailing vessels built in the United States from 1782 to 1849, inclusive.

(b) One hundred transatlantic packet ships of the early period.

(c) The later clippers and reputed clippers, 1850 to 1860 inclusive, listed under year of launching.

NOTE: Vessels are ship rigged unless otherwise specified. Fractional tonnage not given. Dimensions are (in order) tonnage, length, breadth and depth, given in feet and inches (not, as use of period might indicate, in feet and tenths). Where depth is omitted, it was reported, in accordance with early legal rules for computing tonnage, merely as one-half the breadth.

Many well-known craft are omitted from part (a) to conserve space, the primary purpose of this list being to afford the reader a reasonably clear conception of the character, variety and distribution of early fast vessels. The years from 1830 to 1845 in particular witnessed the construction of a large number of remarkably fine, fast Indiamen, China packets and fruit and coffee traders, only a few of which are noted here. These craft were small in size, rarely measuring much over 500 tons, but were very heavily sparred and occasionally made remarkable passages.

The triangular route between New York, Charleston, S. C., and Europe also developed fast ships during the eighteen twenties. According to tradition, the *Corsair, Lalla Rookh* and several others of that day and trade were decidedly clipperly in appearance and performance.

Vessels listed in part (c) include a majority but not all ship rigged craft usually referred to as "clippers" during the fifties. Many of these were quite full-built, and had no legitimate claim to a clipper rating. They appear, however, to have been heavily rigged in characteristic clipper style, and when loaded could only be distinguished from the true clipper by the expert. A few of the better known clipper barques are also included in this list.

APPENDIX I

(a)

FAST SAILING VESSELS, 1782–1849, INCLUSIVE

SHIP, MEASUREMENTS AND MASTER	PLACE AND DATE OF CONSTRUCTION	OWNER
Abaellino, Caleb Grozier, 606.30: 144.6 x 30.3½ x 22	J. T. Foster, Medford, Mass., 1848	James Tirrell et al, Boston
Akbar, Philip Dumaresq, 642.89: 148.10 x 30.7	Samuel Hall, East Boston, 1839	John M. Forbes, Samuel Cabot et al, Boston (Condemned at Valparaiso 1854)
Alert, Dixey Wildes, 377: 108 x 28	Daniel Briggs, Milton, Mass., 1810	Theodore Lyman, Boston (This was second fast ship of the name)
Alert, Scudder, 398: 113.4 x 28	Noah Brooks, South Boston, 1828	Theodore Lyman, et al, Boston (Burned by *Alabama*, 1862)
America, Jacob Sarley, 654	Formerly French frigate *Blonde*	Purchased in Bordeaux, 1797, by Geo. Crowninshield et al, Salem—Resold in France, 1802
America, Elias Davidson, and later Joseph Ropes, James Cheever, Jr. et al, 473: 114 x 31	Salem, 1804	George Crowninshield et al, Salem (Altered to 331 tons in 1812 by removal of upper deck)
America, Stephen E. Glover, 418: 118.9 x 27.11	Newbury, Mass., 1822	Wm. Goddard, Boston (Her dimensions illustrate tendency to lengthen and refine lines)
America, Warren Fox 346.3: 107 x 26–9/10	Portsmouth, N. H.	Geo. A. Talbot, et al, New York
America, Wm. Howell, 561: 123.10 x 31.11	New York, 1788	Isaac Gouverneur, Peter and Robert Kemble, et al, New York
There were many other early vessels named *America*.		

SHIP, MEASUREMENTS AND MASTER	PLACE AND DATE OF CONSTRUCTION	OWNER
Amity, Sewall Parsons, 499.11: 134 x 28.5	Newbury, 1843	Robt. B. Forbes & John M. Forbes, Boston
Andalusia, Francis W. Wilson, 771.71: 151.4 x 33.5	Baltimore, Md., 1848	David S., Thomas I., and Henry R. Wilson, Baltimore
Ann & Hope, Olney, 550:98 keel x 32 x 19.4	Providence, R. I., 1798	Brown & Ives, Providence (Lost Block Island, 1805, after which Brown & Ives built a second vessel of the same name)
Ann McKim, Joseph Martin, 494: 140.7 x 27.6	Kennard & Williamson, Baltimore, 1833	Isaac McKim, Baltimore (Dismantled at Valparaiso 1852)
Anstiss, Joseph Steele, 595: 140 x 30.5 x 20.6	Hayden & Cudworth, Medford, 1847	Wm. S. Wetmore, New York
Schr. *Antelope*, Enoch Conklin, 266.8: 102.8 x 26 x 11.2	Christian Bergh, New York, 1812	Wm. Bayard, Herman Le Roy, Isaac Iselin et al, New York
Architect, Adams Gray, 520: 140 x 30 x 13.6	L. B. Culley, Baltimore, 1848	Adams Gray, Baltimore (Sold Hong Kong, 1854)
Argonaut, William Knott, 575.40: 147.5 x 29 x 21	Samuel Lapham, Medford, 1849	John Ellerton Lodge, Boston
Ariel, John Copp, later Geo. S. Brewster, 572: 136.4 x 30.4	Currier & Townsend, Newburyport, 1846	Minot & Hooper, et al, Boston (Sold Shanghae, 1857)
Bk. *Asa Fish*, Thos. E. Wolfe, 320.29: 107.7 x 27.11 x 12	Irons & Grinnell, Mystic, 1849	Amos Grinnell and a number of others of Stonington & Groton
Asia, Thos. B. Hollis, 474.69: 133.2 x 27.10½	Gad Leavitt, Boston, 1834	Lot Wheelwright, Boston
Astrea, John Gibaut, 360: 110 x 27 x 13.6	Pembroke, Mass., 1782 (A smaller *Astrea* was built at Bradford, Mass., 1795, for E. H. Derby)	Elias Hasket Derby, Salem (An early example of the long narrow model)
Atahualpa, Dixey Wildes and later Wm. Sturgis, 209: 85.5 x 23.7 x 11.10	Kennebunk, Mass., 1800	Theodore Lyman, Kirk Boot and Wm. Pratt, Boston
Beaver, John Whitten, 447: 111 x 29.6	Eckford & Beebe, New York, 1805	John J. Astor, New York

SHIP, MEASUREMENTS AND MASTER	PLACE AND DATE OF CONSTRUCTION	OWNER
Belisarius, Geo. Crowninshield, 209: 94.6 x 25 (Apparently raised to two decks in 1795)	Salem, 1794	Geo. Crowninshield & Sons, Salem (Tonnage changed to 261 tons in 1795—Lost near Tunis, April 1810.) This is possibly the *Bellesarius* referred to in Joshua Humphrey Jr.'s notebook.
Bk. *Behring,* Benj. F. Snow, 275.50: 103 x 24.4	Currier & McKay, Newbury, 1842	Wm. H. Boardman, et al, Boston
Schr. *Boxer,* Samuel C. Reid, 275.85: 105.4 x 25.6 x 11.5	John Lozier, New York, 1813	Frederick Jenkins, et al, New York
Braganza, Rogers, 469: 111.6 x 31	Forman Cheeseman, New York, about 1801	A. Gracie & Sons, New York (In Liverpool run 1819–21 &c)
Buena Vista, Simeon Howard, 660.84: 142.5 x 31.11	Richmond, Me., 1848	Mott & McCready, New York
Cabot, Wm. A. Lowry, 338.8: 116.10 x 25.1½	Duxbury, Mass., 1832	Chas. A. Hecksher & Edward Hecksher, New York
Calumet, Richard Cole, 188.59: 81.6 x 23	Charlestown, Mass., 1803	Wm. R. Gray, Boston
Bk. *Candace,* E. C. Gardner, 398: 117.6 x 27.4	Warren, R. I., 1845	Bucklin & Crane, New York
Canton, Murphy, 518: 116.3 x 31.10	Brooklyn, 1799 (Another *Canton,* 408.52: 106 x 29.8 was built in N. Y. 1808, owned by the Bayards)	Thos. Willing Francis et al, Philadelphia. (Said to have been built by Christian Bergh)
Carrington, Abbott, 641: 136 x 32.4	Warren, R. I., 1847	Edward Carrington, Providence
Brig *Chasseur,* Paul Durkee, 356, 115.6 x 26.8 x 12.9	Baltimore, 1812	Wm. Hollins et al, Baltimore
Cincinnati, Samuel C. Howes, later John D. Holbrook, 607.-58: 140 x 30.10	Jas. Curtis, Medford, 1839	Israel Lombard et al, Boston. Sold 1840 to Jas. Wilson et al, Baltimore
Clothier, Matthew Strong, 308.41: 94 x 27.6	Philadelphia, 1791	James Oldden et al, Philadelphia

SHIP, MEASUREMENTS AND MASTER	PLACE AND DATE OF CONSTRUCTION	OWNER
Cohota, W. B. Gerry, 691: 145.6 x 32.3 x 20	Wm. H. Webb, New York, 1843	N. L. & G. Griswold, New York
Commerce, Sam'l Ashton, 430.82: 123 x 28	Philadelphia, 1832	John McCrea, Philadelphia
Congress, 363: 102 x 28.6	Mr. Prince, Baltimore, 1809	Wm. A. Moores, Baltimore, 1820 (Sharp model)
Congress, Allen Miner, 376: 112 x 27.4	Brown & Bell, New York, 1831	E. K. Collins, New York
Bk. *Coquette*, Oliver Eldridge, 457.26: 116 x 29.9 x 16.3	Samuel Hall, Boston, 1844	Russell & Co., Canton, China
Corinthian, Hall, and later Golden Dearth, 503: 123.9 x 30.1	Baltimore, 1822	Wm. H. De Wolf, Bristol, R. I. (Sharp model)
Corsair, Simon V. Peabody, 301.05: 115 x 23.10 x 18.10	Medford, 1845	Augustus Hemenway, Boston
Courier, Wm. Wolfe, 381.10: 103.6 x 29	Mr. Wright, New York, 1817	Andrew Foster, New York (Used for a time as a Black Ball packet)
Courier, Geo. Dewhurst, 391.61: 116 x 27.4	Currier & McKay, Newburyport, 1844 (In addition several other *Couriers* were built)	Foster & Elliott, New York
Covinton, Holbrook, 350: 104.6 x 27.6	Baltimore, 1825	James Wilson et al, Baltimore
Delaware, Thomas Truxton, 390½: 105.8 x 29	Philadelphia, 1791	Robert Morris et al, Philadelphia, and Wm. & James Constable, New York
Dromo, De Wolf, 493: 122 x 30	Amesbury, Mass., 1804	George De Wolf et al, Bristol
Esther May, Levi Stevens, 499.21: 129 x 29.2	Bristol, R. I., 1847	Morrill & Baker, Boston (Lost in Yang Tse River, 1860)
Ketch *Eliza*, Stephen Phillips, 184: 93 x 25 x 9	Enos Briggs, Salem, 1794	Elias H. Derby, Salem (The *Eliza* had one deck and quarter galleries)
Empress of China, John Green, 360	Boston (also given as Baltimore) 1783	Robert Morris et al, New York

SHIP, MEASUREMENTS AND MASTER	PLACE AND DATE OF CONSTRUCTION	OWNER
Equator, Russell E. Glover, 398.19: 124.3 x 26.5	Charlestown, Mass., 1830	Russell Glover, New York, and Stephen Glover, Roxbury, Mass.
Euphrates, Nash De Cost, 364.49: 103. 9½ x 28.3	New Bedford, 1809	Cornelius Grinnell, Wm. Howland et al, New Bedford
Factor, Josiah F. Caldwell, 299.72: 95.8 x 26.9	New York, 1792	Albert Wyckoff, New York (Josiah Adams and Daniel Cotton of **New** York were first owners)
Fama, Woodward, 362.84: 110.3 x 27.1	Newburyport, 1819	Benj. T. Reed, Boston
Fame, Jeremiah Briggs, 363: 102 x 28.6	Salem, 1802	Geo. Crowninshield et al, Salem. In 1815, John H. Hill, Robt. Ainslie et al, New York, Thos. Mix, master
Fanny, Daniel H. Brain, 238¾: 85.11 x 25.4	Samuel Ackerly, New York, 1792	Lenox & Maitland, New York. (Thos. Buchanan, New York, first owner)
Bk. *Fanny*, Isaac D. Gates, 341.20: 113 x 29.4 x 11.7	P. Forsyth, Mystic, Conn., 1849	Charles Mallory, et al, Mystic
Brig *Findorf*, M. P. Cottle, 216: 92 x 25 x 10.8	Matthews Co., Virginia, 1813	Thos. Higenbotham, Baltimore
Flora, Jacob De Hart, 306.29	Scituate, Mass., 1801	Sam'l Meeker, Philadelphia, 1803–4
Brig *Fox*, John Cowman, 224.61: 90 x 23.5 x 12	Henry Eckford, New York, 1809	John J. Astor, New York. (Sold to Henry Hammond, New York, May 25, 1910)
Frances Henrietta, Jared Goodrich, 411: 104.9 x 30	Philadelphia, 1803	Isaac Clason, New York
Friendship, Philip P. Pinel, 366.36: 105 x 28.1	Portland, 1815 (Same owners had a *Friendship* 343.17 102 x 27.7 built at Salem in 1797)	Jerathmiel Pierce, et al (Captured by Malays Feb. 7, 1831 at Quallah Battoo, Sumatra & recaptured. Sold to Fairhaven for a Whaler, 1831)
Bk. *Gallego*, Silas D. Washburn, 372.56: 114 x 26.10¾ x 13.5½	Fairhaven, Mass., 1847	Warren Delano, New York, and later Matthew P. Game, U. S. Consul at Quayaquil
Ganges, James R. Callender, 524	Thomas Penrose, Philadelphia, 1795	Thomas W. Francis et al, Philadelphia

SHIP, MEASUREMENTS AND MASTER	PLACE AND DATE OF CONSTRUCTION	OWNER
Gen'l Brown, James Copeland, 899.20: 147 x 37	Adam & Noah Brown New York, 1815	Several other large ships were built at New York about this time.
Gentoo, Abel Coffin, 435.48: 124.1½ x 27.9	Herman Holmes, Boston, 1834	Daniel C. Bacon, Boston
George, Samuel Endicott, 328.63: 110.10 x 27	Salem, 1814, built for a privateer	Joseph Peabody, Salem (Condemned at Rio Janiero 1837)
George Washington, Patrick Hayes, Jonathan Donnison, et al, 624: 130.9 x 32.8	Providence, R. I., 1794	John Brown, et al, Providence, and later Lewis Clapier et al, Philadelphia, in 1803 (Later frigate *George Washington*)
Georgiana, Geo. G. Gardner and later John Land, 553.88: $133\frac{5}{16}$ x $30\frac{2}{16}$, 7.6 between decks, 14.6 hold	Pogelt & Pearson, Philadelphia, 1836	C. A. & E. Hecksher, New York
Brig *Gipsey*, Geo. Main, 207.29: 89 x 24 x 11	Christian Bergh, New York, 1809	Geo. Main & Ebenezer Stevens, New York
Glide, Samuel Tucker, 306: 97.9 x 26.8	Salem, 1811	Joseph Peabody and master, Salem (Wrecked at Tacanova, South Seas, March, 1832)
Golden Age, Stephen Phillips, 219: 85.8 x 24 x 12.2	Philadelphia, 1796	Elias H. Derby, Salem
Grand Turk, William Loring, 270.50: $90\frac{6}{16}$ x $26\frac{2}{16}$	New Market, N. H. 1806	Jacob P. Girand, New York, and Andrew Foster, merchants
Grand Turk, Benj. Hodges, 564: 124 x 32	Enos Briggs, Salem, 1791	Elias Hasket Derby, Salem (Derby also had *Grand Turk* about 300 tons, built 1781, for a privateer)
Brig *Grand Turk*, Holton J. Breed, 309: 102 x 28 x 12.4	Wiscasset, 1812	Francis Boardman et al, Salem (Sold Havana, 1816)
Bk. *Greenpoint*, J. H. Wardle, 500.39: 131.8 x 28.10	Jabez Williams, New York, 1849	Thomas Wardle, New York
Grey Eagle, John Power, 479: 132.6 x 27.6 x 14.3	Abraham & Cooper, Baltimore, 1848	John B. McKeever et al, Philadelphia (One deck, Square stern, billet head)

SHIP, MEASUREMENTS AND MASTER	PLACE AND DATE OF CONSTRUCTION	OWNER
Grey Hound, John Claypoole, 536: 137.5 x 28.9 x 14.8	Henry Meads & Thos. Horney, Baltimore, 1848	David Stuart et al, Baltimore
Haidee, Joseph S. Soule, 647.56: 142 x 31.7½	Freeport, Me., 1843	Isaac T. Smith, New York
Hazard, Richard Gardner, 325: 101 x 27	Salem, 1799	Richard and John Gardner, Salem
Bk. *Hazard*, Andrew Barstow, 403.75: 122.6 x 27.4 x 13.2¾	Samuel Hall, Boston, 1849 (337 tons under new rules)	Henry Gardner, Salem, 1866
Helena, Deliverance P. Benjamin, 598: 134.6 x 31.4 x 20	Wm. H. Webb, New York, 1841	N. L. & G. Griswold, New York (Missing 1857)
Heber, John W. Patterson, 434.79: 126.8 x 27.4½ x 19.9	Medford, Mass., 1844 Waterman & Ewell	Daniel C. Bacon et al, Boston
Herald, Zachariah Silsbee, 326: 101 x 27 x 14.6	Falmouth, Mass., 1797	Ebenezer Preble et al, Salem (Captured by British, 1808)
Herald, Foreman, 395: 111 x 28.3	New York, 1823	George Law, Baltimore, 1838
Hibernia, Hugh Graham, 327: 97 x 27.10	Foreman Cheeseman, New York, 1811	Samuel & Wm. Craig, New York (Wm. Martin, Baltimore, 1826)
Hindoo, James F. Miller, 580.48: 136 x 30.6½	Portsmouth, N. H., 1835	Daniel Bacon et al, Boston, (Francis Burritt, New York, 1850)
Hope, James Barr, 282.45: 95.9 x 26	Salem, 1805	John Barr and James Barr, Salem (Sold New Bedford, Dec. 1829)
Hope, 416: 108.6 x 29.6	Talbot Co., Md., 1805	Jacob Adams, et al, Baltimore, 1816
Horatio, Howland, 470: 119.10 x 29.8 x 17	Hillman, New Bedford, 1833	Grinnell & Minturn, New York
Horsburgh, Jos. Osgood, 543: 141 x 28.10 x 20.9	Hayden & Cudworth, Medford, 1847	Daniel C. Bacon et al, Boston
Houqua, Philip Dumaresq, 339: 104.2 x 27.1	Noah Brooks, Boston	Thos. H. Perkins et al, Boston

SHIP, MEASUREMENTS AND MASTER	PLACE AND DATE OF CONSTRUCTION	OWNER
Houqua, N. B. Palmer, 582.84: 142.4 x 29.10 x 16.8	Brown & Bell, New York, May 3, 1844 (Launched)	A. A. Low & Bro., New York
Bk. *Inca*, Thos. M. Cook, 376.58: 116 x 26.9	Baltimore, 1840	Thos. M. Cook, of Baltimore, and Sampson & Tappan, Boston
Indian Chief, Wm. Cochran, 401.47: 105.3 x 29.4	Portsmouth, Va., 1812	Granville S. Oldfield, Baltimore
Bk. *Isabelita Hyne*, Samuel F. Dewing, 350	Philadelphia, 1846	(Lost near San Francisco, Jan. 8, 1856)
Jamestown, Trask, 1151.40: 176.2 x 37.2 x 22.9	Perine, Patterson & Stack, New York, 1847	Slate, Gardner & Co., New York (Quite fast—arrived New York May 15, 1854 in 91 days from Manilla)
Bk. *Jennett*, J. O. Barclay, 247.61: 105 x 27.6 x 9.8	Saybrook, Ct., 1847	Chas. Peterson, New Haven, Ct.
Jenny Lind, Lauchlan McKay, 532.62: 141.6 x 28.6 x 22	Donald McKay, East Boston, 1848	Geo. M. Fairbanks, Joseph P. Wheeler & D. McKay, Boston
Brig *John Gilpin*, Jos. Eyre, 283: 104 x 25.10 x 11.9	St. Michaels, Md., 1826	Matthew Kelly et al, Baltimore
Brig *John Gilpin*, Jos. Couthbouy, 248: 99.6 x 24.3	F. & H. Rogers, Medford, 1826	Daniel Parker, Boston
John G. Coster, D. P. Benjamin, 714: 141 x 33.6 x 21.9	New York, 1841	Joshua Atkins, later Howland & Aspinwall, New York
John Q. Adams, Edward C. Nickels, 622: 144.4 x 31.8 x 21.3	Paul Curtis, Medford, 1844	Daniel P. Parker, Boston
John W. Cater, John R. Crane, 217.31: 89.4 x 24.2 x 11.5	Dan'l Buell, Killingworth, Ct., 1831	Jacob Fowler & Charles Morgan, New York
Joshua Bates, Thos. C. Stoddard, 620.26: 143.1 x 30.9	Donald McKay, Newburyport, 1844	Train & Co., Boston
Lady Adams, Robt. Benthall, 274.31: 100.6 x 24.8	Baltimore, 1825	Hugh Birckhead, Baltimore

SHIP, MEASUREMENTS AND MASTER	PLACE AND DATE OF CONSTRUCTION	OWNER
Lady Madison, 450.21: 112 x 30.2	Scituate, Mass., 1810	Jacob Barker, New York
Brig *Lady Monroe*, Forbes, 240: 90.6 x 24.6	Baltimore, 1817	Jacob Adams & Wm. H. Conkling, Baltimore
Lantao, Joseph P. Johnson, 593.36: 135.6 x 31.0½ x 20.3	Samuel Hall, East Boston, 1849	Daniel N. Spooner, Boston (Missing 1857—Capt. Andrew Barstow)
Brig *Leander*, Samuel Rea, 233.30: 91.4 x 23.5 x 11.8½	Salem, 1821	Joseph Peabody, Salem (Condemned & sold Gambia, 1844)
Liberty, Samuel Singleton, 252.24	Philadelphia, 1795	Stephen Girard, Philadelphia
Liberty, Moses Starbuck, 303.36: 104 x 25.6	Chatham, Ct., 1799	Geo. Howland, Jas. Howland et al, New Bedford, and Samuel Hicks, New York
Living Age, Robt. P. Holmes, 727: 150.3 x 32.6 x 23.4	Jotham Stetson, Medford, Mass., 1848	Edward D. Peters & Co., Boston (Wrecked Pratas Shoals, Dec. 31, 1854) Owned first by Wm. Appleton, John H. Reed, et al, Boston.
Mandarin, N. D. Symonds, 296: 108 x 24.6	Salem, 1828	David A. Neal et al, Salem
Mandarin, Nash, 320: 98.4 x 27.3	Amesbury, Mass., 1803	Jos. King et al, Baltimore, 1824
Manhattan, John B. Lasher, 667: 130 x 35 x 17	Samuel Ackerly, New York, 1800	Phillip Rhinelander et al, New York
Margaret, Samuel Derby, 295: 91 x 27.5	Salem, 1800	John Derby et al, Salem (Made voyage to Japan in 1801. Lost 1810)
Maria, Griswold, 344.04: 102 x 27.8 x 13.10	Richard Hayden, Saybrook, Ct., 1811	Geo. Griswold & Nathaniel L. Griswold, New York, Richard & Ebenezer Hayden
Maria, Green, 397.33: 127.4 x 25.10 x 13.1	Isaac C. Smith, Hoboken, N. J., 1849	Chas. W. Swift, New York
Maria & Eliza, Francis Boardman, 215: 83 x 24.6 x 12.3	Dover, N. H., 1789	Francis Boardman, Nathaniel West, Salem
Mars, Matthew Rogers, 296.57: 95.3 x 26.8	Stratford, Ct., 1800 (Another *Mars*, 260 tons, was built in Mass., 1795)	Thos. Carpenter, New York, and Liffert Lifferts, Philadelphia

SHIP, MEASUREMENTS AND MASTER	PLACE AND DATE OF CONSTRUCTION	OWNER
Martha, Henry Waddell, 340.67: 105 x 27	Salem, Mass., 1796	Thomas Salter, New York, part owner
Maryland, Jonathan Perry, 464.45: 114 x 30.4	Baltimore, Md., 1799	Wm. Taylor, Baltimore, and later Wm. Bayard, Hermann LeRoy and many others, New York
Massachusetts, Wm. Hutchins, 615.76: 125.9 x 33.3	Newbury, Mass., 1799	T. H. Perkins, Stephen Higginson, Thos. C. Amory et al, Boston
Mechanics Own, Humphrey Seabury, 540.58: 128.2 x 30.7	Bishop & Simonson, New York, 1849	An Association of Mechanics
Memnon, Joseph Gordon, 1068: 170 x 36 x 21	Smith & Dimon, New York, 1847	F. A. Delano, New York
Meridian, 388: 105 x 29	Anne Arundel Co., Md., Nov., 1816	(Sharp Model)
Messenger, James Buffington, 277.49: 93.8 x 26	Salem, 1805	Simon Forrester, Salem (Sold Boston, 1831)
Milo, Stephen Glover, 398: 107.3 x 29	Newburyport, 1811	David Hinckley, Boston
Bk. *Mimosa*, Jerome B. Hildreth, 240.81: 104 x 25.4 x 10.2	Baltimore, 1848	Edward C. Bates et al, Boston, and Jerome B. Hildreth
Minerva, Richard Ward, Jr., 224.27: 84 x 24.10 x 12.5	Haverill, Mass., 1798	Richard Crowninshield et al, Salem
Montauk, McMichael, 505.19: 128 x 29.6	Wm. H. Webb, New York, 1844	Wm. S. Wetmore, New York
Mount Hope, Breeze, in 1810, 602	Newport, R. I., 1800-1801	Gibbs & Channing, Newport —Later owned by Gen. Derby
Mount Vernon, Walter Kerr, 431.59	Philadelphia, 1796	Samuel & Wm. Meeker, Philadelphia
Napier, 470: 123.6 x 29	Baltimore, 1833	Robert Hancock et al, Baltimore
New Jersey, James Cooper, 402	Philadelphia, 1795	Geo. Plumstead, et al Philadelphia
North Point, Pawson 480: 113 x 31	Wm. Price, Baltimore, May, 1816	(Sharp Model)

SHIP, MEASUREMENTS AND MASTER	PLACE AND DATE OF CONSTRUCTION	OWNER
Oliver Ellsworth, Wm. Henry, 410: 111.6 x 28.9	Norwich, Ct., 1801	William Henry and Wm. M. Polymert, New York
Oneida, James F. Cressy, 420.35: 116.1 x 28.4¾	New Bedford, 1832	Francis S. Hathaway et al, New Bedford and Gideon Nye, Jr., New York
Oneida, Wm. Cressy, 793: 150.6 x 34 x 22.3	Westervelt & Mackey, New York, 1841	Boyd & Hincken and Grinnell & Minturn, New York
Ontario, James N. Brown, later Depeyster, 527.73: 124.6 x 30.9	A. & N. Brown, 1812	Grinnell & Minturn, New York Thos. C. Butler, New York (In Rotterdam trade 1816)
Oriental, T. D. Palmer, 1003: 185 x 36 x 21	Jacob Bell, New York, 1849	A. A. Low & Bro., New York (Lost in River Min China, February 25, 1854)
Orpheus, N. Cobb, 573: 132 x 31	C. Bergh & Co., New York, 1832	N. Cobb, New York
Pacific, Wm. Bowne, 385: 110 x 28	A. & H. Brown, New York, 1807	Isaac Wright and Francis Thompson, New York
Packet: Benj. Beckford, 229.89: 89 x 24.6 x 12.3	Portland, 1803	Wm. Gray, Jr., Boston
Paladin: John White, 341.66: 103.9 x 27.3	Salem, 1816	Joseph White and a large number of Salem men. Built by an association for a Liverpool & Salem packet but idea was never carried out and ship sold to Boston, December, 1817.
Panama, D. P. Benjamin, 612: 135 x 31.8 x 20	W. H. Webb, New York, 1844	N. L. & G. Griswold, New York
Panther, Chas. Bartling, 407.27: 108 x 29.3	Providence, R. I., 1819	Edward Carrington, Jr., Providence, and later, Jonathan Ogden and John Ferguson, New York
Paul Jones, N. B. Palmer, 624: 144.6 x 30.8	Waterman & Ewell, Medford, Mass., 1842	John M. Forbes and Russell & Co., Boston
Paul Sieman, 443: 107.10 x 30.10	Hunley Gayle, Mathews Co., Va., 1800	Wm. Taylor, Baltimore (Sold in Amsterdam, 1803)
Perserverance, James Silver, 241.10: 90.1 x 24.8	Salem, 1809	Richard Wheatland et al (Condemned Madagascar, 1827)

SHIP, MEASUREMENTS AND MASTER	PLACE AND DATE OF CONSTRUCTION	OWNER
Pigou, Benj. Loxley, Jr., 359: 100.3 x 28.8	Philadelphia, 1783	John Field, Jesse Wake, Pattison Hartshorne, et al Philadelphia
Brig *Pilgrim*, Thompson 181: 86.6 x 37.7 x 10.9¾	Sprague & James, Medford, 1825	Joshua Blake, Boston
Ploughboy, Wm. Jones, 286.78	Philadelphia, 1801	Wm. Jones, Sam'l Clark, John Savage, Jos. Dugan & Jas. Barclay, Philadelphia
President Washington, Jacob Sarly, 958.14: 145 x 38.8	Providence, R. I., 1791	John Brown & John Francis, Providence
Probus, Charles Sumner, 647: 143 x 31.6	Jotham Stetson, Medford, 1841	Daniel P. Parker, Boston and Wm. S. Wetmore, New York
Raduga, Thomas Leach, 587: 150 x 29	Currier & Townsend, Newburyport, 1848	John E. Lodge, et al, Boston, and later H. Prince, et al, Boston (Lost 1890)
Rainbow, John Land, 752: 159 x 31.10 x 18.4	Smith & Dimon, New York, Launched Jan. 22, 1845	Howland & Aspinwall, New York (Missing 1848)
Rattler, Stump, 538.9: 137 x 29.3	Baltimore, 1852	
Rebecca Sims, Brewton, 400.15	Sam'l Bowers, reported builder, Philadelphia, 1807	Joseph Sims, Philadelphia (Sunk to blockade Charleston in Civil War)
Reindeer, John Lord 800.26: 156.6 x 33.5 x 22	Donald McKay, East Boston, launched June 9, 1849	J. M. Forbes, Geo. B. Upton & Sampson & Tappan, Boston (Wrecked in South Seas, February 12, 1859)
Resolution, Benj. Sherburne, 324.61: 104.6 x 26.4½	Norwich, Conn., 1801	Alpheus Dunham, Boston
Restitution, John Derby, 247.73: 89.4 x 25.2¼	Newbury, 1803	Simon Forrester, Salem (Sold at Boston, 1832)
Brig *Richard Alsop*, Wm. McMichael, 282.52: 90 x 26	Mathews Co., Va., 1831	Richard Alsop, Philadelphia
Richard Alsop, John Kenney, 835.85: 157.2 x 34.1	Bath, Me., 1847	N. L. & G. Griswold, New York
Stmr. *Robert Fulton*, Inott, 702: 159 x 33.9 x 14.3	Henry Eckford, New York, 1819	David Dunham & Co., New York (First large ocean steamer-converted into a sloop-of-war and sold to Brazil)

SHIP, MEASUREMENTS AND MASTER	PLACE AND DATE OF CONSTRUCTION	OWNER
Robert Fulton, Evans Dubs, 561.94: 129 x $31\frac{1}{16}$	John Bowly (or Buely?) Philadelphia, 1836	Charles Blight, Philadelphia
Roman, Heolyn Benson, 492.20: 118.10 x 30.6	New York, 1825	Talbot & Olyphant, New York
Rousseau, Myles McLeven, 305.87: $92\frac{9}{16}$ x $28\frac{8}{16}$ x $18\frac{8}{16}$	Philadelphia, 1802	Stephen Girard, Philadelphia
Bk. *Rover*, Horatio Nelson, 358: 112.11 x 26.6	Jacob Bell, New York, 1848	Jacob Bell, New York
Sabina, Sylvester Matison, 412.17: 111.6 x 28.10	New York, 1823	Robt. L. Taylor, Abraham Richards, et al, New York
Sally, Richard E. Orne, 322.58: 97.6 x 27.6	Boston, 1803	James Cook, Timothy Bryant, Jr., et al, Boston Lost on Bahama Bank, 1825
Samarang, Geo. Abbott, 377.59: 120.6 x 26.2 x 13.1	Boston, 1833	Levi H. Brigham, Geo. Abbott, et al, New York
Samuel Appleton, Samuel Kennedy, 780.67: 156.6 x 32. $10\frac{1}{2}$ x 21.9	Paul Curtis, Medford, 1849	Daniel P. Parker, Boston
Samuel Russell, N. B. Palmer, 957: 173.6 x 34.6 x 19.11	Brown & Bell, New York, Launched Aug. 14, 1847	A. A. Low & Bro. (Wrecked Gaspar Straits, November 23, 1870)
Bk. *Saxonville*, Wm. Reed, 422: 125.6 x 27.1 x 20.6	John Taylor, Medford, 1847	Josiah W. Blake, et al, Boston
Sea, Wm. Edwards, 807: 149.6 x 34.6	Baltimore, 1838	Reuben Fisher, et al, Norfolk
Sea Witch, Robert H. Waterman, 908: (192, o.a.) x 34 x 19; also 907.53: 170.3 x 33.11 x 19	Smith & Dimon, New York, Launched December 8, 1846	Howland and Aspinwall, New York (Wrecked near Havana, March 28, 1856)
Severn, John Cowman, 279.24: 91.6 x 26.6	New York, 1792	John J. Astor, New York (Elijah Pell and Thos. Pearsall, New York, were first owners)
Severn, Pitkin Page 572.61: 140.2 x 29.10	Sprague & James, Medford, 1837	Josiah Macy, New York, Wm. H. Macy, et al

SHIP, MEASUREMENTS AND MASTER	PLACE AND DATE OF CONSTRUCTION	OWNER
Sooloo, Very, 440: 131.7 x 26.11	Salem, 1840	Benj. W. Silsbee, et al, Salem
Splendid, John Land, 1843, 473: 126.6 x 28.10	Baltimore, January, 1832.	N. L. & G. Griswold. Later Hudson Foster, Philadelphia (Was a whaler in 1868)
Brig *Sphynx*, Henry Richards, 286.11: 108.8 x 26.8 x 11	Henry Eckford, New York, 1812	John Whetten & Robt. Dickey, New York
Superb, 527: 117 x 32	Baltimore, 1817	John Carrere, Baltimore
Susquehanna, Dixey, 583: 129 x 32.6 x 20	Philadelphia, 1833	H. & A. Cope, Philadelphia (Rated by Lloyds, 1869— "a sharp model")
Swift, Joseph Wheldon, 320.91: 100.4 x 26.11	New Bedford, 1805	Jerah Swift, et al, New Bedford
Schr. *Swift*, 315: 110 x 25.11	Baltimore, 1814	Phillip Mercier, Baltimore (Sharp model)
Tam O'Shanter, 777	Enos Soule, Freeport, Me., 1849	Enos Soule, Freeport (Foundered off Cape Cod, December, 1853)
Tartar, Gerry, 401: 108 x 29	Salem, 1811	Wm. Sturgis et al, Boston
Tartar, Benoni Lockwood, 573: 140 x 30.6 x 19.3	Mr. Hammel, Philadelphia, 1845	Booth & Edgar, New York
Thomas B. Wales, David Crocker, 599.59: 141.6½ x 30.5½ x 22.6	Waterman & Ewell, Medford, 1844	Geo. W. Wales, et al, Boston
Thomas Wattson, Thomas, 349: 121.6 keel x 26.8 x 12.10	Caleb Goodwin & Co., Baltimore, 1848	Thomas B. Wattson, Philadelphia
Trescott, James Haile, 341.43: 111.16 x 22 x 13	Medford, 1825	A. M. Lawrence, et al, New York
Trident, Curtiss Blakeman, 461: 111 x 30.9	A. & N. Brown, New York, 1805	Isaac Bell, et al, New York
Brig *Troubadour*, Rains, 198: 92.6 x 23.5 x 10.2	Baltimore, 1833	John Hutson, Hugh Jenkins & Thomas Reyburn, Baltimore
Tsar, Thomas Leach, 470.37: 131 x 27.11½ x 14	Currier & Townsend, Newbury, Mass., 1847	Wm. Ropes, Boston (Sold to Russian-American Fur Co.)

SHIP, MEASUREMENTS AND MASTER	PLACE AND DATE OF CONSTRUCTION	OWNER
Brig *Tweed*, Robinson, 307: 105 x 25.6 x 12.9	Baltimore, 1834	Hugh Jenkins, et al, Baltimore
Uriel, Dennis Janvrin, 799.28: 156.4 x 33.4½ x 24.5	Wm. Hall, Boston, 1847	Kirby Page, Uriel Crocker, John Waldron et al, Boston and John Wade, Woburn, Mass.
Bk. *Valparaiso*, Ben. Lockwood, 402: 117.6 x 27.6	Baltimore, January, 1836	Wm. Platt, et al, Philadelphia. Later Howland and Aspinwall, New York
Valparaiso, Thornton B. Rennell, 697.28: 147 x 32$\frac{2}{10}$	Philadelphia, 1847	John R. Wilmer, et al, Philadelphia
Venus, 465: 125.4 x 28.9 x 14.3	W. & Geo. Gardner, Baltimore, 1838	Lambert Gittings, Baltimore (Sharp model—sold abroad immediately)
Bk. *Vernon*, John McKay, 306.77: 107.9 x 25	Medford, Mass., 1839	Warren Delano, New York
Voltaire, Ezra Bowen, 305	Philadelphia, 1795	Stephen Girard, Philadelphia
Venice, John Power, 558: 135$\frac{8}{10}$ x 30	Philadelphia, 1839	Robert Burton, and Edward Clement, Philadelphia
Schr. *Viper*, 303: 105 x 25.3	Chatham, Conn., 1812	Wm. Sturgis et al, Boston
Wisconsin, Oliver R. Mumford, 925: 157 x 39 x 21	New York, 1847	B. A. Mumford, et al, New York. Owned in South America, 1869
Woodrop Sims, Hess, 305: 94 x 27.4	Philadelphia, 1794	Joseph Sims, Philadelphia
Schr. *Yellot*, Murphy, 179: 93 x 22 x 9.8	Baltimore, 1823	Isaac McKim, Baltimore
Schr. *Zebra*, Lemuel Bourne, 244: 104.4 x 25.7 x 10.2	A. & N. Brown, New York, 1812	Wm. Dunlap, et al, New York

APPENDIX I

(b)

ONE HUNDRED EARLY PACKET SHIPS

SHIP, MEASUREMENTS AND MASTER	PLACE AND DATE OF CONSTRUCTION	OWNER
Acasta, Augustus H. Griswold, 330.15: 99 x 27.7	Athens, New York, 1818	John Griswold, New York

SHIP, MEASUREMENTS AND MASTER	PLACE AND DATE OF CONSTRUCTION	OWNER
Ajax, Chas. A. Heirn, 627.7: 132-$\frac{8}{10}$ x 32$\frac{5}{10}$	Kensington, Pa., 1826	Robt. Kermit & Stephen Whitney, New York
Albion, John Williams, 434.25: 113.6 x 29.4	Sidney Wright, New York, 1818	Wm. Wright, New York
Amethyst, John M. Robertson, 359: 109.10 x 27	Boston, 1823	Wm. Appleton, et al, Boston
Amity, John Stanton, 382.17:106.6 x 28.6	Forman Cheeseman, New York, 1816	Francis Thompson, et al, New York
Ann Maria, 367.87: 104-$\frac{8}{10}$ x 28-$\frac{2}{10}$	Philadelphia, 1811	John Flack, New York
Aurora, John Taubman, 346.75: 105.1 x 23.3	Baltimore, 1823–1824	Robt. Kermit & Jas. Mowatt, et al
Baltic, T. G. Bunker, 409.83: 110 x 29	Brown & Bell, New York, 1822	Sam'l Hicks, New York
Baltimore, James Funck, 658.8: 139 x 32.6 x 22	Westervelt & Roberts, Williamsburg, N. Y., 1836	Robt. Carnley, Jacob A. Westervelt, et al, New York
Bayard: Henry Robinson, 339.18: 99 x 28	New York, 1819	Daniel Van Dyke, New York
Belfast, Elijah Bunker, 491.2: 122 x 30.1	Belfast, Mass., 1811	S. T. Jenkins, S. Hicks, et al, New York
Birmingham, N. Cobb, 571.31: 128.10 x 31.5	Chas. Porter, New York, 1825	N. Cobb, Jas. Buckley, Jas. & Richard Loines, New York
Braganza, Jas. Brown, 469.82: 111.6 x 31 x 15.6	Forman Cheeseman, New York, 1813	Wm. & Archibald Gracie & Chas. King, New York
Brighton, Wm. S. Sebor, 350.23: 105.6 x 27.6	Wm. Crockett, New York, 1824	John Griswold, Peter Crary, et al, New York
Britannia, Wm. Sketchley, 630.4: 132.10 x 32.6	Brown & Bell, New York, 1826	Wm. Wright, Isaac Wright, Jos. Walker, New York
Caledonia, James Rogers, 647.61: 136 x 32.6	Brown & Bell, New York, 1828	Black Ball Line, New York
Canada, Seth G. Macy, 545.86: 131.6 x 30.3	Brown & Bell, New York, 1823	Black Ball Line, New York

SHIP, MEASUREMENTS AND MASTER	PLACE AND DATE OF CONSTRUCTION	OWNER
Carroll of Carollton, Jas. B. Ingersoll, 695.92 : 136.10 x 33.8 x 16.10	Baltimore, Md., 1829–30	John S. & Peter Crary, New York, and James S. Brander, Petersburgh, Va.
Champlain, A. A. Ritchie, 624.46 : 131.10 x 32.6	New York, 1834	Wm. Platt, Hugh F. Hollingshead, et al, Phila.
Cincinnatus, Augustus H. Griswold, 373.23 : 98 x 29.9	Chas. Browne, New York, 1818	S. W. Coates, John Griswold, et al, New York
Columbia, Jas. Rogers, 490.30 : 123 x 29.10	Sidney Wright, New York, 1821–2	Black Ball Line, New York
Corinthian, Geo. Davis, 401.32 : 112.6 x 28.3	Blossom, Smith & Dimon, New York, 1822	T. Phelps, Peter Crary, Jr., John Taylor, New York
Cortes, Nash De Cost, 381.24 : 106.6 x 28.6	New Bedford, 1819	John Griswold, et al, New York
Courier, Wm. Bowne, 381.10 : 103.6 x 29	Sidney Wright, New York, 1817	Black Ball Line, New York
Courier, Robt. Marshall, 388.53 : 111 x 28	Medford, Mass., 1815	Jeremiah Thompson, New York
Crisis, Wm. Skiddy, 336.76 : 103 x 27.2	Sam'l Story, Norwich, Ct., 1819	S.S. Howland, et al, New York (Was in John Griswold's London Line several voyages)
Desdemona, F. Naghel, 331.93 : 98.7 x 26.4	Middletown, Ct. 1823	J. J. Boyd, Wm. Bayard, et al, New York
Edward, Josiah Macy, 346.46 : 102.5 x 27.8	Hanover, Mass., 1815	S. T. Jenkins, et al, New York
Edward Bonaffe, James Funck, 325.50 : 102 x 26.10	Christian Bergh, New York, 1824	John J. Boyd, C. Bergh, Jacob Westervelt, et al, New York
Edward Quesnel, Elnathan Hawkins, 380.10 : 106 x 28.10	C. Bergh, New York, 1824	Robt. Bayard, et al, New York
England, Geo. Maxwell, 729.66 : 140.4 x 34	Smith, Dimon & Comstock, New York, 1834	Geo. T. Trimble, Sam'l Hicks, Silas Wood, et al, New York
Emerald, Philip Fox, 359 : 109.10 x 27	John Wade, Boston, 1822	Wm. Appleton, et al, Boston

SHIP, MEASUREMENTS AND MASTER	PLACE AND DATE OF CONSTRUCTION	OWNER
Europe, Edward G. Marshall, 618.17: 137.4 x 31.6	New York, 1833	Chas. H. Marshall, Jonathan Goodhue, et al, New York
Florida, White Matlack, 522.83: 123 x 30.10	Blossom, Smith & Dimon, New York, 1822	Willis Hicks, Silas Hicks, et al, New York
France, James Funck, 411.37: 116.6 x 28	C. Bergh & Co., New York, 1827	Andrew Norwood, Christian Bergh, et al, New York
Francis Depau, Henry Robinson, 595.82: 133 x 31.6	Brown & Bell, 1833	Sam'l M. Fox, Francis A. Depau, Miles R. Burke, Mortimer Livingston, et al, New York
Francois 1st., Wm. Skiddy, 496.53: 127.3 x 29.4	C. Bergh & Co., New York, 1828	Miles R. Burke, Francis Depau, Isaac Bell, New York
Garonne, Daniel L. Porter, 296.45: 95 x 26.9	Milford Ct., 1815	Wm. Whitlock, Jr., et al, New York, 1825
Garrick, Wm. Robinson, 895.56: 157.6 x 35.4 x 21	New York, 1836	Edward K. Collins, Jas. Foster, et al, New York
Great Britain, Francis French, 724.93: 138.6 x 34.2	Brown & Bell, New York, 1826	Jeremiah Thompson, New York
Hannibal, Jas. Watkinson, 440.31: 117 x 29	Fickett & Crockett, New York, 1821–2	John Flack & Jas. Watkinson, New York
Hercules, Seth G. Macy, 334.85: 103 x 27.1	John Lozier, New York, 1816	Thomas S. Byrnes, James Somes, Geo. T. Trimble, Jas. Buckley & Richard Somes, New York
Hercules, Henry Austin, 497.2: 124 x 29.10	Henry Eckford, New York, 1822	David Leavitt & Henry Eckford, New York
Hibernia, Geo. Maxwell, 551.4: 132 x 30.4	New York, 1830	Jos. Walker, Wm. Wright, & estate of Isaac Wright, dec'd., New York
Hudson, H. L. Champlin, 368.6: 106 x 28	Scott & Francis Fickett, New York, 1822	John Griswold, New York
Huntsville, Chas. Stoddard, 522.77: 130.8 x 29.8 x 14.10	S. & F. Fickett, New York, 1831	Amos Palmer, New York, Jas. Foster, Jamaica, N. Y., and Jas. Foster, Jr., New Orleans

SHIP, MEASUREMENTS AND MASTER	PLACE AND DATE OF CONSTRUCTION	OWNER
Illinois, John Bunker, 413.43: 117 x 28 x 14	New York, 1826	Silas Holmes, Robt. Waterman, Chas. H. Marshall, et al, New York
Independence, Ezra Nye, 732: 140 x 32 x 20	Stephen Smith, New York, 1834	Swallow Tail Line, New York
Isaac Hicks, Joseph Macy, 495.45: 119.6 x 30.6	Jas. Morgan & Son, New York, 1824	Samuel Hicks, et al, New York
James Cropper, Wm. Bowne, 495.43: 120 x 30.5	Sidney Wright, New York, 1821	Wm. Bowne, Francis Thompson, et al, New York (Sam'l C. Reid, master, 1822)
James Monroe, Jas. Watkinson, 424.41: 118 x 28.3	Adam Brown, New York, 1817	Black Ball Line, New York
John Jay, James Goodday, 502.85: 124.2 x 30	New York, 1827	Howland & Aspinwall, New York
Leeds, Wm. Stoddard, 408.52: 112.8 x 28.6	Scott & Francis Fickett, New York	Thaddeus Phelps, J. Grinnell, Peter Crary, Jr., et al, New York
London, Francis Allyn, 407.71: 112 x 28.7	Scott & Francis Fickett, New York, 1822	Samuel Candler, Robt. N. Waite, New York
Louisville, Peter Price, 516.60: 129.4 x 29.8 x 14.10	Scott & Francis Fickett, New York, 1831	Jas. Foster, New Orleans, Amos Palmer, Peter Price, N. Y., Jas. Foster, Jamaica, New York
Manchester, Wm. Lee, Jr., 561.36: 126.11 x 31.5	Noah Brown & C. Porter, New York, 1825	Black Ball Line, New York
Manhattan, F. W. Marshall, 390.79: 110 x 28.3	New York, 1818	Geo. T. Trimble, Thos. Byrnes, dec'd., James Loines, et al, New York
Marmion, Elnathan Hawkins, 277.73: 94.4 x 25.10	Baltimore, 1811	Jacob Le Roy, Wm. Bayard, et al, New York
Meteor, Nathan Cobb, 325.40: 106.5 x 26.1	Newbury, Mass., 1819	T. S. Byrnes, G. T. Trumble, et al, New York
Montano, Miles R. Burke, 365.74: 104.6 x 28.2	Christian, Bergh, New York, 1822	Isaac Bell & Francis Depau, New York

SHIP, MEASUREMENTS AND MASTER	PLACE AND DATE OF CONSTRUCTION	OWNER
Montreal, Christopher H. Champlin, 542.72: 132 x 30.1	C. Bergh & Co., New York, 1833	E. E. Morgan, H. L. Champlin, C. Bergh, et al, New York
Nashville, John Rathbone, 513.81: 131.8 x 29.3 x 14.7½	C. Bergh & Co., New York, 1831	John Rathbone, New York, & Thomas Banks, James Pench & John Bien, New Orleans
Natchez, Hartwell Reed, 523.72: 130.3 x 29.9 x 14.10½	Webb & Allen, New York, 1831	Thos. L. Servoss & Thos. Barron, New York, & Nath'l Dick, Wm. J. McLean, et al, New Orleans
Nestor, Daniel Sterling, 481.87: 114.9 x 30.10 x 15.5	John Lozier, New York, 1815	Levi Coit, Jos. Howland, et al, New York
New York, Geo. Maxwell, 516.30: 127 x 30	Brown & Bell, New York, 1822	Black Ball Line, New York
North America, Robt. I. Macy, 610.69: 134.5 x 31.5	Brown & Bell, New York, 1831	Black Ball Line, Wm. Wright, Isaac Wright & Benj. Marshal, New York
Ontario, James N. Brown, 527.73: 124.6 x 39.9 x 15.1½	A. & N. Brown, New York, 1812	Benj. G. Minturn & John T. Champlin
Orbit, Josiah Macey, 384.46: 108 x 28.4	Brown & Bell, New York, 1821	Sam'l Hicks, et al, New York
Oxford, John Rathbone, 752.47: 147.6 x 33.6 x 21.6	Webb & Allen, New York, 1836	Chas. H. Marshall, Jonathan Goodhue, Pelatiah Perit, et al, New York
Pacific, Solomon Maxwell, 586.86: 133.6 x 31.6	Brown & Bell, New York, 1823–4	Black Ball Line, New York
Panthea, Jonathan Eldridge, 370.4: 106 x 28.1	Sam'l Fickett & Wm. Crockett, New York, 1821	T. S. Byrnes, Jas. Buckley, New York
Paris, Henry Robinson, 338.61: 103 x 27.3	Christian Bergh, New York, 1823	Henry Robinson, Wm. Bayard, et al, New York
Pennsylvania, John P. Smith, 808.10: 148 x 34.9 x 21	Webb & Allen, New York, 1836	Moses H. Grinnell, Robert B. Minturn, et al, New York
Philadelphia, Henry L. Champlin, 542.72: 132 x 30.1	C. Bergh & Co., New York, 1832	Chas. C. Griswold, New York

SHIP, MEASUREMENTS AND MASTER	PLACE AND DATE OF CONSTRUCTION	OWNER
President, Henry L. Champlin, 468.71: 125 x 28.9	C. Bergh & Co., New York, 1831	Chas. C. Griswold, New York
Rhone, Wm. Hathaway, 471.17: 127.11 x 28.5	C. Bergh & Co., New York, 1831	Benj. Aymar, Henry Kneeland, Henry K. Bogert, et al, New York
Robt. Bowne, John Holdrege, 504.92: 123 x 30.3	Stonington, Ct., 1832	Grinnell & Minturn, et al
Robert Fulton, Hugh Graham, 340.19: 103.11 x 27.2	Boston, 1818	Abraham Bell & Abraham Thompson, New York
Roman, Jeremiah Dickenson, 492.20: 118 x 30.6	Brown & Bell, New York, 1825	Sam'l Hicks, et al, New York
Sapphire, Joseph Callender, 366: 112.6 x 26.10	E. & H. Rogers, Medford, 1825	Wm. Appleton, et al, Boston
Siddons, Edward B. Cobb, 895.56: 157.6 x 35.4 x 21.4	New York, 1837	Edward K. Collins, et al, New York
Silas Richards, Henry Holdredge, 450.13: 120 x 29	Isaac Webb & Co., New York, 1824	Thaddeus Phelps, et al, New York
Silvanus Jenkins, Josiah Macy, 547.24: 127.4 x 30.11	Jas. Morgan & Sons, New York, 1825	Samuel Hicks, Henry Hicks, John Hicks, et al, New York
Silvie de Grasse, Wm. C. Thompson, 641.23: 140.6 x 31.8	New York, 1834	Samuel M. Fox, Isaac Bell, Mortimer Livingston & Curtis Bolton, New York
South America, Chas. H. Marshall, 605.59: 133.9 x 31.8	New York, 1832	Wm. Wright, et al, New York
Splendid, John W. Sterling, 642.48: 134 x 32.8	Isaac Webb & Co., New York, 1823	Chas. Hall, New York
Stephania, Miles R. Burke, 315.18: 97 x 27.3	Noah Brown, New York, 1819	Francis Depau, et al, New York
Superior, Geo. R. Dowdall, 575.56: 126 x 32	Isaac Webb, New York, 1822	Chas. Hall, New York

SHIP, MEASUREMENTS AND MASTER	PLACE AND DATE OF CONSTRUCTION	OWNER
Topaz, 363: 110 x 27.1½	Thatcher Magoun, Medford, 1822	Wm. Appleton, et al, Boston
Toronto, Robt. Griswold, 631.42: 135.3 x 32.6	C. Bergh & Co., New York, 1835	John Griswold, New York
United States, James L. Wilson, 675.79: 130.6 x 34.2	Brown & Bell, New York, 1825	Jonathan Trimble, New York
United States, George C. DeKay, 984.74: 149.4 x 38.6	Henry Eckford, New York, 1831	Henry Eckford, New York
Utica, Frederick F. Depeyster, 525.49: 131.3 x 29.8	C. Bergh & Co., New York, 1833	James Funk, Jacob Westervelt, C. Bergh, et al
Ville De Lyon, Chas. Stoddard, 791¼	Webb & Allen, New York, 1837	Sam'l M. Fox, Mortimer Livingston, et al, New York
Virginian, Isaac Harris, 616.44: 133.7 x 32 x 16	Smith Dimon & Comstock, New York, 1832	Silas Wood, Geo. T. Trimble, Sam'l Hicks, et al, New York
Washington, Edward Rossiter, 741.60: 141.9 x 34.1	Brown & Bell, New York, 1825	Charles Hall, New York
William Byrnes, N. Cobb, 517.70: 123 x 32.8	Noah Brown, New York, 1823	Geo. Trimble, et al, New York
William Tell, Chas. Clark, 367.21: 103 x 28.6	Brown & Bell, New York, 1821	Sam'l Hicks, et al, New York
William Thompson, Wm. Thompson, 495.43: 120 x 30.5	Sidney Wright, New York, 1821	Black Ball Line, New York
York, Wm. Baker, 433.46: 118.6 x 28.8	Wm. Crockett, New York, 1824	Jos. Grinnell, Peter Crary, et al, New York

APPENDIX I (c)

NOTE: The following list includes nearly, but probably not quite all ships built in the United States from 1850 to 1859, inclusive, which are entitled to clipper classification. It also includes a considerable number which unquestionably were not of clipper model, but which were heavily sparred, and ably commanded, and by reason of excellent passages contributed somewhat to the fame of the clipper period.

Wherever obtainable the measurements have been taken from custom house records. When, owing to loss, destruction or misplacement of records, such data was not available, it has been taken from the marine columns of contemporary newspapers. It will be noted that measurements herein do not always agree with those heretofore published. It may be said, in partial explanation of this fact, that various custom house records relating to the same ship are by no means in agreement, even when due allowance has been made for the more obvious errors. The personal equation, both in surveying ships and in transcribing records, was of course always present.

Many ships had a succession of well known masters and owners. It has been the intention here to give the first master and owner, wherever such information has been obtainable.

Much data has been omitted of necessity in order to keep the present volume within a reasonable compass.

APPENDIX I

(c)

THE LATER CLIPPERS AND REPUTED CLIPPERS, 1850–1860, INCLUSIVE

SHIP, MEASUREMENTS AND MASTER	PLACE AND DATE OF CONSTRUCTION	OWNER
1850		
Alert, Francis Bursley, 764.22: 152.6 x 33.1	Metcalf & Norris, Damariscotta	Crocker & Warren, New York (Lost Formosa—1858)
Bk. *Black Squall*, John Codman, 400: 127 x 30.2½ x 12.2½	C. B. Butler, Cape Elizabeth, Me.	John Codman, New York (Bought by New York firm for San Francisco trade)
Bk. *Dragon*, Dunn, 290: 110 deck x 24	Currier & Townsend, Newburyport	Williams & Daland, Boston
Celestial, E. C. Gardner, 860.10: 158 x 34 x 19	Wm. H. Webb, New York	Bucklin & Crane, New York ("Sharpest ship built at time." Made two passages in English tea trade—Sold Spanish 1858)

SHIP, MEASUREMENTS AND MASTER	PLACE AND DATE OF CONSTRUCTION	OWNER
Eclipse, Jos. Hamilton, 1222.92: 194.10 x 36.8 x 21.6	Jabez Williams, Williamsburgh, New York	Geo. Buckley, et al, N. Y. and later Thos. Wardle & Booth & Edgar, New York (Lost Ypala, Oct. 11, 1853)
Game Cock, Lewis G. Hollis, 1392: 1119 N. 190.6 x 39.10 x 22	Samuel Hall, East Boston	Daniel C. Bacon, Robt. L. Taylor, et al, New York (Condemned—Good Hope, 1880)
Bk. *Geo. E. Webster*, Jesse G. Cotting, 354.24: 121.6 x 27 x 11.10	Hayden & Cudworth, Medford, Mass.	Reuben S. Wade, Samuel G. Reed, et al, Boston
Grey Feather, Daniel McLaughlin, 586.82: 138.4 x 30.5 x 19	C. S. Husten, Eastport, Me.	L. H. Sampson & Co., New York (Sold Bremen, 1862)
John Bertram, Frederick Lendholm, 1080: 180 x 37 x 20—778 N.	Elwell & Jackson, East Boston	Glidden & Williams, Boston & Flint, Peabody & Co., San Francisco. (Sold 1855 to Wm. F. Schmidt, of Hamburg.) Abandoned at sea Mar. 17, 1883.
Bk. *Kremlin*, Bearse and later Wm. I. Rogers, 504: 127 x 27.5 x 19.6	Paul Curtis, Medford	J. S. Emery & Co., Boston Was at Boston, May, 1868
Mandarin, Thomas C. Stoddard, 776: 151.6 x 33.6 x 19.3	Smith & Dimon, New York	Goodhue & Co., New York (Lost on uncharted reef in China Sea, Aug. 9, 1864)
Bk. *Paladin*, Murphy, 460: 126 x 28.6 x 14.6	J. Gardner, Baltimore, Md.	Sold Buenos Ayres
Nicholas I, Thomas Leach, 596: 133 x 31.6 x 17.6	Smith & Dimon, New York	Richard M. Weston, Robt. C. Goodhue, et al, New York
Bk. *Race Horse*, David S. Babcock, 530: 125 x 30 x 16	Samuel Hall, East Boston	I. Goddard & Co., Boston
Roman, Wm. E. Putnam, 774.56: 152-$\frac{7}{10}$ x 33-$\frac{3}{10}$ x 16.6½	Geo. Raynes, Portsmouth, N. H.	Joseph D. Taylor, David W. C. Olyphant & Robt. M. Olyphant, New York
Bk. *Rosario*, Caleb Sprague, 498.73: 130.1 x 29 x 15.6	Capt. J. M. Hood, Somerset, Mass.	Amos & Mulford Howes, New York

SHIP, MEASUREMENTS AND MASTER	PLACE AND DATE OF CONSTRUCTION	OWNER
Seaman, Jas. Myrick, 546: 136 x 23.10 x 15	R. & E. Bell, Baltimore	Thos. Handy, New York (Burned at sea Feb. 6, 1855, Capt. Daniels)
Sea Nymph, Phillip M. Hale, 526.25: 131 deck x 29.4$\frac{1}{2}$	Adams Gray, Baltimore	(Condemned Hong Kong, December, 1860)
Sea Serpent, Wm. Howland, 1402.21 (975 new) 196$\frac{9}{10}$ x 39$\frac{2}{10}$ (actual depth 20.8)	Geo. Raynes, Portsmouth, N. H.	Grinnell, Minturn & Co., New York
Stag Hound, Josiah Richardson, 1534.10: 215 x 39.8 x 21 Length also given 209	D. McKay, East Boston	Geo. B. Upton & Sampson & Tappan, Boston (Burned off Pernambuco, Oct. 12, 1861)
Surprise, Philip Dumaresq, 1261.62:183.3 x 38.8 x 22	Samuel Hall, East Boston	A. A. Low & Bro. New York (Lost on Plymouth Rocks, Japan Feb. 4th, 1876)
White Squall, Benoni Lockwood, 1119: 190 x 35 x 21	Jacob Bell, New York	Wm. Platt & Son, Phila. (Sold at Montevideo in distress Sept. 1856, French ship *Splendide*. Reported beached in sinking condition, 1877)
Witchcraft, Wm. C. Rogers, 1310.18: 187 x 39 x 22	Paul Curtis, Chelsea	Wm. D. Pickman, Richard S. Rogers, Salem. (Bought by T. Magoun & Sons, Boston, about Mar. 1–10, 1854) Lost near Hatteras Apr. 8, 1861
Universe, Thomas J. Bird, 1297: 186 x 38.7 x 28.6	Smith & Dimon, New York	Williams & Guion's Liverpool Line. (Early clipper packet)

1851

Antelope, Tully Crosby, 507.42: 132 x 29 x 19	J. O. Curtis, Medford	Wm. Lincoln & Co., Boston Frederick H. Whitmore. N. Y. (in 1855)
Aramingo, Capt. John Sylvester, 760: 152.6 x 34.6 x 22.6	Aaron Westervelt, New York	Chamberlain & Phelps, New York (Was German ship Matador, 1875)
Challenge, Robert H. Waterman, 2006.51: 230.6 x 43.2 x 26	Wm. H. Webb, New York	N. L. & G. G. Griswold (Sold 1861 to Thos. Hunt & Co. *Golden City*. Lost off French coast, 1876)

SHIP, MEASUREMENTS AND MASTER	PLACE AND DATE OF CONSTRUCTION	OWNER
Comet, E. C. Gardner, 1836: 228 x 40.4 x 22	Wm. H. Webb, New York	Bucklin & Crane, New York (Burned 1865—80 passengers and crew lost—18 saved.)
Coringa, Symmes Potter, 777: 153 x 35 x 22	Jotham Stetson, Medford	N. B. Goddard & Co., Boston (Was in Boston 1874— rated A 1½)
Courser, A. L. Richardson, 1024: 176 x 35 x 24	Paul Curtis, Medford	Richardson & Co., Boston (Lost Pratas Shoal April 4, 1858, Capt. Cole and crew saved)
Eagle, J. S. Farran, 1296: 192 x 38.10 x 22	Perine, P. & Stack, Williamsburgh, N. Y.	Harbeck & Co., New York (Sold India, 1862)
Eliza F. Mason, 582: 127 x 30 x 15	Baltimore	(Sold, Chili, 1863)
Eliza Mallory, J. E. Williams, 649.12: 130 x 33.6	Chas. Mallory, Mystic	E. D. Hurlburt & Co., New York Lost on coast of Florida
Empire, E. A. Thorndike, 1272: 189 x 38	Thomaston, Me.	Foster & Nickerson, New York
Eureka, Auchincloss, 1041: 171 x 36.5 x 21.6	Jacob A. Westervelt, New York	Chambers & Heiser, New York (Bought by N. L. & G. G. 1859, Sold Br. 1863, Condemned Calcutta, 1866)
Bk. *Falcon*, John A. Phipps, 509.45: 137.7 x 28.4	Newburyport	John E. Lodge, Boston
Flying Cloud, Josiah P. Cressy, 1782.48: 229 x 40.8 x 21.6 1139 British: 219 x 40 x 21	D. McKay, East Boston	Grinnell, Minturn & Co., New York (Sold Br. 1862—lost 1874)
Flying Fish, Edward Nickels, 1505: 207 x 39.6 x 22	D. McKay, East Boston	Sampson & Tappan, Boston (Wrecked River Min, Nov. 23, 1858—condemned and sold.)
Gazelle, Robert Henderson, Jr., 1244: 182 x 38 x 21	Wm. H. Webb, New York	Taylor & Merrill, New York (Dismasted and condemned 1854, Later, 1861, British ship)
Golden Gate, Truman, 1340.8: 193.6 x 38.8 x 21.6	J. A. Westervelt, New York	Chambers & Heiser, New York (Burned Pernambuco, May 26, 1856)

SHIP, MEASUREMENTS AND MASTER	PLACE AND DATE OF CONSTRUCTION	OWNER
Governor Morton, John A. Burgess, 1429.86: 196.6 x 39.8 x 26	Jas. M. Hood, Somerset, Mass.	Handy & Everett, New York (Burned, 1877 S. W. Pass. below New Orleans)
Harriet Hoxie, P. E. Rowland, 678	Irons & Grinnell, Mystic, Ct.	Post, Smith & Co., Mystic (Sold Antwerp, 1859)
Hoogly, John Chadwick, 1304.4: 190 x 38.4 x 25	Samuel Hall, East Boston	D. C. Bacon & Sons, Boston (Lost in river below Shanghae August 20, 1852)
Hornet, Lawrence, 1426.62: 203 x 38.10 x 21.10	Westervelt & Mackay, New York	Chamberlain & Phelps, New York (Burned at sea 1866)
Hurricane, Samuel Very, Jr., 1608: 215 x 40 x 22	Isaac C. Smith, Hoboken	C. W. & A. Thomas, New York
Ino, R. E. Little, 895: 160.6 x 34.11 x 17.5 673 N.	Perine, Patterson & Stack, New York	Siffkin & Ironsides, New York 1859—Goddard & Thompson, Boston. (Resold by U. S. Government, 1867, to Samuel G. Reed, Boston and named *Shooting Star*)
Invincible, H. W. Johnson, 1769: 238 x 42.10 x 25.6	Wm. H. Webb, New York	Jas. W. Phillips, New York 1860—Spofford & Tileston, New York (Burned at New York, 1867)
John Stuart, Watson Ferris, 1653.83: 228 o.a. 206 x 41.8 x 28.2	Perine, Patterson & Stack, New York	B. A. Mumford, Jas. Smith et al, New York (Sold British, 1863)
John Wade, Geo. H. Willis, 639: 145 x 32 x 16.6	Hayden & Cudworth, Medford	Reed, Wade & Co., Boston (Sold 1854 to J. J. Dixwell, Boston, for "Augustine Heard Line," to China) Lost Gulf of Siam, Mar. 28, 1859
Kate Hayes, Miner S. York, 700: 149.1 x 33 x 22	Trescott, Maine	Stephen W. Dana, et al, Boston
Mercury, Richard D. Conn, 1350.83: 193.6 x 38.10 x 22.2	Westervelt & Mackay, New York	Boyd & Hincken's Line of Havre packets. New York

SHIP, MEASUREMENTS AND MASTER	PLACE AND DATE OF CONSTRUCTION	OWNER
Bk. *Mermaid*, George J. O. Smith, 533.22: 138.6 x 28.11 x 15	Samuel Hall, Boston	Edward R. Hall, Edward Gassell and John J. May, et al, Boston
Monsoon, L. Winsor 773: 158 x 32.7 x 21	Trufant & Drummond, Bath, Maine	Geo. Hussey, N. Bedford
N. B. Palmer, Chas. P. Low, 1399.52: 1124 N. 202.6 x 38.6 x 21.11	Westervelt & Mackay, New York	A. A. Low & Bros., New York (Abandoned at sea 1892)
Nightingale, John H. Fiske, 1066: 722 N. 185 x 36 x 20	Samuel Hanscom, Jr., Portsmouth, N. H.	Sampson & Tappan, Boston (Abandoned at sea 1893)
Northern Light, Freeman Hatch, 1021: 171.4 x 36 x 21.9	E. & H. O. Briggs, South Boston	James Huckins, Boston (In collision and abandoned at sea, January 2, 1861)
Racer, Henry W. Steele, 1669: 207 x 42.8 x 28	Currier & Townsend, Newburyport	Red Cross Line, E. E. Morgan, D. Ogden et al, (Lost coast of Ireland, May 6, 1856)
Raven, Wm. W. Henry, 712: 158 x 32.8 x 17	James M. Hood, Somerset, Mass.	Crocker & Warren, New York (Condemned at Rio Janeiro 1863 sold and repaired as Bk. *Bessie* Listed Spanish 1875)
R. B. Forbes, Justus Doane, 757: 156 x 32 x 19.6	Samuel Hall, East Boston	J. S. Coolidge & Co., Boston (Sold 1861 Hong Kong)
Rip Van Winkle, Capt. Baker, 1094.83: 175.5 x 36.10 x 21	Jas. M. Hood, Somerset, Mass.	Eagle & Hazard, New York
Roebuck, Walden, 815: 170 x 33 x 815	Bourne & Kingsbury, Kennebunk, Me.	Thaddeus Nichols & Thos. Curtis, Boston (Lost off Cohasset Jan. 28, 1859)
Seaman's Bride, Joseph Myrick, 668: 152 x 31 x 19	R. & E. Bell, Baltimore (carried three moon sails)	Thos. J. Handy, New York (Sold Hamburg, 1855— *Carl Staegoman*)
Shooting Star, Judah P. Baker, 903: 164 x 35 x 18.6	Jas. O. Curtis, Medford (designed by Capt. John Wade)	Reed, Wade & Co. (Sold Siam, 1856—wrecked Formosa 1867)

SHIP, MEASUREMENTS AND MASTER	PLACE AND DATE OF CONSTRUCTION	OWNER
Snow Squall, Isaac Bursley, 742.63: 157 x 32 x 16.6	Alfred Butler, Cape Elizabeth, Me.	Chas. R. Green, New York (Condemned Port Stanley, 1864)
Southern Cross, Levi Stevens, 938.48: 168.6 x 34.9 x 21	E. & H. O. Briggs, East Boston	Baker & Morrill, Boston (Burned by the *Florida*, June 6, 1863)
Bk. *Springbok*, S. L. Hurd, 370: 120 deck x 27 x 13.3	Geo. Thomas, Rockland, Me.	Seccomb & Taylor, Boston
Staffordshire, Josiah Richardson, 1817: 230 (243 o.a.) x 41 x 29	D. McKay, East Boston	Enoch Train & Co., Boston (Lost Dec. 25, 1853, near Cape Sable)
Stilwell S. Bishop, Wm. E. Derrickson 595: 156 deck— 140.1 x 31.4 x 15	Wm. Cramp, Kensington, Pa.	Henry Simons, Jr., Philadelphia (Sold 1856 to Rutter, Newell & Co., Baltimore—renamed *Grey Eagle*)
Sword Fish, David S. Babcock, 1036: 169.6 x 36.6 x 20	Wm. H. Webb, New York	Barclay & Livingston, New York (Sold 1854 to Crocker & Warren. Lost in Yang-Tsze, July, 1862)
Syren, Geo. Z. Silsbee, 1064.37: 179 x 35.10 x 22	John Taylor, Medford	Silsbee, Wm. D. Pickman et al, Salem. (Condemned at Rio Janeiro, 1888. Sold, repaired. Listed 1920 as Bk. *Margarida* of Buenos Ayres)
Telegraph, Kimball Harlow, 1068.60: 178.2 x 36 x 21.6	J. O. Curtis, Medford	P. & S. Sprague & Co., Boston (Burned, repaired, 1857— renamed *Henry Brigham*— Sold Peru, 1865—burned at sea 1868)
Trade Wind, W. H. Osgood, 2045: 29 245.6 x 42 x 30.2	Jacob Bell, New York	Booth & Edgar, New York & Wm. Platt & Co., Philadelphia. (Lost in collision June 26, 1854)
Typhoon, Chas. H. Salter, 1611: 207 x 41 x 23	Fernald & Pettigrew, Portsmouth	D. & A. Kingsland, New York (Sold Singapore, 1863—Listed 1869, British Ship *Indomitable*)
Union, B. Buxton, 1012: 184 x 35.7 x 21.8	Baltimore	S. Lurman & Co., Baltimore (Sold French 1863—condemned 1872)
Victory, Oliver G. Lane, 669.66: 151 x 31	Benjamin Dutton, Newburyport, Mass.	Benj. A. Gould et al, Boston (Lost near Cape Henry Feb. 9, 1861)

SHIP, MEASUREMENTS AND MASTER	PLACE AND DATE OF CONSTRUCTION	OWNER
Warner, Luther Ripley, Jr., 500.10: 138 x 28	Cape Elizabeth, Me.	Wm. H. Merritt, New York
Wild Pigeon, Geo. W. Putnam, 996: 178 (189 o.a.) x 35 x 20	Geo. Raynes, Portsmouth	Olyphant & Co., New York (Put under British flag 1863. Abandoned 1892 in N. Atlantic)
Witch of the Wave, J. Hardy Millet, 1498: 220 x 40 x 21 997 N.	Geo. Raynes, Portsmouth	Glidden & Williams & Hunt & Peabody, Boston (Sold about 1857, Amsterdam, *Electra*, listed 1871)

1852

Alboni, N. R. Littlefield, 917: 156 x 37.6 x 21	Mason C. Hill, Mystic, Ct.	Charles Mallory, and later Jas. Bishop & Co., New York (Sold Germany 1863— Disappears 1874)
Alexander, J. A. Baxter, 596: 143 x 29 x 20	Hayden & Cudworth, Medford	J. A. Baxter & Co., Boston
Antelope, Robert Shinn, 1186: 188 x 39 x 21.4	Perine, Patterson & Stack, New York	Henry Harbeck & Co., New York (British ship in 1870)
Archer, Francis A. Bursley, 1095.87: 182 x 36 x 21.6	James M. Hood, Somerset, Mass.	Crocker & Warren, New York (Foundered Feb. 12, 1880, from New York to Havre.)
Atalanta, William Williams, 1288.79: 193.9 x 37.10 x 21.6	Gardner & Palmer, Baltimore	Montell & Co., Baltimore (Sold Spain, 1856— *Marguerita*)
Australia, Clough 1447: 192 x 40 x 27	Wm. H. Webb, New York	Williams & Guion, New York (Wrecked Ayab, May, 1864)
Bald Eagle, Philip Dumaresq, 1703.62 215.8 x 41.2 x 23.6	D. McKay, East Boston	Geo. B. Upton, Boston (Missing 1861 on voyage from Hong Kong to San Francisco)
Beverly, Perry Jenkins, 676: 151.6 x 31.1 x 21.9	Paul Curtis, Medford	Israel Whitney & Wm. Perkins, Boston (Disappears 1874)
Carrier Pigeon, Azariah Doane, 844: 175 x 34 x 21	Hall, Snow & Co. Bath	Reed, Wade & Co., Boston (Lost first voyage, 50 miles South of San Francisco)
Celestial Empire, Sumner Pierce, 1395.20: 193 x 39.7 x 29	Jotham Stetson, South Boston	C. H. Parsons & Co., New York (Abandoned Feb. 20, 1878, North Atlantic)

SHIP, MEASUREMENTS AND MASTER	PLACE AND DATE OF CONSTRUCTION	OWNER
Charles Mallory, Chas. Hull, 698: 155 x 33 x 18	Chas. Mallory, Mystic	Charles Mallory, Mystic (Lost 1853, Brazil)
Bk. *Comet*, 536.11: 144 x 29 x 13.6	Pembroke, Me.	Edward C. Bates, et al, Boston
Contest, William Brewster, 1098.92: 181.4 x 36 x 21	Jacob A. Westervelt	A. A. Low & Bro., New York (Burned by Alabama, 1863)
Dauntless, James Miller, 791: 175 x 33 x 21½	Benj. F. Delano, Medford	W. N. Goddard, Boston (Lost 1853 with all hands)
Defiance, Robert McCerren 1690.87: 204 x 42.5 x 29	Geo. Thomas, Rockland	Mr. Wm. T. Dugan, New York, to 1854. Bought by McCreedy Mott & Co., 1854 (Condemned Canary Isles, 1856, *Teide*)
Ellen Foster, Capt. Scudder, 996: 180 x 37 x 24	Joshua T. Foster Medford	J. & A. Tirrell, Boston (Lost Neah Bay, Wash., December, 1867)
Fleetwood, Frank Dale, 663.47: $146\frac{7}{10}$ x $31\frac{4}{10}$	Geo. Raynes, Portsmouth	Sewall, Johnson & Co., Boston & Capt. Frank Dale (Lost in ice off Horn, May 3, 1859—5 saved.)
Flying Arrow, Charles T. Treadwell, 1092: 170.8 x 37.10 x 23.4	Isaac Dunham, Frankfort, Me.	Manning Stanwood & Co., Boston (Condemned and sold Melbourne 1856)
Flying Childers, Jeremiah D. D. White, 1125: 183.9 x 36.4 x 22.6	Samuel Hall, East Boston	J. M. Forbes & Cunningham Bros., Boston—Later James Baines & Co. (Coal Hulk at Port Jackson many years)
Flying Dutchman, Ashbel Hubbard, 1257.46: 191 x 37.8 x 21.6	Wm. H. Webb, New York	George Daniels, et al, New York (Lost Brigantine Shoals, February, 1858)
Flying Eagle, W. Parker, $1004\frac{25}{100}$: $184\frac{9}{10}$ x $34\frac{6}{10}$ x $22\frac{8}{10}$	Wm. Hitchcock, Newcastle, Me.	Frederick Nickerson & Co., Boston (Condemned Mauritius 1879)
Bk. *Francis Palmer*, 302: 125 x 25 x 11.9	J. M. Balkesn, Robbinstown, Me.	Kesing & Brown, San Francisco (1869)
Bk. *Gazelle*, Geo. Ward, 253: 108 x 25.4 x 10.3	Lane & Jacobs, New Haven, Ct.	H. Trowbridge & Sons, St. Croix

SHIP, MEASUREMENTS AND MASTER	PLACE AND DATE OF CONSTRUCTION	OWNER
Gem of the Ocean, Freeman Crosby, 702: 152 x 31.8 x 20.6	Hayden & Cudworth, Medford	Wm. Lincoln, Boston (Sold 1867 to McPherson & Witherbee, San Francisco) (Wrecked on Vancouver, 1879)
Golden City, Samuel F. Dewing, 810.49: 154.10 x 33.10 x 20.10	J. A. Westervelt, New York	Chambers & Heiser, New York (Sold British 1863—Lost South Pacific, December 1, 1879)
Golden Eagle, Samuel A. Fabens, 1120.82: 194.4 x 35.6 x 21.6	Hayden & Cudworth, Medford	Wm. Lincoln & Co., Boston. Later E. M. Robinson, New Bedford & John A. McGaw, N. Y. (Burned by Alabama, Feb. 21, 1863)
Golden Fleece, Freeman, 968: 173 x 35 x 21	Paul Curtis, Boston	Weld & Baker, Boston (Wrecked San Francisco April 22, 1854)
Golden Racer, Benj. M. Melcher, 837: 196 x 34 x 19	J. C. C. Morton, Thomaston, Me.	Owned in Boston—Sold to Roberts & Williams, N. Y. 1855 (Lost in River Min, 1856)
Golden West, Samuel R. Curwen, 1441: 196 x 39 x 23.4	Paul Curtis, East Boston	Glidden & Williams, Boston Later J. A. & T. A. Patterson (Sold Br. 1863—Listed 1866)
Hippogriffe, Anthony Howes, 671.36: 155.6 x 30.6	Shiverick Bros., East Dennis, Mass.	Capt. Christopher Hall, Prince S. Crowell, et al, Dennis (Sold British, 1863)
Hussar, Isaac S. Lucas, 721: 151 x 32 x 23	G. W. Jackman, Newburyport	Bush & Wildes, Boston (Sold 1854 to G. Hussey, New Bedford—Sold Singapore, 1864)
Island City, P. Saunders, 700 (about)	Silas Greenman & Son, Westerly	Stanton & Thompson, New York
Jacob Bell, Kilhaur, 1381: 200.11 x 38.5 x 22	A. C. Bell, New York	Bought by A. A. Low & Bro., New York, 1856 (Burned by the *Florida*, February 13, 1863)
John Gilpin, Justus Doane, 1089: 195 x 37 x 22	Samuel Hall, East Boston	Pierce & Hunnewell, Boston (Abandoned off Horn, January 30, 1858)
Josephine, Wm. Jameson, 947	Samuel Hanscom, Jr., Eliot, Me.	Gen. Jos. Andrews, Salem (Burned in St. Louis Harbor, Mauritius, June, 1859)
Kate Napier, Capt. Morton, 700 (about)	Baltimore, Md.	Reported "new clipper" but possibly an old ship

SHIP, MEASUREMENTS AND MASTER	PLACE AND DATE OF CONSTRUCTION	OWNER
Lady Franklin, Nagle, 463.62: 133 x 27.6 x 18	Jarvis (or Jairns) Pratt, East Boston	Wm. Ropes, Boston (Abandoned October 1856)
Lady Suffolk, Adams Gray, 529.80: 130 x 28.8 x 15.7	Baltimore, Md.	Adam Gray, Baltimore
Levanter, Wm. A. Follansbee, 868: 182 x 33 x 22 also 849.76: 161.6 x 33.10	Metcalf & Norris, Damariscotta, Me.	B. F. Metcalf and R. W. Trundy, and later Smith & Boynton & Naylor & Co., New York—Sold 1863 E. Wheelwright, Boston
Line Gale, 536	Willets & Bishop, Sag Harbor	(Name possibly changed when sold)
Lotus, John Leckie, 660.14: 154.6 x 30.4 x 19.6	J. Taylor, Chelsea	Dabney & Cunningham, Boston (Sold French 1863—Listed 1871)
Malay, Nat Brown, Jr., 868: 178 o.a. 167 x 33.2 x 19.1	John Taylor, Chelsea	Silsbee, Stone & Pickman, Salem (Condemned Tahiti, Oct., 1891)
Messenger, Frank Smith, 1350.49: 200.6 x 38 x 21.8	Jacob Bell, New York	Slate & Co., New York—Sold to Wm. Platt & Co., Phila. 1853 (Condemned and sold Mauritius, 1879)
Bk. *Messenger Bird*, Doane, 418.54: 120.6 x 27.8 x 13.2	Kingston, N. Y.	Francis Danielson, Boston
Meteor, Samuel W. Pike, 1068: 195 x 36 x 24	E. & H. O. Briggs, South Boston	Curtis & Peabody, Boston (Sold British, 1862)
Mountain Wave, John Paine, 633.5: 144 x 31 x 21	Joshua Magoun, Charlestown	Alpheus Hardy & Co., Boston (Sold Fayal 1865)
National Eagle, Knott Pedrick, 1095: 179 x 36 x 24	Joshua T. Foster, Medford	Fisher & Co., Boston (Lost in the Adriatic 1884)
Ocean Spray, Chas. A. McLellan, Warren, Me., 1089: 174 x 37 x 23	Geo. Dunham, et al, Frankfort, Me.	Veasie & Co., Bangor, Me. & Ralph C. Johnson (Abandoned at sea, 1857)
Onward, Jesse C. Cotting, 874: 167 x 34.6 x 20.6	J. O. Curtis, Medford	Reed, Wade & Co., Boston, 1857—John Ogden, New York (Sold Callao, Nov., 1884)
Bk. *Pathfinder*, J. Madison Hill, 373: 15 draft	Jas. M. Hood, Somerset, Mass.	Sold 1852 to Ogden & Haynes, San Francisco & Capt. J. N. Reed

SHIP, MEASUREMENTS AND MASTER	PLACE AND DATE OF CONSTRUCTION	OWNER
Peerless, Caleb G. Babson, 632.91: 145 x 30.10	Patten & Sturdevant, Richmond, Me.	E. E. Davidson, Boston and Edward Babson, Gloucester, Mass.
Phantom, Harry Devens, 1174: 195 x 37.11 x 21.6	Samuel Lapham, Medford	Crocker & Warren, New York & Crocker & Sturgis, Boston Later D. C. & W. B. Bacon, Boston (Lost near Pratas Shoals, July 13, 1862)
Polynesia, Jacob G. Homer, 1084: 177 x 36 x 22	Samuel Hall, East Boston	Pierce & Hunnewell, Boston (Burned San Francisco, March 1, 1862)
Queen of the East, Freeman Bartlett, 1275: 184 x 38 x 28 Also 1237.75: 187 x 37.10	Metcalf & Norris, Damariscotta, Me.	Crocker & Warren, New York (Lost So. Pacific, April 1872)
Queen of the Pacific, Wm. Reed, 1356.61: 197 x 39.6 x 26.8	Isaac Ewell, Pembroke, Me.	John M. Mayo, Boston and later Reed, Wade & Co., Boston (Condemned 1857—repaired—Lost 180 miles north Pernambuco September 19, 1859)
Queen of the Seas, Elias D. Knight, 1356: 195.6 x 38.8 x 22	Paul Curtis, Medford	Glidden & Williams, Boston (Supposed foundered in Formosa Channel about Sept. 21, 1860—all hands)
Rattler, Stump, 538.9: 137 x 29.3	Baltimore	Reported lost near Norfolk in 1853, but listed in 1869 as owned in Palmero
Rattler, Richard Brown, 1120.77: 192 x 35.1 x 21	Geo. Thomas, Rockland, Me.	Wm. Whitlock, Jr., New York (Broken up 1890)
Red Rover, Wm. O. Putnam, 1021: 172 x $35\frac{9}{10}$ x 23	Fernald & Pettigrew, Portsmouth	R. L. Taylor, et al, New York Sold early 1861 to Jas. Baines & Co. (Wrecked Moreton Island near Brisbane, May 31, 1872)
Sea Lark, Chas. L. Willcomb, 973.52: 172 x 35 x 17.6	Trescott, Me.	Sam'l G. Reed, Boston & E. Mott Robinson, New Bedford
Simoon, Martin Smith, 1436: 205.7 x 38.8 x 22.6	Jabez Williams, Williamsburg, N. Y.	Benj. A. Mumford & Co., New York—(Sold Lamport & Holt, October, 1863—Listed 1912)
Sirocco, J. L. Sanford 1130.51: 175.3 x 37.6 x 22.6	Wm. & Geo. Gardner, Baltimore	Damon & Hancock, Philadelphia (Sold British about 1860) Lost at sea 1873

SHIP, MEASUREMENTS AND MASTER	PLACE AND DATE OF CONSTRUCTION	OWNER
Sovereign of the Seas, Lauchlan McKay, 2420.83: 258.2 x 44.7 x 23.6	D. McKay, East Boston	Bought soon after launching by Andrew F. Meinke of Funch & Meinke, New York—Sold 1854 to J. C. Godeffroy & Son, Hamburg (Lost Sts. of Malacca, 1859)
Star of the Union, George H. Willis, 1057: 200 x 35 x 21.6	J. O. Curtis, Medford	Reed, Wade & Co., Boston—Sold to I. H. Bartlett & Son, New Bedford, 1854 (Reported condemned and sold 1866)
Bk. *Storm,* John Roberts, 545.15: 131 x 30.3	Sag Harbor, New York	Slate Gardner & Howell, New York. Also Tucker, Cooper & Co.
Tinqua, Jacob D. Whitmore, 668: 145 x 31.9 x 19 Also 142 x 31.7	Geo. Raynes, Portsmouth	Olyphant & Co., New York (Lost on Hatteras, Jan. 12, 1855)
Tornado, Oliver R. Mumford, 1801.56: 222.2 x 41.8 x 28	Jabez Williams, Williamsburg, N. Y.	W. T. Frost & Co., & Benj. A. Mumford, New York—Sold British 1863 (Burned, 1875)
Western Empire, Chas. F. Winsor, 1397.76: 191.11 x 39.9	Abner Stetson, Newcastle, Me.	Wm. Sprague, et al, Boston
Westward Ho, Johnson, 1650: 210 x 40.6 x 23.6	D. McKay, East Boston	Sampson & Tappan, Boston (Sold Peru, 1857—Burned Callao, 1864)
Whirlwind, Wm. H. Burgess, 960.62: 170 x 35 x 21.6	Jas. O. Curtis, Medford	W. & F. H. Whittemore, Boston
Bk. *White Wing,* Sherman, 293.15: 108.8 x 25.9 x 11.7	Kingston, Mass.	Thos. & John Dallet, et al, Philadelphia
Winged Arrow, Frank Bearse 1052: 176.6 x 36 x 22.	E. & H. O. Briggs, South Boston	Baker & Morrill, Boston (Sold to Russo-American Fur Co. 1868).
Winged Racer, Wm. Homan 1767: 210 x 42.6 x 23	Robt. E. Jackson, East Boston	Seccomb & Taylor, Boston. Shortly sold Sampson & Tappan, Boston, 1857. Sold to W. L. Taylor. (Burned Nov. 7, 1863 by Alabama).
Wings of the Morning, H. A. Lovell, 915.64: 166.10 x 34.6	Edwin Achorn, Waldoboro, Me.	Talbot & Olyphant, New York. (Sold French 1856—Listed 1868).

SHIP, MEASUREMENTS AND MASTER	PLACE AND DATE OF CONSTRUCTION	OWNER
Young Australia, 766: 172.6 x 36 x 20	Fernald & Pettigrew, Portsmouth, N. H.	Sold British

1853

Amphitrite, Oliver Eldridge, 1687: 206 x 39 x 24—also Boston Register: 221 x 40.4 x 26.3	Samuel Hall, East Boston	(Sold to Richard Green, London, September, 1853.)
Anglo Saxon, John Leeds, 868.71: 160 x 34.5	F. W. Rhodes, Rockland, Maine	Henry A. Kelley, Robt. B. Coleman, et al, New York, and later E. M. Robertson, New York
Aurora, Nathaniel Brown, Jr., 1396: 202.4 x 38.6 x 24	John Taylor, Chelsea	Stone, Pickman, Silsbee & Allen, Salem. (Sold British, 1863.)
Belle of the West, Wm. F. Howes, 936.24: 167 x 34.11 x 17.5½	Shiverick Bros. East Dennis, Mass.	Capt. Christopher Hall, Glidden & Williams, Boston. (Sold India 1864. Foundered 1868)
Black Hawk, 1579.16: 213 x 39.10 x 26.10	Hall & Teague, Fairfield, Ct. Black Rock, Ct.	Owned by builders. (Foundered 1854).
Black Warrior, Murphy, 1828: 234 x 42 x 23.8	Austin & Co. Damariscotta, Me.	Wm. Wilson & Son, Baltimore. (Sold 1862, Jas. Baines & Co. *City of Melbourne*.)
Bonita, Chas. F. Winsor, 1127: 182 x 36 x 22.6	E. & H. O. Briggs, South Boston	Capt. James Huckins, Boston. (Condemned Algoa Bay, 1857)
Boston Light, Callaghan, 1154: 189.5 x 36.4 x 22.6	E. & H. O. Briggs, South Boston	Jas. Huckins & Sons, Boston. Later Henry Hastings, Boston (Sold India, January, 1863.)
Challenger, T. Hill, 1334:206 x 38.4 x 23	Robt. E. Jackson, East Boston	W. & F. H. Whittemore, Boston. Later Samuel G. Reed & Co., (Sold Peru, 1863. Abandoned 1875.)
Chariot of Fame, Allen H. Knowles, 2050: 220 x 43 x 27.6	D. McKay, East Boston	Enoch Train & Co., Boston. Sold 1868 to Wilson & Chambers, Liverpool. (Disappears 1874).
Cleopatra, Samuel V. Shreve, 1562: 220 o. a. 206.6 x 41.6 x 23.3	Paul Curtis, East Boston	Benj. Bangs, Boston. (Lost Sept. 26. Struck wreck & foundered Sept. 23–25, 1855).
Climax, Wm. F. Howes, 1051: 180 x 36 x 22.9	Hayden & Cudworth, Medford	Howes & Crowell, Boston. (Sunk at Callao April, 1855 & sold).

SHIP, MEASUREMENTS AND MASTER	PLACE AND DATE OF CONSTRUCTION	OWNER
Competitor, Moses Howe, Jr., 871, 175 o. a., 169 x 33.5 x 20.2	J. O. Curtis, Medford	W. F. Weld & Co., Boston. (Sold abroad 1863. Was owned Finland 1901 *Edward*).
Cyclone, Nathaniel Ingersoll, Jr., 1109: 173.3 x 35.7 x 22.6	E. & H. O. Briggs, South Boston	Curtis & Peabody, Boston (Sold British 1863 *Avon* Disappears 1874).
Dashing Wave, John B. Fiske, 1180: 181.8 x 39.6 x 21.3	Fernald & Pettigrew, Portsmouth, N. H.	Samuel Tilton & Co., Boston. (Was a barge in fishery business. Hull in first class condition 1920. Lost same year.)
David Brown, Geo. S. Brewster, 1715.47: 218.6 x 41 x 22.9	Roosevelt & Joyce, New York	A. A. Low & Bro., New York. (Abandoned at sea 1861 in No. Atlantic.)
David Crockett, Capt. Spencer, 1679: 215.10 x 40.6 x 27	Greenman & Co., Mystic, Ct.	Handy & Everett, New York. Later by Lawrence Giles & Co. (Converted into a barge 1890 by Peter Wright & Son, Phila.)
Director, 850	Hayden & Cudworth, Medford	Crowell, Brooks & Co., Boston (Possibly renamed *Fleetwing*, see 1854)
Don Quixote, Wm. Nott, 1429: 207 x 38.5 x 23.9	Samuel Lapham, Medford	John Ellerton Lodge, Boston
Dreadnought, Samuel Samuels, 1413.72: 200 x 39 x 26.6	Currier & Townsend, Newburyport	David Ogden, et al, New York, Red Cross Line. (Lost off Cape Horn, July 4, 1869).
Eagle Wing, Eben H. Linnell, 1174: 198 x 39 x 23	James O. Curtis Medford	Chase & Tappan, Boston. (Lost 1865, all hands, from Boston to Bombay.)
Edith Rose, Crowell, 510: 129 x 28 x 18	Hayden & Cudworth, Medford	Yates & Porterfield, New York
Edwin Forrest, Braddock W. Crocker, 1141: 186.6 x 36.4 x 23	Daniel D. Kelly, East Boston	Crosby, Crocker & Co., New York. (Missing 1859–60).
Flectric, Gurdon Gates, 1273.81: 185.1 x 38.8 x 21.6	Irons & Grinnell, Mystic	G. Adams, New York. (Sold Germany 1860. Abandoned, 1872).
Elizabeth Kimball, Freeman, 998.	Edward Dutton, Marblehead	Edward Kimball, Marblehead. (Beached on Easter Island, 1873.)
Emerald Isle, Henry E. Scott, 1736.10: 215 x 41.8 x 28	Trufant & Drummond, Bath	W. & J. T. Tapscott, Line of Liverpool & New York packets

SHIP, MEASUREMENTS AND MASTER	PLACE AND DATE OF CONSTRUCTION	OWNER
Empress of the Seas, W. E. Putnam, 2197: 230 x 43 x 27	D. McKay, East Boston	Wm. Wilson & Son, Baltimore. (Burned Port Phillip, Dec. 19, 1861.)
Euroclydon, Bennett, 1410: 191 x 34 x 22	Messrs. W. & J. Gardner, Baltimore	Hancock & Dawson, Philadelphia
Fearless, Nehemiah Manson, 1184: 191 x 36.5 x 22	A. & G. T. Sampson, East Boston	Wm. F. Weld & Co., Boston. (Sold Germany for Norwegian a/c 1878).
Flora Temple, Meyers, 1915.65: 233.9 x 41.9	J. Abraham, Baltimore	Abraham & Ashcroft, Baltimore (Lost China Sea October 15, 1859—868 lost).
Flyaway, M. Sewall, 1274: 190 x 38.3 x 21.6	Wm. H. Webb, New York	Schiff Bros. & Co., New York. (Sold Spanish 1859. Listed 1875).
Bk. *Flying Cloud,* 350	Perine, P. & S., Williamsburg, N.Y.	H. Harbeck & Co., New York.
Flying Dragon, Judah P. Baker, 1127: 187 x 38 x 22	Trufant & Drummond, Bath	Reed, Wade & Co. and later, Samuel G. Reed & Co., Boston. (Wrecked off San Francisco, 1862)
Flying Scud, Patten, and later Warren H. Bearse, 1713.41: 220.6 x 40.9 x 23.9	Metcalf & Norris, Damariscotta, Me.	R. W. Cameron, New York (Sold British April, 1863 *Cestrian*—Listed 1871)
Frigate Bird, Perry C. Cope, 567: 155 x 33 x 19 Also given 805.27: 156.5 x 33.6	J. A. Robb, Baltimore	C. H. Cummings & Co., Philadelphia (Sold British 1861)
Gauntlet, Sam'l G. Borland, 1854: 230 x 42 x 23 Also given 240 x 40.5 x 21.2½	Thos. J. Southard, Richmond, Me.	Stephenson & Thurston (Sold British 1860 *Sunda* Burned 1878)
Bk. *Gem of the Sea,* A. Bowen, 371.91: 116 x 26.2 x 13.5	Chase & Davis, Warren, R. I.	Sold to New York House for Australian trade
Geo. Peabody, Pousland, 1397: 195 x 39 x 27	J. O. Curtis, Medford	Wm. F. Weld, & Co., Boston (Condemned Valparaiso 1881)
Golden Light, Chas. E. Winsor, 1140: 182 x 36 x 22½	E. & H. O. Briggs, South Boston	James Huckins & Sons, Boston (Burned Feb. 22 on 1st voyage)

SHIP, MEASUREMENTS AND MASTER	PLACE AND DATE OF CONSTRUCTION	OWNER
Golden State, L. F. Doty, 1363: 188 x 39.8 x 21.6 (944 new)	J. A. Westervelt, New York	Chambers & Heiser, New York A. A. Low & Bro. (Lost Cape Elizabeth, Portland, Me., December, 1886)
Granite State, John Chase, 1108: 174 x 34 x 24	Samuel Badger, Portsmouth, N. H.	Edw. Size and Capt. John Chase (Wrecked 1868)
Bk. *Grapeshot*, E. J. Parker 345: 120.2 x 26.3 x 11.11	Cumberland, Me.	Sebastian Lawrence, et al, New London
Gravina, Caleb Sprague, 818.2: 165.3 x 32.8 x 18	Isaac C. Smith, Hoboken	Messrs. Howes & Co., New York
Great Republic, Joseph Limeburner 3356.59, 2751 N.: 302 x 48.4 x 29.2 (4555: 335 x 53 x 38, originally)	D. McKay, East Boston	A. A. Low & Bro., New York Foundered 1872, as *Denmark* British ownership
Guiding Star, Eliphalet Hale, 900: 165 x 33 x 23	J. Currier, Newburyport	Moses Davenport, et al, Newburyport (Condemned Hong Kong 1870)
Herald of the Morning Otis Baker, Jr., 1294: 203 x 38 x 23.6	Hayden & Cudworth, Medford	(Listed British ship 1890)
Highflyer, Gordon B. Waterman, 1195: 183 x 38 x 25	Currier & Townsend Newburyport	D. G. Ogden, et al, Red Cross Line (Missing with all hands 1855)
Hound, E. Spicer, Jr. 714: 143 x 33 x 17	Charles Mallory, Mystic, Conn.	Charles Mallory, Mystic
John Land, Peleg Howes, 1054: 176 x 36 x 22	E. & H. O. Briggs, South Boston	Baker & Morrill, Boston (Abandoned at sea Mar. 25, 1864)
Juniper, Parsons, 514: 141.3 x 28	Robbinston, Me.	Aymar & Co., New York (Lost on reef below Pernambuco Nov. 12, 1857, Capt. Lefevre)
Kate Hooper, John J. Jackson, 1488.76: 205 x 39.6 x 24	Hunt & Wagner Baltimore	J. A. Hooper, Baltimore (Burned Hobson's Bay 1862)

SHIP, MEASUREMENTS AND MASTER	PLACE AND DATE OF CONSTRUCTION	OWNER
Kathay, Thomas C. Stoddard, 1438.48: 209 x 38.4 x 21.6	J. A. Westervelt, New York	Goodhue & Co., New York (Put under British flag 1863— Lost Howland's Island Jan. 20, 1867)
Kingfisher, William Freeman, 1286: 217 x 37 x 21	Hayden & Cudworth, Medford	Wm. Lincoln & Co., Boston Later—Samuel G. Reed & Co. (Condemned Montevideo, 1871)
Lightfoot, Sumner Pierce, 1996: 233 x 42.9 x 23	Jackson & Ewell, East Boston	Howes & Co., et al, Boston (Wrecked at Saugor, 1855)
Live Yankee, Thorndike, 1637: 212 x 40 x 23.6	Horace Merriam, Rockland	Geo. W. Brown, et al, New York Sold almost at once to Foster & Nickerson, New York— Later Lawrence, Giles & Co. (Wrecked on coast of Galicia, 1861)
Lookout, John G. Joyce, 1291: 198 x 38.4 x 21.9	Chase & Davis, Warren, R. I.	E. Buckley & Sons, New York (Wrecked in Japan Sea, 1878)
Matchless, Symes Potter, 1033.5: 177 x 35.6 x 22	Isaac Taylor, Chelsea	Nathaniel & Benj. Goddard, Boston (Lost Oct., 1857, after leaving Anjier, N. Y., for Manila)
Miss Mag, Josiah S. Arey, 727.29: 153.6 x 32.1 x 16	Geo. Pierce, Farmingdale, Me.	Sam'l C. Grant, Farmingdale, Maine, and Pierce & Bacon, Boston (Name changed to *Beaver*)
Mischief, Martin Thompson, 560.69: 144 x 29 x 16.6	Jas. M. Hood, Somerset	W. H. Merrill & Capt. Martin Townsend, New York (Sold San Francisco, 1853)
Morning Light, E. D. Knight, 1713: 220 x 43 x 27	Toby & Littlefield, Portsmouth, N. H.	Glidden & Williams, Boston 1863 Jas. Baines & Co.— *Queen of the South*
Morning Light, Benj. Johnson, 938: 172 x 34 $\frac{3}{10}$ x 19	Wm. Cramp, Kensington, near Philadelphia	Stilwell S. Bishop, et al, and later Bucknor & McGammon, Phila. (Captured and burned 1863)
Morning Star, Wm. L. Foster, 1105: 183.6 x 36 x 24	J. T. Foster, Medford	T. B. Wales & Co., Boston (Said variously to have been lost 1890 and late 70's. Sold British, 1863, *Landsborough*)
Mystery, Peter Peterson, 1155: 185 x 37 x 23	Samuel Hall, East Boston	Crocker & Sturgis & D. C. & W. B. Bacon, Boston (Sold British, 1854)

SHIP, MEASUREMENTS AND MASTER	PLACE AND DATE OF CONSTRUCTION	OWNER
Neptune's Car, Forbes, 1616: 216 x 40 x 23.6 (length also given 206)	Page and Allen, Portsmouth, Va.	Foster & Nickerson, New York (Sold British, 1862)
Nonpareil, Edward Dunn, 1431: 220 x 41.6 x 22.5 1097 new: 192 x 39 x 22.6	Dunham & Co., Frankfort, Me	Thos. Richardson & Co., New York
North Wind, J. D. Hildreth, 1041: 177 x 35.8 x 21	A. C. Bell, New York	Grinnell, Minturn & Co. (Possibly sold British, 1861)
Ocean Herald, Spencer, 2135.6	Col. Cyrus Cotter, Damariscotta	Everett & Brown, New York (Sold French, 1856, *Malabar*)
Ocean Pearl, Winthrop Sears, 847: 170 x 32.8½ x 23	J. Magoun, Charlestown, Mass.	Alpheus Hardy & Joshua Sears Boston (Wrecked Tarragona, 1864)
Oracle, Chas. E. Ranlett, 1196	Chapman & Flint, Thomaston, Me.	(Sold British, Nov., 1862)
Pampero, Calvin Coggin, 1375: 202.6 x 38.2 x 21	Chas. Mallory	J. Bishop & Co., New York (Sold Government, 1861— resold October 1, 1867)
Panama, W. P. Cave, 1139: 867 new: 192.4 o.a. x 35.7 x 19.4	Thos. Collyer, New York	N. L. & G. Griswold, New York (Condemned and sold Bahia, 1867)
Peerless, 1100	Messrs. Sampson, East Boston	Wm. F. Weld & Co.
Phoenix, Crabtree, 1458: 217 o.a. x 41.6 x 24	Thos. E. Knight, Cape Elizabeth, Me.	N. Blanchard & Sons—later Chas. Carow, Portland, Me. (Burned Feb. 28, 1860, Melbourne)
Portland, Wm. Leavitt, 997.93: 173.9 x 35.3	Cape Elizabeth. Me.	N. F. Deering, et al, Portland, Me.
Pride of America, Hawthorne, 1826: 213 x 38 x 22	Patten & Sturdevant, Richmond, Me.	Patten & Sturdevant (Sold British, March, 1854— foundered, 1883)
Pride of the Ocean, Washington Read, 1525: 196 x 42.2 x 24	Daniel Foster, Warren, R. I.	Cady & Aldrich, Providence, R. I. (Sold British, 1854, *Belgravia*)
Progressive, 1119: 180 x 36.5 x 22	F. W. Rhoades, Rockland, Me.	

SHIP, MEASUREMENTS AND MASTER	PLACE AND DATE OF CONSTRUCTION	OWNER
Queen of Clippers, John A. Zerega, 2360.58: 248.6 x 45 x 28	Robt. E. Jackson, East Boston	Seccomb & Taylor, Boston— Soon sold to Zerega & Co. & D. Fowler, New York (Sold France, 1856)
Quickstep, Cook, 823.35: 159.6 x 33.9	Enos Soule Freeport, Me.	Dunham & Dimon, New York (Sold British, 1863)
Radiant, Allen H. Bearse, 1318: 197 x 37.11 x 24.4	Paul Curtis, East Boston	Baker & Morrill, Boston— (Sold Calcutta 1863)
Rapid, Richard S. Corning, 1115: 176.9 x 36.8 x 20	Roosevelt & Joyce, New York	Jas. Bishop & Co., New York (Sold Danish 1859—Listed 1866)
Red Gauntlet, Thomas Andrews, 1038: 178 x 35.6 x 22	James W. Cox, Robbinston, Me.	F. Boyd & Co., Boston, & James W. Cox (Burned by *Florida*, 1863)
Red Jacket, Asa Eldridge, 2305: 251.2 x 44 x 31, also given 2434.86: 250 x 45.7 x 24	Geo. Thomas, Rockland	Seccomb & Taylor, Boston (Sold Liverpool, 1855)
Reporter, Octavius Howe, 1474: 207.5 x 39 x 24.6	Paul Curtis, Boston	David Snow, Boston (Lost off Horn Aug. 17, 1862)
Resolute, John W. Perry, 786.80: 151.6 x 33.9 x 19.4	Westervelt & Sons, New York	A. A. Low & Bro., (Sold British 1862—Listed 1875)
Ringleader, Richard Matthews, 1156.54: 189.8 x 36.2 x 22.9	Hayden & Cudworth, Medford	Howes & Crowell, Boston (Lost on Formosa Banks, 1863)
Romance of the Seas, Philip Dumaresq, 1782: 240.9 x 39.6 x 20	D. McKay, East Boston	Geo. B. Upton, Boston (Missing Hong Kong to San Francisco early 1863)
Rover's Bride, J. D. Nason, 376: 135 x 29 x 11.4	Foster & Booz, Canton, near Baltimore	J. D. Nason, San Francisco (Sold Australia, 1854—Abandoned Dec. 24, 1856, from Savannah to Liverpool)
San Francisco, Isaac T. Sitzer, 1307.23: 194.10 x 38 x 22	A. C. Bell, New York	Rich & Elam & Thos. Wardle, New York (Lost entering San Francisco, Feb. 8, 1854—1st voyage)

SHIP, MEASUREMENTS AND MASTER	PLACE AND DATE OF CONSTRUCTION	OWNER
Sea Nymph, Chas. D. Harding, 1215: 188 x 37.4 x 22	Reuben Fish & Co. Fairhaven	Edward Mott Robinson, N. Bedford (Wrecked May 4, 1861, Point Reyes, Calif.)
Skylark, Wm. W. Henry, 1209.27: 190 x 37 x 22	James M. Hood, Somerset	Crocker & Warren, New York (Sold Hamburg, 1865–60)
Bk. *Snap Dragon*, Fred'k Sherwood, 618.74: 142.2 x 30.10 x 18.2	W. H. Webb, New York	Wakeman, Dimon & Co. New York
Spark of the Ocean, Willard J. Treat, 895.42: 171 x 33.7 x 16.9½	Waldoboro, Me., 1853	Alfred Blanchard, Wm. H. Greely, et al, Boston
Sparkling Wave, John C. Hubbard, 665: 136.3 x 32.6 x 22	Mason Barney, Swansea, Mass.	Eben H. Balch, Boston Sold British, 1864
Spirit of the Times, Klein, 1206: 191.7 x 36.8 x 21.6 Also 1206.18: 191 x 31.10 x 18	Cooper & Slicer Baltimore	Aymar & Co., New York (Sold Hamburg—1861— broken up about 1871)
Spitfire, John Arey, 1520.1: 206.2 x 39 x 20	James Arey & Co., Frankfort, Me.	Thos. Gray & Manning & Stanwood, Boston (Sold British 1863—Listed 1869)
Star of Empire, Albert H. Brown, 2050: 220 x 43 x 27.6	D. McKay, East Boston	Enoch Train & Co. (Under Capt. French put into Algoa Bay from Rangoon for Falmouth June 28, 1856, and condemned)
Storm King, Henry Devens, 1399.69: 195.6 x 39.4 x 23	John Taylor, Chelsea	Dana, Dana & Co., Boston (Sold British 1863—Listed 1875)
Stornaway, 750	Samuel B. Keyes, Orland, Me.	Welles & Gowan, Boston
Strelna, Thomas Leach, 713.75: 155.11 x 31.5½	Richmond, Me.	Wm. Ropes, Boston
Sweepstakes, George E. Lane, 1735: 216.4 x 41.6 x 22	Daniel & Aaron Westervelt, New York	Chambers & Heiser, New York (Ashore in Sts. of Sunda and condemned at Batavia May, 1862)

SHIP, MEASUREMENTS AND MASTER	PLACE AND DATE OF CONSTRUCTION	OWNER
Undaunted, Wm. Freeman, 1371: 198 x 38 x 23	Hall, Snow & Co., Bath, Me.	W. H. Foster & Co., Boston (Condemned Rio, Sept., 1863, *Halden*, 1867)
Viking, Zenas Winsor, Jr., 1349.54: 230 o.a. x 41.9 x 22.9	Trufant & Drummond, Bath	Geo. Hussey, New Bedford (Lost Princess Island off Simoda, June 4, 1863)
Water Witch, Washington Plummer, 1204: 182 x 37.9 x 18.9½	Fernald & Pettigrew Portsmouth	Stephen Tilton, et al, Boston (Lost at Ypala, June 1, 1855)
Waverley, Wm. F. Clark, 749: 161 x 34 x 22	Joshua Magoun, Charlestown, Mass.	Thos. Curtis, Thaddeus Nichols, et al, Boston (Missing on voyage to Calcutta, 1862)
West Wind, G. W. Elliott, 1071: 180 x 36.6 x 24	Joshua Foster, Medford	J. & A. Tirrell, Boston (Sold British 1863 *Lord Clyde* of Calcutta)
Western Continent, Stephen Higgins, 1272	Hon. S. C. Foster, Pembroke, Me.	John M. Mayo & Co., Boston
Whistler, Capt. Chas. H. Brown, 820: 171 x 36 x 22	Geo. W. Jackman, Jr., Newburyport	Bush & Wildes, Boston (Lost on King's Island, Bass Straits, 4 days out of Port Phillip for Singapore May 23, 1855)
White Falcon, Ryan 1372: 190 x 38 x 23	Pittston, Me.	M. O. Roberts, New York (Sold Peru 1864—Burned 1866)
White Swallow, F. W. Lovett, 1192: 186 x 37 x 22.10	Hayden & Cudworth, Medford	Wm. Lincoln & Co., Boston Later Jos. Nickerson, Boston (Abandoned near Fayal, 1871)
Wide Awake, Smith, 758: 168.6 x 31 x 17.10	Perine, P. & S., Williamsburg, N. Y.	Siffkin & Ironsides, New York (Sold Siam, 1857)
Wild Duck, A. G. Hamilton, 860: 175 x 35.4 x 22.8, also given 165 x 33.6	Geo. Raynes, Portsmouth	Olyphant & Co., New York (Lost River Min., 1856)
Bk. *Wildfire*, 338.30: 128.4 x 27.4 x 10.6	Amesbury, Mass.	Peter A. Hargous, New York
Wild Ranger, J. Henry Sears, 1044: 177 x 35.4 x 22.8	J. O. Curtis, Medford	Sears & Thatchers (Libelled and sold British after collision Jan., 1862—foundered after collision, 1872)

SHIP, MEASUREMENTS AND MASTER	PLACE AND DATE OF CONSTRUCTION	OWNER
Wild Rover, Hamilton, 1100: 187 x 36 x 22	Austin & Hall, Damariscotta	Alpheus Hardy & Co., Boston (Lost on Long Island, 1871)
Wild Wave, Josiah N. Knowles, 1547	G. H. Ferrin, Richmond, Me.	Benj. Bangs, Boston (Wrecked 80 miles from Pitcairn Island, Mar. 5, 1858)
Wizard, Shungar H. Slate, 1601: 210 x 40.6 x 25.9	Samuel Hall, East Boston	Slate & Co., New York (Sold British 1862 *Queen of the Colonies*, Mackay, Baines & Co. Reported wrecked 1874)
Woodcock, Frederick M. Ranlett 1091.17: 187.1 x 35.4	Achorn & Gleason, Waldoboro, Me.	Dunham & Dimon, New York (Went ashore Dungeness, Lambert master, and bilged)
Young America, David S. Babcock, 1961: 243 x 43.2 x 26.9	Wm. H. Webb, New York	Geo. B. Daniels, New York 1860—Abram Bell's Sons (Sold Austria 1882—missing 1886)
Young Brander, 1467: 194 x 36 x 24	Jotham Stetson, Chelsea	Brander, Williams & Co., Boston Later Edward Matthew, New Orleans (Sold British 1855—Abandoned at sea 1873)

1854

Adelaide, Joseph Hamilton, 1831.45: 214 x 43 x 28.2	A. C. Bell, New York	Thos. Wardle, New York
Asterion, Moses Gray, 1135: 188 x 36 x 24	Abner Stetson, Chelsea	David Snow, et al, Boston 1860—Bucklin & Crane (Lost Bakers Island, 1863)
Belle Wood, Joseph T. Tucker, 1399.69: 195.6 x 39.4 x 29	Greenman & Co., Mystic	John A. McGaw, N. Y., and later Williams & Guion, Liverpool
B. F. Hoxie, Stark 1387: 187 x 40 x 23	Maxson, Fish & Co., Mystic, Ct.	N. G. Fish & Co., Mystic (Burned by *Florida* June, 1862)
Blue Jacket, Eldridge, 1790: 235 o.a. x 41.2 x 24 1442 new: 195 x 39.2 x 23	Robt. E. Jackson, East Boston	Seccomb & Taylor, Boston (Burned off Falklands 1869—Sold 1854 to John James Frost London.)

SHIP, MEASUREMENTS AND MASTER	PLACE AND DATE OF CONSTRUCTION	OWNER
Bostonian, Chas. B. Brookman, 1099.85: 183.6 x 35.11 x 23	Boston	Henry D. Brookman, et al, Boston
Bk. *Bounding Billow*, Levi Smith, 353.6: 120.6 x 26.6 x 12.1	Jotham Stetson, Chelsea	Ephraim Lombard, Josiah F. Conant, et al, Boston
Canvas Back, Clark, 731: 153 x 32 x 19.6	Abraham & Ashcroft, Baltimore	Oelrich & Lurman, Baltimore (Sold British, 1863)
Champion of the Seas, Alexander Newlands, 2447: 252 x 45.6 x 29.2	D. McKay, East Boston	Jas. Baines & Co. (Abandoned off Horn Jan. 3, 1876)
Charmer, I. S. Lucas, 1055: 181.1 x 35.5 x 23.2	Geo. W. Jackman, Jr., Newburyport	Bush & Wildes, Boston (Sold 1863 Liverpool—still Listed 1875)
Cœur de Lion, Geo. W. Tucker, 1098: 178.4 x 36.2 x 21.6	Geo. Raynes, Portsmouth, N. H.	W. F. Parrott, Boston & Capt. Geo. W. Tucker, Portsmouth (Sold Hamburg, 1857)
Bk. *Cossack*, H. A. Ballard, 586.33: 138.8 x 30.5 x 17.9	E. & H. O. Briggs, Boston	Curtis & Peabody, Boston
Crest of the Wave, Wm. S. Colley, 942: 175 x 34 x 21	Hon. Joshua Patterson, Thomaston, Me.	M. R. Ludwig, Baltimore (All hands lost prior to April 14, 1870—Wrecked on Wreck Island 15 miles North Cape Charles)
Crystal Palace, Benj. F. Simmons, 653.41: 149.9 x 30.9 x 19	Eastport, Me.	E. M. Robinson, et al, New Bedford
Dashaway, 1012: 177 x 35 x 23	J. Rideout, Hallowell, Me.	Read, Page & Co., Hallowell (Sold British 1863— *Mauritius Merchant*)
Driver, Nich. Holberton, 1594.49: 209 x 40.6	Newburyport	David Ogden, et al, New York
Elizabeth F. Willets, Charles E. Sisson, 825: 156 x 34 x 19	Chas. Mallory, Mystic	Charles Mallory (Sold Shanghae, 1864)
Eloisa, Ybargany, 725.21:151$\frac{3}{10}$x32$\frac{3}{10}$	Currier & Townsend Newburyport	Built for a house in Valparaiso, and sailed at once for that port

SHIP, MEASUREMENTS AND MASTER	PLACE AND DATE OF CONSTRUCTION	OWNER
Emily Farnum, 1119: 194 x 35 x 23	Geo. Raynes, Portsmouth	W. Jones & Co., Portsmouth (Lost Cape Flattery, Nov., 1875)
Euterpe, Geo. W. Brown, 1985: 224 x 43.8 x 24.6	Horace Merriam, Rockland	Foster & Nickerson, New York (Abandoned off Brazil 1871)
Express, T. M. Weeks, 1072.51: 183 x 35$\frac{5}{10}$	Fernald & Pettigrew Portsmouth	Peter Marcy, New Orleans, et al
Fanny McHenry, Alfred F. Smith, 1237: 194 x 39 x 23 Also given 1237.36: 191 x 37.4 x 24	A. & G. T. Sampson East Boston	G. McHenry & Co., Philadelphia. Later Thos. Richardson & Co. (Renamed *Philadelphia*.)
Fatherland, Gardner, 1180: 194.3 x 38.6 x 23.7	Wm. Hall, East Boston	M. Green, London, Oct., 1854, *Sanspareil*
Fleetwing, Laban Howes, 896: 167 x 34 x 21.8	Hayden & Cudworth, Medford	Crowell, Brooks & Co., Boston (Condemned Melbourne 1885)
Francis A. Palmer, A. Richardson, 1425.6: 201.5 x 39 x 28.1	Wm. Perine, Greenpoint, L. I.	E. D. Hurlburt & Co., New York
Galatea, Henry Barber, 1041: 182 x 36.6 x 23	Joseph Magoun, Charlestown, Mass.	W. F. Weld & Co., Boston Prendergast Bros. & Co., 1875 (Sold Nor. 1882)
Golden Rule, 1194 New: 185 x 37.7 x 23.6	Wm. Hitchcock, Newcastle, Me.	Frederick Nickerson. et al, Boston
Grace Darling, S. H. Doane, 1197: 185.5 x 37 x 23.6	E. & H. O. Briggs, South Boston	Chas. B. Fessendon, Boston Bought by Baker & Morrell, 1858 (Missing 1878—18 lost)
Haidee, Jos. H. Tillinghast, 395.84: 137 x 27.1 x 11.6	Allen & Simpson, Providence, R. I.	1857—sold to E. Sanchez Doiz, New York (Scuttled off Montauk, 1858, while a slaver)
Harvey Birch, Wm. Nelson, 1482: 196 x 40.6 x 28	Irons & Grinnell, Mystic	J. H. Brower & Co., New York (Burned by *Nashville*, 1862)
Indiaman, McCallum, 1165	Hugh McKay, East Boston	Sampson & Tappan, Boston
Isaac Jeanes, Chipman, 843: 157 x 35 x 21.6 Draft 20 Also given 159 x 34	Wm. Cramp, Philadelphia	Isaac Jeanes & Co., Philadelphia

SHIP, MEASUREMENTS AND MASTER	PLACE AND DATE OF CONSTRUCTION	OWNER
James Baines, Chas. McDonnell, 2515: 266 o.a. x 44.9 x 29	D. McKay, East Boston	James Baines & Co., Liverpool (Burned Liverpool April 22, 1858)
King Lear, Asa Eldridge, 1936.24: 231.10 x 42.2 x 29.3	R. E. Jackson, East Boston	Seccomb & Taylor, Boston (Sold to London)
King Philip, Eleazer C. Taylor, 1486.47: 203.3 x 39.8 x 23	Geo. Thomas, Quincy, Mass.	Patrick Grant & Wm. B. Reynolds, Boston
Lightning, James Nicol Forbes, 2083.88: 243 x 42.8 x 23	D. McKay, East Boston	James Baines & Co., Liverpool
Mary, Wm. Churchill, 1148: 179 x 37 x 21	Benj. Dutton Marblehead, Mass.	Edward Kimball, Salem, et al, 1862—J. P. Turner (Condemned Callao 1867—Repaired and sold British)
Mary Ogden, Samuel Loveland, 969: 159 x 36.8	Chase & Davis, Warren, R. I.	G. Bulkley, New York
Mary Robinson, Frederick Crocker, 1371: 215 x 38.6 x 22.6	Trufant & Drummond, Bath, Me.	E. M. Robinson, New Bedford (Lost Howland's Island 1864)
Midnight, Jas. B. Hatch, 962: 175 x 36 x 20.10	Fernald & Pettigrew Portsmouth, N. H.	Henry Hastings, Boston (Condemned 1878 at Amboyna)
Morning Glory, 1119: 182 x 36.6 x 26.9	Portsmouth, N. H.	J. Goodwin, Portsmouth
Nabob, Dewhurst, 1246: 193 x 38 x 24	John Taylor, Chelsea, Mass.	Wm. Appleton & Co., and their successors, Hooper & Co. (Lost on Luzon Nov., 1862)
Napier, J. L. Sanford, 1811: 216 x 42.6 x 28	Wm. & Geo. Gardner, Fell's Point, Balt.	Dawson & Hancock, Phila. (Sold British Nov., 1863—Lost Baker's Island, 1871)
Neptune's Favorite, Oliver G. Lane, 1347: 194.4 x 39.8 x 23.8 Also given 210 x 38 x 24	Jotham Stetson, Chelsea	H. A. Kelly & Co., Boston (Sold British 1863 *Mataura* Listed 1874)
Nor' Wester, Frank C. Eldridge, 1267: 185.6 x 38.6 x 23	S. Lapham, Medford	J. T. Coolidge & Co., Boston 1864—R. F. C. Hartley, et al, Boston (Burned Key West, 1873)

SHIP, MEASUREMENTS AND MASTER	PLACE AND DATE OF CONSTRUCTION	OWNER
Northern Eagle, Joshua F. Grozier, 664.88: 146.10 x 31.5 x 21.6	Andrew Burnham, East Boston	J. & A. M. Tirrell & Wm. Dillaway, Boston
Ocean Express, Thos. Cunningham 1697: 240 x 41 x 24.5 1495 new: 215 x 41.2 x 24.6	J. O. Curtis, Medford	Reed, Wade & Co. and their successors Sam'l Reed & Co. (Sold Peru, 1872)
Ocean Rover, Tucker, 777: 162 x 33 x 23 823 new: 157 x 33.10 x 22.10	Tobey & Littlefield, Portsmouth, N. H.	R. H. Tucker, et al, Boston
Ocean Telegraph, Geo. H. Willis, 1495: 212 x 40 x 23 1214 new: 201 x 40 x 23	J. O. Curtis, Medford	Reed, Wade & Co., Boston (Sold 1863 to James Baines & Co. *Light Brigade*—Coal Hulk at Gibraltar after 1883 for many years)
Osborn Howes, Nehemiah D. Kelly, 1100: 186 x 35.9 x 23.9	Hayden & Cudworth, Medford	Howes & Crowell, Boston (Sold British 1864—Listed 1870)
Panther, N. G. Weeks, 1278: 193.7 x 37.5 x 24	Paul Curtis, Medford	R. C. Mackay & Sons, Boston, 1868—Pope & Talbot (Wrecked Vancouver Island, Jan., 1874)
Pride of the Sea, Hooper, 1600: 218 x 41 x 23	Foster & Booz, Baltimore	Jas. Hooper & Co., Baltimore (Burned off Barnemouth, 1854, with cotton from New Orleans to Liverpool)
Rambler, Allen Baxter, 1119: 182 x 37 x 23	Hayden & Cudworth, Medford	Baxter Bros. Yarmouth Mass. & Israel Nash, Boston (Sold Germany 1863 *Fanny*)
Robin Hood, Richard Bearse, 1181.63: 186 x 37 x 23.6	Hayden & Cudworth, Medford	Howes & Crowell, Boston (Burned Aug. 20, 1869, at Baker's Island)
Santa Claus, Bailey Foster, 1256: 194 o.a. x 38.6 x 22.11	D. McKay, East Boston	Jos. Nickerson & Co., Boston (Lost at sea Aug. 9, 1863)
Saracen, J. Barry, 1266.15: 189.4 x 38 x 24	E. & H. O. Briggs, East Boston	Curtis & Peabody, Boston (Sold San Francisco, 1865, to go under Italian flag *Teresa*)

SHIP, MEASUREMENTS AND MASTER	PLACE AND DATE OF CONSTRUCTION	OWNER
Sierra Nevada, Penhallow, 1942: 222.2 x 44.4 x 26.4	Tobey & Littlefield, Portsmouth	Glidden & Williams, Boston (Lost on coast Chile, 1877)
Sparkling Sea, Nehemiah Rich, 893.34: 167.3 x 34 x 17	Bristol, Me.	Alfred Blanchard, et al, Boston
Starlight, Josiah Chase, 1153: 190 x 37 x 23	E. & H. O. Briggs, South Boston	Baker & Morrill, Boston (Sold Peru, 1864 *Proto Longo*)
Starr King, Geo. H. Turner, 1171: 200 o.a. x 39 x 22.6	Geo. W. Jackman, Jr., Newburyport	Baker & Morrill & Bates & Thaxter, Boston (Lost June, 1862, on Pt. Rourania between Hong Kong and Singapore)
Stingray, Nicholas Kirby, Jr., 985	Eckford Webb, Green Point, L. I.	Wakeman & Dimon, New York (Lost on Fire Island, Jan. 9, 1856, from Canton, Sept. 30)
Sunny South, Michael Gregory, 702.5: 144.8 x 31.4 x 16.6	Geo. Steers, Williamsburg, N. Y.	Napier, Johnson & Co., New York (Aug., 1860, captured by British with 800 slaves and sold as British cruiser)
Swallow, Benj. W. Tucker, 1435: 210 x 38.6 x 23.6 (Registered New York as 200.7 in length)	Robt. E. Jackson, East Boston	Dugan & Leland, New York, & Seccomb & Taylor, Boston (1862 sold to Thatcher Magoun. Abandoned at sea 1885)
Talisman, Francis Bursley, 1237.72: 194.8 x 36.11 x 23.6	Metcalf & Norris, Damariscotta	Crocker & Warren, New York (Burned 1863 by *Alabama*)
Bk. *Tejorca*, 470: 140 x 28 x 12	Isaac C. Smith & Son, Hoboken	Wm. A. Sale, Jr.
Troubadour, Knott Pedrick, 1200 (about)	Currier & Townsend, Newburyport	Fisher & Co., Boston
Virginia, Freeman G. Sparks, 959.43: 175.3 x 34.4 x 212	Rose, Robbinston, Me.	Geo. W. Hunter, Boston
Windward, Whiting, 818: 159 x 35 x 21	Trufant & Drummond, Bath	R. W. Cameron, New York, Agts., (Wrecked Whidby Is., Puget Sound, Dec., 1875)

SHIP, MEASUREMENTS AND MASTER	PLACE AND DATE OF CONSTRUCTION	OWNER
Wizard King, J. Cobb, 1398: 199.6 x 38.10 Draft 21	T. J. Southard, Richmond	T. J. Southard, Richmond, Me.
Yankee Ranger, 707.78: 162.6 x 30.6	Rockland, Me.	Gustavus Moler, Wm. Heye, et al, New York
Zephyr, J. B. King, 1184.11: 193.8 x 36.2 x 25.10	Daniel D. Kelly, East Boston	T. B. Wales & Co., Nathaniel Emmons, et al, Boston

1855

Abbott Lawrence, Benj. Hale, 1497.68: 202.6 x 39.11 x 24.4	D. McKay, East Boston	Geo. B. Upton, John M. Forbes, et al, Boston
Andrew Jackson, John E. Williams, 1679.37: 222 x 40.2 x 22.2	Irons & Grinnell, Mystic, Ct.	J. H. Brower & Co., New York
Beacon Light, Robt. Simonson, 1376.10: 194.6 x 39.1 x 24	Jotham Stetson, Chelsea	Jotham Stetson
Black Sea, 791: 150 x 34 x 24.4	Messrs. Lupton, Greenpoint, New York	Funch & Meinke, New York (Sold Br. 1863—*Jupiter*, London)
Brewster, Albert Dunbar, 984: 171 x 35 x 23	Currier & Townsend, Newburyport	W. Clark et al, Boston (Sold Norway *Fama* 1886. Disappears 1890)
Carrier Dove, Corner, 1694.35: 207.8 x 42 x 24	Jas. Abraham, Baltimore	Montell & Co., Baltimore (Lost near Tybee Mar. 3, 1876)
Cherubim, Smith, 1796: 217 x 43 x 24	J. Abraham, Baltimore	David Currie, et al, Richmond, Va. (Sold Cox Bros. Dundee, 1863. Disappears about 1870)
Courier, Wm. Wolfe, 554: 135 x 30	Currier & Townsend Newburyport	Foster, Elliott & Co. New York
Criterion, 1386.92: 198.3 x 38.9 x 28	Wm. Hitchcock & Co., Damariscotta	F. Nickerson & Co., Boston (Sold Moravia, 1882)

SHIP, MEASUREMENTS AND MASTER	PLACE AND DATE OF CONSTRUCTION	OWNER
Daring, Robt. Simonson, 1094: 181 x 36 x 23	Geo. W. Jackman, Jr., Newburyport	Bush & Comstock, Boston (Partly dismasted 1865—condemned Valparaiso—sold British. Disappears 1874)
Defender, Beauchamp, 1413: 184 x 38 x 23	D. McKay, East Boston	Kendall & Plimpton, Boston (Lost Feb. 27, 1859, on Elizabeth Reef, South Pacific)
Derby, Hutchinson, 1062: 180 x 36.9 x 23.5	John Taylor, Chelsea	Pickman, Silsbee, et al, Salem (Was German ship *Derby*, 1881)
Dictator, T. Everett, 1293: 189 x 38.5 x 23.8	Jas. W. Cox, Robbinston, Me.	Samuel Train, Medford (Burned by *Georgia* April, 1863)
Donald McKay, H. Warner, 2595: 266 x 46.3 x 29.5	D. McKay, East Boston	Jas. Baines & Co., Liverpool
Electric Spark, Laban Howes, 1216: 184 x 40 x 24	Hayden & Cudworth, Medford	T. Magoun & Son, Boston (Lost coast Ireland, 1869)
Fair Wind, Allen, 1299: 195 x 36.10 x 24	E. & H. O. Briggs, South Boston	Henry S. Hallet & Co., Boston (Sold British 1866—Reported to 1875)
Ganges, Evans, 1254: 192 x 39 x 23	Hugh McKay, East Boston	W. S. Bullard, Boston (Sold British, 1863)
Goddess, Zenas Crowell, 1126: 182.10 x 36.5 x 23.9	Hayden & Cudworth, Medford	Baxter Bros., Boston (Sold British 1864—Was at Pensacola June, 1886)
Golden Fleece, Alfred M. Lunt, 1535: 210 x 37.9 x 25	Paul Curtis, East Boston	Weld & Baker, Boston (Condemned Montevideo, 1877)
Good Hope, 1295: 187 x 38 x 25	J. O. Curtis, Medford	R. L. Taylor, New York—later Geo. F. Burritt, New York—later E. E. Morgan's Sons (Lost near Quebec, 1881)
Harry Bluff, Redman, 1244: 184 x 37 x 24	Jotham Stetson Chelsea	Chas. R. Green, New York (Lost Nantucket Shoals 1869)
Harry of the West, 1050: 182 x 36 x 23	Robt. E. Jackson, East Boston	Calvin Adams, New York (Burned Mouth of Mississippi, Nov., 1865)
Bk. *Helen Mar*, E. T. Lowe, 510.92: 134.7 x 28.4 x 14.7	Baltimore, Md.	George Logan, New York

SHIP, MEASUREMENTS AND MASTER	PLACE AND DATE OF CONSTRUCTION	OWNER
John Milton, Ephraim Harding, 1444.79: 203.6 x 39 x 19	Fairhaven, Mass.	G. Hussey, et al, New Bedford (Lost Feb. 20, 1858, with all hands (26), near Montauk)
Kit Carson, Seth Crowell, 997: 173 x 36 x 22	Shiverick Bros., East Dennis, Mass.	Prince S. Crowell, East Dennis (Sunk off Rio during Brazilian war)
Leah, Jonathan Latham, 1438.23: 180 x 42 x 21	Geo. Greenman & Co., Mystic	J. A. McGaw, New York (Lost with all hands 1st voyage)
Mameluke, Elisha Whitney, 1303: 195 x 38.10 x 24	E. & H. O. Briggs, South Boston	Curtis & Peabody, Boston (Sold British 1863 *Milton* Listed 1874)
Manitou, Elliot Honeywell, 1401.56: $199\frac{8}{10}$ x $38\frac{3}{10}$	Wm. Cramp, Petty's Island, N. J.	Bishop, Simons & Co., Phila. (Missing 1859)
Mary Whitridge, Robt. B. Cheesebrough, 978: 168 x 34 x 21	Hunt & Wagner, Baltimore	Thos. Whitridge & Co., Balt. (Cut down to barge before 1886—Lost 1902)
Noonday, W. B. Gerry, 1189: 200 o.a. x 38.6 x 23.6	Fernald & Pettigrew, Portsmouth	Henry Hastings, Boston (Lost on uncharted Rock near San Francisco, Jan. 1, 1863)
Bk. *Quick Step*, J. Smith, 523.35: 142.11 x 28.1 x 18.9	Samuel Hall, Boston	Daniel C. Bacon, et al, Boston
Rival, Eben Sears, 983.50: 177 x 34.7 x 23	Hayden & Cudworth, Medford	Howes & Crowell, Boston (Missing Rangoon to Falmouth, E. 1872)
Sancho Panza, J. B. Hildreth, 876: 152.6 x 34 x 21.5	Samuel Lapham, Medford	John Ellerton Lodge, Boston (Sold British 1863—Listed 1890)
Star of Hope, Abraham Somerville, 1197.83: 191 x $36\frac{7}{10}$	Portsmouth, N. H.	Chas. H. Coffin, et al, Newburyport (Abandoned June 13, 1861)
Stephen Crowell, Burgess, 936: 174 x 35.6 x 24	Burgess & Clark, Warren, Me.	Snow & Burgess, New York
Titan, Oliver Eldridge, 1985	Roosevelt & Joyce, New York	Capt. Daniel C. Bacon, Boston (Abandoned at sea Feb. 18, 1858)

SHIP, MEASUREMENTS AND MASTER	PLACE AND DATE OF CONSTRUCTION	OWNER
Vitula, Samuel K. Leach, 1187.87: 183 x 37.6 x 24	E. & H. O. Briggs, East Boston	Williams & Daland, Boston Nov. 1859 Samuel G. Reed, Boston (Condemned Rio June, 1867—Later repaired as British ship *Bessie & Annie*—Later *James Rowen*)
War Hawk, Lemuel B. Simmons, 1067: 182 x 35.6 x 23	Geo. W. Jackman, Newburyport	Bush & Comstock, et al, Boston Sold 1871 to S. L. Mastick & Co., San Francisco (Burned 1883)
Whistling Wind, 1800 (about)	Wm. & Geo. Gardner, Falls Pt., near Balt.	(Name probably changed almost immediately)
Wild Hunter, Joshua Sears, 1081: 178.7 x 36.2 x 22.6	Shiverick Bros., East Dennis, Mass.	Capt. Christopher Hall, et al, East Dennis—Soon bought by Bush & Wildes, Boston (Listed 1875, Not listed 1884)
Young Mechanic, H. Freeman, 1375: 199.6 x 38.6 x 22.6	T. W. Rhoades, Rockland	Wm. McLoon, Rockland (Burned at sea 1866)
Bk. *Zephyr*, 534.44: 155.6 x 27 x 14.10	S. G. Bogert, New York	Chamberlain & Phelps, New York

1856

Alarm, Nathaniel Matthews, 1184: 182 x 37.6 x 23	E. & H. O. Briggs, South Boston	Baker & Morrill, Boston (Lost 1863—3 days out of Akyab for Singapore)
Arey, Samuel J. Sewall, 1123.35: 179.7 x 36.11 x 23	Williams & Arey, Frankfort, Me.	Sold to Wakeman, Dimon & Co., New York
Asa Eldridge, Moses R. Coleman, 1324: 192 x 38.10 x 25	E. & H. O. Briggs, South Boston	Henry Hallet, Boston. Sold to W. F. Weld & Co., 1865 (Owned Liverpool 1880)
Aspasia, John Green, 632: 145 x 31 x 20	Maxson, Fish & Co., Mystic, Ct.	N. G. Fish & Co., Mystic Later Bucklin Crane & Co., N. Y. (Sold England 1863)
Atmosphere, John S. Pray, 1485.52: 190 x 41.4 x 20.8	George Greenman, Mystic, Ct.	John A. McGaw, New York to 1863—Wm. Tapscott & Co., Liverpool—1863 (Sunk off Pernambuco 1882)
Beaver, Smith	Formerly ship *Miss Mag*—name changed	

SHIP, MEASUREMENTS AND MASTER	PLACE AND DATE OF CONSTRUCTION	OWNER
Black Hawk, B. P. Bowers, 1175: 178 x 38.5 x 23.9	Wm. H. Webb, New York	Bucklin & Crane, New York
Black Prince, Chas. H. Brown, 1061: 180 x 36 x 22	Geo. W. Jackman, Newburyport	Bush & Wildes, Boston (Lost N. Atlantic, Feb. 1865)
Caroline	Same ship as the *Arey* (See above)	
Charger, Luther Hurd, 1136: 190 x 38.1 x 23.4	E. G. Pearce, Portsmouth, N. H.	Henry Hastings, Boston (Wrecked near Cuba Dec. 14, 1873)
East Indian, Wm. Le Craw, 897.20: 172 x 33.6	Currier & Townsend, Newburyport	Stephen Tilton & Co., Boston (Sold Calcutta April, 1864)
Empress, Joseph Morrell, 1293.85: 193.1 x 38 x 24	Paul Curtis, East Boston	H. Harbeck & Co., New York (Sold British, 1863. German ship *Elizabeth*, 1886)
Endeavor, Doane, 1137: 184.6 x 36.6 x 22.2	Robt. E. Jackson, Boston	Cunningham Bros., Boston— Later Frank Hathaway, New Bedford (Burned Japan 1875)
Expounder, Foster 1176: 171 x 37 x 23	Joshua Magoun, Charlestown, Mass.	Paul Sears, Boston (Made into barge, 1881— Disappears, 1906)
Bkn. *Fairy*, Blish, 629: 141.3 x 31.6 x 18.2	Roosevelt, Joyce & Co., New York	Gordon, Talbot & Co., New York
Florence, Philip Dumaresq, 1045.21: 171.7 x 36.6 x 22.6	Samuel Hall, East Boston	J. M. & R. B. Forbes, Boston (Sold British 1862. *Hypatia* Lost, 1887)
Flying Mist, E. B. Linnell, 1183: 200 o.a. x 39 x 24	Jas. O. Curtis, Medford	Theodore & Geo. B. Chase, Boston. (Lost Bluff Harbor, New Zealand, Aug. 26, 1862)
Glad Tidings, Horatio Nelson, 898: 163.8 x 34.6 x 22	Roosevelt, Joyce & Co., New York	Wm. Nelson & Son, New York
Hesperus, John Lewin, 1019.73: 176 x 35.5 x 24	J. T. Foster, Medford	Thos. B. Wales & Co., Boston (Burned at Woosung, 1861)
Intrepid, E. C. Gardner, 1173.45: 179.9 x 37.8 x 23	Wm. H. Webb, New York	Bucklin & Crane, New York (Lost on Belvidere Reef, 1860)

SHIP, MEASUREMENTS AND MASTER	PLACE AND DATE OF CONSTRUCTION	OWNER
Joseph Peabody, Edward Weston, 1198.2 : 184 x 37.6 x 24	E. & H. O. Briggs, South Boston	Curtis & Peabody, Boston (Sold British, 1863—Listed 1874 bk. *Dagmar*)
King Philip, Gardner, 1194: 182 x 36.6 x 24	D. Weymouth, Alna, Me.	Glidden & Williams, Boston (Agents)
Logan, Eleazer C. Taylor, 1541.5: 207 x 40 x 26.7	Geo. Thomas, Quincy	Wm. Whitlock, Jr., New York
Mary Bangs, Somes, 958 : 177 x 36 x 23	Paul Curtis, East Boston	W. H. Bangs & Co., Boston (Wrecked near Altata, Mex., 1874)
Mary L. Sutton, P. E. Rowland, 1448: 216 o.a. 192 x 40.8 x 23	Chas. H. Mallory	Chas. H. Mallory (Lost Baker's Island, Nov. 20, 1864)
Mastiff, Wm. O. Johnson, 1030.70 168.10 x 36.6 x 22	D. McKay, East Boston	Warren Delano, New York (Burned 5 days out of San Francisco Sept. 10, 1859)
Minnehaha, Beauchamp, 1698: 209 x 41.10 x 28.4	D. McKay, East Boston	R. W. Cameron & Co., New York (Agents)
Norseman, Haskell, 812	Robt. E. Jackson, East Boston	Cunningham Bros. & Co., Boston (Sold Siam, 1863)
Orpheus, Laban Howes, 1272: 200 o.a. x 42 x 23 1067 new: 191 x 38 x 21	Rice & Mitchell, Chelsea, Mass.	W. F. Weld & Co., Boston (Wrecked Nov., 1875, near Puget Sound)
Reynard, Drew, 1051: 182.6 x 37 x 23	Geo. W. Jackman, Newburyport	Bush & Comstock, Boston (Sold 1871 to D. D. Kelly, Boston—Listed 1886)
Rising Sun, Orr, 1310: 207 x 39 x 27	G. Skolfield, Brunswick, Me.	G. Skolfield & Co.
Bk. *Roebuck*, Anthony Chase, 455.77: 135 x 27 x 14.6	Thos. Collyer, New York	Reynolds & Cushman, New York
Seaman's Bride, A. B. Wyman, 758.43: 139.3 x 32.1 x 16.6	Carter & Co., Belfast, Me.	Enoch Benner, Daniel Lewis, et al, Boston
Silver Star, Thomas F. Wade, 1195.29: 184 x 37.6 x 24	J. O. Curtis, Medford	Reed & Wade, later S. G. Reed & Co. (Lost Jarvis Island, 1860)

SHIP, MEASUREMENTS AND MASTER	PLACE AND DATE OF CONSTRUCTION	OWNER
Sportsman, Wm. Thompson, 626.3: 142.2 x 31 x 21	Belfast, Me.	J. Pierce & Co., Boston, R. W. Cameron & Co., New York, Agts.
Stephen R. Mallory, G. J. Lester, 959: 164 x 35 x 23	Bowne & Curry, Key West	Benner & Brown, New York
Thatcher Magoun, Alexander Baxter, 1248: 190 x 40 x 24	Hayden & Cudworth, Medford	T. Magoun & Son, Boston (Sold Nor. about 1874—Lost off Africa early '80's)
Uncowah, N. Kirby, Jr., 988.21: 169 x 35.8 x 22	Wm. H. Webb, New York	Wakeman, Dimon & Co., New York (Sold Peru, 1865— Burned 1870 in Pacific)
Webfoot, Milton P. Hedge, 1091: 180 x 37.6 x 22	Shiverick Bros., East Dennis	Prince S. Crowell, et al, Boston (Stranded at Dunkirk April 8, 1864 and sold British— Beached and broke up Cape Flattery, Nov., 1886)
Witch of the Wave, Bachelder, 1020: 190 x 33.2 x 22.1	Geo. Raynes & Son, Portsmouth, N. H.	Messrs. Titcomb and Chas. H. Coffin, Newburyport

1857

SHIP, MEASUREMENTS AND MASTER	PLACE AND DATE OF CONSTRUCTION	OWNER
Bk. *Dawn*, Levi B. Chase, 387: 126 x 27.10 x 12.1	Thos. Collyer, New York	Geo. Savory, et al, New York (U. S. Government in 1863)
Belle of the Sea, Christopher Lewis, 1255: 189.4 x 37.7 x 23.6	Ewall & Dutton, Marblehead	T. B. Waters & Co., Boston— Later Edward Kimball, Wenham (Sold Liverpool, 1864)
Belvidere, Isaac N. Jackson, 1321.58: 189 x 38 x 24.3	Paul Curtis, Boston	Richard Baker, Jr., Wm. F. Weld, et al, Boston
Fortuna, Hanson, 659: 147.8 x 31.2 x 20.9	Paul Curtis, East Boston	Israel Lombard & Co., Boston
Bk. *Gemsbok*, Simeon Mayo, 622.11: 141.7 x 31 x 17	R. E. Jackson, East Boston	E. I. Cleveland, et al, Boston
Hotspur, Potter, 862: 154.9 x 35 x 20	Roosevelt & Joyce, New York	Frank Hathaway, et al, New Bedford (Lost on Paracels Reef, 1863)
Richard Busteed, Daniel S. Stanwood, 661.92: 148.8½ x 31.1 x 21	Emery Sawyer, Quincy Pt., Mass.	Jacob Stanwood, Boston

SHIP, MEASUREMENTS AND MASTER	PLACE AND DATE OF CONSTRUCTION	OWNER
Twilight, Gurdon Gates, 1482: 196 x 40.4 x 22.7	Chas. Mallory, Mystic	Gates & Co., Mystic (Condemned at San Francisco 1877—Sold Mystic 1863 and later in 1864 to Peru)
Victory, James Ainsworth, 1313.65: 180 x 40	Currier & Townsend, Newburyport	David Ogden, et al, New York
Bk. *Wild Gazelle*, John Humphrey, 490.22: 133.8½ x 28.3 x 17.6	James O. Curtis, Medford	Joshua W. Davis, Boston Alpheus Hardy, et al

1858

Industry, Robt. H. Waters, 1106: 180 x $37\frac{4}{10}$ x $23\frac{8}{10}$	J. O. Curtis, Medford	Theo. Chase, Boston
Memnon, Perez Jenkins, 789.34: 158.3 x 32.11 x 23	E. & H. O. Briggs, South Boston	E. & H. O. Briggs, Henry S. Hallet, Oliver Eldridge, et al, Boston
Prima Donna, John S. Pray, 1529: 203.6 x 42 x 24	Greenman & Co., Mystic	John A. McGaw, New York— U. S. Government during war. 1875—Chas. Mallory (Sold Austrian 1883)
Sirius, Poope, 851: 165 x 34.2 x 19	Cooper & Butler, Baltimore	Sold to Bremen
Star of Peace, F. M. Hinckley, 941	N. Currier, Jr., Newburyport	Chas. Hill & Co., & M. Davenport, Boston (Burned by *Florida*, 1863)
Templar, Martin, 946 new: 160 x 32 x 23	J. T. Foster, Medford	T. B. Wales & Co., Boston

1859

Haze, Forsyth, 862 *new:* 151 x 34 x 21.8 18.6 draft	C. Mallory, Mystic	C. Mallory, Mystic
Maid of the Sea, D. S. Stanwood, 661: 155 x 30.2 x 21.6	M. Simpson, Bath, Me.	Jacob Stanwood, et al, Boston
Shooting Star (2nd), L. H. Drinkwater, 947: 182 x 36.6 x 23.6	Geo. Raynes, Portsmouth, N. H.	Reed, Wade & Co., Boston (Burned by Chickamauga, Oct. 31, 1863)

APPENDIX II

AUSTRALIAN PASSAGES

Liverpool to Melbourne   63 days

James Baines—Captain Charles McDonnell. Arrived at anchor Hobson's Bay (inner harbor) Feb. 12, 1855, from Liverpool Dec. 10, 1854. Spoken off Rock Light near Liverpool, Dec. 11. Reported she was held by head wind and did not clear the land (Irish Channel) until Dec. 16, and ran from land to land (Cape Otway) in less than 58 days, the record.

Melbourne to Liverpool   63 days

Lightning—James N. Forbes. Arrived Liverpool October 23, 1854, taking her pilot the 22nd from Melbourne August 20, in 63 days pilot to pilot and 64 days, 3 hours port to port. (N. Y. H., November 13, 1854.)

New York to Melbourne   70 days

Mandarin—J. W. C. Perit. Arrived at Melbourne March 1, 1856, from New York. December 21, 1855, in 70 days. (See log.)

Liverpool to Melbourne   71 days

Young America—D. S. Babcock. Arrived June 29, 1858, from Liverpool April 18th in 71 days. (The Argus [Melbourne], June 30, 1858.)

New York to Melbourne   74 days, 8 hours

Panama—W. P. Cave. Arrived at Melbourne July 10, 1856, from New York. (N. Y. H., November 3, 1856.)

Equator to Melbourne   44 days

Red Jacket—Milwood. From London September 20, 1855. Arrived at Melbourne, December 4th, reporting 44 days from Atlantic Equator to Melbourne. (N. Y. H., April 8, 1856.)

London (Downs) to Port Phillip   66 days
   North Wind—W. S. Morton.   Downs, November 10, 1859.
Port Philip, January 15, 1860.   (N. Y. H., April 24, 1860.)

Sydney to Hampton Roads   75 days
   Flying Dragon—Horace H. Watson, Jr.   Arrived Hampton
Roads October 28, 1860.   Seventy-five days from Sydney.   (N.
Y. H., November 2, 1860.)

Anjier to Melbourne   21 days
   Whistler—Charles H. Brown.   Passed Anjier April 24 and
arrived at Melbourne May 15, 1855, in 21 days.   (N. Y. H.,
August 25, 1855.)

Rio Janeiro to Port Phillip   36 days
   Bk. *Nimrod*.   Nichols.   Arrived at Port Phillip August 21,
1853, in 36 days, from Rio Janeiro.   (N. Y. H., November 18,
1853.)

CALIFORNIA PASSAGES

San Francisco to Boston   76 days, 6 hours
   Northern Light—Freeman Hatch.   Arrived Boston May 29,
from San Francisco March 13, 1853, in 76 days, 6 hours.   (See
log.)

San Francisco to Philadelphia   82 days
   Messenger—Frank Smith.   Arrived at the Delaware Capes
January 23, and at Philadelphia January 26, 1854, from San
Francisco, 82 days.   (N. Y. H., January 27, 1854.)

Round trip between New York and San Francisco   195 days
   Contest—Wm. Brewster.   Sailed from New York November
16, 1852, remained at San Francisco 15 days and arrived back at
New York May 30, 1853, in the net sailing time of 180 days.
(N. Y. H., June 1, 1853.)

Round trip between New York and San Francisco
                                                6 months, 24 days
   Flying Dutchman—Ashbel Hubbard.   Arrived New York
May 8, 1853, having gone to San Francisco and back in 6 months,
24 days, including detention in port.   (N. Y. H., May 9, 1853.)

New York to Equator   15 days, 19 hours
    Great Republic—Joseph Limeburner. Sailed from New York,
December 7, 1856, crossed the Line December 23, in 15 days, 19
hours, the record.   (Monthly Nautical Magazine, 1857, vol. 7,
page 363.)
New York to Equator
    Tinqua—J. D. Whitmore. From New York, November 24,
1852, for San Francisco. Reported December 7th in latitude 2.33
North, longitude 31.10 West, having run to within 153 miles of
the Equator in 13 days. (N. Y. H., February 2, 1853.)
            NOTE: Captain Clark's report of a run of the *Stag*
        Hound in 1858 from Boston to the Equator in 13 days was
        probably due to a misprint, as the run in question appears
        to have occupied 18 days.
San Francisco to Equator   12 days
    Comet—E. C. Gardner. Sailed from San Francisco and dis-
charged pilot 6 P. M., February 13, 1853. Crossed the Line
February 25, approximately 11½ days out. (See log.)
San Francisco to Equator   12 days
    Flying Dutchman—Ashbel Hubbard. Sailed from San Fran-
cisco for New York, discharging pilot at 7 P. M., February 12,
1853. Crossed the Equator during the early part of February
24th, in 12 days. (See log.)
San Francisco to Equator   13½ days
    Comet—E. C. Gardner. Leaving San Francisco December 27,
1853, for New York. Ran to the Equator in 13½ days. (N. Y.
H., March 15, 1854.)
Equator to San Francisco   12 days
    Comet—Arquit. Arrived San Francisco February 25, 1856,
reporting 122 days and 12 days from the Line. (N. Y. H.,
March 28, 1856.)
Equator to San Francisco   14 days
    Seaman—Myrick. Arrived at San Francisco March 10, 1851,
from New York and 14 days from the Line. (N. Y. H., April 22,
1851.)
50 South Pacific to the Equator   15½ days
    Meteor—Melville. Arrived at San Francisco July 23, 1859.

reporting 15 ½ days from 50 South Pacific to the Equator. (N. Y. H., August 20, 1859.)

Equator to New York   15 days

    Comet—E. C. Gardner. Arrived New York March 14, 1854, from San Francisco in 15 days from Equator crossing. (N. Y. C. A., March 15, 1854.)

Equator to New York   16 days

    Swordfish—H. N. Osgood. Arrived at New York March 2, 1860, in 81 days from Shanghae and 16 days from the Line. (N. Y. H., March 4, 1860.)

New York to San Francisco   89 days, 4 hours

    Andrew Jackson—John E. Williams. Arrived at pilot ground, San Francisco, 4 P M., March 23, 1860, from Sandy Hook, New York, December 25, 1859, at noon, in 89 days, 4 hours, Sandy Hook to pilot station. (See log.)

New York to San Francisco   89 days, 8 hours

    Flying Cloud—Josiah Cressy. Arrived San Francisco night of April 20, 1854, from anchor at New York, 12 noon, January 21, in 89 days, 8 hours. As the time she arrived during the night of April 20, is not at present ascertainable, it is uncertain whether the reported passage is from anchor to anchor or not. She does not appear to have been in sight off the coast at sun down, the 20th, 89 days, 6 hours from her anchor in New York, although further information on this point may come to light.

New York to San Francisco   89 days, 21 hours

    Flying Cloud. Josiah P. Cressy. Arrived San Francisco August 31, 1851, from New York, June 2, 1851, in 89 days, 21 hours, anchor to anchor. (See log.)

San Francisco to New York   76 days

    Comet—E. C. Gardner. Arrived New York March 14, 1854, from San Francisco December 27, in 76 days, 7 hours, from wharf to anchor at Sandy Hook. (N. Y. C. A., March 15, 1854.)

San Francisco to New York   78 days

    Bald Eagle—Caldwell. Arrived New York May 19, 1854, from San Francisco in 78 days. (N. Y. C. A., May 20, 1854.)

San Francisco to New York

    David Crockett—P. E. Rowland. Arrived New York January 16, 1860, from San Francisco October 15, 1859, 93 days. (N. Y. C. A., January 17, 1860.)

San Francisco to New York   83 days

Andrew Jackson—John E. Williams. Arrived New York August 21, 1859, 83 days from San Francisco. (N. Y. H., August 22, 1859.)

Rio Janeiro to San Francisco   67 days

Hurricane—Samuel Very, Jr. Arrived at San Francisco April 15, 1852, from Rio Janeiro February 8, in 67 days. (See log.)

San Francisco to Rio Janeiro   58 days

John Bertram—Frederick Lendholm. Arrived at Rio Janeiro September 2, 1851, from San Francisco July 5, in 58 days. (N. Y. H., October 19, 1851.)

Rio Janeiro to San Francisco   62 days

Witchcraft—Wm. C. Rogers. Arrived at San Francisco August 11, 1851, from New York via Rio Janeiro June 10, in 62 days, the record. (N. Y. H., September 21, 1851.)

Rio Janeiro to San Francisco   65 days

Spitfire—John Arey. Arrived San Francisco February 20, 1854, from Rio Janeiro December 16, 1853, in 65 days. Said never to have been beaten by any loaded ship except *Witchcraft*. (N. Y. H., March 26, 1854.)

San Francisco to Cape Horn   35½ days

Comet—E. C. Gardner. Leaving San Francisco December 27, 1853, for New York, ran to Cape Horn in 35½ days, the record. (N. Y. C. A., March 15, 1854.)

San Francisco to Cape Horn   38 days

Messenger—Frank Smith. At Philadelphia January 26, 1854, from San Francisco. Reported 38 days from San Francisco to Horn. (N. Y. H., January 29, 1854.)

San Francisco to Cape Horn   38 days

Northern Light—Freeman Hatch. Left San Francisco March 13, 1853, passed Cape Horn April 20th. (See log.)

Cape Horn to Chesapeake Bay   37 days

Flying Mist—Eben H. Linnell. Arrived at New Point, Chesapeake Bay October 13, 1857, from Caldera, Chile, August 23, in 51 days, and reporting 37 days from Cape Horn. (N. Y. H., February 9, 1859.)

NORTH PACIFIC TO NORTH ATLANTIC PORTS

Lahaina to New Bedford   89 days

Elizabeth F. Willets—Gates. Arrived New Bedford March 3, 1860, 89 days from Lahaina, claimed as the record. (N. Y. H., March 7, 1860.)

Honolulu to New York   82 days

N. B. Palmer—Charles P. Low. Arrived New York, July 14, 1854, in 82 days from Honolulu. (Morning Courier [N. Y.], July 15, 1854.)

INDIA PASSAGES

New York to Bombay   74 days

Sweepstakes—George E. Lane. Arrived at Bombay July 22, 1857, from New York May 9th, in 74 days, the record. (N. Y. H., September 15, 1857.)

New York to Bombay   77 days

Jacob Bell—Charles F. W. Behm. Arrived off Bombay in a fog June 1, 1856, from New York, March 16th, in 77 days. (See log.)

New York to Bombay   81 days

Flying Scud—Rodney Baxter. Arrived at Bombay, July 4, 1856, from New York April 14th, in 81 days. (N. Y. C. A., August 28, 1856.)

Bombay to New York   81 days

Sweepstakes—George Lane. Arrived New York March 21, 1858, from Bombay December 30, 1857, in 81 days, the record. (N. Y. C. A., March 22, 1858.)

Calcutta to Boston   81 days

Witch of the Wave—Benjamin Tay. Arrived Boston July 3, 1853, from Saugor April 13th in 81 days, the record. (See log.)

Calcutta to Boston.   82 days

Staffordshire—Josiah Richardson. Anchored at Boston 9 A. M. April 20, 1853, from Saugor 8 P. M., January 26th, reported 82 days. (See log.)

Calcutta to New York   85 days
    Webfoot—Hedge. Arrived New York March 21, 1859, 85 days from Sand Heads. (N. Y. C. A., March 22, 1859.)
Boston to Calcutta   85 days, 16½ hours
    Beverly—Chase. Took pilot November 23, 1857, off Sand Heads at 11.30 A. M., from Boston Light 7 P. M. August 30, in 85 days, 16½ hours from pilot to pilot. (See log.)
Calcutta to Boston   88 days
    John Land—Warren H. Bearse. Arrived Boston February 24, 1857, from Saugor November 28, 1856, in 88 days. (N. Y. H., February 24, 1857.)
Boston to Calcutta   86 days, 21½ hours
    Nor'Wester—Frank O. Eldridge. Arrived off Sand Heads midnight September 17, 1855, from Boston Light, 3.30 A. M., June 23, in 86 days, 21½ hours. (See log.)
Lizard (Eng.) to Calcutta   80 days
    Typhoon—Samuel Goodhue. From Deal, May 13, 1854, reported 80 days from the Lizard to Sand Heads. (N. Y. H., October 20, 1854.)
Calcutta to Liverpool   77 days
    James Baines—Charles McDonnell. Arrived Liverpool April 16, 1858, from Sand Heads, 77 days. (See log.)
Calcutta to England   79 days
    Hurricane—Samuel Very, Jr. Took pilot off Falmouth April 2, 1856, from Sand Heads, January 10th, 83 days out and "79 sailing days." (See log.)
England to Calcutta   84 days
    Hurricane—Samuel Very, Jr. Arrived at Sand Heads November 5, 1855, from off Portsmouth, where pilot was dropped August 12, in 84 days 12 hours, pilot to pilot. (See log.)

INDIAN OCEAN

Calcutta to Cape of Good Hope   37 days
    Witch of the Wave—Benjamin Tay. Sailed from Saugor April 13, 1853, and passed the Cape of Good Hope May 20th in 37 days, a record. (See log.)

Anjier to Cape of Good Hope   25 days

    Kathay—Thomas C. Stoddard. Arrived New York January 8, 1856, from Shanghae 93 days, reporting 25 days from Anjier to Cape of Good Hope. (N. Y. H., January 9, 1856.)

    (Equalled by *Sea Witch* and several others.)

Anjier to Cape of Good Hope   25 days

    Young America—David S. Babcock. Passed Cape of Good Hope October 30, 1858, from Anjier October 5th. (N. Y. H., December 14, 1858.)

Java Head to Cape of Good Hope   26 days

    Ino—Plummer. On a 91 day voyage from Woosung to New York. Ran from Java Head December 14, 1858, to Cape of Good Hope January 9, 1859, 26 days. (N. Y. C. A., February 21, 1859.)

MANILLA PASSAGES

Manilla to New York   84 days

    Wizard—Woodside. Manilla January 11, 1861. Arrived at New York April 5, in 84 days, the record. (N. Y. H., April 6, 1861.)

    Manilla to Boston   86 days

    Fearless—Nehemiah Manson. Arrived Boston May 21, 1855, from Manilla February 24, in 86 days. (N. Y. H., May 23, 1855.)

Manilla to Boston   90 days

    John Bertram—Frederick Lendholm. Arrived Boston January 30, 1855, from Manilla, November 1, 1854, in 90 days. (N. Y. C. A., February 1, 1855.)

Cape of Good Hope to New York   38 days

    Courser—Wm. Cole. Arrived New York December 30, 1852, from Canton and 38 days from the Cape of Good Hope, passing that point November 22nd. (N. Y. H., December 31, 1852.)

Cape of Good Hope to New York   36 days

    N. B. Palmer—Higham. Arrived New York January 16, 1859, from Shanghae and longitude of Cape of Good Hope December 11, 1859, 36 days from the Cape. (N. Y. H., January 17, 1859.)

TRANSATLANTIC PASSAGES—EASTWARD

New York to Liverpool   15 days, 16 hours

New York—George Maxwell. Arrived Liverpool morning of January 1, 1824, from New York December 16, 1823, in 15 days, 16 hours from city to city. (N. Y. C. A., February 14, 1824.)

Boston to Liverpool   12 days, 6 hours

James Baines—Charles McDonnell. Arrived Rock Light, Liverpool, September 25, 1854, from Boston September 12, in 12 days, 6 hours from Boston Light to Rock Light.

New York to Liverpool   13 days

Red Jacket—Asa Eldridge. Arrived Liverpool January 23, 1854, from New York January 11, in 13 days, 1 hour, 25 minutes, dock to dock. (N. Y. H., February 11, 1854.)

Baltimore to English Channel   12 days

Mary Whitridge—Robert B. Cheesebrough. From Baltimore June 20, 1855, for Helvoet. Landed passengers in England in less than 12½ days from the Chesapeake. (N. Y. H., August 6, 1855.)

(Distance considered probably best run across the Atlantic ever made.)

Portsmouth, N. H., to Liverpool   13½ days

Typhoon—Charles H. Salter. Arrived Liverpool in the early morning March 26, 1851, from Portsmouth March 12, in 13½ days port to port. Was off Holyhead, detained by fog, in less than 13 days. (N. Y. H., April 11, 1851.)

New York to Falmouth, England   13 days, 12 hours

Southampton—E. E. Morgan. Arrived Falmouth June 22, 1850, from Sandy Hook, 11 P. M., June 8, in 13 days, 12 hours. (London Ship Gazette, July 2, 1850.)

New York to Liverpool   14 days, 8 hours

Memnon—Gordon. New York, November 6, 1848, to pilot off Pt. Lynas night of November 20th, at 12.30 o'clock, 14 days, 8 hours. (N. Y. H., January 24, 1853.)

Savannah, Ga., to Cork   14 days, 9 hours
   Phœnix—John Hoxie. Arrived Cork January 24, 1859, in 14 days, 9 hours from Savannah. (N. Y. H., February 20, 1859.)

New York to Liverpool   14 days, 12 hours
   Independence—Ezra Nye. Just returned from Liverpool, made her outward passage in 14½ days. (N. Y. C. A., June 15, 1836.)

Hampton Roads to Liverpool   15 days
   Sierra Nevada—Penhallow. Arrived at Liverpool April 11, 1855, in 15 days from the Chesapeake. (N. Y. H., April 30, 1855.)

Charleston, S. C., to Liverpool   16 days
   Caroline—Conner. Arrived at Liverpool July 18, 1853, from Charleston, July 2, at 12.20 P. M., in 16 days. (Charleston Mercury, August 10, 1853.) Not noted by Liverpool papers.

Boston to Gibraltar   14 days
   Bk. *Wildfire*—Mosman. From Boston May 13, 1853. Passed Gibraltar in 14 days, the record. (N. Y. H., July 10, 1853.)

New York to Marseilles   19 days, 20 hours
   Flying Scud—Rodney Baxter. Arrived Marseilles January 9, 1856, from New York December 20, 1855, in 19 days, 20 hours. (N. Y. H., February 5, 1856.)

TRANSATLANTIC PASSAGES—WESTWARD

Liverpool to New York   16 days
   Yorkshire—D. G. Bailey. Arrived off Sandy Hook November 17, 1846, and at the city at noon the 18th, from Liverpool November 2, in a passage of less than 16 days. (N. Y. H., November 19, 1846.)

Liverpool to New York   15 days
   Andrew Jackson—Johnson. Arrived Sandy Hook, N. Y., November 18, 1860, from Liverpool November 3rd, in 15 days. (N. Y. H., November 20, 1860.)

Portsmouth to New York   15 days, 18 hours
   Columbia—J. C. Delano. Arrived at Sandy Hook, N. Y., night of April 16, 1830, from Portsmouth, England, at noon April 1, in 15 days, 18 hours. (N. Y. C. A., April 19, 1830.)

Liverpool to New Orleans   26 days
    Unicorn—Spring of 1824, 26 days. (N. Y. E. P., April 29, 1824.)   Beaten several times by later ships.

TRANSPACIFIC PASSAGES

Honolulu to Hong Kong   19 days
    Memnon—Joseph Gordon. Arrived at Hong Kong December 16, 1850, a few hours over 19 days from Honolulu. (N. Y. H., March 8, 1851.)
    (The above run was equalled by the *Red Gauntlet* April 24 to May 14, 1856.)
        NOTE: On the run of the R. B. Forbes over the same course in 1852 in 21 days 13 hours Captain Justus Doane made his distance 5400 miles, averaging over 250 miles per day. (N. Y. H., May 6, 1852.)
Coast of Japan to San Francisco   20 days
    Golden West—Putnam. Arrived at San Francisco June 2, 1856, from the coast of Japan May 13, having averaged above 243 miles per day for 20 days. (N. Y. H., May 6, 1852.)
Hong Kong to San Francisco   33 days
    Challenge—John Land. Arrived San Francisco April 22, 1852, in 33 days from Hong Kong. (N. Y. H., June 4, 1852.)
    (On this run the *Challenge* was 18 days from opposite Japan, a record.)
Shanghae to San Francisco   34 days
    Schooner *Sierra Nevada*—L. B. Edwards. Early in 1851 ran from Shanghae to San Francisco in 34 days, averaging 7½ knots for the trip. (N. Y. H., March 21, 1851.)
San Francisco to Shanghae   32 days
    Swordfish—Charles Collins. Anchored off the port July 19, 1853, from San Francisco June 16th, 32 days, 9 hours out.
        (NOTE: *Celestial*, Palmer, was reported as arriving at Hong Kong in 1852 in 33 days from San Francisco, but it has been impossible to verify this. She cleared at San Francisco March 6th for Hong Kong and was next reported at Shanghae April 22nd, 1852.)

San Francisco to Woosung   36 days

Golden City—Richard Canfield. Arrived Woosung April 5, from San Francisco February 28, in 36 days. (N. Y. H., June 28, 1854.)

San Francisco to Whampoa   36 days

Memnon—Gordon. San Francisco November 9, 1850, Canton December 15th, 36 days. (N. Y. H., January 24, 1853.)

San Francisco to Shanghae   43 days

Bk. *Gallego*—Thos. M. Johnson. Arrived Shanghae October 26, 1850, from San Francisco September 13, in 43 days, then called the shortest time known. (N. Y. C. A., February 20, 1851.)

San Francisco to Singapore   43 days

Onward—E. A. Luce. Arrived Singapore December 15, 1856, from San Francisco, 43 days. Stated to be a record. (Singapore Times, December 23, 1856.)

   Note: Apparently the shortest passage across the Pacific was that of the barque *Mermaid*, which arrived at San Francisco August 23, 1865, from Shanghae, reporting 31 days. (N. Y. H., August 30, 1865.)

San Francisco to Honolulu   8 days, 8½ hours

Flying Cloud—Josiah Creesy. From San Francisco September 26, 1852, passed Honolulu 8 days, 8½ hours out. (N. Y. H., February 10, 1853.)

San Francisco to Honolulu   9 days, 22 hours

Flying Eagle—Bates. Arrived at Honolulu July 19, 1858, from San Francisco July 9, in 9 days, 22 hours. (N. Y. H., August 12 and September 13, 1858.)

San Francisco to Honolulu   10 days

Hurricane—Samuel Very, Jr. Passed Honolulu September 30, 1854, in 10 days from San Francisco. (N. Y. C. A., November 25, 1854.)

San Francisco to Calcutta   56 days

Southern Cross—Levi Stevens. Arrived Sand Heads, December 25, 1851, in 56 days, net, from San Francisco. (N. Y. H., March 5, 1852.)

Sydney to Valparaiso   31 days
   Rover's Bride—Arrived at Valparaiso June 18, 1855, reporting 31 days from Sydney. (N. Y. H., August 12, 1855.)
Melbourne to Valparaiso   32 days
   Carrier Dove—Corner. Arrived Valparaiso October 23, 1856, from Melbourne, 32 days. (N. Y. H., December 15, 1856.)
Port Phillip to Callao   35 days
   Bk. *Gem of the Sea*—Bowden. Reported a run of 35 days early in 1854 from Port Phillip to Callao, and an average of 242 miles for 22 successive days. (Portland, Me., Advt., May 2, 1854.)
     NOTE: *Challenge.* Land reported run from San Francisco to Honolulu in 8 days in 1852, and from San Francisco to within 400 miles of Hong Kong in 27 days.)

SOUTH AMERICAN PASSAGES

New York to Rio Janeiro (off port)   23 days
   Phantom—Alvin H. Hallett. Sailed from Boston January 6, 1853, and passed Rio Janeiro on the 23rd day out. (N. Y. H., May 26, 1853.)
Rio Janeiro to Delaware Capes   23 days
   Grey Eagle—W. P. Whipple. Arrived at Quarantine below Philadelphia, June 9, 1852, from Rio Janeiro May 17, in 23 days. (See log.)
Rio Janeiro to Philadelphia   25 days
   Courier—Olmstead. Arrived at Philadelphia June 29, 1859, 25 days from Rio Janeiro. (N. Y. H., June 30, 1859.)
New York to Rio Janeiro   29 days
   Snow Squall—Gerard. Arrived Rio Janeiro March 21, 1856, from New York the afternoon of February 21st, in 29 days. (N. Y. H., May 13, 1856.)
Lat. 36 S. Atlantic (S. E. of Montevideo) to New York   27 days
   Warner—Luther Ripley, Jr. Arrived New York July 9, 1853, in 67 days from Valparaiso, reported 27 days from lat. 36 South Atlantic. (N. Y. H., July 11, 1853.)
Buenos Ayres to New York   36 days
   Cl. Bk. *Dawn*—Chase. Arrived New York at 2.00 A. M., June 11, 1860, 36 days from Buenos Ayres. Distance 6500 miles.

Average, 180 miles per day. Said to be a record. (N. Y. H., June 12, 1860.)

Callao to Rio Janeiro   32 days

Phantom—Alvin H. Hallett. Arrived at Rio Janeiro in distress October 18, 1853, in 32 days from Callao. (N. Y. H., December 24, 1853.)

Talcahuano to New York   50 days

Wild Pigeon—P. N. Mayhew. Arrived New York April 28, 1860, 50 days from Talcahuano, the record. (N. Y. H., April 29, 1860.)

Pisagua, Peru, to New York   51 days

Wild Pigeon—P. N. Mayhew. Arrived at New York October 21, 1858, from Pisagua August 31, 51 days. (N. Y. H., October 22, 1858.)

Caldera, Chili, to Chesapeake Bay   51 days

Flying Mist—Arrived New Point, Chesapeake Bay, October 13, 1857, from Caldera August 23, in 51 days and 37 days from Cape Horn. (N. Y. H., February 9, 1859.)

Chincha Islands to Hampton Roads   52 days

Defiance—John Kendrick. Arrived at Hampton Roads April 20, 1855, from Chincha Islands February 27, in 52 days. (N. Y. H., April 26, 1855.)

Callao to Hampton Roads   58 days

Panama—Girard. Arrived Hampton Roads January 19, 1854, and at New York on the 25th of January in a passage of 6 days from Hampton Roads. (N. Y. H., January 26, 1854.)

Valparaiso to Boston   58 days

Telegraph—G. W. Pousland. Arrived Boston August 20, 1853, from Valparaiso June 20th, in a passage reported as 58 days. (N. Y. H., August 11, 1853; Boston Atlas, August 21, 1853.)

Callao to New York   58 days

Ocean Telegraph—George H. Willis. Arrived New York June 25, 1855, from Callao April 28, in 58 days. (N. Y. H., June 26, 1855.)

Callao to New York   61 days

Andrew Jackson—John E. Williams. Arrived New York August 21, 1860, from Callao, June 21, 1860. (See log.)

Callao to Hampton Roads   60 days
    Adelaide—Wakeman. Arrived New York November 14,
1859, 60 days from Callao. (N. Y. H., November 17, 1859.)

Talcahuano, Chile, to Boston   61 days
    Magellan—J. H. Millet. Arrived Boston May 28 from Talca-
huano March 28, 1850, in 61 days, and from land to land in 59
days. (B. A., May 29, 1850.)

Chincha Islands to Hampton Roads   64 days
    Edwin Forrest—Crocker. Arrived at Hampton Roads No-
vember 22, 1857, in 64 days from Chinchas. (N. Y. H., November 23, 1857.)

New York to Valparaiso   59 days
    Sea Witch—George Fraser. Arrived Valparaiso June 11,
1850, from New York April 13th, in 59 days. (N. Y. H., August
7, 1850.)

New York to Valparaiso   62 days
    Eclipse—Joseph Hamilton, at Valparaiso prior to March 13,
1852, from New York, January 5th, reporting 62 days' passage.
(N. Y. H., April 17, 1852.)

San Francisco to Callao   33 days
    Hornet—Wm. Knapp. Arrived at Callao October 7, 1853,
from San Francisco September 4, in slightly more than 33 days.
(See log.)

Valparaiso to San Francisco   34 days
    Telegraph—Kimball Harlow. Arrived at San Francisco
April 16, 1854, in 34 days from Valparaiso. (S. F. Daily Herald,
April 18, 1854.)

San Francisco to Valparaiso   35 days
    Seaman. Myrick. Arrived Valparaiso May 23, 1851, from
San Francisco April 18, in 35 days. (Baltimore Sun, August 21,
1851.)

Montevideo to New York   36 days
    Eagle—J. S. Farren. Arrived New York July 8, 1854, from
Montevideo June 2, in 36 days. (N. Y. C. A., July 10, 1854.)

Montevideo to San Francisco   61 days
    Sparkling Wave—John C. Hubbard, Jr. Arrived San Fran-

cisco April 14, 1855, from Montevideo, reporting 61 days, said to be the record. (N. Y. H., May 14, 1855.)

NOTE: Record from Callao to San Francisco (28 days) made by Rockland built *Rattler,* 1878.

CHINA PASSAGES

Hong Kong to New York   74 days, 14 hours

Sea Witch—Robert Waterman. Arrived New York March 25, 1849, from Hong Kong, January 8, in a passage of 74 days, 14 hours. (The China Mail, January 11, 1849; N. Y. C. A., March 26, 1849.)

Macoa to New York   78 days

Natchez—Robert Waterman. Arrived at New York the morning of April 3, 1845, from Canton and Macoa January 14, in 78 days. (N. Y. C. A., April 4, 1845.)

Hong Kong to New York   79 days

Sea Serpent—J. D. Whitmore. Arrived at New York March 22, 1856, from Hong Kong January 3, in 79 days. (N. Y. C. A., March 24, 1856.)

Hong Kong to New York   82 days

Eagle Wing—Worth. Arrived New York June 3, 1859, 82 days from Hong Kong. (N. Y. H., June 4, 1859.)

New York to Hong Kong   81 days

Oriental—Theo. D. Palmer. Arrived Hong Kong August 8, 1850, from New York May 18, in 81 days. (N. Y. H., November 8, 1850.)

Anjier to New York   62 days

Sea Witch—Robert Waterman. Arrived at New York July 25, 1847, from Canton May 3, in 81 days and 62 days from Anjier, the record. (N. Y. H., July 26, 1847.)

Anjier to New York   67 days

Panama—Wm. P. Cave. Arrived New York January 21, 1855, from Anjier November 15, 1854, in 67 days. (See log.)

New York to Anjier   73 days, 20 hours

Helena—Eyre. Arrived Java Head February 14, 1846, from New York November 1, 1845, in 73 days, 20 hours, the shortest at that time. (N. Y. H., June 9, 1846.)

Anjier to London   69 days

    David Brown—George S. Brewster. Arrived at Gravesend October 28, 1854, from Shanghae July 11, via Anjier August 20, 1854, in 69 days from Anjier with copper torn and cutwater twisted from being aground. (See log.)

Anjier to London (Deal)   65 days

    Challenge—Pitts. From Whampoa August 5, 1852. Arrived Anjier September 13, and arrived at Deal November 18, in 65 days from Anjier, a record.

London (Downs) to Hong Kong   83 days, 12 hours

    Eagle Wing—E. H. Linnell. Left Downs 8 A. M. April 17, 1855. Arrived Hong Kong July 10, in passage of 83 days, 12 hours from pilot 9.30 A. M., April 17, to pilot off Hong Kong. Was anchored inside the Ladrones, becalmed the night of July 9th.

Portsmouth, England, to Anjier   72 days

    Nightingale—Samuel W. Mather. Sailed from Portsmouth February 10, 1853, and passed Anjier April 23, in 72 days, said to be a record then. (N. Y. H., July 10, 1853.)

Liverpool to Hong Kong   84 days

    Comet—E. C. Gardner. Arrived Hong Kong September 9, 1854 (took pilot September 7), from Liverpool June 17, in 84 days, 16 hours, anchor to anchor, and 83 days, 21 hours, pilot to pilot. (The China Mail, September 14, 1854; N. Y. C. A., November 11, 1854.)

New York to Singapore   78 days

    Wizard—S. H. Slate. Arrived Singapore October 27, 1854, from New York August 10, in 78 days. (N. Y. H., January 26, 1855.)

Shanghae to New York   81 days

    Swordfish—Crocker. Shanghae December 12, 1859, to New York March 2, 1860, 81 days, the record. Becalmed on the Equator in the Atlantic 5 days. (N. Y. H., March 4, 1860.)

Shanghae to New York   82 days

    Surprise—Charles Ranlett. Arrived New York March 24, 1857, from Shanghae January 1, in a few hours over 82 days. (See log.)

Shanghae to New York   82 days

N. B. *Palmer*—Higham. Arrived New York January 16, 1859, from Shanghae October 25, 1858, making the run to Sandy Hook in 82 days. (N. Y. C. A., January 17, 1859.)

Woosung to New York   84 days

Eagle Wing—Eben H. Linnell. Arrived New York February 15, 1856, from Woosung November 23, 1855, in 84 days. (N. Y. H., February 20, 1856.)

Shanghae to New York   85 days

Panama—Wm. P. Cave. Arrived New York January 20, 1855, from Shanghae October 27, in 85 days. (See log.)

Shanghae to New York   90 days

Golden State—Barstow. Arrived at New York April 1, 1855, from Shanghae January 1, in 90 days. (N. Y. C. A., April 2, 1855.)

Shanghae to England   86 days

Golden Gate—S. F. Dewing. Arrived off Beachy Head, England, February 23, 1855, from Shanghae November 22nd, 1854, in 86 days, net, having been in collision in the China Sea and losing several days by putting in to Batavia. The record from Shanghae to this point. (N. Y. H., February 17 and March 19, 1855.)

Shanghae to London   91 days

Nightingale—Samuel W. Mather. Arrived off Beachy Head 11 A. M., May 18, 1855, from Shanghae the afternoon of February 16th in 91 days, pilot to pilot. (See log.)

Hong Kong to Bankok   6 days

Kathay—Thomas C. Stoddard. Arrived at Bankok December 31, 1857, from Hong Kong December 24, in a few hours over 6 days, said to be "the quickest run on record." (N. Y. H., March 15, 1858.)

Hong Kong to Singapore

Hurricane—Samuel Very, Jr., November 21 to 27, 1854. Six days, 12 hours, anchor to anchor—an average of slightly less than 10 miles an hour. (See log.)

Shanghae to Anjier   10 days

    Swordfish—Crocker. Shanghae December 12, 1859, to Anjier December 22, 10 days. (N. Y. H., March 4, 1860.)

      NOTE: *Golden Gate*, Dewing, reported 9½ days from Shanghae to Batavia in November, 1854. (N. Y. H., February 17 and March 19, 1855.)

New York to China via San Francisco   126 days

    Flying Cloud—Josiah P. Creesy. Arrived Hong Kong June 7, 1854, from New York, via San Francisco, in 126 sailing days, a record. (N. Y. H., August 27, 1854.)

Round Voyage, between New York and Canton

                                                          6 months 16 days

    Rainbow—John Land. Arrived New York April 16, 1846, in 79 days from Macao, crossing Equator 60 days from Macao. She left New York October 1, 1845, and returned in 6 months and 16 days, the record. (N. Y. C. A., April 16, 1846.)

Since the original publication of this volume in 1930 a number of record passages, day's runs, and hourly rates of speed have come to light, or have been verified, and have been listed in *Five Hundred Sailing Records of American Built Ships*, published by the Marine Historical Association, Inc., Mystic, Connecticut, in 1952. By far the most notable of these is the 465-mile noon-to-noon run of the *Champion of the Seas*, Alexander Newlands, master, made on Dec. 12, 1854, while running her easting down on a voyage from Liverpool to Melbourne. Complete navigational data was furnished by the master and published in the *Champion of the Seas Gazette*, the ship's weekly newspaper. The essential facts reported were as follows:

Noon position by observation:
Dec. 11. Lat. 47.01 S. Long. 88.31 E.
Dec. 12. Lat. 49.58 S. Long. 99.15 E.
Making good a course of S. 67½ E. Distance 465 miles.

The 438-mile noon-to-noon run of the *Marco Polo* was also made on a voyage from Liverpool to Melbourne in 1854, on Jan. 7. An account of the run was published the same day in the weekly *Marco Polo Chronicle*. This run antedated the 436-mile run of the *Lightning* by more than a month.

APPENDIX III

LIST OF 139 VOYAGES MADE BY SHIPS REPORTED AMERICAN,
IN THE CHINA-TO-ENGLAND TRADE BETWEEN
1850 TO 1860, INCLUSIVE

NOTE: Inaccuracies in Far East marine reports and delays in noting transfer of registry of American-built vessels to other flags, may operate to decrease or increase this list very slightly, but it is submitted with the confidence that it offers a substantially accurate record of the trade during the fifties. A number of vessels erroneously reported as American have been eliminated from the list and none reported as foreign have been included, even when built in America. In this and the following appendix, marine reports are occasionally in conflict as to dates of sailing and arrival. Such conflicts rarely appear in important sailings, but where they do, care has been taken to list the date which, everything considered, appears most nearly correct. During the period covered by this abstract a number of other American built ships engaged in the trade under foreign registry.

VOYAGES MADE BY AMERICAN SHIPS FROM CHINA TO ENGLAND IN THE TEA TRADE

1850

SHIP AND MASTER	SAILED	ARRIVED
Jeanette, Ward	Whampoa, Aug. 25	London—Jan. 20, '51
Oriental, Theo. Palmer	Whampoa, Aug. 27 Anjier, Sept. 18	London—Dec. 4, '50
Argonaut, Nott	Whampoa, Aug. 27	London—Jan. 17, '51
Roman, Putnam	Whampoa, Sept. 11 Anjier, Oct. 7	London—Jan. 17, '51
Carlo Mauran, Tillinghast	Canton, Nov. 1	Deal—March 14, '51 London—March 17

SHIP AND MASTER	SAILED	ARRIVED
Mohawk, Morrison	Canton, Nov. 1 Anjier, Nov. 28	Deal—March 14, '51 London—March 17
Wisconsin, Mumford	Whampoa, Dec. 4	London—March 13, '51
Bk. *Nautilus*, Gardner	Whampoa, Dec. 14	London—Aug. 4, '51

1851

Susan G. Owens, Barclay	Hong Kong, Jan. 11	London—May 6, '51
Georgia, Talbot	Hong Kong, Feb. 6	Deal—July 17, '51
Rose Standish, Pearson	Hong Kong, Feb. 11	London—June 13, '51
Far West, Briard	Whampoa, March 8	Downs—Aug. 15, '51 London—Aug. 16
Inca, Goodrich	Hong Kong, March 22	Deal—Aug. 9, '51
Sheridan, Cornish	Canton, March 21 St. Helena, June 12	Deal—Aug. 14, '51 London—Aug. 16
W. H. Harbeck, Shinn	Hong Kong, April 17	Liverpool—Aug. 21, '51
Charles, Andrews	Whampoa, June 30	London—Dec. 10, '51
Oriental, Palmer	Woosung, July 15	London—Nov. 20, '51
Roman, Putnam	Woosung, July 23 Anjier, Sept. 1	Deal—Nov. 28, '51 London—Dec. 1
Surprise, Dumaresq	Whampoa, July 28	Brighton—Nov. 10, '51 London—Nov. 12
Memnon, Gordon	Whampoa, Aug. 16	London—(Lost in Gasper Straits, Sept. 14)
White Squall, Goodwin	Whampoa, Sept. 8 At anchor 2 days off Anjier	Isle of Wight—Dec. 16, '51 London—Dec. 22, '51
Jamestown, Homan	Whampoa—Oct. 13	Deal—Feb. 17, '52—London
Bk. *Green Point*, Wardle	Canton, Nov. 14 Anjier—Dec. 6	London—May 3, '52
Remittance, Mooers	Shanghae, Nov. 15	London—May 3, '52
Bk. *Behring*, Thompson	Canton, Dec. 13	London—April 3, '52
Witch of the Wave, Millet	Canton, Jan. 5 Anjier, Jan. 12	London—April 6, '52

1852

Helen McGaw, Lunt	Canton, Jan. 19 Anjier, Feb. 7	London—May 24, '52
Prescott, Spear	Shanghae, Jan. 25	Liverpool—June 13, '52
Joshua Bates, Easterbrook	Shanghae—Jan. 28	London—June 11, '52

SHIP AND MASTER	SAILED	ARRIVED
Heber, Patterson	Woosung, Feb. 24	Deal—July 22, '52 London—July 23
Telegraph, Harlow (Kimball)	Whampoa, March 29 Anjier, April 21	London—July 20, '52
Bk. *Inca*, Wylie	Canton, March 31 Anjier, May 6	Liverpool—Aug. 30, '52
Celestial, Palmer	Shanghae, May 8 Anjier, May 17	Liverpool—Sept. 22, '52
Versailles, Frost	Shanghae, June 25 St. of Sunda, Sept. 12	Deal—Dec. 9, '52 London—Dec. 13
Bk. *Race Horse*, Porter	Whampoa—July 15 St. of Sunda, Aug. 20	Liverpool—Nov. 17, '52
Surprise, Ranlett	Canton, July 19 Anjier, Aug. 18	Downs—Nov. 2, '52 London—Nov. 3
Nightingale, Fiske	Shanghae, July 31	Deal—Dec. 10, '52 London—Dec. 11
John Bertram, Lendholm	Shanghae, Aug. 3 St. of Sunda, Oct. 18	London—Jan. 10, '53
Challenge, Pitts	Canton, Aug. 5 Anjier, Sept. 12	Deal—Nov. 18, '52 Gravesend—Nov. 19
Eclipse, Hamilton	Shanghae, Aug. 23 Anjier, Oct. 9 St. Helena, Dec. 3	Deal—Jan. 5-6, '53 London—Jan. 10
Invincible, Johnson	Whampoa, Sept. 15 St. of Sunda, Oct. 11 Cape Good Hope, Nov. 17	Gravesend—Jan. 2, '53 London—Jan. 5
Wisconsin, Scott	Shanghae, Oct. 3	London—Feb. 5, '53
Andalusia, Wilson	Shanghae, Oct. 23 St. of Sunda, Nov. 16	London—Feb. 24, '53
Bk. *Kremlin*, Deane	Shanghae, Nov. 19 Anjier, Dec. 15	Deal—April 4, '53 London—April 5

1853

Samuel Appleton, Doane	Shanghae, Feb. 9 Anjier, March 4?	St. Helena—April 22, '53 London—May 31
S. V. Given, Given	Woosung, March 15 (Also given March 11)	London—July 16, '53
Erie, Lewis	Woosung, March 27	London—Aug. 20, '53
Racer, Steele	Shanghae, June 11 Anjier, Aug. 31	Off Scilly—Dec. 2, '53; Deal— Dec. 8; London—Dec. 12
Architect, Potter	Whampoa, June 25	London—Oct. 10, '53

SHIP AND MASTER	SAILED	ARRIVED
Challenge, Pitts	Canton, July 13 St. of Sunda, Aug. 10 Put in Fayal, Oct. 20, very leaky	Deal—Dec. 20, '53 London—
Nightingale, Mather	Woosung, Aug. 8 Anjier—Sept. 11	Deal—Nov. 28, '53 London—

Celestial, Palmer	Foo choo foo—Re-
	  ported there Nov. 4,
	  apparently an error
		London—Jan. 31, '54
		Reported 96 days

Tsar, Schibye	Foo choo foo, Aug. 31 Anjier, Oct. 17	London—Jan. 16, '54
Bk. *Old Hickory*, Potter (late Haskell)	Hong Kong, Sept. 28	Deal—Jan. 30, '54
Torrent, Copp	Woosung, Oct. 6 Anjier, Nov. 8	Deal—Feb. 24, '54 London—Feb. 25
Golden State, Doty	Shanghae, Oct. 24	Deal—Feb. 9, '54; Gravesend— Feb. 12; London—Feb. 13
Typhoon, Salter	Shanghae, Nov. 4 Anjier, Nov. 24	Deal—Feb. 16, '54 London—Feb. 21
Flying Childers, White	Whampoa, Nov. 9 Anjier—Dec. 1	London—Feb. 23, '54
Mystery, Peterson	Shanghae, Nov. 14 Anjier, Dec. 6	Deal—March 14, '54 London—March 15
Argonaut, Hale	Shanghae, Dec. 1 Hong Kong, Dec. 8	London—April 3, '54
Resolute, Perry	Canton, Dec. 8	London—April 4, '54
Vancouver, Lunt	Foo choo foo, Nov. 24 Anjier, Dec. 14	London—March 31, '54
Bk. *Jennett*, Mix	Shanghae, Dec. 15 Hong Kong, Dec. 21 Anjier—Jan. 3, '54	London—April 3, '54
Oriental, Fletcher	Canton, Dec. 22	London—Lost Feb. 25 coming out of River Min

1854

Snow Squall, Bursley	Shanghae, Jan. 6 Anjier—Jan. 18	London—May 5, '54
Flying Dutchman, Hubbard	Canton, Feb. 12 Anjier, March 3	Gravesend—May 24, '54 London—May 25
Onward, Wade	Shanghae, April 11	London—Aug. 28, '54
Romance of the Seas, Dumaresq	Whampoa—June 9 Anjier, July 2	London—Sept. 21, '54
Gravina, Caleb Sprague	Foo choo foo, June 23	Downs—Oct. 23, '54 London—Oct. 25

SHIP AND MASTER	SAILED	ARRIVED
Architect, Potter	Canton, July 9 Anjier—Aug. 13	London—Oct. 30, '54
David Brown, Brewster	Shanghae, July 11 Anjier, Aug. 18	London—Oct. 28, '54
Queen of the East, Bartlett	Shanghae, July 11 Anjier	Deal—Dec. 28, '54 London—Jan. 1, '55
Eagle Wing, Linnell	Foo choo foo, July 31 St. Helena, Oct. 25	Off North foreland—Dec. 4, '54
Lightfoot, Pierce	Whampoa—Aug. 7	Off North foreland—Dec. 2, '54 Gravesend—Dec. 5; London—
Archer, Thomas	Shanghae, Sept. 4	London—Jan. 9, '55
Bk. *Jenny Pitts*, Israel L. Snow	Shanghae, Oct. 17 Anjier, Nov. 12	Gravesend—March 4, '55 London
Cygnet, Booth	Foo choo foo, Nov. 10 Anjier, Dec. 2	London—April 7, '55
Golden Gate, Dewing	Shanghae, Nov. 25 Anjier, Dec. 10	London—Beachy Head—Feb. 23, '55

1855

SHIP AND MASTER	SAILED	ARRIVED
Oracle, Ranlett	Shanghae, Jan. 7 Anjier, Jan. 26	London—May 9, '55
Nightingale, Mather	Shanghae, Feb. 8 Anjier, March 5	Beachy Head—May 18, '55 London—May 21
Rapid, Corning	Shanghae, March 15 Anjier, April 1	London—Deal, July 1, '55
Staghound, Behm	Woosung, April 8	Deal—Aug. 27, '55—London
Nabob, Dewhurst	Shanghae, April 28	Dungeness—Sept. 12, '55 London—Sept. 14
Roebuck, Walden	Shanghae, May 13	London—Oct. 10, '55
Sovereign of the Seas, Muller	Shanghae, May 23	London—Nov. 9, '55
Torrent, Trundy	Shanghae, June 6 Batavia, Aug. 4	London—Nov. 12, '55
Storm King, Devens	Foo choo foo, June 23	Deal—Nov. 7, '55 London—Nov. 12
Neptune's Favorite, Oliver P. Lane	Woosung, July 5	Deal—Oct. 25, '55 London—Oct. 29
Wild Pigeon, Hanson	Foo choo foo, July 12 St. Helena, Oct. 9–10	London—Dec. 6, '55
Eureka, Whipple	Foo choo foo, July 22	London—Dec. 14, '55
Frigate Bird, Cope	Foo choo foo, July 23	London—Dec. 27, '55
Spitfire, Arey	Foo choo foo, July 24 St. Helena, Oct. 8	Plymouth—Nov. 28, '55 London—Dec. 4
Don Quixote, Nott	Foo choo foo, July 24	London—Nov. 7, '55

SHIP AND MASTER	SAILED	ARRIVED
North Star, Smith	Canton, Aug. 12	Deal—March 7, '55
Sparkling Wave, John C. Hubbard, Jr.	Shanghae, Aug. 17 Anjier, Sept. 18	London—Dec. 26, '55
Neptune's Car, Patten	Foo choo foo, Sept. 29	London—Jan. 22, '56
Flying Dutchman, Hubbard	Shanghae, Oct. 8	Deal—Jan. 24, '56 London—Jan. 26, '56
Kingfisher, Crosby	Canton, Macao, Oct. 20; Anjier, Nov. 7	Deal—Jan. 24, '56 London—Jan. 28
Romance of the Seas, Henry	Shanghae, Nov. 1 Anjier, Nov. 29	Deal—March 7, '56
Narragansett, Edmonds	Shanghae, Nov. 1	London—April 5, '56
Swallow, Tucker	Shanghae, Nov. 9	Scilly—Mar. 14, '56; Deal—March 21; London—March 24

1856

Challenger, Burgess	Canton, Jan. 10	Deal—April 28, '56 London—April 30
Invincible, Graham	Hong Kong, Jan. 21	London—May 15, '56
Galatea, Barber	Canton, Feb. 5 St. of Sunda, Feb. 21	Deal—May 17, '56
John Wade, Harding	Foo choo foo, June 9	Deal—Nov. 20, '56 London—Nov. 22
Bk. *Maury*, Fletcher	Foo choo foo, June 9	London—Oct. 15, '56
Ringleader, Matthews	Foo choo foo, June 17 St. of Sunda, Aug. 9	Gravesend—Oct. 31, '56 London—Nov. 1
Spitfire, Jackson	Canton, July 23 St. of Sunda, Aug. 30	Deal—Nov. 21, '56
Lorenzo, Morrow	Canton, Aug. 10	Deal—Nov. 28, '56 London—Dec. 1
Rolling Wave, Crawford	Canton, Aug. 16	Liverpool
Kingfisher, Crosby	Foo choo foo, Oct. 4 Anjier, Nov. 1	London—Jan. 21, '57
Bk. *Arctic*, Lane	Canton Anjier, Nov. 9	Queenstown—March 6, '57 Liverpool—March 11
Bonita, Freeman Hatch	Shanghae, Nov. 30	London—March 15, '57

1857

Competitor, White	Shanghae, Jan. 9 Anjier, Feb. 5	London—June 21, '57
Swallow, Tucker	Shanghae, Jan. 19 Anjier, Feb. 7	Lands End—April 29, '57 Gravesend—May 4—London

SHIP AND MASTER	SAILED	ARRIVED
Neptune's Favorite, Lane	Shanghae, Feb. 13 Anjier, March 6	London—June 8, '57
Bk. *Maury,* Fletcher	Foo choo foo, July 3	Off Dartmouth—Oct. 14, '57 London—Oct. 17
Bk. *Fairy,* Blish	Foo choo foo, July 4 Anjier, July 29	London—Oct. 19, '57
North Wind, Gove	Foo chow, Aug. 1	London—March 25, '58
Celestial, Palmer	Foo choo foo, Aug. 27 Anjier, Oct. 12	London—Jan. 11, '58
Spitfire, Arey	Foo chow, Oct. 25 Anjier, Nov. 22	Plymouth—Feb. 15, '58 London

1858

Bk. *Snapdragon,* Davis	Whampoa, May 1 Anjier, May 20	Gravesend—Aug. 12, '58 London—Aug. 13
Florence, Dumaresq	Woosung, Dec. 26 Anjier, Jan. 8, '59	Deal—April 2, '59 London—April 4

1859

Ringleader, Matthews	Foo chow, Feb. 24	Deal—June 11, '59 London—June 13
Golden City, Leary	Foo chow, March 30 Anjier, May 6	Deal—Aug. 17, '59 London—Aug. 18
Grace Darling, Baxter	Shanghae, June 7 Anjier, June 26	London—Oct. 24
Sea Serpent, Whitmore	Foo chow, June 19 St. of Sunda, Aug. 4	Off Plymouth—Oct. 27, '59 London
Charmer, Lucas	Foo chow, June 28	Liverpool—Nov. 11, '59
Rapid, Belcher	Foo chow, July 30	London—Dec. 8, '59
Bald Eagle, Treadwell	Shanghae, Aug. 6 Anjier, Sept. 13	Portsmouth—Dec. 4, '59 Liverpool
Crystal Palace, Simmons	Macao, Aug. 30	Plymouth—Oct. 27, '59 London—Oct. 29
Sultan, Berry	Shanghae, Oct. 22	London—Feb. 2, '60
Brig. *Nankin,* Moseley	Foo chow Anjier, Oct. 27	Queenstown—Feb. 23, '60 Gravesend—March 3
Florence, Wadsworth	Whampoa, Dec. 12 St. of Sunda, Dec. 24	London—March 23, '60
Alboni, Barnaby	Foo chow, Dec. 24 Anjier, Jan. 8, '60	Start Point—April 12, '60 London—April 16

1860

Lawrence Brown, Bearse	Foo chow, Feb. 29 Anjier, March 21	London—July 18, '60

SHIP AND MASTER	SAILED	ARRIVED
Bk. *Saxonville*, Gardner	Hong Kong, March 5	Deal—Aug. 19, '60—London
Flying Cloud, Winsor	Foo chow, Aug. 6	London—Dec. 7, '60
Bkn. *Fairy*, Blish	Hong Kong, Aug. 10 Anjier, Aug. 30	London—Dec. 3, '60

APPENDIX IV

NOTE: The information relating to the California clipper voyages, hereinafter listed, has been compiled from Custom House records, log books and the marine columns of contemporary newspapers. In general, it may be stated that anyone desiring to verify the dates of a particular passage may do so by consulting newspaper files and shipping records at or about the date of clearance or arrival mentioned herein.

It should be especially noted that reports of the actual time of sailing or arrival are not always available, and when they are, they may be regarded as less generally reliable than the custom house record of clearance. For the convenience of the reader, however, the approximate length of each passage is stated. In the great majority of cases, the elapsed time given is that reported on the arrival of the respective ships. In a majority of cases also—perhaps in all important voyages, possible error in computation aside—the time is correct to a fraction of a day. In some instances, as where the clearance of a vessel is given but no light has been thrown on her actual sailing, it will be understood that the length of passage given is approximately correct, only.

Much information bearing on the actual hours of arrival and departure can and undoubtedly will be supplied in years to come from log books and other records now in private hands. In the end, the facts will be established with a convincing thoroughness impossible in the present state of public records. It is believed, however, that the completely documented story will not differ appreciably from that herein set forth, either in sum total or in important particulars.

SHIP AND MASTER	SAILED	ARRIVED AT SAN FRANCISCO
1848		
Brig. *Mary & Ellen*, Eagleston	Salem, Oct. 28	March 26—150 days
Fanny Forrester, Sweetlin	New York, Nov. 15	April 24—161 days
Silvie De Grasse, Rich	New York, Nov. 20	April 17—149 days—Touched at Valparaiso and sailed thence March 1
Bk. *Whiton*, Roland Gelston	New York, Nov. 22	April 12—142 days
Brig. *Col. Fremont*, Pickett	Baltimore, Dec. 11	May 18—159 days
Sea Queen, Manson	New York, Dec. 13	April 30—125 days net. Touched at Valparaiso and sailed thence March 18
Bk. *Louisiana*, Williams	Philadelphia, Dec. 20	June 2—165 days
Bk. *Eliza*, A. S. Perkins	Salem, Dec. 23	June 2—162 days
Bk. *Carib*, Webb	Boston, Dec. 31	June 23—reported 175 days

NOTE: Other vessels sailing direct for San Francisco toward the close of 1848, included the schooner *Invincible* and barque *John W. Cater* and ships *Florence, Iowa, Rome* and *Henry Nesmith,* all from New York. Schooner *Favorite* from New Bedford; brig *Satillo* and barque *John W. Coffin* from Boston and brig *Sterling* from Salem. Several of the vessels sailing this year carried government supplies and troops. In all 80 vessels were reported as having sailed by the end of the year but this included those going to the Isthmus, etc.

1849		
Greyhound, Claypole	Baltimore, Jan. 10 Capes of Virginia, Jan. 12	June 3—116 days net—Reported off Cape Horn, 46 days out. Also given as 119 days
Tarolinta, Cane	New York, Jan. 13	July 6—175 days
Brig *Pauline*, French	Boston, Jan. 13	Sept. 3—240 days
Brig *Georgiana*, Taylor	New York, Jan. 18	Sept. 7—233 days
Architect, Gray	New Orleans, Jan. 18	June 28—127 days net
Grey Eagle, Bower	Philadelphia (Delaware Capes) Jan. 22	May 18—113 days net, via Valparaiso. Also given as 117 days
Schooner, *A. Emery*, Clay	New York, Jan. 25	Sept. 6—220 days
Orpheus, Freeman	New York, Jan. 30	July 8—159 days
Bk. *Drummond*, Pierce	Boston, Feb. 1	Sept. 1—210 days

SHIP AND MASTER	SAILED	ARRIVED AT SAN FRANCISCO
Bk. *Hebe*, Stetson	Baltimore, Feb. 3	Sept. 13—218 days
Bk. *Touro*, W. H. Low	New Orleans, Feb. 3	Sept. 7—214 days
Clarissa Perkins, Goodrich	New York, Feb. 7	Sept. 12—216 days
Xylon, Coudra	Baltimore, Feb. 8	Sept. 14—219 days
Bk. *Lanark*, Woodbury	Boston, Feb. 9	Sept. 12—212 days
Schooner *John Allyn*, Brownell	New Bedford, Feb. 12	Sept. 12—214 days
Brig *Col. Taylor*, Lovett	Boston, Feb. 12	Sept. 13—208 days
Audley Clark, Dennis	Newport, Feb. 14	Sept. 1—198 days
Schooner *J. B. Gager*, Halsey	New York, Feb. 14	Sept. 12—208 days
Brig *Henry Lee*, Vail	New York, Feb. 17	Sept. 13—206 days
Bk. *J. A. Jessurum*, Reed	New York, Feb. 24	Sept. 12—200 days
Bk. *Orb*, Moores	Boston, March 1	Sept. 9—189 days
John G. Coster, Durkey (or Durkee)	New York, March 1	Aug. 5—158 days
Bk. *Vernon*, McKay	New York, March 2	Oct. 9—222 days
Bk. *Edward Fletcher*, Holbrook	Boston, March 5	Sept. 9—182 days
Brig *Mallory*, Burden (Also reported as a bark which is probably correct)	New York, March 8	Sept. 13—189 days
Loo Choo, Cushman	New York, March 9	Sept. 16—192 days
Helena, Land	New York, March 10	Aug. 23—166 days
Samoset, Hollis	New York, March 22	Sept. 9—173 days
Brig *Rising Sun*, Hooper	New York, March 24	Sept. 13—165 days
Mayflower, Hicks	New Bedford, March 31	Sept. 13—163 days
Brig *Emma Isadora*, Henry	Boston, March 31	Sept. 13—165 days
Schooner *Planet*, Pratt	Boston, April 2	Sept. 10—160 days
Memnon, J. R. Gordon	New York, April 11	Aug. 28—122 days net
Andalusia, Wilson	Baltimore, April 18	Sept. 17—150 days
Argonaut, Wm. Knott	Boston, Oct. 30	March 18—1850—Reported 133 days

SHIP AND MASTER	SAILED	ARRIVED AT SAN FRANCISCO
Reindeer, John Lord	Boston, Nov. 22	April 2—1850—Reported 122 days net, and 36 days from Valparaiso, claimed as record.
Russell Glover, Frederick G. Ward	New York, Dec. 21	May 6, 1850—"The celebrated ship *Samuel Russell* going in just ahead of us."
Bk. *Green Point*, Wardle	New York, Dec. 21	July 8, via Valparaiso

NOTE: During the first two weeks of September, 23 vessels arrived from Eastern ports at San Francisco, none of which were clippers. The average passage for the entire fleet was 200 days.

1850

Natchez, Duryee	New York, Jan. 4	June 3—Reported 150 days
Samuel Russell, Low	New York, Jan. 15	May 6—109 days, Record
Valparaiso, Osgood	New York, Feb. 7	June 28—142 days
John Q. Adams, Nickels	New York, Feb. 15	July 1—136 days
Wisconsin, O. R. Mumford	New York, Feb. 21	June 24—121 days
Thos. Wattson, Thomas	Philadelphia, Delaware Capes, March 4	June 25—113 days
Houqua, McKenzie	New York, March 14	July 23—130 days
Cohota, Gerry	Boston, April 7	Aug. 13—124 days
Sea Witch, Geo. Fraser	New York, April 13	July 24—97 days Record
Memnon, Gordon	New York, May 27	Sept. 27—122 days
Carrington, Abbott	New York, June 21	Nov.—128 days
Celestial, E. C. Gardner	New York, July 16	Nov. 1, or Oct. 30?—104 days
Andalusia, Wilson	Phila., July 17	Dec. 12—148 days
Mandarin, Stoddard	New York, July 25	Nov. 29—126 days
Sea Queen, Manson	New York, cleared, July 25	Dec. 22—135 days
Bk. *Race Horse*, Babcock	Boston, August 4	November 24—109 days (94 days, 14 hours from land to land)
White Squall, Lockwood	New York, Sept. 5	Jan. 8—126 days—Lost main topmast and 3 top-gallants 3rd day out—124 days via Rio 73 days. (Arrived Rio Janeiro Oct. 18 and sailed on 20th)
Bk. *Geo. E. Webster*, Cotting	Boston, cleared Oct. 5	Jan. 26—113 days—16 days from Line

SHIP AND MASTER	SAILED	ARRIVED AT SAN FRANCISCO
Helena, John Land	New York, cleared, Oct. 29	March 12—132 days
Pilot Boat *Fanny,* Kelly	Boston, Nov. 1	Feb. 15—106 days
Seaman, Myrick	New York, cleared, Nov. 23	March 10—107 days—N.Y.H. April 22nd says she ran from lat. of Valparaiso in 30 days and from Line in 14 days
Uriel, James G. Foster	Boston, Nov. 27	May 3—158 days
Surprise, Philip Dumaresq	New York, Dec. 13	March 18—96 days 15 hours; 16 days and 14 hours from Line
Sea Nymph, Philip M. Hale	New York, Dec. 15	May 21—157 days

1851

SHIP AND MASTER	SAILED	ARRIVED AT SAN FRANCISCO
Bk. *Isabelita Hyne,* Samuel F. Dewing	New York, Jan. 13	May 18—125 days
John Bertram, Frederick Lendholm	Boston, Jan. 10	June 3 — 126 sailing days Sprung main mast and bowsprit March 29th put in Valparaiso. Sailed April 13th.
Sea Serpent, Wm. Howland	New York, Jan. 11	May 17—114 sailing days— Sprung bowsprit 4 days out. Arr. Valparaiso March 25th. Sailed again April 10th. Elsewhere reported 8 days at Valparaiso.
Grey Feather, Daniel McLaughlin	New York, cleared Jan. 11	May 30—138 days
Eclipse, Hamilton	New York, Jan. 15	May 20—125 days—Reported light adverse winds becalmed 31 days (Clark states had to put into Valparaiso 62nd day out—that would be about March 18.)
Stag Hound, Richardson	New York, Feb. 1	May 25—114 days—Clark gives 107 days net. Lost main top and three topgallants 6 days out. Saved everything. Valparaiso April 8 and sailed again 12th. (Took 7 days to get main topsail on her after dismasting owing to gale)
Gazelle, Henderson	New York, March 4	July 17—134 days—Captain blind last 50 days and sick almost whole voyage

SHIP AND MASTER	SAILED	ARRIVED AT SAN FRANCISCO
Ino, R. E. Little	New York, March 12	July 24—Reports 133 days
Joshua Bates, Easter-brook	New York, March 12	October 16—156 days
Alert, Bartlett	New York, March 15	Aug. 21—150 days
Architect, Caspar	New York, March 20	July 30—116 days net. At Talcahuano 13 days
Shooting Star, Judah P. Baker	Boston, March 22	Aug. 14—142 days—Put in to Rio to get main topgallant mast. Sailed May 9th.
Bk. *Greenpoint*, Wardle		Feb. 16 from Talcahuano
Gamecock, Hollis	New York, April 3	Oct. 5—185 days via Rio Janeiro 93 days—greatest day's run 325 miles. Arrived Rio May 10th, main mast sprung. Sailed July 6.
Witchcraft, Rogers	New York, April 4	Aug. 11—127 days, net 103 days. Lost Mizen mast. Arrived Rio prior to May 23. Sailed June 10th. She ran from Rio to San Francisco in 62 days —record.
Eureka, Auchincloss	New York, April 26	Oct. 17—174 days, via Valparaiso 45 days. Arrived Valparaiso Aug. 29th and sailed Sept. 1st.
N. B. Palmer, Low	New York, May 6	Aug. 21—106 days
Southern Cross, Stevens	Boston, May 8	Sept. 22—136 days
Bk. *Mermaid*, Smith	Boston, May 12	Oct. 18—160 days—Put into Pernambuco for repairs— Sailed night of July 19th.
Witch of the Wave, J. Hardy Millet	Boston, May 20	Sept. 20—123 days
Flying Cloud, Cressey	New York, June 2	Aug. 31—89 days
Valparaiso, Kilham	New York, June 17	
Syren, Edward A. Silsbee	Boston, June 30	Nov. 18—141 days
Eagle, Farran	New York, July 10	Nov. 18—131 days
Telegraph, Harlow	New York, July 11	Nov. 15 — 127 days — Spoke *Eagle* on Oct. 31. Lat. 17.27 N., Long. 122 W.

SHIP AND MASTER	SAILED	ARRIVED AT SAN FRANCISCO
Challenge, Waterman	New York, July 13 Anchored at S. W. Spit morning of July 13—Wind was easterly until 15th when it came off westerly.	Oct. 29—109 days—also reported 106 days.
Sea Witch, Fraser	New York, Aug. 1	Nov. 20—111 days (Clark says 110 days from Sandy Hook) Was within 500 miles of port for 5 days.
Typhoon, Salter	New York, Aug. 2	Nov. 18—108 days
Raven, Henry	Boston, Aug. 5	Nov. 19—106 days
Hornet, Lawrence	New York, Aug. 21	Jan. 23—155 days—Calms and head winds. 73 days to Horn —17 days off Horn. Best day 318 miles.
John Wade, Willis	Boston, Sept. 5	Jan. 14—131 days—71 days to Horn—16 days from Line but laid off harbor 3 days—19 days. Had continual head winds.
Comet, E. C. Gardner	New York, Oct. 1	Jan. 14, '52. Reported 103 and 104 days
Trade Wind, Osgood	New York, Oct. 2	Feb. 1—122 days
Wild Pigeon, Geo. W. Putnam, formerly of Packet, *Sunbeam*	New York, Oct. 11	Jan. 28 — 109 days —Captain reported 107 days
Golden Gate, Truman	New York, Oct. 11	Feb. 5—114 days
Reindeer, Lord	Richmond, about Oct. 26	March 22—148 days, via Valparaiso 48 days
Celestial, Palmer	New York, Nov. 1	Feb. 17—108 days (also given 106 days, Herald March 31)
Flying Fish, Edward Nickels	Boston, Nov. 6	Feb. 15—101 days—Anchored off bar Feb. 14—100 days
Versailles, Knowles	Boston, about Nov. 7	March 24—138 days.
Sword Fish, Babcock	New York, Nov. 9	Feb. 10—94 days
Thos. Wattson, Lyle	Philadelphia, Nov. 19	March 6—118 days
Northern Light, Bailey Loring	Boston, Nov. 20	March 8—Reported 110 days
Seaman's Bride, Myrick	New York, cleared and sailed Dec. 10	May 20—152 days—via Valparaiso 42 days. Arrived Valparaiso March 6—lost entire foremast Feb. 28 in squall. 33 days at Valparaiso 119 days net.

SHIP AND MASTER	SAILED	ARRIVED AT SAN FRANCISCO
John Bertram, Lend-holm	Boston, Dec. 12	March 26—106 days
Hurricane, Very	New York, Dec. 17	April 15—120 days—Via Rio 67 days. Lost fore and main top masts.
Mechanic's Own, Burgess	New York, Dec. 17	May 20—150 days
Invincible, Johnson	New York, Dec. 20	April 13—115 days—Said putting into Rio lost 8 days. Put in Rio Jan. 26 water tank leaky—sailed Jan. 28
Union—Buxton	Baltimore, Dec. 20	(Arrived at Rio Jan. 30th)

NOTE: From July 2nd to 10th—13 arrivals from East Coast averaged 197 days.

1852

Courser, Cole	Boston, Jan. 1 and put back	April 28—Reported 108 days net (Note: both *Courser* and *Eclipse* probably sailed Jan. 10, as heavy easterly gale prevailed until that date.)
Eclipse, Joseph Hamilton	New York, Anchored at S. W. Spit, Jan. 3.	April 22—Reported arrived Valparaiso 62 days out and sailed thence March 13, reporting 108 days to San Francisco
Aramingo, Sylvester	New York, Jan. 12	May 29—137 days
Hoogly, Chadwick	Boston, Jan. 18	May 28—Reported 127 days. Lost fore and main top masts 3 days out. Put into Rio Feb. 24 and sailed 27th.
Wisconsin, Scott	New York, Jan. 19	May 22—118 days
Dauntless, Miller	Boston, Jan. 28	Cleared for Valparaiso and arrived there May 2
Kate Hayes, Mauran	New York, Cleared Jan. 30	July 5—Reported 157 days
Andalusia, Wilson	New York, Cleared Feb. 1	June 24—143 days. (Reported from New York.)
Roebuck, Walden	Boston, Feb. 4	July 3—Reported 152 days net
Eastern State, Kilburn	New York, Feb. 13	July 12—149 days
Victory, Lane	Boston, Feb. 17	June 30—Reported 130 days
Argonaut, Nott	Boston, cleared Feb. 17	July 4—Reported 134 days
Bk. *Race Hound*, Copeland	New York, Feb. 17	July 19—154 days, arrived Valparaiso, May 24

SHIP AND MASTER	SAILED	ARRIVED AT SAN FRANCISCO
Tornado, Mumford	New York, Feb. 21	July 1—127 days. Reported very light winds
Stag Hound, Behm	New York, March 1	July 4—125 days. Carried sky-sails 88 days.
Sea Nymph, Hale	New York, March 2	July 4—124 days
Grecian, Ilsley	New York, March 2	August 11—150 days. Put into Rio with small-pox—was quarantined and sailed April 18th.
Samuel Appleton Doane	Boston, March 3	July 21—137 days. Touched at Valparaiso for water May 31 and sailed June 3.
Antelope, Crosby	Boston, March 3	July 30—118 days
Sea Serpent, Howland	New York, March 9	June 30—113 days
Gov. Morton, Burgess	New York, March 11	July 15—125 days
Ino, Smith	New York, March 18	July 12—116 days. Spent 5 days in Rio.
Harriet Hoxie, P. E. Rowland	New York, March 24	August 3—120 days net. Best day 311 miles—16 knots. Put into Valparaiso under jury masts June 2 and sailed June 14
Horsburgh B. W. Crocker	Boston, March 25	August 2—131 days
Empire Eben A. Thorndike	New York, March 29	August 13—128 days. Went into San Francisco dismasted and under jury rig.
North America, Austin	New York, April 3	Sept. 1—151 days. Had 471 pass. Arrived Rio and sailed May 28. Arrived Valparaiso July 5, sailed July 10th
Queen of the East, Truman Bartlett	New York, April 7	Sept. 8—154 days via Callao 41 days
White Squall, Kennedy	New York, April 10	July 29—110 days
Atalanta, Wallace	New York, April 14	Sept. 3—141 days
Bk. *Pathfinder*, J. Madison Hill	New York, April 17	Sept. 16—151 days. Letter from Capt. 13 days out says she made 316 miles and does 13 knots easily.
Staffordshire, Josiah Richardson	Boston, May 3	August 13—102 days, 120 pass. and freight list 13 feet long.
Shooting Star, Judd P. Baker	Boston, May 3	August 17—106 days
Antelope, Shinn	New York, May 8	October 10—155 days
Beverly, Jenkins	Boston, May 10	October 1—144 days

SHIP AND MASTER	SAILED	ARRIVED AT SAN FRANCISCO
Flying Cloud, Cressy	New York, May 14	Sept. 6—113 days
Gazelle, Dollard	New York, May 18	Oct. 1—135 days. In collision off Horn—lost bowsprit, etc.
Hippogriffe, Howes	Boston, May 17	Oct. 20—156 days
N. B. Palmer, Low	New York, May 22	Sept. 30—130 days. (Sailed 390 miles on May 26). See letter about trip. Arrived Valparaiso Aug. 11, 86 days. Sailed 20th—35 days off Horn.
Josephine, Jameson	New York, May 25	Oct. 19—147 days. Arrived Valparaiso Aug. 22, 85 days—sailed 25th
S. S. Bishop, Turley	Philadelphia, Cleared May 27	Sept. 30—121 days
Union, Buxton	New York, June 1	Sept. 28—120 days
Messenger, Smith	New York, June 1	Oct. 3—124 days
Ellen Foster, Grozier	Boston, June 3	Oct. 31—140 days, Via Rio July 23
Racer, Steele	New York, Cleared June 5	October 19—128 days. Anchored at S. W. Spit June 7.
Grey Hound, Pickett	New York, June 13	Oct. 20—125 days
Cohota, Gerry	Boston, June 16	Nov. 2—138 days
Eureka, Welsh	New York, June 22	Nov. 7—138 days
Witch of the Wave, Tay	Boston, June 22	Oct. 19—119 days
Southern Cross, Stevens	Boston, June 25	Nov. 28—155 days—Arrived Montevideo Aug. 23, expected to sail 16th or 17th Sept. Had been on fire.
Defiance, McCerren	New York, June 25	Dec. 2—160 days—Reports 136 days—83 from Rio. At Rio Aug. 29 repairing. 23d. at Rio.
Bk. *Greenfield*, Follansbee	New York, June 29	Oct. 31—122 days
Bk. *Mermaid*, Smith	New York, Cleared July 1	Oct. 18—108 days—Put into Pernambuco and sailed July 20. 22 days from Horn to Line.
Bk. *Gallego*, Ellery	New York, Cleared July 1	Oct. 20, via Rio Janeiro—110 days—But see arr. Jan. 6—187 days
Jamestown, Moore	New York, July 10	Nov. 14—127 days
Mandarin, T. C. Stoddard	New York, Cleared July 11	Nov. 5—116 days
Polynesia, Jacob G. Homer	Boston, July 20	Dec. 8—141 days

SHIP AND MASTER	SAILED	ARRIVED AT SAN FRANCISCO
Warner, Carr (also reported Johnson)	New York, July 22	Dec. 19—140 days, via Rio Janeiro
Buena Vista, Linnell	New York, July 25	Dec. 24—152 days
Onward, Cotting	Boston, July 29	Dec. 1—120 days
Albatross, Knowles	New York, Cleared July 29	Jan. 12—160 days
Bk. *Jeanette*, Mix	New York, July 31	Dec. 27—148 days
Bk. *Black Squall*, Faulkner	New York, Cleared July 31	Jan. 3—156 days, via Valparaiso.
Seaman, Daniels	New York, July 31	Dec. 9—129 days
Bk. *Golden Age*, Strong	New York, Aug. 1	Dec. 27—149 days
Raven, Henry	New York, Aug. 1	Nov. 30—121 days
Sovereign of the Seas, McKay	New York, Aug. 4	Nov. 15—103 days (Dismasted and refitted at sea)
Winged Arrow, F. Bearse	Boston, Aug. 5	Nov. 27—113 days
Samuel Russell, Limeburner	New York, Aug. 12	Dec. 9—119 days
R. B. Forbes, J. C. Ballard	New York, Aug. 13	Dec. 17—126 days (24 days off Horn)
Golden Fleece, Freeman	Boston, Aug. 16	Jan. 4—140 days
Sea Witch, Fraser	New York, Aug. 22	Dec. 9—108 days
Coringa, Mason	Boston, Aug. 23	Jan. 2—132 days
Syren, Silsbee	New York, Aug. 25	Dec. 23—118 days
Bk. *Comet*, Burnham	Boston, Aug. 25	Dec. 19—126 days
Monsoon, Winsor	Boston, Aug. 28	Jan. 5—130 days
Golden City, Samuel F. Dewing (formerly of *Isabelita Hyne*)	New York, Sept. 8	Jan. 4—118 days—Detained 5 days off Farallones in fog.
Bk. *Isabelita Hyne*, Lamson	New York, Sept. 8	Jan. 10—124 days
John Wade, Little	New York, Sept. 11	Jan. 7—117 days
Malay, Brown	Boston, Sept. 14	Jan. 10—118 days
Chas. Mallory, Chas. Hull	New York, Sept. 15	Jan. 8—115 days
Thos. Wattson, Lyle	Philadelphia, Sept. 20	Jan. 29—131 days
Comet, Gardner	New York, Sept. 27	Jan. 18—112 days
Gem of the Ocean, Crosby	Boston, Oct. 4	Feb. 2—121 days
Wild Pigeon, Putnam	New York, Oct. 11	Feb. 7—119 days—118 days

SHIP AND MASTER	SAILED	ARRIVED AT SAN FRANCISCO
Flying Dutchman, Hubbard	New York, Oct. 15	Jan. 27—104 days, via Rio. Was 35 days from 50S.—16 from Line
Dauntless, Miller	Boston, Oct. 15	Feb. 12—118 days net (Was at Valparaiso Jan. 1–3, 39 days from Valparaiso)
Westward Ho, Graves (also given as Johnson)	Boston, Oct. 16	Jan. 31—107 days (Captain Johnson given on arrival)
John Gilpin, Doane	New York, Oct. 28	Feb. 2—93 days—20 hours port to pilot
Northern Light, Freeman Hatch	Boston, Oct. 28	Feb. 23—118 days
Flying Fish, Nickels	New York, Oct. 31	Jan. 31—92 days, 4 hours—Reported on her 88th day she was 156 miles nearer San Francisco than *Flying Cloud* was on her 89 day passage. Was off the Heads 3 days in calms and light airs.
Queen of the Seas, Elias D. Knight	Boston, Nov. 3	March 11—131 days, via Valparaiso
Grey Feather, McLaughlin	New York, Cleared Nov. 4	March 15—126 days
Whirlwind, Burgess	Boston, Nov. 10	March 11—121 days
Trade Wind, Nathaniel Webber	New York, Nov. 13	Feb. 24—103 days—3400 tons measured cargo. 46—1st class passengers. A third deck added recently, probably largest cargo ever taken from New York.
Tam O'Shanter, Soule	Boston, Nov. 15	March 26—130 days
Telegraph, Pousland	Boston, Nov. 15	March 10—115 days
Contest, Brewster	New York, Nov. 16	Feb. 24—100 days
Game Cock, Hollis	New York, Nov. 16	March 10—114 days
Meteor, Samuel W. Pike	Boston, Nov. 17	March 10—113 days
Alboni, Littlefield	New York, Nov. 21	March 31—129 days—Was off Horn 15 days and within 300 miles of San Francisco for 18 days
Tingqua, Whitmore	New York, Nov. 24	March 19—115 days—Was in lat. 2–33 N. in 13 days
Living Age, Holmes	New York, Nov. 25	April 1—127 days
Fleetwood, Dale	Boston, Cleared Dec. 1	April 13—130 days

SHIP AND MASTER	SAILED	ARRIVED AT SAN FRANCISCO
Golden Eagle, Fabens	Boston, Dec. 3	May 9—157 days. Via Rio 78 days. Was off River Platte 36 days in gale and leaky. Put in to Rio Jan. 23. Sailed Feb. 21. (129 days net). This included return to Rio from 36 S.
Golden Gate, Barstow	New York, Dec. 6	March 20—94 days
Jacob Bell, Kilham	New York, Dec. 8	April 10—123 days
Winged Racer, Homan	New York, Dec. 12	March 30—108 days
Golden West, Curwen	Boston, Dec. 13	April 16—124 days
John Stuart, Ferris	New York, Cleared Dec. 17	May 4—136 days
Flying Childers, White	Boston, Dec. 18	April 10—113 days
Red Rover, Putnam	New York, Dec. 18	April 19—117 days (net) 36 days out carried away main-top mast and fore and mizen topgallant masts. Put in Juan Fernandez 2 days for water.
Roman, Hepburn	New York, Dec. 18	April 17—120 days. Reported 115 days
Peerless, Bacon	Boston, Dec. 19	July 20—210 days. Via Valparaiso 60 days. Detained 6 days at Valparaiso
Carrington, French	New York, Cleared Dec. 14	April 20—121 days
Bk. *Storm*, Roberts	New York, Cleared Dec. 20	April 10—110 days. Was 17 days 6 hours to line. Was 16 days without topgallant masts owing to trestle trees breaking down.
Hussar, Lucas	Boston, Dec. 22	April 16—115 days
Bald Eagle, Dumaresq	New York, Dec. 25	April 11—109 days

1853

Esther May, Howes	Boston, Jan. 6	June 1—146 days
Phantom, Alvin H. Hallet	Boston, Jan. 6	April 20—104 days. Reported 23 days to the latitude of Rio Janeiro
Eagle, Farren	New York, Jan. 7	April 30—111 days. Spoke *Celestial* & *John Stuart* off Horn
Celestial, Palmer	New York, Jan. 8	May 8—119 days
Rattler, Brown	New York, Jan. 8	May 9—121 days

SHIP AND MASTER	SAILED	ARRIVED AT SAN FRANCISCO
Tornado, Mumford	New York, Jan. 11	May 2—111 days. Was within 300 miles of port for 7 days. Reported 109 days.
Rattler, Stump	Philadelphia, Jan. 14	May 27—133 days.
Alert, Thomas	Cleared New York, Jan. 15	June 14—148 days
Mountain Wave, Paine	Boston, Jan. 17	May 28—131 days
Simoon, Smith	New York, Jan. 19	June 1—132 days
Flying Arrow, Treadwell	Boston, Jan. 20	(Dismasted and sailed again from New York, Aug. 10.)
Wings of the Morning, Lovell	New York, Jan. 21	July 23—165 days net (Put into Rio March 18 with a loss of topmasts. Sailed April 2nd).
Typhoon, Salter	New York, Jan. 22	June 8—133 days. Was detained off San Francisco by fog—arrived off Heads June 4
Lucknow, Plummer	Boston, Jan. 15	June 4—139 days 22 days to line—off Horn 20 days in westerly gales.
Oriental, Fletcher	New York, Jan. 26	May 7—101 days. (Lost foremast off Horn and repaired at sea.)
Queen of the Pacific, Reed	Boston, Jan. 26	August 9—Via Valparaiso, 193 days
Carrier Pigeon, Doane	Boston, Jan. 28	June 6—132 days. Went ashore below San Francisco. Total loss.
Golden Racer, Melcher	Boston, Jan. 29	June 9, 130 days
Star of the Union, Willis	New York, Jan. 29	June 2—123 days
Mystery, Peter Peterson	Boston, Feb. 6	June 25—135 days net (5 days at Valparaiso).
Northern Crown, Lamb	New York, Feb. 8	July 14—154 days. 39 days from Line to San Francisco.
Governor Morton, Burgess	New York, Feb. 8	June 11—123 days
Golden State, Doty	New York, Feb. 8	July 12—153 days, 132 days net (March 16 put into Rio and sailed April 6). Was 42 days from Line to San Francisco.
Sword Fish, Collins	New York, Feb. 12	May 30—107 days. Best day 340 miles.
Sea Serpent, Howland	New York, Feb. 12	June 1,—109 days
Reliance, Berry	New York, Feb. 12	August 11—180 days

SHIP AND MASTER	SAILED	ARRIVED AT SAN FRANCISCO
Golden Light, Winsor	Boston, Feb. 12	(Burned at sea Feb. 22.)
Sirocco, Sanford	New York, Feb. 15	July 10—145 days. Off Horn 22 days in gales.
Corinne, Joyce (Stickney)	New York, Feb. 17	Dismasted and returned to New York. (Resailed April 28.)
Archer, Bursley	New York, Feb. 20	July 16—146 days
Houqua, Dixey	New York, Feb. 21	July 15—144 days
Flying Eagle, Parker	Boston, February 22	August 10—167 days (142 days net). (Put into Rio April 10 lost main topmast and all gear attached 5 days out). Sailed May 5th.
Courser, Berry	New York, Feb. 24	July 12—138 days
Stag Hound, Behm	New York, Feb. 24	July 1—127 days. Had light winds, skysails 81 days. (Detained 10 days putting into Juan Fernandez for water.)
Snow Squall, Bursley	New York, Feb. 25	August 2—155 days. Reported 60 days off the Horn, being driven to 60 South and carrying away all iron work on bow sprit, steering gear, etc.
Ocean Spray, McLellan	New York, Feb. 26	July 19—135 days
Stilwell S. Bishop, Sherman	Philadelphia, passed the Capes March 5	July 4—121 days
Radiant, Bearse	Boston, March 6	July 14—130 days
Aramingo, Drinkwater	New York, March 10	July 23—133 days
Empress of the Seas Putnam	New York, March 13	July 12—121 days
Storm King, Collier	Boston, March 14	July 27—133 days. Put in to Valparaiso for water June 16 —expected to sail June 18
Surprise, Ranlett	New York, March 15	July 9—116 days
Seaman's Bride, Myrick	New York, March 19	July 17—120 days
Witchcraft, Dudley	New York, March 19	July 8—110 days
Lantao, Bradbury	New York, March 24	July 23—121 days
Competitor, Howes	Boston, March 27	July 20—114 days
Climax, Howes	Boston, March 28	July 21,—115 days
Antelope, Shinn	New York, March 28	July 21—Reported 115 days
Frigate Bird, Cope	Philadelphia, April 1	August 29—150 days

SHIP AND MASTER	SAILED	ARRIVED AT SAN FRANCISCO
Harriet Hoxie, Manwaring	New York, April 5	August 31—140 days. Was 30 days off the Horn losing fore yard.
Highflyer, Waterman	New York, April 7	Sept. 3—148 days. Put into Rio Janeiro prior to June 7 with defective pumps. Sailed again June 9th.
Oxnard, Hinckley	New York, April 14	Sept. 11—150 days
Shooting Star, Kingman	New York, April 14	August 15—121 days
Eclipse, Hamilton	New York, April 18	August 17—119 days
Victory, Lane	New York, April 21	Sept. 3—134 days
John Land, Howes	Boston, April 22	August 26—126 days
Cleopatra, Shreve	Boston, April 20	Sept. 1—130 days
Antelope, Snow	New York, April 25	August 31—128 days
Hornet, Knapp	New York, April 28	August 12—106 days
Flying Cloud, Cressy	New York, April 28	August 12—106 days
Celestial Empire, Pierce	New York, April 28	Sept 21—146 days
Corinne, Stickney	New York, April 28	Oct. 13—165 days
White Squall, Kennedy	Philadelphia, May 6	Sept. 4—121 days
Ino, Smith	New York, May 10	Sept. 8—121 days
West Wind, Elliot	Boston, May 14	Sept. 26—135 days
Anglo-Saxon, Leeds	New York, May 14	Oct. 12—150 days
Reindeer, Bunker	New York, Cleared May 17	Oct. 19—132 days
Mischief, Thompson	New York, May 20	Nov. 9—170 days via Valparaiso 42 days—130 net. (Arrived Valparaiso Aug. 16 for repairs. She sailed Sept. 25 in company with *Pathfinder*—much betting on result. Experts said *Mischief* too heavily sparred. Bk. *Pathfinder*, Lawrence, arrived Nov. 16, reporting 45 days.)
Belle of West, Howes	Boston, May 21	Sept. 29—131 days
Invincible, Johnson	New York, May 21	Sept. 9—110 days
Western Star, Thayer	Boston, May 27	Nov. 11—167 days
White Swallow, Lovett	Boston, May 27	Oct. 24—149 days
Windward, Whiting	New York, May 31	Nov. 3—155 days
Messenger, Smith	Philadelphia, Cleared May 31	Oct. 6—122 days

SHIP AND MASTER	SAILED	ARRIVED AT SAN FRANCISCO
Juniper, Parsons	Boston, June 6	Jan. 4, '54—208 days,—off Horn 49 days. (At Callao 8 days for water, etc.)
Gazelle, Dollard	New York, June 9	Oct. 7—119 days
Young America, Babcock	New York, June 10	Sept. 29—110 days
Grey Hound, Snow	Baltimore, June 13	Nov. 9—132 days
Atalanta, Wallace	New York, June 20	Oct. 24—124 days
Bonita, Winsor	Boston, June 21	Nov. 9—141 days
Wild Ranger, Sears	Boston, June 21	Oct. 25—125 days
Flying Dutchman, Hubbard	New York, June 23	Oct. 7—106 days
Queen of Clippers, Zerega	New York, June 30	Oct. 27—118 days
John Bertram, Lendholm	Boston, June 30	Oct. 24—114 days
Wild Duck, Hamilton	New York, July 3	Nov. 14—130 days
Andalusia, Hall	New York, July 3	November 26—146 days
Arab, Thurston	Boston, July 6	Jan. 6—184 days
Contest, Brewster	New York, July 6	Oct. 24—110 days. Reported 36 days to the Horn
Wisconsin, Scott	New York, July 6	Dec. 21—168 days
Whistler, Brown	Boston, July 16	Nov. 21—130 days
Flying Dragon, Baker	Boston, July 21	Dec. 16—148 days. 31 days off Cape—lost jibboom, sprung bowsprit and fore yard. Captain Baker died on the voyage.
Wizard, Slate	New York, July 24	Dec. 19—148 days
North Wind, Hildreth	New York, July 27	Dec. 12—138 days
Comet, Gardner	New York, Aug. 4	Dec. 10—128 days
Trade Wind, Webber	Philadelphia, Aug. 4	Dec. 10—125 days
Hurricane, Very	New York, Aug. 9	Dec. 12—124 days (*Hurricane* had to anchor at Quarantine 8th with mutiny. Revenue brig *Washington* took off mutineers in irons)
Mandarin, Perit	New York, Aug. 9	Dec. 11—123 days
Flying Arrow, Clark	New York, Aug. 10	Dec. 31—143 days
Raven, Crocker	New York, Aug. 13	Dec. 11—113 days
Northern Light, Hatch	Boston, Aug. 15	Dec. 16—122 days
Witch of the Wave, Miller	Boston, Aug. 16	Dec. 11—117 days
Southern Cross, Paine	New York, Aug. 19	Jan. 11—147 days
Wide Awake, Smith	New York, Aug. 21	Dec. 13—113 days

SHIP AND MASTER	SAILED	ARRIVED AT SAN FRANCISCO
John Wade, Little	Boston, Aug. 21	Dec. 22—120 days
Onward, Wade	New York, Aug. 27	Jan. 25—151 days
Thos. Wattson, Lyle	Philadelphia, Aug. 27	Jan. 29—155 days
Rover's Bride, Phillips	Baltimore, Aug. 27	Jan. 26—152 days
Fearless, Manson	Boston, Aug. 30	Dec. 22—114 days
Bk. *Comet*, Burnham	Boston, Sept. 3	Jan. 14—133 days
Sweepstakes, Lane	New York, Sept. 3	Jan. 6—125 days—Was 4 days in sight of San Francisco Heads—Carried skysails 61 days.
Wild Pigeon, Hanson	New York, Sept. 5	Jan. 11—129 days
Winged Arrow, Bearse	Boston, Sept. 11	Jan. 15—127 days
Ocean Pearl, Sears	Boston, Sept. 12	Jan. 25—135 days
Jacob Bell, Kilham	Philadelphia, Sept. 14	Jan. 14—122 days (also reported sailed 13th)
Bk. *Greenfield*, Follansbee	New York, Sept. 17	Jan. 25—130 days
Flying Fish, Nickels	Boston, Sept. 19	Jan. 11—114 days
Skylark, Henry	New York, Sept. 19	Jan. 15—118 days
Morning Light, Johnson	Philadelphia, Sept. 26	Feb. 9—136 days
N. B. Palmer, Low	New York, Sept. 27	Jan. 26—121 days
Kingfisher, Crosby	Boston, Oct. 3	Jan. 25—114 days
Bald Eagle, Caldwell	New York, Oct. 1	Jan. 25—116 days—Also reported sailed Oct. 2.
Morning Light, Knight	Boston, Oct. 3	Feb. 11—131 days
Eureka, Whipple	New York, Oct. 4	Feb. 6—125 days
Samuel Russell, Limeburner	New York, Oct. 5	Jan. 20—107 days
Pampero, Coggins	New York, Oct. 9	Jan. 25—108 days
Neptune's Car, Forbes	New York, Oct. 15	Feb. 9—117 days
Samuel Appleton, Young	Hampton Roads, Va., Oct. 16	Feb. 21—128 days
Samuel Lawrence, Patten	Boston, Oct. 19	Feb. 23—127 days
Ringleader, Matthews	Boston, Oct. 21	Feb. 8—110 days
Matchless, Potter	Boston, Oct. 21	Feb. 8—110 days
Golden City, Canfield	New York, Oct. 23	Feb. 8—108 days
Spitfire, Arey	Boston, Oct. 23	Feb. 20—Arrived Rio Nov. 27. Sailed 16th Dec. Was off Horn 15 days in gales—was 380 miles from San Francisco 87 days out.

SHIP AND MASTER	SAILED	ARRIVED AT SAN FRANCISCO
San Francisco, Setzer	New York, Oct. 25	Feb. 8—106 days (Lost at the entrance of San Francisco harbor)
Cyclone, Ingersoll, Jr.	Boston, Nov. 2	Feb. 24—114 days
Eagle, Farren	New York, Nov. 4	Feb. 16—104 days
Westward Ho, Hussey	New York, Nov. 14	Feb. 27—105 days—Off Horn 3 weeks in heavy weather.
Syren, Allen	New York, Nov. 16	March 30—131 days
Don Quixote, Nott	Boston, Nov. 22	March 28—126 days
Dashing Wave, Fisk	Philadelphia, Nov. 26	March 28—118 days—Arrived Valparaiso Feb. 16 and proceeded same day.
Coringa, Bates	New York, Nov. 30	May 4—155 days
Lightfoot, Pierce	New York, Cleared Nov. 30	March 25—113 days—Sailed Dec. 2. Had a spritsail yard carried away and lost a man—Had to tack more than 75 times off Horn.
Telegraph, Harlow	Boston, Dec. 1	April 16—Arrived Valparaiso, Feb. 20—remained March 1. Lost bowsprit and fore topgallant mast. Delayed 15 days. Ran from Valparaiso to Pt. Reyes 34 days. Said to be fastest record at that time.
Aurora, Brown	Boston, Dec. 3	April 10—128 days—Put in to Rio, Jan. 25—mutiny
Golden Fleece, Freeman	New York, Dec. 4	April 10—128 days
David Brown, Brewster	New York, Dec. 13	March 23—99 days
Romance of the Seas, Dumaresq	Boston, Dec. 16	March 23—96 days
Eagle Wing, Linnell	Boston, Dec. 20	April 5—115 days
Polynesia, Watson	New York, Cleared Dec. 24	April 10—104 days—Was off Horn 49 days out.
Look Out, Joyce	New York, Dec. 29	May 4—126 days
Game Cock, Osgood	New York, Cleared Dec. 29	April 23—115 days

1854

Monsoon, Baker	Boston, Jan. 4	May 4—120 days—Sailed Jan. 4
National Eagle, Matthews	Boston, Jan. 6	May 20—134 days

SHIP AND MASTER	SAILED	ARRIVED AT SAN FRANCISCO
Archer, Thomas	New York, Jan. 12	April 28—106 days—Sailed Jan. 12. Was 16 days from Horn to Line
Herald of the Morning, Baker	Boston, Jan. 21	May 7—106 days—Was within 180 miles of port for 6 days.
Flying Cloud, Cressy	New York, Cleared Jan. 19	April 20—89 days 8 hrs. Sailed Jan. 21 at noon in tow. Made sail and cast off from tug 3.30 P.M. 17 days to line.
Red Rover, Putnam	New York, Jan. 22	May 24—122 days
Winged Racer, Gorham	Boston, Jan. 24	May 23—119 days
Seaman's Bride, Mayo	New York, Jan. 23	May 23—120 days
John Gilpin, Ring	New York, Jan. 28	May 23—115 days
Union, Buxton	New York, Feb. 3	June 10—128 days
Cœur de Lion, Tucker	Boston, Feb. 4	June 18—135 days
Whirlwind, Burgess	New York, Feb. 4	June 13—129 days
Challenger, Hill	Boston, Cleared Feb. 6	June 9—112 days
Tinqua, Whitmore	Philadelphia, Feb. 9	June 12—123 days
Stilwell S. Bishop, Sherman	Baltimore, Feb. 20	July 2, via San Diego 112 days
Meteor, Pike	Boston, Feb. 22	June 23—122 days
Sea Serpent, Howland	New York, Feb. 24	June 21—118 days
Golden Racer, Nagle	Baltimore, March 2	Aug. 9—151 days
R. B. Forbes, Ballard	New York, March 11	July 26—138 days
Fleetwing, Howes	Boston, March 11	July 11—123 days
Messenger, Kennedy	Philadelphia, Mar. 13	July 17—127 days
Starlight, Chase	Boston, March 16	July 11—118 days
Viking, Winsor	Boston, March 17	July 10 (log)—116 days
Golden Eagle, Fabens	New York, March 21	July 23—125 days
Carrington, French	New York, March 22	July 24—125 days. Crossed Equator 22 days out.
Swordfish, Osgood	New York, March 29	July 23—117 days
Golden Gate, Dewing	New York, Cleared March 29	August 1—126 days. Was 6 days in company with *Surprise* in Straits of La Maire.
Surprise, Ranlett	New York, April 6	Aug. 2—119 days
Alboni, Littlefield	New York, Cleared April 8	Sept. 1—147 days. Arrived out after very hard time off Horn —driven back around the Falklands twice. Hove to for 9 days on one occasion. Carried skysails for 60 days after passing the Horn.

SHIP AND MASTER	SAILED	ARRIVED AT SAN FRANCISCO
Starr King, Turner	Boston, April 19	August 16—120 days
Stag Hound, Behm	New York, April 26	Aug. 14—110 days
John Stuart, Ellery	New York, April 27	Aug. 16—also given Sept. 10—112 days
Robin Hood, Bearse	Boston, May 6	Sept. 10—128 days
Witchcraft, Freeman	New York, May 9	Aug. 15—98 days. Best run 340 miles and was 2 days off Heads in fog. 9 days within 700 miles of San Francisco.
Golden West, Curwen	Philadelphia, May 10	Oct. 2—146 days
Courser, Berry	New York, May 10	Sept. 25—137 days
Northern Light, Hatch	Boston, May 13	Sept. 15 or 17?—126 days
Competitor, Howes	New York, May 23	Sept. 23—122 days
Mary Robinson, Crocker	Boston, May 25	Oct. 12—Was 4 days at Valparaiso, Aug. 22—26
Hurricane, Very	New York, May 26, P.M.	Sept. 4—112 days. Was 77 days to Line—then met calms and was within 500 miles of port for 15 days.
Golden State, Barstow	New York, May 26, A.M.	Sept. 28—125 days
Bonita, Hollis	Boston, May 26	Sept. 26—118 days. Had light airs for 30 days north of Line.
Gazelle, Dollard	New York, June 3	Sept. 27—114 days
Galatea, Barber	Boston, June 4	Sept. 27—114 days
Star of the Union, Stahl	New York, Cleared June 9	Oct. 14—124 days
Nor'Wester, Eldridge	New York, June 13	Oct. 14—123 days
Kate Hooper, Jackson	New York, June 15	Oct. 25—133 days
Victory, Neal	New York, June 17	Dec. 23—190 days Via Valparaiso—Nov. 9
Grace Darling, Doane	New York, June 17	Nov. 7—144 days
Climax, Freeman	New York, June 24	Nov. 8—138 days
Midnight, Hatch	Boston, June 30	Oct. 25—118 days
Live Yankee, Thorndike	New York, June 29	Oct. 20—114 days
Young America, Babcock	New York, July 2	Oct. 20—111 days
Morning Star, Foster	Boston, July 3	Nov. 27—148 days
John Land, Percival	Boston, July 6	May 13 '55 Via Valparaiso Nov. 2 Via Tahiti where was in distress—312 days
Rapid, Corning	New York, July 12	Nov. 25—137 days

SHIP AND MASTER	SAILED	ARRIVED AT SAN FRANCISCO
Contest, Brewster	New York, July 12	Nov. 17—129 days. Started head, lost house, etc., lying to Sept. 22, off the Horn.
Fearless, Manson	Boston, July 18	Nov. 19—125 days. Was 15 days from Line to San Francisco—crossed Line Nov. 4.
Ocean Telegraph, Willis	New York, July 22	Nov. 24—126 days. Becalmed last 6 days.
Thos. Wattson, Lyle	Philadelphia, July 25	Dec. 12—141 days. Also reported arrived Dec. 14.
Celestial, Palmer	New York, July 29	Dec. 8—133 days
Sting Ray, Kirby	New York, July 29	Dec. 8—133 days
Whistler, Brown	Boston, Aug. 1	Dec. 9—11 A. M.—131 days Arrived below
Flying Eagle, Bates	New York, Aug. 11	Dec. 22—134 days
Red Gauntlet, Andrews	Boston, Aug. 12	Dec. 9—120 days
Wild Duck, Hamilton	New York, Aug. 13	Dec. 19—129 days. Had moderate winds—was 600 miles from port for 15 days.
Raven, Hanson	New York, Cleared Aug. 17 for Rio Janeiro.	Feb. 23, via Rio 118 net—84 days.
Antelope, Mooers	New York, Aug. 18	Jan. 2—138 days off Horn 15 days.
Osborn Howes, Kelley	Boston, Aug. 23	Jan. 21—151 days
Hornet, Benson	Philadelphia, Aug. 27	Jan. 9—136 days
Challenge, Kenney	New York, Sept. 4	Jan. 2—120 days. Was 20 days off Horn—16 days from Line to Farallones, Dec. 30, but hauled off a/c fog.
Bk. *Jane A. Falkenberg*, Falkenberg	Boston, Sept. 6	Jan. 2—118 days. 48 days to Cape Horn and 20 days off Horn in Westerly gales.
Wild Pigeon, Hanson	New York, Sept. 17	Jan. 29—135 days
Flying Fish, Nickels	Boston, Sept. 20, Evening	Jan. 10—113 days. Skysails 85 days. Broke rudder head in 53 S. and steered with tackles thereafter. Was 17 days from Line to San Francisco.
Wild Ranger, Sears	New York, Sept. 22	Jan. 26—132 days
Hussar, Winsor	New York, Oct. 11	Feb. 23—135 days

SHIP AND MASTER	SAILED	ARRIVED AT SAN FRANCISCO
Winged Arrow Bearse	Boston, Oct. 15	Feb. 8—115 days. Ran from 50 S. to within one day sail of San Francisco in 34 days—was becalmed 7 days within one day of port. Also spoke *Pampero* off Horn.
Pampero, Coggins	New York, Oct. 18	Feb. 20—126 days
Sweepstakes, Lane	New York, Oct. 25 at 7 A.M.	Feb. 21—119 days. Draws 21 feet 4 inches.
Lotus, Leckie	Boston, Oct. 25	Feb. 25—124 days
Southern Cross, Howes	Boston, Oct. 25	Feb. 22—121 days
Bald Eagle, Treadwell	New York, Cleared Oct. 25	Feb. 23—117 days
Phantom, Peterson	New York, Oct. 26, at 10 A.M.	Feb. 23—120 days. Draws 19 feet 2 inches
Electric, Gates	New York, Nov. 9	March 4—116 days. Was off Farallones March 1 in fog.
Flyaway, Sewall	New York, Nov. 13	March 2—110 days
Morning Light. Johnston	Philadelphia, Nov. 13	March 14—122 days
Cleopatra, Thayer	New York, Nov. 15	March 4—110 days
Saracen, Barry	Boston, Nov. 17	April 12—147 days
Sea Nymph, Harding	New York, Cleared Nov. 16	April 12—148 days
Flying Arrow Treadwell	New York, Nov. 22	April 13—143 days (Dismasted 7 days out)
Sunny South, Gregory	New York, Cleared Nov. 21	April 12—143 days
Mountain Wave, Humphrey	Boston, Nov. 24	May 13—171 days
Tornado, Mumford	New York, Nov. 25	April 10—137 days
Golden City, Canfield	New York, Nov. 27	April 11—136 days. Passed Le Maire Jan. 27 in company with *Spitfire*
Reindeer, Bunker	Boston, Nov. 29	April 14—137 days (Dismasted 6th day out).
Spitfire, Arey	Boston, Nov. 30	March 28—119 days
Aurora, Brown	New York, Dec. 2	April 3—123 days
Sparkling Wave, Hubbard	Philadelphia, Cleared Dec. 6	April 14 via Montevideo 61 days —the present record—130 days
Water Witch, Plummer	New York, Cleared Dec. 6	April 11—127 days

SHIP AND MASTER	SAILED	ARRIVED AT SAN FRANCISCO
Neptune's Favorite, Lane	Philadelphia, Dec. 8	April 2—116 days
Don Quixote, Nott	Boston, Dec. 12	March 29—108 days
Western Continent, Burnham	New York, Dec. 12,	April 11—121 days
Gov. Morton, Burgess	New York, Dec. 15	April 2—104 days. 45 days to Horn—off Horn 12 days.
Charmer, Lucas	Boston, Dec. 15	April 12—119 days
Morning Light, Knight	New York, Dec. 19	April 12—115 days
Telegraph, Harlow	Boston, Dec. 20	April 9—111 days
S. S. Bishop, Shankland	Philadelphia, Dec. 23	April 29—128 days
White Squall — "3 masted brig," Marsden	New York, Dec. 29	Stove cabin bulwarks, broke boom and injured 4 men in squall Dec. 31 and returned.
Boston Light, Callaghan	Boston, Dec. 30	April 11—103 days

1855

John Fyfe, Lawton	Glasgow, Jan. 4	May 21—138 days
Westward Ho, Hussey	Boston, Jan. 12	April 24—101 days. (Reported Jan. 13 on arrival)
Elizabeth F. Willets, Sisson	New York, Jan. 13. Also said to have sailed Jan. 14 in company with *Neptune's Car*	May 10—118 days. Was 15 days within 800 miles of port.
Bk. *Greenfield,* Follansbee	New York, Jan. 14	May 6—113 days
Neptune's Car, Patten	New York, Jan. 14	April 25—122 days
Syren, Allen	Boston, Jan. 23	June 4—133 days
Harriet Hoxie Manwaring	Philadelphia, Jan. 24	May 31—128 days
Adelaide, Hamilton	New York, Jan. 27	May 21—115 days. Said to have made the latitude of Rio Janeiro in 25 days.
Kathay, Stoddard	New York, Jan. 27	May 31—125 days
Kingfisher, Crosby	Boston, Jan. 27	May 30—124 days
Phoenix, Hoxie	New York, Jan. 30	June 5—127 days
Paragon, Drinkwater	New York, Cleared Feb. 1	June 30—145 days

SHIP AND MASTER	SAILED	ARRIVED AT SAN FRANCISCO
Harvey Birch, Nelson	New York, Feb. 3	June 5—123 days
Winged Racer, Gorham	Boston, Feb. 3	June 3—121 days
Herald of the Morning, Baker	New York, Feb. 4	May 15—101 days
Samuel Russell, Yeaton	New York, Feb. 16	June 13—118 days
Flying Cloud, Cressy	New York, Cleared Feb. 15	June 6—112 days
Dashing Wave, Fisk	Boston, Feb. 18	June 19—122 days
White Squall—"3 masted-brig," Burk	New York, Feb. 17	Dismasted and put into Rio Janeiro, re-rigged as a barque and returned to New York
Samuel Willets, Spicer	New York, Feb. 20	June 19—120 days
Atalanta, Montell	New York, Feb. 24	June 30—124 days
Northern Empire, Hill	New York, Cleared Feb. 17	June 30—125 days
Key Stone, Wm. McFarland	Boston, Feb. 23	December 10 (150 days) Went to New York and sailed thence
Red Rover, Logan	New York, Feb. 24	June 13—110 days 20 days to line 48 to Horn
John Milton, McCleaves	Boston, Feb. 26	July 14—136 days
Monsoon, Baker	New York, Feb. 27	Aug. 2—157 days
Lookout, Joyce	New York, Mar. 1	Aug. 2—155 days
Ellen Foster, Scudder	Boston, Mar. 8	Aug. 2—152 days
Polynesia, Watson	Boston, Mar. 6	July 16—133 days
Panama, Cave	New York, Mar. 8	June 29—114 days. Sprung fore topmast split sails, etc., off Horn
Witchcraft, Freeman	New York, Mar. 10	July 13—126 days
Eagle, Farren	New York, Cleared Mar. 13	July 15—117 days
Queen of the Seas, Tay	Boston, Mar. 18	Aug. 2—138 days
Sword Fish, H. N. Osgood	New York, Cleared Mar. 19	July 21—113 days
Shooting Star, Kingman	New York, Mar. 21	July 15—115 days
War Hawk, Simmons	Boston, Mar. 27	Aug. 2—129 days

SHIP AND MASTER	SAILED	ARRIVED AT SAN FRANCISCO
Coringa, Hallet	Boston, Cleared Mar. 31	Aug. 30—153 days
Game Cock, Osgood	New York, April 1	Aug. 24—150 days
Messenger, Kennedy	New York, April 3	Aug. 2—122 days
Cœur de Lion, Tucker	New York, April 6	Aug. 2—119 days
Starlight, Chase	Boston, April 7	Aug. 30—146 days
Sea Serpent, J. D. Whitmore	New York, April 9	Sept. 5—147 days gross. (She was at Rio June 2) Carried away maintop mast—top-gallant mast trusses, yard slings, sails, etc., off River Plate
B. F. Hoxie, Stark	Philadelphia, Cleared April 9	Sept. 17—153 days
Carrington, French	New York, Cleared April 13	Sept. 16—153 days
Starr King, Turner	New York, Cleared April 19	Aug. 26—130 days
Kit Carson, Seth Crowell	Boston, April 24	Aug. 30—129 days
Robin Hood, Bearse	New York, April 25	Sept. 1—130 days
Alboni, Barnaby	New York, Cleared May 5	Oct. 21—165 days. Was 53 days without foretopgallant mast. Off Horn 18 days, 500 miles from port for 19 days in calms
Golden Eagle, Fabens	New York, May 10	Aug. 25—108 days
Meteor, Pike	Boston, May 12	Aug. 30—111 days
Highflyer, Waterman	New York, May 17	Oct. 8—144 days
Competitor, Otis White	Boston, May 28	Oct. 15—141 days
Radiant, Bearse	New York, Cleared May 28	Oct. 12—138 days. Was 8 days from 50 to 50 S.
Challenger, Burgess	Boston, June 2	Oct. 14—135 days
Fleet Wing, Howes	New York, Cleared June 2	Nov. 1—153 days
Bk. *Snap Dragon*, Brown	Philadelphia, June 4	Oct. 8—126 days
Galatea, Barber	New York, Cleared June 15	Oct. 29—137 days
Viking, Winsor	Boston, June 17	Oct. 17—123 days
Fearless, Manson	Boston, June 23	Oct. 19—118 days
Spirit of the Times, Klein	New York, Cleared June 23	Dec. 1—162 days

SHIP AND MASTER	SAILED	ARRIVED AT SAN FRANCISCO
Golden West, Putnam	New York, June 28	Dec. 22—178 days. Arrived Valparaiso Oct. 17. Sailed Nov. 10—Sprung bowsprit, lost main topsail, etc.
Thos. Wattson, Lyle	Philadelphia, passed Capes, July 5	Nov. 30—149 days
West Wind, Elliot	Boston, July 13	Nov. 22—133 days
Andrew Jackson, Williams	New York, Cleared July 13	Nov. 20—131 days
Sirocco, West	Philadelphia, Cleared July 14	Nov. 23—133 days
Hornet, Benson	New York, Cleared July 20	Nov. 12—116 days. Was 49 days to 50 S. and 7 days from 50 to 50 S.
Grace Darling, Doane	Boston, July 25	Dec. 1—130 days
Flying Dragon, Little	New York, Cleared July 28	Nov. 23—119 days
Midnight, Hatch	New York, Aug. 6	Dec. 29—146 days
Wild Rover, Taylor	Boston, Cleared Aug. 6	Dec. 21—138 days
Matchless, Potter	Boston, Aug. 9	Dec. 19—133 days
Ocean Telegraph, Willis	New York, Aug. 10	Dec. 8—121 days
Morning Star, Foster	New York, Aug. 18	Jan. 4—140 days
Samuel Appleton, Deshon	Boston, Aug. 18	Jan. 9—145 days
Red Gauntlet, Andrews	New York, Cleared Aug. 18	Mar. 1—194 days. Put into Valparaiso Dec. 19 to repair. Sailed Jan. 11—Was 50 days to line—80 to Horn
Winged Arrow, Bearse	Boston, Aug. 30	Jan. 4—128 days
Defender, Beauchamp	Boston, Sept. 1	Jan. 14—136 days
John Stuart, Chamberlin	New York, Sept. 4	Jan. 16—135 days
Black Warrior, Murphy	New York, Sept. 6	Jan. 8—125 days. Off Horn 15 days—light winds and calms except off Horn—300 miles from port for 8 days.
Flora Temple, Meyers	New York, Sept. 8	Feb. 19—164 days. 40 days off Horn—under storm sails all the time.
Flying Fish, Adams	Boston, Sept. 12	Dec. 27—107 days
Flying Eagle, Bates	New York, Sept. 20	Jan. 21—124 days

SHIP AND MASTER	SAILED	ARRIVED AT SAN FRANCISCO
Competitor, Hildreth	New York, Cleared Sept. 18	H. & M. says sailed May 28th
Sky Lark, Dow	New York, Cleared Sept. 19	Feb. 13—146 days
Gladiator, Whitfield	Baltimore, Cleared Sept. 22	Mar. 29—188 days
Wings of the Morning Lovell	Philadelphia, Cleared Sept. 26	Feb. 18—146 days
Wild Ranger, Sears	Boston, Oct. 3	Feb. 15—130 days
Mameluke, Whitney	Boston, Oct. 3	Feb. 19—139 days. Was off San Francisco 10 days in calms and fog
Carrier Dove, Corning	New York, Oct. 5	April 28 via Rio 98 days— Arrived Rio Janeiro Dec. 2. 8 days out she had carried away main mast 5 feet from eyes of rigging and fore and mizen topgallant masts with all attached—was at Rio 7 weeks
Sancho Panza, Hildreth	Boston, Cleared Oct. 11	Mar. 8—147 days. Put into Juan Fernandez for water, was there 4 days
Charmer, Lucas	New York, Oct. 15	Mar. 8—139 days
Noonday, Gerry	Boston, Oct. 17	Mar. 5—139 days
Resolute, McKenzie	New York, Cleared Oct. 16	Mar. 11—144 days
Comet, Arquit	New York, Cleared Oct. 24	Feb. 25. Reported 33 days to line, 77 to Horn—crossed line 110 days out. Arrived San Francisco *122 days*, which if correct would give her 12 days from Line?
Ringleader, Matthews	Boston, Oct. 27	Feb. 13—107 days
Victory, Drew	New York, Cleared Oct. 29	April 1—153 days
Wild Duck, Ellery	New York, Oct. 30	Mar. 9—132 days
Rival, Eben Sears	Boston, Nov. 8	Mar. 31—143 days
Southern Cross, Howes	Boston, Nov. 8	Mar. 8—120 days
Ocean Express, Cunningham	New York, Nov. 13	Mar. 27—133 days
Golden Racer, Wilson	New York, Cleared Nov. 15	Mar. 13—117 days
Anglo-Saxon, Mayo	New York, Nov. 16	Mar. 16—118 days

SHIP AND MASTER	SAILED	ARRIVED AT SAN FRANCISCO
Corinne, Stickney	Boston, Nov. 16	Mar. 31—155 days
Bk. *Greenfield*, Follansbee	Liverpool, Nov. 21	Mar. 13—111 days. (New York harbor Dec. 8, '55) Was 87 days to line—then light northerly winds
Daring, Simonson	Boston, Nov. 22	Mar. 13—112 days
Fair Wind, Allen	New York, Nov. 22	April 11—138 days
Brewster, Clark	New York, Nov. 23	Mar. 28—126 days
Star of the Union, Stahl	Boston, Nov. 26	May 11—113 net. Twisted rudder head off and went to Falklands to repair—47 days lost
Isaac Jeans, Chipman	Philadelphia, Cleared Nov. 28	April 11—129 days
Bk. *Hollander*, Millett	Boston, Cleared Nov. 30	April 12—133 days
Tornado, Mumford	New York, Dec. 6	Mar. 27—110 days
Antelope, Cole	New York, Cleared Dec. 7	Mar. 15—97 days
Reporter, Howes	New York, Cleared Dec. 8	Mar. 27—106 days
S. S. Bishop, Lindsay	Philadelphia, Cleared Dec. 14	April 11—113 days
Golden Fleece, Lunt	Boston, Dec. 17	April 9—112 days
Red Rover, Logan	New York, Dec. 17	April 7—110 days
Mary Whitridge, Cheesebrough	New York, Cleared Dec. 18	April 11—112 days
Flyaway, Sewall	New York, Dec. 22	April 8—106 days
Electric Spark, Laban Howes	Boston, Dec. 24	April 9—106 days
Adelaide, Wakeman	New York, Dec. 27	April 29—123 days
Osborn Howes, Kelly	New York, Dec. 27	April 30—124 days
Rambler, Lothrop	Boston, Dec. 31	May 22—142 days

1856

Wild Hunter, Sears	Boston, Cleared Jan. 5	April 29—108 days
Aurora, Clough	New York, Jan. 7	April 29—112 days
Golden City, Avery	New York, Cleared Jan. 7	May 1—113 days
David Brown, Bradley	New York, Jan. 15	April 28—103 days
Phantom, Peterson	New York, Jan. 18	April 29—101 days
Alexander, Holway	New York, Jan. 20	May 22—123 days
Sultan, Wyman	New York, Jan. 20	May 21—122 days
Derby, Hutchinson	Boston, Jan. 22	May 21—120 days

SHIP AND MASTER	SAILED	ARRIVED AT SAN FRANCISCO
Nabob, Bartlett	Boston, Jan. 29	May 21—112 days
Sea Nymph, Harding	New York, Feb. 1	May 25—113 days
Lotus, Leckie	New York, Cleared Feb. 1	July 5—146 days. Off Horn 20 days
Empress of the Seas, Wilson	New York, Feb. 8	June 3—115 days
Don Quixote, Elwell	Boston, Feb. 10	May 31—110 days
Star of Hope Sowerby	New York, Feb. 10	Dec. 7—via Montevideo 80 days. On fire April 14 at Montevideo. May 10 discharged. Still there July 13
Sweepstakes, Lane	New York, Feb. 20	May 25—93 days. Spoken March 25—latitude 32—20 South, 49 West.
White Swallow, Brown	New York, Feb. 20	July 5—136 days. Arrived Line 17½ days out. Heavy weather off Horn. Lost 3 men overboard—sprung bowsprit, etc.
Goddess, Crowell	Boston, Feb. 25	June 8—135 days
Storm King, Callaghan	New York, Feb. 26	July 3—124 days. Was 17 days to line—48 to Straits le Maire —10 days off Horn.
Wizard, Slate	New York, Feb. 29	June 27—117 days. Off Horn 15 days—crossed line 86th day out.
Mastiff, Johnson	Boston, March 7	July 19—133 days
Sierra Nevada, Penhallow	New York, March 9	July 15—129 days
Syren, Foster	New York, March 12	July 25—130 days
Flying Cloud, Reynard	New York, Cleared, March 13	Sept. 14—185 days via Rio. Put into Rio Janeiro June 5, partly dismasted and sailed again June 22nd.
Morning Light, Johnson	Philadelphia, March 17	Aug. 12—144 days
Eagle Wing, Waters	New York, March 25	July 23—118 days
Young America, Babcock	New York, Cleared March 26	July 14—107 days. 49 days to Horn. Struck by sea May 18— broke jibboom 3 pcs. Stove bulwarks, started two cheeks, etc.
Alarm, Matthews	Boston, April 4 (Log)	Aug. 16 (Log) 130 days
Mary L. Sutton, Rowland	New York, April 5	July 26—110 days

SHIP AND MASTER	SAILED	ARRIVED AT SAN FRANCISCO
Neptune's Favorite, Lane	Boston, April 8	July 31—115 days
North Wind, Gove	New York, April 8	July 31—115 days
Polynesia, Perkins	New York, Cleared April 11	
Cœur de Lion, Tucker	New York, April 18	Aug. 26—131 days
Competitor, Wade	Boston, Cleared April 19	Sept. 13—139 days (Barometer went to 27—80 days off Horn.)
Eureka, Canfield	New York, April 26	Aug. 26—120 days
John Gilpin, Ring	New York, Cleared April 28	Sept. 22—140 days
Santa Claus, Foster	Boston, May 1,	Sept. 21—140 days
Sea Serpent, Whitmore	New York, May 4	Sept. 12—129 days
Napier, Stafford	New York, May 4	Sept. 23—141 days
Onward, Luce	New York, Cleared May 6	Oct. 15—158 days
Nor' Wester, Gregory	Boston, May 7	Sept. 22—132 days
John E. Thayer, Pousland	New York, May 11	Sept. 22—130 days
Flying Dutchman, Hubbard	New York, May 18	Sept. 19—124 days
Robin Hood, Bearse	New York, May 20	Sept. 22—125 days
Thatcher Magoun, Baxter	Boston, Cleared May 20	Sept. 22—140 days
Endeavor, Doane	New York, May 21	Sept. 26—128 days
Western Continent, Burnham	New York, May 22	Nov. 15—176 days via Valparaiso 49 days.
Rapid, Winsor	New York, Cleared May 26	Jan. 5, 57 via Rio 225 days
Euterpe, Arey	New York, June 2	Sept. 22—112 days
Reindeer, Bunker	New York, Cleared June 2	Nov. 18—162 days
B. F. Hoxie, Crary	New York, Cleared June 5	Nov. 6—149 days
Black Prince, Brown	Boston, June 9	Nov. 6—151 days
Norseman, Haskell	New York, June 10	Oct. 31—144 days
Kate Hooper, Jackson	New York, June 11	Oct. 25—131 days
Archer, Osgood	New York, Cleared June 13	Nov. 5—135 days
Silver Star, Wade	New York, Cleared June 17	Nov. 19—148 days
Fearless, Manson	Boston, June 25	Oct. 31—127 days
Romance of the Seas, Henry	New York, Cleared June 30	Oct. 24—113 days

SHIP AND MASTER	SAILED	ARRIVED AT SAN FRANCISCO
Northern Eagle, Hill	Boston, June 30	Dec. 16—168 days
Intrepid, Gardner	New York, Cleared June 30	Nov. 26—145 days
Neptune's Car, Patten	New York, Cleared June 30	Nov. 15—134 days
Fleet Wing, Howes	New York, Cleared July 3	Dec. 13—158 days
Oriental, Whipple	New York, Cleared July 8, Reported for Benecia	Nov. 24—135 days
Snow Squall, Lloyd	New York, July 9	Jan. 30—via Montevideo 60 days. Arrived Montevideo Sept. 15 in distress. Lost suit of sails, topgallant masts, main topmast, etc.
Joseph Peabody, Weston	Boston, July 14	Dec. 6—145 days
Bald Eagle, W. H. Treadwell	New York, July 18	Nov. 15—120 days
Tsar, Fales	New York, Cleared July 25	Jan. 15—168 days
Aspasia, Green	Philadelphia, Cleared July 22, and went to sea from Lewes, July 25	Dec. 8—134 days
Golden Eagle, Fabens	New York, Cleared July 26	Dec. 1—112 days
Ocean Telegraph, Willis	New York, Cleared Aug. 1	Jan. 3—154 days
Ocean Pearl, Crowell	New York, Cleared Aug. 6	Jan. 14—157 days
Midnight, Hatch	New York, Aug. 12	Jan. 3—142 days
Bostonian, Maling	Boston, Aug. 12	Jan. 3—142 days
Cyclone, Osgood	Boston, Aug. 22	Jan. 10—140 days
Starlight, Matthews	New York, Aug. 21	Jan. 3—135 days
Reynard, Drew	Boston, Sept. 3	Jan. 22—140 days
Dashing Wave, Young	New York. Cleared Sept. 9	Jan. 10—120 days
Undaunted, Freeman	New York, Cleared Sept. 8	Jan. 20—132 days
Winged Arrow, Bearse	Boston, Sept. 15	Jan. 12—119 days
Hound, Stevens	New York, Cleared Sept. 17	Aug. 26 '57—via Rio 115 days— Put into Rio. Sailed April 28

SHIP AND MASTER	SAILED	ARRIVED AT SAN FRANCISCO
Galatea, Barber	New York, Cleared Sept. 29	Jan. 28—116 days
Flying Fish, Nickels	Boston, Oct. 4	Jan. 19—106 days
Edwin Forrest, Crocker	New York, Cleared Oct. 11	Feb. 25—132 days
Harvey Birch, Nelson	New York, Oct. 16	Mar. 3—139 days
West Wind, Hatch	Boston, Oct. 19	Mar. 2—135 days
Beaver, Smith	New York, Cleared Oct. 23	Mar. 2—131 days
War Hawk, Freeman	New York, Cleared Oct. 23	Mar. 2—131 days
Morning Light, Knight	Boston, Oct. 28	Mar. 2—126 days
Defender, Robinson	New York, Cleared Oct. 31	Mar. 30—148 days
Andrew Jackson, Williams	New York, Nov. 13	Feb. 28—102 days
Flying Mist, Linnell	Boston, Cleared Nov. 15	Mar. 12—113 days. Becalmed 15 days in Atlantic and 11 days in Pacific
Flying Dragon, Little	New York, Cleared Nov. 24	Mar. 5—102 days
Uncowah, Kirby	New York, Nov. 28	Mar. 26—116 days
Morning Star, Foster	Boston, Dec. 4	Mar. 16—101 days
Great Republic, Limeburner	New York, Dec. 5	Mar. 9—92 days. Was 15 days 18 hours to line; 46 days to Horn, best day 413 miles. 3 days off harbor in fog.
Flying Eagle, Bates	Boston, Dec. 5	April 4—118 days
Westward Ho, Hussey	New York, Cleared Dec. 6	Mar. 26—101 days
John Milton, Harding	New York, Dec. 8	May 6—149 days
Wild Rover, Crowell	Boston, Dec. 17	April 24—127 days
Reporter, Howes	New York, Dec. 25	April 17—110 days. Passed Horn 50 days out. Line 84 days, and was within 700 miles of San Francisco for 17 days.
Webfoot, Hedge	New York, Dec. 26	April 23—119 days

1857

Charger, Hurd	Boston, Jan. 4	May 8—124 days
Stag Hound, Peterson	Boston, Jan. 4	April 22—108 days
Asa Eldridge, Coleman	New York, Jan. 5	May 8—122 days

SHIP AND MASTER	SAILED	ARRIVED AT SAN FRANCISCO
Electric Spark, Titcomb	New York, Jan. 7	May 7—118 days. 21 days to Line—54 to Horn.
Mameluke, Whitney	New York, Jan. 13	July 5—173 days
Noonday, Brock	Boston, Jan. 15	May 13—113 days
Comet, Arquit	New York, Jan. 30	June 22?—142 days. Returning to New York she reported 98 sailing days from San Francisco and 92 from Elide I. Lower California and 14 days from Line in the Atlantic to New York
Courser, Cole	New York, Jan. 30	July 4—154 days
Southern Cross, Howes	Boston, Feb. 4	June 22—138 days
Lookout, Hamilton	New York, Feb. 9	June 5—116 days
Golden Fleece, Lunt	New York, Feb. 10	June 21—124 days
Cowper, Stevens	New York, Feb. 12	July 2—134 days
Ringleader, Matthews	Boston, Feb. 17	June 21—122 days
Red Rover, Logan	New York, Feb. 28	July 4—124 days
Osborn Howes, Kelly	New York, Mar. 3	July 30—147 days
Wild Hunter, Sears	Boston, Mar. 7	July 15—129 days
David Crockett, Spencer	New York, Mar. 10	July 19—122 days
E. F. Willets, Holmes	New York, Mar. 25	Aug. 1—130 days
Mary L. Sutton, Sisson	New York, Cleared Mar. 28	Aug. 19—143 days
Black Hawk, Bowers	New York, April 2	July 30—119 days
Fair Wind, Stroot	Boston, April 1	Sept. 9—158 days
Aurora, Clough	New York, Cleared April 4	Nov. 6—via Rio 105 days—Carried away rudder head near Falklands—went back to Rio—in port 40 days. Sailed July 24
Daring, Simonson	New York, Cleared April 9	Aug. 22—131 days
Charmer, Lucas	New York, April 18	Sept. 2—133 days
John Land, Bearse	Boston, April 16	July 30—102 days
Belle of the Sea, Lewis	Boston, April 25	Aug. 31—128 days
Storm King, Callaghan	New York, Cleared April 25	Sept. 2—123 days
Panama, Cave	New York, Cleared May 5	Sept. 2—117 days

SHIP AND MASTER	SAILED	ARRIVED AT SAN FRANCISCO
Belvidere, Jackson	Boston, May 7	Sept. 11—127 days
Mastiff, Johnson	New York, Cleared May 11	Sept. 29—140 days
Flora Temple, Cole	New York, May 12	Sept. 14—123 days
Indiaman, Smith	Boston, Cleared May 22	Sept. 9—124 days
Adelaide, Wakeman	New York, May 25	Sept. 29—127 days
Flying Dutchman, Hubbard	New York, Cleared May 30	Sept. 10—102 days
Sancho Panza, Bird	New York, Cleared June 2	Nov. 16—141 days
Talisman, Thomas	New York, Cleared June 2	Oct. 24—140 days
Lotus, Leckie	New York, Cleared June 4	Oct. 19—133 days
Herald of the Morning, Lathrop	New York, Cleared July 6	Nov. 15—130 days
Sierra Nevada, Penhallow	Boston, June 16	Nov. 5—140 days
Panther, Gannett	Boston, July 8	Nov. 30—144 days. Was off Horn all September
Goddess, Crowell	Boston, July 9	Nov. 16—129 days
Empress of the Sea, Wilson	New York, July 12	Nov. 14—124 days
Conquest, Sears	New York, Cleared July 18	Dec. 20—156 days
Atmosphere, Lunt	New York, Cleared July 18	Dec. 23—150 days
Frigate Bird, Cope	Philadelphia, Cleared July 21	Jan. 6—165 days
Polynesia, Perkins	Boston, July 28	Dec. 15—130 days
Flyaway, Sewall	New York, Aug. 6	Dec. 14—125 days
Sparkling Sea, Ryder	Boston, Aug. 19	Jan. 22—150 days
Thatcher Magoun, Baxter	New York, Aug. 20	Dec. 25—125 days
Neptune's Car, Bearse	New York, Cleared Aug. 29	Mar. 4—180 days. Arrived Rio Nov. 8—foremast sprung
Golden Rule, Mayo	Boston, Aug. 29	Jan. 8—114 days
Wild Wave, Knowles	New York, Cleared Aug. 31	Jan. 23—140 days
Kit Carson, Dillingham	New York, Cleared Sept. 11	Feb. 11—147 days. Was 30 days off Horn
Flying Fish, Nickels	Boston, Sept. 28	Jan. 20—114 days

SHIP AND MASTER	SAILED	ARRIVED AT SAN FRANCISCO
Santa Claus, Foster	New York, Cleared Oct. 8	Feb. 21—128 days
Bostonian, Burnham	New York, Cleared Oct. 17	Mar. 4—140 days
Starlight, Matthews	Boston, Oct. 21	Feb. 17—118 days
Challenger, Windsor	New York, Oct. 23	Feb. 17—111 days
Webfoot, Hedge	New York, Cleared Nov. 12	Mar. 15 '58—119 days
Don Quixote, Hale	New York, Nov. 15	Mar. 4—108½ days
Vitula, Hubbard	Boston, Nov. 20	April 1—128 days
Ocean Telegraph, Willis	New York, Cleared Nov. 24	Mar. 15, '58. Passage reported as 105 days—20 hrs.
Fleetwing, Howes	Boston, Cleared Dec. 3	Mar. 28—113 days
Mary Robinson, Harding	New York, Dec. 7	April 10—122 days
Esther May, Clark	Boston, Dec. 8	May 19—165 days
Viking, Winsor	New York, Dec. 10	Mar. 30—108 days
Chatsworth, Horne	Boston, Dec. 19 (Also reported sailed 20th)	April 18—118 days

1858

Dashing Wave, Young	Boston, Jan. 1	April 18—107 days
Twilight, Gates	New York, Jan. 5	April 16—100 days. 45 days to Horn and within 900 miles of port for 12 days
Lookout, Sherwood	New York, Jan. 5	April 27—112 days. 47 days to Horn
Chariot of Fame, Knowles	New York, Jan. 7	May 13—125 days
Ocean Express, Hotchkiss	New York, Jan. 8	May 13—124 days
Richard Busteed, Stanwood	Boston, Jan. 10	July 8—178 days
Andrew Jackson, Williams	New York, Jan. 16	April 27—102 days. 47 days to Horn—off Horn 13 days moderate weather
Black Prince, Brown	Boston, Jan. 19	July 6—160 days, via Rio—105. Arrived Rio Feb. 27—mutiny —left Mar. 9
Edwin Forrest, Crocker	New York, Jan. 25	June 8—133 days

SHIP AND MASTER	SAILED	ARRIVED AT SAN FRANCISCO
Edwin Flye, Weaver	New York, Cleared Jan. 25	June 12—135 days
Golden Eagle, Harding	New York, Jan. 27	June 12—135 days
Flying Eagle, Bates	New York, Feb. 5	June 23—132 days
E. F. Willets, Holmes	New York, Cleared Feb. 5	June 11—122 days
Stag Hound, Hussey	Boston, Feb. 6	June 7—121 days. Reported in 7 S. latitude 21 days out
Southern Cross, Howes	Boston, Feb. 12	July 4—140 days
Phantom, Peterson	New York, Feb. 15	June 21—127 days
Star of the Union, Stahl	New York, Cleared Feb. 23	July 5—124 days
Raduga, Burditt	Boston, Feb. 24	Aug. 16—174 days via Rio
Gauntlet, Borland	New York, Feb. 27	Aug. 9—161 days
Charger, Hurd	Boston, March 2	July 1—117 days
Rattler, Almy	New York, March 9	July 3—115 days
Black Warrior, Murphy	New York, Mar. 10	July 2—114 days
Defender, Robinson	New York, Mar. 13	Aug. 13—150 days
Witchcraft, Boott	Boston, Mar. 13	Aug. 30—via Valparaiso 170 days
Oracle, Wood	New York, Mar. 14	July 1—109 days
Flying Dragon, Little	New York, Mar. 25	July 30—126 days
David Crockett, Spencer	New York, Mar. 24	July 17—116 days
West Wind, Baxter	Boston, Mar. 25	Aug. 11—137 days
Morning Star, Foster	New York, Mar. 31	Aug. 4—125 days
Ringleader, Matthews	New York, April 3	July 27—114 days (Spoke *John Land* 10 days before arrival)
John Land, Bearse	Boston, April 6	July 24—108 days
Anglo-Saxon, H. Manter or Munter?	New York, April 10	Sept. 21—164 days
Sky Lark, Follansbee	New York, April 14	Aug. 9—116 days
Harvey Birch, Nelson	New York, April 17	Sept. 24—159 days
War Hawk, Simmons	New York, Cleared April 30	Sept. 24—142 days
Radiant, Hallett	New York, May 4?	Sept. 23—143 days
Horsburg, Oakes	Boston, May 5	Oct. 1—128 days
Hound, Baker	New York, Cleared May 11	Sept. 22—131 days

SHIP AND MASTER	SAILED	ARRIVED AT SAN FRANCISCO
Reynard, Freeman	Boston, May 12	Sept. 24—132 days
Juniata, Wilson	Baltimore (Cape Henry), May 15	Nov. 12—150 days
Mary L. Sutton, Spicer	New York, Cleared May 25	Sept. 24—116 days
Renown, Smith	Boston, May 26	Oct. 1—127 days
Reporter, Howes	New York, June 3	Oct. 15—130 days
Alboni, Barnaby	New York, Cleared June 8	Nov. 8—150 days
Grace Darling, Bearse	Boston, June 10	Oct. 15—125 days
Endeavor, Doane	New York, June 15	Oct. 16—122 days
Asa Eldridge, Coleman	New York, June 23	Nov. 17—147 days
Golden City, Leary	Boston, June 24	Nov. 16—144 days
Indiaman, Smith	Boston, June 30	Nov. 17—140 days
Eagle Wing, Worth	New York, Cleared June 30	Nov. 10—131 days
Silver Star, Wade	New York, July 4	Nov. 30—140 days. Also reported as arrived Nov. 21 by Overland mail.
Queen of the Pacific, Dubois	New York, July 8	Nov. 17—131 days. Put into Pernambuco for water, 126 days net.
Challenge, Fabens	New York, July 17	Nov. 12—117 days
Golden Fleece, Manson	Boston, Cleared July 24	Nov. 15—112 days
Rambler, Lothrop	New York, Cleared July 27	Jan. 17—173 days
Henry Brigham, Young	New York, July 27	Dec. 6—131 days
Wandering Jew, Stackpole	New York, Aug. 6	Jan. 17—163 days
Euterpe, Arey	New York, Sept. 1	Jan. 14—135 days
Great Republic, Limeburner	New York, Aug. 30	Dec. 28—120 days
Adelaide, Wakeman	New York, Aug. 30	Jan. 10—133 days. Was in company with *Great Republic* for 10 days up to Cape St. Roque.
Superior, Soule	New York, Cleared Aug. 27	Jan. 18—140 days
Memnon (2), Jenkins	Boston, Aug. 30	Jan. 18—159 days
Talisman, Thomas	New York, Cleared Sept. 4	Jan. 17—136 days

SHIP AND MASTER	SAILED	ARRIVED AT SAN FRANCISCO
Stephen R. Mallory, Lester	New York, Cleared Sept. 4	Feb. 2—146 days
Polynesia, Morse	Boston, Sept. 9	Mar. 25—198 days
Mary Whitridge, Cressy	New York, Sept. 13	Jan. 29—136 days
Fleetwing, C. Howes	New York, Sept. 18	Feb. 11—145 days
Galatea, Lunt	New York, Cleared Sept. 23	Feb. 18—144 days. Arrived San Francisco Feb. 8—Osborn Howes, Boston Feb. 10
Seaman's Bride, Wyman	New York, Sept. 25	April 4—185 days
Carrier Dove, Montell	New York, Cleared Oct. 1	Mar. 8—155 days
Archer, Crowell	New York, Cleared Oct. 7	Feb. 10—127 days
Robin Hood, Matthews	New York, Oct. 14	Feb. 11—119 days
Ocean Belle, Brown	New York, Cleared Oct. 18	Mar. 27—157 days
Crest of the Wave, Colley	New York, Cleared Oct. 20	April 8—163 days 36 days off Horn
Intrepid, Gardner	New York, Cleared Oct.20	Mar. 5—132 days
Manitou, Honeywell	New York, Cleared Oct. 23	April 10—168 days
Sea Nymph, Whiting	New York, Cleared Nov. 1	Mar. 22—137 days
Grey Feather, Harford	New York, Cleared Nov. 3	Mar. 19—128 days
Ocean Telegraph, Potter	New York, Cleared Nov. 3	Mar. 17—125 days
Moonlight, Breck	New York, Cleared Nov. 4	April 7—150 days
Fearless, Devens	Boston, Nov. 13	Mar. 17—125 days
Kingfisher, Harlow	Boston, Cleared Nov. 2	Mar. 18—128 days
Industry, Waters	Boston, Cleared Nov. 2	April 4—146 days
Ivanhoe, Lane	New York, Nov. 11	Mar. 30—138 days
Prima Donna, Pray	New York, Nov. 20	Mar. 20—119 days
Herald of the Morning, Baker	Boston, Nov. 22	Mar. 18—116 days
Neptune's Favorite, Emmerton	New York, Nov. 24	Mar. 23—117 days

SHIP AND MASTER	SAILED	ARRIVED AT SAN FRANCISCO
Midnight, Brock	Boston, Dec. 2	April 5—121 days
Starlight, Howes	New York, Dec. 6	April 3—118 days
Golden Rocket, Pendleton	Boston, Dec. 8	May 18—158 days
Nonpareil, Green	New York, Dec. 11	April 7—115 days
Comet, Todd	New York, Dec. 15	April 7—112 days
Nightingale, Peterson	Boston, Cleared Dec. 27	May 18—148 days
Andrew Jackson, Williams	New York, Dec. 23	April 5—103 days. Wind south with rain at sunset
Aspasia	New York, Dec. 23	May 31—158 days
Storm King, Callaghan	New York, Dec. 28	May 18—138 days
Queen of the Seas, Crowell	Boston, Dec. 28	May 17—138 days

1859

Derby, Hutchinson	New York, Jan. 2	May 18—135 days
Hurricane, Sherman	New York, Jan. 9	May 30—142 days
Hornet, Mitchell	Boston, Jan. 18	May 28—128 days
Flying Childers, Horton	Boston, Cleared Jan. 22	May 28—117 days
Sweepstakes, McGill	New York, Jan. 23	May 8—106 days
Lookout, Sherwood	New York, Jan. 24	May 17—112 days
Northern Eagle, McKinney	New York, Jan. 25	Aug. 1—via Rio 190 days
Challenger, Winsor	New York, Jan. 26	Returned to New York Feb. 16 partly dismasted
Young America, Brown	New York, Jan. 30	July 24—174 days. Dismasted and put into Rio Janeiro. Left Rio May 15th and came out in 69 days—2nd best on record.
Wizard, Woodside	New York, Jan. 31	June 24—144 days. Had very rough voyage, rolled masts out—filled cabins, etc., four days out
Whirlwind, Giet	New York, Cleared Feb. 3	May 5—120 days
Belvidere, Jackson	Boston, Cleared Feb. 8	July 17—157 days
Flying Mist, Linnell	New York, Feb. 20	June 26—123 days
Cyclone, Millet	Boston, Feb. 28	June 30—122 days
Flying Eagle, Bates	New York, Feb. 28	Aug. 1—153 days

SHIP AND MASTER	SAILED	ARRIVED AT SAN FRANCISCO
Kathay, Stoddard	New York, Mar. 10	July 9—121 days
Belle of the West, Howes	Boston, Mar. 11	July 25—136 days
Ocean Express, Willis	New York, Mar. 13	Aug. 1—140 days
Amos Lawrence, Nickerson	New York, Mar. 13	Aug. 1—140 days
David Crockett, Rowland	New York, Mar. 16	July 27—131 days
White Swallow, Crosby	New York, Mar. 16	July 27—128 days
Sparkling Wave, McCort	New York, Mar. 18 Cleared	Feb. 6—324 days via Rio—163 days—Valparaiso 56
Nor' Wester, Savory	Boston, Mar. 19	July 28—129 days
Rattler, Almy	New York, Mar. 21	Aug. 30—160 days
Meteor, Melville	New York, Mar. 26	July 23—114 days
Waverley, Reed	Boston, Mar. 31	Sept. 12—166 days
Dashing Wave, Lecraw	Boston, April 4	Aug. 3—120 days
E. F. Willets, Gates	New York, Cleared April 4	July 27—111 days
Chariot of Fame, Knowles	New York, April 7	Aug. 3—117 days
Orpheus, Howes	New York, April 8	Aug. 1—114 days
Challenger, Windsor	New York, April 16	Aug. 15—120 days
Charger, Hatch	Boston, April 20	Aug. 23—124 days
Witch of the Wave, Todd	New York, April 24	Sept. 7—135 days
Viking, Winsor	New York, April 30	Sept. 12—133 days
B. F. Hoxie, Crary	New York, May 2	Sept. 16—138 days
Flying Dragon, Watson	Boston, May 8	Sept. 6—119 days
Cherubim, Skinner	New York, May 9	Nov. 19—193 days via Valparaiso—43 days
Northern Light, Doane	Boston, May 16	Sept. 16—124 days
Webfoot, Hedge	New York, Cleared May 17	Oct. 22—159 days. Probably weather bound and sailed when *Golden Eagle* did—May 23
Golden Eagle, Luce	New York, May 23	Dec. 24—217 days. Was 90 days off Horn in heavy gales
Wild Rover, Sparrow	New York, May 25	Nov. 20—173 days
Uncowah, Kirby	New York, Cleared June 2	Oct. 22—143 days

SHIP AND MASTER	SAILED	ARRIVED AT SAN FRANCISCO
Twilight, Gates	New York, June 3	Sept. 26—114 days
Daring, Simonson	New York, Cleared June 8	Nov. 5—151 days
Southern Cross, Howes	Boston, June 10	Oct. 22—134 days
Endeavor, Truman Doane	New York, June 23	Nov. 6—137 days
Anglo Saxon, Cavarly	New York, Cleared June 24	Nov. 12—142 days
War Hawk, Simons	Boston, Cleared June 25	Nov. 19—148 days
Shooting Star, Hotchkiss	New York, June 28	Nov. 19—142 days
Lotus, Leckie	New York, Cleared June 30	Nov. 19—143 days
Arey, Wilson	New York, July 11	Jan. 1, '60—170 days
Golden Fleece, Manson	New York, July 14	Nov. 12—118 days
Queen of the Pacific, Dubois	New York, Cleared July 27	Lost 190 miles north of Pernambuco, Sept. 19th
Mary Robinson, McCleave	New York, Aug. 2	Dec. 24—144 days
Talisman, Thomas	New York, Cleared Aug. 15	Jan. 6, '60. Reported 142 days
Don Quixote, Nott	New York, Cleared Aug. 17	Jan. 4, '60—141 days
West Wind, Baxter	New York, Aug. 20	Feb. 10—170 days
Malay, Wilcomb	New York, Sept. 4	Jan. 31—149 days
Black Hawk, Bowers	New York, Cleared Sept. 6	Jan. 25, '60—142 days
Panther, Gannett	Boston, Cleared Sept. 14	Feb. 3—139 days
Francis A. Palmer, Allen	New York, Sept. 15	Mar. 5—164 days
Asa Eldridge, Coleman	New York, Sept. 29	Feb. 10—132 days
Reynard, Freeman	New York, Sept. 30	Dismasted 6 days out. Put into Boston and sailed thence Nov. 4. Arrived at San Francisco Mar. 13—130 days
Prima Donna, Pray	New York, Cleared Oct. 3	Feb. 10—126 days
Eagle Wing, Worth	New York, Oct. 6	Feb. 3—120 days
Noonday, Henry	Boston, Oct. 6	Feb. 10—126 days

SHIP AND MASTER	SAILED	ARRIVED AT SAN FRANCISCO
Good Hope, Miller	New York, Oct. 19	Mar. 12—144 days
Henry Brigham, Potter	New York, Oct. 20	
Zephyr, King	New York, Cleared Oct. 21	April 5—168 days
Napier, Keith	New York, Oct. 22	Feb. 19—119 days
Expounder, Knowles	Boston, Oct. 25	Mar. 12—138 days
Europa, Robertson	New York, Oct. 31	Feb. 27—117 days
Lookout, Sherwood	New York, Nov. 3	Feb. 20—109 days
Reynard, Freeman	Boston, Nov. 5	2nd sailing having been dismasted, shortly before
Reporter, Holt	New York, Nov. 20	Mar. 17—123 days
John Land, Bearse	Boston, Nov. 25	Aug. 21—271 days. Arrived Valparaiso Feb. 23, leaky
Great Republic, Limeburner	New York, Nov. 23	Mar. 12—109 days
Ocean Telegraph, Little	New York, Nov. 24	Mar. 12—109 days
Archer, Schibye	New York, Cleared Nov. 29	Mar. 71—110 days
Robin Hood, Matthews	New York, Dec. 8	Mar. 25—107 days
Sea Nymph, Whiting	New York, Dec. 19	April 23—130 days
John Stuart, Bernsee	New York, Dec. 21	April 23—124 days
Fleetwing, Howes	New York, Dec. 23	May 1—131 days
Sierra Nevada, Jas. G. Foster	Boston, Dec. 24	Mar. 31—98 days
Andrew Jackson, Williams	New York, Dec. 25	Mar. 24—89 days
Neptune's Car, Sprague	New York, Dec. 31	April 23—115 days

1860

Morning Star, Foster	Boston, Jan. 7	April 22—106 days
Galatea, Wendell	New York, Jan. 14	May 27—135 days
Midnight, Broeck	Boston, Jan. 17	May 17—111 days
Morning Light, Johnston	Philadelphia, Jan. 17	June 7—140 days
Starlight, Howes	New York, Jan. 19	May 19—121 days
Vitula, Bursley	New York, Cleared Jan. 19	May 29—130 days
Mary L. Sutton, Spicer	New York, Cleared Jan. 26	May 12—103 days. 22 to line —50 to Horn—off Horn 15 days

SHIP AND MASTER	SAILED	ARRIVED AT SAN FRANCISCO
Carrier Dove, Montell	New York, Feb. 3	June 8—127 days
Herald of the Morning, Mitchell	Boston, Feb. 7	May 25—108 days
Silver Star, Wade	Baltimore (Hampton Rds.), Feb. 10	
Ocean Pearl, Crowell	New York, Feb. 17	June 29—132 days
Euterpe, Arey	New York, Cleared Feb. 25	June 25—118 days
David Crockett, Burgess	New York, Mar. 2	July 3—123 days
Comet, Todd	New York, Mar. 9	June 30—113 days
Witchcraft, Boott	New York, Mar. 20	July 29—131 days
Jacob Bell, Frisbie	New York, Mar. 20	July 15—117 days
Storm King, Callaghan	New York, Mar. 27	Aug. 21—148 days
Pampero, Lester	New York, April 2	July 31—121 days
B. F. Hoxie, Crary	New York, April 5	Aug. 24—142 days
Nonpareil, Green	New York, April 17	Aug. 24—130 days
White Swallow, Crosby	Boston, April 18	Aug. 7—112 days. Was off the Heads 6 days in fog.
E. F. Willets, Barrett	New York, Cleared April 18	Sept. 30—166 days
Hornet, Mitchell	New York, April 19	Sept. 2—137 days
Electric Spark, Candage	Boston, April 21	Sept. 10—142 days
David Brown, Berry	New York, Cleared April 27	Aug. 30—126 days
Derby, Hutchinson	New York, May 15	Oct. 19—155 days
Black Prince, Brown	New York, May 25	Oct. 19—148 days
Neptune's Favorite, Emerton	New York, May 26	Oct. 12—140 days
Challenger, Winsor	New York, May 29	Oct. 4—128 days
Meteor, Melville	Boston, May 30	Oct. 12—133 days
Panama, Soule	New York, June 2	Oct. 1—121 days
Winged Arrow, Berry	Boston, June 18	Nov. 16—150 days
Golden Fleece, Manson	New York, June 22	Oct. 29—130 days
Golden State, Ranlett	New York, June 22	Oct. 29—128 days
Southern Cross, Howes	Boston, July 6	Nov. 15—133 days
Ocean Express, Haley	New York, Cleared July 10	Nov. 30—144 days

SHIP AND MASTER	SAILED	ARRIVED AT SAN FRANCISCO
Fair Wind, Elkanah Crowell	New York, Cleared July 27	Dec. 7—133 days
Nor'Wester, Almy	Boston, July 28	Dec. 14—140 days
Morning Light, Thomas	New York, Aug. 8	Dec. 14—129 days
Orpheus, Howes	New York, Cleared Aug. 11	Dec. 31—141 days
Dashing Wave, Lecraw	Boston, Aug. 15	Jan. 5—141 days
Aurora, Clough	New York, Cleared Aug. 30	Jan. 19—139 days
Web Foot, Hedge	New York, Cleared Sept. 8	Jan. 24—134 days
Flying Childers, Horton	New York, Cleared Sept. 8	Jan. 6—115 days
Ringleader, Matthews	Boston, Sept. 10	Jan. 14—115 days
Shirley, Brown	Boston, Sept. 15	Feb. 23—160 days
Ocean Telegraph, Little	New York, Cleared Sept. 22	Jan. 30—125 days
Skylark, Bursley	New York, Sept. 29	Feb. 18—142 days
Eagle Wing, Colby	New York, Cleared Oct. 8	Feb. 11—122 days
Lookout, Sherwood	New York, Cleared Oct. 11	Feb. 22—130 days
Malay, Wilcomb	Boston, Oct. 18	Feb. 21—125 days
Radiant, Matthews	Boston, Cleared Oct. 20	Mar. 12—137 days. Sailed, put back and remained 23rd
Great Republic, Limeburner	New York, Oct. 24	Feb. 6—104 days
Sierra Nevada, Foster	New York, Cleared Oct. 26	Mar. 2—117 days. Reported 116 days
Anglo-Saxon, Cavarly	New York, Cleared Nov. 5	Mar. 15—137 days
Flying Eagle, Walden	New York, Cleared Nov. 7	April 18—160 days. Anchored off Bedloes Island, Nov. 10— via Montevideo, 84 days
Mary L. Sutton, Spicer	New York, Nov. 20	Mar. 11—110 days
Mary Robinson, McCleave	New York, Nov. 28	Mar. 29—120 days
Belle of the Sea, Sigsbee	New York, Nov. 28	April 19—134 days
Grace Darling, Bearse	Boston, Nov. 30	April 8—129 days

SHIP AND MASTER	SAILED	ARRIVED AT SAN FRANCISCO
Golden Eagle, Swift	New York, Cleared Dec. 5	Mar. 28—110 days
Racer, J. D. Gates	New York, Dec. 14	May 8—144 days
Spitfire, Leach	Boston, Dec. 21	April 8—107 days
Black Hawk, Bowers	New York, Dec. 21	April 8—107 days
Talisman, Thomas	New York, Cleared Dec. 18	April 13—112 days
Morning Star, Foster	New York, Cleared Dec. 22	April 23—118 days
Romance of the Seas, Clough	Boston, Dec. 28	April 13—105 days

APPENDIX V

Flying Cloud, JOSIAH P. CRESSY, FROM NEW YORK TO
SAN FRANCISCO, 1851

June 3   Lat. 39.27 N.   Lon. 70.47   W   WNW   SW   NW
Moderate breezes   fine weather.   Left foot of Maiden Lane at 2
P.M. & pilot at 7 off the Hook

June 4   Lat. 38.49   Lon. 67.47   NW   WNW   W   Moderate breezes   fine weather

June 5   Lat. 37.25   Lon. 63.17   WNW   WNW   NW   Moderate breezes   fine weather

June 6   Lat. 36.36   Lon. 57.15   NW   NW   NW   Good
breezes   fine weather   Lost Main & Mizen Topgallant mast &
Main Topsail yard

June 7   Lat. 36.09   Lon. 55.18   NW   WSW   WSW   Good
breezes   fine weather   Sent up topgallant Masts & Yards.

June 8   Lat. 35.34   Lon. 51.07   SSW   S½E   S½E   Gentle
breezes   fine weather   Sent up Main Topsail Yard & Set all possible sail.

June 9   Lat. 33.59   Lon. 45.39   S½E   S½E   S by W   Gentle breezes   Hazy weather

June 10   Lat. 32.16   Lon. 40.59   S by W   S by W   SSW
Gentle breezes   Hazy weather

June 11   Lat. 30.48   Lon. 39.52   SSW   SSW   SSW   Very
light breezes   fine weather

June 12   Lat. 29.54   Lon. 39.47   S by W   S by W   S by E
Faint Airs and Calms   fine weather

June 13   Lat. 27.41   Lon. 40.22   SSE   SE by S   Calm
Faint Airs & Calms   fine weather

June 14   Lat. 24.50   Lon. 40.23   SE by E   SE by E   SE by
E   Light breeze   fine weather   Discovered Main Mast badly
sprung 4 feet below the hounds

June 15   Lat. 21.21   Lon. 40.10   SE by E   SE by E   SE by E   Gentle breeze   fine weather with passing Clouds

June 16   Lat. 17.10   Lon. 39.12   SE by E   SE by E   SE by E   Gentle breeze & Puffy Middle & Latter fresh & puffy

June 17   Lat. 12.50   Lon. 37.54   SSE   E by S   E   Fresh with light Rain Squalls & Cloudy weather

June 18   Lat. 9.29   Lon. 35.18   E by S   E by S   ENE   Fresh & squally with frequent showers

June 19   Lat. 6.49   Lon. 32.33   NE   NE   SE   Fresh & squally with Rain.   Latter faint Airs

June 20   Lat. 6.04   Lon. 34.03   S   SSE   Calm   Baffling Airs & fresh Squalls,   tacked ship 6 times,   Ends Calm

June 21   Lat. 5.27   Lon. 32.50   Calm-SSW   NW   Calm Middle Light Squalls with Rain—40 miles easterly current

June 22   Lat. 5.11   Lon. 32.00   Calm   Calm   Calm   Occasional faint Airs   weather fine—20 miles Easterly Current

June 23   Lat. 4.33   Lon. 31.23   Calm   E   Calm   Middle faint Airs & Squalls with Rain

June 24   Lat. 1.37   Lon. 32.50   SE   SE by S   SE by S Faint Airs,   Middle & latter   Gentle breezes   fine weather

June 25   Lat. 1.56 S   Lon. 33.26   ESE   ESE   ESE   Gentle breezes   fine weather

June 26   Lat. 4.39   Lon. 33.26   ESE   ESE   ESE   Gentle breezes   fine weather   Midnight tacked ship to clear Rocas Shoal at 2 A. M.   Tacked South

June 27   Lat. 7.27   Lon. 33.20   ESE   ESE   ESE   Very light breezes   fine weather

June 28   Lat. 9.45   Lon. 34.31   ESE   ESE   S   Very light breezes   fine weather   Latter squally with Rain

June 29   Lat. 10.59   Lon. 35.16   SSW-Calm   S   SSE   Fresh with heavy Squalls,   one Reef in Main topsail,   tacked twice

June 30   Lat. 12.54   Lon. 37.20   S   SSE   S   Fresh with heavy Squalls   tacked twice

July 1   Lat. 13.49   Lon. 37.02   S   Calm   S by E   Light baffling & squally   tacked twice

July 2   Lat. 15.10   Lon. 38.00   Light & baffling with fine weather   tacked twice

July 3 Lat. 17.27S Lon. 38.35W SE by S ESE ESE Very light Airs & fine weather Land in sight all Day

July 4 Lat. 19.16 Lon. 38.29 E by S E ENE Very light Airs Calm at times with occasional showers, 2 P. M. 20 fathoms water, at 6—17 fathoms from 17 fathoms to 35 fathoms & down to 20 fathoms up to midnight, at 1 A. M. 35 fathoms.

July 5 Lat. 21.33 Lon. 38.50 ENE ENE ENE Very light breezes fine weather Latter Cloudy with Light showers & squally appearances

July 6 Lat. 24.22 Lon. 40.00 NE NE NE Very light breezes thick Hazy weather—Latter fine weather

July 7 Lat. 26.59 Lon. 42.17 NE NE NNE Very light breeze Hazy weather

July 8 Lat. 29.33 Lon. 44.36 NNE NE NE Very light breezes Hazy weather

July 9 Lat. 32.50 Lon. 49.00 NNE N NNW Very light breezes thick Hazy weather. Middle fresh, Latter unsteady with thunder, lightning & Much Rain, Ends faint baffling Airs

July 10 Lat. 34.58 Lon. 51.24 NW NW W Very light breezes with thunder Lightning & Rain: Middle very heavy Squalls with Much & very severe thunder & Lightning Double Reefed the Topsails; Latter part blowing hard Gale—No Observations

July 11 Lat. 36.32 Lon. 49.36 WSW SW SW Heavy Gales, Close Reefed Topsails split fore Staysail & Main Topmast Staysail at 1 P. M. Discovered Main Masthead Sprung (same time Brig in Company to leeward lost fore & Main topmast) sent down Royal & Topgallant Yards & Booms off Lower & Topsail Yard to releave the mast, very turbulent sea Running Ship Laboring hard & shipping large quantities of Water over lee Rail, Middle & Latter parts hard Gales & Harder squalls. No observations.

July 12 Lat. 37.02 Lon. 50.09 SW SW S Heavy Gales & sea 3 P. M. wore ship to NW after running off an hour in consequence of Laubourd hawse stopper getting adrift & filling fore castle full of water, after getting round Carpenter discovered two auger holes had been boared in the Deck close to the after sill of the fore Castle & to the side, under the after birth, which has been done by some one of the sailors, on Enquiry found the man under whose birth the hole was had been seen coming out of the fore Castle with an auger in his hand   put him in Irons—Also a man who was seen to work at the holes digging with a marling spike which led to its discovery—then holes are about 3½ or 4 inches apart and the interveening space Dug away to all appearances with a marline spike making one Large hole—say 4 inches long by 1 or 1½ wide; During the time of washing away the Hause stopper and getting the ship on Lauboard tack the water over this hole was from two to three feet Deep consequently must have admitted a large quantity of water into the between Decks on & among the Cargo, at 4 having secured Hawse Stopper & hole in Deck wore ship again to Southward through the night hard gales & harder squalls   Latter moderating & veering to Southward Wore ship at 7 A.M. out   Reefed and made Sail,   Ends fresh breezes   fine weather   ship making 5 inches more water than usual.

July 13   Lat. 36.43 S   Lon. 53.53 W   SSW   SW   SW by S Fresh breezes & Cloudy,   6 P. M. Carried away Main Topsail tie & truss band round the mast,   single Reefed Topsails,   Middle fresh & Pleasant Moon eclipsed at 3 Hour 30 Minute A.M. Latter moderate & Clear   19 inches of water in the ship that being 6 more than usual.

July 14   Lat. 37.55   Lon. 57.23   S by E SSE ESE Moderate & Pleasant—ship making same water as before the Gale.

July 15   Lat. 41.28   Lon. 61.07   NW NW WNW Moderate & Pleasant   4 P M Saw the Land WNW 25 miles;   Middle fresh & Cloudy with light Rain Squalls,   Latter light breezes & cloudy with light Rain Squalls   No observations

July 16   Lat. 44.23   Lon. 63.29   Calm SE NE Faint Airs & Calms,   Middle & Latter fresh & baffling with cloudy weather Spoke ship Harriet Erving 79 days from Boston for Valparaiso

July 17   Lat. 47.32   Lon. 64.55   NE   ESE   ESE   Light breezes   thick weather   Latter moderate   No observations

July 18   Lat. 48.56   Lon. 65.30   SE   ESE   ESE   Faint airs

& drizzling Rain, 4 P M in Studding Sails,   10 hours 30 minutes
Sounded 65 fathoms

July 19   Lat. 49.39   Lon. 66.17   Calm   N^d   N^d   Mostly
Calm thick weather sometimes Rain

July 20   Lat. 54.25   Lon. 65.00   ENE   ENE   NE   Light
increasing breezes from Northward & veering gradually to ENE,
Winds cloudy, 3 hours 30 minutes set Lauboard Studding Sails, at
10 in studding sails, weather Rainy with sleet & Squally Mid^t in
topgallant sails, at 4 A M close Reefed Topsails & furled Courses
wind blowing a hard gale with thick Weather & snow, at 11 A M
obliged to wave ship & haul off to Northward Cape St. Diego
bearing by Estimate S 9 degrees W 16 miles, no observations.

July 21   Lat. 54.02   Lon. 65.00   NE   NE   SE   Blowing
hard with snow & Rain, at 1 A M saw a large ship standing NE
with loss of Foresail

July 22   Lat. 54.41   Lon. 64.50   ESE   SE by S   E   Hard
Gale with Rain & sleet shipping much water bad sea Running,
at 4 P M Weather fair Saw Cape St. Diego bearing SE 15 miles,
wore ship at 5 P M to NE, at 6 A M wore ship to Southward at
10 saw the land South 20 miles, at meridian St. Diego W 10 miles
Weather moderate & Cloudy

July 23   Lat. 56.04   Lon. 68.16   E   E   E   Moderate all
set sail passed through St. Le Marie & Cleared the Land at 6 P M,
Strong tide setting to Northward Middle Rainy, Latter fair
Cape Horn N 5 miles at 8 A M, the whole coast covered with
snow—wild Ducks numerous,

July 24   Lat. 55.43   Lon. 72.51   ENE   NE   NW   Gentle
breezes light snow Squalls; middle & Latter moderate & Clear
weather, all sail set.

July 25   Lat. 53.36   Lon. 78.04   N   N   NE   Moderate
breezes with Rain & snow squalls

July 26   Lat. 50.57   Lon. 80.33   S   S   SW   Light breezes
& Cloudy Latter fine breeze & Clear weather

July 27   Lat. 47.55   Lon. 84.06   SSW   SSW   S by E   Light
breezes & Cloudy Sent up Main topgallant & Royal Yards set
all possible sail.

July 28   Lat. 46.58   Lon. 85.06   SSW   WSW   SW by W

Light airs & Cloudy All sail set, Middle Light Rain Squalls; Latter fine weather

July 29 Lat. 46.06 Lon. 87.46 Calm Calm N First & Middle Calm, Latter good breeze with fine weather

July 30 Lat. 41.58 S Lon. 91.00 W ENE ENE E Fresh breezes fine weather. Latter part unsteady all studding sails set

July 31 Lat. 36.58 Lon. 95.46 SE SE SE Fresh breezes fine weather 2 P M wind SE, at 6 squally, In lower & topgallant studdingsails at 7 in Royals, at 2 A M in Fore topmast studdingsail, Latter part High sea running ship very wet, fore & aft, Distance Run this Day by observation 374 miles, an average of 15 7/12 knots per hour, during the Squalls 18 knots of line was not sufficient to measure her rate of speed, Topgallantsails set stro

August 1 Lat. 31.28 Lon. 96.25 SE SSE S Strong Gales & Squally at 6 P M In Topgallantsails, Double Reefed Fore & Mizen Topsails, bad sea Running, at 4 A M made sail again Ends all Lauboard studdingsails set

August 2 Lat. 27.29 Lon. 98.35 S S S Fresh breezes fine weather, Latter moderate & Cloudy

August 3 Lat. 24.47 Lon. 100.56 SE ESE ESE Light breezes fine weather Middle light squalls & cloudy, Latter fine weather

August 4 Lat. 21.51 Lon. 102.56 ESE ESE ESE Light breezes fine weather Middle passing Clouds

August 5 Lat. 19.12 Lon. 105.31 ESE ESE ESE Light breezes fine weather Middle passing Clouds

August 6 Lat. 16.24 Lon. 108.08 ESE ESE ESE Light breezes fine weather Middle passing Clouds

August 7 Lat. 13.34 Lon. 110.53 ESE ESE ESE Light breezes fine weather Middle passing Clouds

August 8 Lat. 10.42 Lon. 113.42 ESE ESE ESE Light breezes fine weather Middle Squally; Latter fine weather

August 9 Lat. 7.47 Lon. 116.36 ESE ESE ESE Light breezes fine weather Middle Fresh Squalls with Rain weather fine

August 10 Lat. 5.24 Lon. 118.56 SE by E SE by E SE

by E   Light breezes   fine weather   Middle Fresh Squalls with Rain   Ends fine

August 11   Lat. 2.55   Lon. 121.50   ES E   SE by E   ESE Light breezes   fine weather

August 12   Lat. 0.27   Lon. 124.12   ESE   ESE   ESE   Light breezes   fine weather

August 13   Lat. 2.35 N.   Lon. 125.20   ESE SE by E   ESE Light breezes   fine weather   Latter Cloudy with light showers, Ends fine

August 14   Lat. 6.21 S   Lon. 126.17   E   E   E   Moderate breezes   fine weather

August 15   Lat. 9.39   Lon. 127.04   SSE   SSE   SSE   Light Squalls of Rain   Weather Cloudy   fine at intervals

August 16   Lat. 12.01   Lon. 127.13   S   S   S   Faint breezes Fine weather

August 17   Lat. 12.46   Lon. 125.50   NW   NW   NW   Faint breezes   Squally appearances in the NW—at 6 P M heavy Squalls with much Rain   Ends Calm with fine weather

August 18   Lat. 14.20   Lon. 127.09   Calm   NNE   NNE Cloudy with occasional Rain Squalls; Middle & Latter pleasant

August 19   Lat. 16.52   Lon. 129.07   NNE   NNE   NNE Light breezes & Cloudy weather

August 20   Lat. 19.56   Lon. 131.36   NNE   NNE   NNE Light breezes & puffy   fine weather

August 21   Lat. 23.40   Lon.134.56   NNE   NNE   NNE Fresh breezes & puffy   Royals furled

August 22   Lat. 27.46   Lon. 138.02   NNE   NNE   NNE Fresh breezes & Squally Reefed Main Topgallant sail.

August 23   Lat. 31.30 N.   Lon. 140.07   W NE by N   NE by N   NE by N   Good breezes   fine weather

August 24   Lat. 34.40   Lon. 142.15   NE by N   NE by N NE by N   Passing Clouds & Pleasant weather,   Middle Squally, Latter light & Unsteady

August 25   Lat. 35.23   Lon. 141.48   NE by N   NE by N NE by N   Light unsteady breezes   fine weather   Latter Gentle breezes & Pleasant.

August 26 Lat. 36.03 Lon. 141.06 NNE NE ENE Light Baffling & pleasant

August 27 Lat. 36.09 Lon. 137.17 NNE ENE NE by E Light Baffling & Pleasant Latter fresh breezes & Cloudy

August 28 Lat. 36.36 Lon. 135.00 N by E NE by N NE by N Fresh breezes & squally with Rain; Latter Gentle breezes & Pleasant

August 29 Lat. 36.10 Lon. 131.48 NNE N by E NNE Light breezes & pleasant; Latter squally lost Fore topgallant mast

August 30 Lat. 36.29 Lon. 127.17 NNW NNW NNW Strong breezes & heavy squalls with high sea 26 miles southerly Current

August 31 NW NW NW Light breezes & Pleasant; Middle strong & Squally at 2 A M hove ship too for Daylight at 6 A M made South Farallone NE 2 degrees E 6 miles, at 7 took a Pilot, at 11 hour 30 miles came to anchor in five fathoms water off North beach San Francisco Harbor.

APPENDIX VI

ABSTRACK OF A VOYAG FROM NEW YORK TOWARDS SAN
FRANCISCO WITH REMARKS ON THE WEATH &C.

Ship—*Andrew Jackson*—5th Voyag—J. E. WILLIAMS, Master

Dec. 26—At 1 P.M. high Lands Light Bore West Distant about 15 miles from which I take my Dep

Monday, Dec 26. No Obs. SW, WSW, WSW, First part Modrat Breeze Middle Cloudy with Squalles Latter part Modrat with Heavy Clouds & Lightning in SW.

Tuesday, Dec 27. Lat. 38.45, Lon. 65.26, W to N, W to NE, WNW, First part Modrat and Baffling Middle part Light and Baffling with Rain Latter part Strong breeze and Clearing up Sume.

Wednsday, Dec 28. Lat. 37.32, WNW, NW to WNW, NWlyN First part Strong Breeze & Squally with a Bad Sea Middle part a Gale with Hevey Squalles and High Sea Ship Rouling very bad At 3 AM Furled Four & Main Top Gallant Saile Latter part more Modrat At 7 AM sot main Top Gallant Saile At 10 AM Pased a Brig under Clost Reefs Runing Ship makes sume water The Sea is very cross from West and from North Great quant of Gulf weed.

Thursday, Dec 29. Lat. 36.30, Lon. 54.40, NW to WNW, WNW, WNW, First part Strong Gale from WNW with Hevey Rain Squalles Middle part the Same Latter part Clearing up Sume High Sea.

Friday, Dec 30. Lat. 34.41, Lon. 49.50, WNW, WNW, NW, First part Strong Breeze with Hail Squalles At 7 PM sot Top mast Studingsails Middle part Strong & Squalley Latter part more Modrat Sot maine Royol & Mizin Top G Sail Sea going down Sume.

Satarday, Dec 31.   Lat. 33.03,   NNW, N to NW, N to SW, First part Modrat   Middle part Light and Baffling from N to SW   Latter part Strong Breeze and Cloudy.

Sunday, Jan 1. Lat. 29.57, Lon. 42.26, SW, WSW to W, W, First part Strong Breeze At Reef the Main top G Saile & Furled Four & Mizin   Middle part more Modrat   Latter part Modrat   Royol Studing Sailes Sot.

Monday, Jan 2. Lat. 28.00, Lon. 40.40,   W to NNW, WNW, W, These 24 houers Light and Baffling from W to NNW & Cloudy.

Tuesday, Jan 3. Lat. 27.05, Lon. 39.50, WSW, SW & Calm, S & Calm These 24 Houers Light winds and Calms Clouds coming from the South.

Wednsday, Jan 4. Lat. 26.04, Lon. 39.40, Calm, SSW to SSE Baffling, ESE & SE, First part Calm Middle part Baffling Airs Latter part Modrat 3 ship in Sight.

Thursday, Jan 5. Lat. 23.13, Lon. 38.40, ESE, E by S, East, First part Modrat with Sume Rain Squalles Middle part Strong and Squalley Furled Royols Latter part Strong with Hevey Squalles and Bad Sea from the SE Reef main Top G Sail Sot Pased 4 ship Bound North.

Friday, Jan. 6. Lat. 19.59, Lon. 37.43, E by S, E by S, E to ESE, First part Strong Breeze, At 7 Sot Reef Four T G Sail Middle part more modrat Sot Mizen T G Sail Latter part Strong 3 T G Sail Sot.

Satarday, Jan 7. Lat. 16.10, Lon. 36.25, ESE, East, E to E by S, First part Modrat at 2 PM Sot 3 Royoles Middle part Strong Breeze and Squalley at 8 Furled Royoles at 12 Furled Four & Mizin T G Sails and Reef the Main Ther is a very Bad Sea Runing & the most wind I ever Saw on the Last Latter part more Modrat Sot Four & Mizin T G Sails.

Sunday, Jan 8. Lat. 12.30, Lon. 34.40, East, East, E to E by S, First & Middle part Strong with Sume Rain Squalles Latter Less Squalley at 8 A M Sot main Royol Bad Sea Runing Ship Rouly Bad.

Monday, Jan 9. Lat. 8.50, Lon. 32.20, E by S, E by N, East, These 24 houers Strong Breeze Latter part Sea and Wind going down Sume   At 6 Sot Four and Mizin Royoles   the uper Cloud Comes from SW.

Tuesday, Jan 10,   No obs.   (Lat. 5.35,   Lon. 30.55)   East, E by N.   East,   First and Middle part Strong Breeze   Latter part Light and Squalley with Sume Rain and Thunder and Lightning I am afrad that we have lost ouer good wind.

Wednesday, Jan 11,   Lat. 4.55,   Lon. 30.35,   Calm, Allround, ENE to E,   First part Calm and Rain Squalles   Middle part high Airs and Baffling   Latter part Light with Rain Squall.

Thursday, Jan 12,   Lat. 3.05,   Lon. 29.32,   East,   ESE to SE, E to S,   First part Rain Squalles   Middle part more wind   Latter part Strong Breeze in the Squalles   One Ship in Company   Wind very Baffling.

Friday, Jan 13,   Lat. 2.31,   Lon. 30.48,   South,   S by E,   S by E to S by W.   These 24 houers Light Airs Calms and Squalles Tacd East 3 houers.

Satarday, Jan 14.   Lat. N. 1.20,   Lon. 31.30,   Calm,   SE, SE by S,   First part Calm   Middle part Strong Breeze in Squalles with Rain   Latter part Modrat Breeze with Passing Clouds.   (20 Days & Twelve houers)

Sunday, Jan 15,   Lat. S. 1.35,   Lon. 32.40,   SE,   SE by E, SE by E & SE,   First part Modrat Breeze and Cloudy   Middle part Clear   Latter part Squalley and Baffling   It look Kind a hard for Cap St Rook this time.

Monday, Jan 16,   Lat. 4.06,   Lon. 33.38,   SE by S,   SE, SE by E,   First part at Noon & 30 minutes Hevey Squalls   Royols in at 2 Modrat.   Middle and Latter part modrat   Stud 1 houer to the E by N.

Tuesday, Jan 17.   Lat. 4.49,   Lon. 33.42,   SE by S,   SE by S, SE by S,   These 24 houers Strong Treads   At 1 PM tack to the E by N   at 5:30 tack to SW by S   at 6:30 tack to E   at 10 tack to S W   at 3 AM tack E   at 6 tack to SW.

Wednesday, Jan 18.   Lat. 6.14,   Lon. 34.16,   SE by S,   SE by S,   SE by S & SSE,   First and Middle part Strong with Squalles At 3 PM tack to the East   at 11 tack to SW by S   Latter part more modrat   all Saile

Thursday, Jan 19, Lat. 7.45,   SE by S, SE by S, SE by S

Baff, First part Rain Squalles At 1 tack to the East at 8 tackd to SW Middle part Modrat Latter part Light at 8 AM made the Land at Noon tackd to the ENE Fort Purnebuco in Sight Bering SW by S. (The Chronometer Put the Ship about 8 miles to fare West).

Friday, Jan 20, Lat. 9.39, Lon. 35.15, SE by S, SE by E, SE by E, This Day Modrat Breeze Tacking about at 6:30 P M Pernambuco Tower Bore SW by S Latter part at 5:30 Land in Sight at Noon Cant see Land.

Satarday, Jan 21, Lat. 13.12. Lon. 36.00, SE by E, ESE, ESE to E, First part Modrat Middle part the same with Sume squalles Latter part Modrat at 11 AM Hevy Squalles Wind Canting E Ends Light.

Sunday, Jan 22. Lat. 16.54, Lon. 36.16, SE by E, SE by E, ESE & SE by E, These 24 houers Strong Breeze with Frequant Squalles wind Baffling.

Monday, Jan 23. Lat. 20.31, Lon. 37.28, SE by E, SE by E, SE to East, These 24 Houers Modrat with passing Squalles Latter part Sot Studing Sails.

Tuesday, Jan 24. Lat. 22.39, Lon. 38.38, East, E to ENE, ENE to NE, These 24 Houers Light Winds and Cloudy A Large Curkel Round the Sun.

Wednsday, Jan 25. Lat. 24.44, Lon. 39.55, NE, NE by E, NE, Thise Day Modrat Breeze from the NE with Quear Looking Clouds at times A Mackrel Sky and Mears Teiles & Read in the Morning.

Thursday, Jan 26. Lat. 27.10, Lon. 41.46, ENE, NE by E, NE, First part Light Middle part Modrat Lightning in the East & in the West with Hevy Clouds Round the Horizin Latter part the Same Saw a Bark Bound North.

Friday, Jan 27. Lat. 29.08, Lon. 43.35, NE to NNE, NE by E, NE & NE by E, First part Hevy Cloud Coming up from the N & West and go off to the SW Middle & Latter part Modrat and Clear Pased a Brig Bound SW.

Satarday, Jan 28, Lat. 31.27, Lon. 45.42, NE by E, NE to N, North, These 24 houers Modrat Breeze and plesant Weather Hevy Deue Last Night.

Sunday, Jan. 29. Lat. 34.15, Lon. 48.27, NNW, NW, WNW o NNW, First part plesant with Modrat Breeze   Middle part Strong with Fogg Squalle   Latter part Strong to 8 AM then Light   Ends Very Light   Glass goes down.

Monday, Jan 30, Lat. 35.35, Lon. 50.38, NW to SSW, S by E, SSW, First part Light and Canting to the South   at 7 PM tacked to the WSW   Middle part Modrat   Latter part Light and Baffling   Sea Coming from the South.

Tuesday, Jan 31. Lat. 36.43, Lon. 51.53, S to SSE, SE by S, E to NE, First part and Middle part Light   Latter part Light, Airs and Baffling   ther has been a Hevy Roule from the South all this Day.

Wednsday, Feb. 1, Lat. 38.49, Lon. 53.06, NE, North, NW to WNW, First part Light   Middle part Modrat Breeze and plesant   Latter part Modrat   the Sea has gon Down and the water is Light Colour   this is Remarkable weather for these lattetude   Strong Curent to the South S East   (We have had a Strong Curent to Day   it Must have benn from the River)

Thursday, Feb 2. Lat. 41.30, Lon. 56.05. WNW, NW by W, NW by W, First part Modrat and plesant.   Middle part modrat with thick Foggs   Latter part Fogg at times.

Friday, Feb 3. Lat. 43.27, Lon. 57.56, NW to WSW, NW to N, First part Light and Canting to WSW   Middle part Light and Canting back to the NW   Latter part Breezing up from the North   It is Smoth as a mile pond.

Satarday, Feb 4. Lat. 46.04, Lon. 59.00, N to W, W to SW, SW, First part Modrat Breeze and canting to the West at 4 PM   Hold in Top Gallant Studing Sails   Middle part Squalley Lightning in the SW   Furled Sky Sail & Royols   Hold in Top Mast Studing Sail   Latter part Breezing up with the Sun   at 9 Furled Top Gallant Sailes   at 6 AM the Glass Started up   The Sea is Makin fast and Hevy Whit Clouds Coming up in the SW.

Sunday, Feb. 5. Lat. 46.49, Lon. 58.42, SW, SW to South, S & Baffling, First part a Gale   at 7 Made a Sail a head   Middle part Modrating fast and Sea going Down   at 12 tackd Ship the sail Bering ENE   Sot Top Gallant Sail   Latter part Light Airs

and Calms   The Ship is about 8 miles a Starn.   The Glass is going
up and down to fast for good weather.

Monday, Feb. 6,   Lat. 49.10,   Lon. 62.08,   NNW,   NW by
N,   WNW,   First part at 2 P M a Breeze from the North Middle
part Strong Breeze with Rain Squalles   Latter part Blowing hard
and Canting to the WSW   at 11 AM Furled Top G Sail.   43 and
a Hafft Days.

Tuesday, Feb 7.   Lat. 51.17,   Lon. 63.20,   West,   W to NW,
W to E by S,   First part Modrating   at 3 Sot Top Sails   Middle
part Light and Baffling   Latter part Breezing up Strong   Ends
Strong and Cloudy.

Wednsday, Feb 8,   Lat. 55.20,   Lon. 63.45,   E by S,   E by S,
E by S to ESE,   First and Middle part Strong with Smoth Sea
Latter part Modrat and Foggy   at 8 AM passed Cap St. John
Ends modrat Wind Canting to SE.

Thursday, Feb 9.   Lat. 56.31,   Lon. 66.31,   S to NE,   NE,
NE to West,   First part Modrat.   Middle part Light with Fogg
Clouds   Latter part Breezing up and Rainey   at 10:30 Made
Cap horn   at 11 Wind Canted to the West   Holed in Studing
Sailes   End Clear and Light Airs   *Cap Horn Bering N W*   3 Sails
in Company.

Friday, Feb 10.   Lat. 56.46,   Lon. 69.50,   Baffling,   North,
N to WNW,   First part Light Airs and Calm   at 8 a Breeze from
the North   Middle part Modrat breeze   at 2.30 Made *Diego
Ramires at 4 A M passed them*   Latter part wind Dieing away and
Canting to the WNW & Rainy   at 6 holed in Top Studing Sail
Ends Light & Baffling Clouds Coming up in the NW

Satarday, Feb 11,   Lat. 56.58,   Lon. 70.20,   Calm,   Calm,
WNW Baffling,   First and Middle part Light Airs and Calms
Latter part Light Breeze and Baffling   at 8 AM tackd to the NW
at 11.30 tackd the SSW   Hevy Clouds all Round.

Sunday, Feb 12,   Lat. 56.55,   Lon. 74.69,   NW,   North,   N
by E to NW, First part Light   at 5 P M Spok the *Weling Bark
Covington Boun to Warren R I*   Middle part Breezing up   at 12
Strong Breeze with Sume Rain Squalles   Latter part Strong
Breeze with Rain Squalles   at 11 AM Cleard up Fine.   At Noon
the Bar Began to go Down Fast   at 3 PM 29.22   at 4 29.17   at 5

29.15 at 6 29.15 at 7 29.13 at 8 29.12 at 5 AM 29.05 at 8 29.07 at 10 29.10   Ther has not been as mush wind I expect with the Glass as Low as it has been   Bad Sea from North.

Monday, Feb 13.   Lat. 56.38,   Lon. 78.22,   NW & NNW, NW to NNW, NNW to WSW, First part at 2 PM thicking up at 3 Hevy Squalls   Furled Top Gallant Sailes   at 4 Reefed the Main Sail   at 6 Reefed the Top Sailes   wether Looking very Bad Middle part Rain and Hale Squalles at 3 AM Cleard up Sume   at 4 AM Sot Hole Top Sailes and Main Sail   at 6 wind Light and Canting to the West   sot three Top Gallansail & Cragack   at 8 tack to the NW   at 10 Reefd Four & Main Top G Sailes   Hevy Clouds coming up in SW.

Tuesday, Feb 14.   Lat. 55.58,   Lon. 80.56,   WSW to NW, NWE to NW,   NW to WSW,   First part Modrat   at sot Mizin Top G S   at 3.30 PM tackd to SW   Wind Canting to NW   at Strong Breeze Furled Top G S   at 8 Hevy Squalles with Rain Reef the Top Sailes and Courses   at 9 Furled the Main Saile and uper Top Sailes   Blowing Verey Hevy   Wind Cantin to NE   at 10 PM Wind Holed Sudanly to NW and Moderating Sume Through the Middle part Hevy Looking Clouds   Latter part Modrating   at 6 Sot Hole Top Sail & Reefd Main Sail & Spanker at 8 AM Tackd ship to NW   at 9 AM sot main Top G S   Ends with Strong Breeze and Very Bad Sea   at 11 Furled Main Top G S   Very Bad Sea from NW & NNW.

Wednesday, Feb 15.   Lat. 52.50,   Lon. 81.09,   WSW to W, W by N,   W by N to WNW,   First part Strong and Squalley Four & Maine Top G S   Sot Sume of the times   Middle part the Same   Latter part Strong Breez with Sum Rain Squalles   Reefed Four & Main Top G S Sot   Ther is a Very Bad Sea from NNW and West.

Thursday, Feb 16.   Lat. 51.40,   Lon. 80.13,   WNW to NW, NW & Baffling,   Calm,   First part Modrating   wind canting to NW   Sot Royol & Staysailes   Middle part Light and Baffling Latter part Calm   Hevy Clouds in the West.   53 and hafft Days The Barometer is going up Nicely and I am in hope to havey a good Run Yeat.

Friday, Feb 17.   Lat. 48.37,   Lon. 81.56,   SW,   SW by W,

WSW to W, First part at 3 P M a Breeze from the WSW at 6 PM Going 8 knots with Studingsaile Sot Middle part Modrat Breeze Latter part Strong Breeze with Hale Squalles at 5 AM Holed in Studingsailes Wind Canting to the West. the Clouds Look Rather quear it is Clay Color and I think it mines Eastwardly.

Satarday, Feb 18. Lat. 44.41, Lon. 81.57. WNW, WNW, WNW to W, First part Strong Breeze and Squalley at 8 PM Furled Royoles Middle part Strong and Squalley Mizen Top G Sail in from 9 to 1 AM Latter part Modrating and Clearing up at 5 AM Sot Royoles & StaySailes at 7 Sot SkySale End Modrat.

Sunday, Feb 19. Lat. 41.04, Lon. 84.12, West, West, W to WSW, First part Strong Breeze Middle part Strong & Cloudy Latter part Modrat.

Monday, Feb 20. Lat. 38.38, Lon. 85.25, West, W to WNW, W to WNW, First part Modrat Middle and Latter part Light and Baffling Cloudy Swell from SW.

Tuesday, Feb 21. Lat. 36.22, Lon. 82.48, WNW, W by N, SW & West. First part and Middle part Light & Baffling Latter part more Studdy and Clearing up Sea Smoth Swell from SSW.

Wednesday, Feb 22, Lat. 34.40, Lon. 88.20, SW to SSE, SSE & SE by S, SSE & South, These 24 Houers Light Winds and Baffling swell from SW & South Cloudy weather.

Thursday, Feb 23. Lat. 32.56, Lon. 89.40, SSE to SE, SE, SSE to SE, These 24 Houers Light Winds and Baffling Swell from SE & SW.

Friday, Feb 24. Lat. 30.52. Lon. 91.20, SE by S, SE by S, SE, First part Light Middle & Latter part Modrat and Cloudy Sea Making fro SE.

Satarday, Feb 25. Lat. 28.12, Lon. 93.08, SE by E, SE & E, East, First and Middle part Modrat and Cloudy Latter part Strong and Clear Swell from SW.

Sunday, Feb 26. Lat. 25.40, Lon. 95.12, E & ESE, E & ENE, E & ENE, These 24 Houers Modrat Breeze and Cloudy most of the time.

Monday, Feb 27. Lat. 23.11, Lon. 97.40, E to NE, N & E,

N & E,   First part Modrat   Middle part Strong with Baffling Squalles from E to North   Latter part Strong with Baffling Squalles from N to East   Hevy Clouds Round.

Tuesday, Feb 28. Lat. 21.17, Lon. 99.07, E to N Calm, N & SE, E to NE, First and Middle part Light Airs Calms and Baffling Squalles, Latter part Clearing up   wind more Studdy.

Wednsday, Feb 29. Lat. 18.52, Lon. 101.00, East, ENE, East, First part Modrat Breeze   Middle part the Same   Latter part Strong   Treads & Cloudy   a Curkel Round the Sun.

Thursday, Mar 1. Lat. 16.20, Lon. 102.56, E, E, E, These 24 houers modrat Breeze and plesant weather   Swell from South.

Friday, Mar 2, Lat. 13.52, Lon. 105.00, E & ENE, E to NE, E & ENE, This Day Modrat Breeze and plesant weather High Swell from South.

Satarday, Mar. 3. Lat. 11.10, Lon. 107.10, ENE, E, E, This Day Modrat Breeze and Cloudy   the up Clouds Comming from NW.

Sunday, Mar 4. Lat. 8.05, Lon. 109.09, E to ESE, ESE, ESE & E, First and Middle part Modrat Breeze and Cloudy Latter part Strong & Clear.

Monday, Mar 5. Lat. 4.48, Lon. 110.45, E to SSE, Baffling, ENE, East, First and Middle part Modrat and Cloudy Latter part Light & Clear.

Tuesday, Mar 6. Lat. S 1.50, Lon. 111.41, SE to NE, ENE to NNE, E to NE, First part Modrat & Cloudy   Middle part Baffling and Squally with Sume Rain   Latter part Baffling and Squalley   Wind from ENE to NNE. 73 Days to the Equator the Shortest but 3 on Record.

Wednsday, Mar 7. Lat. N. 00.12, Lon. 113.08, NE & E, E to NE, E, First part Light Wind with Fine Rain   Middle part Light with passing Clouds   Latter part Very Light and Clear.

Thursday, Mar 8. Lat. 00.55, Lon. 113.53, East, E & ENE, ENE, These 24 houers Light Airs and Baffling. Latter part Scrubed the Ship Out Seide.

Friday, Mar 9. Lat. 3.15, Lon. 115.47, E to NE, NE, NE

by N, First part Light and Squally Middle part Modrat Breeze with passing Clouds Latter part Strong I hope this is the Tread But the Bar Dont go up and I am afrad of it.

Satarday, Mar 10. Lat. 6.52, Lon. 117.24, NE by E, ENE, ENE, First part Strong Middle part More Modrat Latter part Sume Squalles.

Sunday, Mar 11. Lat. 10.30, Lon. 118.54, NE by E, ENE, ENE, First part Modrat Breeze with passing Squalles Middle part Strong Breeze and Cloudy Latter part Strong treads and pleasant weather.

Monday, Mar 12. Lat. 14.23, Lon. 121.05, NE, NE to NE by N, NE by N, First part Strong Breeze and Bad Sea from the NNW Sky Sail in Sume of the Time Middle part More Modrat Latter part Modrat Breeze and plesant weather.

Tuesday, Mar 13. Lat. 16.42, Lon. 124.05, NNE, N by E, NNE, First part Modrat and plesant Middle part Strong Breeze Latter part Strong Breeze Not a Cloud to be Seene the Sun went Down & Came up Very Read.

Wednsday, Mar 14. Lat. 20.07, Lon. 126.36, NNE, NE by N, NE & NE by N, these 24 houers Strong Breeze and Clear Bad Sea from NNW Sky Sail in from 8 PM.

Thursday, Mar 15. Lat. 23.37, Lon. 128.10, NE by N, NE, NE by E, First part Strong Middle part Modrat Latter part Light and Clouding up.

Friday, Mar 16. Lat. 24.52, Lon. 129.26, NE to NNE, NNE, N by E, First and Middle part Very Light and Baffling Latter part Breezing up the End is going fast *I am in hopes yeat to Do as well as the Flying Clouds time.*

Satarday, Mar 17. Lat. 26.50, Lon. 131.46, NNE, NE by N, N by N to NE by E, First part Modrat Breeze & Bad Sea coming from NE Middle part Modrat and Cloudy Latter part Little Squalley Very Bad Sea Wind Baffling.

Sunday, Mar 18. Lat. 29.34, Lon. 132.26, NE by E, NE & NE by E, NE by E, Baffling, First part Fine Rain Squalles Middle part Thick but more Study Latter part Modrat and Clearing up Sum Bad Sea from NW and Long Roule from the West.

Monday, Mar 19. Lat. 32.49, Lon. 133.56, NE, NE & NE by E, NE to NNE, First part Breezing up Strong at 7 PM Furled Sky Sail Middle part Strong Breeze with Bad Sea Latter part wind Baffling and Puffey I am in hopes the wind will Come to the west Soone.

Teusday, Mar 20, Lat. 34.05, Lon. 134.50, NE to NNE, NNE to N, N to NNE Calm, First part Strong Breeze and Puffy and Baffling 3 points Middle part Light and Baffling at 3 AM tackd to the ENE Latter part Light airs and Calm.

Wednsday, Mar 21. Lat. 35.00. Lon. 133.17, WSW to SW, SW, First part Calm Middle part Light Latter part Breezing up Strong with Sume Rain.

Thursday, Mar 22. Lat. 36.10, Lon. 138.44, SW to W, SW to W, WSW, First part Strong and Squalley at 6.30 holed in Studingsailes at 8 Furled Royoles and Top G Sailes Blowing Strong in Squalles Middle part Hard Squalles with Rain Latter part Modrating with Sume Hail Squalles Ends with Main Royol Sot. *On the 22 we are good for the Flying Cloud Yeat*

Friday, Mar 23. Lat. 37.26, Lon. 124.35, WSW & W, WSW to SW, SW to South, First part Modrat with Baffling Rain Squalles Middle part modrat & Baffling Latter part Modrat and Baffling Coulord water at Day Light. First part Modrat Breeze at 4 PM Made the Farallons Middle part Light & Calms Latter part Light at 7 AM tuck pilot

89 DAYS AND 4 HOURS FROM NEW YORK

APPENDIX VII

SHIP AND SAIL PLANS FROM ORIGINAL MODELS AND PLANS

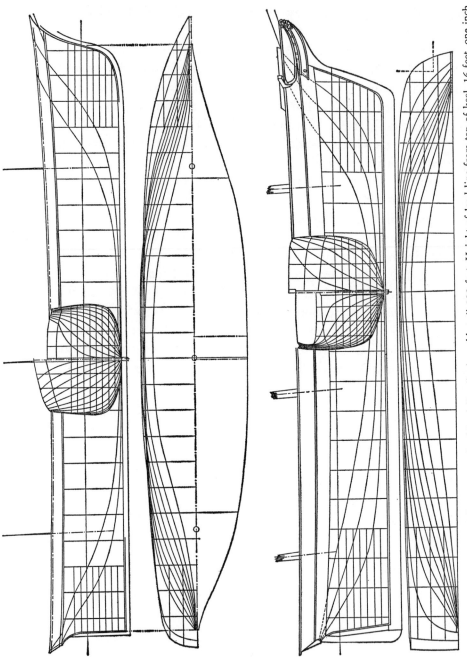

UPPER: Lines of the ship *Lightning*. Length of load line "twixt rabbets," 228 feet. Height of load line from top of keel, 16 feet, one inch.

LOWER: Lines of the New York and Canton packet *Rainbow*. Length of the keel, 148 feet, six inches. Length of the waterline, 154 feet, three inches. Moulded beam, 31 feet, eight inches. Depth from innerside planking to underside deck, 20 feet, one and one half inches. Draft forward, 17 feet, six inches; aft, 18 feet.

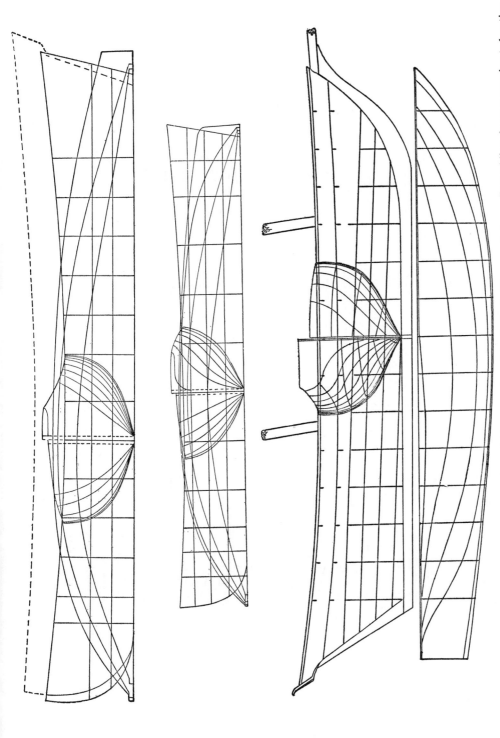

UPPER: Lines of ketch *Eliza* from original builder's model in possession of the Peabody Museum, Salem. Dotted line shows approximate location of bulwarks.

CENTER: Lines of sloop-of-war *Wasp*, from original builder's model in possession of the New York Historical Society.

(These two models, constructed about 1794, are said to be the earliest examples known of the "water line model.")

LOWER: Lines of a Baltimore clipper, period of 1820. Original drawing by M. Marestier (see op. cit.)

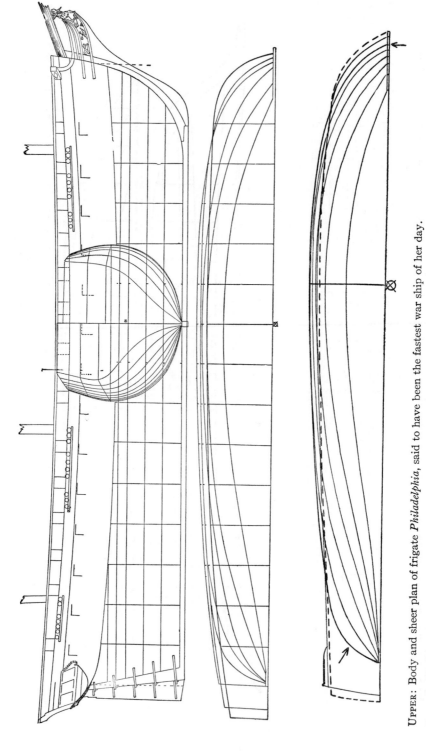

UPPER: Body and sheer plan of frigate *Philadelphia*, said to have been the fastest war ship of her day.

CENTER: Half-breadth plan of the *Philadelphia*.

LOWER: Half-breadth plan of the frigate *Constitution*. It will be noted that the entrance lines of the *Philadelphia* are somewhat sharper than those of the *Constitution*. Arrow indicates load water line of *Constitution*.

From plans furnished by courtesy of the U. S. Navy Department, Washington, D. C.

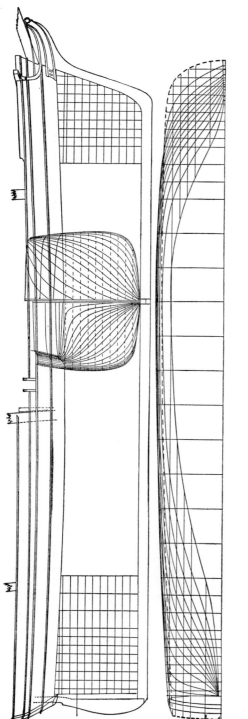

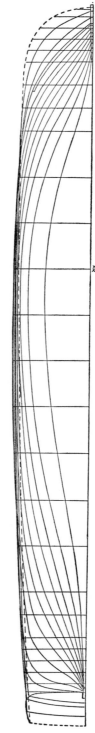

UPPER: Body, sheer and half-breadth plans of the packet *Yorkshire* ("The fastest packet of her day").

LOWER: Half-breadth plan of the China packet *Helena*, which proved capable of making as fast passages as the Baltimore clippers, while stowing a much greater tonnage.

It will be noted that the *Helena* did not differ materially from the *Yorkshire*, except for the fact that she was somewhat sharper.

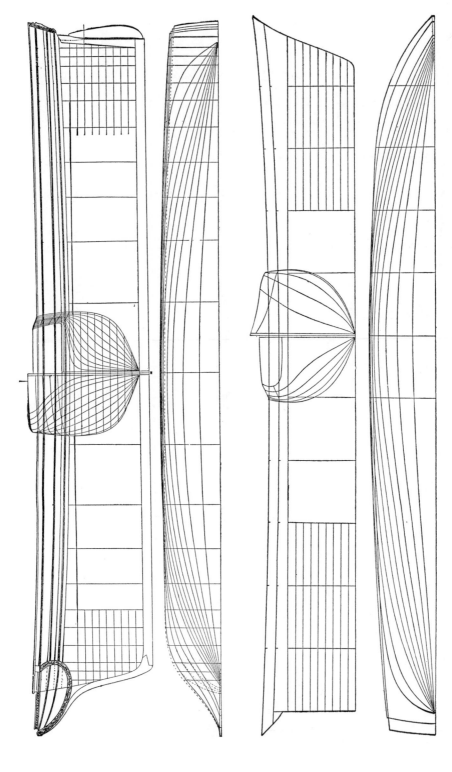

UPPER: Body, sheer and half-breadth plans of the early China clipper *Samuel Russell*, which combined the principal features of the new packet design, greatly lengthened and sharpened, with the pronounced dead-rise of earlier fast sailing theory.

LOWER: Body, sheer and half-breadth plans of the clipper *Nightingale*, showing an extreme example of the theory of design responsible for the more conservatively drafted *Samuel Russell*. Lines from the *Monthly Nautical Magazine*.

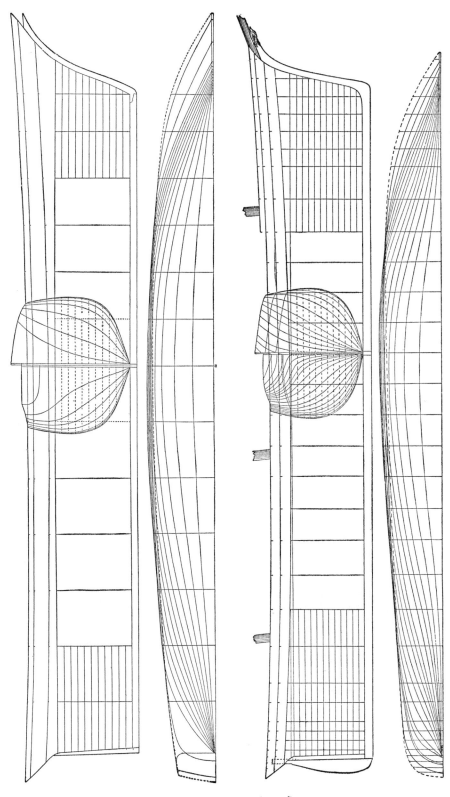

UPPER: Body, sheer and half-breadth plans of the extreme clipper *Witch of the Wave*, a fast and beautiful example of the early clipper school. Lines from original builder's model in possession of Mariners' House, Boston.

LOWER: Body, sheer and half-breadth plans of the extreme clipper *Challenge*, one of the most notable examples of the early clipper school.

In his finest clipper, the *Young America*, built a couple of years later, Webb modified these lines materially, and in particular gave the *Young America* a flat floor, bringing her in line with the later or "packet school" of design developed by Pook and others.

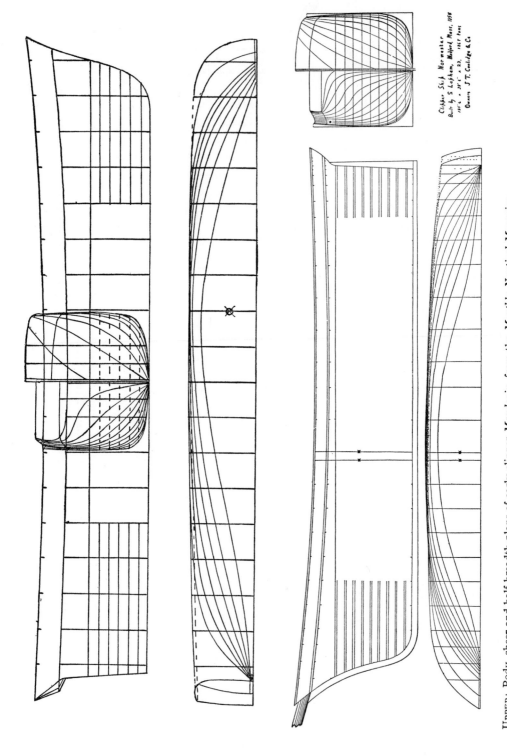

Clipper Ship *Nor'wester*
Built by S. Lapham, Medford, Mass, 1854
185⁴ · 36′ ⁶″ · 22, 1168 tons
Owners J. T. Coolidge & Co.

UPPER: Body, sheer and half-breadth plans of early clipper *Mandarin*, from the *Monthly Nautical Magazine*.

LOWER: Body, sheer and half-breadth plans of the medium clipper *Nor'Wester*, from the original model by courtesy of the Boston Marine Museum.

It is obvious that both vessels are true lineal descendants of the flat-floored packet school of theory. Both ships have records of very fast runs.

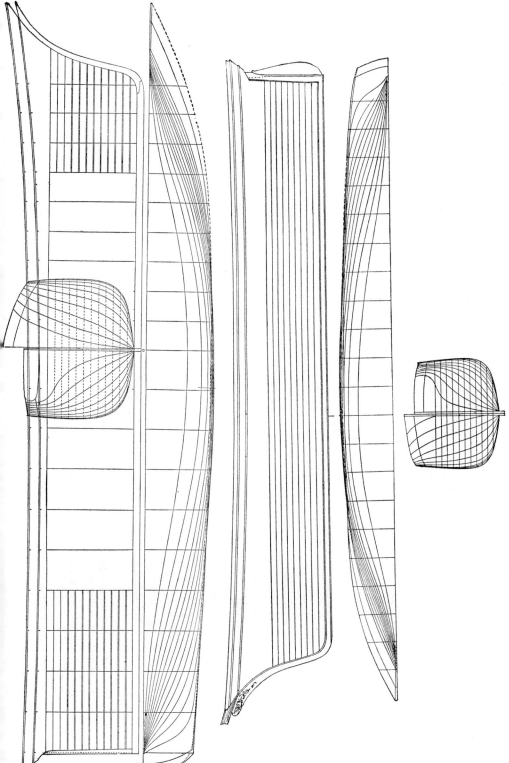

UPPER: Lines of extreme clipper *Belle of the West.* Designed by Pook.

Lines taken from builder's model in the possession of the Mariners House, Boston.

LOWER: Lines of the *Herald of the Morning.* Designed by Pook.

An excellent example of the very fast flat-floored type of clipper ship—a good carrier and a handsome craft. Lines from the *Monthly Nautical Magazine,* 1856.

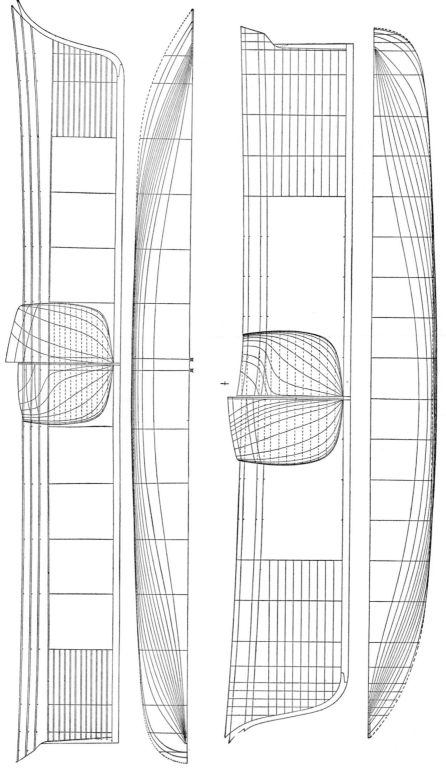

UPPER: Body, sheer and half-breadth plans of the *Sovereign of the Seas*, from the original model in possession of the Mariners House, Boston. Lines lengthened to conform to ship as built.

LOWER: Body, sheer and half-breadth plans of the medium clipper *Andrew Jackson*, from the original builder's model in possession of Mr. Brower Hewitt, grandson of the owner.

Both models represent examples of the "flat-floored packet school" of theory at its best, in the development of fast and burdensome carriers.

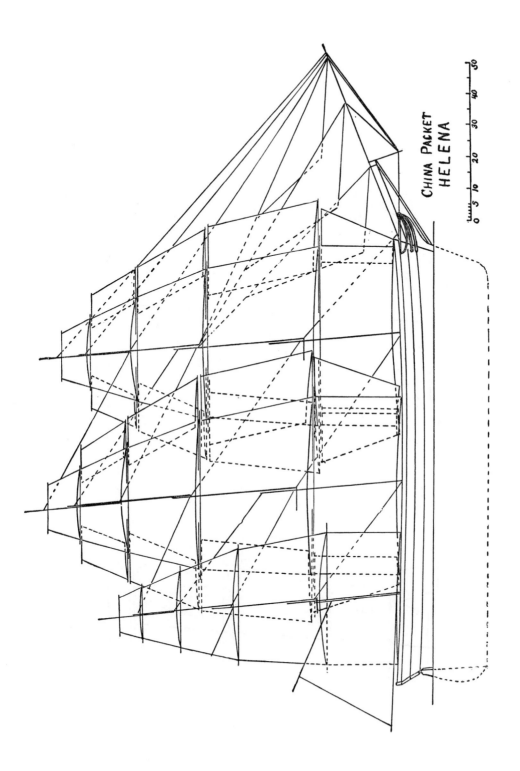

CHINA PACKET
HELENA

0 5 10 20 30 40 50

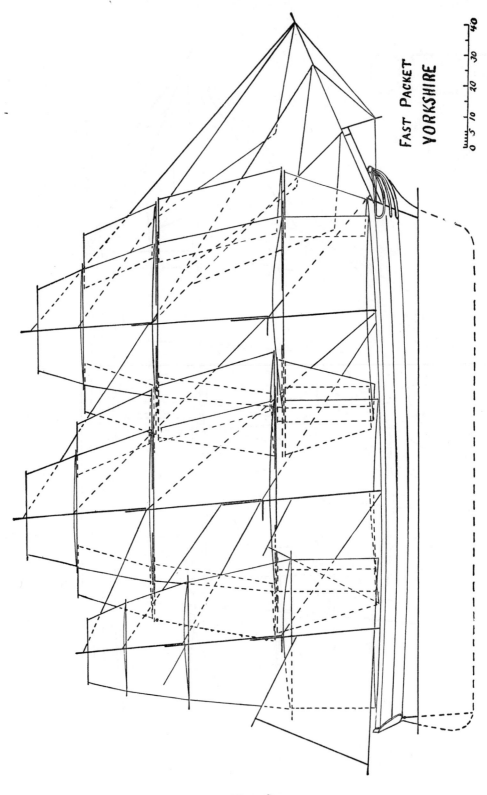

FAST PACKET
YORKSHIRE

0 5 10 20 30 40

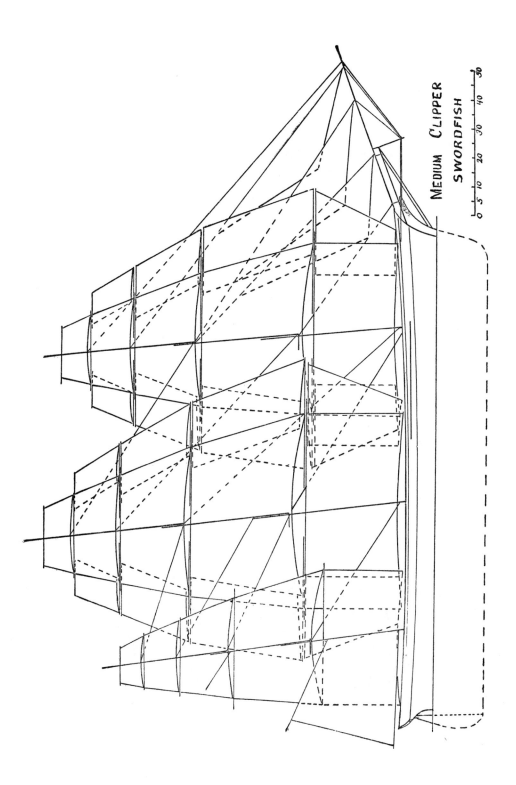

MEDIUM CLIPPER
SWORDFISH

0 5 10 20 30 40 50

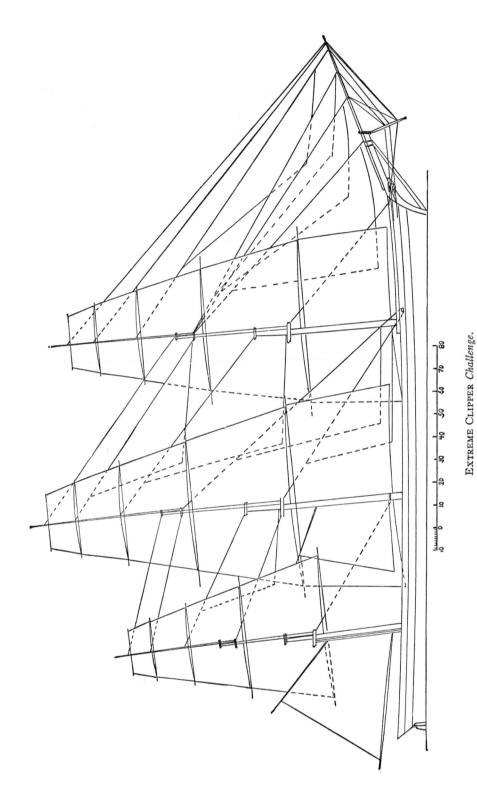

EXTREME CLIPPER *Challenge.*

Showing sail plan after upper spars had been cut down eight feet.

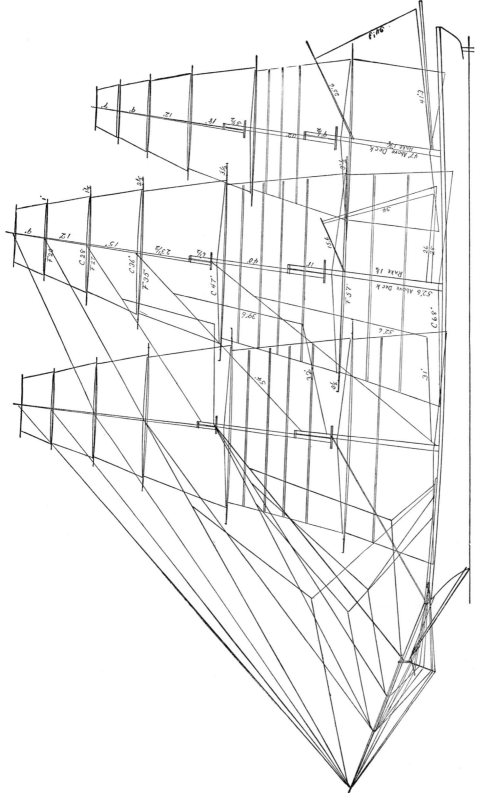

BALTIMORE CLIPPER *Seaman's Bride* (668 tons).

From the original sail plan in possession of the Maryland Historical Society showing three moon sails. Jibs and part of foremast restored.

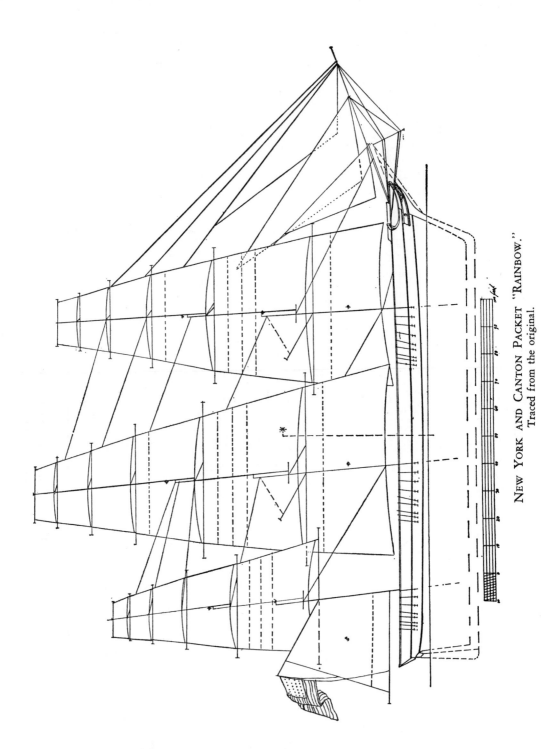

New York and Canton Packet "Rainbow."
Traced from the original.

BIBLIOGRAPHY

Bibliography and Source Material

Maritime interests formed so important a part of American life for many years that data concerning it are to be found scattered through a wide range of literature. References which might appropriately be included in a bibliography of sailing ship history would constitute an unwieldly mass of questionable value. It has seemed advisable, therefore, to give here a few only of the principal repositories of source material and supplement this with a list of some of the more important and readable secondary works and articles.

Log Books, Sea Journals, etc.

Since these contain the daily record of the ship at sea, and frequently also the business transacted in port, they comprise one of the most important bodies of source material. Aside from a large number of such manuscripts in private hands, nearly all historical societies, museums and libraries in the North Atlantic states have some of these records. The largest public collections of merchant ship logs are those in the Marine Division of the United States Weather Bureau at Washington, and in the Essex Institute at Salem. The W. B. has the logs and official abstracts collected by Lieut. Maury and his predecessors. They are bound in upwards of 500 volumes, each volume containing several—the number in a single binding frequently exceeding 20. Altogether, there are several thousand covering voyages from the closing years of the 18th century to 1860. The collection of the E. I. comprises some 1500 logs, ranging from the middle of the 18th to the latter part of the 19th century. These two collections constitute a great, and in the former case, a largely undeveloped mine of information.

Closely allied to the log books are the letters, records, and account books of persons and firms connected with the shipping industry. Manuscripts of this character are to be found in every historical society of the seaboard towns from Maine to Maryland. A number of such manuscripts have been reprinted in whole or part in the Proceedings of the Mass. Hist. Soc., and the publications of the Essex Institute.

Models, Lines, Tables of Measurement and *Sail Plans,* in the last analysis, are the only authentic sources of information regarding the type, appearance and rig of early ships. They also constitute the best means for studying the evolution of nautical craft.

The Smithsonian Institute, in Washington, has, perhaps, the largest American collection of original builder's ship models in existence, although it is not conveniently arranged for examination. Many private collections—principally in Massachusetts and Connecticut—contain from a dozen to sixty models. The Naval Academy, at Annapolis, has a large number of early warship models. The Webb Institute of Naval Architecture, in New York, has a considerable number of Wm. H. Webb's models of all types, together with sail plans, lines and tables of measurement. The Boston Marine Museum, Peabody Museum, at Salem, and the Portsmouth Athenæum have important collections. Fine old builders' models are scattered among old sailors' boarding houses and homes, such as the Mariner's House, Boston, and the Sailors' Snug Harbor in New York. The Maryland Historical Society, in Baltimore, has some half-models and original sail plans. Scattered plans, lines and models are to be found in numerous institutions, libraries, etc., along the coast. An occasional old ship-yard still has some of its original models, but the number of these is lessening from year to year. Several yacht clubs have collections, principally of yachts and small, fast sailing craft. The model room of the New York Yacht Club is noteworthy in this respect.

Perhaps the best published collection of ship's lines is *Plans of Wooden Ships* in two large folio volumes, by Wm. H. Webb (N. Y.)

The *Memoire sur les bateaux a vapeur des Etats-Unis,* etc., by Jean Baptiste Marestier (Paris, 1824) contains the lines and sail plans of a number of early Baltimore brigs and schooners.

John Willis Griffiths, in his *Treatise on Marine and Naval Architecture* (London, cir. 1856) gives lines and tables of measurement of contemporary vessels.

Various numbers of *The Monthly Nautical Magazine,* published at New York from 1855 to 1858, inclusive, show lines of famous clippers.

Henry Hall, in his *Shipbuilding Industry of the United States* (1882) gives plans of several clipper ships.

There are several recent publications on ship models. The *Ship Model Builders Assistant,* by Charles G. Davis, published by the Marine Research Society at Salem, is very good on the general subject, while Prof. F. Alexander Magoun's, *The Frigate Constitution and Other Ships,* from the same press, is one of the best works of its kind extant.

Custom House Records constitute source material of the highest order. There appear to be virtually none in America prior to 1789. During the Revolution and prior to the adoption of the Constitution there appears to have been little attempt to keep such records. Earlier files have largely disappeared and it seems probable that many were removed to England during the Revolution. In general, existing custom house records are fragmentary and in some ports the quantity remaining is almost negligible. Records of arrivals and clearances, imports and exports, crew and passenger lists, registers, enrolments and "carpenter's certificates" (*i.e.,* the certificate of the builder of the ship in question) comprise most valuable documents for the student of history and allied subjects. Most ports appear to have preserved parts only of one or two of these various files. None have files which approximate completeness. All ship registers between 1793 and 1800 were deposited in the Treasury Building, Washington, D. C., some years ago in connection with the French spoliation claims, and are still there.

Fragmentary as these files are, they constitute the sole authentic source of information regarding many phases of the shipbuilding industry and maritime trade of the country. If preserved, they will prove also, in years to come, prolific sources of genealogical records. They appear, however, to be in a gradual process of disintegration by loss, mutilation, neglect, improper storage or deliberate destruction. In view of this, it seems proper to make the tentative suggestion that since these early records have now no other than an historical value, they should be removed to institutions such as universities and historical societies, where they will receive proper care.

Newspaper Files supplement, and in many cases their "marine columns" virtually duplicate important customs information. In certain years and places they furnish the sole remaining contemporary records of local shipbuilding and maritime activities. The papers of Boston, Salem, New York, Philadelphia and Baltimore, and for the very early period, Newport, are especially important. Many of these are cited elsewhere in this volume. It can serve no useful purpose to catalogue such papers here, since all American files accessible to the public are now listed in a voluminous printed index which may be consulted at any of the larger libraries, and which gives the information as to where they may be seen. As a whole, the coastal papers constitute a secondary source of information of high order in marine matters. Accuracy was essential to their usefulness, and where errors crept in, they appear to have been painstakingly corrected in subsequent issues. In reviewing or giving résumés of events of preceding years, however, they are much less reliable.

In the foreign field, *Lloyds* (London) *List* is indispensable. In China waters, beginning with 1845, shipping was excellently reported in the *China Mail,* which also published periodically the *China Overland Mail* and the *Supplement* to the *China Overland Mail.* These were issued at Hong Kong, where the *Hong Kong Register* was also printed for several years. *The Chinese Repository* was also published at Canton from 1832 to 1851, but I have been unable to examine its files. Australian movements are well reported by *The Empire* (Sidney) and *The Argus* and *The Morning Herald* (Melbourne). The best files of foreign issues of this character are to be found in the Congressional Library and the British Museum.

Statistics

American State Papers, Commerce and Navigation (1789–1821) and thereafter entitled *Commerce and Navigation Reports*. These give detailed reports from year to year of registered tonnage, volume of trade, ships built, etc.

Merchant Marine Statistics (No. 5, 1928). A pamphlet of 76 pages issued in 1928 by the U. S. Department of Commerce, Bureau of Navigation. A compact but very complete summary of official reports on tonnage, etc., from August 1789, to June 30, 1928.

Hunt's Merchants Magazine and *Niles Register* give many valuable figures on the volume of entrances and clearances and tonnage.

The volume of entrances and clearances for various ports are also to be found from time to time in the local newspapers, and are usually published early in January of each year. During the Forties and Fifties some papers (notably the *New York Herald*) published several times a year a résumé of local and occasionally outside shipbuilding activities, giving tonnage launched and on the stocks, etc.

Beginning with 1858, the yearly volumes of *American Lloyds Register of American and Foreign Shipping,* and for later years, *The Record,* and still later *The Blue Books* of the U. S. Bureau of Navigation, afford a vast amount of information regarding the size, tonnage, type, etc., of individual vessels. The E. I. has one of the most complete files of these earlier registers.

Shipbuilding

L. Vernon Briggs, *History of Shipbuilding on the North River* (Boston, 1889).

J. J. Currier, *Historical Sketch of Shipbuilding on the Merrimac River* (Newburyport, 1877).

Joshua Humphreys' Book. Original manuscript notebook in the possession of the Pennsylvania Historical Society. Contains the British Naval Establishments for 1719 and 1745, giving the principal dimensions for each class of warship. Also gives the lines of several early American warships, beginning with the frigate *Randolph,* in 1776. Very valuable for the early period.

John H. Morrison, *History of New York Ship Yards* (N. Y., 1909). An excellent and comprehensive work on the subject.

Hunt's Merchants Magazine, Ships, Models and Shipbuilding, February, 1848.

R. W. Meade, *A Treatise on Naval Architecture and Shipbuilding* (Phila. 1869).

Pennsylvania Annual Report of the Secretary of Internal Affairs, 1891, Official Documents, No. 10. Throws some light on shipbuilding in Philadelphia during the obscure period from 1781 to 1800, but sources of information are not indicated.
(See also on early Philadelphia shipbuilding, *Scharf & Westcott, History of Philadelphia*).

The Monthly Nautical Magazine (1855–8) contains valuable articles on shipbuilding from time to time. In connection with the general subject, see, *e.g.*, the account of Geraus' rig in the issue for Mar., 1857, which appears to be quite similar in principle to the Marconi rig.

Consult also *List of References on Naval Architecture* in the New York Public Library, by Rollin A. Sawyer, Jr.

William Hutchinson Rowe, *Shipbuilding Days and Tales of the Sea in Old North Yarmouth* (Portland, 1925). Also *Shipbuilding Days in Casco Bay,* 1727–1890 (Yarmouth, Me., 1929). Full and interesting accounts of important centers of Maine shipbuilding activities.

See also John Willis Griffiths (op. cit.) and Henry Hall (op. cit.).

Local Histories, Biographies, Memoirs, etc.

Rev. Charles Brooks, *History of Medford* (Boston, 1855).

Augustus C. Buell, *Memoirs of Charles H. Cramp* (Phila.). An interesting account of the life work of one of Philadelphia's greatest ship builders.

E. P. Collier, *Deep Sea Captains of Cohasset.*

Thomas G. Cary, *Vigilance Committee in 1851.* A manuscript record of events in California during the early days of the Gold Rush. (Library of Congress).

R. B. Forbes, *Notes on Ships of the Past* (p.p. Boston, 1888).

Frank Gray Griswold, *Clipper Ships and Yachts.* (N. Y., 1927).

Benjamin J. Lindsay, *Old Marblehead Sea Captains.* (Marblehead, 1915).

William Gilman Low, *A. A. Low & Brothers' Fleet of Clipper Ships.* (N. Y., 1922).

Richard C. McKay, *Some Famous Sailing Ships and Their Builder Donald McKay.* A very complete and readable account of the life and work of that rare old master-builder, Donald McKay.

Ralph D. Paine, *The Ships and Sailors of Old Salem.* (N. Y., 1908). An interesting and thorough work based on contemporary documents, log books, etc.

Francis William Sprague, *Barnstable and Yarmouth Sea Captains and Ship Owners.* (p.p. 1913).

Benjamin C. Wright, *San Francisco's Ocean Trade.* (S. F., 1911). Very good on the early period.

In addition to the above, nearly all town and county histories along the North Atlantic coast contain a chapter or two on ship building and sea-faring activities. There are also a number of very good and interesting books, pamphlets and articles on special topics, among which may be mentioned *The Log of the Grand Turks,* by Robert E. Peabody; *Salem Vessels and Their Voyages,* by George G. Putnam; the numerous articles on Salem ships by F. B. C. Bradlee in the E. I. H. C.; the pamphlets of the State Street Trust Company (Boston) on the ship owners and sea captains of old Boston, and *Ships and Shipmasters of Old Providence,* published by the Providence Institution for Savings.

One of the best collections of sailor songs, chanties, etc., is that compiled by Johanna C. Colcord and published by Bobbs-Merrill Co., in 1924 under the title of *Roll and Go.* Miss Colcord is herself a "square rig" seaman of no mean experience, having been born at sea and having spent nearly eighteen years in deep water sailing ships.

Histories and General Sailing Ship Literature

Willis J. Abbot, *American Merchant Ships and Sailors.* (N. Y., 1908). An account of many phases of nautical life.

Robert Greenhalgh Albion, *Forests and Sea Power.* (Harvard University Press, 1926). Develops the interesting theory that the loss of American mast timber during the Revolution resulted in a wide-spread condition of unseaworthiness throughout the British Navy—a fact which played an important part in bringing about peace.

James Burney, F.R.S., *History of the Buccaneers of America,* (London, 1816). An interesting account shedding light on American colonial conditions.

Arthur H. Clark, *The History of Yachting.* (N. Y., 1904). Gives a good account of the early development of small fast sailing craft.

Arthur H. Clark, *The Clipper Ship Era.* (N. Y., 1910). The outstanding account of the clipper ship period—written by a clipper ship sailor.

George Coggeshall, *History of the American Privateers and Letters-of-marque, During Our War With England in the Years 1812, '13 and '14.* (2nd ed., N. Y., 1856). One of the most worthwhile books on the subject—written by a famous captain of American privateers.

Commander E. Hamilton Currey, R.N., *Sea Wolves of the Mediterranean.* (N. Y., 1910). A readable story of the fast craft of the Mediterranean and their work.

Joseph Esqnemeling. *The History of the Bucaniers, Freebooters and Pyrates of America.* Ed. (1741, 2 vols.). Compiled from various Journals, accounts of eyewitnesses, etc. A very interesting contemporary account, apparently written or compiled mainly by Esqnemeling.

Fitzhugh Green, *Our Naval Heritage.* (N. Y., 1925). One of the best short histories of the American Navy and American Privateers.

C. S. Hill, *History of American Shipping*. (N. Y., 1883). Good on the early period.

Howe & Matthews, *American Clipper Ships*. (2 vols., Salem, 1926). By far the best compendium of clipper ship information, compiled principally from contemporary sources.

W. S. Lindsay, *History of Merchant Shipping and Ancient Commerce*. (4 vols., London, 1874). A voluminous general treatise on trade and shipping in which much of the work is devoted to British shipping. An important but not always reliable work.

Edgar S. Maclay, *A History of American Privateers*. (N. Y., 1899). A very satisfactory work, showing the results of considerable research.

Winthrop L. Marvin, *The American Merchant Marine, Its History and Romance from* 1620 *to* 1902. (N. Y., 1902). Contains much interesting matter but, owing to the extent of the field covered, necessarily somewhat sketchy.

John Masefield, *On the Spanish Main*. (London, 1906). A very readable account of sea life in colonial times.

Louis F. Middlebrook, *Maritime Connecticut in the Revolution*. (1 vol., 1925). An excellent piece of research.

Samuel E. Morison, *The Maritime History of Massachusetts*. (Boston, 1925). A very thorough work, full of interesting details entertainingly written.

C. B. Norman, *The Corsairs of France*. (London, 1887). Throws light on a picturesque period and on the development of fast craft on the Mediterranean, etc.

William Hutchinson Rowe, has in preparation a *Maritime History of Maine* which promises to be very complete.

John R. Spears, *The Story of the American Merchant Marine*. (N. Y., 1910). A brief but excellent general account, covering the entire period.

Commander E. P. Statham, R.N., *Privateers and Privateering*. (N. Y., 1910). A valuable account of privateering in colonial times and during the War of American Secession and War of 1812.

A Hyatt Verrill, *Smugglers and Smuggling*. (N. Y., 1924). A popular general account of various forms of smuggling.

BIBLIOGRAPHY

Gomer Williams, *History of the Liverpool Privateers and Letters-of-marque, with an Account of the Liverpool Slave Trade*. (London, 1897). Very interesting and apparently done with considerable thoroughness.

In addition to the foregoing, it may be noted that C. P. Wright, of Cambridge, Mass., has in preparation a doctoral thesis on the economic aspects of the packet ships, which promises to be the most thorough study yet made of that phase of American shipping activities, and which will undoubtedly throw much new light on the period.

INDEX

To lessen repetition, the given or Christian names of individuals are omitted for the most part from text and appendices. The index supplies such information by giving full names wherever available, thus making possible complete identification in a majority of instances.

In the matter of names of firms and persons, some discrepancy in spelling, initials, etc., is to be noted in records of every description, official and otherwise. Such names are reported as they were set down in contemporary accounts, in the belief that this course will rarely mislead and, in some instances, may result in more definite identification.

INDEX

Bartlett, J. H. & Son, 424
Bartling, Capt. Chas., 400
Bates, Capt., 459, 496, 501, 507, 511, 514
Bates, Edward C., 399, 420
Bates & Thaxter, 439
Baxter, Capt., 473
Baxter, Capt. (Alexander), 446, 505, 509
Baxter, Capt. Allen, 438, 511, 516
Baxter, Capt. J. A., 419
Baxter, Capt. Rodman (or Rodney), 328, 453, 457
Baxter Bros., 438, 441
Baxter, J. A. & Co., 419
Bayard (Packet), 405
Bayard, Robt., 406
Bayard, Wm., 391, 399, 406, 408, 409
Beacon Light, 440
Beale, Edward Fitzgerald, 132, 142
Bearse, Capt., 473
Bearse, Capt. Allen H., 431, 489, 500, 512, 519
Bearse, Capt. (Frank or Franklin), 290, 300, 424, 485, 492, 497, 501, 506
Bearse, Capt. Richard, 300, 413, 438, 495, 500, 505, 509
Bearse, Capt. Warren H., 300, 301, 427, 454, 508, 511, 517
Beauchamp, Capt. (Isaac), 441, 445, 501
Beaver (Formerly clipper ship *Miss Mag*), 443, 507
Beaver, 82, 131, 391
Beckford, Capt. Benj., 400
Bedford, 14
Behm, Capt. Charles F. W., 453, 471, 483, 489, 495
Behring (Cl. barque), 226, 392, 468
Belcher, Capt., 473
Belfast (Packet), 405
Belisarius (Fast ship), 33, 392
Bell, Abraham, 410
Bell, A. C., 421, 430, 431, 434
Bell, Isaac, 403, 407, 408, 410
Bell, Jacob, 128, 145, 157, 184, 264, 400, 402, 414, 418, 422
Bell & Co. (R. & E. Bell, Balt.), 156, 414, 417
Bell, Abram's Sons, 434
Belle of the Sea, 342, 446, 508, 519
Belle of the West, 46, 273, 333, 354, 355, 375, 425, 490, 515
Belle Wood, 434
Bellesarius (Fast ship—probably same as *Belisarius*), 34
Belvidere, 446, 509, 514
Benjamin, Capt. Deliverance (Pulaski), 83, 100, 101, 103, 143, 323, 396, 397, 400
Benjamin Morgan, 19, 20
Benner, Enoch, 445
Benner & Brown, 446
Bennett, Capt., 427
Bennett, Capt. (David), 35, 65
Bennett (James Gordon), 111, 131, 136, 142, 173, 206
Benson, Capt. (Heolyn), 83, 402, 496, 501
Benthall, Capt. Robt., 397

Bergh, Christian, 391, 392, 395, 400, 406, 407, 408, 409, 410, 411
Bernsee (Also given Bernese), Capt., 517
Berry, Capt., 473, 488, 489, 495, 518, (*Winged Arrow*), 518
Berry, Capt. John Charles, 327
Bessie & Annie (Brit.), 443
Beverly, 85, 333
Beverly (Cl. ship), 317, 419, 454, 483
B. F. Hoxie, 434, 500, 505, 515, 518
Bien, John, 409
Birckhead, Hugh, 397
Bird, Capt., 509
Bird, Capt. Thomas J., 414
Birmingham (Packet), 405
Bishop, James & Co., 419, 430, 431
Bishop, Stilwell S., 429
Bishop & Simonson, 399
Bishop, Simons & Co., 442
Black Ball Line, 56, 57, 64, 65, 66, 405, 406, 408, 409, 411
Black Hawk (of Connecticut), 425
Black Hawk (of New York), 371, 444, 508, 516, 520
Black Hawk (of Newburyport) (Loss), 371
Black Prince, 444, 505, 510, 518
Black Sea, 440
Black Squall (Cl. barque), 157, (Record), 235, (Reg.), 412, 485
Black Warrior, 425, 501, 511
Blake, Joshua, 401
Blake, Josiah W., 402
Blakeman, Capt. Curtiss, 403
Blanchard, Alfred, 432, 439
Blanchard, N. & Sons, 430
Blight, Charles, 402
Blish, Capt., 335, 372, 444, 473, 474
Blossom, Smith and Dimon, 406, 407
Blue Jacket, 434
Boardman, Capt. Francis, 395, 398
Boardman, Wm. H., 392
Bogert, Henry K., 410
Bogert, S. G., 443
Bolton, Curtis, 410
Bonita, 262, 333, 425, 472, 491, 495
Boot, Kirk, 391
Booth & Edgar, 403, 413, 418
Boott (or Boolt), Capt., 511, 518
Borland, Capt. Saml. G., 427, 511
Boston (Frigate), 9, 10
Boston (Log), 326
Bostonian, 435, 506, 510
Boston Light, 318, 360, 425, 498
Boston & Liverpool Packet Company, 68
Bk. *Bounding Billow*, 435
Bourne, Capt. Lemuel, 404
Bourne & Kingsbury, 417
Bowden, Capt., 460
Bowditch, Capt. Ebenezer, Jr., 7
Bowen, Capt. A., 427
Bowen, Capt. Ezra, 404
Bower, Capt., 143
Bowers, Capt. B. P., 444, 508, 516, 520
Bowers, Samuel, 35, 401
Bowly, John, 402
Bowne, Capt. William, 57, 58, 406, 408

INDEX

INDEX

INDEX

The text of this book is set in Linotype Garamond. It is twelve point, with three points of leading. The chapter titles are in twelve point Linotype Garamond small caps.

The book is printed on fifty-pound White Warren's Olde Style paper. The black-and-white illustrations are printed on seventy-pound White Woodbine Folding Enamel, with the full-color plates on eighty-pound White Lustro Gloss. The cloth is White Lynnene, natural finish. The printing and binding are by the George Banta Company, Incorporated, Menasha, Wisconsin.

CLIPPER SHIP

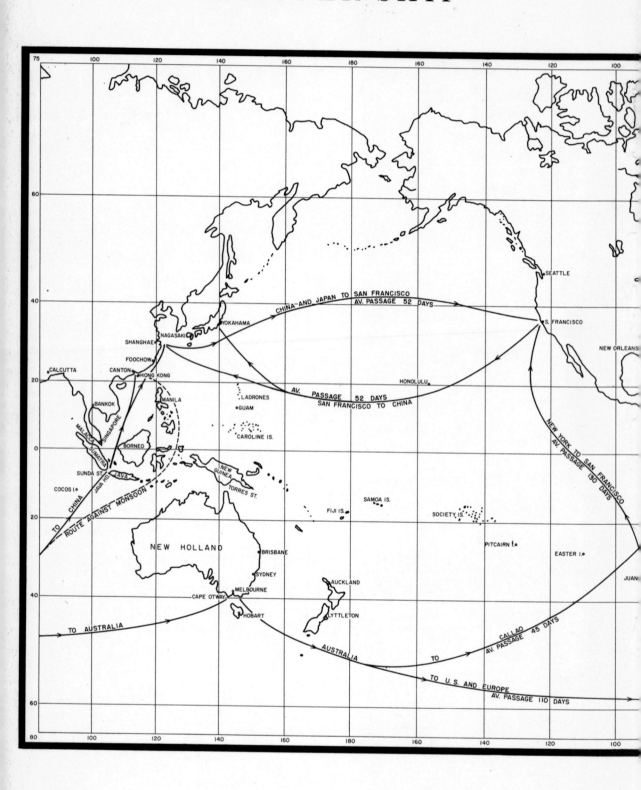

COMPILED FROM VARIOUS EDITIONS